ORGANIZATION THEORY AND DESIGN

**The Irwin Series in Management and
The Behavioral Sciences**

Consulting Editors
L. L. CUMMINGS   E. KIRBY WARREN

Advisory Editor
JOHN F. MEE

Organization Theory and Design

Robert A. Ullrich, D.B.A.
*Professor of Management and
Associate Dean
Vanderbilt University*

George F. Wieland, Ph.D.
*Consultant
Ann Arbor, Michigan*

1980
Revised Edition

Richard D. Irwin, Inc.
Homewood, Illinois   60430

*Irwin-Dorsey Limited
Georgetown, Ontario   L7G 4B3*

This book was previously published under the title of
Organizations: Behavior, Design, and Change.

© RICHARD D. IRWIN, INC., 1976 and 1980

All rights reserved. No part of this publication may be reproduced, stored in a retrieval system, or transmitted, in any form or by any means, electronic, mechanical, photocopying, recording, or otherwise, without the prior written permission of the publisher.

ISBN 0-256-02285-2
Library of Congress Catalog Card No. 79-89949

Printed in the United States of America

1 2 3 4 5 6 7 8 9 0 A 7 6 5 4 3 2 1 0

For Our Children

Karl and Eleanor Ullrich
Susan, Sandra, Mike, and Patience Wieland

Preface

Millions of us have seen pictures of the planets on our television sets. These pictures were taken by robot devices that traveled enormous distances to show us alien worlds. Surely, these events will mark a turning point in civilization for future historians.

In many ways, the exploration of the planets symbolizes an era. It demonstrates an unprecedented ability to employ technology and organizational networks. It illustrates humanity's unending desire to explore and learn. Moreover, many of those who saw the pictures in their living rooms were alive before the Wright brothers flew!

Our grandparents remember gas lights in their homes, horse-drawn carts, and crystal radio sets. They went from gaslight to space flight in a lifetime. The progress that permitted them to see the sunrise on Mars is attributable in part to the growth of modern organizations. Understanding these organizations is essential—especially now, when some of the progress they achieve is offset by socially undesirable consequences.

Unfortunately, such understanding is hard to come by. One problem is that these organizations are extremely complex—yet, complexity can be mastered ultimately. More frustrating, from our point of view, is that scientific study of organizations is an infant discipline. Numerous, divergent views and theories of organizations confront the student. Resulting from different traditions and philosophies, they sometimes appear irreconcilable.

We have attempted to describe these major, theoretical positions by presenting selected works that exemplify the various schools of thought. In doing so, we have taken the position that, while the theories are not entirely mutually exclusive, they cannot be fitted together as pieces of a scientific jigsaw puzzle.

Beyond our concern with organizations *qua* organizations, we have emphasized the social processes found in organizations. People's values and socially derived views of the world are important determinants of processes such as conflict, strategic choice, and change. We have described these processes as they are influenced by the interactions of major organizational variables that are described by the various theories.

Chapter 1 provides a brief illustration of the growth of science—of the development of theories and their interaction with the culture. Chapter 2 introduces the major schools of thought on organizations. The remaining chapters in this section of the text are devoted to structure, technology, and control.

Section II explores the relationship of the organization to its environment. Section III provides an analysis of processes—some of which cross organizational boundaries—and their behavioral and rational foundations. The next section is devoted to the problem of evaluating organizations. Finally, Section V deals with the process of organizational change.

We have emphasized the aspects of organizations that are subject to control and manipulation by management *and* that have been studied by one or another of the scientific disciplines. Our aim has been to provide a text which is practical, and yet sufficiently based on scientific evidence to provide the reader a foundation for subsequent, systematic learning.

Our aim has been to describe organizations as we understand them. Thus, we have not provided an exhaustive survey of the literature, but have cited major findings upon which our understanding is based. We have acknowledged the manager's need to take decisive action in areas where the behavioral scientist would prefer to withhold judgment. In doing so we occasionally have weighed the evidence available and advised the reader accordingly. Yet, although we would like to link the fields of organization theory and behavior with the manager's task of designing, controlling, assessing, and changing organizations, we have been reluctant to lead the reader to conclusions in every case. As managers, we can draw conclusions that have no support in the literature on research; as scientists, we cannot.

Finally, we expect that many readers will have had a prior course in organizational behavior. However, we do not consider this to be prerequisite.

January 1980   ROBERT A. ULLRICH
GEORGE F. WIELAND

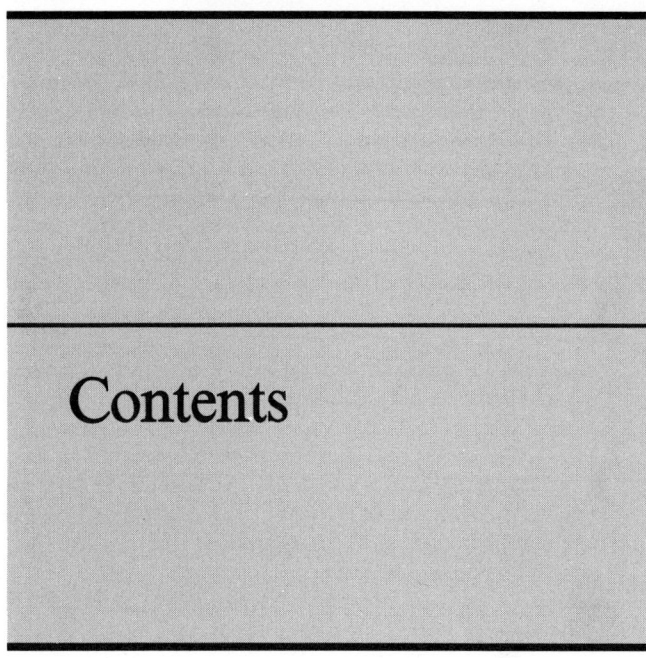

Contents

SECTION I
Fundamental Design Concepts   1

1. Science and Culture   3

THEORY AND CULTURE: Theories as necessities. The functions of theory in everyday life. Systematic modifications of theory. The origins of revolutions in theory. Still more revolutions.

2. Two Views of Organizations   13

THE RATIONAL VIEW: Frederick W. Taylor's scientific management. Principles of management. Max Weber's analysis of bureaucracy. Bureaucratic functions and dysfunctions. Bureaucracy and individual freedom. The human relations movement. Hawthorne in a different light. The contingency approach. Limitations of the rational view. THE SOCIAL SYSTEMS VIEW: The departure from closed-system perspectives. The system rationale. Systems and subsystems. Organizations as subsystems of society. Some consequences of the system view. The location of subsystems in the organizational hierarchy. Social systems. A study plan for organizations.

3. Organizational Structure   36

A REVIEW OF THE CLASSIC CONCEPTS OF STRUCTURE: Structure. Vertical differentiation by authority. Horizontal differentiation by specialization. Departmentalization by function, process, location, and product. Span of control. Line and staff relationships. THE RATIONAL VIEW OF STRUCTURE: Developing structures. Outcomes for the organization. Process criteria. Assumptions about human resources. Additional assumptions. STRUCTURE AND PROCESS CRITERIA: The centralized functional form. The decentralized divisional form. Adaptive structures. The innovative organization. Further considerations for the design of structure. Some behavioral consequences of formal structure. Defensive behavior. PARTICIPATION AND STRUCTURE: Group decision making and group methods of supervision. High-performance goals for the organization. An example of the participative structure. Mutual influence systems. Influence graph. Identifying participative organizations. Attributes of participative organizations. A comparative study of participative structures. Measuring differences in structure. Ideal and actual degrees of participation. Influence and structure. A SYSTEM VIEW OF STRUCTURE: Beyond the rational view. Subunit differentiation. Degrees of differentiation. Differentiation and integration. Managing differentiation and integration. Influencing integration. Dominant competitive issues. Reprise.

4. Technology and Structure   78

RELATIONSHIPS BETWEEN TECHNOLOGY AND STRUCTURE: Job complexity and span of control. Three classes of technology. Technology and organizational strategies. Mechanistic and organic organizations. Technology and variations in formal structure. Technology and critical functions. Technology and production control. The technological imperative. Technology: Diffuseness and specificity. Technology as a process. Technology, structure, and psychological differences. Technology: Certainty and variety. Organizational structure in relation to technology. Structure, subunits, and technology. Technology versus humanism. COMBINING TECHNOLOGY AND STRUCTURE: Changing the fit between social and technical subsystems. The composite system. An experimental sociotechnical system. Toward the design of sociotechnical systems. Technology and interpersonal relationships. Managing the fit.

5. Control   103

RATIONAL CONTROL PROCESSES: Internal and external relations. Controlling external relations. Controlling internal relations. Bureaucratic conflict. "Invisible" rules. The advantages of rules and operating procedures. Rules and centralized decision making. Relationships between centralization and structuring of activities. Determinants of structuring and centralization. Professionals and bureaucracies. Bureaucracy and professionalism as alternatives. Bureaucracy in the service of professional autonomy. Matching organizational requirements with professional needs. Unprogrammed coordination. Developing routine technologies. CONTROL—SYSTEM VIEWS: Interdependence. Managing organizational interdependencies. Between bureaucratic and professional organizations. Location of control as a function of information processing requirements. Mechanisms for developing information-processing capacity. Increasing capacity or reducing processing requirements: A dilemma. From external to internal control. Management by objectives. Positive reinforcement. Compliance structures.

SECTION II
Determinants of Design: Goals, Environment, and Strategy   133

6. Goals   135

CONCEPTS OF GOALS: Organizational Goals. Formal Goals. Behavioristic versus rationalistic study of goals. Operative goals. Output, system, product, and derived goals. Output goals. System goals. Product goals. Derived goals. MANAGING STAKEHOLDER EXPECTATIONS: Stakeholder expectations. Conflict of expectations. Mixed expectations. Reinforcing expectations. Unsupported expectations. Clarity of goals. Communication and goal clarity. Conflicting goals. Limits to rationality in organizations. Decision premises and organizational vocabularies. Constraints. Stabilization of conflict. Side payments. Sequential attention. GOALS AS DETERMINANTS OF DECISIONS: Goals and means as determinants of organizational structure. Computation. Judgment. Compromise. Inspiration. Measures of goal attainment and organizational responses. Organizational problems and goal-setting. Controlling elites and goals. Conclusion.

7. The Organization's Environment   166

KNOWING THE ENVIRONMENT: Routine responses to the environment. A system view of the environment. Causal texture of the environment. The enacted environment. Organization sets. Defining the enacted environment. Interdependence and constraints. MANAGING THE ENACTED ENVIRONMENT: Organizations, society, and the physical environment. Interrelationships and uncertainty. The negotiated environment. Organizational prestige sets. Exchange of personnel. Domain consensus. Boundary roles. Boards of directors. Joint ventures. Autonomy and dependency. The problem of intermediate industrial concentration. Growth and uncertainty. The environment, the organization, and organizational behavior. The residual meaning.

8. Strategy Formulation   189

MODELS OF STRATEGIC DECISION MAKING: Strategic versus administrative planning. Strategy formulation: The normative approach. Descriptive studies. Strategy formulation: The disjointed incremental approach. A contingency approach. Processes of strategy formulation. Coalitions in strategy formulation. Rational or system model for strategy? DECISION MAKING AS A PROCESS: The strategic decision process. Identification phase. Development phase. Selection phase. Political processes. Control and communication processes. Dynamic factors. The behavior of strategy makers. Values. Strategic management. Dissonance reduction and the intractability of managers.

SECTION III

The Functioning Organization: Human Factors — 215

9. People — 217

INDIVIDUAL NEEDS AND BEHAVIOR: Origins of contemporary theories. Drive reduction theories. Maslow's hierarchy of needs. The validity of the hierarchy of needs. A theory of need hierarchies. The two-factor theory. Job enrichment. Limitations to the generality of job enrichment. Motives and subcultural differences. Motives and individual differences. Achievement motivation. Achievement motivation and economic development. Motivation and organizational structure. Motivation and ability. EXPECTATIONS AND BEHAVIOR: Work satisfaction and productivity. Sources of work satisfaction. The expectancy model of motivation. Evaluation of the expectancy model. Applications of the expectancy model. The expectancy model and person-job discrepancies. Combining the expectancy and need theories. Intrinsic motivation. Intrinsic motivation and central nervous system needs. Deci's theory. The path not taken.

10. Organizational Roles and Norms — 245

ROLES, NORMS, AND INDIVIDUAL BEHAVIOR: The fluid nature of organizations. A negotiated order. Shared understandings. Negotiating agreements. Informal structure. J-shaped distribution of behavior. Internalized rules. Roles. Roles, norms, and role senders. The structure of norms. Effects of normative situations. Ambiguous norms. The role episode. Role conflict. Role ambiguity. Sources of role ambiguity. MANAGING ROLE CONFLICT: Organizational roles, innovation, and adaptation. Sources of role conflict. Managing role conflict. Managing stress in boundary roles. Influence, power, and bases of power. Bases of compliance. The power of lower participants. The normative element and power. NORMS AND ORGANIZATIONAL BEHAVIOR: Power and decisions. Power of stakeholders. Normative power and decisions. Normative structure and political processes. Role negotiation. Political processes.

11. Power and Conflict — 274

SOURCES OF CONFLICT: Power as a source of conflict. The process of conflict. Effects of conflict. The effects of bureaucratic conflict in different organizations. A study of conflict in top management. The power of the boss. Shared goals and pressures for conflict resolution. The importance of power in resolving conflict. BUREAUCRATIC CONFLICT: Autonomy and conflict. Activation of commitments and obligations. Integrating individual and organizational goals. Socialization as a means for resolving bureaucratic conflict. Socialization of attitudes and values. Leading control mechanisms. Selective recruitment. Participation as a social control mechanism. The accommodation mechanism for individual and organizational integration. Primary and secondary relations in organizations. SYSTEMS CONFLICTS: Subgoals and conflicts. Goal and style differentiation. Superordinate goals. Moving conflict within units. Incentive systems. Reducing functional interdependence. Dealing with sequential dependencies.

Reducing pressures for compliance. BARGAINING CONFLICTS: Limited resources and conflicts. Distributive bargaining tactics. Pressure tactics. Concessions. Tacit communication. Informal conferences. Intermediaries. The importance of normative structure. Integrative bargaining. Dealing with conflict sequentially. Content specific and equity norms. The norm of mutual responsiveness. PARTISANS: Two perspectives on conflict: Social control and partisans in the subsystem. Getting power. Trust and distrust. Usefulness of distrust. Confidence, neutrality, and alienation. Reactions by authorities. Pitfalls in confrontation and participation. Participation's usefulness to the partisan.

12. Leadership 313

LEADER BEHAVIOR AND GROUP PERFORMANCE: Changing views of leadership. Preliminary definitions of leadership. Two factors in leadership. Leader traits and group needs. Four theories of leadership. STRUCTURAL VARIABLES AND LEADER BEHAVIOR: Conditions and intervening variables in leadership processes. Fiedler's "favorableness" of the situation for leadership. The path-goal theory of leadership. The varying effects of leadership. Leadership in changing situations. Leadership and organizational constraints. Leadership and decision making. Degree of participation. Choosing the appropriate degree of participation. Leadership and power. LEADER BEHAVIOR AND ORGANIZATIONAL PERFORMANCE: Top management and leadership. Selznick's perspective of institutional leadership. Opportunism and utopianism. Leadership and creativity.

13. Behavioral Consequences of Organizational Architecture 345

ARCHITECTURE AND BEHAVIOR: Environmental determinism. Size of work space and group cohesiveness. Westgate and Regent Hill. Confounding social variables. Need fulfillment in the environment. The physiological needs. The need for safety. The needs for love and belongingness. The need for self-esteem and group esteem. The need for self-actualization. DESIGNING WORK SPACES: Guidelines for the design of work environments. Physical design in the larger organization. A contingency approach to design. Physical designs for diagnosis. Physical designs in time and space.

SECTION IV
Criteria for Evaluating Organizations 367

14. Criteria for Evaluating Organizations 369

INTERNAL CRITERIA: The rational and system models. A goal view of organizational effectiveness. Criterion measures. Multiple goals. Empirical approaches to evaluation criteria. Limitations of the empirical approach. Efficiency. Potential and actual efficiency. The system approach to evaluation. EXTERNAL PERSPECTIVES: Profit: Efficiency and political effectiveness. Long-run efficiency. Organizational effectiveness from the perspective of the larger system. Domain consensus. Domains as subsystems. Organizational contributions to the general good. A FRAMEWORK FOR EVALUATION: Operative goals and system needs. Some suggestions for evaluating designs. Relevance of selected criteria. Some operative criteria. Productivity, adaptability, and flexibility. Further criteria. External criteria. No single criterion: Trade-offs and suboptimization. Suboptimization as a virtue. Values.

SECTION V
Changing the Organization   401

15. Introduction to Organizational Change   403

DETERMINANTS OF ORGANIZATIONAL CHANGE: Some determinants of change in organizations. Complexity. Centralization. Formalization. Stratification. Production. Efficiency. Job satisfaction. Systemic qualities of the variables studied. Dynamic organizations. Static organizations. Stable and dynamic environments. Diversification. Scientific management. Organizational affluence. "Everyday" change. Growth. Consequence of growth. Organizational life cycles. Two stages of organizational change. DILEMMAS IN THE PROCESS OF CHANGE: Determining the need for change. Initiation of change. Implementation of change. Routinization of change. Resistance to change. Dilemmas in perspective. ALTERNATIVE CHANGE STRATEGIES: Rational and emotional aspects of change. Depth of intervention. Depth of intervention and client dependency. Deep intervention strategies and social norms. The consultant's dilemma.

16. The Process of Change in Organizations   437

THEORETICAL VIEWS OF CHANGE PROCESSES: Behavioral equilibrium. Unfreezing behavior. Changing behavior. Refreezing behavior. Change and the larger organization. A process for consultants. Developing a need for change. Establishing change relationships. Clarifying the problem. Choosing from alternatives. Transforming intentions into change efforts. Stabilizing change. Ending the relationship. DESCRIPTIVE VIEWS OF CHANGE PROCESSES: Descriptive studies of change processes. Problem recognition. Search for solutions. Arrival of a change agent. Commitment of top management. Collaboration. Creativity. Reality testing. Diffusion. An example of organizational change. Elements of organizational change. Results of the organizational Change. Reorganizing. Introducing structural change. Phases of change processes—Development of the role. Unit integration. System integration. Evaluation of the change effort. Sequencing changes in technology, structure, and people. Postscript.

17. The Future: Some Ways of Thinking   462

MAJOR APPROACHES TO FUTUROLOGY: The inevitability of mishap. Genotypic variables in the social system. Approaches to futurology. SOME GENOTYPIC ORGANIZATIONAL VARIABLES TO CONSIDER: Rationality in organizational life. The limits to rationality. PREDICTIONS BASED ON GENOTYPIC VARIABLES: Theoretical biases toward growth and consensus. Is economic growth inevitable or desirable? A benign decrease in economic growth. The social limits to growth. The growth of individualism and self-interest. The time frame of the observations. A shift toward communal concerns. The state as a mechanism for changing values. Japan as a model. Power and value changes. The dominance and decline of business. New thruster groups. The trouble with futurology. Transformation to a new paradigm. A new transcendent paradigm. Reprise.

References **484**

Index **509**

SECTION I

Fundamental Design Concepts

Chapter 1
Science and Culture

Chapter 2
Two Views of Organizations

Chapter 3
Organizational Structure

Chapter 4
Technology and Structure

Chapter 5
Control

PREMISE

Large, complex organizations constitute a familiar part of our everyday lives. IBM, ITT, and MIT are household words. Yet, familiar as they are, these organizations are not well understood generally. Such institutions, established to fulfill both societal requirements and membership needs, exert forces in their own right. Our text begins, then, with a preliminary study of organizations as entities in society. Following this, we shall examine various parts of organizations—their technologies, goals, formal structures, and the like. We feel this format is useful because the parts of an organization cannot be understood fully outside of the context in which they exist.

1

Science and Culture

INTRODUCTION

On December 29, 1971, Elliot L. Richardson, then Secretary of Health, Education and Welfare, commissioned a study of the quality of work life in America. Unlike other federal task force reports, this one, *Work in America,* was to become something of a bestseller. Part of the reason for the report's popularity is its style. Contrary to what one might expect of a technical study, *Work in America* reads like a novel. More important, perhaps, the report gives authority and apparent validity to a number of popular, contemporary views of work. It suggests a meeting of the minds between academics and intellectuals on the one hand, and the federal bureaucracy on the other.

The report's basic premise appears in the introductory chapter. Drawing on the ever popular writings of Abraham Maslow (1970, 1971), the report states, "... the very success of industry and organized labor in meeting the needs of workers has unintentionally spurred demands for esteemable and fulfilling jobs" (*Work in America,* p. 12). Although Maslow's concept of a need for self-actualization (or self-fulfillment) is not mentioned explicitly thereafter, the study goes to considerable length in advocating the need to redesign jobs to make them more esteemable and fulfilling.

Notably absent from the task force report is any mention of the fact that none of the research conducted over the past 30-odd years has verified either the hierarchy of needs or the need for self-actualization postulated by Maslow (Wahba and Bridwell, 1975). Equally lacking is acknowledgment of research findings published in the late 1960s that seriously question the general usefulness of job redesign (for example, Turner and Lawrence, 1965; Hulin and Blood, 1968; Blood, 1969).

We are not the first to see these apparent flaws in *Work in America,* and it is not our intention to criticize its authors. For one thing, belief in the need for self-actualization is fairly widespread; it is almost part of our culture. For another, this need may exist, even though its existence has yet to be verified. Finally, a good deal of what each of us believes, scientists and lay persons alike, is based on ideas for which there is little or no empirical support. The important points to remember are that the validity of knowledge is problematic; that theories are *believed,* as well as understood, by those who use them; that such belief, when widespread, makes the introduction of new ideas extremely difficult; and that, despite all their faults, imperfect theories can lead to useful thoughts and actions that would not have occurred in their absence. Obviously these observations apply to everyday affairs. Less obvious, perhaps, is the contention that they also apply to scientific endeavor. A brief example from the work of Robert A. Millikan makes this point.

Robert A. Millikan was the second American to win a Nobel prize in physics. His achievements over a long, distinguished career included pioneering research on the nature of subatomic particles, light, and cosmic radiation, as well as administrative and consultative contributions to academia, industry, philanthropic foundations, and the federal government (Kevles, 1979). His research on the photoelectric effect will be of interest here.

One of the classic disputes in physics concerned the nature of light. Some scientists advocated a wave theory of light; others argued for a particle theory. Which was correct? The contemporary view, which says both, was hard to accept. "Why? because it fitted into no pre-existing conceptions; waves are waves and [particles] are [particles] . . . there is nothing in common experience that has the properties of both" (Hebb, 1949, p. 119).

Einstein's work was to resolve this debate, but his formula had not been verified. By 1915, however, Millikan's research ". . . confirmed the validity of Einstein's equation in every detail. [But, Millikan] . . . did not believe he had confirmed the quantum theory of light. . . . Because of the overwhelming evidence for the wave nature of light, he was sure . . . that [Einstein's] equation had to be based on a false (although obviously quite fruitful) hypothesis" (Kevles, 1979, p. 145).

Chapter guide

At the outset of each chapter we shall pose questions to help you organize and understand the ideas that follow. Each question is answered within the following chapter, although not always explicitly.

1. How useful are theories in practical, everyday affairs?
2. How can a hypothesis be false but fruitful at the same time?
3. Why should we look to the past, which may be irrelevant, for an understanding of the contemporary behavioral sciences?

THEORY AND CULTURE

Theories as necessities

Our intent is to describe organizations in terms of theories that are both grounded in empirical data and applicable to the task of management. Yet, our study will also lead us to unproven theories and to research findings based on samples that are miniscule relative to the populations they are supposed to describe. For these and other reasons, it is very important that we understand the strengths and weaknesses of scientific studies in general, and of this field of study in particular. For this, we shall turn to history.

According to Thomas Kuhn (1957), a noted historian of science, we humans do not exist for long without inventing theories. Theory gives meaning to everyday life. Kuhn makes this point by exploring the steps that led to modern astronomy. Although we shall begin, with Kuhn, by looking far into the universe and ancient history (and, in doing so, move as far away from modern, complex organizations as we can), we shall discover analogies that give insights into the process and meaning of the contemporary behavioral sciences.

Textbooks provide a simple, but sometimes erroneous, description of the evolution of science. Scientific discoveries are presented in a sequence that permits the author to make a point, and the reader is led to conclude that scientists discover bits and pieces of the truth that eventually are combined to form a whole truth. Probably nothing is farther from the truth!

The science of astronomy is Kuhn's case in point. People in prehistoric times enjoyed a view we rarely see as clearly today—the night sky. The star-strewn, black velvet sky, untainted by city lights or air pollution, is breathtaking. While you and I are fortunate to see this, our early ancestors marveled at it nightly and were compelled to try to understand it.

Early cosmologies gave comfort to those who lived beneath this awesome spectacle, for they permitted the illusion of understanding. The sky was an inverted bowl; the sun, a god, chariot, or demon; the earth, perhaps, a strip of land between two mountains on which the sky rested. The details are unimportant here. We need only understand such cosmologies as crude theories that gave meaning to everyday experiences.

The problem with cosmologies is that they describe the heavens, but do not account for astronomical data. For example, it was noticed that stars moved predictably (at least most of them did) and that the positions and times of sunrise and sunset changed systematically. These observations became problems for cosmology and led to a search for a more comprehensive understanding of the heavens.

By the fourth century B.C., a more satisfying theory was available. According to Kuhn, this early theory saw the earth as a tiny sphere suspended in the center of the universe. The universe, in this case, was a large, rotating sphere embedded with stars. The sun moved between the earth and heavenly sphere. Beyond the spheres was nothing.

Cosmology was the product of mythology. The two-sphere theory was born of science, for it was deduced from empirical data. Early travelers reported that the circumpolar stars fell below the horizon as they traveled southward, and new stars rose into the nighttime sky. Mariners observed that ships' masts appeared over the horizon before their hulls became visible. Others correctly inferred that the earth's shadow covered the moon during lunar eclipse and saw that it was round. These and other observations, some of which were erroneous, by the way, supported the two-sphere theory.

The functions of theory in everyday life

Theories are extremely practical and are used in everyday life. In fact, the original two-sphere theory still is used today, even though astronomers have replaced it with a better one. We shall return to this point after examining the properties of a theory that make it useful.

A theory is an aid to the memory. It replaces extensive lists of observations with a model from which these observations can be derived. An analogy is that compound interest tables are becoming obsolete now that the compound interest formula has been modeled into the circuits of electronic calculators. This property of theories is called *conceptual economy*.

A second useful property of a theory, as we shall see, is that it enables us to make predictions that would not be made in the theory's absence. In terms of both properties, the two-sphere theory rates extremely well. Its usefulness contributed immeasurably to the progress of civilization. However, the same usefulness impeded further developments in astronomy.

For one thing, the theory was used to develop a fairly accurate calendar, one that served agriculture, commerce, and a host of other activities. Second, early surveying techniques, as well as celestial navigation, were developed from the two-sphere model. In fact, the ancient theory is used today in this context. Celestial navigation, for example, is based on the apparent motion of stars, rather than on their true motion. If we are interested only in the apparent motion of the stars, the two-sphere theory gives predictions of motion nearly as accurate as those provided by contemporary theory. And, the older theory is simpler. For the purpose of teaching celestial navigation, the ancient theory has greater conceptual economy than contemporary theory. As a result, the navigation texts studied by seafarers just 20 years ago began by suggesting that they think of the earth as a tiny sphere suspended in the center of the universe!

Beyond its use in commerce and agriculture, the two-sphere theory led to world-shaking predictions and actions. For example, it suggested that the world could be circumnavigated. In the absence of a theory such as this one, would Columbus have set sail? The theory also suggested that the earth's circumference could be estimated. Such estimates were made, and ironically the one used by Columbus was far too small. Using the available estimate of circumference, Columbus had reason to believe he had reached India. Actually, when you think about it, he had never been farther from India in his life.

Columbus may not have been the first to reach the New World, and he certainly must have been lost when he got there, but these speculations are unimportant to us at the moment. What is important is to see the usefulness of a theory as invalid as the two-sphere theory.

The theory was used in other ways as well. Kuhn tells us it was common for astronomers in those early times to earn their livelihoods as astrologers. While the patrons of early science may have been dilettantes as far as astronomy was concerned, their interests in astrology and its predictions probably were more avid. As it turned out, the astronomers whose observations were most accurate were in greatest demand for their services as astrologers. Obviously, an earth-centered universe is more attractive to the astrologer than is a universe in which the earth occupies a remote corner of a galaxy that is one of billions of galaxies. Later, Christianity was to show a similar preference. A corrupt earth in the center of a perfect, unchanging celestial sphere was preferable to theories of astronomy that were to come later. According to Kuhn, this preference lingered in some quarters as late as 1873.

It is clear that science becomes woven into the fabric of everyday life. The abstract conclusions of early astronomers, for example, were incorporated into many interrelated aspects of their culture. Lay people as well as scientists believed the two-sphere theory. Although some, even in Columbus's day, still believed the world was flat, enough believed the two-sphere theory to make it extremely difficult to challenge. The theory was defended by commerce, the clergy, and, of course, by astronomers who could profit little by changing it. Here is a disconcerting analogy: The astronomer/astrologer has been replaced by the scientist/consultant who is rewarded handsomely by industry and government for his or her mastery of contemporary (but perhaps invalid) theories.

Systematic modifications of theory

If the planets were not visible to the naked eye, Kuhn continues, we still might believe in the two-sphere theory. But the planets gave rise to major problems for ancient astronomers. The word *planet* comes from a Greek word meaning wanderer. The choice of terms is far from accidental. Planets deviate from the motion of the stars—they seem to wander in the sky. One way to reconcile this problem theoretically was to enlarge the number of spheres in the universe. Thus, it was postulated that one sphere held the stars. Additional rotating spheres held each of the planets observed by the ancients. The accuracy of the new, seven-sphere theory was an improvement over the older theory, but additional problems remained. The true planets (but not the sun or moon, which also were considered planets) seem to go backward in the sky at certain times of year. This apparent reversal of motion, called *retrograde motion,* could not be explained even by the revised theory.

Astronomers again rose to the challenge. One revision of the seven-sphere theory suggested that planets orbited points on the rotating spheres. The combined motions of the planets in orbit and the spheres in rotation provided an explanation of retrograde motion, which is illustrated in Figure 1-1.

Unfortunately, this system of compound motion explained only a portion of the observed variation in the planets' positions. Further, as additional, more accurate observational data were gathered by astronomers, greater discrepancies between observed and predicted planetary motion were encountered. This led to more complex theories of compound motion, which we shall not describe here. The result, however, was twofold. First, none of the theories advanced was able to withstand the test of more refined observations. Second, as you may have guessed, the seven-sphere theory, now extremely complex, had lost much of its conceptual economy. Yet, for all its faults, this theory survived for hundreds and hundreds of years.

The origins of revolutions in theory

Now, we must address the notion of the scientist as a finder of pieces that fit and ultimately solve the puzzles of science. This is a comforting notion, and it is not altogether inaccurate. It describes what Kuhn calls "routine science." Routine science must appear somewhat lackluster to the lay person. Existing theories suggest hypotheses that are tested. Results of these tests may confirm the existing theory, suggest minor modifications of the theory, or be ignored and discarded for a variety of reasons. Think about Robert Millikan's research that confirmed Einstein's equation in every detail. Millikan did not discard the wave theory of light in favor of the quantum theory he had verified experimentally, because prior research had provided overwhelming evidence in favor of the (invalid) wave theory.

According to Kuhn, theories not only eliminate the need for collections of observational data, they also explain these data, and allow the scientist to understand them. But this is only the case when the theories are *believed.* Such belief has its roots in psychology as well as logic. Apparently, Millikan's belief in wave theory precluded rejecting it in favor of the quantum theory—a conclusion he should have accepted. This is routine science, the

FIGURE 1-1
An ancient theory of retrograde planetary motion

A. A planet's orbit (epicycle) about a point on a rotating sphere (deferent) gives rise to true, not apparent, retrograde motion:

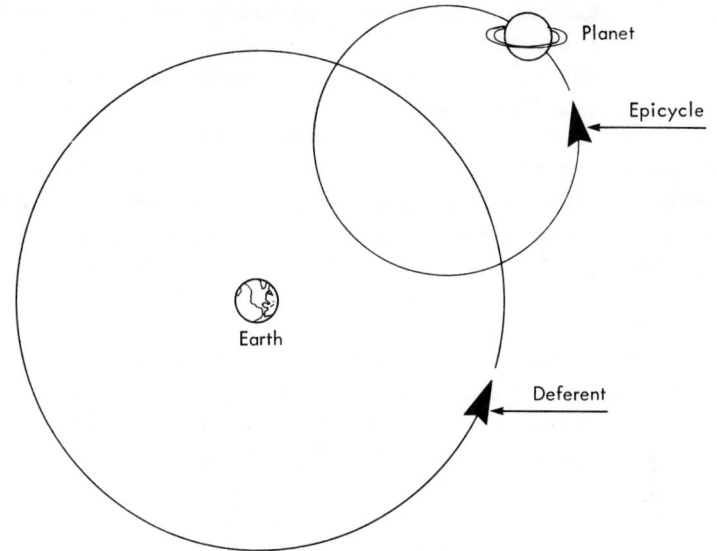

B. The combined motions of the epicycle and deferent would look something like this:

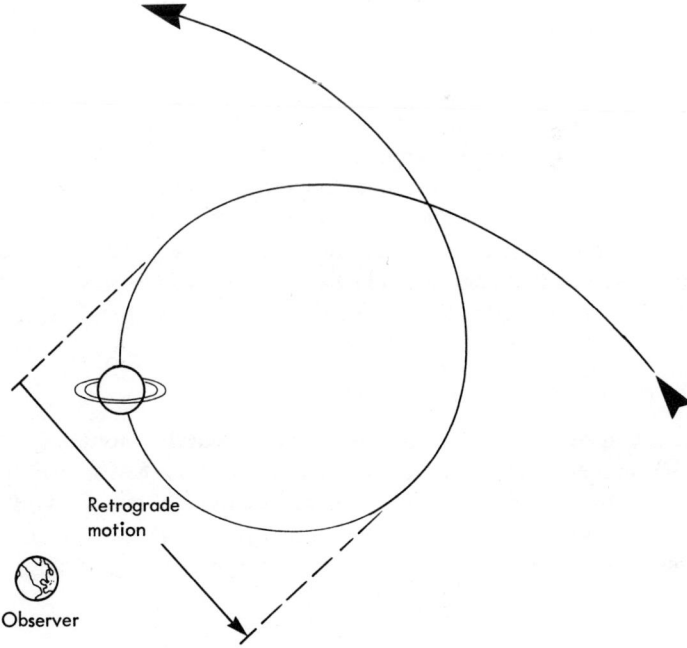

difficult, challenging, and often futile search for support of the status quo in science.

The other kind of science—the kind that replaces accepted theories with radical, alternative models of reality—is a different matter altogether. It calls for a scientist whose belief has been shaken. Oddly, the events that ultimately shatter one's belief in the accepted order of science sometimes occur outside the laboratory in the prosaic comings and goings of ordinary people. Such was to be the case with astronomy.

The close of the Dark Ages was marked by the rediscovery of the writings of ancient scholars: Aristotle, Ptolemy, and others. Academic labors of the Middle Ages comprised translating these works from the various languages in which they had been transcribed and interpreting them. The authority of the ancient scholars, including their views on astronomy, went unquestioned.

Seafarers on voyages of discovery, not scholars, provided evidence that finally brought Aristotle's authority into question. These voyagers discovered new lands and people, proving the ancient geographers to have been wrong. Could it be that the ancient views on astronomy were equally flawed?

A second, more prosaic event set off a chain of responses that concluded the history of early astronomy. As we have said, the two-sphere and seven-sphere theories gave rise to calendars. And good calendars they were, but not good enough. By the 16th century, the cumulative error in the calendar was creating difficulties for commerce, administration, navigation, and the like. Society's activities were becoming more complex, and required more accurate methods for measuring time.

Copernicus, a leading astronomer of his day, was asked to advise the Papacy on calendar reform. Copernicus's response, as related by Kuhn, strikes one as both astonishing and amusing. Copernicus realized that he would need to reform the science of astronomy as a first step in reforming the Julian calendar. He would need to rearrange the universe! As you might imagine, he declined the challenge. But not for long.

You probably know the rest. Copernicus transposed the earth and sun. The earth orbited the sun, the new center of the universe, as did the other spheres and epicycles. Aristotle's universe was hardly changed. But a revolution in scientific theory had taken place, and Kelper, Galileo, Newton, Einstein, and still others moved on from Copernicus's break with Aristotle.

Still more revolutions

The movement was all but smooth and orderly, though. Newton's clockwork universe, after dominating scientific thought for centuries, was replaced by the newer, still strange relativistic views of Einstein. The revolutions continue, for we are still ignorant. Will the universe expand forever, or is it slowing, someday to contract, explode, and begin itself anew?

What are black holes—portals to other universes, as some astronomers think? What are quasars? Pulsars? Antimatter? Quarks? Gravity waves? How little have we learned?

To paraphrase Somerset Maugham, this is not the apex of civilization to which humankind has struggled painfully. This merely is the first day of the rest of the struggle. The college texts we studied some 20 years ago are obsolete. Many contain inaccuracies and misconceptions. Today, we find them amusing. In spite of our efforts and good intentions, many of the facts and theories on which we base our description of complex organizations will be found inaccurate or incorrect some years from now. We hope to be amused by this, as well.

One point we must remember is that science has an undeserved reputation for knowing truth. In actuality, science merely tries to discover truth objectively, and fails as often as any other human endeavor.

A second point concerns belief. Scientists tend to believe the theories with which they work. Such belief is rash, Kuhn reminds us, but essential if we are to take actions based on theories. Such belief is not without cost, however; it may delay and impede the development of more fruitful theories.

Third, these shortcomings of science are not sufficient grounds for cynicism. Imperfect theories lead us to profitable thoughts and adventures we would not have undertaken or even imagined in their absence. Perhaps this is why Millikan thought Einstein's equation was based on a false but fruitful hypothesis.

Fourth, science is not an orderly process in which research results are cumulative. Rather, it is a disjointed effort. Theories are established. Hypotheses are formulated and tested. Some results confirm the theories; others do not. Ultimately, theories crumbled under the combined weight of questions left unanswered and disconfirming data. From the revolution, new theories emerge. Often the proponents of the old are antagonists of the new.

Finally, a generation or more may pass before a newer, better scientific theory finds its place in the culture. If humankind does not exist for long without inventing theories, neither does it surrender familiar ideas willingly. Psychological, economic, and professional interests are vested in the theories that lend meaning to experience.

DISCUSSION QUESTIONS

1. Professor Kuhn's history of a scientific revolution parallels similar histories in other fields. I think you might enjoy reviewing text books written 20 or 30 years ago in light of those you have studied recently. In the same vein, *Scientific American*'s department "50 and 100 years ago" is fascinating reading and could provide interesting material for a class report.
2. Is history a science? How are the methods of science applied to the study of history?

3. Professor Maslow has left a legacy of brilliant, humane concepts, theories, and research studies. One of these studies (Maslow and Mintz, 1972) explored the effects of the environment's aesthetic qualities on subjects' productivity and physical and mental health. His experiment required that he define and alter the aesthetic qualities of an experimental room. How does a scientist define and measure beauty?

competitor used that knowledge and built a shop in which it was possible to throw a heavy stream of water on the tools, and that was a shop started by men who had left the Midvale Steel Works and who knew enough to do this. That shows the slowness of men, in that trade at least, to take advantage of a 40 per cent gain in cutting (Taylor, 1960, pp. 106–7).

Chapter guide

1. Only one of the Midvale's competitors copied the cooling system within the 20-year period cited. Why would presumably rational, intelligent men not take advantage of the efficiencies that had been amply demonstrated to them?
2. Taylor saw organizations as tools for getting work done. Can you think of any misleading assumptions that this view would lead you to make about organizations and their functioning?

THE RATIONAL VIEW

Frederick W. Taylor's scientific management

Prior to the turn of the century, work methods were passed on as part of the culture from parent to child or from craftworker to apprentice. Workers learned their craft or trade differently, and, as a result, similar tasks were performed in a variety of ways. Yet, it stands to reason that some methods were more efficient than others. Taylor (1960) became convinced that efficient work methods could be identified and taught to less efficient workers, and furthermore, as the newly found increases in productivity were shared, labor and management alike would benefit. Thus, he became one of the first practitioners to advocate control of human behavior in organizations and to call attention to the importance of people in the quest for efficiency in organizations.

Taylor reasoned that logic and order existed in the apparent chaos of work organizations if only one could find them. The problem-solving style that he used to rationalize work processes follows:

1. Gather all of the rule-of-thumb knowledge possessed by the work force, classify it, and wherever possible reduce it to laws or rules.
2. Study the workers just as you would study machines.
3. Bring scientifically selected workers and machines together. Inspire the workers to change.
4. Divide the work formerly done by workers into two sections—and turn over one section to management (for example, have managers assign tools to laborers).

The need for Taylor's method was hard to dispute. For example, he noticed that laborers at Bethlehem Steel used the same shovels regardless of whether they were moving a shovelful of rice coal weighing 3½ pounds or a shovelful of wet ore weighing 33 pounds. Which size load, asked Taylor, was more efficient?

Empirical studies showed that laborers were most efficient when the shovel load was 21 pounds. To improve efficiency, Taylor had shovels of different sizes brought to the workplace. Each worker was given a shovel that would hold 21 pounds of the material to be moved. Furthermore, some shoveling techniques were found to be more efficient and less tiring than others. Taylor instructed the laborers in the best techniques, monitored their performance, and retrained them if their performance deteriorated. Taylor's laborers were paid a bonus. Those who could not, or would not, follow his instructions were reassigned to other work at their former wage.

There was more to be done, however. The yard in which these laborers worked was two miles long and one-half mile wide. Between 500 and 600 men were employed in this yard to shovel numerous materials of different densities. How was the problem of getting laborers, shovels, and work properly coordinated to be handled? This became the responsibility of management, along with training the workers and monitoring their performance.

Taylor's approach led to major advances in industrial efficiency, and his work was extended by the works of Gantt (1973) and Gilbreth (1972a, 1972b). The magnitude of his improvements led him to generalize that his principles could be applied to all social activities, including the management of homes, universities, farms, and governmental departments.

Despite its success, however, scientific management (the precursor of operations research) took only one possible view of organizations: as a means toward the attainment of specific goals, that is, as tools. At first glance this may seem a useful and reasonable position. Its shortcomings, however, are readily demonstrated.

Viewing the organization as a rational arrangement of means assembled in the pursuit of specific ends draws out attention directly to the productive process and away from other vital organization functions, as is shown in Figure 2-1. Generally speaking, productive processes are concerned with the ratio of output to input, the criterion of efficiency. Efficiency is gained, in part, through economies of scale and a stable environment. *Yet, organizations reside in turbulent environments characterized by uncertainty and change. Somehow the organization must accommodate itself to its environment and at the same time strive for efficiency in its use of resources. This is a major problem which constitutes a recurring theme in our text.*

Principles of management

Scientific management was not without critics. Some felt that by specifying work methods so precisely, Taylor had eliminated the dignity of labor.

FIGURE 2-1
A systems view of organizations

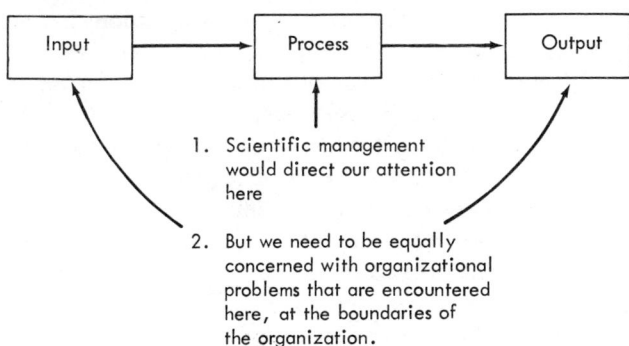

Without the power to decide how to work, laborers were reduced to automatons. Other critics were skeptical of the broader claims made for scientific management. They believed that Taylor was speaking not of principles, but of a collection of axioms and an arbitrary combination of specific mechanisms, such as time study and work methods study. These critics advocated a deeper analysis of organizational phenomena—directed toward exposing the underlying scientific principles of management.

The Frenchman Henri Fayol (1841-1925) did, indeed, go deeper and develop a series of principles of management. These were thought to be scientific prescriptions for the body corporate, which, if applied intelligently, would ensure that an organization would be managed effectively. One of the principles is elaborated below as an indication of the flavor of the times.

Order

> For social order to prevail in a concern there must, in accordance with the definition, be an appointed place for every employee and every employee must be in his appointed place. Perfect order requires, further, that the place be suitable for the employee and the employee for the place—in English idiom, "The right men in the right place" (Fayol, 1960, p. 236).

Other principles included division of work, unity of command (one worker, one boss), subordination of individual interest to the interest of the organization, and span of control (the number of subordinates that are supervised by one person).

Similar writings began to appear: *The Principles of Organization* (Mooney and Reiley, 1939) and *The Elements of Administration* (Urwick, 1943), to name two of the more famous ones. These works attempted to look beyond the production process for a more global understanding of organizations. However, they were simply reflections on the authors' experiences, rather than results of empirical studies. What all had in common with Taylor's work was the notion that one set of prescriptions was superior to all others. Theirs was a rational view.

Max Weber's analysis of bureaucracy

Another, more systematic rational view of organizations is found in the sociological theories of bureaucracy. Bureaucracy, according to German sociologist Max Weber, provides a way of consciously organizing people and activities to achieve specific purposes (Weber, 1958, 1964). It emphasizes the conscious, and correspondingly formal, structural aspects of organizations over the "natural" and traditional forms of organization. Most important, bureaucracy stresses rationality and the efficient organization of means toward a given end. Weber delineated the components of bureaucracy from descriptions of large-scale organizations that were stable, enduring, and efficient. He proposed both to describe these very efficient organizations and to consider the relationship of these organizations to the status of individual freedom in society. Did the growth of large, complex, and efficient organizations foretell the curtailment of individual freedoms?

Weber developed his theory early in this century when our current research technology for studying organizations was nonexistent. The concepts of the theory and their empirical referents, therefore, were derived from the formal structure of organizations that individuals will emphasize in describing their organization to someone else. These concepts included *hierarchy of authority, impersonality, specialization,* and *systems of rules.*

Weber contrasted *legal-rational authority* with authority that stems from either *charisma* or *tradition.* Bureaucracy is based on legal-rational authority, a formally established body of social norms designed to organize behavior in the rational pursuit of specified goals. Obedience in a bureaucracy is owed not to a person (a traditional chief or a charismatic leader) but to an office—to a set of impersonal principles. A person is selected to fill an office because of knowledge and competence, and that person acts according to the duties of the office. Bureaucracy entails a government of laws, not people.

Such legal authority is used to coordinate the specialized elements of the organization in a manner that permits efficient functioning (much as Taylor advocated, too). After a systematic division of labor based on training and expertise, the officials and their tasks are grouped according to technical knowledge and with the aim of attaining maximum task efficiency.

Authority is distributed in a hierarchy of positions, each successive position in the hierarchy embracing in authority all those beneath it. Authority is impersonal, restricted, and delimited according to the specification of the office.

Perhaps the most general way of characterizing Weber's view of bureaucracy is in terms of *rationality:* the use of knowledge to relate various means to organizational ends in the best way possible. Rules, based on technical knowledge, are established with the expectation that they will regulate the organization's structure and processes so as to attain maximum efficiency.

People sometimes confuse bureaucracy with organizational hierarchy and consider them to be synonymous. However, not all hierarchies are bureaucratic. The rational nature of a hierarchy determines whether or not it constitutes a bureaucracy. Bureaucracies, in fact, replaced feudal hierarchies. The traditional authority of the feudal lord was replaced by legal authority, which was legitimated by a belief in the ultimate correctness of its rules.

While Weber's views are useful, a number of studies show that the formal, rational elements of bureaucratic organizations produce inconsistencies and unforeseen consequences. These consequences can lead to changes within the organization that produce conflict between elements within the bureaucracy and generally speaking lead to inefficiencies.

Bureaucratic functions and dysfunctions

A number of criticisms and amplifications of the theory of bureaucracy arise from what is called functional analysis. One may view the bureaucratic organization as being made up of both formal and informal social systems. The formal systems of rules, authority, and hierarchies are purposefully designed. In addition, various spontaneous (human) forces within the organization produce what are known as informal social systems (the informal organization). Since the elements of both the formal and informal systems interact, relationships between elements can be examined in terms of their contributions to the entire organization. One may view the entire organization as having needs (or functional requirements), and any part of the organization may be viewed in terms of its contribution to the fulfillment of these needs—in terms, that is, of its function. Any element of the organization that hinders the fulfillment of these needs is said to be *dysfunctional.*

In a classic report, March and Simon (1958) collate the accounts of a number of students of bureaucracy showing that the functioning of bureaucratic structures creates various conditions that tend to reduce, or at least to inhibit, its expected efficiency. Merton (1940) reasons that over the long run bureaucratic adherence to rules and impersonal behavior are dysfunctional. Rules and impersonality are desirable methods for producing reliable behavior, but ultimately they tend to become overemphasized. Variations in the needs of clients will render impersonal treatment ineffective, which in turn becomes a source of client dissatisfaction. The bureaucrat, faced with dissatisfied clients, will rely increasingly on rules, categorization, and impersonality as defense mechanisms. Thus, rules and procedures become internalized and are followed in an inflexible manner, especially when the ends of the organization, to which the rules are means, are not salient. The rigid behavior that results is not effective in dealing with individual clients or with changing circumstances.

Gouldner (1954) also describes the dysfunctional consequences of rules in bureaucracies. General and impersonal rules are used to decrease the visibility of power relations, to make power less personal and a more rational means of coordination, since it is assumed that people work better in the absence of overt power. However, when detailed rules and regulations are specified, workers learn the lower limits that the organization places on acceptable behavior. They learn what is expected of them and in some cases perform only to that level. One organizational response to minimal performance is to provide closer supervision, which, of course, makes power more visible and creates tensions within the organization.

Selznick (1949) illustrates the dysfunctional consequences of the practice of delegating authority. Since all authority cannot be retained at the top of a complex organization, some must be delegated to lower, more specialized units. With the aim of increased effectiveness, these units specialize further and use the increased delegated authority to respond and adapt to their unique circumstances. However, this can lead to a divergence of interests among specialized units and to the growth and internalization of subgoals. These subgoals are appropriate for the effectiveness of specialists and local units, but conflict with the subgoals of other units and the goals of the organization as a whole.

In general, then, we see that the rational quality of bureaucracy theory encounters problems, not only in failing to account for the changing environment, but also in failing to anticipate the consequences of human behavior in the organization. In attempting to gain control over the organization by using rules, impersonality, categorization, and authority, the controls designed to maintain the subsystem tend to disturb the equilibrium of a larger system (March and Simon, 1958, p. 44). Bureaucracy theory, then, falls short as an explanation of organizations because it fails to consider the unanticipated consequences that can accompany the anticipated outcomes of rational activity.

The rational model views the organization as a mechanical arrangement in which parts may be replaced at will without repercussions on other parts, much as a physical device (Gouldner, 1959). The above examples of dysfunctions indicate the possible advantage of viewing the organization as an organic whole composed of interdependent parts. Each part contributes to the whole, and the whole contributes to the needs of each part.

Bureaucracy and individual freedom

At this point let us return to one of Weber's initial concerns in his study of bureaucracy. To what extent is bureaucracy detrimental to individual freedoms in society? In a study of the internal politics of large-scale organizations, the German sociologist Michels (1915) confirmed the Machiavellian view that those with power will become an elite who dominate and prevent the practice of democracy. From his studies, Michels formulated the "iron law of oligarchy": power inevitably comes to reside in the hands of a few at the top of organizations. Modern large-scale organizations are oligarchic by virtue of their very structure, even when the ideals of the organization are democratic. This phenomenon is evident in his study of the German Socialist party. Despite its ideals, the party retained a facade of democracy only in its official regulations and handbooks. In practice, it was ruled by a small elite. A more recent study of democracy and a two-party political system in a typographer's union (Lipset, Trow, and Coleman, 1956) indicates, however, that oligarchy may not be inevitable.

Obligarchy occurs because true democracy involves direct participation by the governed, which may not be possible when their number is large and when the complexity of problems facing the organization requires extensive knowledge and expertise. The absence of prerequisite knowledge and skills at lower levels in the organization will eventually force decision making to the top.

Furthermore, as the incumbents of top positions gain a near monopoly on power, power itself may corrupt them. Power obtained from hierarchical authority and concentrated at the apex of the organization makes these positions virtually impregnable. The elite can dispense distorted information or withhold information from those at lower levels, as it best serves their own interests. Their overriding interest is to maintain the power they enjoy. Psychologically, the elite may feel that they are indispensable to the organization because of their unique knowledge and experiences. Despite beliefs they may hold about the desirability of democracy, they will find it extremely difficult to relinquish their positions and prerogatives. As a result of these ideas, Michels predicted that the outcome of a Socialist revolution would be a dictatorship. This was several years before the Russian revolution.

At this point it is not clear whether Michels described universal human tendencies to dominate and control resources or merely the properties of a social artifact. Perhaps the iron law of oligarchy should not be viewed as the condemnation of a process that creates elite classes, but as an observation of a simple fact of life: if we are to have complex organizations, we must be willing to live with unequal distributions of power and limitations of freedom in some areas of life. We suggest that the issue may be one of values—our priorities regarding individual freedom in comparison with other values such as affluence.

The human relations movement

Another limitation of the rational view was to emerge in a most curious way. Research on work methods quite naturally led to studies of the work environment. One such study must have led to feelings of consternation, the likes of which few researchers have experienced.

Engineers at the Hawthorne plant, a subsidiary of AT&T, were measuring the effects of lighting intensity on worker productivity. Workers were assembled in a special facility, where illumination could be varied and measured and worker output recorded. A control group was used, as well. Predictably, as illumination was increased, productivity increased. The intensity of lighting then was decreased systematically, with the expectation that productivity would suffer. However, this was not the case. Output continued to increase! It finally fell off when the illumination in the test facility was equivalent to a bright moonlit night. To confuse matters further, the control group's productivity also increased during the experiment, relative to productivity in the plant. The engineers repeated this experiment, twice, with similar results.

To help explain these disconcerting results, scientists working in similar research areas were consulted. Elton Mayo and Fritz Roethlisberger, who previously had investigated the effects of rest periods on worker productivity, were recruited to lead a series of related experiments that were to last for several years (Roethlisberger and Dickson, 1964).

Three major studies were conducted from which much was learned about the behavior and attitudes of people at work. For example, it was found that work groups have their own informal status hierarchies. They sometimes cooperate to restrict production and discipline members who deviate from their norms. These points seem to have eluded organization watchers prior to the Hawthorne studies. The importance of this work should not be underestimated. However, much of what was learned probably was misleading and costly for science as well as for industry, as we shall see.

The most famous of the Hawthorne studies was the relay assembly test room experiment. Five female volunteers, selected on the basis of mutual friendship choices, were assigned to work in a special room where their output and conversations were recorded. Prior to their assignment to the test room, the workers' output had been measured covertly in the plant to obtain baseline data. After their transfer to the experimental room, five weeks were allowed to pass before the experiment was begun. Following this, rest periods of various lengths were introduced, the hours of work were varied, snacks and free lunches were produced, and then all changes were rescinded. The workers were consulted on all changes and were encouraged to work at a comfortable pace.

Regardless of how working conditions were varied, productivity seemed to increase. The explanation was simple. Management had given the women special treatment; it had consulted them and shown consideration for their feelings and interest in their ideas. In other words, the women had been treated as individuals rather than as hired hands. In consequence, their morale increased, which led to improved productivity.

The economist's view—that labor is motivated by wages—gave way to the human relations view. Workers' social and psychological needs, as well as their monetary needs, influence their behavior at work. In the human relations view, satisfaction of these needs, that is, job satisfaction, leads to increased productivity. However, countless research studies conducted over some 40 years since then have failed to demonstrate that more than a few percent of the variance in productivity could be attributed to job satisfaction.

The Hawthorne studies were subjected to a number of criticisms. Some critics suggested that the authors' merely had found another approach to increasing efficiency by manipulating the work force. We feel this criticism has merit, and this is why the human relations school has been included with the rational view of organizations. Other critics objected to the methodological approach taken in the studies. However, 35 years were to pass before the scientific worth of the conclusions was challenged (Carey, 1968).

Hawthorne in a different light

Carey's painstaking analysis of the Hawthorne research casts a different light on the relay assembly test room study. He reports that five weeks after the transfer to the experimental room, an incentive payment scheme was introduced, and work methods were reevaluated using time and motion study. Output increased by 4 to 5 percent. Whether the increase should be attributed to the incentive scheme or to an error in the time and motion study cannot be determined.

Next, rest pauses were introduced and varied, and free lunches were provided. Supervision was friendly, and the women were consulted on menu preferences as well as proposed changes in rest breaks. Throughout this phase of the study, the workers were observed to talk excessively and to pay too little attention to their work. Output did not improve. After numerous warnings from management, two of the "leaders on talking" were removed from the experiment and replaced by substitutes, one of whom was in great need of money and became the group's informal leader and disciplinarian. At this point, output began to increase. However, output was recorded as each worker's maximum productivity in each period, not as her average output for the period.

Replacing subjects whose behavior does not conform to the scientist's predictions and measuring peak rather than average performance clearly are not acceptable practices in a scientific study. Were the researchers dishonest? Why were these grave flaws not seen for 35 years, when they were evident in the original research reports? As we said in the first chapter, honest scientists have believed in false theories and incorrect interpretations of data since ancient times. This is not dishonesty, but the blindness that can accompany conviction. Lay people, too, are susceptible to such blindness. The notion that efficiency can be improved by making workers happy is compelling.[1]

We also suggested that invalid theories can lead to profitable thoughts

---

[1] A later study (Franke and Kaul, 1978), using statistical techniques that were not available to the original researchers, further discredits their conclusions.

and actions. Whether or not they were valid, the Hawthorne studies provided impetus for a new line of scientific inquiry. The informal behavior of workers was studied further. Theories of needs and motivation were tested in the workplace. Techniques such as job enrichment (the attempt to make jobs more esteemable and fulfilling) were proposed, implemented, and evaluated. Sometimes they worked. Sometimes they didn't.

The contingency approach

Eventually, the notion that there is only one best way to plan, organize, and control was abandoned. What seemed to be the best way of doing things in one organization did not work equally well in other organizations. What seemed to apply to one task did not apply to others. The explanation proposed by contingency theorists is that research findings are specific to the setting under study and are not necessarily generalizable to other, dissimilar settings. For example, a theory that applies to routine manufacturing operations may not be applicable to research and development activities and the leadership style found to be effective in R&D labs may not be useful on the battlefield. The best course of action is contingent upon the organization's task and environment.

This view is helpful, as we will demonstrate in the next chapter. It is also an improvement over some of the earlier ideas proposed by organizational theorists. Whether it constitutes a theory or even a departure from the rational view is debatable. First, contingency theory suggests that if we understand the crucial contingencies facing the organization, we should be able to select appropriate research findings (assuming such data are available) to learn how best to proceed. This approach strikes us as being more sophisticated, but philosophically no different than the approaches of Taylor, Fayol, and the others. Second, the contingency view implies that science advances as a result of a continuous process. As new research findings become available, pieces are added to the puzzle, and the solution becomes clearer. This contradicts our understanding of the history of science. In Chapter 1 scientific progress is portrayed as a discontinuous process, in which replacing one paradigm with another constitutes a scientific revolution. If this is so, tomorrow's theories will not arise directly from the contingency approach, but will precipitate from its shortcomings.

Limitations of the rational view

The major limitation of the rational view is that it attempts to understand organizations from a *closed-system* perspective (James Thompson, 1967). Systems are closed when they are isolated from the influences of external variables and when they are deterministic rather than probabilistic. A deterministic system is one in which a specific change in one of the system's variables will produce a particular outcome with certainty. Such systems require, of course, that all the variables are known and controllable (or predictable). If we view an organization in this manner we will agree, as did Fayol, that organizational effectiveness will always prevail if organizational variables are held within known limits; that is, if management follows sets of rules that are assumed to maintain desired relationships among the various parts of the organization.[2]

For reasons to be elaborated below, organizations and, for that matter, all social systems are *open systems*. They are affected by changes in their environments, the so-called external variables. The environment is potentially without bounds and includes many unknown and uncontrollable variables. Rational control, with the selection of the very best means toward the given end, usually is not possible because of the limits of management's knowledge and control.

Second, the outcomes of social systems are probabilistic as opposed to being deterministic (James Thompson, 1967). Human behavior is not altogether predictable. Humans are complex, responding to many variables that are not fully understood, including those pertaining to self-control. Ordering individuals to behave in a particular way or prearranging their relationships with others in the organization by no means ensures that they will act as management desires. By the same token, management cannot assume that customers, suppliers, regulating agencies, and the like will behave predictably either.

However, we shall not abandon completely the rational view in favor of another. Somewhat in keeping with the contingency approach, we suggest that the rational view is an apt, but limited, explanation of organizations. It is not unreasonable to ask if there are optimal solutions to certain kinds of organizational problems.

In one sense, organizations are rational responses to problems. However, the degree of rationality suggested is far from the "preposterously omniscient rationality" ascribed to economic man (Simon, 1976). We intend to behave rationally as managers and workers, but the limitations and problems we encounter leave us short of our intended goal.

THE SOCIAL SYSTEMS VIEW

The departure from closed-system perspectives

As we have already suggested, closed social systems do not exist. However, we need to consider "closed" and "open" as extremes on a continuum

---

[2] The thermostat that regulates a heating system is part of a closed system. Unless the system malfunctions, a particular setting of the device will yield ambient temperatures that remain within known limits. If the temperature of the air circulating through the thermostat falls to the lower limit of this range, we can predict with near certainty that the furnace will be turned on. Furthermore, under normal operating conditions, exogenous variables (variables other than room air temperature) will have no effect on the system.

rather than as mutually exclusive alternatives. In doing so, we will be able to ask whether different parts of an organization ought to be more open or more closed.

James Thompson (1967) suggests that open- and closed-system characteristics tend to vary from one part of an organization to another. This tendency is elaborated in a scheme that divides organizations into three separate levels of responsibility and control: the technical, managerial, and institutional levels (Parsons, 1960). The technical level, which is the lowest in the hierarchy of authority, primarily is concerned with the efficient operation of the organization's technological processes. For example, in a manufacturing firm, those who operate the machines, maintain them, clean the facilities, type reports, schedule work, and their supervisors perform the technical function. An attempt is made at this level to exclude uncertainty and to construct a closed and deterministic system so that efficient production can ensue.

The managerial level is concerned with the administration of the technical level so as to articulate it with the environment, both on the input and output sides. In the manufacturing example, the managerial level comprises those who deal with the procurement of raw materials, the recruitment of personnel, the maintenance of finished goods inventories and their eventual sale, and in general the planning and controlling activities that hold everything together.

Finally, the top, institutional level performs the function of relating the organization to its environment in terms of its right or legitimacy to operate and to acquire the resources that its activities require. At this level, executives will be concerned with changing the company's products in anticipation of forecasted changes in demand, complying with various state and federal regulations, lobbying to influence the nature of future regulations, improving the firm's competitive position in the industry, engaging in public relations activities, and the like. Functioning at this level most resembles an open system.

Parsons' logic suggests that the line of authority, assumed by bureaucratic theory to run from the chief executive to the shop floor, is interrupted where the different levels interface. Furthermore, while the different levels perform dissimilar functions necessary for the system as a whole, they are interdependent as parts of the larger system.

These characteristics predispose the organization to conflict. As Thompson states, "the articulation of levels and of functions rests on two-way interaction, with each side, by withholding its important contribution, in a position to interfere with the function of the other and of the larger organization" (James Thompson, 1967, p. 11). For example, the managerial level may argue for shorter, more flexible production runs that will enable the organization to fill customer orders more quickly. This suggestion may be bitterly opposed by the technical level, since it would decrease the efficiency of the manufacturing process.

FIGURE 2-2
Interruptions in the line of authority assumed by the theory of bureaucracy

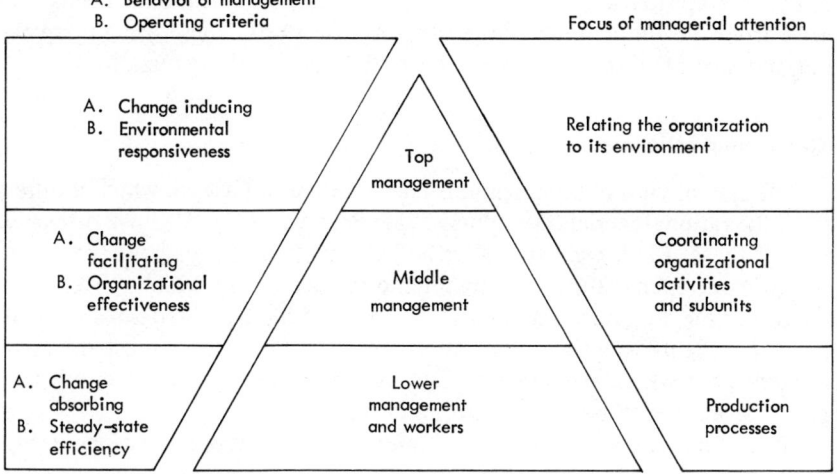

Further exploration strengthens the argument that the bureaucratic model is not a completely valid description of organization functioning. Figure 2-2 illustrates the focus of attention, operating criteria, and generalized behavior that should exist at the three major organizational levels indicated above.

Top levels of management guide the organization to appropriate changes in response to changes in the environment. Top management is change inducing. Accordingly, the criterion against which top management performance is evaluated is responsiveness.

Supervisors, foremen, and workers are engaged in productive processes—the operation and maintenance of what Thompson calls the organization's *technical core*. The criterion of effectiveness for technical and rational systems, as we have said, is efficiency. Since change and uncertainty are detrimental to efficiency, lower level personnel seek to maintain steady-state conditions by resisting or absorbing pressures to deviate from the status quo.

Finally, according to this line of reasoning, the mission of middle levels of management is to coordinate subunits of the organization by mediating between top and lower levels in the hierarchy. These individuals, if they perceive their roles according to this logic, will serve as change facilitators, since organizational effectiveness appears to stem from the coordination of efficiency and responsiveness.

Although this outlook describes a departure from the mechanistic, closed-system perspective, it is still essentially bureaucratic in its assumption that functional subunits can be arranged and coordinated in some rational manner to pursue known objectives. Furthermore, it suggests that the major directions and goals of the organizations flow from the top downward. Finally, this approach offers little analysis of the organizational needs that arise from the functioning of the organization itself. These are among the major concerns of theorists using the system model of organizations.

The system rationale

The system view of organizations has three major bases in which it differs from the rational model (Gouldner, 1959; Perrow, 1972). We have discussed two of these. First, we have described the view that organizations are to some degree open to the environment and to uncertainty, which prevents full control of the "organizational tool." Second, we have pointed out the likelihood that the parts of the organization are often more than a mechanical arrangement in which deliberate changes can be made without affecting other parts, because each is part of an organic whole.

A third major component of the system view is that organizational structures, once created, come to have a life of their own, and behave in unplanned and spontaneous ways. Formal structures, as we saw above in the case of delegation of authority, may lead to pressures for subsystem survival and enhancement, because the very structures that are established to fulfill both membership needs and environmental requirements exert forces in their own right.

The important focus of attention in the system view is not on the deliberately created formal structure but on the actual behavior of individuals and the organization as a whole. Attention, for example, is focused on the fact that subordinates with superior knowledge often make suggestions to their formal superiors that are accepted. The patterning of such behaviors comprises the organizational structure (Katz and Kahn, 1966). The structure of an organization, therefore, is inseparable from the functioning of the organization (Kahn, 1974). Furthermore, because the organization is a structuring of events, as opposed to physical parts, it has no structure apart from its functioning (Katz and Kahn, 1978).

This line of reasoning has a chilling effect on our hopes of understanding organizations by studying their tangible parts—physical apparatus, rule books, and organization charts. It forces us to study intangibles and to ask, What functions must a social system perform to survive? Part of the answer is provided in Figure 2-1. All organizations must acquire *inputs* (such as raw materials and information); *process* these inputs so that their value, however measured, is increased; and dispose of *outputs* (goods and services). Furthermore, if the system is to sustain itself, the disposal of outputs must provide resources sufficient for the renewal of inputs. The obvious example is that income from sales of finished goods is used to purchase raw materials and pay wages. This point is less obvious in other kinds of organizations. For example, we observe that, on average, tuition revenues comprise less than half of the resources needed to operate a private university. Now, the problem is, What is the nature of the university's output, and how does this output influence philanthropic actions upon which the university must rely for some of its resources? We shall return to this problem, but not until we have covered a lot more ground.

A social system that only acquires inputs, processes them, and disposes of outputs will not survive for long. Additional functions must be performed for the system to be viable. The system must *maintain* itself, at least by replacing its worn-out parts. Next, it must be able to *adapt* to crucial changes in its environment. Finally, it must *manage* these functions—control and coordinate them so that each contributes to the ultimate well-being of the system. Any function, if improperly managed, could damage the system. Inadequate maintenance, for example, can have an obvious detrimental effect. Excessive maintenance also can be detrimental if it interferes with other functions or consumes resources needed elsewhere in the system.

Systems and subsystems

When an organization is formed, its mission and the roles of its members are often stated so generally that they are diffuse. As the members gain experience and strive to meet the established criteria, they focus increasingly on specialized tasks. The more specialized the requirements of tasks, the fewer tasks a single individual will be able to undertake successfully. Thus, the organization will become differentiated into subunits, or subsystems, that have specific, as opposed to generalized, functions. This tendency is termed *progressive differentiation.*

The essential functions of a social system that are described above are preformed by specialized, differentiated subsystems of the larger organization (Katz and Kahn, 1978). It is helpful to think of organizational subsystems as analogies to the systems in the human body. The analogy suggests that subsystems are not necessarily organized into single departments or organizational units. Rather, as is the case with the circulatory or nervous systems in the body, they may run through the entire organization. Five of these organizational subsystems can be identified (Katz and Kahn, 1978).

The *production subsystem* essentially is what we have referred to as the organization's technical core. It comprises the part of the organization that converts inputs into desired outputs. In some cases, such as mass production technologies, it may be useful to isolate the production subsystem from the environment (James Thompson, 1967). If this can be done, we can view the subsystem as a closed system. In turn, this will encourage us to seek increased efficiencies by searching for optimal production techniques.

However, the closed-system approach is not always reasonable. For example, research and development labs employ research technologies. Since the work of R&D labs is characterized by uncertainty, we would expect the research technology to operate best in an open system. Therefore, the optimal production technique suggested by the rational view would not apply.

The *support subsystem* links the production subsystem to the organization's environment. It procures an adequate supply of inputs to be processed and disposes of outputs. The purchasing department in a business and the office of student recruitment in a university belong to support subsystems, as do sales offices and student placement services. In addition to conducting specific transactions with the environment, the support subsystem engages in so-called institutional transactions such as maintaining favorable relationships with customers or organizations that employ graduates.

The *maintenance subsystem* keeps the rest of the organization in good working order, so to speak. It provides routine maintenance for equipment, replaces depleted assets with new ones, or procures additional capacity for the organization as it grows. The equipment for getting work done consists of more than machines, however. As Katz and Kahn observe, this equipment often comprises patterned human behavior. Thus, the maintenance subsystem also recruits, indoctrinates, and socializes new employees, and devises ways to promote teamwork and reward desired behaviors.

As we have said, an organization must change to survive over the long run. Such changes are the province of the *adaptive subsystem*. Research and development, market research, and long-range planning are suggestive of the functions performed by this subsystem. However, in observing that organizations adapt to their environments, we should not conclude that they are adaptive in every instance of environmental change. Most large organizations are bureaucracies that sometimes appear inflexible and capable of withstanding the winds of change for long periods of time. Moreover, large organizations often try to change the environment rather than adapt. Advertising, public relations activities, lobbying (and other political activities, both legal and illegal) can be used by large organizations to change the environment. Such activities are also functions of the adaptive subsystem.

Finally, the activities of these subsystems must be directed, controlled, and coordinated. This is the function of the *managerial subsystem*. Almost inevitably, these subsystems will operate somewhat at variance with one another; for example, the production subsystem is constrained by task requirements in meeting its objectives. Task requirements, however, may exclude the very attributes of work that are intrinsically rewarding to the work force, as when mass production techniques preclude the establishment of more satisfying work roles. Here efficiency is gained at the expense of the objectives of the maintenance subsystem—namely, the satisfaction of workers.

The essential function of the managerial subsystem is coordination of other subsystems in situations like those above. However, rather than taking a long-run approach to reducing sources of conflict in the organization, management often travels the easier route of meeting problems on a day-to-day basis, making concessions first to one part of the organization and then to another. For example, a crash advertising program may be initiated to deal with a sales decline, but at some later point, cost considerations may demand a cutback in employees, including those in the advertising section. By attending to problems sequentially (as opposed to anticipating problems and their interrelatedness with other problems), management causes the organization to move somewhat erratically, first in one direction, then in another.

Organizations as subsystems of society

The system view proposed by Katz and Kahn is appropriate to social systems other than formal organizations. Society, for example, is a social system in which organizations perform the functions of subsystems. The production subsystem of society comprises industries that create wealth, manufacture goods, and provide services. These include firms involved in farming and mining, manufacturing and processing, and communications and other services. Maintenance functions socialize and otherwise prepare people for roles in other organizations and in society at large. The function is direct in the case of training centers and universities and restorative in the case of health and welfare organizations. Presumably, support functions are provided by firms engaged in import and export activities, as well as by branches of the government such as the immigration service. Adaptive functions are served by organizations that create knowledge, test theories, and attempt to find novel solutions for existing problems. Included in this category of organizations are those engaged in the arts and sciences. Finally, the managerial subsystem comprises society's political organizations. Management of other subsystems is accomplished through adjudication, coordination, and the control or regulation of people, resources, and other subsystems.

Some consequences of the system view

Potential uses for the rational theories are obvious. Perhaps this is because much of the rational view was developed from attempts to improve the functioning of actual organizations. The system view is more academic in the sense that it tends toward abstract generalizations that apply to all social systems. Thus, its utility is less obvious. Yet, it can be extremely useful. We shall introduce this argument here and support it in the remainder of our text.

A good theory lets us see things that would go unnoticed without the theory to guide our thoughts. Unfortunately, the same theory may blind us to other ways of seeing things. Katz and Kahn (1978) describe a number of blind spots that develop from the closed-system view that are avoided by the open-system perspective. First, closed-system thinking fails to recognize the full extent to which an organization is dependent on inputs from its environment and the degree to which these inputs fluctuate over time. Second, scientific management and bureaucracy increasingly move toward tighter integration, coordination, and organizational stability. These tendencies prevail regardless of environmental conditions that would indicate that increased flexibility is more appropriate. Third, closed-system theories fail to recognize what Katz and Kahn term *equifinality:* the ability to reach a specific outcome through the application of numerous combinations of means. In other words, equifinality states that, for many problems, there are many acceptable solutions, but no optimal solutions. Fourth, the mechanistic views of organizations would lead us to assume that all irregularities in organizational functioning are error variances that should be treated accordingly. Finally, closed-system thinking does not give adequate emphasis to the need to develop environmental surveillance systems that will monitor environmental changes and provide feedback on organizational functioning.

Another generalization from the system view is that you cannot do merely one thing. The different parts of an organization are interrelated, and a change in one part will affect other parts. The system view disposes us to anticipate the unintended consequences of organizational actions.

The concept of system needs illustrates these points. System theorists maintain that organizations react not only to external forces, but to internal stimuli as well. Systems generate their own needs, and some behavior in organizations is directed toward meeting these needs and managing situations in which subsystem needs conflict.

One such system need experienced by the organization as a whole is the need to preserve the character of the system (Katz and Kahn, 1978). The structure of a social organization, as we have indicated, is based on interrelated sets of activities that are cyclical and fairly consistent over time. If these interactions are disrupted severely, the system will become disorganized and cease to exist. Hence, Katz and Kahn observe the organizational tendencies to achieve both *steady state* conditions and *dynamic homeostasis.*

Steady state, in this instance, refers to the preservation of relationships among the system's subunits and maintenance of predictable modes of cooperation within the organization. Dynamic homeostasis denotes the tendency of systems to grow, adapt, and otherwise change while maintaining the steady state characteristics indicated above. The concept of dynamic homeostasis is an analogy drawn from biology, where it is used to describe such processes as those that maintain your internal temperature at 98.6° F as you travel from Florida to Alaska in the winter.

The location of subsystems in the organizational hierarchy

The models presented earlier in the chapter assume that the functions of management are segregated into different organizational levels. Problems of relating the organization with its environment, for example, have been assumed to fall to top levels of management. Using implications of the system approach, we will begin to question this notion.

Katz and Kahn are in agreement with Parsons (1960) when they observe that, since top levels of management tend to deal solely with institutional problems, the traditional concept of unity of the chain of command is rendered invalid. They conclude, as did Parsons, that there are significant breaks in the chain of command at various levels of management.

However, we can argue that the specific functions of various subsystems are performed in numerous levels in the organization's hierarchy, rather than being segregated at one level or another. Responsibilities for productive processes, for example, frequently rest at vice-presidential levels. Similarly, adaptive functions are performed by sales personnel at the bottom of the hierarchy, as well as by top management. We can argue that the subsystems postulated by Katz and Kahn are located vertically in the hierarchy as well as horizontally. Thus, the organization looks more like a marble cake than a layer cake.

Moreover, we can argue that these subsystems consist of interrelated role requirements rather than particular organizational members. This conceptualization permits us to view the supervisor, whose primary formal responsibility is to the productive subsystem, as a member of the maintenance subsystem as well. Much of a supervisor's work consists of dealing with human problems; that is, with maintaining the motivation and satisfaction of subordinates. By the same token, other organizational members perform multiple functions and operate within more than one subsystem.

This line of reasoning causes us to question the notion that institutional problems, which are resolved via strategic planning and policy formulation, are addressed by top management alone. Rather, we agree with Petit (1972) in his observation that strategies are formulated, in part, by pressures from lower levels of management. Petit suggests that the process of strategy formulation is inductive rather than deductive. Lower levels of management persuade executives to adopt policies that are designed to achieve technical rationality or uncertainty avoidance, depending on whether the managers engage primarily in the productive or adaptive subsystems. Executives, in turn, formulate organizational strategies that respond not only to environmental-institutional concerns, but that also seek to balance various policy decisions that have been urged upon them. This line of reasoning is dissimilar to the bureaucratic model and is closer, in theory, to the open-system model of organizations.

Social systems

Our view is that the system model of organizations is somewhat unrealistic, because it leaves out many of the social qualities of individual human beings. The analogy to dynamic homeostasis and progressive differentiation in biological organisms seems somehow inappropriate to development and change in human organizations. What is needed is a *social* systems view of organizations (Buckley, 1967; Silverman, 1970). The rational model does focus attention on the intentions of human beings and their deliberate acts. The system view of organizations may be inadequate in this regard, for in some situations there is freedom for individuals with their own unique combinations of social characteristics to choose to behave in ways that do not meet system needs (or follow rational plans). Individuals and groups will engage in conflict that is best viewed as self-serving. In short, we suggest that a comprehensive view of organizations must take into account the fact that the sometimes conflicting, sometimes congruent, and sometimes unrelated intentions of human actors are important ingredients of organizations. This leads us to focus on a variety of processes, such as conflict, decision making, and planned change, which develop as a result of rational plans, system needs, and individual choices.

A study plan for organizations

In any event, we have come a long way from the earlier, bureaucratic conceptualization of organizations. Some generalizations we have developed are abstract, and the student who has never had an opportunity to view organizations as social entities may be confused. New ideas and new ways of looking at complex social phenomena often are difficult to assimilate. As we go on, we shall clear some of the water we may have inadvertently muddied.

In this overview, we cannot do full justice to all theories of organizations or to their criticisms. However, we hope that our choice of substantive materials throughout the book reflects our view that useful elements exist in both the rational and the system models. Any one approach is insufficient and blinds us to important aspects of organizations. Use of both approaches is better, although not fully adequate to the task either.

In the next chapter, we shall take the perspective of the rational model and focus on formal structures and organizational designs that have been developed by theorists and practitioners who are disposed toward this approach. They provide an identifiable view of the nature of the organization and its components. The reader should be cautioned, however, that the rational approach is prescriptive. It is a view of the organization that may or may not be reflected in actual behavior. We then shall move toward the system perspective and look in turn at the components of structure, technology, and control systems. Here the view of the organization is more nearly descriptive, based on empirical study of actual behavior, which often fails to conform to the intended, rational model prescriptions.

DISCUSSION QUESTIONS

1. Bureaucrats and bureaucracies frequently are held in contempt in our society. Is this prejudice justified? Under what circumstances would you advocate bureaucracy?

2. Is Michels's iron law of oligarchy inevitable? What implication does your answer hold for democracy in organizations?
3. What evidence is there of conflict between the different levels of an organization (institutional, managerial, and technical)? Can you give examples of organizational conflict that you have experienced? How was this conflict resolved?

3

Organizational Structure

INTRODUCTION

We shall continue our study of organizations by elaborating the rational and system views of organizational structure described in Chapter 2. As noted in the discussion of bureaucracy, the structural aspect of organizations is perhaps more readily identifiable than any other. In addition, it is an artifact that has been part of our culture for thousands of years. Consider, for example, the formal organizational structure that is described in the book of Exodus (*The New English Bible,* 1970).[1]

> The next day Moses took his seat to settle disputes among the people, and they were standing round him from morning till evening. When Jethro saw all that he was doing for the people, he said, "What are you doing for all these people? Why do you sit alone with all of them standing round you from morning till evening?" "The people come to me," Moses answered, "to seek God's guidance. Whenever there is a dispute among them, they come to me, and I decide between man and man. I declare the statutes and laws of God." But his father-in-law said to Moses, "This is not the best way to do it. You will only wear yourself out and wear out all the people who are here.

---

[1] *The New English Bible.* © The Delegates of the Oxford University Press and the Syndics of the Cambridge University Press, 1961, 1970. Reprinted by permission. (Exodus 18: 13–27.)

The task is too heavy for you; you cannot do it by yourself. Now listen to me: take my advice, and God be with you. It is for you to be the people's representative before God, and bring their disputes to him. You must instruct them in the statutes and laws, and teach them how they must behave and what they must do. But you must yourself search for capable, God-fearing men among all the people, honest and incorruptible men, and appoint them over the people as officers over units of a thousand, of a hundred, of fifty or of ten. They shall sit as a permanent court for the people; they must refer difficult cases to you but decide simple cases themselves. In this way your burden will be lightened, and they will share it with you. If you do this, God will give you strength, and you will be able to go on. And, moreover, this whole people will here and now regain peace and harmony." Moses listened to his father-in-law and did all he had suggested. He chose capable men from all Israel and appointed them leaders of the people, officers over units of a thousand, of a hundred, of fifty or of ten. They sat as a permanent court, bringing the difficult cases to Moses but deciding simple cases themselves. Moses sent his father-in-law on his way, and he went back to his own country.

Chapter guide

Similar to the bureaucratic model of organizations discussed in the last chapter, the structure proposed by Jethro implies a direct line of authority from Moses down to the rank and file. This relationship is depicted by the organization chart in Figure 3-1.

1. Why did Jethro suggest that Rulers of Fifties have a span of control of five while Rulers of Hundreds and Rulers of Tens were provided spans of two and ten, respectively?
2. What direct authority did Jethro have over the Rulers of Thousands?
3. What differences are there between the position of Jethro and Solomon? Why are these differences deemed to be appropriate?
4. In Chapter 2, we defined structure as patterns of interactions (Katz and Kahn, 1978). Here we use the term differently. Which use of the term is more efficacious in studying organizations? Why?
5. Would it be possible for a Ruler of Hundreds to have more power in Moses' organization than a Ruler of Thousands?

A REVIEW OF THE CLASSIC CONCEPTS OF STRUCTURE

Structure

Students who have read the classic management theorists will be familiar with the description of formal organizational structure that follows. In fact, so will students who have worked in organizations that became aware of

FIGURE 3-1
Exodus reorganized

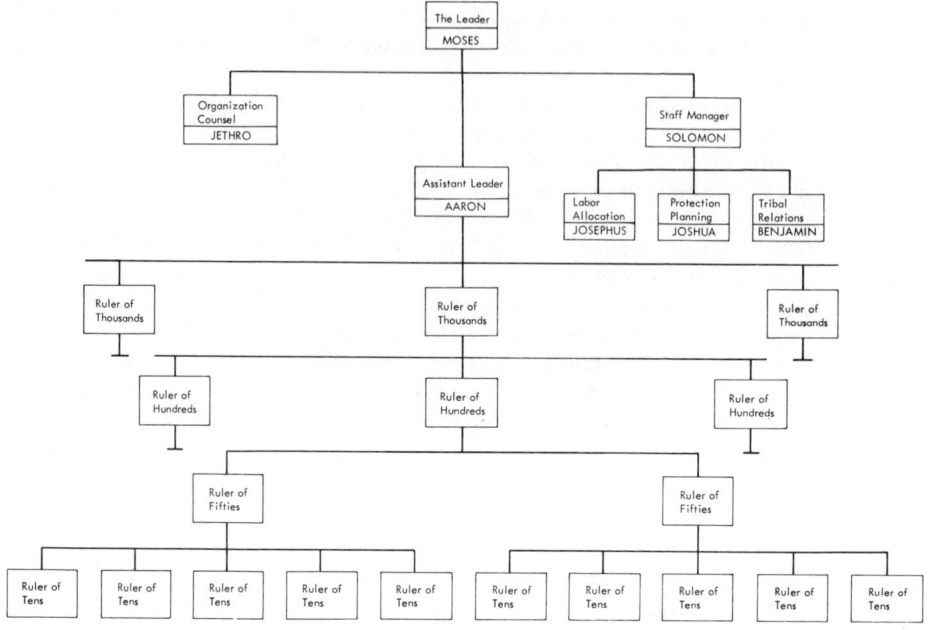

Source: Reprinted by permission of the publisher from *Organization* by Ernest Dale © 1967 by American Management Association, Inc.

their structure through major growth, reorganization, merger, or similar problems. Formal organizational structure generally is the aspect of the organization that management seeks to change to alter its functioning. Attempts to change personality variables, such as attitudes and motives, are less frequent because they require greater degrees of skill, time, and effort. Technology and goal changes are even less frequent, since major alterations of either may change the organization drastically and render it almost a new organization.

Vertical differentiation by authority

Organizational structure may be defined as the network of relationships that exist among various positions (and position holders). Formal structure is a pattern of relationships that has been consciously planned and implemented. For our present purposes formal structure is defined to include the formal hierarchy of authority, as well as rules, formal procedures, and other planned attempts to regulate behavior. Key executives typically decide on basic patterns of structure that, in their opinion, will be most appropriate for themselves, their work, and company goals.

The most common organizational structure is hierarchical, consisting of a vertical dimension of differentiated levels of authority and responsibility and a horizontal dimension of differentiated units, such as departments or divisions. This is the pyramid-shaped organization frequently depicted on organization charts. At the apex of the pyramid are the chief executive officer and perhaps an executive vice president or general manager. At the next level are senior executives, frequently called vice presidents. Below top management are middle managers, generally department or division heads or branch managers. At lower levels of middle management are factory superintendents, branch sales managers, and the like. Supervisory management, composed of various supervisors and section heads, is found below middle management. Individuals whose positions in the hierarchy fall below supervisory management are, of course, not members of management.

Horizontal differentiation by specialization

The horizontal dimension of the formal organization is not diffentiated by degrees of authority, but rather by what is termed *departmentalization*. Employees are organized into groups according to criteria that allow and encourage specialization. According to this reasoning, the organization will be more effective if people with similar abilities and skills work together on specialized tasks, than if all workers are generalists and perform exactly the same set of work—a little bit of everything.

In a very small organization, the top manager may perform all major functions (for example, purchasing, personnel activities, accounting, and supervision of production). As the organization grows, however, the manager will find that time is too limited to deal with the magnitude of problems that have assumed increasing degrees of complexity and that one or more of these functions demands skills and knowledge that the manager does not possess. At this point the manager will most likely create a position for a subordinate manager who specializes in one or more of these areas. In time the manager will organize operations around these subordinates and the functions that they oversee.

Growth is not the sole impetus toward horizontal differentiation. Environmental change can place demands on an organization that its existing personnel are ill equipped to meet. For instance, the advent of the union movement created the need for departments specializing in industrial relations. Similarly, technical innovations require the development of specialized subunits. Scientific management gave rise to departments of industrial engineering, and computer technology spawned today's data processing divisions.

Departmentalization by function, process, location, and product

Departmentalization in organizations takes four major forms: by function, by location, by process, and by product. These four means of departmentalization (or horizontal differentiation) usually are applied in combinations. In fact, some firms are organized according to all of them simultaneously.

Departmentalization by function. In a manufacturing firm, necessary functions include production, finance, sales, personnel, research and development, and purchasing. As we have said, each function will become organized as a department as the organization grows in complexity. For example, the public relations function may be performed by sales representatives through their contacts with the environment, as well as by top managers who give speeches to service clubs and perform related activities. However, if the firm becomes large and complex enough or if special problems arise in the environment, these public relations activities will need both coordination and emphasis. These needs, in turn, provide the rationale for the creation of a separate public relations department.

Departmentalization by process. Departmentalization by process refers to the structuring of an organization according to technological or work processes. A firm that is departmentalized by process may have shipping and receiving departments, a foundry department, a milling department, a machining department, an inspection department, and so on.

Departmentalization by location. Organizational structures can be segregated by territories, districts, regions, and countries. Where locations make a difference (where demands for services, products, and product characteristics vary, for instance, or where labor, energy, or raw materials supplies differ), a rationale exists for departmentalization on this basis. Sears, Roebuck has eastern, mid-western, western, and southern sales divisions each with its own somewhat different purchasing decisions. A large electrical utility with generating facilities in several cities departmentalizes accordingly. Multinational firms often divisionalize by location so that divisions operate in relatively homogeneous taxation, legal, or consumer environments.

Departmentalization by product. Finally, departmentalization by product or product-market is characteristic of organizations that produce a variety of products and sell in different markets. General Motors, of course, is a prime example. Chevrolet cars are produced and marketed in a division that is separate from the divisions producing Pontiacs and Cadillacs. Other examples include firms that segregate divisions working for the government from those serving civilian markets. Presumably, meeting contract specifications, as opposed to consumer expectations, generates dissimilar managerial problems, which justify organizing by product. Similarly, the quality of products manufactured or sold may serve to differentiate the organization. This is true for General Motors, as well as for department stores with bargain basements offering less expensive and lower quality products than are found in the main part of the store.

Span of control

Next to departmentalization, span of control probably is the most important concept in understanding both horizontal and vertical differentiation. As we have said, the term refers to the number of subordinates a manager supervises. Earlier theorists attempted to define the absolute limits of span of control (for example, five to eight subordinates). Subsequently, of course, these limits were found to be unrealistic. The number of individuals that a manager can supervise depends on the complexity of the tasks performed by subordinates, the amount of subordinate-superior interaction required by the task, the abilities of both the subordinates and their manager, and other factors (Barkdull, 1963; Udell, 1967).

The average size of the span of control influences the overall shape of an organization. A large number of employees supervised by a single manager reduces the number of hierarchical levels in the organization below the number of levels found in an organization employing the same number of individuals but having a smaller average span of control. If we draw organization charts for these two firms, we will find that the pyramid shape of the organization with a large average span will appear rather flat, while that of the organization with the smaller span of control will appear relatively tall.

Department-store organizations with tall pyramidal shapes were compared with flat pyramid-shaped department-store organizations in an investigation of the effects of different-sized spans of control (Worthy, 1950). The morale of personnel and the effectiveness of the tall stores seemed poorer than those of the flat stores. In the simple, flat organization, the individual supervisor is free from close control because of the large span and is free to develop initiative and self-reliance. We should take care in generalizing from this study, however, because we shall see in Chapter 4 that the nature of the technology and the task put constraints on structure, including the span of control. Furthermore, studies similar to Worthy's have produced mixed results (Ivancevich and Donnelly, 1975).

Line and staff relationships

Let us return to the basic elements of structure and examine the concepts of line and staff. Line refers to the basic hierarchical person-boss relationship, the line of authority or chain of command that extends from the top to the bottom of an organization.

Because special areas of competence are required in modern organizations, the line must be augmented with staff departments. Whereas "line executives are those who contribute directly to profits, either by producing the product or service or selling it, . . . [T]he staff executives are those who facilitate the work of the line, performing services for it, providing it with advice and information, and auditing its performance in various respects" (Dale, 1967, p. 61).

Large organizations may use a *functional staff arrangement;* for example, when a corporation decentralizes, it may experience difficulties relating staff functions at the home office to the branches and divisions in the field. Locating executives in charge of staff functions at corporate headquarters, while assigning their subordinates to the decentralized units, might remedy this problem; for example, the vice president in charge of personnel might headquarter at the home office while those below the vice president head up personnel departments in the firm's branches. In this form of organization, the general managers of the branches exercise autonomous control over the personnel departments in their branches, subject, of course, to corporate policy and guidance by the vice president for personnel at corporate headquarters. In general, the greater the need for specialized knowledge across the entire organization, the higher the staff unit will be positioned.

In practice, a whole range of authority relationships may be found between a staff specialist and members of the line who are at the same or lower levels. Hellriegel and Slocum (1974) observe at least four types of authority relationships ranging from purely advisory to command authority.

1. "Staff Advice" is purely advisory. The managers may approach the personnel department for help in recruiting a new subordinate, or they may do the recruiting themselves.
2. A "Compulsory Advice" relationship entails a requirement that managers seek advice. However, they are not required to follow the recommendations given. For example, managers may be required to have all prospective secretarial employees complete a typing test administered by the personnel department. However, they need not follow the advice that a particular typing speed is a prerequisite to employment.
3. A "Concurring Authority" relationship requires agreement by both the line manager and the staff specialist that a particular action be taken. Both must agree, for example, that a particular cutoff point on typing speed plus a minimum educational level are essential prerequisites to employment. If agreement cannot be reached on criteria for selecting prospective employees, the decision is moved to a higher level in the organization.
4. Finally, a "Limited Company Authority" relationship entails line authority by the staff unit over a particular delimited area of line functioning. In hiring practices, for example, the personnel department may be granted authority to decree unilaterally the required typing speed, and the line manager must conform to this rule, regardless of compensating or extraordinary factors.

Some organizations depend so much on knowledge and expertise that the staff professionals play dominant roles in the organization. In professional organizations such as hospitals and universities, the professionals (physicians or professors) do the primary work of the organization and have both authority and responsibility for it. They are, as it were, the line. The administrators in hospitals and universities support and assist the professionals, providing facilities, resources, and personnel that enable the professionals to get on with their work. The professionals have general authority over work with their clients, and the administrators have limited staff authority over such matters as selection of clients and purchasing procedures.

THE RATIONAL VIEW OF STRUCTURE

Developing structures

The classic concepts of structure provide a language we can use in thinking about certain aspects of organizations. Unfortunately, these concepts do not tell us how organizations *should* be structured. Moreover, although an organization chart together with rule books and procedures manuals can tell us something about how management intended the organization to operate, whether or not the organization actually behaves as intended is quite another matter—a problem the classic concepts do not address adequately. More important, we need to ask whether the organization depicted on the organization chart functions more effectively than would alternative organizational arrangements. Here, again, we are at a loss for an answer. One approach to answering these questions is to determine the attributes of different structures. Once these attributes have been identified, we can ask what effect a particular attribute has on the organization's functioning. Depending on the nature of the organization's environment, one kind of organizational behavior will be preferable to another, and one type of structure will appear more appropriate than the others.

Outcomes for the organization

All goal- and efficiency-seeking (purposive) organizations theoretically attempt to maximize the return on resources employed over the long run (Ansoff and Brandenburg, 1971). In doing so, the hospital, business firm, or university will enhance its legitimacy in the environment and its claim to resources needed for continued functioning. For example, long-run maximization of return on investment will enhance the business firm's position in negotiating financing arrangements with a lending institution, and excellence, however measured, will provide a competitive advantage for the hospital in obtaining referrals, funds, and personnel.

Yet, this outcome, maximizing return on resources, is too abstract for the purpose at hand. For this reason, Ansoff and Brandenburg postulate a set of near-term objectives that eventually lead to the desired outcome, if pursued successfully. These objectives are (1) maximizing near-term performance, (2) achieving long-term growth, which will develop a posture for successful long-term performance, and (3) protecting the organization from catastrophic risks. These objectives can be met in any number of ways. Furthermore, the most appropriate way of meeting these objectives is determined in part by the organization's environment.

Ansoff and Brandenburg propose a set of organizational performance measures that are process oriented rather than outcome oriented. These performance measures (called *process criteria*) are used to assess organizational behaviors that, in turn, are means to the objectives enumerated above. Performance according to appropriate process criteria is taken as an indication that the organization is (or has been in the recent past) functioning in such a way that it is likely to meet its objectives and eventually maximize the return on resources employed (see Figure 3–2).

Process criteria

The process criteria fall into four general categories: (1) *steady-state efficiency,* (2) *operating responsiveness,* (3) *strategic responsiveness,* and (4) *structural responsiveness.* Each different organizational structure to be studied performs better according to some criteria than to others. The problem of adapting the organization to its environment will cause management's emphasis on certain criteria to be more appropriate than its emphasis on others, depending on the nature of the organization's environment.

FIGURE 3–2
Process criteria, objectives, and outcome

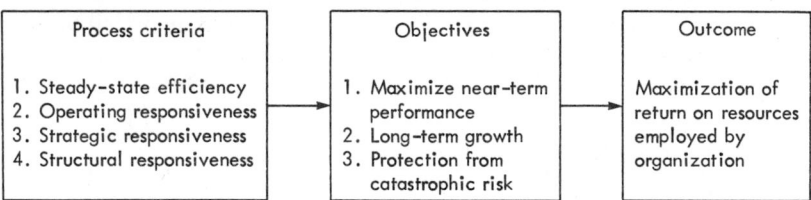

Steady state efficiency. Imagine a firm that produces goods or services that do not change appreciably for long periods of time. These goods or services are sold in markets where demand is constant. The firm in question is in a position to meet its objectives by pursuing steady state efficiency. Maximum steady state efficiency is realized when the unit cost of output is minimized for a constant level of output. To achieve such efficiency, management may employ techniques that establish optimal order quantities and production runs, economies of scale, economies of skills and overheads (*synergy* in the terminology of Ansoff and Brandenburg), and the like.

Operating responsiveness. Operating responsiveness refers to the organization's ability to make quick and efficient changes in its level of output. Instead of emphasizing the ability to handle a specific level of output efficiently, this criterion emphasizes the ability to change levels of production to respond appropriately to variations in levels of demand and competitive activity. Operating responsiveness is measured by standby capacity and information processing capacity—in other words, by the ability to balance inventories and product availability at market locations. Obviously, the costs of maintaining a given level of operating responsiveness—the costs of excess capacity—are borne at the expense of steady state efficiency.

Strategic responsiveness. The third major criterion is strategic responsiveness which measures the organization's ability to respond to changes in the nature, not the volume, of demand. Obsolescence of products, innovations in product technology, changes in markets, and alterations of the legal and social constraints under which the organization operates often require changes in the nature of what is produced. Strategic responsiveness depends on the organization's ability to maintain surveillance of its environment and to act on the intelligence obtained. In maintaining the ability to respond quickly to environmental changes, the organization behaves in ways that are antithetical to the maximization of steady state efficiency. We will return to this dilemma later in the chapter.

Structural responsiveness. If an organization experiences difficulty in attaining steady state efficiency, operating responsiveness, or strategic responsiveness, then a fourth criterion will become relevant, namely, structural responsiveness. Structural responsiveness refers to the organization's abilities to design new organizational structures and to implement them. Structural responsiveness becomes especially vital in an environment that is characterized by rapid technological innovation. As we have said, technology and structure are interdependent, and the nature of their interaction determines organizational effectiveness to a large extent.

Assumptions about human resources

As the appropriate process criteria are met by an organization's structure, the potential efficiency of the organization, according to Ansoff and Brandenburg, will near optimum. In recognizing that human variables are not directly included in any of the criteria, the authors assume that the necessary individual talents are available to the organization, that individuals will accept the positions assigned to them, and that these individuals will be motivated to exercise their talents in the positions assigned. Similarly, we assume that necessary financial and physical resources are available to the organization.

At this point we must ask whether the assumptions concerning human resources are tenable, for there is considerable evidence to the contrary. Reasonable organizational structures are not always accepted by managers. Furthermore, similar organizations are not always equally effective. Then, some organizations with structures that do not seem adequate—that are judged inappropriate by experts—are quite effective.

I. Fundamental design concepts

Apparently the human element makes a difference in cases such as these, and a motivated work force can overcome or compensate for suboptimal structure just as dissident or alienated members can thwart the objectives of even the most skillful designer. However, it will be useful to assume with Ansoff and Brandenburg that the organization's members will behave as they are "supposed to" to limit our attention to the present approach to designing formal structures. We shall consider the human element more carefully in the next section of this chapter.

Additional assumptions

Ansoff and Brandenburg add to these categories of organizational performance criteria a set of criteria that, they argue, are independent of the particular objectives of an organization. For example, they see the quality of decisions and information as critical to organizational effectiveness regardless of the specific objectives pursued. Under this general category we also find criteria such as the timeliness of information, the availability of relevant information, the absence of irrelevant information, the rapidity with which decisions can be made, and the compatibility of authority and accountability.

STRUCTURE AND PROCESS CRITERIA

Having developed four categories of process criteria, Ansoff and Brandenburg illustrate how contemporary structures vary in their ability to satisfy each of the criteria. In the following discussion, note the organizational forms illustrated are not necessarily mutually exclusive. In fact, we frequently find organizations using a combination of two or more structural forms.

The centralized functional form

The centralized functional form of organization gained widespread application throughout American industry during the 1920s and is still widely used both in this country and abroad, especially in smaller firms. This form primarily consists of departmentalization by function. Activities such as marketing, manufacturing, and research and development are grouped under functional executives who report to a central headquarters (Figure 3–3). This structure is effective in terms of steady state efficiency. Grouping individuals by similar functions allows for economies of scale and economies of overheads and skills. Relatively high operating responsiveness also characterizes this form because of its simple communication and decision-

**FIGURE 3-3
The centralized functional form of organization**

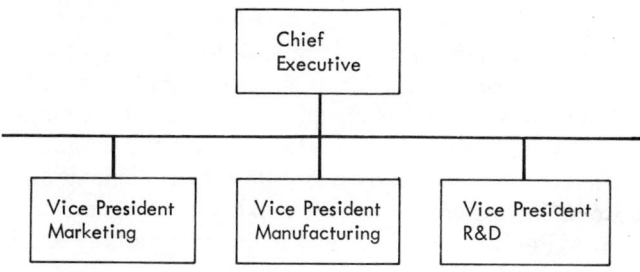

making networks. However, beyond certain limits, increases in the organization's size, number of products or services offered, or number of product-markets served will render the organization relatively ineffective in terms of this criterion.

The centralized functional form seems to result in relatively low strategic and structural responsiveness. The same individuals in top management who are concerned with operating decisions are also responsible for administrative and strategic problems. Since administrative and operating problems frequently are more pressing and visible, strategic problems are likely to suffer from neglect. Strategic responsiveness is also relatively poor because of difficulties in integrating the efforts of dissimilar functions, such as research and development and manufacturing. Again, operating decisions will take precedence over strategic decisions. Finally, and most important, when strategic responsiveness entails adding products or markets, this form of organization may suffer from information overload. For example, there is a limit to the number of decisions a single department can make concerning different products or markets.

The decentralized divisional form

As increases in the size and complexity of centralized functional organizations caused corresponding decreases in operating responsiveness, Du Pont and General Motors pioneered a second, widely used structure in the 1920s (Chandler, 1962; Sloan, 1964). Both firms, having grown quite large with expanded product lines, began to experience difficulty making decisions for numerous different products. In the case of each product, relevant decisions required different information and decision criteria. In switching from one product to another, managers became confused, or at least inefficient. Other firms abandoned the functional form for a variety of reasons, such as difficulties in developing general managers, overemphasis on vertical communications at the expense of horizontal communications between departments needed for coordination, fragmentation of planning and control processes according to the different functions, and encouragement of conflict among functions (Carlisle, 1969). Since World War II, the decentralized divisional form has emerged as perhaps the most widely used structure for large, complex firms.

The decentralized divisional form consists of organizational units (usually called divisions) that address a specific product-market under the direction of a manager who has complete strategic and operating decision-making authority (Figure 3–4). Thus, for a given product-market, the division is able to achieve both steady state efficiency and operating responsiveness because, *within the division,* a functional type of organization similar to that shown in Figure 3–3 exists, although some staff functions may be lodged at corporate headquarters.

FIGURE 3–4
The decentralized divisional form of organization

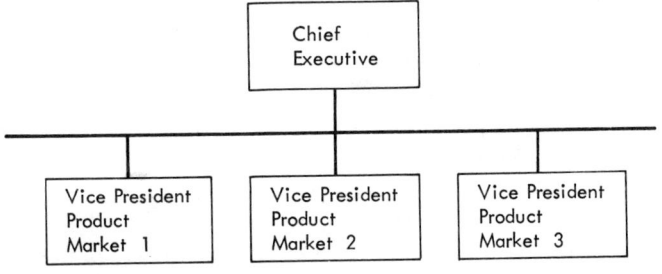

Ansoff and Brandenburg reason that strategic and structural responsiveness can be attained more readily in the decentralized divisional structure than in the centralized functional form in organizations of similar size. Though this appears true in principle, in fact managers in charge of specific product-markets tend to be overburdened, and their strategic responsiveness in expanding their product-market may not be very effective. Strategic responsiveness is further reduced by an inherent characteristic of the structure that compels division managers to compete for limited resources, such as research and development, in a centralized location.

At the corporate level, reduction in top management work load as a consequence of this structure may allow executives to pay greater attention to strategic decisions, as well as to problems relating to overall structure. However, in practice, corporate managements often fail to take advantage of such opportunities. Problems of strategy, being extremely difficult, are driven out of the decision-making process by more immediate, routine, and programmable problems, *unless* management somehow creates special organizational structures for the innovative activities that strategy formulation requires. This generalization suggests that the decentralized divisional form offers only limited improvement over the centralized functional structure.

While operating responsiveness is added to steady state efficiency, improvements in strategic and structural responsiveness are limited.

Before moving to the next type of structure, we should mention a fairly common variant of the decentralized divisional form, one based on geographic area. Large organizations serving major geographic areas frequently decentralize by geographic subdivisions to achieve improved operating responsiveness. Within each geographic unit, one typically finds organization by product-market, and by function within product-market; for example, the large multinational corporations often have separate companies or subsidiaries for different countries, provided the scale of operations is sufficiently large.

Adaptive structures

A third basic organizational structure evolved after World War II in response to increasing needs for structural responsiveness. Organizations, such as firms in the electronics industry, experienced rapid changes in technology, consumer and client demands, and potential demands for innovations in products and services. To exist successfully in such environments, these organizations needed greater degrees of strategic and structural responsiveness. The project management structure is reasonably well suited to meet these requirements. The Manhattan project to develop and produce the atomic bomb demonstrated the effectiveness of project management structure in meeting national needs during World War II. The Department of Defense subsequently required its contractors to use this structural arrangement in the 1950s when strenuous efforts were made to close the missile gap (Carlisle, 1969).

Much of the organizational structure in project management is flexible. The permanent parts of the organization include the corporate office and, below this, certain functional units such as manufacturing, finance, sales, and accounting (see Figure 3–5). The flexible portion of the organization consists of project units that are charged with specific objectives and are disbanded once these objectives have been met. Various members of the organization normally are assigned to the permanent functional areas indicated above, but are reassigned to project teams as the need arises.

For example, a project team may be established to develop a product. The team will continue to operate until divested of its mission by the organization, when members will return to their permanent functional areas. A second team may be charged with developing the organization's long-range strategic plans. Typically, the project group will submit its work to corporate officers for a decision and possible implementation and then disband. Group members then return to their functional divisions until the next planning cycle is begun. These people may play a major role in promoting acceptance of the plan in the organization. According to Cleland (1964), "The project manager acts as a focal point for the concentration of attention on the major

FIGURE 3–5
Project management: An adaptive form of organization

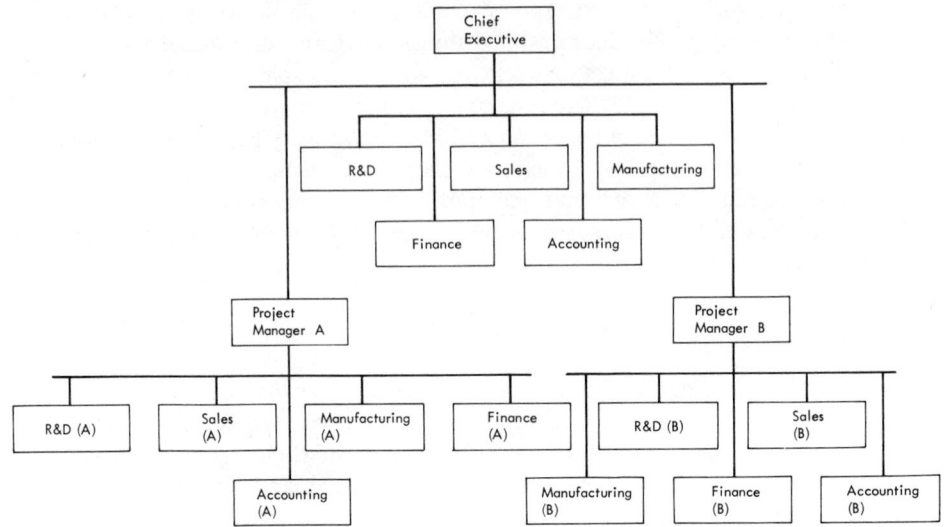

problems of the project. This concentration forces the channeling of major program considerations through an individual who has the proper perspective to integrate relative matters of cost, time, technology, and total product compatibility" (p. 83).

Project teams can be organized in numerous ways. Members of a single functional area may work on some projects, while specialists from diverse functional areas are required for others. Furthermore, at different phases of the project's development, different kinds of arrangements can be introduced.

Matrix organization is a second major class of adaptive structure. This form typically organizes personnel by their functions. For example, an accounting unit may be established as the organizational home for all accountants; an engineering unit may organize the activities of engineering personnel, and so on. As projects are identified and project teams organized to respond to project requirements, specialists from the functional units will be reassigned to these teams when appropriate. These individuals are subject to the authority of both their functional managers and project managers. As was the case with project management, project groups stemming from a matrix organization pursue specific objectives and are disbanded once these objectives have been met. While a traditional hierarchy of formal authority is maintained within project organizations, since project team members are subordinate to their project leader, superior-subordinate relations are less well defined in matrix organizations. Individuals may be responsible to more than one superior, belong to more than one project, or be shifted from

FIGURE 3-6
Matrix organization for project management

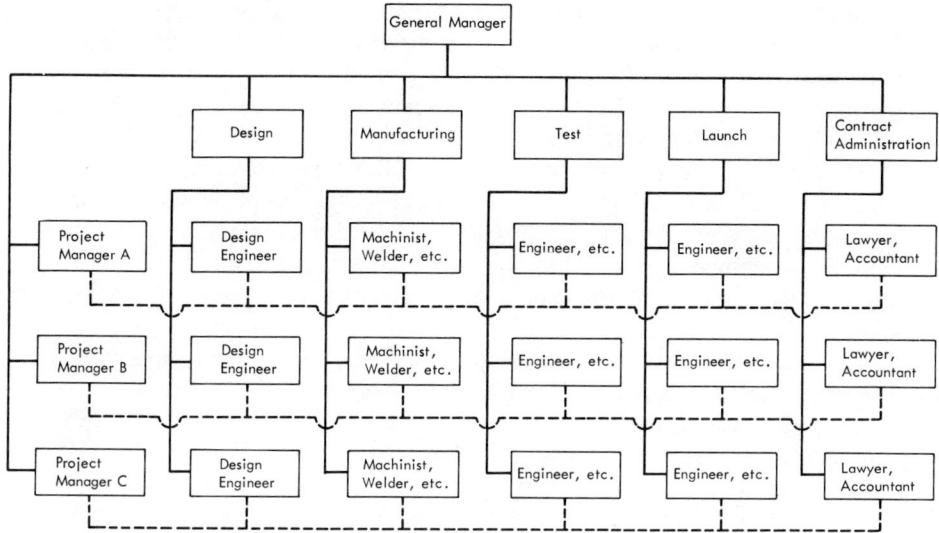

Source: Steiner and Ryan (1968). © Macmillan Publishing Co., Inc. All rights reserved.

one project to another as needed. Furthermore, while the permanent portion of a project organization may be engaged in the pursuit of long-range objectives, matrix organizations may pursue no objectives other than those assigned to ad hoc groups.

In general, having the concern of managers focused on specific tasks improves operating responsiveness and creates a vehicle for the implementation of strategic decisions. Strategic responsiveness is also improved by the matrix organization's ability to create planning groups as the need arises and to decrease the work load of top management by having project teams assume some of the more routine responsibilities of these executives. The predefined cutoff points of projects also facilitate strategic responsiveness.

However, Ansoff and Brandenburg raise two major reservations concerning the limitations of adaptive structures. First, steady state efficiency tends to be poor in adaptive organizations because these structures allow only minimal economies of scale and restrict synergy in the functional competence groups. Each project group tends to duplicate the capacities of the others. The second major disadvantage arises from the need to transfer resources among project groups as projects are created and terminated. If the major resource employed by an organization is the intellectual capacity of its staff, as is the case, for example, in certain research-oriented institutions, then use of an adaptive design is clearly feasible. However, the design will not prove as advantageous in other areas of endeavor such as heavy manufacturing.

An example of the usefulness of matrix organizations is found in the data processing industry. A company that sells or leases computer systems usually markets its services, rather than hardware and programs as such. Thus, each sales presentation must be somewhat tailored for each prospective customer. Typically, experienced personnel from systems design and forms design units will be assigned to a team that includes the sales representative and perhaps one or two trainees. The team will design a package of hardware and software uniquely suited to the prospective customer's needs and may aid the sales representative in making the sales presentation. Similar temporary groups are organized to troubleshoot system problems for present customers and to design new applications for existing computer installations. In each case, the team is disbanded once its objectives have been met.

The firm in question deals with a variety of organizations employing a variety of technologies in different parts of the economy. Opportunities for sales presentations, problems in existing accounts, and requests for help in designing new uses for existing systems arise at random. Each occasion demands the services of a variety of different experts. Most tasks are relatively short-lived. The matrix organization provides the flexibility needed to respond appropriately to this variety of problem situations. However, responsiveness is gained at the expense of steady state efficiency.

The innovative organization

Ansoff and Brandenburg define innovation to include both creativity and its implementation. As we have seen, the preceding adaptive structures may excel at creativity, but may not fare as well at implementation—particularly when implementation requires some degree of steady state efficiency. The *innovative structure* is proposed as an organizational form that is effective in both creativity and implementation—in meeting to some degree all four of the major performance criteria discussed above. Drawing from both the adaptive and decentralized divisional (or centralized functional) forms, this hybrid structure incorporates both strategic and structural responsiveness through the former form and steady state efficiency and operating responsiveness through the latter.

The innovative organization consists of a current business group and an innovative group (see Figure 3–7). The innovative group, organized along the lines of adaptive design principles, emphasizes strategic and structural responsiveness, which are deemed essential to innovation.

Once the innovative group has demonstrated the feasibility of a project, the project is transferred to the current business group, which has a more stable structure.

Organized according to either the decentralized divisional or centralized functional form, the current business group is generally effective in terms of steady state efficiency and operating responsiveness. In other words, this hy-

FIGURE 3-7
The innovative organization

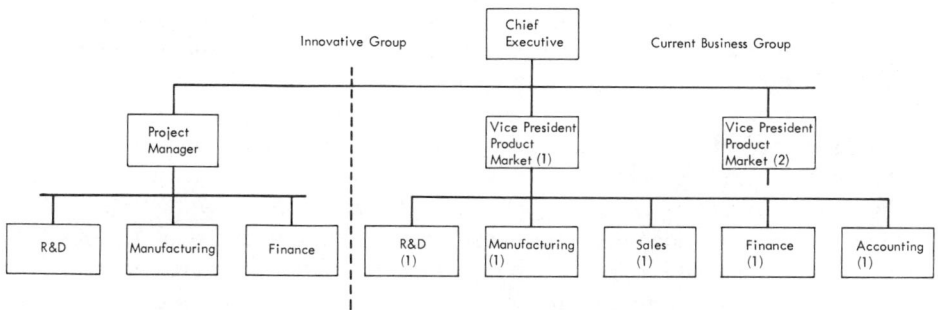

brid structure seeks to obtain the advantages of the strong points of the adaptive and more traditional forms. According to a number of observers, the adaptive and innovative designs will receive increasing attention in the coming years (Davis and Lawrence, 1977).

Further considerations for the design of structure

Although we have found a rationale for designing formal organizational structures that is more useful than the classic principles of management, we are still faced with a number of serious concerns and unanswered questions. First, the approach of Ansoff and Brandenburg, whatever its merits, is based on logic and experience, not on empirical data. Although we shall turn to more systematic research as we proceed with our study, we will neither confirm nor reject their ideas on the basis of available research data. Still, these ideas are useful.

Second, if more than one type of structure is to be used in an organization, as in the case of the innovative structure, how are the dissimilar structures to be integrated so that they function in concert?

Finally, we have assumed that members of the organization will behave as they are supposed to. As we know, this is not always the case. We have left out the distinctly human needs described by Katz and Kahn, and others. At one extreme, Richetto (1970) tells us that "satisfied pyramid dwellers" do exist and that the new adaptive structures can cause them considerable anxiety because of the ambiguity these structures foster. At the other extreme, the severe morale problems that arise in bureaucracies have been reported widely in academic publications and the popular press. In any event, the interdependence of structures and people cannot be ignored. This is the problem we shall turn to next.

Some behavioral consequences of formal structure

By the mid-1960s, the popular and academic presses were awash in articles predicting the demise of bureaucratic organizational structures. The bases of such arguments were that (1) bureaucracies are too inflexible to meet the demands of a rapidly changing environment, and (2) such organizations restrict employee behavior to an intolerable degree. The second argument is of interest at this point for it underlies the development of radically different approaches to organizational structure.

A number of interesting and perhaps valid theories of motivation are based on the notion that people need to realize their full, unique potentialities, just as they need food or love. Moreover, while biological growth ends in the individual's early 20s, psychological growth can continue throughout one's lifetime, provided the environment fosters such growth. Assuming this to be true, one would conclude that mature, self-realizing adults require jobs that are esteemable and fulfilling, as mentioned in Chapter 1. Furthermore, one would ask, What happens when these adults find themselves in jobs that prohibit growth and self-realization? A number of theories have been proposed to answer this question. One of the better known theories illustrates the general line of reasoning.

People are born with predispositions toward psychological as well as biological growth. The infant's state of dependency gives way in childhood to the adult's predisposition toward independence. In the same manner, other infantile characteristics yield to predispositions toward competence, patience, superordinancy, and a potentially long attention span (Argyris, 1957).

Unfortunately, the adult who is predisposed to develop along these dimensions often winds up in a job that restricts further development. At worst, a job may require childlike rather than adult characteristics. This is thought to occur when the degree of formal structure is high. When we think of structure as rules and procedures, as well as the hierarchy of authority, we will expect structure to be greatest at the lowest levels of the organization.

The assembly line provides a graphic but extreme illustration of this point. The procedures employed by assembly-line workers often are prescribed by management. Few of the workers' abilities are used. Tasks are of limited duration. Far from being independent, these workers are subordinate to the organization's technology. They are directed and controlled by supervision and management.

According to Argyris, placing adults in jobs that limit their development produces feelings of severe frustration and anxiety. In attempting to deal with these feelings, the individual can resort to three basic strategies: (1) seek advancement, (2) quit, or (3) engage in defensive behavior. At first glance, advancing within the organization appears a viable remedy for the situation described. As one moves upward in the hierarchy of traditional organizations, practices of directive leadership, task specialization, and unilateral control diminish. Furthermore, seeking better, more satisfying work is consistent with American, middle-class norms. Unfortunately, the practice of hiring college-educated supervisory personnel conspires against individuals seeking to rise from the shop floor if their education ended with high school. Furthermore, the span of control employed by most organizations limits the number of job opportunities available at successively higher levels. For many individuals, then, escape through career advancement from restrictive jobs, such as those on assembly lines, is an empty dream.

The second alternative is quitting. However, given the education and experience of those about whom Argyris writes, it is unlikely that changing employers will result in better jobs. In addition, the longer an employee remains in an organization, the greater will be the cost of quitting. Seniority rights, company pensions, and the like may be lost in changes of employment and, consequently, serve to decrease the likelihood that an individual will change jobs. According to Argyris, the final and most frequently chosen alternative is to cope with feelings of frustration and anxiety through the use of defense mechanisms.

Defensive behavior

All normal people engage in appropriate defensive behavior. People who smoke in the face of the Surgeon General's warning probably deny that *their* use of tobacco constitutes a danger to *their* health. Denial is a form of defensive behavior. We cannot hope to respond directly or effectively to all of the real and imagined physical and psychological threats that life places in our way. If we are to travel by air, we must deny the possibility that our flight will be terminated by disaster. To do otherwise would pave the way for an incapacitating fear of flying. Other defense mechanisms include projection, the tendency to attribute one's own feelings to another; displacement, the shifting of behavior from one object to another (as is the case when individuals who are angry with the boss vent their rage on subordinates); and regression, the tendency to engage in behavior that was effective as a child, but is inappropriate for an adult (as happens when men and women have tantrums or crying fits in the face of frustration).

As we have said, defensive behavior is both helpful and normal. However, a distinction needs to be made between the individuals who can be comfortable while in flight by denying the possibility of disaster and individuals who take things out on innocent bystanders or who react to difficulty with childishness. Healthy people have a repertoire of defense mechanisms from which they draw subconsciously and apply in ways that foster adult behavior. Less healthy are individuals whose defensive behavior impedes their effectiveness in life or those who have learned to meet all contingencies with a limited number of defenses.[2]

Argyris contends that defensive behavior caused by certain work environments, together with apathy toward work that these defenses ulti-

---

[2] For a more complete description of defense mechanisms, see Sarnoff (1962).

mately produce, result in consequences such as goldbricking, restricting output, cheating, and slowing down. Furthermore, employees who engage in these practices form groups that sanction them, and eventually internalize such practices as work norms. As these norms become established, they are likely to gain recognition in the larger organization. Such norms have been termed *psychological work contracts* between supervisors and subordinates. A typical contract may take the form of a mutual understanding that, in return for adequate (but not outstanding) productivity and minimal dysfunctional behavior, the supervisor will stay off everyone's back, that is, interact as little as necessary with subordinates so as not to encroach on their apathy and desires to be uninvolved in their work.

While this definition of a fair day's work for a fair day's pay may prove

FIGURE 3-8
Growth-delimiting organizations

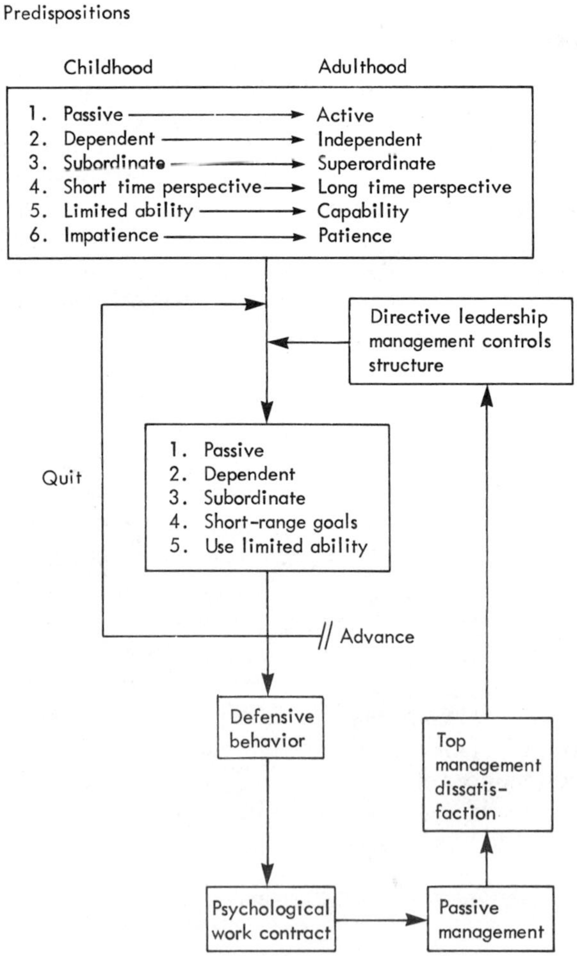

Predispositions

	Childhood	Adulthood
1.	Passive	Active
2.	Dependent	Independent
3.	Subordinate	Superordinate
4.	Short time perspective	Long time perspective
5.	Limited ability	Capability
6.	Impatience	Patience

Directive leadership management controls structure

1. Passive
2. Dependent
3. Subordinate
4. Short-range goals
5. Use limited ability

Quit

Advance

Defensive behavior

Psychological work contract → Passive management → Top management dissatisfaction mutually satisfactory for workers and their supervisor, it is liable to contradict management's expectations of the work force. Managers may diagnose such undesirable behaviors as failings of their employees rather than as inevitable outgrowths of the work environment created by management. This being the case, remedies for the shortcomings of lower level personnel may take the form of increased directive leadership, more stringent management controls, and other activities that, according to Argyris, originally caused the problems for which remedies were sought. Thus, the behavioral system described is self-reinforcing (Figure 3–8).

PARTICIPATION AND STRUCTURE

The way out of this vicious cycle, according to some theorists, is through employee participation. By allowing employees to decide matters directly affecting their work, management will encourage them to develop according to their adult predispositions. To engender effective participation, an organization's structure must create three essential conditions: (1) supportive relationships, (2) group decision making and group methods of supervision, and (3) high-performance goals for the organization (Likert, 1961).

Supportive relationships are created when interactions with both peers and superiors maintain the employee's feelings of importance and worth. Such interactions will be cooperative rather than competitive; employees will help one another in achieving their objectives. Supervisors will demonstrate confidence and trust in subordinates and will help workers reach their goals. Employees will be informed about matters affecting their jobs, and their ideas will be solicited and used when appropriate.

If these kinds of relationships are established, the organization will benefit from having mobilized both the economic and noneconomic motives of its members. Furthermore, Likert suggests, the organization will benefit from the ensuing cooperative action focused on achieving the organization's goals.

Group decision making and group methods of supervision

The organizational structure proposed by Likert is designed to enhance work group involvement in decision making and supervision. In contrast to typical bureaucratic structures that emphasize the authority of superiors over subordinates, the participative organization stresses cooperative groups that include supervisors and their subordinates as members. Subordinates also may belong to a second group comprised of employees at the next level down in the organization. Thus, the organization consists of overlapping groups with managers at every level, except the very highest and very lowest, who serve as linking pins between two groups (Figure 3–9).

FIGURE 3-9
The linking pin function

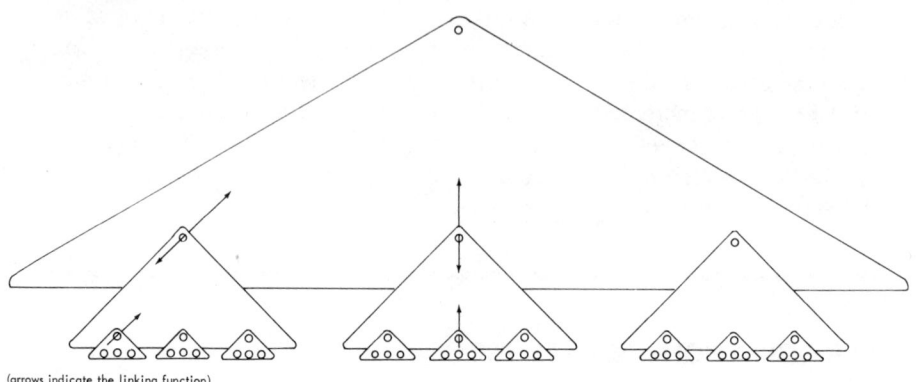

(arrows indicate the linking function)

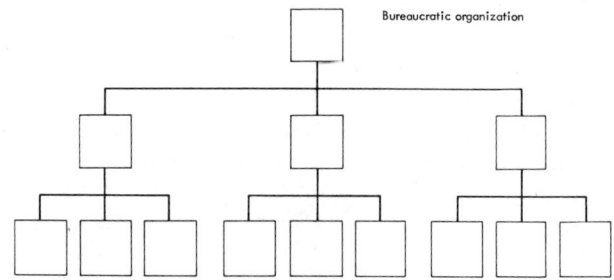

Source: From *New Patterns of Management* by Rensis Likert. Copyright 1961, McGraw-Hill Company. Used with permission of McGraw-Hill Book Company.

All members of a work group who are affected by the outcome of a decision are involved in making and implementing the decision. The superior's role in the group is to coordinate decisions with actions taken at the next level in the organization, the level at which the superior is a subordinate in a similar group. This coordinating, or linking pin, function of the leader serves to inform other group members about organizational matters that affect them and, in turn, to integrate the decisions of various groups. Beyond this, each group leader's responsibility is to help group members identify problems, decide on appropriate courses of action, and, most important, manage their efforts as a group.

High-performance goals for the organization

The third essential condition for the participative organization requires that both superiors and subordinates have high aspirations for the organization's performance. For the organization to function effectively, these aspirations must be goals of the groups who make decisions and manage their implementation. The combination of the first condition, which emphasizes support for individuals and their needs, and the second condition, which involves management by overlapping groups of individuals, provides the means by which the needs and desires of individuals can be met through the achievement of high-performance goals.

An example of the participative structure

Likert illustrates how each of the three essential conditions contributes to the successful functioning of the participative organization. Data from a large sales organization, in which 20 high-producing offices were compared with 20 low-producing offices, showed that when sales managers stressed high-performance goals and exhibited supportive behavior, the sales office invariably performed well. High-performance goals, unaccompanied by supportive behavior, were not effective, nor was supportive behavior without high-performance goals.

Further examination showed that the high-performing sales offices invariably used the group method of supervision. Although the sales personnel in question operated within the same sales district and competed with one another for sales and commissions, they still found the group method useful and, in fact, produced more than sales representatives in other offices who merely competed against one another. An example of the group method is the meetings in which sales representatives described their selling activities so they could be analyzed by their manager and peers.

High-performing sales offices conducted group meetings regularly. Usually the offices were fairly small, consisting of no more than 12 to 15 employees. Typically, sales representatives, in turn, reported in detail their activities since the previous meeting, describing the number and kinds of prospects obtained, calls made, kind of sales presentations used, the closing attempted and their results, the number of sales made, and the volume and quality of the total sales. The other people in the group would then analyze the salesperson's efforts, methods, and results, and from their experience offer suggestions for improving performance. After the analysis by the group, each sales representative, with the group's advice and assistance, proceeded to establish performance goals for the following period. These goals included both the procedures and the results to be realized before the next group meeting.

The manager or supervisor also attended the group meetings and served as the chairperson, whose major role was that of a constructive problem solver. The manager saw that the group supported its members and set high-performance goals that served to achieve both individual and organization aspirations.

As the result of the meeting, sales representatives felt a commitment to the group and to the manager to achieve the goals, which they in concert with the group set for themselves. The aspirations established in the meetings were often reinforced between meetings; sales representatives frequently reminded one another of the goals and commitments to which the group was dedicated. Similarly, salespeople continued coaching one another between meetings; they availed themselves of the technical knowledge and skills of both their colleagues and superiors. From an organizational standpoint, the result was a climate in which important skills and resources could be shared, regardless of the individual's position in the firm's hierarchy.

The manager of an effective group must do more than just act supportively during group meetings. The manager must see that all group members are as well trained in group decision-making and group interaction processes as they are in the technical aspects of their work. Both in group meetings and in day-to-day interaction, the manager must help individuals maintain and realize the goals that they have set for themselves. In this sense, managers are more than just group members; they are responsible for organizing groups effectively and for assuring that planning, scheduling, and related activities support both organizational objectives and individual goals. And, of special importance, through membership in the group at the next higher level in the hierarchy, the manager links this sales unit to the rest of the enterprise.

Mutual influence systems

At this point let us examine the influence relationships in Likert's participative organizations. Likert found that managers who use supportive relationships and group methods of decision making possess more influence in their units than managers who fail to mobilize group resources. Moreover, the subordinates in these organizations enjoy a greater degree of influence than do their counterparts in organizations where the system of management is less participative. At first glance this appears to be an anomaly. We might expect that group participation in management vests influence in subordinates at the expense of the influence possessed by superiors. Apparently this is not the case; people at both levels of the organization experience more influence under participative management than they do under alternative styles of management.

Influence graph

Arnold Tannenbaum (1968) and his associates at the University of Michigan provide us with research findings that greatly extend our understanding of influence processes within organizations. Their research indicates relationship between the nature of the influence process and the organization's effectiveness. Tannenbaum uses a graph to illustrate the influence process (Figure 3-10). The horizontal axis of the graph represents the organization's hierarchy of authority with the president or top manager at one end, rank-

FIGURE 3-10
Influence graph

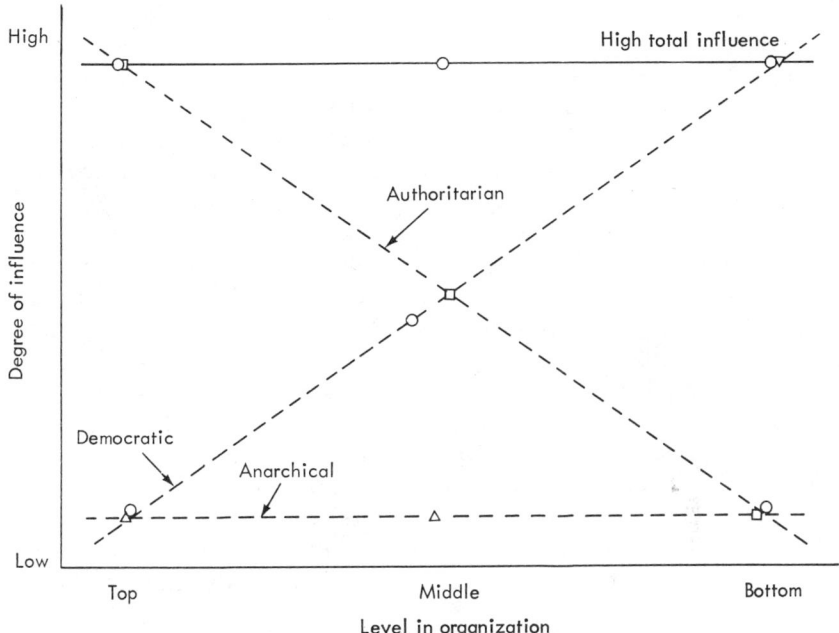

Source: Adapted from *Control in Organizations* by A. Tannenbaum. Copyright 1968, McGraw-Hill Book Company. Used with permission of McGraw-Hill Book Company.

and-file members at the other, and middle managers and supervisors in between. The vertical axis indicates the amount of actual, effective influence that individuals at various hierarchical levels exercise. By plotting the degree of influence exercised at each level of the organization on the graph, a curve, which succinctly illustrates influence relationships within an organization, can be constructed. Such curves as this can be used to compare influence relationships in different organizations, and in a single organization at different points in time.

In practice, four different classes of curves can be identified. If top, middle, and lower management plus rank-and-file members all report they have little influence in the organization, the resulting curve has a relatively flat slope and is situated fairly low with respect to the vertical axis. Adding the degrees of influence reported by each level of the hierarchy indicates that the total amount of influence wielded within the organization is relatively low. Such an organization can be described as somewhat *anarchistic* in that individuals, regardless of their position in the organization, have relatively little influence over what others in the organization are doing.

A more common situation is one in which upper levels of management wield considerable influence, middle levels exercise moderate influence, and lower management and the rank and file, respectively, possess lesser degrees of control. This situation describes an *authoritarian* organization; the degree of influence enjoyed is proportional to the individual's status in the organizational hierarchy.

The opposite condition, in which influence is inversely related to position in the hierarchy, also exists, though much less frequently. One survey of local units of the League of Women Voters, a voluntary organization, indicated that in some units, members were able to exercise more influence than the officers. This relationship might be *democratic,* although the term is used here to describe a rather unusual form of democracy.

Adding the degree of influence exercised at each level of the organization, one finds that the total influence in both autocratic and democratic institutions is only moderate. This finding contrasts with the total influence found in organizations in which individuals at all levels report that they have a high degree of influence over what happens within the organization. When an influence graph for this kind of organization is constructed, the resulting curve is nearly parallel to the horizontal axis and relatively high on the vertical axis. The influence graph for an organization with *high total influence,* in fact, is very similar to the curve for a cohesive group. In cohesive groups and in Likert's participative organizations, leaders and group members alike report that they have a high degree of influence over what happens in the group.

Identifying participative organizations

How does the participative structure fare according to Ansoff and Brandenburg's process criteria? Other than speculate, we can do little else to find an answer. A major obstacle to direct comparison of this structure with those discussed previously is that we have altered our definition of structure. Rather than the classic definition of structure as hierarchy plus rules and procedures, we have switched to Katz and Kahn's definition of structure as a pattern of interactions.

Thus, Likert's approach to structure is to categorize organizations according to the types of interactions they employ. The interactions, or performance characteristics, selected for study are listed in Table 3–1.

TABLE 3–1
Organizational and performance characteristics of different management systems

1. Leadership processes used.
2. Character of motivational forces.
3. Character of communication processes.
4. Character of interaction-influence processes.
5. Character of decision-making processes.
6. Character of goal-setting or ordering processes.
7. Character of control processes.

FIGURE 3-11
Sample questionnaire item

| Extent to which superiors have confidence and trust in subordinates | Have no confidence and trust in subordinates | Have condescending confidence and trust, such as masters have to servants | Have substantial but not complete confidence and trust; still wish to keep control of decisions | Have complete confidence and trust in all matters |

Source: Likert (1967).

A questionnaire comprising 51 items was devised to measure the seven performance characteristics listed in Table 3-1. Each questionnaire item asks respondents to rate their organization on a continuum that measures a dimension of the performance characteristic in question. The left-hand side of each continuum suggests an authoritative approach to management, while its right-hand side suggest a more participative approach. Figure 3-11 shows a sample questionnaire item that is intended to measure one dimension of the leadership processes used in the organization.

Next, each continuum is partitioned into four intervals, each of which suggests a different style of management interaction with subordinates. Responses on all 51 items thus provide a profile of the organization's management style. Profiles that tend toward the right-hand side of the continuum indicate the participative form of organization Likert advocates, which he calls a *System Four organization* (see Figure 3-12).

Attributes of participative organizations

Studies of many different kinds of organizations—ranging from labor unions, to industrial services firms, to industrial products firms, to sales organizations, to voluntary organizations such as the League of Women Voters,—show that organizations with high total influence are more effective in achieving their goals, whatever they may be, than are organizations with lower total influence (Tannenbaum, 1968). Local Leagues of Women Voters, for example, in which both leaders and members report that they have a great deal of influence over what happens are leagues that raise relatively more from their community, have larger proportions of the commu-

FIGURE 3-12
Likert's systems of management

| Exploitative authoritative | Benevolent authoritative | Consultative | Participative group |
| (System One) | (System Two) | (System Three) | (System Four) |

Source: Likert (1967). Copyright © McGraw-Hill Book Company. Used with permission of McGraw-Hill Book Company.

nity as members, and have larger and more active programs than do leagues with lower total influence (Tannenbaum and Kahn, 1958). Labor unions with high total influence are more effective in keeping management responsive to union-related issues than are labor unions that possess lower levels of total influence (Tannenbaum, 1961).

However, studies such as these may overstate the case somewhat. Showing that participative structures are associated with organizational effectiveness is not the same as providing evidence that the former caused the latter. The famous studies at the Harwood Manufacturing Company provide a case in point.

These experiments took place when the Harwood Manufacturing Company, the leading firm in the pajama industry, purchased the Weldon Company, which was second in volume in the industry. The president of the Harwood company is a psychologist who had long practiced the principles of human relations.

As measured by the current research, the management system in Harwood was generally System Three and System Four, that is, consultative or participative management. This was not true for Weldon, which was closer to Systems One and Two, exploitative authoritative or benevolent authoritative management. Weldon Company operations also had been unprofitable for several years, while Harwood had managed to show a profit during the same period.

Although Harwood personnel replaced the corporate management of the Weldon Company, the plant manager and supervisory staff in the Weldon plant were retained. A training program for managers and supervisors was begun to emphasize the principles and skills required by a system of management that approached System Four. The plant manager was helped to use this system and to encourage his subordinate managers and supervisors to do the same. All of these changes were initiated and supported by the company's new top management.

Measurements by the Michigan researchers showed that there were marked changes in the management system year by year after Weldon's acquisition by Harwood. While the improvement did not reach the System Four level of functioning found in Harwood, Weldon did move to a System Three and a Half kind of management. As Likert expected, performance and productivity subsequently improved. The average earnings of piece-rate workers increased by nearly 30 percent in the absence of a change in the basic wage structure. At the same time, total manufacturing costs decreased by about 20 percent. Employee turnover dropped to half of its former level. Length of employee training was reduced substantially. Employees expressed more friendly attitudes toward the company, and finally the organization began to show a profit. Return on investment changed from −17 percent to +15 percent and was still improving at the time of Likert's writing. A full report on how System Four was established at Weldon is found in a book called *Management by Participation* written by the president of the firm, Alfred J. Marrow, and two of the Michigan researchers, David Bowers and Stanley Seashore (1967).

Much to our dismay, these authors may have missed a major point of their study. In accounting for the benefits of participative management, Marrow, Bowers, and Seashore (1967) mention only in passing that many of these improvements may have resulted from the implementation of traditional management practices. When the change in ownership took place, a new plant layout was devised, and new equipment was installed. Control and record-keeping procedures were improved. Industrial engineers began to retrain workers, much as Taylor would have advocated. Workers who, after training, could not produce up to standard were weeded out. Thus, the effect of System Four management is anything but clear. The improvements noted by the researchers might be attributed just as easily to the introduction of changes consistent with the ideas of scientific management.

A comparative study of participative structures

The term *participation* has not been used with much precision so far. What does it mean to encourage work group decision making and management? Do we mean that workers merely have a voice in determining methods and schedules of work, or do we mean that the rank and file will elect plant management and decide major policy issues? Clearly, the latter degree of participation is not likely to be found in business organizations in the United States. Yet, if we are to identify the attributes of participative organizational structures, it will be desirable to study a sample of organizations that range from authoritarian bureaucracies to worker-managed collectives.

Tannenbaum and his associates (1974) studied organizations in five countries having different political and economic ideologies. Firms were studied in five industries: plastics, foundry, canning, metalwork, and furniture.

The ideological differences among the countries in which this study was conducted are dramatic. These differences are reflected in their respective economic systems, as well as in the structures of individual organizations in each economy. In one of the countries, Yugoslavia, economic units are owned by society, not by the state or by individuals. The workers' collective, aided by smaller, elected groups, enables all workers to participate directly and indirectly in major decisions facing the unit. Workers elect managers and supervisors, and they also approve strategic choices such as decisions regarding product changes and major opportunities for investment, divestment, and merger. The managers, who are elected for four-year terms, lack direct formal authority over others. They are responsible for organizing and coordinating the activities of the unit. However, these managers are able to wield considerable influence by virtue of their experience and their ability to set agendas.

The Kibbutzim in Israel were studied as a second, but dissimilar, class of highly participative organizations. The Kibbutz is owned by its members, who control all major activities through the general assembly. Plant managers, as well as various plant committees, are elected and serve for two to three years. Approximately half of the workers gain management experience at one time or another. (It should be noted that many Kibbutzim are agricultural and lack manufacturing facilities.)

Other than petty cash allowances, Kibbutz members receive no wages for their work. Meals are eaten in a communal dining area, and supplies are drawn from stores as needed.

Decision making in the plant takes various forms, depending on the nature of the decision in question. Investment and development plans are proposed by plant management, but subject to the approval of the general assembly that includes all Kibbutz members. Production plans and schedules are proposed by management, but decided by the workers' assembly in the plant. Technical and professional problems are decided by plant management. Thus, the extent of participation varies from full participation to representation, depending on the issue at hand. In general, the structure ensures that the more important the problem, the more direct will be membership participation.

In contrast to the Israeli and Yugoslavian plants, the organizations studied in Austria, Italy, and the United States are bureaucratic. Major policy and strategy decisions are the prerogatives of top management. Subordinate managers and workers are selected by those above them in the hierarchy. Ownership varies from individuals, who may or may not be managers, to shareholders, who occasionally may be employees. While participation is limited in all three countries, it was probably greatest in the American firms and least in the Italian firms.

Measuring differences in structure

Members of each organization studied were asked to describe their organization using Likert's (1967) methodology (see Figure 3–11). The average organizational profiles developed for each country bear out our expectations. A profile of the average extent of participation, which is based on six questionnaire items, is presented in Figure 3–13.

When small plants are considered, the Kibbutzim seem to come closest to Likert's view of System Four management, followed by the Yugoslavian plants. Italian plants seem to be the most autocratic of the group. Similar differences appear in the findings for large plants, although comparisons with Israeli plants cannot be made. There are no large plants in the Kibbutzim.

While these findings do not show one kind of structure to be superior to the others, they do suggest an interesting point: apparently, viable organizations can be formed using a variety of quite dissimilar structures. The question of which form is superior is problematic. What criterion determines superiority? A number of possible criteria come to mind, and we shall look at structure in terms of several of these.

Ideal and actual degrees of participation

If we agree with Likert and Tannenbaum that workers want and benefit from participation, we still are entitled to ask, But how much participation? The present study suggests an answer that may come as a surprise. Respondents were asked to answer a second set of questions similar to those on which Figure 3–13 is based. The second set asked how much participation should there be ideally, rather than how much there is actually. Figure 3–14 indicates the discrepancies between the ideal and actual for items 3, 4, and 6 in Figure 3–13.

FIGURE 3–13
A profile of participation in plant management in five countries

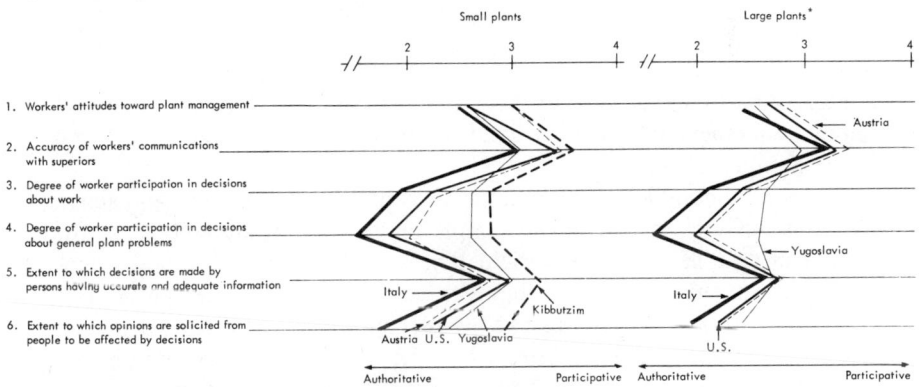

* Large plants are not found in Israeli Kibbutzim.
Source: Adapted from Tannenbaum et al. (1974, p. 52).

Two notable points emerge from Figure 3–14. First, although the actual degrees of participation reported for the Israeli and U.S. organizations differ considerably, the discrepancies between the actual and ideal are quite small in both instances. One explanation of this finding is suggested by differences in the political ideologies of the organizations' members. Participation implies equality. However, equality is valued differently in capitalistic and socialistic thought. Americans value *equality of opportunity*. Although society's rewards are unequally distributed, Americans are unlikely to complain as long as they believe that the opportunity to achieve these rewards is available to all. Socialistic thought emphasizes *equality of outcome*, not opportunity. Society's rewards should be distributed equally. Thus, Tannenbaum's findings suggest that inequality in organizations is acceptable to

FIGURE 3-14
Discrepancies between ideal and actual participation in organizations

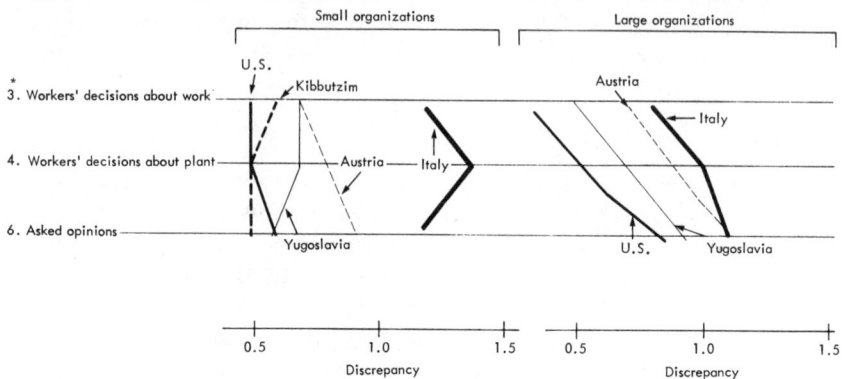

* Item numbers correspond to item numbers in Figure 3-13.
Source: Tannenbaum et al. (1974, p. 56).

American participants who see themselves as potentially upwardly mobile. Kibbutz members, on the other hand, value the equality of outcome found in the Kibbutz.

The second notable point is that the discrepancy between ideal and actual participation was greater in the sample of Italian employees than in the American sample, although participation was relatively low in both countries. We can suggest two possible reasons for this difference. The Italian work force probably encompasses a broader spectrum of political ideologies than is found in the United States. Thus, the emphasis on participation and equality of outcome would vary among Marxists, socialists, and capitalists. The discrepancy could be explained as a function of the larger proportion of communists and socialists in the Italian work force. The second possible explanation for the discrepancy is that the Italian work force is less upwardly mobile than its American counterpart. This is indicated, for example, by the finding that 59 percent of American respondents in large organizations reported that good work would lead to better opportunities for advancement, while only 28 percent of the Italians gave this response (Tannenbaum et al., 1974, p. 66). To the Italian worker, organizations may encompass inequality of both outcome and opportunity.

Influence and structure

An influence graph, similar to the one discussed earlier in this chapter, was developed for the organizations in the five countries. As illustrated in Figure 3-15, the curves for the Israeli and Yugoslavian organizations are flatter than similar curves for firms in the three capitalistic countries. This much was expected. However, contrary to the theoretical influence graphs depicted in Figure 3–10, the flatter curves do not suggest greater total influence than some of the steeper curves. Taken at face value, the curves suggest that total influence is higher in U.S. firms, both large and small, than in either Yugoslavian or Israeli organizations. Possible measurement problems aside, this may reflect the relatively high degree of *informal participation* that typifies many U.S. firms.

In any event, we are now in a position to define broadly some different attributes of bureaucratic and participative structures. Tannenbaum and his associates were unable to demonstrate that one type of structure produced a better return on resources than the others. The economic conditions facing the organizations in the five countries differed, as presumably did the kinds of technologies employed, training of managers and workers, and quality of raw materials. If these varied, differences in steady state efficiency, for example, could not be attributed merely to differences in structure. Thus, we do not have evidence that participative structures are more efficient than authoritative structures. Arguments to the contrary probably are more philosophical than scientific.

However, formal organizations produce more than goods and services; they actualize to some degree the values of their host culture. All other things being equal, we should prefer participation in organizations to the

FIGURE 3–15
Influence graphs for plants in five countries

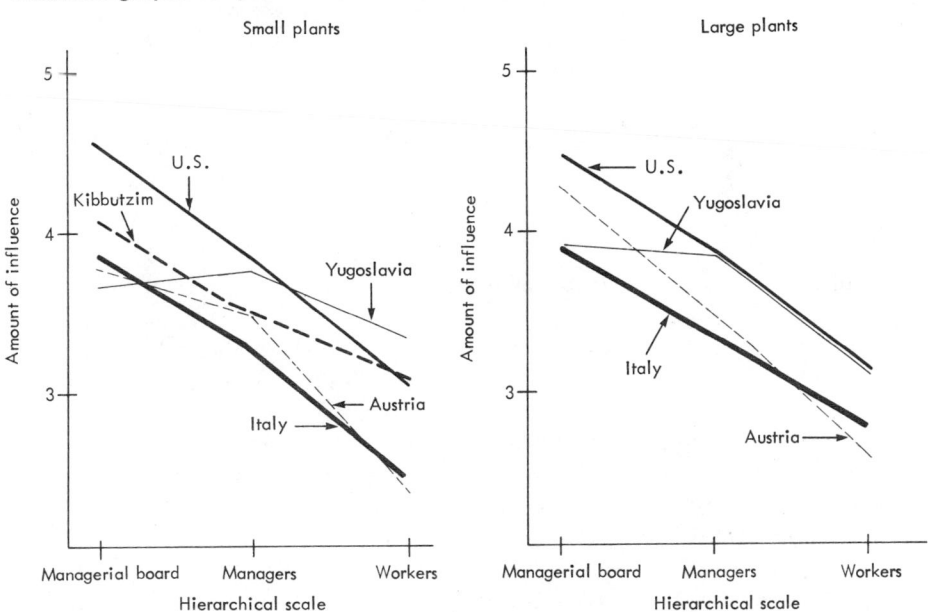

Source: Adapted from Tannenbaum et al. (1974, p. 59).

extent that we value egalitarianism and equality of outcome. Unfortunately, all other things are not equal. We cannot say with certainty that full participation is as efficiently productive as more authoritative forms of structure in all cases, or vice versa. Thus, we are left still wondering whether equality of outcome in organizational life is preferable to the efficiency that might be gained in a more bureaucratic organization. As you can see, the one-best-way approach of the rational theories leaves much to be desired.

A SYSTEM VIEW OF STRUCTURE

Beyond the rational view

With one exception, the approaches to formulating structure presented thus far presuppose that a single form of structure, such as bureaucracy, matrix structure, or System Four organization, is appropriate for an entire organization. The exception is provided by Ansoff and Brandenburg, who argue that an adaptive structure can be grafted to a bureaucracy that performs routine operations. Presumably, the task of innovation is carried out in a different environment (that is, task environment) than is the more routine task of production. Consequently, subunits performing in different task environments require different structures to function effectively.

This raises several major questions. Are there more than two subunits in an organization, and do they operate in dissimilar task environments? Review of the work of Katz and Kahn encourages us to answer each question affirmatively, although somewhat tentatively. These answers lead to still another question, for the implication is that a single organization may employ a number of dissimilar structures. How are units with different task environments and dissimilar structures to be coordinated in the service of some overriding organizational goal?

Subunit differentiation

Progressive differentiation was mentioned in the previous chapter as a characteristic of open systems. We shall now take a closer look at the process of differentiation in organizations by starting with a hypothetical example.

Imagine that a number of us have set out to invent an holographic camera for amateur photographers. Although a good deal has been written about lasers, holography, optics, and photography, we do not know how to build an inexpensive, pocket-sized camera that will produce clear, aesthetically pleasing three-dimensional images. Much will depend on the research we perform and its results. Some of our work will be trial and error, and often we will be guided by insights, intuition, and hunches. In brief, our task environment will be characterized by a high degree of uncertainty. Our planning horizon will be quite long; we know that our task may take years, if it can be accomplished at all. Prescribed work methods, schedules, procedures, and the like have little meaning in this context. How can we plan and schedule problem-solving activities when we are not sure how the problem can be solved? A formal hierarchy of authority will serve little purpose in this context either. Authority will rest with those of us who can answer crucial questions and point to potentially useful problem-solving activities, regardless of our formal status in the group. Overall, we will share an orientation to our task and to the goal of innovation.

Now, suppose that success has not eluded us and that the prototype camera has been turned over to a somewhat larger group of workers who are manufacturing cameras by the thousands and selling them to a distributor. In what respect is this second group different from our R&D team? For one thing, it faces a much more certain task environment. Once a puzzle has been solved, it is no longer a puzzle. The problem facing the manufacturing group is how to produce a reliable product efficiently. Formal structure will be introduced as the group discovers that some procedures lead to more effective production than others. A hierarchy of authority may take form as the need to plan and coordinate routine manufacturing operations becomes apparent. Schedules will become pressing as the manufacturing group faces delivery deadlines. This group will share an orientation toward its task and toward its goals of efficiency and product reliability.

Obviously, the R&D and manufacturing subunits of this hypothetical organization are quite dissimilar. From the system perspective, the differences between the units are as important as the characteristics of each unit.

Degrees of differentiation

The dissimilarities between subunits in the preceding example can be attributed to differences in the degrees of uncertainty in each subunit's task environment. A more formal statement of this relationship appears in Table 3-2.

In their study of firms in three industries (plastics, consumer foods, and standardized containers), Lawrence and Lorsch (1967) found that subunit characteristics varied according to the environmental (task) uncertainty these subunits faced. Subunits operating in highly uncertain task environments were found to have a low degree of formal structure, personnel who were task oriented, and a long time orientation. Where the task environment appeared to be less uncertain, subunits were characterized by extensive formal structure, a short time orientation, and personnel who were task oriented. Goal orientations differed across subunits, not because of uncertainty in the task environment, but because different goals are inherent in different environments. For example, two manufacturing subunits may operate in equally uncertain task environments, but one may pursue the goal of efficiency while the other seeks quality production at the expense of efficiency.

TABLE 3-2
Relationships between uncertainty in the subunit's environment and subunit characteristics*

Uncertainty of the environmental sector	High	Moderate	Low
Subunit characteristics			
Extent of formalized unit structure	Low	Medium	High
Interpersonal orientation	Task	Social	Task
Time orientation	Long	Medium	Short
Goal orientation†	Unspecified		

* Source: Lorsch (1975, p. 260).
† Goal orientations are reported to be inherent in the environment and unrelated to uncertainty. For example, one manufacturing subunit may pursue the goal of efficiency and a second may seek quality at the expense of efficiency, while both operate in environments typified by low uncertainty.

These four characteristics are combined by Lawrence and Lorsch to form an approximate measure of subunit *differentiation*. Differentiation is defined as "... *the differences in cognitive and emotional orientations among managers in different functional departments, and the differences in formal structure among these departments*" (Lorsch, 1975, p. 259).

A major contention of this system approach is that subunits of the larger organization do not necessarily face the entire environment in which the larger organization functions. Instead, subunits may segment the environment. For example, R&D and manufacturing subunits exist simultaneously in many organizations, not sequentially as in our hypothetical illustration. Thus, R&D may face a highly uncertain task environment while manufacturing operates under much more certainty. Effective organizations differentiate subunits according to the extent required by differences in the uncertainty in the task environments of these subunits.

We have used an obvious example to arrive at a less obvious point. Apparently there are organizations in which all subunits face task environments characterized by nearly equal degrees of uncertainty. The task environment of R&D, for example, may be no more uncertain than that of manufacturing. This can be the case when R&D deals with manufacturing problems instead of basic research. Differentiation between these subunits should be low according to the logic presented here. Subunit differentiation should be higher when uncertainty is high for some units and low for others than when it is either high or low for all units.

Differentiation and integration

As we have said, the efforts of different subunits must be integrated if the organization is to be effective. *Integration* is defined as "... *the quality of the state of collaboration that exists among departments that are required to achieve unity of effort by the environment"* (Lorsch, 1975, p. 259). The authors contend that integration becomes more problematic as subunits become more differentiated.

The organizations studied differed across industries in terms of degree of differentiation and the means for accomplishing integration. Important differences were also noted between effective and less effective organizations within the same industry.

Subunits (sales, production, and research) in the container industry operated in task environments characterized by uniformly low degrees of uncertainty. Producing containers involves simple mechanical processes that are well understood. Research in this industry was focused mainly on production problems. Selling in an industry where competitors use identical equipment to produce nearly identical products at approximately the same costs appears to entail little more than taking orders and meeting delivery dates (Lawrence and Lorsch, 1967, p. 92).

Subunits in the plastics industry operated in task environments characterized by more varied degrees of uncertainty. Research subunits were engaged in problems of basic research, for example, altering the molecular structure of substances to create materials with desired properties. The task environment of the production subsystem was less uncertain than that of R&D. Uncertainty in the sales subsystem's task environment fell somewhere in between these two extremes. The diversity of uncertainty facing subunits of firms in the food industry was moderate—neither as varied as in the case of plastics firms nor as uniform as in the case of container manufacturers.

These findings are summarized in Table 3-3, which depicts the characteristics of the *more effective firms* studied in each industry. In all, six plastics firms and two firms from each of the other industries were studied. Change in profits over five years, change in sales volume over five years, and an index of new products introduced during the five years (expressed as a percent of the final year's sales) were combined to form a measure of effectiveness.

Managing differentiation and integration

As Table 3-3 illustrates, the differentiation of subunits in effective firms was directly proportional to the diversity of task environment uncertainty confronting their subunits. However, whether differentiation was high or low, the degree of subunit integration was high in all effective firms.

Where differentiation is low, integration seems to come easily. Since each unit's behavior is somewhat predictable, coordination can be accomplished by plans, procedures, and the hierarchy of authority—by the organization's formal structure. Moderate differentiation is accompanied by the creation of special roles for people who integrate the activities of subunits. Formal structure is also used, but somewhat differently. Activities that are uncertain and differentiated are difficult to predict and plan. For this reason there is

TABLE 3-3
Environmental factors and organizational characteristics of effective organizations

Industry	Environment diversity	Actual differentiation	Actual integration	Integrative devices		Conflict management variables	
				Type of integrative devices	Special integrating personnel as % of total management	Hierarchical influence	Unit having high influence
Plastics	High	High	High	Teams, roles, departments, hierarchy, plans, and procedures	22*	Evenly distributed	Integrating unit
Foods	Moderate	Moderate	High	Roles, plans, hierarchy, procedures.	17*	Evenly distributed	Sales and research
Container	Low	Low	High	Hierarchy, plans and procedures	0*	Top high, bottom low	Sales

* This proportion was constant for the high and low performer within these industries.
Source: Lorsch (1975, p. 263).

less reliance on formal structure and more emphasis on ad hoc coordination. Highly differentiated subunits of the plastics firm were integrated by special departments and teams of integrating personnel, as well as by special roles and formal structure. However, it is important to note that the less-effective organizations also made use of integrating devices such as roles, teams, and plans. The uses to which these devices were put distinguished the more effective firms from their less effective competitors.

Integrating the activities of groups with diverse goals, time orientations, and technical backgrounds implies a potential for conflict. For example, the demands of the sales unit for product modifications may seem unreasonable to the R&D and production units, but for different reasons. The manner in which such disagreements are resolved, according to Lawrence and Lorsch, influences the organization's effectiveness. In effective firms, such conflict was addressed openly, with an attempt to make the resolution of conflicting positions consistent with the interests of the larger organization. In the less-effective firms studied, such conflicts tended to be smoothed over or forced. Smoothing over conflict does not resolve the basis of disagreement, but merely allows the disputing parties to agree to disagree. Forcing suggests unilaterally requiring other units to comply with one unit's position.

The authors also note that the individuals responsible for conflict resolution in the more-effective firms were able to influence the conflicting subunits because of their knowledge of the problem at hand and because they were able to see the problem from several points of view. In less-effective firms, these individuals tended to base their right to influence on their position in the organization rather than on their expertise, and had one-sided points of view. They tended to see the problem from the perspective of one subunit or another, rather than from the organization's viewpoint.

Influencing integration

One of the findings of the present study sheds additional light on Tannenbaum's concepts depicted in the influence graph (Figure 3–10). Influence in the effective container firm was distributed more or less as illustrated by the curve for authoritarian organizations.[3] Top management had the most influence, while those at the bottom of the organization had the least. Faced with relatively little uncertainty, these managers could obtain the information necessary for coordinating subunit activities.

This was not the case in either the plastics or food-producing firms. Faced with more uncertainty and greater subunit differentiation, the effective organizations in these industries operated by distributing power throughout the hierarchy. Influence was wielded by the individuals possessing the knowl-

---

[3] We define terms such as *power, influence,* and *control* at a later, more appropriate point in the text. For the present, please note that the term *influence* is used to mean the ability to influence.

edge relevant to subunit integration, regardless of their rank. While pertinent knowledge was available to high-level managers in the production subsystems, low-level personnel typically possessed such information in the more uncertain sales and research units. For example, the scientists engaged in a research project may be more knowledgeable than their managers about the implications of their research for future sales or production activities. From these observations, we can draw the tentative inference that the more uncertain the task environment, the more we may gain from encouraging high total influence in the organization. Conversely, the less the uncertainty, the more we may benefit from an authoritarian structure.

Differences in the amount of influence wielded by different departments were also noted. Each organization faced crucial problems typified by high uncertainty, and the subunit most knowledgeable about crucial problem areas appeared to have the most influence. Selling activities were subject to more uncertainty than either research or production in the container firm. Thus, it is argued, the sales subunit of the effective container firm possessed more influence than the other two subunits. In the food industry, both sales and research were subject to more uncertainty than the production subunit and consequently enjoyed greater influence than the production subsystem. Finally, integration presumably was the most crucial problem facing the highly differentiated plastics firm. Thus, the integrating unit came to have the highest degree of influence.

Dominant competitive issues

Competition among firms takes different forms in different industries. The nature of competition, furthermore, will affect the degree of integration required between subunits in a firm. In the container industry, for example, production was found to be the dominant competitive issue. Neither container firms nor their customers can afford to maintain large inventories of containers. Yet, to operate efficiently, production processes must operate almost continually. Thus, a precarious balance must be maintained between sales volume and delivery dates on the one hand and production scheduling on the other. In other words, close integration between production and sales is essential in effective container firms. Since products and costs are similar across firms in this industry, the ability to produce and deliver containers when customers need them is a competitive advantage.

A related competitive advantage is product quality. Customers were reported to use containers at rates of up to 850 a minute in mechanized packaging operations. A single, malformed container could easily jam such machinery. Consequently, users were concerned with the uniformity of the containers they purchased (Lawrence and Lorsch, 1967, p. 90). To compete effectively by producing uniformly reliable products, close integration between production and research is required, since research efforts are directed toward solving production problems in this industry. Finally, since competitors' products were nearly alike and product or technological innovations were practically nonexistent, a lesser degree of integration was required between the research and sales subunits.

The food and plastics firms offer marked contrast in this regard. The dominant competitive issue in both industries was innovation in products and production technology. Consequently, close integration was observed between sales and research and between production and research. The problems of integrating sales and production was less crucial.

Reprise

By now, you may have begun to think that the system view has carried the day. It seems to encompass much of the rational view, but goes far beyond it. It seems to indicate where bureaucratic, formal structures are useful as well as where more adaptive structures better serve the organization. It suggests the means for integrating dissimilar units in a single organization. Various theories from the human relations movement—Tannenbaum and Likert—seem to fall into place within a systemic perspective of organizations.

However, despite its conceptual economy, the system view presented here has not been validated. Please recall that Lawrence and Lorsch's sample comprised merely ten organizations, too few to generalize from. Moreover, their research methods were exploratory and tentative, not exact (see Pennings, 1975). Recent studies have attempted to verify their findings, but with mixed, inconclusive results. This is an extremely difficult area in which to conduct research successfully. How does one accurately measure environmental uncertainty, integration, or influence in organizations?

Other system theories have been proposed, but none has been as comprehensive. We shall encounter some of these in other chapters. The point we must make here is that while we may prefer the system view intellectually, it has not been validated scientifically.

DISCUSSION QUESTIONS

1. Do you think that high total influence implies that all members of an organization have equal voice in all decisions?
2. How does one determine the limits of participation in organizational decision making?
3. What costs are incurred by moving to a form of organization that permits high total influence? How can these costs be justified?
4. Describe your school in terms of the concepts presented in this chapter.
5. Does the school's organization fit any of the traditional designs? Does the school have a prepared organization chart? In your opinion does the organization perform as the chart suggests it should?

4

Technology and Structure

INTRODUCTION

Visitors to a world's fair that celebrated "A Century of Progress" were greeted by a sign proclaiming: *Science discovers: Technology executes: Man conforms.* One visitor, a long-time student of the relation of technology to social change, was led to wonder where this strange categorical imperative had come from. How is it, he asked, that humankind has become obliged to surrender to its own creation (Mumford, 1972, p. 4)?

Mumford's question was rhetorical; he had previously supplied the following answer: Early Christian dogma began to crumble when Copernicus removed the earth from the center of the universe. The belief that corrupt humanity, the ultimate focus of God's attention, existed in the center of a perfect, unchanging cosmos had been shaken. "... [S]cience, which had made this shattering discovery by the mere exercise of common human faculties, not divine revelation, became the only trustworthy source of authentic and reputable knowledge" (Mumford, 1970, p. 29). The profound religious reorientation that followed Copernicus's discovery contributed much to the immense authority of science and technology today, according to Mumford.

Does humankind conform to technology? How are organizations affected by the technologies they employ? These and other questions are raised and partially answered in the following illustration.

In 1975, *Technology Review* noted that a technological revolution in manufacturing was long overdue. For every three minutes a part spends in cutting or forming processes in a typical metalworking shop, it spends seven minutes being set up and 40 minutes moving and waiting. Moreover, 75 percent of all metal parts manufactured in this country are made in batches of 50 or fewer. These conditions, together with the fact that output per manhour of labor increased at less than half the rate of increase in average compensation between 1960 and 1973, provide pressures for dramatic technological change (Mattill, 1975, p. 60).

Three years later the same journal noted that the predicted revolution had begun in the form of a program, supported by the U.S. Air Force, to bring computer-aided manufacturing to the aerospace industry. Apparently, many of the parts manufactured in this industry could be made in a computer-managed processing system that would require 50 to 75 percent fewer workers than currently were needed. In addition, the nature of the work force would be changed appreciably. Semiskilled jobs would all but disappear. Remaining would be highly skilled programmers and maintenance personnel and low-skilled workers such as parts-finders and tool-changers. Furthermore, job mobility for low-skilled workers would diminish. The aerospace organizations would become restructured along the lines of firms in the chemical or oil refining industries (Mattill, 1978, p. 20).

Chapter guide

1. In what ways do the different technologies employed in manufacturing and chemical processing organization's cause them to differ?
2. What is technology?
3. Is it possible to make a clear distinction between technology and structure?
4. In the last chapter we suggested that management's freedom to choose a formal structure for the organization is constrained by the nature of the task environments encountered. We will demonstrate the possibility that technology imposes similar constraints in this chapter. Is management passive, then, doing little more than identifying and implementing the course of action remaining when all constraints have been applied? Or are managers really free to choose alternatives that agree with their personal preferences?

RELATIONSHIPS BETWEEN TECHNOLOGY AND STRUCTURE

Job complexity and span of control

A simple example of the technology-causes-structure view is found in the relationship observed between job complexity and span of control (Gerald Bell, 1967). Bell determined that the complexity of the task in which a supervisor and subordinates are engaged is inversely proportional to the supervisor's span of control.

According to Bell, job complexity is a function of the number of tasks associated with the job, the degree of unpredictability associated with these tasks, the individuals' rights to exercise discretion in making job-related decisions, and the amount of responsibility they exercise in the performance of their work. To the extent that one or more of these factors increase for either the supervisor or the subordinates, the supervisor's effective span of control is diminished.

As the degree of job complexity increases, a corresponding increase occurs in the amount of information that the work group will need to process. Biological systems can suffer from information overload (James Miller, 1960); only so much information can be processed by a system in a given period of time. Higher information loads cause the system to break down, to show strain (Wieland, 1965), or to engage in various coping mechanisms, which can produce relative inefficiency. In simple jobs, supervisors and subordinates make few job-related decisions and, consequently, process a relatively small amount of information. Under these conditions a supervisor can manage a fairly large number of subordinates. As job complexity increases, however, supervisors will become overloaded and eventually management will feel pressures to create additional levels of supervision, thus reducing the span of control.

Three classes of technology

Most writers would agree that technology influences much more than the organization's span of control. Some, such as James Thompson (1967), go so far as to argue that both strategy and structure are affected by the kind of technology employed.

Thompson distinguishes three major classes of technological processes. The first, the *long-linked technology,* converts raw materials into finished output by performing a series of operations in a fixed sequence. The assembly line is an example. Step B in the assembly process always follows step A and precedes step C. The successful performance of step C is dependent on the successful performance of step B, but not vice versa. This is known as serial interdependence.

Because long-linked technologies operate repetitively, producing the same standardized products over extended periods of time, most facets of production can be studied and a knowledge base can be developed. Imperfections in the technology can be identified and remedied. Thus, *instrumental perfection,* the ability to inevitably produce a desired outcome, can be approached, and maximum *efficiency* can be sought.[1]

Mediating technologies are used to link clients who wish to engage in specific transactions, but who otherwise prefer to remain uninvolved with one another. Banks do this when they lend the savings of depositors to individual borrowers. The postal service, telephone utilities, and insurance industry also employ mediating technologies. While the units in a mediating technology are not serially interdependent, they must be managed in such a way that the actions of each unit are compatible with the actions of other units. Such compatibility is achieved by *standardizing* the organization's transactions and, in doing so, establishing conformity in client behavior. For example, not only is telephone equipment standardized, but also people who use telephones conform to standard procedures, as do patrons of the postal services and bank customers. Furthermore, standardization rationalizes the processes used to link clients appropriately. For example, depositors' funds are not loaned indiscriminately to borrowers. Rather, potential borrowers are screened by routine, standardized procedures, and are assigned to appropriate risk categories. The interest rate charged to a borrower varies according to the borrower's risk category. Where risk is too high, loan requests are refused. The use of impersonal rules and standardized procedures is consistent with our definition of bureaucracy in Chapter 2.

The third form of technology identified by Thompson is the *intensive technology* employed by hospitals, research laboratories, and certain engineering firms. The use of an intensive technology is determined by the nature of the problem at hand and the variety of problems encountered, which cannot be predicted accurately. For example, a hospital emergency room contains a variety of skills and equipment. Which of these will be used and in what order depends on the unique needs of each patient. Instrumental effectiveness, not maximum efficiency, is the concern of organizations employing intensive technologies. In a sense, these organizations pursue something akin to strategic responsiveness in that they must be prepared to meet a variety of contingencies. In the case of the emergency room, this means that a considerable number of skills and apparatus must be available, even if some of them are rarely used. As mentioned in Chapter 3, this

---

[1] The concept of instrumental perfection becomes clear when contrasted with situations in which it cannot be approached; for example, psychotherapy may produce its desired outcome, but the outcome is far from inevitable.

standby capacity entails costs of a sort not encountered in organizations that seek steady state efficiency.

Technology and organizational strategies

In theory, each step in a long-linked technology can be made predictable and efficient. The major problems of uncertainty that concern management, then, are not to be found in the technical core, but on the input and output sides of the organization. Maintaining a steady supply of raw materials of satisfactory quality may become problematic, as may disposing effectively of outputs. For this reason, organizations emphasizing long-linked technologies tend to grow by acquiring sources of critical supplies and access to markets, where possible and advantageous. This form of organizational growth is termed *vertical integration*. A classic example occurred in the petroleum industry. Originally, the major oil companies operated only refineries. However, they were quick to integrate vertically on the raw materials side by acquiring oil wells, expertise in exploring and drilling for oil, and transportation equipment to move crude and refined products. On the output side, networks were established to market a variety of petroleum products, ranging from fuel oils to insecticides.

A different sort of problem faces managers of organizations employing mediating technologies. Here the major uncertainties cluster around the organization's potential dependency on clients and the risks inherent in client transactions. The banking example used above illustrates both points. First, imagine that the hypothetical bank was able to attract all the deposits it needed from one or a few individuals. Despite the adequacy of deposit balances, bank management would have cause for apprehension, for the bank would become dependent on these individuals. Consequently, the depositors would be in a position to influence management. Obviously, management would prefer to receive deposits from many individuals, whose transactions are too small to constitute sources of dependence. Similarly, managers would rather hold a diversified portfolio of loans than a few, extremely large loan accounts. The larger the number of loans, the less the likelihood that a single default will expose the organization to catastrophic risk, all other things being equal. Thompson's point, then, is that organizations employing mediating technologies expand by *increasing the populations served*.

Since the use of an intensive technology is determined by the nature of the problem at hand, the problem itself constitutes a major source of uncertainty for the organization. The patient in a hospital or inmate in a correctional institution does not merely receive a service, but is expected to participate in a process that is designed to change the individual. In some cases, the technology must be available to clients around the clock, as, for example, in a hospital's intensive care unit. In other cases, clients must be isolated from their usual environment. Presumably, the inmate in a correctional institution has been removed from an environment that fostered behaviors in need of correction. Sometimes clients must be coerced into cooperating in the change process. Some hospital inpatients could be treated as outpatients if they could be trusted to restrict their diets or activity levels. In all of these examples, the organizations employing intensive technologies attempt to decrease uncertainty by *incorporating the object worked on.*

Mechanistic and organic organizations

Thompson's reasoning suggests that an organization's reliance on formal structure will vary, depending on the nature of its core technology. While long-linked and mediating technologies are associated with rules, plans, and standardized operating procedures, intensive technologies are not. The contingencies faced by the latter are too numerous and varied to be planned for and met with predetermined courses of action. This is an important point to remember, for Thompson argues that the nature of an organization's technology will influence its selection of a strategy for reducing uncertainty. Equally important is the notion that the structure that develops around a particular technology will limit the organization's choice of future strategies. This view is supported by the work of Burns and Stalker (1961).

The authors investigated a number of diverse firms that were interested in entering the electronics field. Most of these firms failed to enter this field successfully. Because of their reliance on formal structures, the organizations were mechanistic. Typically, these businesses were unable to deemphasize formal hierarchical structure and develop more equality in influence relationships and greater flexibility. Though relatively successful in previous endeavors, their attempts to enter a new field of operations were unsuccessful.

Burns and Stalker contrasted these firms with a number of relatively successful companies in the electronics industry. Characterized by the authors as organic, the latter organizations paid less attention to formal procedures and encouraged horizontal as well as vertical communication, flexible instead of rigid roles, and decision making at all levels, including lower levels—all very much along the lines that Likert (1967) and Tannenbaum (1962) emphasized.

However, please note that the mechanistic and organic firms originated in different industries with dissimilar technologies and marketing environments. One can infer that the more informal, organic structure suits organizations within dynamic industries (such as the electronics industry), while the more formal mechanistic structure is appropriate for organizations within stable industries. Burns and Stalker's findings reinforce the theory that the nature of the industry (or more precisely, the nature of the organization's technology and environment) determines the appropriateness of the organization's structure. Moreover, an appropriately developed structure may inhibit an organization's entry into industries that are different from the industry for which the structure was developed.

Technology and variations in formal structure

Having indicated the far-reaching consequences that some writers attribute to the use of one technology or another, we shall return to our first example and explore further the effects of technology on span of control and other aspects of formal structure. The relationships between technology, structure, and strategy will be explored further in Chapters 7 and 8.

One of the earliest and best-known works in this area was conducted in England by Joan Woodward (1965). Woodward surveyed 92 firms to examine the applicability of various classic prescriptions for management to actual practice. Woodward was concerned with the usefulness of such concepts as functional departmentalization, line-staff arrangements, the optimal span of control, and the number of hierarchical levels within an organization. After developing general measures of the relative effectiveness of these organizations, she attempted to correlate the occurrence of different structural forms with organizational effectiveness. As we are learning, she found that no single form of organizational structure leads to organizational effectiveness. In fact, only after grouping the firms according to their typical mode of production did relationships between form and effectiveness become apparent.

Woodward categorized the firms according to the type of production system used: (1) the unit or small-batch firms that made one or at most a few kinds of products for special orders (for example, a manufacturer of scientific instruments); (2) the large-batch assembly and mass-production firms (for example, an automobile manufacturer); and (3) the process production firms involved in automated production (such as oil or chemical producers). In Woodward's opinion, the three production systems—the *unit, mass,* and *process systems*—demonstrated increasing degrees of complexity. The survey data, thus categorized, indicated that in the unit-production firms the span of control of the chief executive ranged from 2 to 9 employees, in the mass-production firms from 4 to 13, and in the process-production firms between 5 and 19 employees. Furthermore, the span of control for first-line supervisors also differed according to the type of production system, as did the ratio of workers to managers and other aspects of organizational structure. Apparently, the nature of the firm's technology rendered some forms of structure more appropriate than others.

Now, one might argue that these differences in structure resulted from mistakes made by organizational planners who failed to use the appropriate, classic organizational designs. However, an analysis of the various firms revealed a consistent relationship between success and particular kinds of structure. In the case of spans of control, *those firms with average spans for* their type of production system were successful, whereas firms deviating from the average span in their production system were less successful. Another way of stating this is to say that the same span of control may be successful or unsuccessful depending on whether the firm is using one kind of technology or another.

Technology and critical functions

Approximating Lawrence and Lorsch's findings (Chapter 3), Woodward found that firms employing different technologies had different critical functions. Development was the critical function in unit-production firms, that is, the function on which the success of marketing and manufacturing depended. Many of the products sold by unit-production firms are unique. Marketing such products involves selling the firm's capacity to design and develop the manufacturing procedures for one-of-a-kind items. As an extreme example, we can think of the organizations that produced hardware for the Mars landers. Here, marketing units secured contracts to build items that had never been manufactured before; for example, video equipment that would meet certain size and weight constraints; that could withstand vibration, high g forces, and extreme variations in temperature; and that would operate reliably after months in interplanetary space. Obviously, the greatest uncertainty in this and similar cases lies in product development.

Production was found to be the critical function in mass production firms. The existence of a mass production technology implies that major developmental problems have been overcome. Similarly, facilities for mass production would not be built in the absence of a sufficiently large and stable market. Consequently, problems of efficiency and reliability in production become critical to the organization, as Lawrence and Lorsch found to be the case in the container industry.

Woodward identified marketing as the critical function in process-production firms. Such firms operate almost continuously and produce output that is undifferentiated from competitors' products. Furthermore, once constructed, these facilities must be operated for an extensive period of time, if an adequate return on investment is to be gained. Thus, disposal of output constitutes the organizational activity on which both development and production are dependent.

Regardless of the type of technology they employed, firms that were above average in terms of Woodward's measure of success used status systems that reinforced the importance of the critical function. Furthermore, the chief executives of these firms were found to have been associated with the critical function at one time or another in their careers.

Technology and production control

Using Burns and Stalker's terminology, Woodward described organizations employing mass-production technologies as mechanistic. Firms using unit and process technologies appeared to be more organic. Yet, the latter two types of firms did not have identical structures. They were similar in that they tended to use a single system of production control, but different in terms of the type of control system employed. Unit production depends on the effectiveness of individual contributions, especially when unique products are manufactured. Thus, the control system typically found in unit-production firms was personal. A mechanical control system was the rule in process firms. Processes for controlling and evaluating performance were built into the plants (for example, recording gauges). However, generalizations of this sort could not be made for the mass-production firms, which employed a variety of different control systems.

The technological imperative

Many authors, including Woodward, realize that the technological imperative may be too sweeping a generalization. Organizational behavior is influenced by many forces in addition to those generated by technology. We shall identify the predominant forces throughout the text. For the moment, though, a brief review of three studies will tell us much about what we know and do not know at this point about the forces generated by technology.

We might have hoped that Lawrence and Lorsch, Thompson, and Woodward would have drawn similar conclusions from their studies. Unfortunately, they did not. Although we have indicated a similarity between Lawrence and Lorsch's container firm and Woodward's mass-production organizations, the similarities go no further. For example, Lawrence and Lorsch found research to be the dominant competitive issue in plastics firms. Woodward would have classified plastics firms as users of process technologies. The critical function identified in process firms was marketing, not development (research). Thompson would have grouped process and mass-production firms as organizations using long-linked technologies.

Several problems in comparing the research results are apparent at this point. First, the definitions of technology used by the various authors are incompatible. Furthermore, none seems adequate for the kinds of generalizations we would like to make. Next, when we speak of critical functions or dominant competitive issues, we must ask, critical or dominant for whom—the technical, managerial, or institutional level of the organization? We can make a reasonably sound argument that within a mass-production firm, production problems compete for middle management's attention, while problems related to the need to integrate vertically engage the attention of top management. Finally, with the exception of Thompson, whose work was theoretical and did not arise from primary research, the studies reviewed so far have been limited to business firms. Their results may not be applicable to other kinds of organizations such as schools, hospitals, and governmental agencies. At this point, the need for a broader, more precise definition of technology is obvious.

Technology: Diffuseness and specificity

Although Woodward's work and corroborating replication (Zwerman, 1970) indicate a number of relations between technology and structure, other studies suggest that these relations can be better stated.

Harvey (1968) studied 43 different industrial organizations by using what he calls the dimension of *technical diffuseness and specificity*. Technical diffuseness refers to the technology of firms producing a wide range of products—a range that probably varies over time as well. Technical specificity refers to technologies wherein one product, or at most a limited number of products, is produced consistently. There is a degree of similarity, of course, between technical diffuseness and unit production, that is, "made-to-orderness," just as there are similarities between specificity and process or mass production. However, the dimension of diffuseness and specificity provides a finer instrument to classify technologies and organizations, even within Woodward's classifications. Thus, some unit production firms may be quite diffuse in their technology, while others may be more specific, tending to get orders that, while they are made one by one, are fairly similar to one another.

Using the dimension of technical diffuseness and specificity, Harvey found that four structural characteristics of organizations were related to an organization's position on the dimension. Organizations characterized by technological specificity contained more specialized subunits than organizations characterized by technological diffuseness. Furthermore, they tended to have more levels of authority, greater ratios of managers and supervisors to total personnel, and greater degrees of program specification. Technological specificity, in other words, seems to be associated with Burns and Stalker's mechanical structure, and technical diffuseness with an organic structure.

Technology as a process

Harvey's ideas will lead us in some useful directions. However, we need to broaden them somewhat before proceeding further. Earlier, in discussing the system view, we alluded to Perrow's definition of technology as a means of transforming raw materials (either human, symbolic, or material) into desirable goods and services. Machines, equipment, and supplies, of course, can all be viewed as components of technology, but the most important component by far is the *process* whereby raw materials are transformed into the desired output. Technology, basically, is the technique that brings about this transformation. Such transformation techniques are unlikely to develop in the absence of a supporting body of knowledge. Technology may be found inside one's head, so to speak, for example, the expertise that professionals bring to the job.

In demonstrating this point, Perrow (1965) describes problems in structuring mental hospitals. A fundamental problem is the lack of an effective technology for dealing with most psychiatric illnesses. For many years, shock therapy was used to treat certain forms of psychosis, though no one fully understood how or why it worked. More recently, tranquilizers have come into use, though we lack a theoretical understanding of their effect on mental illness. In general, the same lack of understanding holds true for various forms of psychotherapy, and mental illness still remains a problem. Even though we have a physical apparatus, such as machines for giving shock therapy and pills for tranquilizing patients, the knowledge base that explains the apparatus' intervention in the process of the illness is lacking. As we shall see, the knowledge base is an essential component of technology.

Technology, structure, and psychological differences

Perrow's notion that knowledge, not machinery alone, is a form of technology encourages us to view the research described thus far in a somewhat different light. The works of Harvey, Woodward, and others suggest that a single technology pervades each organization. Obviously, this is not usually the case in complex organizations. Perrow (1967) gives a graphic illustration of the differences among functional subgroups within a single organization. He describes how structural differences can accrue to the marketing, research, and production functions within an organization as a result of each function's preoccupation with different technologies and with problems characterized by different degrees of routineness. The research department generally performs less routine tasks than the marketing department, which performs tasks less routine than the production department. In consequence, departmental structures tend to vary to accommodate the degree of routineness of the tasks.

In addition to having different structures, departments within an organization tend to vary according to the modes of thought that members typically use. Lawrence and Lorsch (1967) found that members of production departments, faced with relatively certain tasks, tended to be more task oriented and less socially oriented than sales department members who faced more uncertain tasks. Sales and production department members, who received fairly rapid feedback, tended to focus more on short-term concerns than research scientists and engineers who did not receive rapid feedback (Table 3–2).

This finding can be explained in several ways. First, individuals who have learned to think in a particular manner may view the thought processes evidenced by members of one functional specialty as more attractive than those evidenced by other specialties. Hence, departments may attract job candidates who are self-selected according to their inclination toward a given cognitive-emotional orientation. Second, on entering a department, individuals possessing varying thinking styles may become socialized to fit in with other members of the department, who ultimately must fit in with the technological requirements of the particular function.

The important point from the Lawrence and Lorsch study is that, in cases where subunit differentiation is appropriately high, the structural and personality differences found among different functions must be allowed to remain if the organization is to be effective. The problem of preserving and integrating such differences can require considerable organizational effort, as was mentioned in Chapter 3. More important, it is unreasonable to view technology as a mechanical process that is independent of psychological and social processes. Lewis Mumford (1970) goes so far as to describe society's technical apparatus as part of the stage setting in which the drama of cultural change is enacted, rather than as the script. We shall return to a sociotechnological view after examining the ideas of Harvey and Perrow in more detail.

Technology: Certainty and variety

Recent work by Perrow (1967, 1970) extends our analysis of technology several steps further. Going beyond Harvey, who examined technology along the single dimension of diffuseness-specificity, Perrow makes use of two separate dimensions in his analysis: (1) the extent to which logical, analyzable search procedures can be used in problem solving (along a dimension running from *well-defined* to *ill-defined* problems), and (2) *task variability* (along a dimension ranging from *variety* in the task to *routineness*).

When faced with a problem for which no previously formulated solution exists, the individual is forced to search for feasible solutions. The nature of the search will vary according to the degree to which the problem is defined. In dealing with well-defined problems, the individual can conduct the search for a solution on a logical, analytical basis. This systematic search for well-established techniques or programs is typical of the problem-solving behavior of mechanical engineers. For example, suppose your car does not start tomorrow morning. Before calling a service station, you may want to find out whether the problem is one you can remedy. Since nothing happened when you turned the ignition switch, you begin to think of logical steps that will isolate the problem. First, is the entire electrical system at fault, or just the ignition system? To answer this question, you will turn on the headlights. If they work, you will know that the problem probably is in the ignition system. The lights do not work, however. Next, you try the horn, which does not work either, to check the possibility that the electrical system is working but that both the starter and lights are defective. Since the probability that three systems have failed independently is low, you accept the premise that the entire electrical system is dead.

Now, how do you analyze the problem? The most logical question to ask is whether the battery has a charge. By touching each end of a jumper cable to the battery terminals, you produce a healthy spark, indicating that the battery holds a charge. Next, you begin to trace the flow of current from the battery, beginning with the battery terminals to which the car's wiring is connected. These are badly corroded. Since corrosion can interrupt an electrical circuit, you disconnect the battery cables, clean both the terminals and cable connectors with a wire brush, and reconnect the battery. When you turn the ignition switch, the car starts. The solution to your problem of getting the car started resulted from a logical, analytical search.

At the other extreme are the so called ill-defined problems. For example, recall the problems of the hypothetical group that decided to invent an holographic camera for amateur photographers (Chapter 3). In dealing with ill-defined problems, the individual, lacking formal search techniques, is forced to draw on unanalyzed experience or intuition and to rely on guesswork and trial-and-error solutions. The physician dealing with a new disease or the researcher faced with a problem in basic research exemplify this kind of problem-solving behavior, as does a glassblower or other artisan.

In addition to the problem-definition dimension, Perrow includes a second dimension that describes the amount of variety experienced in a given job. Some jobs are routine, containing few exceptions from normal, day-to-day practice. Assembly-line and preventive-maintenance jobs are examples. At the other extreme are tasks that inherently contain numerous exceptions and deviations from day-to-day operations. The roles of an electronics technician or a nurse in an intensive care unit exemplify this kind of work. The most variable jobs include those of research scientists and top executives of a growing firm in a new or changing field.

The two dimensions of technology postulated by Perrow can be used to construct a two-by-two table of problem definition and problem variability. We can expect to find classes of organizations that deal with technological processes falling somewhere within the classification scheme presented in Figure 4-1. For our purposes, we will deal only with those that fall at the extremes. Work-related problems vary considerably in some jobs. In addition, solutions to these varying problems cannot be found via logical, analytical search procedures. Jobs fitting this description are located at the upper right-hand corner of Figure 4-1 and are termed *nonroutine*. Many components of firms in the aerospace industry, for example, seem to fit this description.

At the other extreme are tasks that have low variability and few exceptions, the solutions for which can be determined by logical, analytical search. *Routine* jobs, as they are called, are found on assembly lines and in various mass-production technologies such as those used by steel mills. Routine work, to Perrow's way of thinking, is organized very much along the lines of the mechanistic organization. By the same token, organizations that deal with nonroutine work seem similar to the organic firm.

At the upper left-hand corner of Figure 4-1 one finds *craft* industries

FIGURE 4-1
Types of technologies

	Problem variability	
Problem definition	Low variability and few exceptions	High variability and many exceptions
Ill-structured (unanalyzable search)	Craft industries (specialty glass)	Nonroutine (aerospace)
Well-structured (analyzable search)	Routine (steel mills)	Engineering (heavy machinery)

Source: Adapted from Perrow (1967).

which deal, by definition, with problems that are fairly similar over time—low in variability and containing few exceptions. However, even though the problems are fairly similar, their solutions require the application of experience, intuition, and trial and error. Craftsmen, from shoemakers to diemakers, fit into this quadrant of the technology table.

Finally, the lower right-hand corner of Figure 4-1 describes highly variable work that involves many exceptions. In this case though, the variable tasks, including even the exceptions, can be dealt with by means of logical search processes. *Engineering* problems are typical of this class. Every new bridge or building presents problems different from those that an engineer has faced before, but ultimately these problems are solved in a rational, organized manner.

Organizational structure in relation to technology

In making application of two discrete dimensions, Perrow allows us to separate technology into four different kinds and to look at the kind of organizational structure appropriate for each type of technological process. The aspects of structure that Perrow feels should be made congruent with technology are (1) the amount of discretion that can be exercised by high- and low-level staff, (2) the amount of power held by each of these groups, (3) the extent of interdependence between these two groups, and (4) the extent to which these groups coordinate their work using either feedback or the planning of others.[2]

---

[2] Where variability and exceptions to day-to-day operations can be handled through routine procedures and logical, analytical search, the work of subordinates throughout the organizational unit can be coordinated by planning. This is generally true regardless of the rate at which exceptions arise, so long as these exceptions are amenable to analyzable search. In cases where exceptions cannot be handled via analyzable search, planning will not satisfactorily coordinate various work activities. In these instances, the output of a work group as it is subjected to various criteria or as it affects other groups will give rise to feedback from which direction and coordination can be inferred. An example of an individual who derives direction from feedback is the artist whose progress in painting is directed in part by the painting itself as it takes form.

Industries engaged in craft technologies, for example, confront problems that require freedom for low-level personnel to exercise considerable discretion and power in decision making. By the same token, the activities of low-level employees will be subject to coordination via feedback. For these reasons, Perrow suggests that the most effective organizational structure for craft industries is one that is *decentralized*.

Planning can effectively control work that is typified by low variability and analyzable search. An emphasis on planning requires that both high and low levels in the organization exercise little discretion. Furthermore, by virtue of its planning function, top management wields more power than other levels in the organization. Consequently, if they are effective, organizations that use routine technologies tend to employ formal, *centralized* structures.

Nonroutine activities, typified by variability and a large number of exceptions that cannot be resolved by logical, analytical search processes, are amenable to control only through feedback. The ill-structured nature of the work requires that high and low levels of personnel alike exercise considerable discretion in their work. Similarly, both levels, if they are to be effective, must be free to exercise considerable power in the work situation. Because of these characteristics, organizations that engage in nonroutine activities are effective, according to Perrow, when they assume a *flexible, polycentralized* structure.

Finally, the engineering organization operates effectively when it employs a *flexible, centralized* structure. Engineering tasks, although associated with variability and numerous exceptions, are typified by logical, analytical search processes. Thus, the activities of lower levels of management can be controlled by planning. Similarly, lower-level managers need not exercise a great deal of discretion or power. Higher levels of management, however, tend to bear the brunt of the large number of exceptions and planning activities that are implied. Hence, they should exercise significantly more discretion and power than the subordinate levels.

Structure, subunits, and technology

An attempt to verify Perrow's work took the form of a survey of 14 medium-sized manufacturing firms (Magnusen, 1977). Over 3,600 managers responded by describing their work and organizations in terms of Perrow's variables. Modal scores were developed to describe the technology of each organization and of each department in the organization.

Contrary to what might be expected, the organizations clustered into only two categories—routine and nonroutine. However, these tended to fit Perrow's model in terms of the structure they employed.

A possible limitation of Magnusen's research may have been the relative homogeneity of organizations studied; all were manufacturing firms. The inclusion of organizations such as coal-mining firms, music publishers, engineering firms, and art galleries might have produced different results. However, Magnusen draws our attention to a familiar point: organizations typically employ more than one technology. As a result, we may be able to apply Perrow's model to subunits facing problems that are described by a single quadrant of the two-by-two table, but we should not expect to describe entire organizations adequately in this manner.

To demonstrate this point, Magnusen grouped organizational subunits (functional groups) according to the routineness and nonroutineness of their technologies. Figure 4-2 shows that the R&D units studied typically employed nonroutine technologies, as might be expected. Similarly, production subunits typically used routine technologies. Sales units fell somewhere in between, but were more routine than one might have expected.

**Figure 4-2
Percentage of functional groups having routine and nonroutine technologies**

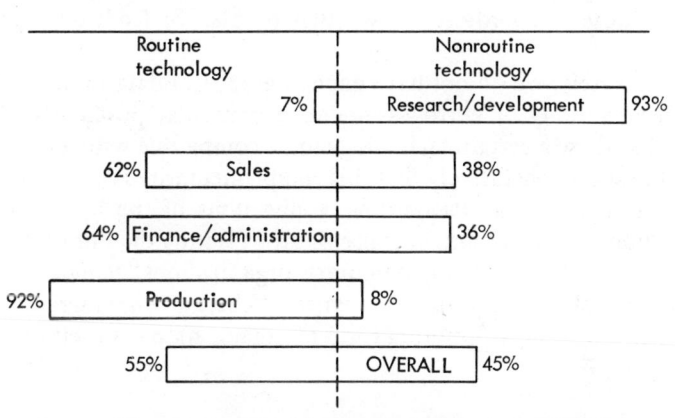

Source: From *Organizational Design, Development, and Behavior* by Karl O. Magnusen. Copyright © 1977 by Scott, Foresman and Company. Reprinted by permission.

Other studies add support for Perrow's position; for example, Hage and Aiken (1969) in a study of 16 health and welfare agencies (rehabilitation, psychiatric services, and services for the mentally retarded) found considerable differences in the variety of work performed. In one organization, the executive director said that the work was so novel and innovative that his staff did not even know which professional organization to join. Another staff member, in reporting his work with highly unpredictable children, said, "We individualize very highly here; we would turn the place upside down for one child—and sometimes we do." This contrasts with organizations having less variable work, consisting mainly of conducting a standard interview with each client to determine eligibility for various types of governmental aid.

As expected, organizations with routine work were more likely to be characterized by centralization of organizational power. According to Hage and Aiken, "If organizational members constantly face a work situation characterized by highly varied clients' needs, then greater organizational power will accrue to organizational members who interact with the clients most frequently." Below we shall explain this in terms of the power accruing to those who can absorb uncertainty for the rest of the organization's members.

Perrow's expectations about the relationship between routineness and discretion were not confirmed, but as expected, the authors did find that routineness was associated with the formalization of roles. Formalization was measured by the existence of rules manuals and job descriptions and by the extent to which the job was highly specified in the description. These are all manifestations of Perrow's "coordination by planning" cited above. In short, Perrow's hypothesis of a relationship between the type of technology and the nature of coordination, whether by plan or feedback, has limited support.

Unfortunately, we do not have enough empirical data to be confident of the general validity of Perrow's model. A particular problem is that even studies that show a certain technology to be compatible with a certain structure fail to show conclusively that this complementarity is essential for organizational effectiveness. Regardless, applications of the model to specific organizations do seem to make sense. Perrow, stating the implications of his model for the design of contemporary organizations, remarks: "Given a routine technology, the much maligned Weberian bureaucracy probably constitutes the socially optimum form of organizational structure" (Perrow, 1967, p. 204).

Technology versus humanism

As logical as Perrow's conclusion seems, it nonetheless raises serious reservations when compared with conclusions implicit in the work of Likert, Marrow, Tannenbaum, and others, who see mutual influence systems and participative management as models for effective organizations of any kind. This dilemma is resolved in part by the observation of Lawrence and Lorsch (1967) that individuals who labor in different specialties tend to think in dissimilar terms. There are, as we have said, satisfied pyramid dwellers. Yet, this begs the question we shall turn to next—Is there a humane way to employ technology in organizations?

COMBINING TECHNOLOGY AND STRUCTURE

Changing the fit between social and technical subsystems

Examples of work successfully combining the rational and system views can be found in the studies of coal mining and textile manufacturing conducted by the Tavistock Institute (Trist, Higgin, Murray, and Pollock, 1963), a research organization in England. The Tavistock researchers dealt with organizations in terms of sociotechnical systems. The technical portion of the system was defined as equipment and work processes; the social portion of the system was defined as the organization of individuals who carry out the necessary tasks of the system. As we shall see, the Tavistock work accommodates both human needs and the technological requirements discussed above.

The Tavistock researchers selected the primary work group as the focus of their investigation. Within the small group of co-workers, they isolated three work-related psychological forces that the sociotechnical system could be designed to foster. The first of these forces is *closure*, the sense of completion one feels on having finished a meaningful unit of work. Psychological research performed many years ago by Zeigarnik (1927) showed that people become frustrated when they are prevented from completing a task and experience the motive to resume and finish work that has been interrupted. Subsequently, it has been demonstrated (Horwitz, 1954; Lewis and Franklin, 1944) that there is a *group Zeigarnik effect*— that members of a group want to complete their task when interrupted but will be satisfied if any member of their group finishes it for them.

The second psychological force arises from the need for *autonomy* in the control of one's activities. This also has a group counterpart. Individual need for autonomy can be satisfied provided that a trusted member of the group possesses the autonomy and decision-making authority to act in one's behalf.

The third psychological force stems from the need for *satisfactory interpersonal relations*. At the risk of oversimplifying, we categorize this need as the workers' desire to be members of cohesive work groups. According to the Tavistock researchers, three group characteristics play major roles in determining a group's cohesiveness: (1) the range of skills required of group members in performing their task must be limited to the extent that each member of the group can understand the group's functioning with respect to the task; (2) to minimize barriers to communication within the group, differences in prestige and status among members of the group must be minimized; and (3) members who become dissatisfied must have the opportunity to leave the group and join another, lest frustration develop and disrupt the group's functioning.

A Tavistock study of the change in coal-mining practices from the traditional "single working" to the "longwall system" (Trist and Bamforth, 1951; Trist et al., 1963) demonstrates the importance of the three psychological forces. In the single-working system, the primary work group consisted of six men, two of them assigned to each of the three shifts. Every member of the primary group possessed all of the skills necessary to perform the three major operations in coal mining, namely, (1) removing coal from the coal face, (2) loading and transporting coal from the face, and (3) erecting roof supports and moving up machinery as the mining proceeded deeper into the coal face. The two miners on a given shift would perform whatever operations were necessary at the time, and the next shift would pick up the task wherever the first pair left off and carry on, as would the members of the third shift. All six men in the group were paid the same wages, the exact amount being determined by the amount of coal the group as a whole mined. Finally, the composition of the group was based on self-selection, with the men selecting their own workmates.

While the single-place working seemed to meet many of the primary group requirements as specified by the Tavistock researchers, the longwall system did not. The longwall system attempted to mechanize the coal-mining process and advance the application of mining technology, and also, in a sense, to make the miners conform to the requirements of the technical system. The installation of new mining equipment required that shifts be manned by fairly large numbers of miners. The workers were divided into three shifts and, most significant, they were assigned to specific functions. The three basic types of mining operations were separated so that the first shift cut into the coal face, the second shift moved the coal to the conveyor, and the third shift brought up the roof supports and conveyor.

The longwall system failed to meet the primary group requirements described above. First, the workers lacked a sense of closure, or completion, since each shift was performing only a fraction of the mining operation. Furthermore, since group cohesiveness was not present among workers across the different shifts, completion of the cycle of mining operations by second or third shifts did not produce the "group Zeigarnik effect." Second, workers on a given shift lacked autonomy and control over their work. Not only were the workers on a particular shift dependent on others in their large group, they were also dependent on the workers of the other two shifts. For example, if the first shift failed to mine a sufficient quantity of coal, the second shift would not have enough coal to load on the conveyor. By the same token, if the second shift did not finish loading the conveyor, the third shift would be unable to move the conveyor up to a new position, and so on. Third, satisfactory interpersonal relations among shift workers failed to materialize because of the existence of major differences in skills and, consequently, in status among the workers. Finally, miners who became dissatisfied with their relationship to their work group were unable to move into a more congenial setting.

As suggested above, the mutual dependency of shifts became a source of intergroup conflict worsened by the lack of social bonds among the groups. This psychological separation was increased by the remuneration system, since miners were no longer paid according to the amount of coal produced by the group as a whole, but rather according to differential rates for specific jobs. Thus, the three specialized shifts were in a position to compete with one another for increases in rates of pay and, consequently, were motivated to blame slowdowns and substandard output on the activities of other groups. Energy was not applied toward increasing the output of the three shifts as a whole but rather toward increasing one group's advantage relative to that of the others.

The composite system

A number of coal-mining operations developed a compromise arrangement for using the new technology, and a study of this arrangement substantiated the analysis comparing the single-place working with the longwall method of mining. The "composite longwall system" comprised a group of 41 men who were divided into three shifts. Rather than having specialized tasks assigned to each shift, the composite longwall method had each shift perform all three of the major mining activities. Furthermore, the group possessed the autonomy to reassign its members as the need arose. Not only did this arrangement provide the work group with a sense of meaningfulness and closure, but because the group organized itself, it was not dependent on external coordination. Thus, the work group exercised considerable autonomy in making decisions that affected its functioning. Finally, the work group in the composite longwall system still selected its membership, and members were paid according to the productivity of the entire group rather than according to the types of tasks that the individuals performed.

The composite longwall system employed a larger number of workers than did the single-place working system. Nonetheless, it was designed so that the work situation reinforced the psychological and group forces that made the single-place system viable. A comparison between the composite longwall system and the conventional longwall system showed the composite longwall system had a lower rate of employee absenteeism, lower operating costs, and a higher rate of productivity.

An experimental sociotechnical system

Similar conclusions can be drawn from a study of the introduction of automatic looms to textile mills in Ahmedabad, India (Rice, 1958). To staff the new automatic looms, 12 different occupational roles were created and assigned among workers. The occupational roles varied from battery filler to weaver, cloth carrier, bobbin carrier, and sweeper. Twenty-nine workers were assigned to the 12 roles and were responsible for the operation of 224 looms. In attempting to fulfill the requirements of the technological system, the 29 workers faced a confusing pattern of interrelationships. For example, three members of one role might serve eight members of another role, but the priorities of the eight for the services of the three were not clearly established. Furthermore, as looms were changed over to produce different types of cloth, the work load and nature of activities associated with different roles were altered. Consequently, it was exceedingly difficult to establish job descriptions for the various roles.

One way to approach the ensuing problems would have been to rationalize further the organizational structure by creating supervisory roles for individuals who would monitor performance and apply controls as necessary. Another approach, which the Tavistock group recommended to management, was to develop an internal work group structure that was related to the demands of both the social and technical systems.

The Tavistock researchers organized the workers into four groups of seven men each—four in a weaving subgroup and three in a maintenance subgroup. The number of work roles was reduced further by an agreement that the new work groups would take over additional tasks previously allocated to only one or two individuals out of the whole group of 29.

Thus the work group was organized so that it bore responsibility for the completion of a meaningful unit of activity. Differences in skills, prestige, and status among the members of the work group were reduced to promote the establishment and maintenance of satisfying interpersonal relationships. In describing the results of the reorganization of the sociotechnical system, Rice tells how the workers now ran as they went about their work, so motivated were they by the psychological work forces. They even attempted to work throughout mealtimes, although Indian labor law prevents this lest it lead to exploitation of the workers. Needless to say, the reorganized portion of the mill proved highly productive, and the organizational structure implemented by the Tavistock group eventually was employed throughout the mill.

Toward the design of sociotechnical systems

A fairly simple conclusion from the Tavistock research would be that the formation and nurturance of cohesive work groups is a palliative for wide-ranging organizational difficulties. Perrow's (1967, 1970) analysis, on the other hand, causes us to agree that different kinds of technologies seem to require different kinds of formal and informal structure. In fairness to Perrow's case, it should be pointed out that coal-mining operations involve tasks with low variability and few exceptional problems. Solutions to these problems, furthermore, are not readily found through logical, analytical search. The natural geological occurrence of coal can require craftsmanlike skills of miners. This being the case, an organizational designer using Perrow's analytical scheme would have recommended that the mines employ a decentralized structure similar to the one that evolved in the composite longwall system.

That the textile workers were engaged in craftsmanlike activities is not clear, however, and there is considerable doubt that Perrow's analytical scheme would have suggested that management employ the form of organization that eventually proved successful. What this seems to suggest is that some organizational designs are logically conceived to meet the technological requirements of a system while others are developed primarily around the social needs of workers.

Both schools of thought contain important elements of truth. Effective forms of organizational design are successful in dealing with organizations as sociotechnical systems; they provide an environment in which the fulfillment of the requirements of the technical system simultaneously allows for the satisfaction of social and individual needs. In Chapter 9 we shall examine approaches to the design process from the beginning, with an emphasis on employees' needs.

Technology and interpersonal relationships

We began this chapter by treating organizations as entities and then moved toward disaggregation by considering functional departments and then individual work groups. To conclude the chapter, we will closely examine an example of the subtle influence that technology can have on relationships between individuals.

A study of restaurants (Whyte, 1949) shows a variety of ways to handle the problem of matching worker characteristics and the technology of work flow. First of all, note that the restaurant is really a rather complex organization, combining both service and production activities. The service end of the business requires that management discern the patrons' tastes so that menus can be constructed and foods stocked accordingly. The time factor in the kitchen is also very critical, as George Orwell so vividly describes in *Down and Out in London and Paris* (1972).

With regard to the flow of work, Whyte found that food-serving personnel who directly initiated work orders for cooks often created tensions and frictions. For this reason, many restaurants use barriers such as a counter (or a spindle) on which written orders are placed for cooks to pick up so that they work at their own pace. Another kind of barrier is the pantry supervisor who collects order slips from waiters and waitresses and passes them out to the cooks.

All this may not seem very relevant to the work of the manager who is far removed from the handling of actual production tasks and physical materials. However, if the problem is conceptualized in terms of handling dependencies, especially dependencies arising from uncertainty in organizations, then we will find parallel phenomena at the managerial level. Uncertainties arise because environmental inputs vary, technology breaks down, or both the environment and the organization's technology give rise to problems that require unanalyzable search. These uncertainties must be handled somehow if the organization is to preserve a semblance of rationality and remain more efficient than an unorganized collection of individuals (James Thompson, 1967). Those roles—managerial or worker—that absorb or buffer uncertainty are the roles on which the rest of the organization becomes dependent.

For example, Crozier (1964) describes how maintenance workers in a French tobacco plant are the only individuals in the organization who can solve the problems of machine breakdowns. Thus, a situation arises in which others become dependent on them, which in turn determines a significant portion of the power relationships in the organization. We shall see in Chapter 6 that the ability to solve critical organizational problems can be a significant element in the determination of organizational goals. However, the important point in the Crozier study is that the power enjoyed by the maintenance workers did not arise naturally. To meet their security needs, the maintenance workers organized themselves into a highly cohesive group and systematically disciplined members who attempted to share their esoteric knowledge with production workers or supervisors.

In other words, social structure may play a significant part in determining the organization's means of production. While many studies take a Marxian viewpoint, one of technological determinism, the reverse is often true. Structure, both formal and informal, as well as human variables can determine technology. The important orientation for the designer of organizations is that of the Tavistock group, which concerned itself with the fit or congruence between technical and social systems, not the sovereignty of one or the other.

The fit between technology and social structure is sufficient, then, to provide guidelines for an organizational design. However, two cautions are in order. First, we have been discussing both technology and structure in very general terms. For example, research findings do indicate that for a nonroutine technology an organic structure is likely to produce greater efficiency than several of the other possible combinations described above; however, within the rather global notion of organic structure and the equally global notion of nonroutine technology, certain kinds of arrangements will work better than others. The discussion of work flow patterns provides one example of such a refined discrimination. Considerable research remains to be done in this area.

Second, the process of fitting the technical system to the social system is dynamic. Depending on the nature of the original technology (or structure), a change to a subsequent technology (or structure) may not be better in spite of the intrinsic merits of the innovation. The sequencing of the technologies (or structures) is critical, too. The classic study of leadership climates (Lippitt and White, 1943), which compares the efficacy of a democratic climate following an autocratic climate with the efficacy of a democratic climate replacing a laissez-faire climate, illustrates the importance of succession dynamics. We shall return to this point in the chapters on organizational change (Chapters 15–16).

Managing the fit

The organizational variables we are discussing are depicted in Figure 4–3. While there is a great deal more to organizations than goals (tasks), structure, technology, and people, as we shall see, managing the fit between them is an important and difficult problem.

FIGURE 4–3
The major variables in organizations

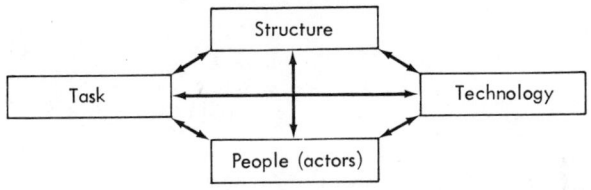

Source: Adapted from Harold J. Leavitt, "Applied Organizational Change in Industry," in James G. March (Ed.), Handbook of Organizations, © 1965 by Rand McNally College Publishing Company, Chicago, Figure 1, p. 1145.

An obvious source of difficulty is that, while we can generalize about appropriate kinds of fits among these variables, research evidence is limited, and we cannot be as specific as we should like to be. A second source of difficulty results from the extent to which these variables change over time. A dramatic example of such change can be found in Whyte's study of restaurants.

In describing Whyte's work, we purposely omitted one important observation; the frictions that arose when food-serving personnel initiated work for cooks were partially attributable to the fact that the high-status male cooks resented taking orders from low-status female food servers. Whyte's study was conducted many years ago, when the individual's sex determined status to some extent. Other studies from the same era indicated similar problems when job status and sex status were incongruent.

We bring this anachronism to light because it illustrates the kind of changes that affect organizations, even though they may neither cause nor anticipate them. Whyte went to great lengths to show that, for a given technology, some arrangements of people caused more problems than others. Yet, Whyte's solutions are irrelevant today, so far as sex influences status in the restaurant business. Nonetheless, this kind of change is unceasing in people, technology, organizational goals, and structure. Managing the fit, as Thompson (1967) said, is aiming at a moving target.

DISCUSSION QUESTIONS

1. What kinds of technologies are employed by:
   a. TV repair shops?
   b. Publishing houses in selecting manuscripts for publication?
   c. Graduate professional schools?
2. Do you think employee morale is higher in organic organizations than in mechanistic organizations? Why?
3. How has the technology that produced the hand-held calculator affected your work as a student?
4. What do slide rule manufacturers do these days?

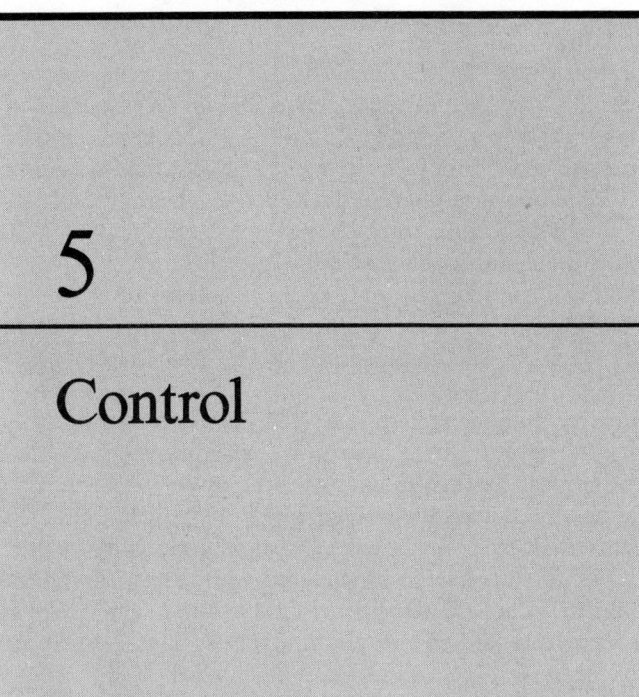

5
Control

INTRODUCTION

Frederick Taylor's work with manual laborers (described in Chapter 2) resulted in what can be described as a control process. As you recall, workers were given the proper shovel for each job and trained to work efficiently. In other words, rules for assigning tools and procedures for using them were devised and implemented. In addition, work standards were established, and individuals were paid a bonus for making quota. Those who failed were retrained in the correct procedures and were rewarded for eventually meeting Taylor's standards. Workers who failed to profit from such training were reassigned to their former, lower-paying jobs.

This simple example contains the essential elements of control processes in closed systems: (1) output is measured and compared with a predetermined standard; (2) when output falls below the standard, the discrepancy (negative feedback) triggers an appropriate corrective action; and (3) corrective actions terminate when output returns to standard. In Taylor's case, the rational approach to controlling behavior seemed to work. Other applications of this approach have not fared as well.

Consider, for example, the practice known as "storming the quota" (Jasinski, 1956). Quota systems still are widely used to evaluate performance in organizations. In manufacturing, for example, departments may have monthly quotas that specify expected levels of output in terms of average labor costs per completed unit. Department supervisors are evaluated monthly according to the percent of quota their departments produce.

Yet, making quota is difficult, and at times almost impossible. Sometimes special orders come through the department, requiring that the line be shut down and machines retooled. Unpredictably, machines break down, raw materials shortages develop, and mistakes are made. Nonetheless, quota must be met! When this happens, the department "storms the quota." Workers are taken off the beginning of the manufacturing process and assigned the jobs near the end to complete as much of the work in process as possible. Routine maintenance of machinery is postponed in the end-of-month rush to make quota, which hastens the equipment's deterioration. At the end of the period, the manufacturing process is unbalanced since workers were taken off the beginning of the line to help meet quota. Thus, raw materials inventories have mushroomed at the beginning of the line, while inventories of partially completed products at later stages of production have been exhausted. A second reassignment of workers takes place at this point, as laborers from the end of the line pitch in to rebuild the work-in-process inventory.

Obviously, the control process depicted here is ineffective. Yet, organizations must be coordinated somehow. Short of living in anarchy, we all must accept controls in one form or another. The rational view suggests that such coordination can be achieved by setting goals and by devising rules, procedures, and hierarchies of authority to focus employees' energies on activities that will achieve these goals. This kind of control is *external,* applied from without. Alternatively, the human relations view indicates that external controls can be minimized to enhance the organization's flexibility and adaptability. Goals and means, it is argued, are most likely to be pursued when *internal* controls of individual behavior are established through collaborative and participative management practices.

Chapter guide

1. Participative management may seem to be a desirable alternative to the forms of external control typically found in bureaucracies, but how can an organization employing a quarter of a million people coordinate employee activities through worker participation?
2. What is positive feedback? How would positive feedback affect a system?
3. Can you identify differences between Taylor's control process and the one used in the manufacturing department that might explain the success of the former and the apparent difficulties in the latter?
4. List some everyday examples of internal and external controls on your behavior.

5. What kinds of problems can accompany the use of external controls in organizations?

RATIONAL CONTROL PROCESSES
Internal and external relations

In the present context, control is defined as the process of obtaining behaviors desired by the organization. We mean human behavior, of course, but also the behavior of inanimate systems such as computing facilities, machine-controlled tools, and automated conveyers. By human behavior, we are referring not only to employees, but also to members of other organizations, including governmental agencies, suppliers, and competitors, as well as unorganized groups such as customers.

Organizations face two distinct, but related, control problems: (1) controlling external relations in the environment and (2) controlling internal relations within the organization. Although the problem of controlling external relations, strategy, will be discussed at length in Chapter 8, we shall introduce it here. However, our major focus for the present will be on the control of internal relations.

Controlling external relations

The rational approach to formulating corporate strategy follows a three-step decision-making process outlined by John Dewey (1910): (1) What is the problem? (2) What are the alternatives? (3) Which alternative is best? Applied to strategy formulation, this logic is elaborated as follows: (1) search the environment for potential threats and opportunities; (2) analyze these; (3) select the threats and opportunities to which the organization needs to repsond; (4) plan, schedule, and implement appropriate responses; and (5) obtain feedback to be used in improving future responses (Ansoff and Brandenburg, 1971). Activities such as these are included in the three uppermost cells of the pyramid of business policies depicted in Figure 5–1.[1] Deciding on major lines of business, products, and markets results in policies that attempt to match the organization's competencies with a need for products or services in the environment.

Controlling internal relations

The organization's strategy, in turn, defines the scope of activities required of lower levels in the organization. Task-related behaviors at lower

---
[1] The terms *policy* and *strategy* are used interchangeably by some authors. Strategic planning typically is viewed as a rational-hierarchical process in which means for obtaining the strategic objectives of the larger organization become subgoals that are assigned to units at lower levels in the hierarchy.

106   *I. Fundamental design concepts*

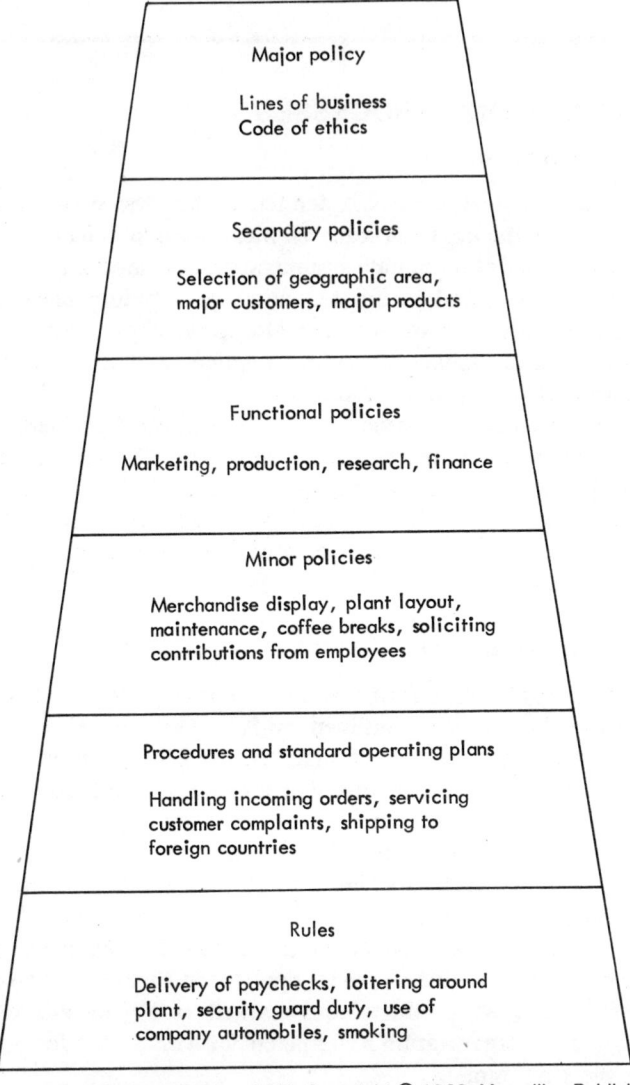

**FIGURE 5-1
Pyramid of business policies**

Source: Steiner (1969, p. 268). Copyright © 1969. Macmillan Publishing Co. All rights reserved.

levels must be coordinated to make the means employed by the organization consistent with the ends it seeks. Such coordination is achieved by devising minor policies, procedures, production plans, schedules, and rules. Minor policies define management's intentions when specific rules and procedures cannot be elaborated for all possible contingencies. For example, standard operating procedures may be specified for loading and discharging fuel at a depot, while policies may govern the organization's employee tuition refund plan. In the first case, management can specify exactly how each step in the fuel transfer operation is to be accomplished to conform to federal safety and pollution regulations. In addition, management may identify a limited number of situations in which exceptions to standard procedures are permissible. Procedures for handling these exceptional circumstances will be explicated as well.

In the second example, management cannot review all courses taught at every educational institution in its area to approve tuition payment for employees ahead of time. Management's policy may be to pay tuition for job-related courses, and the question of whether a particular course is job-related may depend on the employee's job. Thus, a policy is used in place of an indeterminate number of rules that would apply to each course and job category. Each employee's request for tuition refund is considered on its individual merits, and management's judgment in deciding such requests is guided by policy.

Bureaucratic conflict

The formal hierarchy of authority provides a particular type of coordination of individuals, technological processes, and structural elements. Superiors can plan the activities of their subordinates and, by virtue of their authority, issue orders to set them in motion. Direct orders may be issued, but impersonal rules commonly evolve as means of controlling personnel. Unfortunately, this can lead to conflict.

In large organizations in which leaders do not identify personally with subordinates, low-level personnel may find that their goals and aspirations are not considered in decision making. If the organization does not make provisions for the attainment of individual objectives, individuals will seek autonomy as a precondition for arranging their own need-fulfilling activities.

According to Pondy (1967), managers' attempts to gain control of employee behavior limit their freedom to act, make their behavior more predictable, and generally weaken their power in the organization. Unfortunately, the power to exercise autonomy is highly valued in organizations, and the loss of such power is threatening to the individuals involved. As Pondy sees it, subordinates resist attempts to control them, and this resistance, being unpleasant for superiors, generates pressures toward the establishment of impersonal rules and routines. While this may reduce face-to-face conflict (but not necessarily the conflict itself) and lead to fairly predictable behavior, it will also produce rigid behavior. Furthermore, Pondy reasons that: "Rigidity of behavior, which minimizes conflict in a stable environment, is a major source of conflict when adaptability is required" (1967, p. 315).

Various leadership and human relations training programs have been designed as attempts to reduce bureaucratic conflict by replacing rules and direct supervision with appropriate group norms and personal persuasion techniques. However, when they are successful, such practices may decrease, rather than increase, the individual's autonomy. "By heightening the individual's involvement in the organization's activities, (such techniques) actually have provided the basis for the intense interpersonal conflict that characterizes intimate relations" (Pondy, 1967, p. 316). We shall examine this somewhat cynical view of the human relations approach below, for the practices and techniques involved are pervasive in organizations.

"Invisible" rules

Some organizations in which rules and procedures are not codified give the impression of allowing far-ranging freedoms for their employees. However, Perrow (1972) suggests that such organizations can be more binding on employees than those in which rules are more explicit. Although unwritten, rules exist in the organization's culture as norms, agreements, and accepted practices. On joining such an organization, new employees are likely to learn the rules only after transgressing them and suffering consequent sanctions. It is argued that a delineation of rules outlines the employees' areas of freedom and allows them to pursue their endeavors without suffering undue consequences that arise when unwritten restrictions are violated inadvertently.

In other situations, clearly defined rules may be treated temporarily as if they do not exist. In theory, the superior in a bureaucracy will exert control over subordinates and require them to follow regulations. In fact, Blau (1956) shows that supervisors frequently "play ball" with their subordinates, permitting infractions of numerous rules (for example, no smoking rules). In using discretion either to demand compliance or to permit violations of rules, the supervisor exercises what Blau terms *strategic leniency*. Interestingly, the net outcome of strategic leniency is increased (rather than decreased) control over subordinates.

An old Spanish proverb defines the strategy of such leniency: "To receive a favor is to sell your liberty." Supervisors who accommodate subordinates by consulting them before assigning work, by sticking up for them when they get into difficulties with management, and by permitting various infractions of rules create social obligations for their employees. Out of gratitude and, perhaps, the fear that such favors will not be extended in the future, subordinates comply with their supervisor's requests even when the requests exceed the supervisor's legitimate authority. Thus, the supervisor's ability to control subordinates increases as a result of such practices, and may become greater than the formal authority assigned to that position (Blau and Meyer, 1971, p. 64).

The advantages of rules and operating procedures

All types of organizations have their advantages and disadvantages. Yet, bureaucracy has become something of a scapegoat in the literature of organizations and in our culture as well. There is a tendency to elaborate the disadvantages of bureaucracies while overlooking their positive aspects. At the same time, organic and participative organizational forms have been advocated on the basis of the recognition they supposedly pay to the value and dignity of their members. The worth of a particular form of organization in a specific situation, however, is measured according to criteria that far exceed the attention given to member satisfaction.

One advocate of bureaucracy, Charles Perrow (1972), argues that this form of organization is superior to all other types of structure for large, complex organizations. Excessive concerns with attempts to humanize bureaucracies, that is, to apply System Four, participative management, and human relations techniques, have directed our attention away from the contributions of these organizations to society. If bureaucracies are more effective than alternative structures in accomplishing their missions, they are superior. Perrow's argument suggests that in considering a tradeoff between organizational effectiveness and member satisfaction, society should prefer the former to the latter.

Rules and procedures are essential to bureaucracies because they are part of the structure that enables the organization to function effectively. In small groups in which individuals interact face-to-face with one another, coordination may be achieved informally. However, in larger organizations in which members are too numerous to interact directly, turnover among members is significant, and geographic distances between members militate against their interaction, such informal work relationships will not evolve. Instead, rules will be generated to foster coordination.

Rules are also useful because they restrict behavior. Only a limited portion of an individual's repertoire of behavior is appropriate in purposive organizations. In fact, some forms of behavior (for example, social drinking) will impede organizational functioning if allowed on the job. Rules and regulations provide means for proscribing these behaviors.

The routine aspects of a problem can be dealt with fairly automatically through the application of rules, thereby increasing the time and energy available for solving its more difficult aspects. Thus, complex problems can be rendered more simple through categorization.

Favoritism, nepotism, and discrimination on irrelevant grounds are inhibited by rules, according to Perrow. Rules enable individuals to determine where they stand vis-à-vis organizational requirements and can help them organize their activities to benefit both themselves and the organization. In addition, rules protect and enhance the autonomy of subunits within the organization.

Rules are valuable in stabilizing a situation and protecting various kinds of practices, bargains, agreements, and payoffs. They are the organization's memory, according to Perrow. If rules were permanent, problems would arise as the situations to which the rules were addressed changed. However, rules are changed, too, but usually incrementally. Because of the complexity of organizations, drastic alterations of existing rules will "throw everything up for grabs" and create a crisis. So, we are saying that rules can be extremely useful and that one is well advised to proceed cautiously in trying to alter or eliminate them.

Rules and centralized decision making

Although we have said that rules sometimes develop to reduce interpersonal conflict, this tells only part of the story. Other, significant aspects of bureaucratic functioning emerge from a classic study of the dimensions of organizational structures conducted in the Birmingham, England, area by Pugh and associates (1968). A total of 64 structural measures were taken in each of 52 organizations in the research sample. The values obtained were compared across all organizations.

Three of the dimensions studied are of particular interest here: (1) *specialization,* which measures the degree to which labor is divided in the organization; (2) *standardization,* which refers to established routines and procedures, such as those used in personnel selection or promotion decisions; and (3) *formalization,* which measures the degree to which rules, procedures, and instructions are codified in manuals and other documents.

An important conclusion of this study was that measures of *specialization, standardization,* and *formalization* tend to co-vary (to increase or decrease together). Taken together, these three measures indicate the degree to which activities are structured. Hence, the combination is termed *structuring of activities.*

A second important and apparently independent group of measures is termed *concentration of authority.* Primarily, this factor comprises the extent of centralization—the degree to which authority for decision making is localized in a central, high level of line management. Specialization varies inversely with concentration of authority. Generally speaking, authority seems dispersed in organizations that employ relatively large numbers of specialists. A related finding shows that the percentage of employees involved directly in the work flow varies directly with concentration of authority. In general, then, the greater the concentration of authority, the smaller the percentage of employees engaged in staff specialities and the greater the percentage of employees in line positions.

Relationships between centralization and structuring of activities

A number of studies (for example, Blau and associates, 1966; Child, 1972[a]) show a negative relationship between measures of centralization and structuring of activities; that is, organizations having centralized decision-making processes have relatively few rules, standardized procedures, and specializations. Conversely, in organizations in which rules and procedures are relatively numerous, top management tends to delegate decision making to lower hierarchical levels.

In response to findings of still other studies that show the relationship between centralization and structuring of activities to be weak or nonexistent, Mansfield (1973) examined the effect of organizational size on the variables measured. He found that standardization, formalization, and specialization co-vary positively, but that each tends to vary inversely with centralization. His most interesting finding is that relationships between measures of specialization and centralization vary depending on the size of the organization studied.

A direct relationship between measures of specialization and centralization is found in relatively small centralized organizations having about 150 employees on the average; that is to say, where control is concentrated in high, line-management positions, many specialists are employed, presumably to serve as advisers to decision makers. Small decentralized organizations employ relatively fewer specialists (Figure 5–2).

In contrast, an inverse relationship is found between specialization and centralization in relatively large, centralized organizations employing over 6,000 personnel on an average. In organizations in which control is centralized, specialists are relatively few in number. Conversely, in large organizations having decentralized control, specialists are relatively numerous. It is suggested that specialists are used to advise line managers in handling problems brought about by the use of rules and regulations and the need to coordinate large, decentralized units. Finally, organizations that are medium-sized (that employ more than 150 but fewer than 6,000 employees on an average) generally show no significant relationship between measures of centralization and specialization.

Determinants of structuring and centralization

A study by Khandwalla (1974) examined the effects of technology, vertical integration, and sophisticated managerial controls on the relations among organizational size, structuring of activities, and centralization. To operate a mass-production technology (as defined by Woodward, 1965—Chapter 4) efficiently, fluctuations in the environment must be buffered.[2] One likely means to this end is vertical integration. However, vertical integration leads to increased organizational differentiation and, consequently,

---

[2] Buffering refers to practices that protect the organization's core technology from environmental uncertainties so that efficiency and instrumental effectiveness can be maintained (see Chapter 4). Inventory management is an example. Raw materials and finished goods inventories buffer the core technology on the input and output sides, respectively, from fluctuations in raw materials supplies and demand for finished goods.

FIGURE 5-2
The use of specialists in large and small, centralized, and decentralized organizations

Size of organization	Form of organization	
	Centralized	Decentralized
Large	Few specialists	Many specialists
Small	Many specialists	Few specialists

to delegation of authority (decentralization), which in turn give impetus to the introduction of "sophisticated control mechanisms."

Khandwalla defines sophisticated management controls as control systems that require considerable information processing skills of the managers employing them (for example, statistical quality control systems, scheduling techniques, internal audit procedures, and the like).

Professionals and bureaucracies

Approximately one quarter of today's work force comprises managers and professionals (Ginsberg, 1979). How do dimensions of bureaucracy, such as structuring of activities and concentration of authority, affect the work of professionals, whose orientations toward internal controls may conflict with external direction? Here the commonly assumed evils of bureaucracy come most into focus.

The issue of professionals in bureaucracies first surfaced in Talcott Parsons's (1947) discussion of Weber's concept of bureaucracy. Since superiors in the hierarchy may possess less *technical* competence than those below them, Parsons reasoned that bureaucratic structures contained an inherent source of conflict. The dependence of superiors on subordinates for technical advice is asymmetrical with status, authority, and other relationships. Differentiation between line and staff personnel arises, in part, to deal with this problem, but does not alleviate it entirely.

Using the dimensions of bureaucracy described above, Richard Hall (1968) explored relationships between professionals and this type of organization. He approximated the extent of professionalization of a variety of occupational roles by measuring the degrees to which incumbents of the various roles subscribed to the following professional values:[3]

---

[3] The occupational roles included physicians, nurses, accountants, teachers, lawyers, social workers, stockbrokers, librarians, engineers, personnel managers, and advertising account executives.

1. The use of a professional organization (either a formal organization or an informal grouping of colleagues) as a major source of ideas and judgment of professional work.
2. A belief in service to the public, including the notion that the profession is indispensable and benefits both the public and the practitioners.
3. A belief in self-regulation which holds that fellow professionals are best qualified to judge professional work.
4. A sense of calling or dedication to the field of professional endeavor—a dedication that is exercised even at the expense of material rewards.
5. Autonomy—the freedom to make decisions without direction or pressure from clients, the public, or the organization that employs the professional.

Extent of professionalization was compared to the degree of bureaucracy found in organizations employing various occupational roles. On the whole, Hall found bureaucratization inversely related to professionalization; for example, occupational roles in which members reported strong feelings of autonomy were found in organizations characterized by a relative absence of hierarchical authority, division of labor, rules, procedures, and impersonality. Conversely, practitioners who expressed weak feelings of autonomy were found in occupations that served more bureaucratic organizations.

While Hall found fairly systematic, negative relationships, it should be noted that none was of particularly great magnitude except the relationship between autonomy and bureaucracy. In the case of other aspects of professionalization, the relationships were not statistically significant. Therefore, Hall argues that the conflict assumed between bureaucracy and professionals may not be inherent at all. In fact, it may be that for a particular level of professionalization, a certain degree of bureaucratization is essential to the stability and control of organizational functioning.

Bureaucracy and professionalism as alternatives

For the moment, we shall explore the possibility that organizations can employ bureaucracy and professionalism as *alternative* means for regulating and coordinating behavior. Both bureaucratic structures and professional orientations serve to organize, stabilize, and regularize the execution of organizational roles. Rules and procedures restrict and direct the behavior of employees. The same is true of professional norms, ethics, standards, and practices. In the latter case, however, restrictions are internalized. Within limits, an organization can employ either as a means of achieving control.

The limits that constrain choice seem fairly straightforward. In an organization employing professionals, excessive bureaucratization is likely to be dysfunctional. Conversely, the values, beliefs, attitudes, and motivations of nonprofessional workers may limit the efficacy of attempts to cause them to behave somewhat as professionals.

Be that as it may, Hall argues that in the choice of professional (or craft) standards, as opposed to organizational rules or procedures, the former is neither morally superior nor more efficacious than the latter. Many studies of professionals in organizations "... seem to imply that the professional standards are somehow better than those of the organizations. Unless there are available specific criteria of what the organization and the professionals are trying to accomplish, such an assumption is unwarranted" (Richard Hall, 1977, p. 171). For example, it has been noted in the area of health care that professional standards of medicine learned in a teaching hospital may be inappropriate in private general practice or in a community clinic. Treating a patient as an object and looking primarily for esoteric physical diseases may fit a professional model, but standards that emphasize responsiveness to the patient's expressed (and often psychological) problems may prove more appropriate (Duff and Hollingshead, 1968). Still other critics suggest that the prerogatives claimed by professionals occasionally serve vested interests rather than technological requirements. An illustration is that physicians sometimes refuse to explain their practices to patients to protect their monopoly on specialized knowledge (Friedson, 1970[a]).

Bureaucracy in the service of professional autonomy

From a study of physicians employed by three organizations that were bureaucratized to varying degrees, Engel (1969) found that bureaucracy was in some ways beneficial to professional autonomy. She studied physicians in solo and small group practices in which the bureaucratic elements of hierarchy, rules, and regulations were absent. In addition, she studied other physicians in moderately, as well as highly, bureaucratic organizations. The moderately bureaucratic setting was a privately owned, closed-panel medical organization. The highly bureaucratic organization was a governmental medical facility.

A comparison of the degrees of professional autonomy reported by physicians in the three different kinds of settings showed that autonomy was generally highest in the moderately bureaucratic organization and approximately equal in the nonbureaucratic and highly bureaucratic settings.

Engel explains the finding that a relatively high degree of professional autonomy occurs in a moderately bureaucratic (as opposed to a nonbureaucratic or highly bureaucratic) setting by noting that bureaucracy can foster attainment of the professionals' goals. She suggests that autonomy is becoming less relevant to many professions. As knowledge and professional specialization increase, so will interdependence among professionals, technicians, and other nonprofessionals. For example, many kinds of medical care cannot be obtained from physicians in solo or small group practice, but require the services of a large clinic or hospital where a variety of medical specialties and technical and paramedical services are employed and where the appropriate supplies, equipment, and skills to operate equipment are available. Large organizations can mobilize considerable resources for the professional by means of bureaucratic structures. While hierarchies of authority, rules, regulations, and the consequent requirement of organizational loyalty may have detrimental effects, these do not necessarily outweigh the advantage of being able to coordinate resources.

Matching organizational requirements with professional needs

In a study of 125 teachers, researchers, and administrative personnel employed by a small liberal arts college, Gouldner (1958) identified two major role orientations—*cosmopolitans* and *locals*. The cosmopolitan staff, as compared to the local staff, placed higher emphasis on the value of research as a source of job satisfaction, were more likely to feel that there were relatively few people in the college with whom they could share research interests, had more education, published more, were less loyal to the organization, were more likely to gain intellectual stimulation from outside sources, were less happy with their salaries, and were less rule oriented. In short, the cosmopolitan staff had standards derived from the profession, from outside the organization. Employees with local orientations identified more with the institution and its goals and regulations than did cosmopolitans.

There is some evidence that institutional loyalty and commitment to professional standards can be compatible in certain kinds of organizations (Thornton, 1970). Using a sample of nearly 400 teachers from eight Florida junior colleges, Thornton identified faculty members as cosmopolitans and locals. A small negative correlation was found between the organizational and professional orientations; that is, teachers who viewed external control of teaching activities as desirable tended not to have a professional orientation. However, the incompatibility of these two orientations varied, for in some organizations individuals could accept external structuring and also display high professional commitment. This was true in organizations that gave special emphasis to (1) professional performance criteria (for example, recognizing research contributions in performance appraisals); (2) professional autonomy (using expertise as a basis for authority over students); and (3) professional supervision (using only professionally qualified staff to supervise other professionals). Apparently, organizations that attempt to structure the work of professionals need not confront them with a choice between organizational and professional commitment. As standards, regulations, and criteria within a bureaucracy approach and exemplify the norms and values of the professionals it employs, the two commitments will become congruent.

Having noted this, we must take a caution from Engel's study. There is a limit to the extent that professional organizations can be bureaucratized successfully. A relatively weak profession may permit professional and organizational congruence to be achieved by the domination of bureaucratic requirements over most of the professionals' activities. An alternative to this state of affairs is a relatively weak organizational structure that permits congruence to be achieved via domination by the profession. Such appears to have been the case in the studies of scientific laboratories reported by George Miller (1967). Conflict was found between scientists and engineers on the one hand and the administrative hierarchy on the other when the former were located in departments that were part of the larger organization. Laboratories that were more or less autonomous evidenced a lack of conflict between professional and administrative staff.

Unprogrammed coordination

A plausible explanation of Miller's finding is contained in Perrow's taxonomy of technological processes (see Chapter 4). Rules, regulations, procedures, programs, and the like are appropriate for tasks that have analyzable solutions and that vary within reasonable limits. All work roles contain tasks having these characteristics, but some roles, such as those found in the professions, contain fewer than others. In the professional organization, the usefulness of bureaucracy is limited by the extent to which problems can only be solved using judgment or constructs.

However, the organization must be coordinated even in instances in which planning, rules, procedures, and the like are inappropriate. In such cases unprogrammed coordination occurs. The importance of unprogrammed coordination in complex organizations is demonstrated by a study of ten Michigan community general hospitals by Georgopoulos and Mann (1962). A major aim of the study was to ascertain whether differences in the quality of patient care were associated with differences in the adequacy of coordination.

The study revealed that both programmed and unprogrammed coordination were related to the quality of patient care delivered, but that unprogrammed coordination was the more important of the two. As one might expect, unprogrammed coordination has many of the attributes discussed under participative management (Chapter 3). Georgopoulos and Mann refer to these attributes as *sharedness of expectations, complementarity of expectations,* and *cooperation.*

Developing routine technologies

Our previous discussion of technology suggests that our analysis of formal, bureaucratic structure as a control mechanism applies more to units employing routine and engineering technologies than to those using nonroutine or craft technologies (Perrow, 1967). Yet, as we have said, a combination of technological processes typifies complex organizations. The task of controlling nonroutine or craft technologies is far more problematic than the bureaucratic approach discussed above. In fact, the difficulty of the task can move an organization to search for ways of simplifying the problems encountered by these technologies to bring them under the control of its formal structure. James Thompson (1967) argues that a good deal of an organization's behavior can be explained in terms of its attempts to avoid uncertainty. The problem raised here illustrates this point.

Perrow's four types of technologies are depicted in Figure 5-3, along with strategies for simplifying problems associated with each technology and reducing the uncertainty they create for management (Ullrich, 1976, p. 206). Craft technologies, developed in response to ill-structured, relatively invariant problems sometimes can be transformed by modeling techniques into well-structured problems that are amenable to routine technologies. An example is provided by the development of inventory management techniques in the late 1950s. Prior to this, the problem of managing inventory levels for thousands of line items required considerable experience with seasonal fluctuations in demand as well as longer-term trends. The task of holding down inventory carrying costs while carrying sufficient inventories to prevent stockouts was essentially the same for each of the items carried. However, each line item carried in inventory was characterized by somewhat different usage rates, cost, and seasonal fluctuations in demand. The large number of line items carried precluded a logical, analytical approach to inventory management on an item-by-item basis.

However, once the inventory modeling techniques developed by operations research analysts were programmed into electronic data processing systems, the nature of the problem changed. Now, techniques such as the economic order quantity model provided a logical, analytical approach to each reorder decision, and the computer's speed made such an approach practical. In terms of Perrow's model, inventory management moved from a craft to a routine technology.

Modeling is not as useful a technique for simplifying problems associated with nonroutine technologies because of the far greater variability in the

FIGURE 5-3
Means for developing routine techniques

← Control over the environment

Problem definition	Problem variability	
	Low variability and few exceptions	High variability and many exceptions
Ill-structured (unanalyzable search)	Craft industries (specialty glass)	Nonroutine (aerospace)
Well-structured (analyzable search)	Routine (steel mills)	Engineering (heavy machinery)

↓ Modeling

← Differentiation

Source: Adapted from Perrow (1967).

problems encountered. Presumably, the organization cannot appropriately model each of the many different problems it must address. An obvious response in this case is to gain control over the environment to limit variability or eliminate ill-structured portions of the organization's task. For example, a correctional institution founded to rehabilitate inmates (an ill-structured problem) may serve merely to incarcerate them (a well-structured problem), if society can be persuaded not to evaluate the institution on its performance at the former task (Etzioni, 1964). Similarly, a mental hospital formally chartered and publicly supported as a restorative agency may provide custodial rather than therapeutic services (Warriner, 1965). In either case, manipulation of the environment's expectations and demands permits the organization to operate a more or less routine technology. Attempts to influence consumer taste, to control inputs through vertical integration, to socialize employees, and to influence legislation are suggestive of business organizations' approaches to controlling the environment.

Engineering technologies are the easiest to simplify because the problems encountered are well structured. As programmatic solutions to problems are developed, subroutines that are repetitive by virtue of their commonality with other programs are delegated to individuals or groups who perform these tasks routinely.

Obviously, we cannot simplify every problem using the strategies illustrated above—nor should we want to. This leaves the complex organization with a number of crucial areas of uncertainty, problems that are ill-structured and variable. Such problems and the tasks they create do not lend themselves to bureaucratic control techniques. Thus, we have come to the system approach to controlling organizations.

CONTROL—SYSTEM VIEWS

Interdependence

To understand how an organization is controlled, we must identify the kinds of interdependencies the organization faces (James Thompson, 1967). The simplest form of interdependence occurs when subunits depend on each other for survival, but do not interact directly. For example, Chevrolet dealers across the country do not carry on routine transactions with one another. However, the success of each dealership is dependent to some extent on the success of the others. If numerous dealerships provide poor customer service, all may suffer a loss of their good reputation. By the same token, if many lose sales, the loss in revenue experienced in turn by General Motors ultimately will affect other dealers. This type of alliance entails *pooled interdependence.*

Sequential interdependence arises when one organizational unit depends on another for input. A plant that assembles Ford automobiles is dependent on the Ford glass plant for windshields and windows. Please note that the interdependence of the two units is asymmetrical in the case of sequential interdependence; the glass plant is not dependent on the automobile assembly plant for input. However, sequential interdependence is always accompanied by pooled interdependence, which is symmetrical. The well-being of each plant is linked to the well-being of the other.

Reciprocal interdependence arises when the output of one unit becomes the input of another, and vice versa. According to Thompson's logic, the aircraft maintenance unit of an airline and its operations unit are reciprocally interdependent. The maintenance unit's output is serviceable aircraft, which become inputs to the operations unit. Meanwhile, the maintenance unit's input consists of aircraft in need of service—an output or by-product of the operations unit. Reciprocal interdependence invariably is accompanied by sequential and pooled interdependence.

Managing organizational interdependencies

Pooled interdependence is managed by standardizing the activities of interdependent units; for example, enforcing compliance with standard maintenance and repair procedures will ensure that all General Motor's dealerships provide uniform, acceptable quality service for customers. Similarly, accounting systems, advertising and sales efforts, and personnel selection policies will be standardized to maintain an acceptable quality of performance across units.

Plans and schedules are used to manage sequential interdependencies among units. The argument here is much the same as in the case of long-linked technologies (Chapter 4).

Reciprocal interdependence is handled by mutual adjustment of the parties involved. In the airline example, the operations manager must plan the use of aircraft so that routine maintenance can be performed on them. Simultaneously, the maintenance manager must perform routine maintenance and emergency repairs according to a schedule that keeps an adequate number of aircraft at the disposal of the operations unit. Consequently, problems encountered by either group will affect and require adjustment of the other. Please bear in mind that reciprocal interdependence is the most costly to manage, while pooled interdependence is the least costly.

Thompson argues that organizations give the highest priority to managing the costliest form of interdependence. Thus, when organizations contain reciprocally interdependent elements, these elements are grouped into semiautonomous units to enhance mutual adjustments. Obviously, when teamwork is required, management creates teams. However, reciprocal interdependence often is a permanent characteristic of organizations, and rather than ad hoc teams, we shall think of these units as departments or divisions. Furthermore, since the difficulties encountered in making mutual adjustments increase in proportion to the number of elements in the unit, management will restrict the number of elements assigned to each unit. This observation parallels our discussion of span of control in Chapter 3.

Similar groupings will be made of elements that are sequentially interdependent to reduce the organization's planning costs. Obviously, it is more difficult for one unit to make detailed plans for all other units than it is for each semiautonomous unit to create its own plans.

After the organization has horizontally differentiated itself into units to control reciprocal and sequential interdependencies, elements that confront pooled interdependencies are grouped into semiautonomous units. In this case, differentiation occurs so that standard procedures can be developed and applied locally only to those elements that share pooled interdependence.

Because coordination costs limit the size of units thus created, all interdependencies cannot be handled by horizontal differentiation. Thompson reasons that, "When reciprocal interdependence cannot be confined to intra-group activities, organizations ... link the groups involved into a (semiautonomous) second order group ..." (1967, p. 59).

Finally, residual pooled interdependencies among units are handled with standardized rules and procedures that blanket the organization—that con-

FIGURE 5-4
Managing interdependencies in organizations

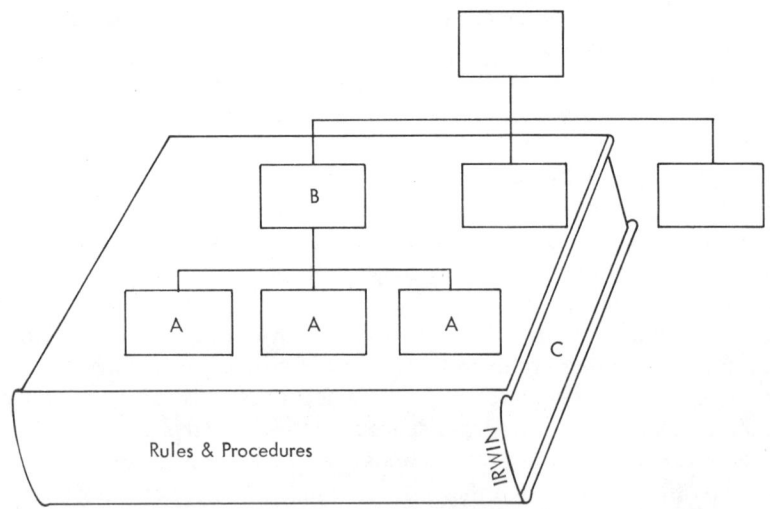

A. The costs of coordinating reciprocal, sequential, and pooled interdependencies are minimized by grouping interdependent organizational elements into semiautonomous units.
B. When reciprocal interdependence cannot be confined to intraunit activities, the units involved are linked by a semiautonomous second-order group.
C. Remaining pooled interdependencies are controlled with standardized rules and procedures that blanket the units involved.

trol the activities of all affected units (see Figure 5-4). Standardization that applies to multiple units typically is accompanied by the formation of liaison (staff) positions that link the rule-making body to the rest of the organization.

Here, then, is a theoretical explanation of the growth of formal organizational structure that is considerably more elegant than the rational view of structure described in Chapter 3. Bureaucratic structures are developed in response to the kinds of interdependencies faced by various elements in the organization. Variations in the structures employed by organizations are to be expected, since interdependencies will vary according to each organization's task.

The conceptual economy of Thompson's approach will be demonstrated shortly. We will find that an elaboration of his ideas explains how organizations control both routine and nonroutine technologies.

Between bureaucratic and professional organizations

There seem to be two basic design principles for adaptive systems such as organizations (Emery, 1974). These systems must contain redundancy either in the form of easily replaceable parts or in the form of parts that contain redundant functions. In the former case, one may design an organization to accommodate workers who perform very simple tasks and who may be replaced with little difficulty (for example, assembly-line workers). In contrast, building potentially redundant functions into the parts is exemplified by professionalism, where, for instance, all attorneys are assumed to possess the same basic skills.

Following this logic, one will find resolution of the mechanistic-rational-organic-system dilemma. To design adaptiveness into the system while avoiding sacrifices of operating efficiency and the lengthy process of professional education (as well as the possible scarcity of requisite intelligence, skill, and interest in the general population), Emery suggests the use of autonomous work groups such as those designed by the Tavistock Institute (Chapter 4). These seem to fall between the two different forms of organization (see Figure 5-5).

The groups consisted of individuals who were relatively similar in terms of status and skills—who consequently were able to communicate freely and interchange work roles as the job required. Viewed as a whole, the groups operated somewhat as professionals do, trying out different techniques and approaches to problems and being flexible as the need arose. In this regard, our discussion of sales representatives engaged in helping their colleagues deal with sales problems may be recalled (Chapter 3).

Rather than being completely autonomous on the one hand or directed by external, organizational controls on the other, individuals are controlled by the group of which they are members. In this form of organization, par-

FIGURE 5-5
Forms of organization and individual control and participation

	Type		
	Bureaucratic	Group	Professional
Locus of control of the individual	External (plans, schedules, rules, etc.)	Group (group norms, plans, rules, etc.)	Internal (individuals, professional standards, etc.)
Degree of participation by the individual	Low (centralized)	Bounded (varying degrees of participation depending on organizationally prescribed limits)	High (decentralized)

ticipation may be full within the group, but it is bounded by external rules and policies that leave individuals with something less than complete autonomy.

Location of control as a function of information processing requirements

We have been careful thus far not to take an inflexible position regarding the optimal location of control, for this will vary. We shall now review a scheme for appropriately changing the locus of control in organizations as problem complexity changes.

Using a sample of 16 health and welfare agencies, Hage and Aiken (1969) studied relationships among centralization and formalization (as they are discussed above), task complexity (as measured by the degree of professional training required of employees), and routineness of technology. They found that the more routine the technology, the greater the tendency toward centralized decision making and policy formulation, codified rules manuals, and job descriptions. Hage and Aiken also found that the more routine the technology, the less the average amount of professional training required of employees.

A related point comes from an analysis by Jay Galbraith (1973). Building on James Thompson's theory of organizations (1967) and a number of studies that examine predictability of organizational tasks, Galbraith concludes that task predictability is a primary determinant of organizational structure.[4] As tasks become more unpredictable, the amount of information that must be processed increases; for example, individuals engaged in uncertain tasks must communicate frequently to make the mutual adjustments that feedback from the task suggests.

The amount of information processing required by task performance depends on three basic factors. The first is *task uncertainty,* which arises be-

---
[4] For example, Burns and Stalker (1961), Woodward (1965), and Harvey (1968).

cause programs and routines for accomplishing the task are unavailable and because the task itself varies (see Chapter 4). Second, information-processing requirements increase with the *number of elements* involved in the decision-making process, as these are determined by *(a)* the size of the organization, *(b)* the complexity or diversity of occupations involved in decision making, and *(c)* the number of products or services produced. The third factor is *reciprocal interdependence* among elements in the decision-making process.

Mechanisms for developing information-processing capacity

Jay Galbraith (1973) provides a taxonomy of organization design strategies that seeks to balance information-processing capacity with the requirements of the organization's tasks (see Figure 5–6). The taxonomy answers the question: How does a large, functionally structured organization cope with information-processing requirements that increase in response to increases in task uncertainty, interdependence, and the number of subunits engaged in task accomplishment?

The simplest way to coordinate interdependent departments is to (1) specify requisite actions in advance with plans, rules, and programs. The need for communication among departments will be reduced to the extent that planning adequately delineates each department's function. However, when the degree of problem complexity increases beyond the point where planning can cope with all contingencies, the organization will (2) resort to the use of its hierarchy of authority. Exceptions that cannot be planned for are referred to higher levels of management for resolution. Such *management by exception* is feasible so long as the exceptions are not of a magnitude that overloads the hierarchy with communications and decision making. When overload does occur, the organization generally turns to coordination that is achieved by (3) specifying goals and outputs (as opposed to planning specific activities that are means to these ends). At any one level of management, planning is concerned with the objectives of that level and not with specific means. The decentralization that is achieved by granting discretion in the choice of means to lower levels of the organization reduces the amount of information processed at higher levels. In addition, higher levels can differentiate the goals they establish for lower levels to reduce the interdependence of the latter. Galbraith provides the following example:

> An example of the way goals are used can be demonstrated by considering the design group responsible for an aircraft wing structure. The group's interdependence with other design groups is handled by technical specifications elaborating the points of attachment, forces transmitted at these points, centers of gravity, etc. The group also has a set of targets (not to be exceeded) for weight, design man-hours to be used, and a completion date. They are given minimum stress specifications below which they cannot design. The group then designs the structures and assemblies which combine to form the wing. They need not communicate with any other design

group on work-related matters if they and the interdependent groups are able to operate within the planned targets (1972, p. 58).

Increasing capacity or reducing processing requirements: A dilemma

In the event that the three alternatives described above prove inadequate to the task of managing uncertainties, an additional series of strategies can be employed. According to Figure 5–6, management can create either (4) slack resources and (5) self-contained organizational units in an attempt to reduce the need for information processing, or develop (6) vertical and (7) lateral systems to increase information-processing capacity. Each strategy has inherent costs and advantages.

Organizational slack (4) can be created by delaying target or completion dates so that exceptions can be managed without straining the capacity of the organization, by relaxing budget and technical specifications to reduce the interdependence of various design groups, and by a number of similar tactics. The costs of organizational slack are measured in delayed delivery dates, backlogs of orders, inventory carrying costs, reduced standards of performance, and the like.

A second method of reducing task-required information processing is to modify the authority structure to allow greater *self-containment* (5) of subunits involved in the task. Interdependence is reduced by dividing the task into several smaller problems that are addressed by units having their own facilities and resources. An example is reorganization from a centralized functional structure to project management (see Chapter 3). In this example, information-processing requirements are reduced by the delegation of decision-making authority to levels at which required information exists.

FIGURE 5–6
Organization design strategies

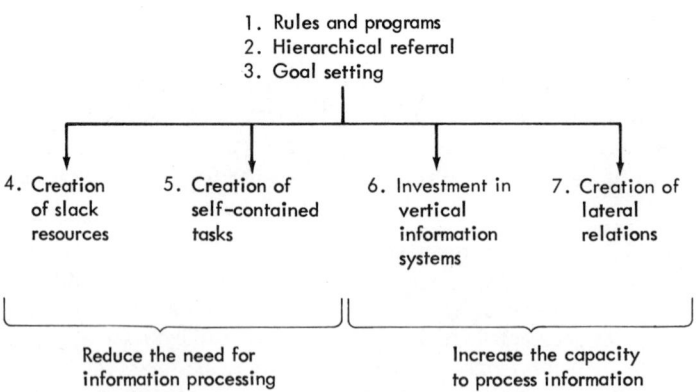

Source: Jay Galbraith, *Designing Complex Organizations*, 1973, Addison-Wesley, Reading, Mass., p. 15. © 1973 Addison-Wesley. Reprinted with permission.

The costs of self-containment include the duplication of effort and resources that are inevitable when separate projects require separate personnel and equipment. Hence, economies of scale are reduced. In addition, project managers necessarily make decisions within all of the functional areas as they pertain to the project. Consequently, they must be generalists. Because of this, the organization foregoes the depth of expertise enjoyed by specialists.

The development of what Galbraith calls *vertical information systems* (6) enables the organization to increase its information-processing capacity to match the requirements of the tasks it encounters. Essentially, these systems provide reduced planning cycles. Once a plan is made, exceptions occur as the environment changes or as inadequacies in the plan itself are discovered. The older the plan becomes, the more exceptions arise. At some point, it will be easier for management to revise the original plan than to deal with increasing numbers of exceptions. Alternatively, by reducing the planning cycle (for example, by planning monthly rather than quarterly) management will avoid many of the exceptions with which it would be faced otherwise. The costs associated with improving the vertical information system include increased numbers of staff specialists on the organization's payroll who are employed in the planning process, as well as perhaps computers and various sophisticated peripheral data processing devices.

The capacity to process information can also be increased through the creation and improvement of *lateral relationships* (7). The simplest of these is direct contact between peers. Rather than send exceptions up the hierarchy for coordination by a superior, the manager can contact the manager of an interdependent unit and deal with the exception directly. This is similar to Likert's concept of linking pins discussed in Chapter 3. Obviously, one cost of this approach is the increased number of time-consuming interpersonal relationships that must be developed among colleagues.

Another approach is the creation of task forces—temporary groups of full- or part-time members who serve as surrogates for higher level managers. Task forces may achieve permanent status in the organization when the problems to which they are addressed are complex and enduring; for example, a functionally organized firm may designate representatives from each function to deal with coordination problems that arise with respect to a particular product.

It should be evident that we are closing the loop, so to speak. Galbraith's suggestions parallel those of Ansoff and Brandenburg (1971) presented in Chapter 3. Ansoff and Brandenburg address four criteria of organizational performance: (1) steady state efficiency, (2) operating responsiveness, (3) strategic responsiveness, and (4) structural responsiveness. Galbraith addresses the problem of managing increasing information and decision flows. One approach seems to verify the other. This is most evident in Galbraith's recommendation that extreme information processing requirements be met with a matrix form of organization. Here, the trade-off is strategic responsiveness gained at the expense of steady state efficiency and operating responsiveness.

From external to internal control

One way to interpret Galbraith's taxonomy is to observe the progression from external controls (rules, plans, and so on, that are advocated for the co-ordination of relatively simple tasks) to increasingly internalized controls that are recommended for tasks of increasing complexity. Goal-setting provides subordinates with the autonomy to select their own means. Increasing slack resources increases lateral autonomy in the organization by decreasing interdependence between departments. The creation of self-contained tasks serves much the same purpose. Reducing the planning cycle causes the operating unit to become more responsive to feedback, since it is feedback in its various forms that suggests modifications to the plan. Finally, the establishment of lateral relationships places the responsibility for coordination of interdependencies in the departments themselves instead of with higher levels of management. This appears to pave the way for unprogrammed co-ordination as well as cooperation between colleagues.

Implicit in Galbraith's taxonomy is the notion that internal control is increased as autonomy is expanded; for instance, commitment to a goal serves to control the choice and employment of means. The taxonomy also assumes that the individuals and groups to whom autonomy is extended are competent to exercise their discretion in the organization's interest. We will digress for a moment to review two management techniques (goal-setting and gaining compliance with rules and programs) that make one portion of the model operational.

Management by objectives

Management by objectives (MBO) can be traced to Peter Drucker's *The Practice of Management,* written in 1954. Drucker advises managers to work toward clear objectives that reflect and support those of their immediate superiors. Furthermore, he suggests that they work with their immediate superiors in establishing higher level objectives, enabling all managers to know and understand the goals of the organization and their superiors as these are related to their own performance. With clearly defined objectives, managers will be in a position to control their own performance and thereby achieve higher levels of motivation.

George Odiorne (1965) termed this philosophy "management by objectives" and provided systematic means for its implementation. His work emphasizes making objectives operational and specifying quantitative measures of progress toward their attainment. Managers work as a pair with each of their subordinates to agree on both the subordinate's objectives in the next time period and the means by which progress will be evaluated at the end of the period in question. Used properly, MBO will include every manager, from the chief executive officer to the last line supervisor, in a dyad of this sort. Furthermore, it is each manager's responsibility under this system to help subordinates meet their objectives.

At first glance, this appears the epitome of the rational view of organizations. In practice, MBO is compatible with the system view as well. Goals other than those of the formal organization are included in the objective-setting process; for example, the subordinate and the boss may develop a program of objectives intended to result in the former's promotion within the organization. Thus, ways of meeting individual and system needs can be made congruent with the pursuit of organizational goals.

Research shows that specific goal-setting, knowledge of results, and participation enhance performance when goals are established at the proper level of difficulty, reasonable time limits are set, and sufficient energy is available for their attainment (Carroll and Tosi, 1973). Other studies (Carroll and Tosi, 1973; Meyer, Kay, and French, 1965; Raia, 1966), generally indicate that MBO results in improved planning, control, and motivation.

However, no system is without its faults. Raia (1966) reports managers' dissatisfactions with the paper work required by MBO and with the apparent overemphasis of quantitative measures. Some managers report attempts to beat the system by fudging reports. Other studies indicate that the benefits of MBO may deteriorate over time (Ivancevich, 1972). Rather than panaceas, techniques of this sort are remedies for organizational problems that occur in specific, limited circumstances. Abuses, failures, and unmet expectations are to be anticipated when they are applied across the board.

Positive reinforcement

We shall comment briefly on one of the most unusual attempts to achieve control found in recent history of organizations—one that will add fuel to the debate over the "superiority" of internal versus external controls. In *Beyond Freedom and Dignity,* Skinner (1971) argues that freedom exists only as the "feeling of freedom." We are all controlled, but feel free when pursuing our own valued ends. We feel controlled (the absence of freedom) when avoiding punishment. In either event, we behave as we have learned (been conditioned) to behave. The professional's internal control was external at one point. The scholar was not born loving truth, but learned, or was taught to love truth in the process of becoming a scholar. Skinner states this more eloquently in his novel *Walden Two:* "A *laissez-faire* philosophy which trusts to the inherent goodness and wisdom of the common man is incompatible with the observed fact that men are made good or bad and wise or foolish by the environment in which they grow" (1970, p. 273).

Internal control is neither good nor bad. Means, such as self-discipline, and the ends they serve are to be evaluated in terms of the effects they produce ultimately. Animals can be conditioned to behave according to the desires of their trainers. At first, the desired behaviors are rewarded to establish consequences that are contingent on their repetition. As the desired behaviors are repeated, the rewards are reduced and eventually eliminated as the learned behaviors become internalized.

Emery Air Freight is presently attempting to improve performance by applying this type of conditioning to its work force (American Management Association, 1973). The "positive reinforcement program," as it is called, starts with an audit of performance to determine how well employees are doing. Where performance is found to warrant improvement, work standards are established by superiors. Following this, employees are required to maintain continuous records of their own performance in relation to the standards. These are submitted to superiors who recognize and praise specific improved performances and avoid censuring lesser efforts.

In theory, reinforcement comes in three stages. First, the superior gives frequent positive reinforcement based on the continuous feedback data received from subordinates, thus shaping their behavior. Later, reinforcement is given infrequently on an unpredictable schedule. Finally, supervisory reinforcement is reduced to a negligible level, and feedback in the form of task accomplishment takes over as the major source of reward for the worker.

In practice, Emery has yet to achieve the stage envisioned where natural reinforcers replace those that are contrived. Supervisors have reduced the amount of recognition they give, but they continue to receive progress reports from their subordinates. Such reporting seems necessary to prevent decreases in productivity. It is argued that keeping progress reports and submitting them to supervisors augments the natural reinforcers—the satisfaction of having completed an assignment or of having given a fair day's work for a fair day's pay. This argument seems rather transparent, however, since submitting forms to supervisors implies evaluation and implicit disapprobation in the case of unfavorable reports.

Be that as it may, Emery Air Freight's positive reinforcement program seems to be quite successful so far. For instance, customer service standards have been 95 percent achieved, as opposed to 35 percent prior to the experiment. Through improvements such as this, the firm apparently has saved over $3 million in a three-year period (American Management Association, 1973).

There is something chilling and Orwellian about the use of behavior modification, perhaps because it appears overly manipulative. It could be argued that this entire book is about manipulation, but we are convinced that other means of control preserve more of the employee's options. For example, the participants in a job enrichment scheme or other form of reorganization are probably aware of their reactions to changes in the organization and are able to exercise whatever power they enjoy to comply with or resist them. This is not the case in behavior modification which generates forces the employee is not likely to understand. It may be that this approach is tainted unfairly by its origins.

Skinnerian systems of behavior modification were developed using subjects who had little control over their behavior. They were deviates who either lacked self-control or were deprived of control by the institutions to which they were committed. It would seem that behavior modification is suited to those whose control is weak and who cannot join coalitions that magnify their limited powers. It makes the assumption that the interests and values of the behavior shaper and the subject are congruent when such an assumption cannot be taken for granted. These kinds of reservations must be weighed against the fact that the technique does seem to work with normal subjects in industrial settings, who do not seem to have suffered any loss of moral responsibility as a result of their conditioning. It may be that we are all conditioned as Skinner suggests.

Compliance structures

Are the ideas presented by Thompson and Galbraith applicable to all institutions—penal, religious, and educational, as well as economic? One could argue affirmatively, but the argument would mask important differences among such organizations, including differences in the way members are controlled. If we define membership to include inmates as well as guards, parishioners as well as clergy, and students as well as faculty, we will find that variations in the ways organizations control their members can be attributed to more than interdependencies, uncertainties, and the like.

According to Etzioni (1961), the forces that determine how members are controlled so that they comply with organizational requirements are implicit in the organization's choice of goals. Organizational goals fall into three broad categories: (1) *order goals,* which refer to the control of deviates; (2) *economic goals,* which specify the production of goods or services for consumption in the marketplace; and (3) *cultural goals,* which are pursued by organizations that create or preserve symbolic objects, apply them, and promote commitment to them.

Organizations that pursue order goals are termed *coercive organizations.* These are typified by prisons, correctional institutions, and custodial mental hospitals. Cultural goals are sought by universities, religious organizations, and political parties, which are classified as *normative organizations.* Business and industry have economic goals and are grouped together as *utilitarian organizations.*

Each type of organization holds a different kind of power over its members (Table 5-1). Coercive organizations, involved in the control of deviates, exercise *coercive* power; for example, they apply physical sanctions or restrict members' satisfaction of needs. Utilitarian organizations, having the means to give or withhold material rewards, are said to use *remunerative power. Normative power* exercised by normative institutions comprises the allocation and manipulation of symbolic rewards; for example, religious symbols or symbols of academic achievement.

TABLE 5-1
Organizational goals and compliance relationships

Type of organization	Goal	Kind of power	Type of member involvement		
			Alienative	Calculative	Moral
Coercive	Order	Coercive	1*	2	3
Utilitarian	Economic	Remunerative	4	5*	6
Normative	Cultural	Normative	7	8	9*

* Efficient compliance relationships.
Source: Reprinted with permission of Macmillan Publishing Co., Inc. from *A Comparative Analysis of Complex Organization* by Amitai Etzioni. Copyright © 1961 by The Free Press of Glencoe, Inc.

The reason that each type of organization tends to use a single form of power is found in the relationship between the organization's goal and the nature of its members' involvement in the organization. The involvement of prisoners and members of other coercive organizations is said to be *alienative*. Were they not alienated from society's fundamental moral values or otherwise maladjusted, they presumably would not be inmates of these institutions.

Because their involvement in the organization is alienative, the organization will not profit from exercising normative power. How can appeals to moral obligations influence an individual who is alienated from the values on which they rest? By the same token, remunerative power is of limited value in cases such as this, since there is little justification for paying deviates to comply with society's moral obligations. This sort of reasoning leads Etzioni to conclude that successful organizations evolve effective compliance relationships with their members. In the case of coercive organizations, this relationship takes the *coercive-alienative* form (Table 5-1).

Members of normative organizations tend to have a *moral* involvement in their institutions. Teachers believe in education, members of religious organizations serve their God, and scientists value the objective pursuit of knowledge. In other words, these individuals find intrinsic value in the goals sought by their organizations and need not be coerced into contributing their labors. Neither will remunerative power be particularly effective in this case. As Etzioni suggests, it is unseemly to offer payment for the exercise of moral duty. Consequently, we are not surprised to find that members of normative organizations such as teachers, social workers, nurses, and clerics are paid less than employees of business firms, who are similar in terms of their education, experience, and rank in the organization. The effective compliance relationship in normative organizations then is *normative-moral*.

Participants in economic organizations tend to seek a quid pro quo. Their involvement is described as *calculative*, since they are willing to contribute their services in return for adequate material rewards. With few exceptions, they are neither alienated from nor morally committed to the enterprise, and neither coercion nor normative persuasion will be effective in gaining their compliance. Rather, the compliance relationship that evolves is *remunerative-calculative*.

Etzioni's ideas round out some of the prescriptions elaborated above. For example, while Thompson or Galbraith may suggest that a particular situation is most effectively governed by rules and procedures, Etzioni tells us that the nature of compliance with such rules will differ among organizations as a function of their goals.

Yet, this distinction is not as great as it might appear. For example, Thompson and Galbraith seem to agree that complex organizational tasks typically are performed by diverse, relatively autonomous occupational roles. Furthermore, because these roles are diverse and autonomous, it is extremely difficult to coordinate them using external control techniques. Some form of internal control, whether commitment to the task, dedication to scientific methods, or adherence to professional norms, is more appropriate.

But, on whom shall the organization rely to exercise self-control in the performance of complex tasks? Clearly, the answer must be, on those who have internalized attitudes, norms, and values that make them appear, in Etzioni's terms, morally committed to the task, organization, or profession. In this sense, the conclusions of Etzioni and Galbraith seem to converge.

In another sense, though, a major distinction remains, for in selecting a goal the organization can render its tasks either simple or complex. Please recall our earlier observation that a mental hospital, formally chartered as a restorative agency, may pursue a goal of providing custodial rather than therapeutic services. Therapeutic services of the type suggested comprise a number of complex, ill-structured tasks that theoretically would be coordinated by feedback and various forms of internal control. Conversely, the custodial function requires relatively simple, well-structured tasks, that typically are amenable to external controls. Thus, the hospital need not recruit internally controlled (morally committed) employees. Furthermore, maintaining custody over inmates usually requires coercion. Coercion, in turn, produces alienation that renders remunerative or normative power less effective. Thus, Etzioni's theory may provide a useful way to describe organizational processes that underlie the observations of Galbraith and Thompson. Apparently, the choice of goals has substantial effects on the organization in other ways as well. This is the topic of our next chapter.

DISCUSSION QUESTIONS

1. What parallels can you draw between Jay Galbraith's work and the ideas of Ansoff and Brandenburg (Chapter 3)?
2. What consequences can the coercive-alienative compliance relationship have for a correctional institution's goal of rehabilitating inmates?
3. What possible shortcomings can you identify in the rational view of strategic planning?
4. What goals do colleges and universities typically pursue?

SECTION II

Determinants of Design: Goals, Environment, and Strategy

Chapter 6
Goals

Chapter 7
The Organization's Environment

Chapter 8
Strategy Formulation

PREMISE

If either the rational or system model of organizations was completely valid, the management of complex organizations would be less arduous than it is. However, as we have seen, neither model describes reality adequately for the simple reason that the two views are not mutually exclusive. While we agree that social systems are open, we must also argue that they are controlled to some extent by rational orderings of events and relationships. Beyond this, we suggest that the organization can be directed toward predetermined outcomes and that instead of being entirely at the mercy of events, the organization exerts some degree of control over its environment.

The organization is much more than an adaptive system. Certainly, management attempts to make appropriate adaptive responses to significant changes in its environment. At the same time, however, the orga-

nization's powers are focused on portions of the environment it wishes to change. Thus, in addition to viewing stategy as a vehicle for adaptation, we must also learn how large organizations use their immense powers in the pursuit of their interests. We must understand the interests or goals of organizations, their environments, and the behavior of the relatively few individuals in whose hands these powers rest.

6

Goals

INTRODUCTION

In an intriguing study of American universities, Edward Gross (1968) obtained rankings of university goals from a sample of faculty members and administrators located at 68 institutions of higher learning. Subjects were provided with a set of 47 goals and asked to indicate the relative degree of importance that their university assigned to each goal, as well as the relative degree of importance that *should* be assigned to each. Partial results of the study are reproduced below:

		Existing goals		*Goals that should be*
Top goals*	1.	Protect the faculty's right to academic freedom	1.	Protect the faculty's right to academic freedom
	2.	Increase the presitge of the university	2.	Train students in methods of scholarship and/or scientific research and/or creative endeavor
	3.	Maintain top quality in those programs we feel to be especially important	3.	Produce students who, whatever else may be done to them, have had their intellects cultivated to the maximum

	Existing goals		Goals that should be
	4. Ensure the continued confidence and support of those who contribute substantially to the financial and other material resource needs of the university	4.	Maintain top quality in all programs in which we engage
	5. Keep up to date and responsive	5.	Serve as a center for the dissemination of new ideas that would change society, whether those ideas are in science, literature, the arts, or politics
	6. Train students in methods of scholarship and/or scientific research and/or creative endeavor	6.	Keep up to date and responsive
	7. Carry on pure research	7.	Maintain top quality in those programs we feel to be especially important
		8.	Assist students to develop objectivity about themselves and their beliefs, and hence examine those beliefs critically
		9.	Make sure the university is run by those selected according to their ability to attain the goals of the university in the most efficient manner possible
	* * * * *		
Bottom goals* 44.	Emphasize undergraduate instruction even at the expense of the graduate program		
45.	Involve students in the government of the university	45.	Make a good consumer of the student
46.	Keep this place from becoming something different than it is now	46.	Involve students in the government of the university
47.	Make a good consumer of the student	47.	Keep this place from becoming something different than it is now

* "Top" and "Bottom" goals have been determined by arranging the actual average scores on a single distribution, separating the distribution into standard deviation units, and selecting goals that fell in the top and bottom standard deviation.
Source: Edward Gross (1968, pp. 529-30).

Chapter guide

Obviously, there is some congruence between existing goals and those that should be goals. More revealing, perhaps, are the discrepancies between the two lists. These similarities and discrepancies begin to take on the meaning when the following questions are raised:

1. How are faculty/administration interests reflected in the actual and desired university goals?
2. How do you imagine students would have responded to questions about desired university goals? Board of trustees members? Townspeople? Hourly paid university employees? Alumni?
3. Are the goals of a university what the faculty and administration perceive them to be, or do students, townspeople, other employees, and members of the board of trustees influence the organization's behavior according to their own objectives and desires?
4. What are goals? Do organizations have goals, or are we speaking of a negotiated consensus of the objectives of the organization's members?

CONCEPTS OF GOALS

Organizational Goals

We often hear an organization's goal described as the end that an organization selects and to which it applies its energies and resources in a constructive, purposive manner. The trouble with this line of thinking is that it may conceive the organization as a sentient being. Furthermore, recognition of the numbers of different constituencies to which a given organization must respond renders this statement of organizational goal-setting more a fiction than a description of reality. For example, cadres of professional managers, labor unions, stockholders, and the board of directors can be numbered among the various constituencies that comprise a business firm. In addition, consumers, suppliers, competitors and regulatory agencies can constrain the firm's range of behavior and consequently its selection of goals. The numerous goals, which these constituencies would have the organization serve, can even be counterproductive.

For a number of reasons, including the existence of multiple constituencies, both students of organizations and managers themselves began to turn from the rational view of a specific organizational purpose or purposes to view organizational objectives in broader terms. Long-run profit maximization came into vogue as a legitimate goal in the profit sector. Some writers, such as Drucker (1963), began to advocate long-run survival, as opposed to profit maximization, as the ultimate objective of the firm. Clearly, if the firm survives over the long run, it will have done so because it managed to satisfy a reasonable number of the demands of its major constituencies.

As debate raged over the merits of survival versus long-run profit maximization, a third school of thought emerged. Cyert and March (1963) concluded that organizations do not have objectives; only people have objectives. Therefore, what we have been calling the objectives of the organization are, in essence, no more than a negotiated consensus of the individuals who play major roles in the organization's affairs.

Finally, a number of researchers came to view the entire concept of organizational goals with suspicion. Katz and Kahn (1978), for example, begin their study of organizations with the observation that organizations typically include both more and less than is intended by their founders or leaders. For this reason, the study of organizations ". . . should begin with the input, output, and functioning of the organization as a system and not with the rational purposes of its leaders" (p. 20).

This view flows readily from the system model of organization described in Chapter 2. While agreeing with Katz and Kahn about the problems in a rational view of organizational goals, we shall not take quite as strong a position. We shall attempt to infer the goals of the organization from a variety of sources: its formal goals; the actual purposive behavior of members; the goals for the organization held by stakeholders; and the constraints and negotiated arrangements arising from conflict between various groupings in the organization. The notion of organizational goals is a difficult one, but with these various perspectives as bench marks, we hope to provide a more or less accurate and useful picture of the organization's goals—of where it is heading.

Formal Goals

An organization's formally stated goals are interlaced with the informal goals and agendas of individuals, groups, and organizational units. This observation lends a measure of order to the apparent chaos in the literature cited above. In contrast to Cyert and March, we contend that organizations do have goals, however ambiguously stated, that are also part of the organization's culture and that transcend the needs and motives of individuals and influential groups. The fact that these goals, which are generally vague in the first place, are clouded further by informal goals leads writers such as Katz and Kahn to despair justifiably of ever understanding an organization through its stated, formal objectives.

By focusing our attention primarily on the *determinants of goals* and the *goal-setting process* we will steer clear of normative statements—statements about what the goals of an organization should be. We will not concern ourselves with whether a firm ought to establish long-run profit maximization or survival as its goal. Rather, we will attempt to describe the manner in which goals are determined through analysis of theory and empirical data, including case histories.

We can begin our inquiry by acknowledging the existence of formal goals which usually are recorded in the organization's charter, annual reports, public statements by key executives, and other authoritative pronouncements. They range, according to the type of organization in question, from profitability in the business sector to the celebration of life in one religious organization with which the authors are familiar. Usually they are purposely vague and general, allowing different constituencies to collaborate in the same organizational framework. Their ambiguity provides a philosophical framework for organizational decisions rather than a system of criterion measures against which day-to-day performance and decisions can be checked. After all, how does one decide whether a particular action will eventually lead to the long-run maximization of the firm's profits?

The formal goals of an organization are not only vague, but according to a number of sociologists, may even be positively misleading. In some cases, such goals are part of the organization's culture and are not meant to be realized (Etzioni, 1964, p. 260). Sociologists have provided a number of examples of such contrasts between formal purposes and actual functioning: a financially profitable community service club whose service is an incidental part of its activities as measured by allocations of time and money to these activities (Warriner, 1965); prisons with the stated aim of rehabilitation that spend very little time or money on such services and instead primarily function in a custodial fashion, putting walls between the prisoner and society (Zald, 1963); and political organizations that espouse democracy but are internally ruled by leaders who do not countenance their own replacement by any democratic procedures (Michels, 1959).

As Warriner (1965) suggests, "Statements of purpose, thus, must be treated as fictions produced by an organization to account for, explain, or rationalize its existence to particular audiences rather than as valid and reliable indicators of purpose" (p. 141). Much as some overseas companies are reputed to have different sets of accounts for the tax collector, the shareholders, and management, organizations are likely to have one or more sets of purposes for different constituencies.

Behavioristic versus rationalistic study of goals

The rational model portrays the organization as focusing its energies on goals such as profit-maximization and long-run survival. It assumes that top management identifies alternative means for achieving these ends and selects from among the alternatives those that are most productive. The means thus chosen become the lower order goals for the next level of managers, who in turn set means for the accomplishment of their goals. This latter set of means gives rise to a set of goals for the next lower level of management, and so on. Following this logic, many studies of organizational goals emphasize the goals that are formally articulated and consciously held by individuals or subgroups within the organization. Unfortunately, while this type of study may describe the goals of individuals within an organization, the sum of individuals' goals may not equal the goal of the entire organization.

Here we shall take a lead from Etzioni (1964): "An organizational goal is a desired state of affairs which the organization attempts to realize..." (p. 6). But *whose* desired state of affairs? We do not mean the multitude of aspirations that various individuals have *for* the organization (for example, "I think this organization should..."), although certain individuals or groups may influence the selection of goals. A view of goals as norms is not sufficient either—the view that the "... group goals represent an operating consensus about a desirable state of a given task" (Thibaut and Kelley, 1959, p. 257). In contrast, we emphasize goals *of* the organization, which are more than the sum of private, individual goals and which are usually different from the publicly espoused purpose(s) of the organization.

Pointing the way, Warriner (1965) looks first at the organization's activities. After determining the amount of member time (resources) devoted to these, he focuses on the most prevalent and important in terms of resource utilization. For Warriner, the assumed functions (that is, the assumed consequences or results) of these activities illustrate the organization's goals.

> Thus a particular mental hospital is judged to be a custodial rather than a therapeutic institution because, taking each of its activities separately, the staff attitude toward and conception of each activity is that it is designed and carried out either (1) to protect the staff, (2) to protect the patient, (3) to keep the patient manageable, or (4) to keep him physically in the institution (Warriner, 1965, p. 142).

Warriner focuses first and foremost on behavior, and ascertains individuals' intentions or understandings of such behaviors. Much as the psychologist develops the construct "attitude" from, and as an explanation of, individual behavior, we suggest that one can observe purposive organizational behavior and infer a scientific construct of organizational goals. In the course of this chapter, we hope to show by examination of examples of goal behavior and the inferred organizational construct how a suprapsychological approach to understanding organizational goals is feasible and useful.

Operative goals

Because of their generality, formal goals, according to Perrow (1970), are likely to obscure two major influences on organizational behavior: (1) the many choices that must be made among *alternative means* for achieving formal goals, including the priorities that must be set in the presence of multiple goals, and (2) the *unofficial goals* pursued by groups and individual members of the organization. Perrow combines these two forces under the rubric *operative goals*—the ends that are sought through the actual functioning of the organization.

Operative goals may specify the manner in which certain formal goals are to be attained; for example, profit goals can be met by pursuing operative goals such as the attainment of economies of scale or market penetration.

The study of operative goals is worthwhile for several reasons. First, they frequently suggest the criteria against which subsequent organizational performance is evaluated. Related to this is the tendency for the organization, or subunits of the organization, to embrace the operative goals as surrogates for the organization's formal goals. This phenomenon has been referred to as *suboptimization*, or functioning at a less than optimal level because a subset of the ultimate goal serves as a focus of efforts. The marketing department may push for a high volume of sales, even though one of the items marketed may cost most to make and sell than the price at which it is sold. A production subunit comprising highly skilled craftsmen may spend a great deal of effort on finishing a product to very close tolerances and producing a quality product when its use by customers does not require such high tolerances and, in fact, the product's price is more important to customers than quality.

Finally, some operative goals are tied to individual or group interests and occasionally become irrelevant to, if not subversive of, the organization's formal goals; for example, a key executive may hold financial interests in an organization that is a supplier to his own. Similarly, the prestige associated with the possession of heart-lung machines and other forms of sophisticated technology has been known to lure some hospitals away from their stated goal of providing excellent patient care. In cases such as these, pressures for policies and operating decisions are based primarily on the interests of the parties involved.

This last observation will free us from the dilemma raised earlier. On one hand, we are disinclined to reify organizations as systems, that is, to conceive the system as a sentient being having a goal. On the other hand, we have disclaimed the notion that an organization's goals are the sum of individual members' goals. Obviously both formal and operative goals are shaped by people, but the people involved are limited to the "... individuals who collectively have sufficient control of organizational resources to commit them in certain directions and to withhold them from others" (James Thompson, 1967, p. 128). We shall follow Thompson in referring to this collection of individuals as the *dominant coalition*. We will elaborate this idea in Chapter 8. For the moment, however, it is sufficient to note that the control of resources can rest outside as well as inside the organization.

Output, system, product, and derived goals

Unlike Drucker (1963), and more in line with the reasoning of Katz and Kahn (1978), Perrow assumes that goals can be inferred directly from the organization's behavior. In one organization, the goal of maintaining certain product characteristics may be the single most influential determinant of the organization's behavior, over and above profitability. Alternatively, another organization may take growth as its primary concern. In developing his study of operative goals, Perrow attempts to categorize such areas of endeavor. This categorization in turn gives rise to four distinct classes of goals.[1]

1. *Output goals.* The kinds of output produced, such as consumer goods, services for other organizations, health care, and education.
2. *System goals.* System characteristics, such as growth, stability, profitability, decentralization, centralization, and efficiency.
3. *Product goals.* The characteristics of goods or services produced, such as quality, quantity, styling, availability, uniqueness, and innovativeness.
4. *Derived goals.* The uses to which organizations put the power that they generate, such as political aims, employee development, and community service.

Output goals

A study of organizations' output goals directs our attention to boundary phenomena, particularly to the influence systems that exist between organizations and their environments. An historical view of universities, for example, brings our attention to changes in output goals that have occurred in response to society's shifting preferences for the output of various educational programs. Agricultural, business, and teacher-training programs have found legitimacy in academia largely as a result of society's demand for individuals who possess advanced knowledge and skills in these areas. Similarly, firms once interested primarily in the manufacture of goods have undertaken to enhance the work-related skills of individuals hitherto unemployable.

Thus, in response to perceived pressures, threats, and opportunities, organizations alter and expand their goals. In terms of expansion, law enforcement agencies may provide social services; businesses may engage in planning and developing new towns; and universities, which once were aloof and isolated centers of learning for the intellectual elite, may now supply public entertainment through their athletic departments. Yet, this tendency toward the expansion of output goals often runs afoul of an apparent societal norm that holds that output functions should be widely distributed among independent organizations (Perrow, 1965). The resistance of conservatives and business executives to the formation of the TVA was founded, in part, on their reluctance to permit a governmental agency to produce such commodities as electricity and fertilizer (Selznick, 1949). Similar fears have been expressed concerning the military-industrial complex. Such fears no doubt have their roots in our culture's aversion to centralized power and authority and a concomitant belief in Adam Smith's "invisible hand."

Finally, Perrow brings to our attention the magnitude of organizational

---

[1] Perrow's (1970) categorization scheme, in fact, includes five goals. We have omitted from our discussion the category of societal goals, which, in Perrow's words, "... has little to do with functioning organizations" (p. 135).

change that is implied in altering output goals. Management skills required for a given type of output may not be directly appropriate to the production of a dissimilar type of product. Perrow cites the example in which the management and organizational skills that served Ford's purposes so well apparently were less effective in the management of the Philco Corporation, which Ford purchased in an attempt to diversify its output goals (Siekman, 1966). We recall from Chapter 4 that different technologies are likely to influence the nature of the organization's structure and behavior. Thus, the behavior that an organization finds effective in managing one technological process may be less than satisfactory in dealing with a different technology adopted through the introduction of a new output goal.

System goals

System goals refer to characteristics of the organization as an organization rather than to its products or services. Organizations are systems, and to function and survive they must be concerned with more than output (Etzioni, 1964). Included as system goals are growth, stability, profitability, and efficiency. These refer to aspects of the system that may receive top priority beyond that of producing one or another kind of output. Growth in research funding, rather than production of quality research may be a goal for a research center. By way of illustration, Perrow points to the history of Eastern Airlines. This company, which for many years held a near monopoly on the most profitable routes, pursued the goal of cost reduction with the consequence of reducing customer service. This situation served the company well for many years until two events occurred. First, the Civil Aeronautics Board decided to strengthen the smaller lines by giving them access to the more profitable routes. Second, the newly encouraged competition began to make inroads into Eastern's business by attracting customers with improved services. After suffering a substantial setback, Eastern, by this time under a new top management, altered its system goals to become more like its competitors.

In terms of such organizational goals as profit-maximization and long-run survival, Eastern may have been poorly managed. Even if this statement is true, it tells us very little. Through his analysis of operative goals, however, Perrow lends considerable insight into the company's history. It does not make much sense to say that competing lines were poorly managed while Eastern was profitable or that Eastern was mismanaged when competitors made inroads into its market. "The other companies simply had different goals, and when their goals of growth and product innovation began to pay off, Eastern had to change its goals, too" (Perrow, 1970, p. 150).

An organization is open to its environment and must alter its goals and behavior appropriately as the environment changes. The study of cybernetic systems tells us that responses to feedback and other external stimuli must be damped, that is, restrained. Instantaneous response is something never found in nature, and for good reason. An organism or machine that responds immediately to each and every change in the signals to which it must ultimately respond will quickly overload and break down. Damping allows the organism to remain unresponsive within tolerable limits. Thus, a thermostat will allow room temperature to vary several degrees around the desired temperature before activating the heating system.

As a cybernetic system, Eastern overdamped. Responses to changes in the environment were delayed until a crisis became evident. In studying goals as they affect organizational behavior then, we must remember that goals ultimately are related to the environment. This not only implies that their initial formulation must be responsive to environmental factors, but that periodic monitoring of the environment is essential to the maintenance of viable goals. In doing so, management employs theoretical constructs that indicate the significant variables in the environment and the kinds of effects that changes in these variables are likely to produce in the organization's relationship to environment.

Product goals

That most organizations have product goals becomes most apparent when one observes the occasional organization that has none. This type of organization is typified by the firm that will handle any product as long as it is profitable, helps the organization grow, or is a means to some other kind of goal. Thus, some supermarket chains have turned to nonfood items as means to their system goal of profit. Against this kind of organization, we can contrast those whose behavior is centered around some readily identifiable product goals. The A&P nicely illustrates product goal behavior in its emphasis on providing high-quality, low-priced foods. Most of A&P's capital has been invested in their own plants for producing A&P baked goods, dairy products, meats, fruits and vegetables, while competitors have been investing in larger stores to handle more profitable nonfood items and to operate more efficiently by means of higher volumes at lower overheads.

An even more striking example of an organization's behavior being shaped by specific product goals is Volkswagen. Early in 1972, Volkswagen's production of the familiar Beetle passed the 15 million mark and with that the long-standing record for production runs set by the Ford Model T. In observing this remarkable achievement, Ball (1972) drew other similarities between Volkswagen and Ford during the Model T era. While the buyer of a Beetle had a choice of a variety of colors, the car's styling and its rear-mounted, air-cooled engine rendered successive years' models indistinguishable, except to the practiced eye. The company expanded its product line by introducing the VW Transporter in 1950, the Karmann Ghia in 1955, and the larger Type Three in 1961. The next new model, the 411, was clearly an attempt to apply the basic Volkswagen engineering and design principles to a car that would appeal to buyers in the middle-income bracket. Ball's appraisal of this tactic is that, "By 1968, however, the auto world was becoming tired of the formula. Wags greeted the 411 with the gibe that it was so named because it had four doors and was introduced eleven years too late" (Ball, 1972, p. 98).

One implication that can be drawn from Volkswagen's experience is that certain design characteristics (especially the air-cooled rear engine) of the Beetle came, in time, to assume the proportions of product goals. Yet, as it turned out, the basic formula that served the company so well over a production run of 15 million cars became incompatible with the changing market for economy cars. Toyota, Datsun, and others made substantial inroads into Volkswagen's U.S. market by producing economy cars that came closer to reflecting consumer preferences. It soon became apparent that the product goals manifested in the ubiquitous Beetle were ill-suited for the design of a car for the contemporary middle-class market.

The introduction of the Audi 100 was the initial departure from Volkswagen's former product goals—but there is an interesting story behind the car. Volkswagen acquired Auto Union to use its productive capacity to manufacture Beetles. After the acquisition, though, the Volkswagen management assigned to the company, together with former Auto Union personnel, collaborated on the design of an automobile that had been on Auto Union's drawing board prior to the takeover. Work on the Audi 100 was carried out without the direct knowledge of top management at Volkswagen. Surprisingly, Volkswagen's management approved the final design, and the Audi 100 became a runaway success (Ball, 1972).

Derived goals

Finally, it is important to recognize that organizations wield considerable power in areas other than their marketplace, and the use of this power may become a central issue for the organization, a matter of interest to management, and an organizational goal. Profit-making corporations, for example, not only contribute large sums of money to universities, public service agencies, and the like, they also may use their philanthropy as leverage to modify the organizations they support. By the same token, lobbies, in behalf of their constituents, exert pressure on legislators to influence legislation affecting them.

In more subtle ways, organizations can change the quality of life around them by erecting buildings that fail to conform to existing architectural themes or by altering the flow of traffic within these areas. Supporting political parties, altering the public's tastes through advertising, and providing or withholding goods and services from the marketplace are only a few of the ways in which organizations strive toward the realization of derived goals.

As important as these phenomena are to our understanding of organizations, we must conclude that much ignorance still prevails in this general area of social responsibility.

MANAGING STAKEHOLDER EXPECTATIONS

Stakeholder expectations

How can goals vary so greatly from one organization to another? How do operative goals come to be? One way of explaining the genesis of organizational goals is suggested by an examination of *stakeholder expectations*. By stakeholders, we mean the individuals and groups who collectively can influence the organizations in question. Such control may be contingent on membership (managers or workers), investments in the organization (owners, benefactors of various kinds), contractual arrangements (suppliers), norms of reciprocity (competitors and other organizations in the environment), or ultimate sovereignty (the nation). Each class of stakeholders has somewhat different expectations *for* the organization that are related to the goals and interests of the various stakeholders themselves. The goals *of* the organization are likely to emerge from the interaction of these various goals *for* the organization.

Conflict of expectations

The example provided in Figure 6-1 illustrates expectations of the stakeholders in a professional graduate school. Example 1 brings to light a familiar illustration of the town-gown problem. In attempting to provide its students with a broad, balanced view of current social issues, a school may invite guest speakers who, in the eyes of more conservative members of the community, are subversive of the community's values.

When the two sets of expectations come into conflict, as they do in the hypothetical example provided above, several tactics may be undertaken.

1. Initially, administrators tend to view problems such as this as the result of misunderstandings. Consequently, a public relations program may be implemented under the assumption that once members of the community understand the role of such speakers in the educational process they will view their activities in a favorable light, that is, in the same way that educators view them. Failing this, several alternative tactics can be undertaken depending on the predispositions of the parties involved.

2. Cooptation can be attempted by inviting the major critics of the school's programs to join (in limited numbers) the groups that are responsible for their planning and implementation.

3. Alternatively, the school may withdraw from contact with the community and proceed in insularity.

4. Other administrators may choose to meet community opposition with force. One administrator, who was opposed by an influential banker in matters affecting the operation of his school, appointed one of the banker's larg-

FIGURE 6-1
Intersections of stakeholder expectations

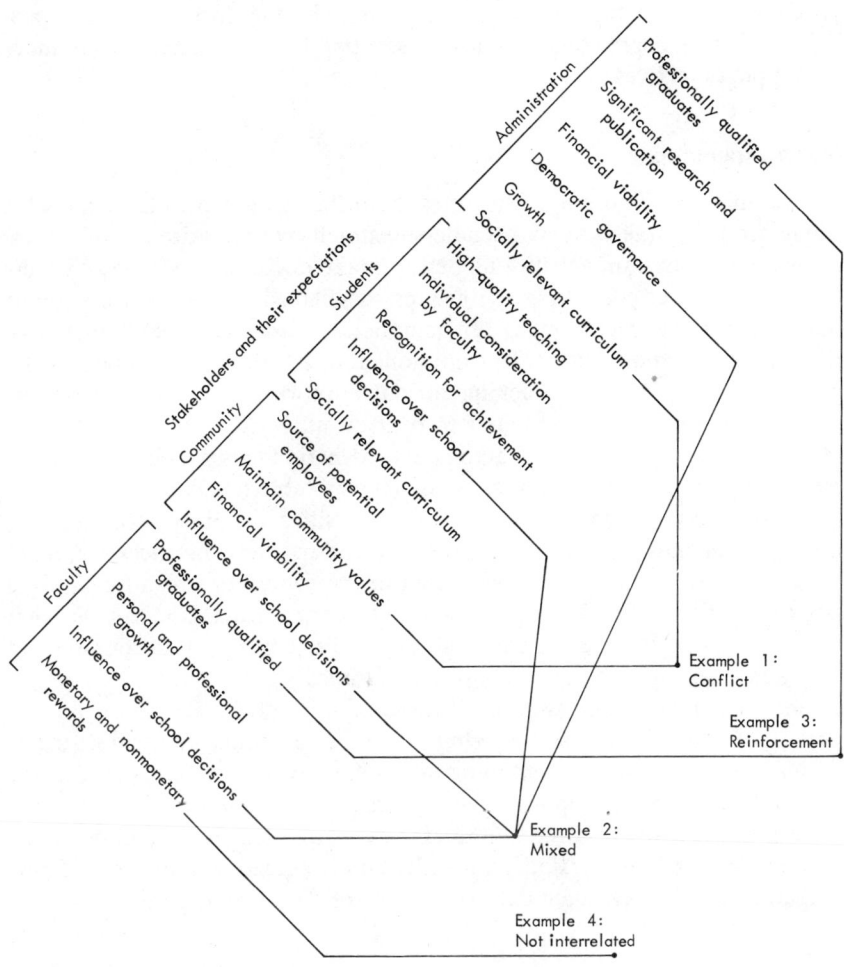

est customers to his advisory council. Finding him to be in sympathy with the school's aims, the administrator arranged for the depositor to influence the banker in matters that had hitherto been sources of conflict.

Throughout dealings of this sort, the community maintains the power to withhold its support (usually financial) from the school. It is interesting to note that, while the organization is subject to threat (loss of community support), the typical responses noted above possess the common thread of altering the environment, or the organization's relationships with the environment, so that organizational goals can be attained in unaltered form.

5. It is sufficient to note here that such responses are in contradistinction to adaptation to the environment, which should be used with caution as a

tactic for handling conflict. Obviously, the many constituencies and interest groups in the environment are prone to disagree on many matters. Thus, to yield to the expectations of one group is to invite the displeasure of others. Furthermore, a degree of autonomy is essential if the organization is to meet its unique objectives.

Mixed expectations

Example 2 in Figure 6-1 illustrates the instances in which the goals of a single group of stakeholders become subsumed by the entire organization. Prior to the 1960s, universities tended to make decisions that affected their members without consulting the groups so affected. However, throughout the 1960s rising expectations among members of various student bodies gave rise to the demands that student opinions and interests be included in the decision-making process. Lacking formal authority or sanctioned power, students united to bring pressures to bear on university administrators. By building cadres of supporters among sympathetic faculty members and by resorting to direct action politics, students were able to cause their goals to be adopted by other stakeholders in the universities. Administrators and faculty members alike give at least lip service and in many instances organizational support to student representation in the formal organization. This is not to say that all stakeholders viewed student participation in decision making as a legitimate system goal. However, while certain alumni and community groups may have abhorred, for instance, the university's acquiescence to student requests for coeducational dormitories (and even student participation in the decision-making process in general), unequal distributions of power between the administration, faculty, and students on the one hand and alumni and community members on the other virtually precluded the expectations of the latter. Nor does the example suggest that all members of the faculty, administration, and student body agreed with the goal of participatory democracy. Such disagreements are typical of organizations.

Reinforcing expectations

Example 3, Figure 6-1, illustrates expectations that are reinforcing in that they are shared by a number of stakeholders. The output goal of a graduate school is likely to be shared by members throughout the organization because it is a major determinant of individuals' motivations to join the organization. Because such goals are widely held, they tend to remain unquestioned and unaltered except in times of organizational crisis.

Unsupported expectations

Finally, Example 4 illustrates an expectation held by only one group of stakeholders that is consequently unlikely to become an organizational goal.

While the faculty may view salaries and other incentives as legitimate goals, administrators tend to view them as means or inducements to other organizational ends. Students and members of the community may view the matter with benign indifference. Thus, unlike an entrepreneurial venture, the university does not exist to provide a financial return to some of its stakeholders, but rather views remuneration as an activity that is necessary to the accomplishment of other goals.

Clarity of goals

The discussion of stakeholder expectations provides a static rather than a dynamic picture of goals; it does not describe the ways in which expectations become shared among stakeholders. A study of the activities that clarify organizational goals contributes to our understanding of this process. Wieland (1969) defines goal clarity to include both relatively widespread goal information and agreement on the information (that is, agreement about the goals).

In contrast, lack of goal clarity may result from ambiguous or insufficient information about goals, or from conflicts between alternative goals. A lack of clarity may be undesirable for a number of reasons. Goals that are unclear can prevent members from using the organization effectively (March and Simon, 1958); the combined efforts of an organization's members may be no more productive than the sum of the efforts of the same individuals were they not organized.

Unclear goals are also subject to displacement by more tangible means. Governmental bureaucracies that do not have clear and specifiable objectives may overemphasize organizational means, such as rules for keeping records or procedures for dealing with clients, at the expense of organizational goals, such as helping the client (Merton, 1957). Perrow (1970) makes the most telling point: goals are an important resource to an organization; they are a form of structure around which efforts are organized and thereby made relatively efficient. They keep the organization from wavering because of vagrant pressures, internal or external, and keep it directed to the task. Not all goals are "good"—some may be inappropriate; some we may disagree with. But clear goals help an organization employ its resources efficiently.

Communication and goal clarity

A study of organizational goals in 12 liberal arts colleges (Wieland, 1969) reveals that communications and influence processes may play important roles in determining goal clarity. Communication was found to be important for clarity, but interestingly enough, the *frequency* of use of various channels of communication was for the most part not associated with clarity. The amount of contact between faculty and department heads and between faculty and the dean was not related to perceived goal clarity. However, it was found that (1) the interest of the dean in faculty ideas, and (2) the frequency of off-campus, noncollege contacts between various ranks in the college were positively associated with clarity of the goals of the college.

If one views clear goals as organizational norms or forms of social structure, then the human relations literature explored in Chapter 3, particularly Likert (1967) and Tannenbaum (1968), provides an insight into the general process whereby goals can be established in an organization. Communication obviously is essential to the process. However, the sharing of information in itself is insufficient. The information that is shared must be *influential.* Individuals must communicate in such a way that they influence and convince the recipients of the communications. As we saw in Chapter 3, an organization with high total influence is one in which various groups are able to influence one another and the organization as a whole. In such an organization, one might expect to find strong social norms, including a normative structure from which we can infer a goal.

Conflicting goals

This analysis of the determinants of goal clarity is based on an assumption that clarity is desirable to improve efficiency. However, one should not overlook the possible value of conflicting goals to an organization. In fact, conflict in goals may be consciously created to improve organizational performance in certain areas, particularly organizational flexibility (Wilson, 1966) and organizational innovativeness and even efficiency (Buck, 1966). Buck suggests that mutually exclusive goals may be purposefully induced by a superior. Subordinates are simply instructed to maximize every dimension of their job (and sufficient resources are not made available): produce at a high level; adhere to the safest procedures; reduce wastes and other costs to a minimum; and so on. Subordinates may respond by using a sequential approach, first maximizing one, then another dimension (Cyert and March, 1963), especially if subordinates can determine which particular dimension the superior is interested in at the moment. Buck (1966) describes other wasteful ways of dealing with such goal conflict: "Just in case the boss asks me" files and "boilerhoused" records. On the other hand, individuals who are capable and motivated may come up with a solution to the problem of conflicting goals, and thereby make the organization more efficient by introducing improved procedures.

In our discussion of goals we have touched several times on the existence of conflict in the goal-setting process—in discussing both stakeholders and the advantages of having unclear goals. At this point, we must introduce the view that conflict is endemic in the goal-setting process and in organizations generally.

On the psychological level of analysis, this view suggests that organizational activities are subject to a great deal of control and coordination in ways that are not immediately visible to the outside observer (Perrow, 1972). It further suggests that the organization must control decision premises, for not only do human beings have their own interests that may deviate from the interests of others and of the organization, but they also have limited rationality.

Limits to rationality in organizations

The traditional economics literature assumes a degree of rationality in decision making that cannot be achieved in actual organizations. Managers are faced with too many decisions and too little relevant information to maximize the return on their resources. Despite their intention to behave rationally, the degree of rationality achieved by managers is bounded by the nature of their work (Simon, 1976).

Life in organizations is extremely complex, and problem solving is time-consuming. Thus, managers may settle for the first adequate solution they find to a problem (satisfice, a term coined by March and Simon), rather than search further for the best one (maximize). As March and Simon (1958) point out, searching the haystack for a needle sharp enough to sew with may be better than persevering in the search for the sharpest needle in the haystack.

Theoretically, management is faced with innumerable decisions. Each prior decision, rule, and operating procedure could be examined, for example, in a continuing search for improvement. This is not the case, however. March and Simon argue that the search for improvements begins only when existing solutions are seen as inadequate. Among other things, this suggests that organizations deal with problems sequentially, as they are identified. Please recall that a similar conclusion was reached by Katz and Kahn (Chapter 3). In addition, many decisions are made by relatively low-level managers, who are not necessarily aware of the impact of their decisions on organizational units other than their own.

Finally, decisions that affect several units often result from bargaining among these units. In the absence of an omniscient decision maker, problems of integrating differentiated units may be resolved in negotiation, as Lawrence and Lorsch suggest (Chapter 3).

The combined effect of these decision-making practices is that policy commitments made to different parts of the organization at different points in time may be imperfectly rationalized and somewhat incompatible. In attempting to meet its objectives, each unit of the organization may interfere with the performance of other units. Thus, the way is paved for intraorganizational conflict.

Decision premises and organizational vocabularies

Numerous practices have evolved to contain this type of conflict; for example, organizations typically employ vocabularies that direct their members' attention toward certain aspects of the organization and away from others. Discussing productivity in terms of monthly quotas (Chapter 5) causes employees to view their work in a particular way. In the contexts of other work settings, the term *quota* has little meaning, and work is viewed differently.

In a similar vein, management may provide or withhold information according to the attention-set it wishes to create. Colleagues and subordinates may not question the propriety of decisions if contradictory information is suppressed. Alternatively, by publicizing carefully selected information, management may instill a uniform set of premises—assumptions on which future decisions will be made—in the organization.

Constraints

According to Simon (1964), individual decision makers' behaviors can also be understood in terms of the constraints imposed on their decisions. Individuals are subject to sets of constraints imposed by various units in the organization which their decision making must satisfy. A constraint may not seem like a goal, but according to Simon: "If you allow me to determine the constraints, I don't care who selects the optimization criterion" (1964, p. 6). Thus, one who can impose a constraint that reduces the set of possible behaviors for others will influence the organization's behavior, regardless of the conscious goal that the bosses may have in mind.

Simon suggests that goals usually are multiple and that establishing *sets of goals* entails two different functions: (1) synthesizing proposed solutions (alternative generation) and (2) testing the quality of a proposed solution (alternative testing). The former is quite important, since alternatives must be generated before they can be tested, and the sequence in which the decision maker generates alternatives greatly affects the alternative finally chosen. Satisficing behavior entails selecting the first workable alternative found. Therefore, assuming there is more than one workable alternative, the order in which alternatives are tested can affect the ultimate selection. However, as Simon suggests, if the constraints or tests for quality are set strongly enough, they can have the most influence on the organization's behavior.

The alternatives generated in one part of the organization can become the tests in another part, and vice versa. Marketing attempts to sell a high-quality product that is attractive to customers, while production attempts to produce a high volume of goods at minimal cost. The marketing department's goal of high quality becomes a constraint for production, and quality controls are established so that a certain standard is reached, even though production costs are increased. The production department's goal of efficiency is likely to serve as a constraint for marketing, which refrains from promising to sell a customer a modified version of the product because it requires a costly change in production setup.

Such sets of "widely shared constraints" become the goals of the organization. Thus, one such constraint, profit, may not enter directly into the decision making of most members of a business organization; yet, it may influence members either directly or indirectly and influence the behavior of the organization as a whole. If one looks only at the alternatives generated, suggests Simon, one may see very different goals throughout the organization, but the behavior of individuals and the organization as a whole is determined by both alternatives and tests—by a "widely shared set of constraints" or premises. We shall see below that these premises pertain not only to goals, but also to the means by which goals are achieved.

Stabilization of conflict

Not all organizational life is characterized by high levels of conflict and tense bargaining, of course. To spare members negotiating every single matter, which would be wasteful, the organization creates certain relatively enduring patterns of behavior (Thibaut and Kelley, 1959). Standard operating procedures, for example, have the effect of reducing conflict. Once embedded in the organization's culture, they tend to go unquestioned. Were this not the case, the agreements, commitments, and decisions they represent would be subject to continuous renegotiation.

Conflict also can be stablized by decentralization. Centralizing all problem solving in the hands of a few individuals usually is not possible; organizations must be decentralized to some degree. Some decisions are made and some goals are attended to at lower levels, others at higher levels. Similarly, departments or divisions primarily attend to one goal, while other subsystems attend to other goals.

While some conflict exists between these subsystem goals, it is stabilized because of the premise-setting described by Simon and by the negotiated order in which some of the goals of one system serve as the constraints of another, and vice versa. Beyond this, conflict is reduced by *loose coupling* the subsystems (Glassman, 1973). When subsystems have relatively few variables in common, they are somewhat independent, or loosely coupled. As a result, each can pursue its goal without affecting greatly the performance of the others.

Side payments

According to Cyert and March, the goals of the organization are created by the side payments or exchanges made by individuals and subsystems in the process of forming coalitions. A number of these side payments go beyond the simple rewards given for accepting coalition desires and take the form of policy commitments. In the bargaining over side payments, Cyert and March see many of the organization's objectives being defined and established. This negotiated order does not result in complete agreement across the organization regarding the organization's goals. First of all, members may agree to disagree: production may allow marketing to do whatever it wants in certain selling activities as long as the volume of orders and the demands for product changes remain within certain limits; marketing may accept "deviate" behavior on the part of production as long as customer-determined quality standards and delivery times are met. Sometimes these agreements to disagree are not conscious. Subsystems go their separate ways within very wide, overall organizational limits. In other words, there can be considerable suboptimization because of divergent subsystem goals. There is local rationality and at best only quasi-resolution of conflict. This is especially feasible if the organization is loosely coupled.

Sequential attention

Conflict between goals can also be handled by segregating them in time, that is, by giving sequential attention to goals (Cyert and March, 1963). Cyert and March suggest that various control systems, such as budgets and allocation mechanisms, are created in part to lessen conflict. The organization's objectives, as stabilized by these structures, generally are renegotiated periodically, sometimes at specified times. Thus, at budget-setting time, the organization reexamines past expenditures and considers whether more or less ought to be expended on each program or department. The budget-setting process either directly or indirectly brings into question expenditures on particular objectives to determine whether these objectives should be modified in light of experience. At this point, the potential for conflict is great. The total of departmental demands for additional resources may exceed available resources. Some departments will be threatened by cutbacks. Competition for resources may become severe. In between budget-setting periods these questions tend not to be raised, and there is a relative absence of conflict about the nature of the organization's goals. In a sense, cutting off discussion of the next period's budget terminates competition for resources—at least until the next budget is prepared. In a similar vein, the potential for conflict can be reduced by using sequential attention, much as the individual does in problem solving, attending first to one problem, then another, rather than all of life's problems at once. The organization may devote extra resources first to one department (subsystem) and its problems and goals, then to another. The department receiving attention will attempt to enforce its constraints on other departments, and its constraints on other departments will take precedence. In terms of the five usual operational goals given by Cyert and March, the organization may focus attention first on (1) a production goal (smoothing or leveling production), then on (2) an inventory goal, then on (3) a (level of) sales goal, and (4) a market share goal, and finally (5) a profit goal. Of course, the order of sequential attention may be rearranged, depending on the emergence of environmental or internal problems, or perhaps new power coalitions.

GOALS AS DETERMINANTS OF DECISIONS

Goals and means as determinants of organizational structure

Beliefs about two basic dimensions of organizational performance have been used by James Thompson and Tuden (1956) to characterize the various decision-making processes that organizations adopt: (1) beliefs about means (beliefs about the differential consequences of the several alternative courses of action that can be undertaken in attempting to achieve a goal), and (2) beliefs about goals (evaluations of the potential outcomes of these courses of action on some scale of desirability). Beliefs regarding means imply specific assumptions about causal relationships between activities and their eventual results. Such assumptions about causation in turn imply knowledge of both historical and empirical evidence concerning relationships between means and ends, as well as assumptions about the future of these relationships. The selection of goals, furthermore, indicates the preferences of individuals and groups for the various outcomes toward which their organization may strive. We can analyze the manner in which decisions are made by noting whether or not there is consensus among the organization's members regarding both causal relationships and preferences for specific outcomes.

Computation

When an organization's members agree on both causation and preferences (or the dominant coalition can get others to agree on their premises), decision making becomes a mechanical process (see Figure 6–2). In the most simple cases, such decision making merely requires the application of routine formulae. At the other extreme, data and alternatives are so numerous that sophisticated computer techniques may be needed to perform the required computations. In any event, when an organization deals solely with decisions that can be achieved via computation, it needs simply to identify problems according to the type of specialists required to perform the computations indicated and to route these problems to the appropriate departments.

This is the heart of what Max Weber termed the "pure type" of bureaucracy. An organization with a *computational* strategy, in which decision making is merely a matter of discriminating the proper routine problem-solving sequences, is quite rare. Such an organization would have the classic pyramidal power structure, with overall coordination emanating from the omnipotent and omniscient boss at the top. There would be few of the coalitions arising from uncertainties and resulting interdependencies or conflicts over scarce resources that have been described by Cyert and March. But, in fact, even the apparently omnipotent boss of such an organization will be subject to some uncertainty and will be dependent on outsiders, if not on someone within the organization. That boss may need to form coalitions with outsiders, as we shall see below.

FIGURE 6-2
Goals and means as determinants of organizational design

Beliefs about causation	Preferences about possible outcomes	
	Agreement	Disagreement
Agreement	Computation	Compromise
Disagreement	Judgment	Inspiration

Source: Reprinted from *Comparative Studies in Administration* by James D. Thompson, edited by the staff of the Administrative Science Center, by permission of the University of Pittsburgh Press. © 1956 by the University of Pittsburgh Press.

Judgment

Where preferences for goals are agreed upon but uncertainty or disagreement exists concerning means, the decision-making process is more complex. This situation can arise because sometimes it is impossible to prove that a given course of action will provide a specific outcome. Some of the uncertainty regarding cause and effect relationships may be found in the environment, as, for example, when a marketing department deals with possible reactions of competitors to a price change. However the uncertainty comes about, it is likely to afford opportunities for certain groups in the organization to gain power; this power may be used to gain entry into the dominant coalition, and may well be used then to specify the cause and effect premises of other organizational members. The organization's members are left to rely on their collective *judgment* in selecting the most appropriate means. Organizations that rely on their members' judgment and get out the vote on important issues include voluntary organizations, trade unions, and numerous forms of university governments.

While it is not difficult to find examples of organizations that make judgmental decisions, the literature of the behavioral sciences has failed to provide a general systematic model for this type of organizational behavior. However, as we noted in Chapter 4 in connection with Perrow's scheme for technology, a nonroutine technology may be most compatible with a "flexible, polycentralized" structure, or an "organic" structure based on high total influence. In such organizations, individuals are likely to relate to one another in terms of a problem-solving mode in which there is collaboration and sharing of information.

Compromise

In some organizations, members agree on the nature of the consequences that can be expected from the implementation of the various alternatives from which they can choose, but disagree in their preferences for these consequences. In such cases, collective judgment cannot adequately overcome disagreements, for the alternatives may be mutually exclusive in that the decision to implement one course of action rules out the possibility of realizing outcomes associated with other courses of action. According to Thompson and Tuden, the appropriate strategy for selecting organizational goals in this situation is *compromise*. Often, while the rank orderings of goals differ among members of the decision-making unit, each member's set of rank-ordered goals contains at least one goal that is common to the sets of the other (or at least the majority of the other) members. Typical of formal bodies that compromise are those whose memberships comprise elected or appointed representatives, such as the United Nations Security Council.

Discussions of negotiation and bargaining and zero-sum games begin to provide a structural model for this kind of decision strategy. Walton and McKersie (1965) have attempted to integrate variable-sum problem-solving processes with zero-sum bargaining to develop mixed models that reflect varying degrees of conflict over outcomes and varying opportunities for integrative problem solutions.

The dominant coalition may attempt to manipulate the premises of the parties that are disagreeing about goal preferences, but often this is difficult to do since many such disagreements have their basis in the external environment.

Inspiration

Finally, on occasion, organizations are faced with situations in which their decision makers disagree on both the nature of the consequences that can be expected from various alternative courses of action and their preferences for the alternative consequences. The anomie that can easily result in this sort of setting is alleviated when *inspiration,* innovation, or a novel interpretation of the situation at hand restructures the situation so that overlooked alternative means, goals, or values emerge and, in so doing, permit agreement. Obstacles to decision making often are removed by a charismatic leader who:

> ... offers a new set of ideals or preferences which rally unity out of diversity, by shifting attention. Pointing to a real or fancied threat from outside is one ancient device for this. (Thompson and Tuden, 1956, p. 202).

Thompson and Tuden propose that, while the situations they illustrate may occur with varying frequency, organizations as a rule tend to be inflexible; they adopt one of the four decision-making strategies as their dominant strategy. Furthermore, they base their structure on the strategy chosen despite the fact that different situations require different strategies and structures.

When one considers that the process of goal-setting can include the selection of a decision-making strategy, as well as problems of reconciling stakeholder expectations, it becomes apparent that this process abounds in complexity. To add still another dimension to the process of goal-setting, we shall consider problems associated with measuring goal attainment and the effect such problems can have on goal selection.

Measures of goal attainment and organizational responses

The question of agreement on means and goals affects not only the organization's structure, but also the organization's relationships with the environment. Following Thompson's logic, we find that the beliefs held by members of the dominant coalition can range from complete to incomplete knowledge of cause and effect relationships (see Figure 6–3). At one extreme, members may believe that knowledge of the means to desired ends is complete. At the other extreme, such knowledge may be presumed to be incomplete. Coalition members also may differ in the standards of desirability they apply to organizational performance. Obviously, we will agree on certain preferences or standards of desirability. We prefer a well-paid work force to one that is poorly paid. We would rather have higher than lower profits, and we would like to charge clients as little as necessary. A problem arises, however, when we consider these preferences simultaneously. Are we disposed toward earning lower profits to pay higher salaries, or are we willing to increase prices to clients instead?

The problem of satisfying multiple goals when trade-offs are inevitable is typical of organizations. If the members of the dominant coalition agree on

FIGURE 6–3
Tests of organizational performance

Standards of desirability	Beliefs about cause and effect knowledge	
	Complete	Incomplete
Crystallized	Efficiency test	Instrumental test
Ambiguous	Social test	Social test

Source: Adapted from James Thompson, *Organizations in Action.* Copyright 1967, McGraw-Hill Book Company. Used with permission of McGraw-Hill Book Company.

appropriate trade-offs, their standards of desirability are said to be cyrstallized—if not, they are described as ambiguous.

From management's point of view, life is least problematic when standards of desirability are crystallized and beliefs about cause and effect knowledge are complete. Management will know exactly what to produce and how to go about producing it. Much as in the case of a routine or long-linked technology, management will be evaluated in terms of the organization's *efficiency*.

When standards of desirability are crystallized, but cause-and-effect knowledge is incomplete, the organization will be evaluated in terms of its *instrumentality* in meeting the standards. The dominant coalition may ask whether a desired state of affairs has been achieved, but it cannot logically determine whether this has been accomplished at the least possible cost. Instrumental tests are appropriate, for example, in evaluating the performance of intensive or nonroutine technologies.

The interesting cases occur when standards of desirability are ambiguous, regardless of whether cause and effect knowledge is complete or incomplete. At best, the dominant coalition cannot agree on what constitutes desirable organizational performance. At worse, such disagreement is accompanied by the inability to specify cause and effect relationships for any of the goals the organization might pursue. In both cases, *social tests* are applied to organizational performance.

Social tests apply measures of performance that, at best, are indirectly related to the organization's mission and goals; for example, management may publish various kinds of information showing historical improvements as surrogates for more direct measures of goal attainment. Organizational growth or the ratio of successful to unsuccessful undertakings may be emphasized, especially in comparison with the growth of other, similar organizations. Yet, such information may tell little if anything about the organization's progress toward its goals. Growth in research funding does not measure the quality of research conducted in a laboratory, nor does a decline in prison escapes tell us how well the penal institution rehabilitates inmates.

A similar tactic is to stress criteria that are quantifiable and highly visible, although not necessarily related to the organization's objectives. A social service agency may stress the number of clients served, but tell us nothing about the benefits of these services to clients. Business schools may publicize their students' average GMAT scores, but provide no evidence of the quality of education they receive. Furthermore, recruiting efforts may be directed toward further increasing such scores. When a school's average GMAT passes 600, it is not clear whether better students or greater organizational prestige is being sought. Prestige is still another surrogate measure of organizational performance to be used in the absence of a mutually agreed on set of objective criteria.

What all these tactics have in common is that on occasion they have little to do with the mission of the organization. Nonetheless they can influence the way the organization is evaluated and consequently can affect its relationship with the environment. They can assume the status of goals and lead to suboptimization. Thus, the organization's goals, consensus about these goals, and understanding of how such goals are achieved can lead management to seek efficiency at one extreme or to suboptimize at the other.

Organizational problems and goal-setting

We have seen that the process of goal-setting is complicated by the influence of (as well as the organization's influence on) structure, technology, and the predispositions of the individuals who control critical resources. In addition, the environment and the problems created by the environment are important in the goal-setting process (Perrow, 1961).

Perrow suggests that the problems facing an organization determine which individuals or groups of individuals will come to dominate the organization. The fact that a group is able to handle major uncertainties for the organization (as described in Chapter 4) may provide sufficient power for that group to dominate the organization, even though the group may lack the formal authority to do so. Furthermore, the expectations of these controlling elites, which presumably are directly related to current problems of the organization, are likely to become the goals of the organization.

Perrow suggests four major problem areas that confront organizations during various stages of their existence; namely, securing capital, securing acceptance by the environment, marshaling skills necessary for the performance of organizational activities, and achieving coordination both among the activities of the organization's members and between the organization and its environment. The relative importance of each of these problem areas is likely to vary over time. As different problem areas emerge, different members of the organization with different skills, experience, training, and outlooks acquire power and authority. They are either formally elevated to positions from which they influence the organization's goals consistent with their particular expectations, or they maintain their former positions and acquire power because of their ability to handle organizational problems and uncertainty, and thereby make others more dependent on them.

Perrow suggests that an organization engaged in fairly routine manufacturing, with a secure market position, may well emphasize coordination and, in doing so, yield control to an experienced administrator. Alternatively, an organization engaged in research and development or in nonroutine production activites is likely to be concerned with the development and utilization of specific skills. Under these conditions, one would expect the organization to be dominated by engineers and other professionals. Although it is by no means conclusive, Perrow's analysis does lead us to consider the possibility that technology influences the power structure of an organization, and the power structure in turn is a major determinant in the process of goal selection.

Controlling elites and goals

Perrow (1961) provides an interesting description of a hospital that changed its goals over time (including system goals and product goals). The case shows how the hospital's dominant coalitions changed as a result of changing organizational problems and illustrates the resultant ascendancy of groups able to handle the related uncertainty. As new problems emerged, computational strategies became obsolete, and groups able to implement a judgmental or compromise strategy gained ascendancy either by striving for primary leadership or joining the dominant coalition, usually replacing to some degree the formerly dominant groups.

At the outset, financial problems dominated the attention of the organization. As a result, the hospital's goals and consequent directions were controlled by the organization's board of trustees. Trustees of nonprofit organizations often are selected because of their ability to make financial contributions to the organization or because of their access to other sources of philanthropy.

Because of their ability to deal with financial problems, the trustees were able to dominate the hospital, for example, by controlling the appointments of physicians and setting policies and goals. Perrow suggests that the goals of an organization can be inferred from the predominant characteristics of the controlling group. Since the role of the trustee requires an emphasis on community responsibility, conservative financial policies are likely to be emphasized by the trustees and consequently by the organization as a whole. If the trustees represent particular social groupings in the community, providing services for these religious, ethnic, or economic groups may become an important goal as well.

These kinds of organizational goals can be contrasted with those of the hospital in a later stage of its development. With the growth of medical science early in the 20th century, hospitals began to emphasize certain professional skills. Obviously, hospitals that failed to provide up-to-date medical care could not expect to keep up with the competition. Because decisions increasingly were based on medical expertise, trustees found they lacked competence in new areas of decision making. Although some equipment purchases required the skills of trustees in obtaining financing, the most critical tasks of the hospital fell to the physicians, who solely were competent to decide on the kinds of equipment and, especially, the kinds of medical skills required.

During this period of development, physicians assumed dominant roles and were able to control the directions in which the hospital moved. Extensive facilities were emphasized, together with low hospital charges, both of which were in their interest. Hospital activities were organized to provide services for the medical staff. High technical standards of patient care were emphasized, as well as excellence in research and medical training. Community needs and financial solvency assumed lesser status in the hospital's hierarchy of goals. Preventive medicine and new forms of medical organization tended to be slighted in favor of improving the kind of medical care already provided by the hospital.

By the middle of the 20th century, the continuing growth of medical science and technology tended to overwhelm physicians; they had come to depend on the services of specialized personnel, some of whose jobs were quite complex, rendering their administration beyond the competence of the physician.

In addition to changes in the technology of medicine, changes in the environment further eroded the physicians' position. Blue Cross and other prepayment schemes grew rapidly and were, at times, able to influence hospitals to improve their efficiency. This, of course, was in the direct interest of the former. Furthermore, hospitals joined other kinds of health care organizations to form systems for providing health care. This required better cooperation and articulation beyond the walls of the hospital. For these reasons, the hospital administrator came to be in a critical position—able, by virtue of specialized training, to coordinate increasingly complex hospital activities, to attend to problems of economy of operation, and to manage coordination with other organizations.

The goals of most hospitals in this third stage of development arose, no doubt, from the need to meet environmental pressures. The ascendancy of hospital administrators with different kinds of backgrounds and interests made it possible for a variety of new goals to emerge. Financial solvency, budgetary controls, efficiency, and a minimal development of services became the new directions for the hospital. A professionally trained hospital manager could well emphasize the use of up-to-date computer technology, the use of human relations principles, and other practices taught in hospital administration programs. Their professional training enabled them to feel equal in many respects to physicians and, as a result, competent to interact with physicians on an equal basis about some of their concerns—including referral systems, the lack of proper quality controls, and other procedures of questionable merit. Other goals that might emerge under the aegis of administrator domination include publicity-seeking innovations (at the possible expense of medical services), the conservative financing emphasized by the trustees, and the goal of using the hospital for career advancement to a larger hospital by expanding the hospital regardless of community needs.

At first glance, one might view this analysis as being limited to hospital organizations where ends are multiple and vague and where numerous potential power centers exist. However, this same approach to the determination of goals can be applied to the business firm, despite its apparent emphasis on the unitary goal of profit and the apparent power of the small group at the very top of the organization. Thus, Perrow suggests that the goals of a firm may change over time in much the same manner as did those of the hospital. In the beginning, the owners will be in a dominant position. Subsequently, a new generation of the founding family may rise to leadership. Eventually, professional executives with particular skills may, by virtue of their ability to solve increasingly complex problems, assume dominant roles in the firm and in so doing determine many of its goals. At each of these stages, one can examine the interests and backgrounds of the particular dominant group to learn the directions the organization may take. It is possible, for example, for the marketing department to play a dominant role because its skills are required at a particular stage in the firm's development. This dominance may become a significant determinant of the behavior of other departments and of the firm as a whole. Some firms tend to select their chief executives from within the organization. Because of the chief executive's lingering identification with the goals of his or her former department, the goals of the entire firm may be similarly influenced.

The notion that different groups can dominate an organization and consequently determine its goals is consistent with the system view. Conversely, the rational view holds that the boards of directors or governing boards of corporations set overall policy, including the directions the organization is to take. In a study of voluntary organizations, Zald (1969) shows that the role of the board in influencing the organization can vary considerably. It is likely that the same factors that determine the power of the board in these voluntary organizations also operate in determining the power of the board of directors of a firm—the important factors being stock ownership, community legitimation, the possession of detailed knowledge of the organization and its problems, the socioeconomic status of the individual board member, and finally board opportunity to influence by virtue of certain crises or transition points arising in the life of the firm.

Conclusion

In summary, we have seen that understanding the behavior of an organization and designing an organization that performs as desired requires that we look beyond its formal goals. We examined operative goals categorized as output, system, product, and derived goals. We have seen that one fruitful method for identifying the goals of an organization is identifying the stakeholders and, among these, especially the dominant coalition. Their expectations for the organization, as well as their own particular interests and desires, influence the selection of goals. Such dominant groups are not invariably found at the top of the formal structure, nor are they necessarily members of the organization.

To identify these dominant groups, we ought to look for critical problems in the organization's technology and the environment, for these problems determine in large measure which groups will become dominant and establish directions for the organization.

From a conflict perspective, many of what appear to be organizational goals are part of a set of decision premises that are negotiated between the various power centers and stabilized by budgets and other control mechanisms. While the organization may employ widely shared sets of decision premises, these may not be evident to the outsider, since they serve as constraints within which the more visible optimizing functions operate. Nevertheless, these shared sets of constraints may comprise a more influential component of the organization's goals than the more visible optimizing functions. Furthermore, conflicting constraints or goals may coexist in an organization through suboptimization and sequential attention to problems. Such conflicting objectives often are an important part of the organization's goals. The extent of agreement on means, as well as on ends, is likely to lead to distinctive patterns of decision making in the organization—computational, judgmental, compromise, and inspirational.

In what sense, then, are goals more than a summing up of individual intentions for the organization? How do constraints created by the goals affect the power one group or individual has over another? While it is true that such intentions or constraints in part determine the organization's goals, organizational members may not be aware of them as constraints or goals for decision making.

This, in part, is what the system view of goals attempts to explain (Etzioni, 1964; Katz and Kahn, 1978). From the structure and functioning of organizations, theorists have attempted to specify system needs. These are not goals in the sense that they are consciously chosen (or negotiated) by the organization, and yet organizations—as organizations—behave as if they have these goals; that is, if one part of the organization does not concern itself with the system need of flexibility, then another part of the organization will—or else the organization will not survive. Many of the university goals listed in the introduction to this chapter, such as academic freedom, prestige, and ensuring confidence and support of contributors, are system needs that are salient and occasionally become more important than the formal goal of producing educated graduates. We shall return to this matter when we discuss the evaluation of organizations and the problems of changing organizational character.

As we discussed technology in Chapter 4, we found that problems arise from the environment. Specifically, Perrow suggests that the variability of raw material imputs has a basic role in the decision processes of the organization relative to its technology. In this chapter we have had even more cause to refer to the environment, in terms of stakeholders outside of the organization who may become part of the dominant coalition that determines goals. In our discussion of the changing goals of a hospital, the uncertainty that arose from new problems led to changes in the dominant coalition and to consequent changes in the goals of the organization. In the next chapter, we shall study the environment of organizations more systematically.

DISCUSSION QUESTIONS

1. What are the formal goals of your college or university?
2. How do organizational goals change over time?
3. Can a new employee who is not part of the organization's dominant coalition affect the organization's choice of goals?
4. Economists argue that an agent's (professional manager's) decisions will deviate somewhat from the decisions that the firm's owners would make in maximizing their welfare. The dollar equivalent of the difference between the agent's decisions and the owner's is part of the cost of an agency relationship. This implies that professional managers do not always operate in the best interests of the firm's owners. Why should this be the case?

7

The Organization's Environment

INTRODUCTION

The past quarter century gave rise to unprecedented awareness of humanity's tenuous existence on a rather small planet. An increasing world population has magnified its impact on the environment through the application of technology. We are now concerned with environmental problems that are aggravated daily.

But what do we mean by environment? The common use of the word is residual—environment means everything but the particular entity under study. This is a valid, but not particularly useful, meaning. Applied to its logical extreme, systems analysis tells us that everything is related systemically to everything else and that to understand one thing is to understand all things. Such understanding is beyond our ken.

Managers, therefore, must restrict their view of the organization's environment to a limited number of important systemic relations. Yet, even this is no easy task. Consider the auto maker's view of transactions between this industry and important segments of the environment.

Chapter guide

According to the 1978 Statistical Abstract of the United States, 823,000 miles of designated federal-aid highway system existed in 1976. Eight thousand miles of the system were completed that year at a cost of $5.24 billion. In 1976, Americans bought 8,498,000 new automobiles. Car notes totaled $66.1 billion that year. The estimated cost of operating each new car for ten years exceeds $17,900. A sample of 1,000 vehicles shows that 69 percent of them were operated at speeds in excess of 55 mph—32 percent were driven faster than 60 mph. Deaths due to motor vehicle accidents exceeded an estimated 46,000 for the year in question. (American casualties in all of World War I were 53,402.) Lost wages, insurance payments, property damage, hospital fees, and the like place the cost of these fatal accidents at $40,889,000. Polluting spills from vessels and transportation-related facilities released 14,967,000 gallons of oil and other substances in U.S. waters. About 800,000 Americans were employed in the manufacture of motor vehicles and equipment. So it goes.

1. What is the impact of financing 8½ million automobiles bought in 1976? As we use credit for more and more of what we purchase, will financial institutions come to hold title temporarily to most of the durable goods in this country? How will they acquire the resources to do so?
2. How many acres of tillable land are consumed annually by road and highway construction? How many more highways can we afford in the face of worldwide food shortages?
3. What alternatives are there to a transportation system that kills 46,000 users a year? Is the average driver skillful enough to handle a car at speeds in excess of 55 mph?
4. What is the automobile's impact on society? How has it altered family life? How have shopping centers affected urban areas?
5. What new forms of competition will the automotive industry face in the next ten years? Public mass transportation? Turbine-powered cars? Rotary engines? Will the industry experience greater federal regulation?

These questions are a tiny fraction of the environmental concerns auto makers have. Yet, managers can respond to only a few of the myriad concerns these questions represent. *How does management define its environment in terms of a limited number of vital concerns to which it must respond?*

KNOWING THE ENVIRONMENT

Routine responses to the environment

We summarized Parson's (1960) description of the organization as three separate levels in Chapter 2. The technical level is concerned with operating the organization's technical process and is buffered from the environment as much as possible. The managerial level articulates the technical level with the environment on both the input and output sides. Finally, the institutional level attempts to relate the organization to its environment.

Ideally, the organization's input and output would naturally flow at constant rates. Since this rarely happens by itself, organizations take steps to ensure a constant flow of work through the technical core. James Thompson (1967) suggests that when the availability of raw materials is problematic, organizations *buffer* the input side of the technical core from fluctuations by stockpiling inventories of raw materials. Such inventories are costly to maintain, but can be less expensive than stockouts, which would interrupt production. Preventive maintenance and routine replacement of equipment are scheduled for similar reasons—to reduce uncertainty in the technical core. Moreover, markets for finished products can fluctuate, as can raw materials supplies. Thus, buffering also occurs in the form of finished goods inventories.

While buffering protects the technical core from environmental uncertainties, *smoothing* attempts to lessen them. Smoothing includes practices such as offering reduced prices to encourage use of the technology during slack periods; for example, reducing long-distance telephone rates after 5:00 P.M. Similarly, airlines offer bargain fares for off-peak travel. Careful scheduling of nonemergency admissions can smooth the demand for hospital services. Essentially, smoothing techniques are inducements to patronize the organization at the organization's convenience.

A third technique for reducing uncertainty is called *anticipation*. When neither buffering nor smoothing can protect the technical core, the organization will attempt to predict fluctuations and adapt to them. If variations in sales are cyclical—for example, if they vary seasonally—the organization can look for additional, countercyclical lines of business. Thus, the technical core can be operated at a fairly constant rate, producing first one product and then the other. Alternatively, if countercyclical products or services cannot be identified, the organization may use forecasts of demand to build up or reduce its capacity appropriately. The Postal Service does this before and after the Christmas holidays.

Finally, when none of these techniques proves effective, organizations resort to *rationing*. If the technology needed to meet peak demand cannot be operated economically between such peaks, the organization may choose to invest in less capacity than peak demand requires. However, in doing so, it will be unable to satisfy demand at all times and, therefore, will ration its output. An ancient example is the wartime practice of *triage* in which the injured were separated into three groups on the battlefield. The mortally wounded as well as those who might recover without medical care were left unattended, while soldiers who would die unless treated were given medical attention. Today, priority services, one-to-a-customer sales, and back orders suggest industrial uses of rationing.

A system view of the environment

Using Parson's logic, buffering, smoothing, anticipating, and rationing appear to be general classes of *managerial-level responses to uncertainty*. Important as they are, they describe only a fraction of the organization's relations with the environment. The problems encountered at the institutional level are far more complex—and much more interesting. Before we look at these, however, we will need a more precise definition of the organization's environment.

Emery and Trist (1965) provide the basis for a definition in the following matrix of relationships pertinent to an organization and its environment:

$$L_{11}, L_{12}$$
$$L_{21}, L_{22}$$

where: L represents some potentially lawful connection, the suffix 1 refers to the organization, and the suffix 2 refers to the environment.

L_{11} represents processes within the organization—interdependencies of internal units. Presumably, these would be observed most frequently in the technical level, which is isolated from the environment. L_{21} and L_{12} represent interdependencies between the organization and its environment. They refer to *input* and *output* processes, respectively. Finally, L_{22} represents interdependencies in the environment that are independent of the organization in question.

Causal texture of the environment

Emery and Trist's matrix directs our attention to the *evolution* of the environment. Changing and increasing interdependencies within the environment constitute its *causal texture*. For the most part, we have dealt with *boundary problems* in our previous discussions of transactions with the environment. We have been concerned primarily with input and output phenomena related to the focal organization. Yet, as Emery and Trist tell us, suppliers and customers frequently are related independent of the focal organization. Other organizations are interrelated, too, and these relationships can affect the focal organization indirectly. Increasing interdependencies (causal texture) cause the environment to behave as a system. This is of crucial relevance to organizations.

The authors describe four types of causal texture, the simplest of which is the *placid, randomized environment*. Here, opportunities and threats are relatively unchanging and randomly distributed. The environment of a nomadic tribe is a crude illustration. The land over which the tribe roams has changed little in the span of tribal memory. Food, shelter, beasts of prey, and other hazards do not change and are more or less randomly distributed. Under such conditions, there is no need to distinguish between tactics and strategy. The best strategy for the tribe is the perfection of local or tactical approaches to each situation as it arises.

A second, more complicated form of environment is the *placid, clustered environment,* in which opportunities and threats are still relatively static, but are clustered rather than randomly distributed. Suppose that the tribe in our previous example gave up its nomadic existence to mine copper, which it bartered for food with a neighboring, agrarian village. While remaining unchanged, the opportunities and hazards facing the tribe now occur in clusters or, in our example, in copper mines. Strategy will now supersede tactics in importance; for example, a search for new sources of copper must be undertaken prior to exhausting current supplies.

The next stage of environmental evolution is termed the *disturbed-reactive environment.* In addition to being placid and clustered, this environment includes one or more organizations in competition with the focal one. *Operations* become an adjunct to tactics and strategy. While strategy identifies an objective to be reached in the future and tactics refer to short-term means to this objective, operations (a term used by German and Soviet military theorists) are attempts to draw off the competition. Now that the tribe is faced with competition from another copper producer, it is important to know the second tribe's strengths, weaknesses, intentions, and information sources. Our tribe may now be forced to think in terms of long-term contracts with customers, price and product strategies, and the threat of industrial espionage.

According to Emery and Trist, the present stage of evolution yields an environment containing *turbulent fields.* In the former stages, the focal organization made changes in its environment and reacted to changes caused by other organizations and unorganized entities with which it had direct contact, for example, competitors and customers. In the turbulent environment, we find changes that affect, but are independent of, the behavior of the focal organization. Our tribe, having forever abandoned its placid existence, is now an auto maker concerned with safety legislation, fuel shortages and consequent price increases, federal antipollution legislation, expected competition from public mass transportation facilities, rising expectations in the labor market, and a myriad of other problems.

Emery and Trist suggest that a number of trends contribute to the emergence of these dynamic forces in the environment. These include (1) increasing interdependencies between the economic sector and other parts of the environment, (2) the increasing tempo of research and development activity, and (3) the increasing growth and complexity of organizations; that is, as organizations achieve greater size, the environment comes to react to the largeness of these institutions per se.

The enacted environment

Emery and Trist draw a clear distinction between two separate parts of an organization's environment: the set of organizations, including the focal organization, that interact directly, and the larger environment in which the set resides. Using this distinction as a point of departure, Pfeffer and Salancik (1978) provide an even more useful definition of the environment.

From the organization's point of view—that is, from the view at the institutional level—the environment comprises three nested levels. The broadest level consists of all individuals and organizations who are related (directly or indirectly) to one another and to the focal organization through its transactions. This view is in some contrast to Emery and Trist's, for Pfeffer and Salancik have not defined the environment to include the entire population. Every event in the environment does not affect the focal organization. Thus, from the organization's perspective, many of the so called L_{22} relationships are irrelevant. Moreover, while some L_{22} relationships can affect outcomes for the organization, they do not necessarily affect its behavior. For example, calculators identical to those purchased by a laboratory two years ago can be bought at considerably lower prices today. However, while changes in the calculator industry have reduced the value of some of the laboratory's assets (an outcome), the lab will not alter its functioning as a result.

The second level is restricted to the individuals and organizations that *interact directly* with the focal organization. According to Pfeffer and Salancik: "... It is on this level that the organization can experience its environment" (1978, p. 63). But this is not the level of the environment that determines the organization's actions.

For the environment to affect an organization's actions, it must be observed and registered (enacted) by the organization. An analogy will clarify this point. Of the many individuals with whom I come into contact, relatively few can influence my behavior. We are not necessarily talking about people who actually influence me, but about my somewhat subjective perceptions of how I am influenced. Thus, my social environment is not defined objectively, as encompassing all of the people who interact with me, but as my subjective experience of people who affect me. In a similar vein, the organization's environment is subjectively enacted. This is the third level of the environment—the organizations and individuals *recognized* by the focal organization as being crucial to its functioning. Such entities may comprise only a fraction of the second level of the environment.

Organization sets

The third level of the environment has been described by some authors as an organization set. Goods, services, information, influence, and even personnel flow among members of an organizational set.

The interactions between organizations usually are conducted by boundary personnel, whose contacts include the boundary personnel of other organizations. For example, in addition to relating to members of one's own production department, a purchasing agent must also interact with salespersons of supplier organizations.

Interorganizational relations develop for a number of different reasons. Some are based on legislation and others on tradition. Occasionally, an organization develops new programs that overlap those of other organizations and require coordination; for example, internship programs require cooperation between the university and other organizations in the field. Alternatively, personnel may hold positions in several organizations, creating overlap, as is the case when professionals link their employers with professional organizations. Finally, most relations stem from reliance on a common pool of resources. Organizations frequently interact as they compete for (or cooperatively allocate) clients and customers, financial resources, raw materials, and the like.

A simple way to analyze an organization set is to diagram it; for example, Richard Hall (1977), concerned with the ways in which society attempts to control problem youths, diagrammed the organization set of a police department. Figure 7-1 depicts this organization set in terms of the frequency of interaction between the focal organization and other elements of the set.

Analyses of this sort direct the manager's attention to the variety of interactions between the organization and others in the set, and raise questions of whether these relationships should be purposely coordinated and managed by the organization or reacted to in a passive way. They should cause the manager to ask whether the organization is designed to handle the relationships effectively. Should separate boundary roles be created for each different relationship? Should staffing and work load decisions be made on the basis of the number of relationships or their nature (for example, cooperative or competitive)? Can formal procedures reduce the need for boundary personnel?

Defining the enacted environment

Answers to the foregoing and other questions hinge on the degree of importance attributed to such relationships by the focal organization. By importance of the relationship, we really mean the importance of the resources exchanged in the relationship and the extent to which the organization is dependent on the relationship for these resources.

Two factors contribute to the *importance of a resource* to the focal organization, according to Pfeffer and Salancik. The first factor is the relative magnitude of the exchange; that is, the percentage of total inputs or outputs exchanged. If the organization purchases a particular raw material from many suppliers, the magnitude of the exchange with any one supplier and,

FIGURE 7–1
The organization set and interaction frequency

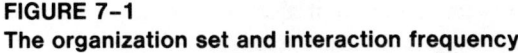

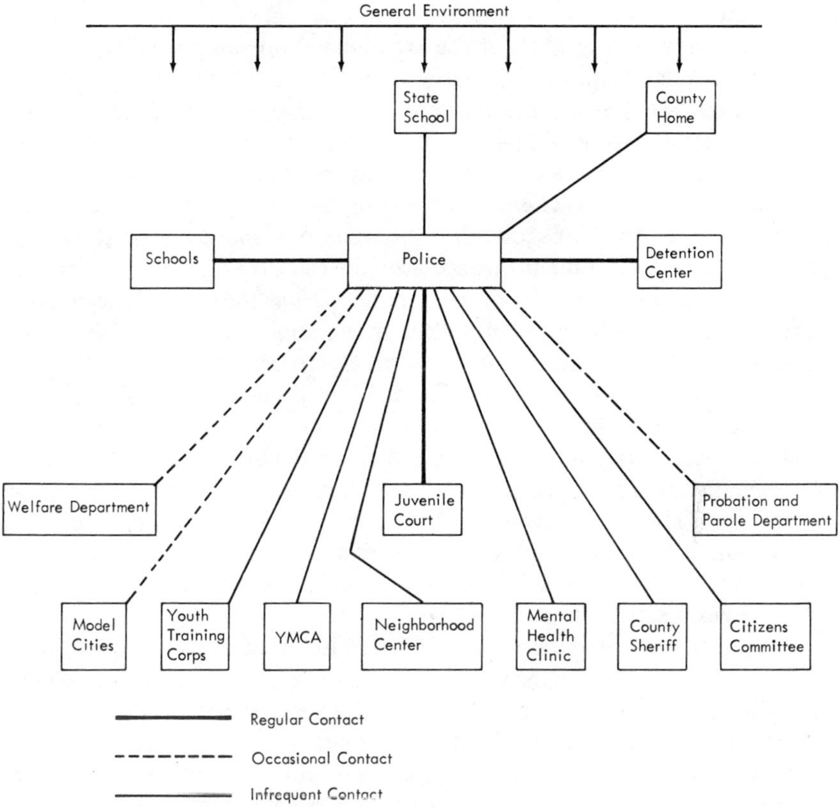

Source: Richard H. Hall, *Organizations: Structure and Process*, © 1977, p. 323. Reprinted by permission of Prentice-Hall, Inc., Englewood Cliffs, New Jersey.

consequently, the relative importance of the resource obtained from the supplier are likely to be slight. This situation is similar to the economists' concept of perfect competition.

The second factor in importance of a resource is the essentiality of the resource. Essentiality, or criticality in Pfeffer and Salancik's terms, is a measure of the organization's ability to continue functioning without the resource. Please note that the resources in question include inputs, such as raw materials and information, as well as markets for outputs. Thus, we can think of relationships with both suppliers and customers in these terms.

The *importance of a relationship* with another organization is related to, but not necessarily determined by, the essentiality of the resources provided by the organization *and* the relative magnitude of the exchange. For example, the resources provided by a single organization, even though essential, may be perceived as relatively unimportant if the magnitude of the exchange in question is slight and the essential resources can be obtained from other sources.

This brings us to the heart of the argument. You can probably think of examples of relationships between organizations that are relatively unimportant, even though the magnitude of the exchange is great and the resource exchanged is essential. The relationship between the corporate headquarters of an insurance company and the local electric power utility provides an illustration. The insurance company could not light its offices, operate its office machines, or run its computers without electricity. Thus, from the perspective of the insurance firm, the resource is essential. Furthermore, since the firm buys all of its electricity from the utility, the relative magnitude of the exchange is high. Yet, the relationship between these two organizations is unimportant; for all practical purposes, it does not affect the insurance company's action. It is probably fair to add that the utility is not even included in the firm's enacted environment.

The insurance company is not dependent on the utility, or to put it more precisely, the interdependence between the firm and the utility is slight and symmetrical. The utility cannot refuse to supply electricity under normal circumstances as long as the firm pays its bills. It cannot raise its prices arbitrarily or sell to the highest bidder. For its part, the insurance firm cannot purchase electricity from a competitor.

As you can see, the importance attributed to an interorganizational relationship by the focal organization is a function of the focal organization's dependence on the second organization relative to the dependence of the second organization on the focal one. When interdependence becomes asymmetrical, the more dependent organization can be influenced by the less dependent one. The dependence of one organization on another, furthermore, rests on the importance of the resources exchanged (that is, on the magnitude of exchange and essentiality of resources). Interorganizational relationships typified by relatively high degrees of asymmetrical interdependence are most likely to become part of the focal organization's enacted environment.

Interdependence and constraints

A study conducted by Salancik puts the foregoing argument in more concrete terms (Pfeffer and Salancik, 1978, pp. 56–59). Beginning with a sample of the nation's top 100 defense contractors, Salancik explored the following line of reasoning:

1. The larger, more visible the firm, the more likely it is to come under pressure to comply with government regulations.
2. The more dependent the firm is on the government as a customer, the more responsive it will be to such pressures.

3. The more dependent the government is on a firm as a supplier, the less likely it is to pressure the firm for compliance with regulations.
4. The more dependent the government is on a firm as a supplier, the less responsive the firm will be to such pressures.

For a number of reasons, only 78 of the 100 firms could be used in Salancik's study. Of these, the third with the largest total sales to nongovernment customers were designated as large, visible organizations. Each firm's degree of dependence on the government was assumed to be proportional to the percentage of the firm's total sales accounted for by government purchases. The government's degree of dependence on each firm was assumed to be proportional to the firm's contribution to total government expenditures for the resource in question; for example, Colt firearms was found to supply 50 percent of the government's small arms purchases (Salancik refers to the government's dependence on a firm as the firm's "control of production of items"). To measure responsiveness to pressures for compliance with government regulations, each firm was contacted by letter and asked about its plans to hire female MBAs the following June. The length of time each firm took to respond to the letter as well as the extent to which its reply encouraged women to apply for positions in the firm were used as measures of responsiveness.

Salancik grouped the firms in his sample into four cells: (1) large, visible firms on which the government was not dependent; (2) large, visible firms on which the government was dependent; (3) small, less-visible firms on which the government was not dependent; and (4) small, less-visible firms on which the government was dependent. For each cell, he correlated the firms' responsiveness to inquiries about employment opportunities for women with measures of the firms' dependence on the government.

Salancik's findings, shown in Table 7-1, illustrate the previous observations about asymmetrical interdependencies and the importance of re-

TABLE 7-1
U.S. defense contractors' responsiveness to inquiry about employment opportunities for women as a function of proportion of sales to the government, firm size, and control of production

Type of firm	Correlation	Sample size
Large, visible firm, not controlling production of items	.84[a]	13
Large, visible firm, with control of production of items	.46[b]	13
Small, less-visible firm, not controlling production of items	.02	26
Small, less-visible firm, with control of production of items	.67[a]	26

[a] $p < .01$.
[b] $p < .05$.
Source: Pfeffer and Salancik (1978, p. 59).

sources. "[W]hen enforcement pressures are assumed to be greatest, responses evidencing concern for affirmative action are strongly related to the degree of the organization's dependence on the government ($r=.84$)" (Pfeffer and Salancik, 1978, p. 58). However, this relationship diminishes for the remaining three cells. As firms experience less enforcement pressure, they appear to be less responsive. Furthermore, firms on which the government is dependent apparently feel less pressure to comply with regulations and, consequently, become less responsive. Thus, in the case of small, less-visible firms that controlled production of items, the correlation was found to be negative.

MANAGING THE ENACTED ENVIRONMENT

Organizations, society, and the physical environment

Our point of view is that environmental problems are organizational problems more frequently than are societal or biological/geological ones. The scarcity of raw materials, such as crude oil, is not so much a problem of the physical environment as it is a problem of misallocation by individuals and organizations. While there is a fixed, short supply of such raw materials, the problem is not how to increase nature's supply, but how to use it more efficiently and, ultimately, how to develop substitutes.

Similarly, social problems confronting organizations may evolve from the activities of other organizations rather than from independent societal trends. The significant environment of organizations is probably other organizations rather than society. According to Perrow, it is society that adapts to large, powerful organizations, rather than the opposite. To think of these organizations as continually adapting to a turbulent environment is misleading. "The environment of most powerful organizations is well controlled by them, quite stable, and made up of other organizations with similar interests, or ones they control" (Perrow, 1972, p. 199).

Following this reasoning, we can attribute part of the crude oil shortage to the collaboration of OPEC nations; part to the interaction of oil producing, auto manufacturing, and highway construction firms that all stood to benefit as petroleum usage increased; part to federal legislation that served the interests of these organizations; part to our own energy consumption habits that were encouraged through advertising; and so on. We agree with Perrow that large organizations affect society and the physical environment to a greater extent than the latter two affect the former in industrialized nations. For this reason, we shall continue our investigation of interorganizational relationships as they constitute the environment of the focal organization.

Interrelationships and uncertainty

Problems do not arise merely because the organization must depend on its environment, but because the other organizations that comprise the environment are not dependable (Pfeffer and Salancik, 1978). This lack of dependability, furthermore, gives rise to uncertainties that constitute the most crucial problems facing management.

Uncertainty, according to Pfeffer and Salancik, is related to *industrial concentration*. Economists measure industrial concentration as the percentage of the market served by the largest four (or eight) organizations in an industry. At one end of this yardstick is pure competition in which each organization in the industry is so small that none can affect prices. Obviously, industrial concentration is minimal in purely competitive markets. At the other end of the yardstick is monopoly in which a single firm controls the entire market.

Where concentration is low, the actions of any single firm will not affect others in the industry. Thus, uncertainty—the inability to predict accurately a competitor's behavior—is inconsequential. Up to a point, the more concentrated an industry becomes, the more crucial the unpredictable actions of competitors become for the focal organization. However, when concentration is high—when relatively few firms dominate their market—uncertainty tends to be low because these firms will coordinate their actions to stabilize their environment. Such coordination can take numerous forms, and results in what Pfeffer and Salancik call a negotiated environment.

The negotiated environment

For many organizations, especially those that require a steady flow of inputs and outputs to operate effectively, the problem of maintaining a stable environment may constitute the single, most important task facing management. Where relatively few firms dominate a market, instabilities arising from the behavior of competitors can be reduced through intrafirm cooperation. If it is legal to do so, organizations in highly concentrated industries may form cartels to restrict price competition and other forms of undesirable (from the firms' point of view) competition. Where cartels are illegal, similar results may be obtained through tacit coordination. This can range from conspiracy and collusion to the establishment of industrywide norms that restrict certain forms of competitive behavior. Unwritten, and sometimes illegal, reciprocity agreements, referral practices, and the coordinating functions of trade associations all can stabilize an environment, particularly when concentration in the industry is high. We shall examine some of these practices in detail.

Organizational prestige sets

Caplow (1964) defines *prestige sets* as organizations of the same type that engage in similar activities and view themselves as a set. "The sociology departments of major universities constitute a set. So do the Protestant churches in a small city, the baseball teams in the American League, the teenagers' clubs at a settlement house, or the leading manufacturers of electrical equipment" (Caplow, 1964, p. 201).

A consequence of this type of set is the emergence of a prestige order. Members of certain sociology departments see their departments as higher or lower in prestige than other departments, and so do members of certain churches, baseball teams, and manufacturing organizations. While complete consensus on rank orderings usually is lacking (members of an organization are prone to exaggerate the prestige of their own organization relative to that of others), a general consensus can be found. This consensus is also apparent to individuals who do not belong to organizations in the set.

High rank in the prestige set is useful in a number of ways. Prestige constitutes a source of power (James Thompson, 1967) that can be used to influence the behavior of lower members of the set. High-ranking members establish standards (which they can achieve readily) that ultimately become the standards by which lesser members are judged.[1] Prestige facilitates recruitment of new personnel, since a new recruit will be compensated, in part, by the prestige and social stature conferred by employment. By the same token, prestige can be used to pay others for needed resources, such as grants and contracts, and constitutes a competitive advantage over lower members of the set.

A number of studies indicate that organizations in prestige sets are linked together informally by exchanges of personnel. Gross (1970) reports that among the top 20 sociology departments in this country, 86 percent of the faculty members received their Ph.D.s from one of the 20 departments, leaving only 14 percent with degrees from universities having lesser ranked departments. Looking at the top 5 departments, he finds that 73 percent of the faculty members are alumni of one of the 5, 21 percent are alumni of the next 15 departments in the top 20, while only 6 percent come from lesser ranked doctoral programs.

Exchange of personnel

Comparable exchanges of executives occur among firms in certain industries, and Pfeffer and Leblebici (1973) argue that it is mutually advantageous

---

[1] One is reminded of the philosophy of Friedrich Nietzsche. "... [T]he judgment of *good* does not originate with those to whom the good has been done. Rather it was the "good" themselves, that is to say the noble, mighty, highly placed, and high-minded who decreed themselves and their actions to be good ..." (Nietzsche, 1956, p. 160).

to interlock firms in the same industry. Stabilized interaction patterns yield a reduction in uncertainty that enables the organizations to behave more rationally and efficiently. They find that exchange of personnel is related to the number of firms in an industry (and to the concentration in the industry). Where many firms compete, it is difficult for managers to disburse themselves to each other's firms. The study of top executives of five firms within each of 20 major industries shows that, where an industry comprises relatively few firms, executives are more likely to have (1) had their last job in the same industry, (2) undergone a large number of job changes, and (3) experienced a relatively shorter average tenure in the company before obtaining the chief executive position than is the case when the industry contains many firms.[2] Exchanges of personnel, whether among members of the organization set or between the former and feeder organizations are expected to lead to similarities among these institutions. However, the prestige set itself also contributes to these similarities. According to Caplow (1964), members of a prestige set come to resemble one another because:

> ... each organization in a set functions as a partial model to those below it while continuously imitating those above. The leading organization in any set ... comes to be regarded as the embodiment of the pattern. Since other organizations in the set lose prestige by deviating from the procedures of the leading organization, the latter may exercise an influence over its followers and competitors that at times approaches outright control (p. 206).

One frequently criticized form of personnel exchange used to stabilize the environment occurs, not within an industry, but between industry and government. Evan (1972) provides several examples of such practices. He analyzes organization sets by aggregating members of the set according to whether they relate to the input or output functions of the focal organization. However, in the examples to follow, the practices Evan illustrates occur because organizations on the output side are also sources of input, namely personnel and information.

The organization set for the Securities and Exchange Commission (SEC) is depicted in Figure 7-2, which can be interpreted as follows: Congress votes annual appropriations for the SEC; the President appoints its commissioners; the courts review some of its decisions; it obtains information and personnel from numerous other agencies. The SEC's output set is extremely large, consisting of thousands of corporations issuing securities to be scrutinized, thousands of brokerage firms that sell these securities, 14 stock exchanges, and the National Association of Securities Dealers, which regulates the conduct of corporations dealing in over-the-counter stock. Equally im-

---

[2] In industries comprising very few firms (for example two), the level of job changes was low, argued Pfeffer and Leblebici (1973) because "... uncertainty was reduced easily with such tactics as price leadership and the development of stable patterns of expectations without communication" (pp. 452–53).

FIGURE 7-2
An organization set analysis of the SEC

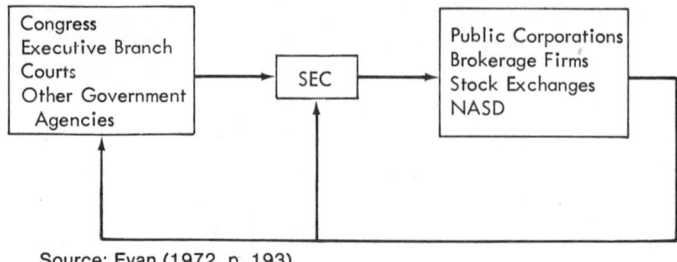

Source: Evan (1972, p. 193).

portant, however, is the observation that many employees of the SEC were former employees of the organizations it regulates, and vice versa.

More complicated is the Interstate Commerce Commission (ICC), which has an input set similar to that of the SEC, but an output set consisting of approximately 17,000 common carriers that do not have self-regulatory agencies. Although several influential trade associations exist (for example, American Association of Railroads), there is no organization in the ICC's organization set to represent consumers' interests.

In light of this, Evan suggests that the ICC's effective performance as a regulatory agency is hampered by the tendency for organizations on the output side of the set to make significant *inputs* to the ICC. He states, for example, that:

> Through ... informal and formal contacts, members of the output-set become, in the course of time, members of the input-set, influencing information gathering as well as policy formation.
>
> Promoting this type of feedback effect is a frequent flow of ICC employees to industry. Of the last eleven Commissioners to leave the ICC, six became top executives of companies in the transportation industry, three became ICC practitioners, and two retired (Evan, 1972, p. 195).

Similar problems have been observed in other agencies; for example, the Food and Drug Administration, which regulates about 50,000 food manufacturing firms, over 1,000 pharmaceutical firms, and a number of trade and professional associations including the American Medical Association, has been criticized for the:

> ... subtle and potentially most dangerous aspect of the FDA setup ... the well traveled, two-way street between industry and Washington. Men from the drug industry have gone on to FDA jobs and—more important—FDA specialists have gone on to lucrative executive jobs in industry. ... It does not seem desirable to have in decision-making positions, scientists who are consciously or unconsciously always contemplating the possibility that their futures may be determined by their rapport with industry (Mintz, 1965, p. 177).

Domain consensus

Another form of tacit coordination results in what is called *domain consensus*. "Domain consensus defines a set of expectations, both for members of an organization and for others with whom they interact, about what the organization will and will not do. It provides, although imperfectly, an image of the organization's role in a larger system, which in turn serves as a guide for the ordering of action in certain directions and not in others" (James Thompson, 1967, p. 29). In terms of Pfeffer and Salancik's argument, domain consensus incorporates a series of unwritten agreements that reduce uncertainty in the environment by delimiting the areas in which rivalry and competition take place.

Organizations compete with one another to be sure, but the establishment of domain consensus provides a shared understanding of the delimited areas in which particular organizations will take their competitive stances in the industry; for example, the competitive arenas of motorcycle manufacturers are fairly evident. The serious rider who tours long distances will be attracted to BMW or Harley-Davidson. Each has unique characteristics that set it apart from the other. The BMW will appeal to the more conservative rider, for instance. Individuals wanting motorcycles for basic, around-town transportation are likely to purchase Hondas, Suzukis, or Yamahas. Some enthusiasts are loyal to four-stroke machines and, consequently, to Honda. Those who like two-cycle engines will find substantial differences between Suzuki and Yamaha machines. The really serious street rider will probably own a Triumph rather than one of the three above. Finally, dirt and competition bikers look to manufacturers such as Bultaco and Husqvarna for their machines. Although they may seem in competition for a large, unsegmented market, these firms exert the bulk of their competitive efforts in unique market segments.

Boundary roles

An example of practices intended to reduce uncertainty in relations with customers is provided by a study of industrial sales representatives (Pruden and Reese, 1972). This study indicates how the external and internal power of boundary personnel can be related and how both seem necessary for effective performance (our descriptions of power in the goal-setting process in Chapter 6 should also be recalled).

Pruden and Reese studied a sample of 91 outside sales representatives employed by a national producer and distributor of wood products to sell a broad line of building materials to retailers, contractors, and industrial users throughout the nation. These customers are powerfully situated vis-à-vis the sales representatives, because they can choose among competing suppliers, all of whom deal with relatively undifferentiated products. Pruden and Reese found that a sales representative's performance was associated with his or her identification with the customer; that is, there was a perception of considerable similarity between high-performing sales representatives and their customers, and they tended to know their customers not only as business acquaintances, but also as friends.

Pruden and Reese argue that salespeople are effective to the extent they have power in a number of areas. Compared to low-performers, the high-performing sales representatives had greater authority over inside salespersons and procedures for the collection of credit, and greater influence over delivery times. Power and authority apparently enabled the successful sales representatives to protect their familiarity with customers, to modify irritating behavior of inside salespersons, and to control very crucial (for the building industry, particularly) delivery times, and thereby differentiate themselves from competing suppliers. Sales representatives apparently are able to use their power to increase discretion over certain functions, ones that are essential to consummating transactions between the organization and the customer (that is, credit, delivery, price, and product functions). At the same time, power is used by sales representatives to build up good relationships with customers, giving them some leverage in the exchange between organization and customer. By offering friendship and a modicum of control over important elements of the seller's organization, the sales representatives are able to offer a good exchange for the buyer's willingness to purchase. Ideally, such relationships are regularized with time, and the organization can depend on such environmental linkages and perform more effectively.[3]

Boards of directors

Boards of directors or trustees sometimes are selected for their expertise in a particular industry or field of endeavor and for their ability to keep abreast of developments in the organization's environment. Board members also are selected for their ability to provide resources—for their potential influence on the environment. In Chapter 6, we described how trustees initially were influential in determining a hospital's goals because they were able to (or had contacts who could) provide financial resources that were needed as the hospital was starting up. Pfeffer (1973) studied some 57 boards in a variety of hospitals and showed that voluntary, community hospitals tended to have larger boards than Veterans Administration hospitals. Voluntary hospitals need community support (in terms of finances and also in terms of patients). The larger the board, the greater the support provided or mediated by board members. VA hospitals depend on the government for funds and have a designated source of patients. Thus, smaller boards, comprising members with administrative expertise, are used. In general, one

---

[3] See also the study of the political economy of organizations (Walmsley and Zald, 1973; Zald, 1970).

might say that board members are likely to be selected according to the degree the organization is dependent on the environment for various inputs (see also Pfeffer, 1972b; Zald, 1967, 1969).

When tacit coordination of several organizations is desired, interlocking boards of directors may be employed (Pfeffer and Salancik, 1978). Such arrangements can link organizations in a way that permits mutual adaptation and cooperation.

Beyond linking individual organizations, some studies point to groups of powerful individuals who influence far broader segments of the environment. Hunter's (1953) classic study of Atlanta, as well as other early studies, show a structure comprising elite business leaders who single-mindedly preserved the city's institutions in their own image. This view has given way to a more complex and pluralistic view of the power structure of communities. A study of New Haven (Dahl, 1961), for example, shows that a large number of individuals have power, depending on the particular issue, with the dynamics of power and the interfaces of groups being important.

While recent studies of community power structures often reveal them to be complex and pluralistic, communities differ in their power structures. The dispersion of power in a community is found (Aiken, 1970) to be associated with (1) location in the North, (2) a high degree of absentee ownership, (3) heterogeneous populations, and (4) lower socioeconomic status populations. Cities with more concentrated power structures were found outside the North, had lower absentee ownership, and so on.

Still other studies question this view of pluralism and suggest that power structures such as Hunter identified link cities, foundations, universities, and corporate boards across the country. Community power relations have been found to extend to the nation as a whole in studies of the American upper class (Domhoff, 1967; 1970). Domhoff investigated the social registers of large American cities such as New York, New Orleans, and San Francisco, and found that there were many overlaps in membership and, as other studies have shown, high levels of overlapping membership on governing boards of corporations, foundations, certain universities, and other organizations. Domhoff concludes that there is a ruling circle of upper class individuals who dominate industry, government, and other important institutions in this country. This is a relatively closed circle, and entrants are only admitted after a considerable period of socialization during which their values become congruent with those of the ruling elite.

Although socialization appears to be a prerequisite to membership in the controlling elite described by Domhoff, it is sometimes a goal of other, similar groups. In such cases it is termed *co-optation*. For example, a local school board, usually elected by voters in a school district, may pose a threat to the school superintendent and school administrators (Kerr, 1964). However, school board members often are easily co-opted. Because they lack expertise in education (for example, curriculum and the like), administrators are sometimes able to control the flow of information to board members and thus mold their views or premises (Chapter 6). As a result, board members are socialized to support the administration's views. Also, because the members often do not represent an organized group (constituency), they are free to modify their views and behavior along the lines suggested by the information provided by the administration. The result of these processes is, as Kerr indicates, that the school board comes to legitimate the administration's policies rather than represent the community to the school administration. The latter, when questioned regarding various policies, can point to the duly elected representatives who have set policy for the school system.

Similar forms of co-optation are used to socialize members of interlocking boards of directors and other controlling bodies. If the consensus resulting from co-optation is carried back to each member's organization, intraorganizational norms and unwritten agreements, such as domain consensus, are likely to result.

Joint ventures

A final example of techniques for achieving a regulated environment is the creation of joint ventures. Presumably, organizations will undertake cooperative ventures when the talents required by the venture are unavailable in a single organization, the resources needed are in excess of what a single firm can provide, or the risk is great enough to warrant pooling interests.

However, Pfeffer and Salancik argue that joint ventures can stem from other motivations as well. When two competitors pool their resources and talents to form a joint subsidiary, they create both the basis for coordination between the parent companies and a rationale for restricting competition between these firms. Typically, executives and other personnel from the parent firms are assigned to management of the joint venture. By maintaining their contacts in their respective parent companies while managing the newly formed enterprise, these individuals link the parent firms. Furthermore, as they work together, each manager learns how managers from the other parent company operate. Such information, when communicated to the parent organizations, can reduce uncertainty regarding competitor behavior. Finally, because of their joint interest in the subsidiary, particularly when the joint subsidiary operates in the same industry as the parent firms, the parent companies will be somewhat constrained in competing directly with one another.

Autonomy and dependency

Regardless of whether we examine sets or domains, we observe that transactions between organizations contribute to their dependencies. A manufacturing organization that depends on a single, large supplier or customer will become dependent and subject to that supplier's influence. Organizations that maintain diversity in their suppliers and customers remain more autonomous.

The nature of interorganizational relations, as well as their number, determine these dependencies. Organizations wishing to preserve their autonomy (as do most) seek ways of coordinating their activities and creating a negotiated environment that limits dependency. All other things being equal, industrywide norms that serve these purposes are preferable to other means, such as cartels or joint ventures, that entail greater dependency. The move from low-dependency techniques to alternative techniques that result in greater dependency is undertaken reluctantly, as the situation requires (Klongan et al., 1972).

Please recall, though, that we have been discussing techniques used in industries typified by relatively high degrees of industrial concentration, where intrafirm coordination is possible. Next, we shall look at ways of reducing environmental uncertainty when techniques such as these are inappropriate.

The problem of intermediate industrial concentration

According to Pfeffer and Salancik, when the number of firms in an industry is too great to permit intrafirm coordination but too small to resemble perfect competition, competitive uncertainty is highest. Firms in industries having this characteristic of intermediate concentration attempt to decrease the number of competing firms and consequently reduce competitive uncertainty by acquiring or merging with competitors. Horizontal integration, as such patterns of organizational growth are known, can lead to higher concentration in the industry and result in possibilities for establishing a negotiated environment.

In Chapter 4, we reported Thompson's conclusion that the uncertainties associated with mediating technologies can also lead to horizontal integration as an attempt to enlarge the population served by the organization. While this argument is not identical to Pfeffer and Salancik's, it is related in that both view this form of organizational growth as a response to uncertainty rather than merely as a means toward higher profits. As evidence of this, Pfeffer and Salancik report that, contrary to what we would predict as economists, the tendency for firms to merge with organizations in their own industry is greatest in industries that are relatively unprofitable.

The reasoning behind this argument will become clearer once we have examined other forms of merger and their impetus. Vertical integration, the acquisition of organizations that exchange resources with the focal organization, is a form of growth associated with firms in highly concentrated industries. Because concentration is high, competitive uncertainty is low. Thus, interdependencies between the focal organization and its suppliers will be relatively more important then interdependencies arising from the behavior of competitors.

A third form of growth is diversification in which the focal organization merges with or acquires firms outside of its own industry. Diversification is particularly attractive when the industry to which the focal organization sells its output is highly concentrated. A manufacturer of automobile parts may sell all or most of its output to a single automobile manufacturer. As we have said, such asymmetrical interdependence is problematic for the focal organization. The uncertainty inherent in the buyer-seller relationship can be lessened, in this case, if the parts manufacturer expands into other industries. By doing so, the proportion of total sales made to a single firm can be reduced. Consequently, the focal organization's dependence on the auto manufacturer will decline.

Research has shown that firms pursuing strategies involving mergers were no more profitable than firms engaged in less merger activity (Reid, 1968). The author concludes that merger apparently is not a successful means toward greater profit, although it provides a vehicle for organizational growth. However, when we look at each form of merger separately, it turns out that firms acquired in attempts to diversify are more profitable than firms acquired for either horizontal or vertical integration. The reason, according to Pfeffer and Salancik, is that acquisition decisions cannot be based on profit considerations alone. If a firm is to merge with or acquire a competitor, for example, the number of candidates for merger will be relatively small. The same case can be made with respect to vertical integration. In either situation, it appears that once the decision has been made to reduce uncertainty through the appropriate form of merger, profitability can only be a secondary concern.

The case of diversification is different. Since it is less constrained in its choice of candidates for merger, the focal organization will have a larger set of organizations from which to choose. Thus, the profitability of the merger may have greater significance for decision makers.

Growth and uncertainty

A somewhat similar observation can be made about organizational growth in general, regardless of whether it results from direct capital investment or merger. Ostensibly, organizations grow to achieve economies of scale. However, a number of studies of organizational growth indicate that "... firms' average profit rates increase until some relatively modest size is achieved and then remain roughly constant or decline slightly. Moreover, considering only those corporations that report positive net income, average profits actually decline as size increases" (Pfeffer and Salancik, 1978, p. 135). What does result as size increases is stability; for example, larger firms experience less variance in profit rates than smaller firms (Caves, 1970). Again we are led to ask whether the impetus for growth is uncertainty avoidance or the profit motive.

The obvious answer is, probably both. Uncertainty avoidance is a means to long-run survival, without which long-run profitability cannot be achieved. Yet, we must impute still other motives to organizational growth—the power needs of managers, the advantages of having society dependent on the organization, and the increases in salary, status, and security that typically accompany growth. Nonetheless, the role of the enacted environment in influencing management decisions and the resulting organizational behavior should not be underemphasized.

The environment, the organization, and organizational behavior

In introducing their book, Pfeffer and Salancik argue that most of the literature on organizations takes the organization for granted and merely asks how its resources can be employed effectively. Thus, such topics as motivation, communication, leadership, and organization design are explored in detail. This approach seems to have two major shortcomings. Although such topics are important, they divert us from the essential task of learning how the organization acquires resources and survives. Existence is problematic for the organization and cannot be taken for granted. As Thompson remarked, the organization is always under attack. This brings us to our second point. As the organization responds to the problems of survival, it makes decisions that affect greatly the behavior of its members. Thus, in addition to studying organizational behavior from the perspective of individuals or small groups it is useful to ask how such behaviors are influenced, directed, and constrained by the organization. Which will account for more of an individual's behavior at work, a theory of individual motivation or the worker's job description? Obviously, the question is intended only to dramatize a point.

With the next chapter, we shall begin to move away from the organization-as-entity perspective that we have maintained so far, to study the human factors for which theories of organizations ultimately must account. Our approach will be to describe behavior that results in complex social systems. Thus, in Chapter 8 we will ask two questions: How does the organization respond to its enacted environment, and how are such responses decided by management?

The residual meaning

We have argued that the environment to which organizations respond consists of other organizations. To an extent this position is viable—but only to a limited extent. Lest we appear to indulge in sleight of mouth, our omissions must be acknowledged.

There is no doubt that other portions of the environment (exclusive of organizations) affect and are responded to by organizations. Yet, it is impossible to write a chapter, or even a book, about "Everything Except the Focal Organization and Its Effects on the Focal Organization." We have omitted much in the hope of providing a lucid analysis of that portion of the environment that accounts for a significant amount of the variance observed.

In cataloging our sins of omission, please add organizational responses that are essentially nonrational. Attending to the norm of organizational rationality, we have ignored responses to the environment such as denial and rationalization. Presumably, the gist of these phenomena has been presented elsewhere in a form that translates easily from individual to organizational responses. With this, we shall close Pandora's box, as it were, and proceed to the more manageable topic of strategy.

DISCUSSION QUESTIONS

1. Thompson argues that vertical integration occurs in industries employing long-lined technologies. Pfeffer and Salancik suggest that high industrial concentration is the impetus. Are these views compatible?
2. How can you tell whether an organization faces high or low competitive uncertainty? Can such uncertainty be measured?
3. In what ways has the environment of higher education changed over the past 25 years? How have colleges and universities responded to these changes?

8

Strategy Formulation

INTRODUCTION

The means that enable the organization to attain its goals in the environment are referred to as *strategy*. A firm may strive for profits by aggressive marketing of new products or by efficient production and price competition in the marketplace. A hospital may provide health care by collaborating with other organizations in a broad network of referrals and contracts, or it may attempt to be comprehensive and self-contained. As the system view states, there is any number of means to an end.

However, not all means are appropriate. Among other things, a strategy should be developed with the organization's strengths and limitations in mind. More important, it should conform to the organization's future environment.

Here we find one of many limitations that make strategy formulation problematic. For example, we can review strategy decisions made by Sears and Montgomery Ward in the 1940s to illustrate the importance of environmental uncertainty in the strategy-making process.

Top management of Montgomery Ward expected a severe, worldwide economic depression to follow World War II, just as the Great Depression came on the heels of the First World War (Steiner and Miner, 1977). Anticipating such conditions, Ward postponed plans to expand after the war to build its cash reserves. Following the predicted downturn in the economy, Ward reasoned, land values and construction costs would be depressed. At this point, Ward's strong cash position would enable it to expand its operations at bargain prices as the nation recovered from the depression. Please note that while economists differed at the time on whether an economic downturn would follow the war, the belief that it would was fairly widespread. Furthermore, had circumstances differed, a severe depression could have ensued.

Sears seems to have accepted the more optimistic forecast, for it began to expand aggressively following the war, moving into suburban locations as part of the middle-class exodus from the cities. Thus, Sears left Ward at the starting gate and has been ahead ever since.

Chapter guide

1. Difficulties in accurately forecasting changes in the environment make strategy formulation problematic. What additional difficulties appear to be inherent in the strategy-making process?
2. Do all formal organizations have strategies?
3. Is strategy formulation solely the prerogative of top management?

MODELS OF STRATEGIC DECISION MAKING

Strategic versus administrative planning

Throughout earlier chapters we have described planning as part of the organization's formal structure. What we meant, however, was not strategic planning, but routine, administrative planning that is used for control purposes. Such planning takes strategic goals as given and deals with the problem of using the organization's resources to meet them. In Parson's terms, administrative planning is a function of the managerial level and concerns merely the acquisition and transformation of raw materials and the disposal of output. Even long-range planning fits this category. "A five-year plan usually is a projection of the costs and revenues that are anticipated under policies and programs *already approved,* rather than a device for consideration of, and decision on, new policies and programs." (Anthony, 1965, p. 57).

Strategic planning involves devising new programs and policies that improve the fit between the organization and its environment. Planning for the mergers and acquisitions described in the last chapter is an example. Returning to Parson's model, strategic planning is defined as a function of the institutional level.

FIGURE 8-1
Examples of activities in a business organization

Strategic planning	Management control
Choosing company objectives	Formulating budgets
Planning the organization	Planning staff levels
Setting personnel policies	Formulating personnel practices
Setting financial policies	Working capital planning
Setting marketing policies	Formulating advertising programs
Setting research policies	Deciding on research projects
Choosing new product lines	Choosing product improvements
Acquiring a new division	Deciding on plant rearrangement
Deciding on nonroutine capital expenditures	Deciding on routine capital expenditures
	Formulating decision rules for operational control
	Measuring, appraising, and improving management performance

Source: Anthony (1965, p. 19).

Figure 8-1 provides examples of activities found at the managerial and institutional levels. Activities required by strategic planning are complex, unstructured, and nonroutine, as opposed to management control activities, which tend to be simpler and more routine.

Some authors take issue with definitions that treat strategy as a plan or an explicit set of guidelines developed in advance of the activities they seek to direct. Mintzberg (1972), for instance, argues that this view limits our focus to abstract, normative aspects of the phenomenon. He suggests that we study strategy as *a pattern in a stream of significant decisions.* This definition can be clarified with a simple example. Early in his presidency, Richard Nixon made a number of decisions that appeared to enhance Republican voting support in the South. The press labeled those decisions Nixon's "southern strategy." In Mintzberg's terms, the implication is ". . . simply that, in spite of the fact that Nixon never announced such a strategy, there appeared to be a pattern in his decisions" (1972, p. 90). Using Mintzberg's perspective, our focus will be directed to the process through which strategy is formulated and to its continuous nature.

Strategy formulation: The normative approach

Mintzberg (1967) identifies two basic approaches to strategy making and likens one to the biblical portrayal of creation and the other to Darwin's theory of evolution. The biblical approach to strategy is normative and rational. It describes how strategy *ought* to develop by following the systematic steps advocated by certain decision theorists. For example, Glueck (1972) suggests that once the organization's goals and objectives are established, the following steps are appropriate: (1) appraisal of the company's status in terms of strengths and weaknesses, (2) the generation of a set of alternative strategies consistent with the strengths and weaknesses, and (3) selection of the best alternative. Ansoff's (1965) approach is similar.

Unfortunately, there is little empirical research on the normative approaches to strategy formulation. For one thing, it is extremely difficult to develop samples and control groups of similar, representative organizations. For another, until recently few firms had special planning departments or made use of formal strategic planning systems (Ringbakk, 1969). Indeed, as Hofer (1973) indicates, most studies of the normative approach to strategic planning have investigated the planning process itself, rather than the relationships between various processes and organizational performance. Rather than describing the effectiveness of different forms of strategy making, these studies tell us how to make the process more rational.

Descriptive studies

The few studies that have attempted to relate the use of strategic and long-range planning to organizational performance have produced mixed results. Thune and House (1970) studied 36 firms and found that some companies with formalized, companywide, long-range planning systems were more successful, according to five criteria of financial performance, than companies without these systems. These findings were obtained for firms in the drug, chemical, and machinery industries, but not for those in steel, oil, or food processing. Ansoff and colleagues (1970) investigated relationships between formal planning for acquisitions and subsequent improvement in financial performance. Approximately 30 percent of the firms studied engaged in formal acquisitions planning and were found to be more successful than the remainder of the sample. However, these findings are limited to acquisitions planning, which may constitute only a fraction of the broader activity of strategic planning. Vancil (1970), on the other hand, studied the accuracy of long-range planning and found no relationship between the accuracy with which sales revenues were projected and the firm's rate of return on investment.

In a later study, Rue and Fulmer (1973) examined 386 organizations in an attempt to relate planning to financial performance. Interestingly, at the time of the study, the majority of firms having five-year plans had engaged in the planning process for only five years or less. Using four different performance criteria (sales growth, growth in earnings, earnings to sales ratio, and return on investment), Rue and Fulmer found no straightforward relationship between the completeness of long-range planning and performance. In the service industries, nonplanners outperformed planners in all cases. Planners outperformed nonplanners in the durable goods industries. According to the authors: "Obviously, such variables as timing, luck, and the immeasurable quality of 'overall managerial competence' have a more direct relationship to a firm's performance success than the formality of its long-range planning activity" (Rue and Fulmer, 1973, p. 72).

Unfortunately, matters can be complicated still further. Despite Thune and House's (1970) finding that planning is related to performance in certain industries, it is not clear that planning caused the improvement noted. Improved performance may lead to subsequent initiation of long-range planning, as Thune and House (1970) found in the case of firms in the food and petroleum industries. It is also quite possible that some third factor, a causal variable, contributes both to improved performance and to the installation of planning systems; for example, changes in top management may (1) cause increases in performance and (2) introduce various new management techniques, such as strategic planning. Although these factors may be associated, neither is necessarily the cause of the other. Finally, numerous other factors contribute to performance. Schoeffler and colleagues (1974) found that 37 factors accounted for 80 percent of the variation in profitability in a study of more than 600 firms.

Strategy formulation: The disjointed incremental approach

The second approach to strategy making, the evolutionary approach, has been termed *disjointed incrementalism*—a term borrowed from political scientists who find it descriptive of the way policies are formulated in our democratic society (Braybrooke and Lindblom, 1963; Lindblom, 1965). However, in addition to being descriptive, disjointed incrementalism is viewed by some as the way in which such decisions ought to be made. In large measure, this argument is offered in the belief that the normative (rational) approach is infeasible. The rational approach assumes a decision maker who is nearly omniscient and omnipotent. In reality, decisions of the sort described here frequently are made by groups of intendedly rational satisficers who cannot agree on objectives and priorities that are complex, interrelated, and have no clear implications for self-interest. Furthermore, no single individual has sufficient power to ensure that the chosen alternative(s) will be implemented properly (Bauer, 1968; Friedman and Hudson, 1974; Schoettle, 1968).

If there is no simple problem statement; no single decision-making unit with a single set of interests, values, and goals; no way to calculate the rank ordering of alternatives; and no assurance that chosen alternatives will be implemented, how are policy and strategy decisions made? Essentially, strategy is a matter of tactics and of starting with specifics and muddling through (Lindblom, 1965). Braybrooke and Lindblom's disjointed incrementalism has been summarized as follows:

1. Choices are made at the margin of the status quo ("the politically feasible").
2. A restricted variety of policy alternatives are considered in a social system, those which differ from existing policies only incrementally.
3. Only analyses of incremental differences in consequences are considered.
4. Means and ends are intermingled. Ends adjust to means, as well as means to ends.
5. Identification and evaluation of alternatives is fragmented, taking place at a large number of disjointed points in the social system.
6. Identification of policy alternatives occurs in response to emergent problems rather than being the result of a positive search for meeting a preconceived set of goals (Guth, 1973, p. 5).

Disjointed incrementalism may be illustrated by decision making on budgets (Wildavsky, 1964; Wildavsky and Hammond, 1965). Generally, the current budget of an agency or organizational unit is taken as given, and what are closely examined are changes at the margin. Since there would be considerable uncertainty about the consequences of major changes in the budget (such as removing several items completely or adding major new items), the consequences of marginal changes are evaluated instead. Decisions are not made on the whole package, but rather according to incremental changes and their implications for the interests and values of other units politically involved with the unit whose budget is being considered.

Budgetary changes may be approved as much for the means or activities proposed as for the objectives sought. Decisions are not made rationally in terms of selecting objectives and choosing the most appropriate means because the budgeted activities may be valued by decision makers for their own sake. If decision makers value the budgeted activities, the ends may have to adjust to the means.

Because organizations generally lack sufficient time and expertise, the full range of alternatives to existing policy is rarely considered. Only if a major budgetary change is proposed are time and effort expended in evaluation and explicit decision making. Moreover, this search occurs in response to proposals and sequentially, proposal by proposal, rather than being comprehensive, synoptic, and rational with regard to the objectives of the unit being budgeted.

A contingency approach

Contingency theorists argue that there is no single, best way to formulate strategy. Initially, strategy dictates technology, which in turn determines structure, as Perrow argues (Chapter 4). A routine technology requires comprehensive, detailed, operational planning, while a nonroutine technology can be served by planning that covers the main points and not the details. If management structures (for example, operational planning, leading, organizing) are contingent on technology and strategy in this manner, an efficient fit will have been achieved. However, as indicated by the feedback arrow in Figure 8-2, existing technology and management structure ultimately restrict the range of future strategies available to the organization (Chandler, 1962) by making some strategies easier to implement than others.

FIGURE 8-2
A contingency view of strategy formulation

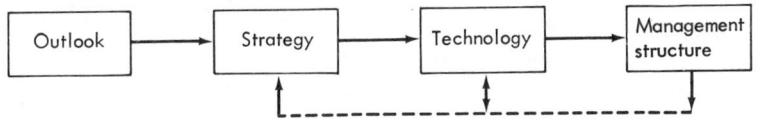

Source: Newman (1971, p. 61).

An extension of this approach is provided by Kast and Rosenzweig (1973) who categorize organizations according to their location on a continuum ranging from "closed/stable/mechanistic" at one extreme to "open/organic/adaptive" at the other. This approach suggests that organizations residing in placid environments are well served by the rational approach to strategic decision making, while those in turbulent environments are better served by disjointed incrementalism. Kast and Rosenzweig see the closed organization as having (1) a single, clear-cut set of goals; (2) a goal-setting process that resides solely with top management; (3) a decision-making apparatus that is autocratic, programmed, and computational; and (4) an information system that supplies primarily quantitative data. These characteristics seem to fit the rational planning process. In contrast, Kast and Rosenzweig describe the open organization as a system having (1) multiple goal sets determined by the need to satisfy numerous constraints; (2) lower-level personnel involved in goal-setting processes; (3) decision-making processes that are satisficing, heuristic, and grounded in disjointed incrementalism; and (4) information flows comprising qualitative data.

At this point, we must caution against embracing the contingency model wholeheartedly. "Hypotheses about these relationships have not been proven via substantial empirical research [and] in fact, it is doubtful whether or not they can ever be proven conclusively" (Kast and Rosenzweig, 1973, p. 319). We would like to be somewhat incremental ourselves for this reason. The contingency models describe extremes that some organizations may experience, but these models do not deal adequately with the world faced by most organizations. We would like to suggest that the average manager works somewhere between open and closed systems; placid and turbulent environments; and rational and disjointed incremental planning processes. An environment falling between these extremes may merely set broad perimeters within which the organization must operate if it is to succeed.

For one thing, organizations have a degree of choice over the environment in which they operate (John Child, 1972a); for example, one strategic choice confronting management may be whether to enter a growing market or a mature one. Similarly, choice concerning geographic location enables management to select from alternative labor sources and taxation policies. Moreover, organizations can exert considerable control over their environment. John Kenneth Galbraith's (1967) discussion of the *technostructure* and its ability to create and manipulate demand for its products is an example of this point. Finally, as we noted earlier, organizations exert political influence. Given sufficient political leverage, an organization can survive and even prosper regardless of whether it fits the requirements of the contingency model or whether its stated objectives are achieved.

Processes of strategy formulation

Strategy formulation involves more than the cognitive or intellectual exercise emphasized so often in management literature, for this type of decision making is embedded in social processes. According to Bower (1970), the study of high-level decision making confronts us with the need to understand psychological phenomena such as individual perception, evaluation, and choice. The process of changing individual and group behavior in organizations becomes salient as well, since strategic change implies a change in organizational behavior. Finally, the strategy-making process must be understood in the context of environmental changes and changes in the organization's resources.

An illustration of the usefulness of this general approach is found in a study by Allison (1971) which describes the United States government's strategy formulation process during the Cuban missile crisis. Three different models are used to describe different facets of the process. Model 1 views the American and Russian governments as unitary actors seeking to determine each other's strategies and objectives, much as two opponents in a colossal, macabre chess match. Khrushchev had told Robert Frost several months earlier that the American people were "too liberal to fight," and emplacement of the missiles was interpreted as a test of the United States's and Kennedy's intentions to stand fast. This analysis is in keeping with the rational approach and is useful in studying organizations as complex as nation-states. It assumes that members of a particular nation-state share common values, beliefs, and ideologies that constitute the parameters of actual policy making—that serve as constraints to the processes described by the second and third models.

The predictive power of the first model is simple to demonstrate in theory. A common American value is the desirability of separating church and state. Suppose that the government were approached by a religious leader with the suggestion that that sect be given official recognition. Predictably, the government would respond as a single individual. This is not because such decisions are made by a single individual, but because all parties to the decision act within a common frame of reference, in this case within a shared value.

Model 2 views strategy as an organizational output that can be inferred from past performance. Organizational constraints, procedures, and routines yield outcomes that are similar to past outcomes produced by the organization in question. Thus, when U–2 flights over Cuba showed that missile installations were being laid out in readily identifiable, trapezoidal patterns, the patterns were compared to those observed in Russian missile sites and found to be identical. Presumably, faced with a novel situation, Russia responded with the application of routine procedures. Similarly, one could presume Russia's Cuban strategy to be an extension of past strategies.

Model 3 views the problem of strategic choice in much the same way that we viewed goal selection in Chapter 6. Coalitions, trade-offs, and the like complicate the process. Focusing on distributions of formal and informal power, Model 3 examines the roles of individuals and groups in the strategy formulation process. Applied to the Cuban missile crisis, the model draws out attention to President Kennedy's role. Apparently predisposed to agree with the military, who were in favor of firm military action in response to the missile sites, Kennedy was swayed by the opinions of his brother and other influential individuals whom he perceived to be on his side. The latter, of course, favored the military blockade that was established eventually.

All three models—the rational "unitary actor," "organizational output," and "political maneuvering" models—provide some "truth" about how strategy is made by nations and by organizations.

Coalitions in strategy formulation

Factors entering into strategy formulation in complex organizations exceed the comprehension of the individual chief executive. No single individual is likely to comprehend adequately the organization's structure, technology, goals, personnel, and environment and their interrelationships and contingencies. Thus, the executive must depend on others in the decision-making process. Participants in this process form what James Thompson (1967) calls the *dominant coalition*—those who act together by pooling their separate knowledge and separate sources of power.

Recalling Thompson and Tuden's (1956) analysis of goals and means as determinants of organization design (Chapter 6), we argue that complete agreement among coalition members on the outcomes of means is rare in complex organizations in changing environments. For this reason, strategic decisions are made judgmentally. Those who make these judgments are important to the organization since they reduce uncertainty, which, if unchecked, will impair the rational functioning of the technical core. Thompson suggests: "The more numerous the areas in which the organization must rely on the judgmental decision strategy, the larger the dominant coalition" (1967, p. 136). The dominant coalition must co-opt those groups or individuals on which it is dependent, so as to amass sufficient power to control decision premises and the functioning of the organization.

We have presented a static view of the dominant coalition but, as Thompson suggests, "a coalition inevitably is *in process*" (1967, p. 138). Because each member enjoys information that is vital to the others, all are interdependent. The interdependence typically is asymmetrical, however, for the knowledge and power of one member may be greater than that of another. Other differences between members accrue in different ways. Some members may be recalcitrant, having outcome preferences that are idiosyncratic and different from those of the majority of coalition members. Some members may hold boundary positions in the organization and represent the outcome preferences of external bodies in addition to those of the focal organization. Other members have *cosmopolitan* orientations that conflict with the preferences of *locals* (Chapter 5).

These observations cast a melancholy pall over the expectation that dominant coalitions can achieve internal coordination. According to the terms used in Chapter 6, compromise is necessary, as well as judgmental decision making. The problem is resolved, however, through the creation of an *inner circle* that conducts the business of the coalition (Thompson, 1967). Out of disagreement, conflict, confusion, and frustration a small group is formed by election, appointment, or self-selection—a smaller coalition within the dominant coalition.[1] Only a small group of individuals who meet face-to-face can deal with the uncertainties and disagreements inherent in the strategy formulation process. According to Thompson, the larger, dominant coalition is limited in its problem-solving activity to judgmental strategies. Sheer numbers of participants militate against the success of compromise strategies. The inner circle, however, is small enough to pursue negotiation and bargaining strategies that lead to compromise. In the inner circle, individuals can get to know each other well enough so that the normative structure, tacit communication, and other subtle processes of compromise can be used.

At first glance, the dominant coalition may appear to make decisions and reconcile differences among members. According to Thompson, what appears to be decision-making behavior is more likely the ratification of decisions made by the inner circle. Thompson points to curriculum revision processes as an example. Changing a curriculum alters each faculty member's work load, subjects taught, and perhaps even career opportunities, not to mention outcomes for students and the university as a whole. Such

---

[1] Where the inner circle is self-appointed, its activities may be covert—hidden from the remainder of the dominant coalition.

changes cannot be achieved by the faculty acting as a whole, but are determined in advance by an individual or small group that proceeds to influence the remaining members of the faculty so that general agreement is reached eventually. Consequently, the faculty votes as a whole to ratify the change, but as a rubber stamp rather than as a decision-making body. At least, this is what happens when the inner circle does its homework effectively.

Rational or system model for strategy?

According to Thompson, organizations tend to reflect the rational orientation imposed by their technical cores, where efficiency and the reduction of uncertainty are emphasized. Nevertheless, the system model is applicable to subsystems that are in direct contact with the environment—those that must deal with uncertainties and contingencies as they import resources, export products and services, and develop political support. As suggested in Chapter 2, these subsystems comprise the managerial level of the organization.

Members of the managerial level must cope with both environmental uncertainty and the steady state requirements of the technical core. They are coordinated in these activities by members of the institutional level. Top executives and their staff coordinate and integrate the activities of departments in the managerial level so that each group makes the concessions essential to effective organizational performance. Leaders of these critical units usually are members of the dominant coalition, and it is their interaction, as managed by top executives, that determines strategy.

This view of organizations clearly is a departure from the rational view that holds strategy making to be an executive function. Petit (1972) argues that:

> ... the middle technical managers attempt to persuade executives to adopt policies designed to achieve technical rationality and middle environmental managers do the same on behalf of uncertainty avoidance. The executives develop corporate strategies that balance these policies. This reverses the cause-and-effect relationships in the [rational] model. Policies are the causes rather than the effects of corporate strategy (Petit, 1972, p. 106).[2]

This bottom-up analysis of strategy formulation suggests that middle-level managers influence top executives to adopt policies that are favorable to their respective subsystems. Carried to an extreme, this will give way to suboptimization. It is top management's responsibility to see that this does not occur by managing the conflict that emerges between different coalition members as they attempt to pursue subsystem ends at the expense of system goals.

Obviously, strategy formulation is not entirely a bottom-up proposition;

---

[2] The term *policy* is used here to suggest a class of decisions that serve as precedents for similar decisions that become routine responses to reoccurring problems.

rather, it is merely influenced by lower participants in the organization. In Petit's view, top management maintains a responsibility for determining what the organization must do to survive as an institution. Strategy formulation, then, consists in part of balancing the demands of the technical core with environmental pressures via leadership exercised by the institutional level.

DECISION MAKING AS A PROCESS

The strategic decision process

Mintzberg and associates (1976) provide a plausible model of the strategic decision-making process. They characterize strategic problems as novel, complex, open-ended, and ambiguous. Rarely do decision makers have more than a vague idea of the problem or how it will be evaluated once it is developed. Unlike the textbook description of decision making under uncertainty, the bane of strategic decision making is the ambiguity of not knowing either outcomes or their probabilities of occurrence.

Mintzberg and associates directed teams of students who had studied organizations for periods ranging from three to six months to identify strategic decisions, to describe the decisions and to program their development. In all, 25 strategic decisions were studied. Typically, the decision-making processes spanned relatively long periods of time. While a third of the decisions required less than a year, another third spanned one to two years, and the remaining third took two years or more. More than half of the resulting decisions yielded custom-developed solutions, a quarter relied on existing programs, and the remaining quarter generated customized modifications to existing programs. The decisions included an airline choosing a new type of aircraft, a radio station firing a star announcer, a hospital instituting a new and controversial form of treatment, and a consulting firm negotiating a merger after losing its major client.

A major outcome of this study was the identification of patterned problem-solving behaviors that accompany strategic decision making. Although the problems studied were ill structured according to our definition (Chapter 4), management's approaches to such problems are patterned and somewhat repetitious and predictable.

Classic models of decision making that follow in the tradition of John Dewey do not adequately describe the patterned behavior observed by Mintzberg and his associates. Such models depict decision making as a linear process—each step in decision making leads to the next in an orderly sequence. The behavior observed in the present study is better described by March and Simon's work (Chapter 6). Satisficing and bounded rationality were apparent. Furthermore, the problem-solving behavior tended to be cyclical rather than linear.

This is easily explained with an analogy. In Chapter 5, we described Jay Galbraith's (1972) view of specified goals as control mechanisms. Please recall that the activities of separate design groups developing a new aircraft were coordinated by specified design characteristics and targets. For example, as long as the group designing the lifting surfaces produced a wing with specified points of attachment, lift, and centers of gravity and stayed within targets for weight, cost, and delivery date, it could work more or less autonomously.

Suppose, however, that the group hit a snag; for example, found that to provide the required lift, weight specifications would have to be violated. Presumably, the group would *recycle* through prior decisions. The problem of wing design contains *nested* subproblems. The major problem is to design an airfoil that meets all specifications. Nested within this, however, is the problem of designing the structure of the wing—the configuration of parts that comprise it. Nested within the structural problem are still other problems; for example, selecting materials that do not violate strength, weight, or cost constraints. These and other nested problems may be reexamined in the hope that alternative solutions will alleviate the problem of excess weight.

Failing this, the weight problem may cause other design groups to begin recycling their prior decisions. The heavier wing may imply that more powerful engines are needed, and this will send the power plant designers back to their drawing boards. Unfortunately, more powerful engines will weigh more than those originally selected, and the additional weight contemplated will require greater lift and, thus, a still heavier wing. Fuselage design may be affected next, since a heavier wing will require stronger points of attachment.

This is essentially what is meant by cyclical problem-solving behavior. It illustrates what we described earlier as mutual adjustment to problems of reciprocal interdependence.

Identification phase

The problem-solving behavior described by Mintzberg and associates begins with an *identification* phase, which includes *recognition* that strategic action is required and a *diagnosis* of the situation in which action is to occur (see Figure 8-3). In one way or another, from the continuous bombardment of information they receive, managers identify situations requiring strategic decisions and mobilize resources to deal with them.

These situations tend to fall into three categories. At one extreme, there are *crises*—situations that portend dire outcomes for the organization. At the other extreme are *opportunities,* or situations from which the organization can benefit. Between these extremes are *problems* that lack both the urgency

FIGURE 8-3
A general model of the strategic decision process

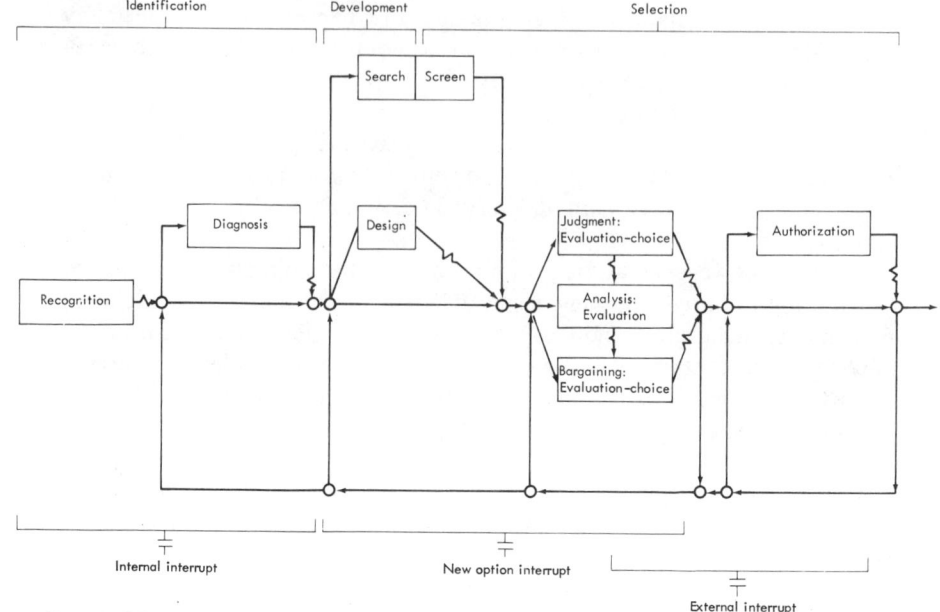

Source: Adapted from Mintzberg et al. (1976, p. 266).

of crises and the appeal of opportunities but are nonetheless important to the organization.

Problems, crises, and opportunities seem to be recognized as a result of threshold phenomena. From the abundance of data received by managers, specific kinds of information exceed a threshold of perception and galvanize strategic responses. From the work of Pounds (1969), we deduce that these thresholds may be exceeded when information deviates from management's expectations. Managers may look for deviations from the expected by employing any of five comparative models:

1. Historical (comparison of current data with past trends).
2. Planning (comparison of current data with projected trends).
3. Extraorganizational (comparisons with other organizations).
4. Other people's (comparisons with the expectations of others).
5. Scientific (comparisons with theoretical predictions).

Apparently, crises as well as opportunities the organization can exploit are recognized following the perception of a single stimulus. Problems, though, seem to be recognized only after repeated stimuli are received. This observation may be explained by management's reluctance to act on problems when solutions are not readily available. For crises and opportunities, reluctance is obviated by necessity in the case of the former and desire for gain in the case of the latter.

Mintzberg and colleagues suggest that, when faced with a crisis, the manager's threshold of perception increases for stimuli generated by opportunities or problems, making their recognition less likely and causing the manager to behave reactively instead of proactively. Conversely, managers confronted by minor problems and relatively light work loads have lower thresholds for problems and, particularly, opportunities. These managers enjoy the prerequisites to proactive behavior.

The diagnostic phase of the identification process serves to define and structure the situation. Stimuli and cause-and-effect relationships are clarified in an attempt to place the issue within a conceptual framework. However, these activities vary according to the nature of the issue at hand. For example, Mintzberg and associates find that opportunities, serious problems, and crises generate less diagnostic activity than do milder problems. Apparently, opportunities do not require extensive investigation because response is not mandatory. Crises and very serious problems displace formal diagnostic techniques by virtue of their immediacy. In any event, unlike later phases of the decision-making process, where reiteration is common, diagnostic procedures are almost never repeated and, consequently, initial diagnoses are rarely revised.

Development phase

After identification comes *development,* the heart of the entire decision-making process and recipient of the bulk of available time and effort. *Search* and *design* procedures constitute the development phase. The former are used to find ready-made solutions (existing programs) while the latter seek custom-tailored solutions or modifications of existing programs.

Search activities generally precede design efforts. Even when existing programs are found lacking, search provides a useful service by reducing design alternatives and, perhaps, identifying existing programs that can be rendered appropriate by modification.

The design phase itself is extremely complex, consisting of interrelated, nested subdecisions that are iterative. Furthermore, each subdecision contains its own search and design activities. The decision maker starts out with a vague image of an ideal solution. Different elements of the roughhewn solution are refined by reiterations of nested cycles of search and design activities until a workable solution takes form. "Thus a solution crystallizes, as the designers grope along, building their solution brick by brick without really knowing what it will look like until it is completed" (Mintzberg et al., 1976, p. 256).

As the concept of satisficing would lead us to predict, design activities yielded a single solution in all situations requiring customized responses. The design of custom-made solutions may be so expensive that only one can be made. Alternatively, a single innovation may exhaust the creative capacities of decision makers. Finally, it may be that psychological closure prohibits the exploration of further alternatives. Conversely, search generally produces any number of ready-made solutions owing, perhaps, to the slight costs entailed by search and alternative generation. Modified solutions, in which moderate custom-design efforts are invested, fall somewhere between the two extremes. Typically, two solutions are generated, one of which ultimately is rejected in the subsequent selection phases of decision making.

Selection phase

Viewed from a rational perspective, *selection* ought to follow identification and development. However, in some cases, subdecisions resulting from development activities are evaluated and subjected to selection prior to the conclusion of the total development phase. Thus, selection may occur any number of times throughout the decision-making process.

Selection itself is a multistage, iterative process. The three basic programs within the selection phase, *screening, evaluation-choice,* and *authorization,* may be applied sequentially. Alternatively, each of the three steps may be multistaged or nested. In sequential selection, screening is used to reduce alternatives to a feasible number. Evaluation then identifies the best alternative, which is chosen and authorized for implementation. Alternatively, the selection phase can be nested, with alternatives evaluated in toto, next evaluated in more detail, and then subjected to intense scrutiny. At each step, alternatives can be eliminated as they fail to meet successively rigorous criteria.

Mintzberg and associates found that screening is not very evident in the strategic decision processes studied, presumably because it is implicit in the search process. As ready-made alternatives are found, they are screened, and the infeasible are eliminated without further ado.

In analyzing the *evaluation-choice* phase of the process, Mintzberg and associates employed portions of the decision-making topology of Thompson and Tuden (1959): *judgment* (a single individual making choices), bargaining (selection by a group of individuals, having conflicting goals and using individual judgments), and *analysis* (computation—a systematic evaluation of relevant data). Judgment is used, Mintzberg found, when decision situations are characterized by centralized responsibility, a lack of rigorous data, and relatively urgent time pressures. When forced to exercise judgment, managers frequently rely on surrogate criteria. For example, one organization in the study chose IBM equipment because of the company's reputation. Analytic (computational) problem solving would have begun by comparing specific, competing data processing devices with the organization's information processing requirements. Bargaining is found to be common, appearing in half of the strategic decisions studied. Computational decision strategies are found in larger business organizations, especially where strategy is contingent on technical considerations.

The final phase of the process, *authorization,* consists of approval by top management, the board of directors, or those vitally concerned with strategy decisions—often because they have the authority to commit or withhold resources. Even when accepted, the decision may be subject to further iterations of authorization at even higher organizational levels.

Authorization decisions are difficult to make in practice. Typically, the executive who is in a position to authorize the implementation of a proposal lacks detailed knowledge of both the proposal and the situation to which it is addressed. Compared with the proponents of the proposal as well as its critics, the executive is relatively ignorant of the problem. Thus, the executive will be unable to recognize biased or distorted reports of either proponents or critics. Coupled with this are the other pressures of the executive's job that rule out the possibility of studying the proposal in detail. The combined effect is that authorization decisions often result from political processes rather than analytic comparisons of alternatives.

Political processes

According to the present study, organizational politics accompany the entire decision-making process depicted in Figure 8–3. In a sense, they run parallel to it.

Organizational politics, the art of determining who gets what, comes into being in part because organizations do not function in an economically rational manner. For instance, if members were remunerated according to their contribution to the organization's overall performance, presumably all would cooperate in the organization's best interests. Unfortunately, this seems not to be the case. A study of 150 financial executives reported in *The Wall Street Journal* indicates that six key factors account for most of the variance in their base salaries. Of these, the number of levels of management reporting to the executive and the executive's age each explained more of the variance observed than any of the remaining four factors. Level of education (having an MBA) ranked third, and was followed by proximity in the hierarchy to the chief executive officer (CEO). Fifth was increasing profitability (a 15 percent increase in profit was associated with a mere 4 percent increase in combined salary and bonus). Finally, the article reported a finding (typical of other, similar studies) of a negative correlation between pay and length of service (Crystal, 1978).

What such findings suggest is that an executive's salary and, as we shall see, power and status can be affected by the courses of action resulting from strategic decisions. A particular course of action may add or delete a level of management reporting to an executive, create or disband an operating division along with its CEO and vice presidents, or reallocate budgeted resources. Thus, a proposed solution to a problem may be supported or resisted for reasons unrelated to the solution's efficacy in resolving the problem.

Moreover, strategic changes can impose additional work on certain departments. Similarly, such changes may make obsolete previous accomplishments, thus destroying a department's sense of achievement. Philosophical disagreements can arise if the organization contemplates placing greater emphasis on one set of goals than on another. For these and other reasons, political pressures can be experienced throughout the decision-making process, and bargaining, attempts at co-optation, and mediation can be observed from the recognition step through implementation of the authorized solution.

Control and communication processes

Two additional processes were observed to run parallel with the decision-making process. The *decision control process* consists of "meta-decision making"—decision making about the decision-making process itself. Included in such activities are planning the planning process and allocating resources to implement it.

Decision-communication processes also continue throughout the decision process. These comprise efforts to collect and disseminate information relevant to decisions under study and arising from the decision-making process itself. Some of this information is essential to decision making, but much is disseminated for political purposes—to pave the way for strategic change.

Dynamic factors

Finally, Mintzberg and his associates observed a set of *dynamic factors* that are characteristic and distinguishing features of the strategic decision-making process. In brief, these factors can be described as follows:

1. *Interrupts* consist of unexpected constraints that may cause delays, and force an organization to cycle back to the development phase. The three most common types are shown in Figure 8–3. *Internal* (political) interrupts occur in the identification phase, when there is disagreement about the existence of problems requiring decisions. *External* interrupts occur when elements in the organization's environment resist the implementation of proposed solutions. *New Option* interrupts arise as alternatives to the proposed solution come to management's attention.

2. *Scheduling delays* may follow each step of the decision process because top managers, extremely pressed for time, must turn their attention to other matters. *Feedback delays* occur because the decision maker must await the results of previous actions. *Timing delays and speedups* occur when a manager purposely stalls or presses ahead to take advantage of special circumstances.

3. *Comprehension cycles* occur in the process when issues are complex and require time to be understood.

4. Finally, there are *failure recycles* in which the decision maker is faced with no acceptable solutions and must either delay until one appears or ultimately end the decision process. Commonly, it was found that organizations faced with failure in finding or designing an acceptable solution recycled back to the development phase.

The complexity added to the decision-making process by these dynamic factors is illustrated in the following example, which is also depicted in Figure 8-4.

FIGURE 8-4
A dynamic design decision process (facilities)—A new plant for a small firm

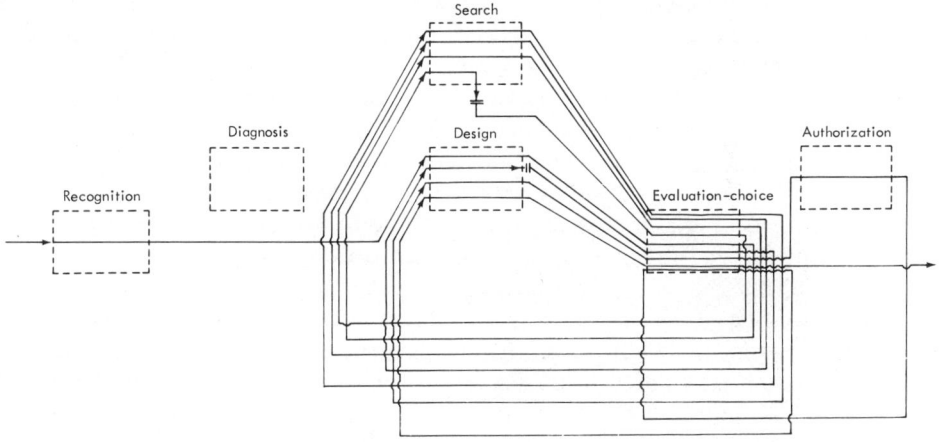

Source: Mintzberg et al. (1976, p. 273).

... a small manufacturing firm was faced with a series of pressures that indicated that its plant was obsolete. A proposal to sell the building was developed (design), and a real estate agent then contacted (search), but no buyers were found. It was then realized that the city might expropriate the land (interrupt), and an agent was hired to negotiate a good price should that occur. Meanwhile, a neighboring firm moved out, and their adjoining parking lot was acquired to provide room for expansion or to increase the expropriation value of the property (evaluation-choice). At the same time, the firm employed architects to investigate two alternatives, but rejected both proposals as too expensive (evaluation-choice), and attention was then focused on moving. Three alternative sites were found (search), and employees were polled and road networks investigated (evaluation). One area proved to be the most desirable, and when an existing facility was found there at a good price (search), it was identified as a favorite candidate and purchased (evaluation-choice). The company planned the modification of the building (design), and commenced the alteration. Two months later, however, the provincial government expropriated at the same time both the old plant and the new and gave the firm a short time to vacate (interrupt). Now the firm faced a crisis. It did, however, have a considerable source of funds from the expropriation and could consider buying land and building a new plant. Only one area was investigated, and a suitable site was located (search). The firm obtained rezoning sanctions from the municipal government, a mortgage from the bank (design), and the assurance that this property would not be expropriated (authorization). The site was purchased (evaluation-choice), and the engineering department, in consultation with the architect, prepared building plans, (design); the plans were quickly finalized (evaluation-choice) (Mintzberg et al., 1976, p. 273).

The behavior of strategy makers

The little empirical evidence we have seems to corroborate Mintzberg's view of strategy making as a complex design process rather than as an exercise in formal, rational planning. Going a step further, Wrapp (1967) suggests that good managers (those able to move their organizations toward the goals they have set) actually do not make policy decisions. Instead of spelling out explicit policy statements or detailed sets of objectives, these managers provide their organizations with a general sense of purpose, develop opportunities as they arise, and generally "muddle through with a purpose."

By muddling, Wrapp does not mean an artless, confused reaction to problems, but rather a style of management that is proactive, but indirect. An illustration of the latter is what he calls "the art of imprecision." Proficient managers know how to satisfy their subordinates, as well as the public and stockholders clamoring for statements on objectives, by making very general and imprecise announcements such as "growth and profit." While the managers do have objectives, they do not get committed publicly to a specific set of objectives, since such specific objectives could constrain the organization when it needs, as it will, to change direction. The successful manager seldom makes a forthright statement of policy despite claims of management textbooks that well-defined policies are essential to a well-run organization. The spelling out of detailed, written objectives, as in management by objectives, is really only useful at lower levels of management.

And as Wrapp sees it, it is impossible to communicate objectives to the entire organization anyway. Organizational members will perceive the statements differently, according to their various positions in the organization. Wrapp suggests that objectives for the organization can only be communicated over time by means of consistency, or a pattern in its operating decisions. He reminds us that decisions linked to actions are more meaningful than mere words.

According to Wrapp, these managers tend not to force entire programs through the organization. Rather, they settle for more modest, indirect progress. One piece of a program is installed in one part of the organization;

later, another piece is implemented elsewhere. Gradually, the entire program falls into place without having been presented in its entirety and subjected to debate and opposition.

Such gradual progress toward program implementation often is accomplished by moving through the organization's *corridors of comparative indifference*. In tallying the likely positions of the organization's power structure (dominant coalition) with respect to a new program, the manager will identify pockets of firm opposition as well as support. Between these extremes are individuals who are comparatively indifferent to the proposal. Rather than pit supporters against the opposition, Wrapp's successful manager will begin to implement portions of the program on neutral ground, so to speak, where there is indifference. As more and more pieces are put into place, opposition to the remaining changes may decline. The various kinds of interdependence we have described will create pressures on unaltered portions of the organization to change. For example, the use of new testing equipment in product quality control may exert pressure on manufacturing to improve its methods. If the result of such changes is improved product quality, marketing may be affected as well. Thus, in our hypothetical example, changes in production and marketing sought by the manager result from the innocuous decision to install improved quality control devices.

A more recent study by Mintzberg (1973) provides details for this portrait of strategic decision makers. Chief executives in five relatively large organizations (a consulting firm, a consumer goods manufacturer, a technology firm, a hospital, and a school system) were studied by recording their activities during week-long periods of intensive observation. The most evident aspect of the executives' jobs was the immense work load entailed. Evenings as well as weekdays were absorbed by the executives' concerns for their organizations. Even when pauses occur in the hectic schedules of these individuals, there are always unanswered letters and unscheduled appointments to fill their time.

Furthermore, the chief executive's work was found to be discontinuous, fragmented, and full of variety. Significant issues were interspersed with trivial ones. Half of all activities were completed in less than nine minutes. The realities of the job, then, encourage the manager to "make decisions abruptly, to maintain the hectic pace, to avoid wasting time" (p. 25).

Chief executives typically are not planners, not contemplative, abstract thinkers, because of the great pace of work and its discontinuous nature. In addition, Mintzberg feels that they gravitate toward, and prefer, hectic, concrete work styles. Mintzberg's study shows that the chief executives gave little attention to routine operating reports, participated in few regularly scheduled meetings, and almost never took part in general, abstract discussion. "The job breeds adaptive information manipulators, men who work in an environment of stimulus-response and who prefer live action.... [the typical chief executive] becomes conditioned by his pace and workload. He tries to keep all his activities brief, actively encouraging interruption in his work in order to maintain the rapid pace and the flow of information . . . " (Mintzberg, 1973, pp. 24–25).

This descriptive study of top managers' work conforms to our view of the strategy maker as a participant in a complex process rather than as a comprehensive, rational planner. As Wrapp points out so well, the top manager is motivated to participate in many operating situations (although not necessarily in making operating decisions) to obtain information and make use of opportunities to influence subordinates as is required by the complex process of strategy making.

In a prescriptive addendum to his report, Mintzberg suggests that the manager (engaged in the complex and frantic activities described above) must gain control of time. The effective top managers apparently do this by taking advantage of what they are obligated to do in any event.

> . . . success derives from turning to their own advantage those things they must do. The shrewd top manager treats the chaos of a crisis as an opportunity to make some necessary changes. A mutiny in a department may be the opportunity to effect a needed reorganization; a drop in sales is a chance to overcome opposition to the dropping of old product lines. He uses a ceremonial speech as an opportunity to lobby for a cause; every time he meets a subordinate, no matter what the reason, he encourages him in his work; and every time he must meet an outsider, he tries to extract some useful information" (Mintzberg, 1973, p. 28).

Values

On the basis of both observation and systematic studies of top managers in business organizations, Guth and Tagiuri (1965) conclude that "personal values are important determinants in the choice of corporate strategies" (p. 123). As used here values mean conceptions of what is valued or desirable, lying somewhere between very general, positive attitudes and a philosophy toward life. They may be viewed as a part of personality, acquired early in life from the socialization practices of parents and from peers and schooling. Values are inculcated by one's society, subculture, and family through systematic applications of sanctions and models. Because they are verbalized infrequently and pervasive, we typically do not become aware of our values until faced with a strange set of values or a value conflict.

The values studied by Guth and Tagiuri were measured by the Allport, Vernon, and Lindzey *Study of Values* (1960) which is based on Spranger's (1928) "six types of men."[3] The *Study of Values* scale has a total of 240 points and is scored so that an average response yields 40 points for each value. Administration of the scale to high-level U.S. executives attending an

---

[3] Descriptions of the six values measured by *A Study of Values* can be found in Ullrich (1972).

advanced management program at the Harvard Business School (Tagiuri, 1965) yielded the average value profile in Table 8-1.

We see that these executives are high on economic and political values, as one might expect, and also on theoretical values, for, as Tagiuri indicates, the high-level executive needs theories to sift through details and abstract what is going on in the organization

TABLE 8-1

Value	Score
Economic	45
Theoretical	44
Political	44
Religious	39
Aesthetic	35
Social	33
Total	240

Adapted from Guth and Tagiuri (1965, p. 123). © 1965 by the President and Fellows of Harvard College. All rights reserved.

However, while Guth and Tagiuri argue that managers' values affect their stategic choices, it is equally plausible that the value systems of business executives are relatively homogeneous compared to the values measured for members of other occupations (Allport, Vernon, and Lindzey, 1960), and that the homogeneity of values held by business executives restricts the range of alternative choices they will entertain. Moreover, conformity to such a homogeneous value system may contribute to the executive's success. England (1973), for example, found that successful managers exhibit pragmatic, dynamic, achievement-oriented values, whereas less successful managers adhere to more passive, static values.

It is not entirely clear whether we are discussing values or motives at this point—the two are quite different in theory, but distinctions between them become blurred in research methodologies. Nonetheless, the theoretical relationship between the executive's value system and strategic choice is important, and deserves further consideration.

In one of the few studies of the effect of values on a number of organizations, Hage and Dewar (1973) examined the value of change among top people in 16 health and welfare organizations providing rehabilitation services. A five-item scale of values favorable to change was administered to the staff of these organizations. Hage and Dewar were interested to see whether the values of (1) the leader (executive director) alone, (2) the "formal elite" (executive director and department heads), (3) the "behavioral elite" (the leader and all staff members who reported that they participated in decisions about policy, programs, personnel, and promotions—clearly critical to strategic decisions), or (4) the "entire staff" would best predict actual subsequent change in the organization over the following three years.

Change was measured in terms of addition of new programs (such as a stroke clinic for a rehabilitation agency or a program for unwed mothers in an agency that had never handled these clients before). Expansion of or change in existing programs were not considered a change. The study sought to answer the question: Whose values determine strategic decision making (inferred) and subsequent implementation of the strategic changes decided on?

The leader's values, or course, did predict the amount of change. What was rather interesting, however, was that the behavioral elite predicted even better. Those of the formal elite predicted less well, and the values of the entire staff not at all. One might conclude that a general predisposition favoring change is not sufficient for creating change, nor is the valuing of change by formally designated top staff. The values of the leader and the behavioral elite (corresponding to what James Thompson [1967] terms the "dominant coalition") seem to affect the implementation of strategy.

Strategic management

Clearly, strategy consists of more than devising a strategic plan, or any other formal, static product such as an environmental forecast or listing of marketing and production options. In contrast, as Gerstner (1972) suggests it is "... fundamentally a creative process. It cannot be programmed or systematized" (p. 6). We would add, however, that engaging in planning and undertaking the strategic exercises offered by management consultants can be a valuable educational exercise, sensitizing managers to the problem of strategy, helping them think abstractly, conceptualize, and model the systemic relations between organizational goals and objectives, environmental threats and opportunities, and organizational strengths and weaknesses. The danger is that the specific plans thus developed may displace the more diffuse management activity needed to create an organizational strategy. Recognition is now given to this danger by the increased emphasis on strategic management rather than strategic planning (Ansoff, Declérck, and Hayes, 1976).

Some of the recent research on business organizations reflects this changing emphasis. Rather than determine whether strategic planning makes a difference in performance, researchers are relating different strategies to different levels of profitability. Hofer (1974), in reviewing this research, suggests that "firms perform best by relating all their product/market activities to some distinctive competence and/or common theme" (p. 8). Rumelt (1974) found that among the 246 companies listed in the *Fortune 500* in 1949, 1959, and 1969, firms that were vertically integrated or that engaged in unrelated businesses were the poorest performers. The best performers were somewhat diversified, but related all of their activities to some central skill or strength. Similarly, Gutman's (1964) study of manufacturing firms with high rates of growth showed that they concentrated on a few segments of the industries in which they competed. These observations bear directly on the work of Pfeffer and Salancik (1978) that was discussed in the preceding chapter.

Some successful business strategies seem to center around the notion of maintaining a strong market share. Chevalier (1972), studying cookie manufacturers, cement producers, and the automobile industry, emphasizes (1) domination of market segments in which the firm operates, (2) divestment in market segments where the share is small, and (3) dominance in a small market (rather than being a follower in a larger market). Similarly, Fruhan (1972) reports how, in the grocery business, National Tea and a number of other firms attempted to get a toehold in many markets (cities) nationwide, while Winn-Dixie aimed at market depth in a limited area, the Southeast. The latter strategy has been shown to be related to higher profits. Obviously, it is the strategy, not the planning process used, that is important.

Dissonance reduction and the intractability of managers

Managers are risk takers, and those who make strategy decisions bear the greatest risks. There is abundant evidence that strategy decisions do not emerge from neat, scientific inquiry, but from judgments and bargains formulated from data that are anything but well understood. The need to make strategy decisions is unavoidable. As the world changes, organizations must change. But managers who make these changes can commit millions of dollars and man-hours to activities designed under conditions of overwhelming uncertainty.

In strategy formulations, especially as portrayed by Mintzberg and associates, an accepted diagnosis of the problem may be less accurate than those rejected, for all the manager knows—or the solution accepted may be inferior to the alternative rejected—and this is a source of *cognitive dissonance*.

In everyday terms, cognitive dissonance arises when our perceptions do not "fit" with one another; for example, imagine an individual faced with a choice of attending either of two universities, each as attractive as the other, for all the prospective student knows. Although the individual may waiver, agonize, and fret, he or she eventually chooses one over the other. This is where cognitive dissonance sets in, for there is a basic incongruity in rejecting an alternative as attractive as the one selected. Festinger (1957) explains that such dissonance is "uncomfortable" and is normally reduced by the individual. For instance, he or she may revise earlier opinions of the rejected university to make it seem inferior to the other. This can occur in the absence of additional information, and may be nothing more than self-delusion. Alternatively, the individual can seek additional selective information that confirms the decision. Other mechanisms can be employed as well. The point is that eventually dissonance will be reduced to the extent that the choice *appears* rational.

Such is also true of managers. Mintzberg and associates suggest that the typical manager enters the decision situation in a relatively unbiased state. The manager is out to get what he or she can, and "will choose any alternative that provides a lot of something, anything, reasonable" (Mintzberg et al., 1976, p. 33). But having made a choice, the manager must reduce the dissonance generated by alternatives foregone. Corroborating Soelberg (1967), Mintzberg and associates suggest that there is a confirmation process in which the implicit choice is subsequently rationalized. Having been rationalized, the choice is announced as a decision. It is no wonder, suggest Mintzberg and associates, that a manager often is not open to suggestions and reason once a decision has been made (announced). Having completed the difficult task of forging choice from ambiguity, the manager has "created the reality" in which to work, rendering it extremely difficult to alter that position.

DISCUSSION QUESTIONS

1. How do strategic decisions differ from tactical decisions? Give examples of each.
2. List some examples of disjointed incrementalism.
3. The Planning, Programming, and Budgeting System (PPBS) was developed as an alternative to disjointed incrementalism. What is BBPS? Why is it no longer popular?
4. Do you agree with Wrapp's statement that Management By Objectives is useful only at lower levels in the organization?

SECTION III

The Functioning Organization: Human Factors

Chapter 9
People

Chapter 10
Organizational Roles and Norms

Chapter 11
Power and Conflict

Chapter 12
Leadership

Chapter 13
Behavioral Consequences of Organizational Architecture

PREMISE

For the most part, recent research on organizations has dealt with individual and small group behavior. This is an important line of inquiry, for it attempts to tell us about the behavior of people in organizations and the subsequent effects of such behavior.

Our interests are somewhat different, for we are involved in a study of organizations and how they are affected by other organizations. This does not mean that we will ignore research on human behavior in organizations, but merely that we will look at the problem with the organization, rather than the individual, in mind.

In the next five chapters, we shall explore three interwoven themes: (1) how the behaviors of individuals and groups affect organizations; (2) how various organizational practices attempt to influence these behaviors for the better; and (3) how organizations come to affect their members in the long run.

9

People

B INTRODUCTION

By 1960, American management was quite familiar with the theoretical inclinations of behavioral scientists such as Maslow, Likert, and McGregor, but few of these theories found their way into accepted practice. The following summary of a story that appeared in *Business Week* in 1965 describes one exception.

Andrew Kay, president of Non Linear Systems, a San Diego-based electronics firm, had read widely the literature on employee motivation and decided to put theory into practice. Here is what happened in Kay's firm when workers managed themselves.

In 1960, Kay assembled his employees and announced plans for reorganization. All workers were to be put on salary at the equivalent of 60 cents per hour more than the prevailing wage rate in the area. Assembly lines were removed and replaced by 16 independent production units of six to seven workers each. Each unit was to be headed by a team captain and was free to determine its own means of production.

When put into effect, the plan yielded an immediate boost to employee morale. Productivity suffered, however, and some workers quit of their own accord. Within three months, though, productivity was at its former level, and by 1965, it was 30 percent higher than it had been prior to the reorganization. Rejected work fell almost to nil, and customer complaints fell 70 percent. The job of quality control inspector was eliminated. Flexibility increased. Where it had once taken eight to ten weeks to tool up for a new product, it now took just two to three weeks.

Below is a summary of a follow-up story that appeared in the January 20, 1973, issue of the same magazine. It provides a surprise ending to a unique chapter in management history and one that seems to contradict many contemporary theories of employee behavior. Whether or not this is actually the case remains to be seen.

In the midst of a slump in the aerospace industry, NLS revenues fell to $3.5 million in 1971 from $6 million in 1965. Aerospace firms, major customers of NLS, cut their orders by half in 1970, but NLS was unprepared to respond accordingly. Six months late in reducing production, the firm accumulated a year's supply of inventory.

Commenting on these events, Kay, president of NLS, remarked that he may have lost sight of the purpose of business, which is not to develop new theories of management. Kay returned the company to traditional budgetary and management techniques and, according to the *Business Week* article, predicted NLS would revert to its former profitability.

The management consultants who worked with Kay over the years said that the motivational programs used in NLS were sound and that the company's misfortune stemmed from other causes. Kay felt differently. Preoccupied with behavioral techniques and long-range planning, top and middle managers lost track of day-to-day operations. Furthermore, close personal ties between management and the work force hindered layoffs necessitated by the aerospace slump. Kay reported that when the crunch came he was still trying to be a nice guy. Eventually he reduced the work force by over half.

Changes in production techniques accompanied the reimplementation of traditional business practices. According to Kay, the independent production units did not accommodate individual differences in the work force. Some workers, he suggested, need repetitive tasks. Salaries have also been brought in line with prevailing rates.

Chapter guide

1. Why did production improve above what it had been in the days of the assembly line? In tearing down the assembly line, did the firm not move to a less efficient method of production? How can you account for this seeming paradox?
2. Assuming that the introduction of tightened financial controls was appropriate under the circumstances, do you think it was also essential to abandon the firm's behavioral innovations? What assumptions have you made in arriving at your answer?
3. Do you agree with Mr. Kay that some employees need to work at repeti-

tive tasks? In responding to this question, did you refer to research data with which you are familiar, to a theory of behavior that you have learned, to your own observations about human nature, or to your reactions to the thought of working at a repetitive task?

INDIVIDUAL NEEDS AND BEHAVIOR

Origins of contemporary theories

Most people have heard of Pavlov and his pioneering work on stimulus-response phenomena. In his most widely known studies, Pavlov presented dogs with food and simultaneously exposed them to the sound of a metronome. In time, the sound of a metronome alone would cause the dogs to salivate—a response normally paired with exposure to food.

The notion that animals can be conditioned to respond to stimuli of the experimenter's choice seems rather simple and straightforward. However, the implications of Pavlov's findings gave rise to some difficult and important theoretical problems. Hull (1930, 1943), on reading an English translation of Pavlov's work, asked in effect, How can a response (salivation), associated with exposure to food, precede the stimulus to which it is appropriate? Does Pavlov's work suggest that the dogs anticipated eating; that is, acted with foreknowledge of an event that had yet to occur?

We shall not describe the line of research Hull pursued to answer these questions because this would take us far beyond the scope of our text. However, we shall look at two major conclusions of Hull's work, since they lie at the heart of subsequent developments in motivation theory. First, Hull came to see behavior as motivated by the organism's needs; for example, the longer an animal goes without water, the greater its drive and, consequently, the higher its motivation to drink. However, motives are neither drives nor behavior. Rather, a motive is a force to behave in a way that results in drive reduction. This leads us to Hull's second conclusion. The behavior an organism uses to reduce its drives are learned. The more often such behaviors are repeated, the more habitual they become. Such reasoning led Hull to conclude that motivation, the force to behave in a particular way, is a function of drive and habit. The theory is expressed by the equation

$$M = f(D \times H).[1]$$

The concepts of drive and habit have been incorporated into many contemporary theories of human motivation. The first is found in *drive reduction theories,* while the second is associated with *learning theories* of

---

[1] The function proposed by Hull is multiplicative, since if either drive or habit is zero, the force experienced by the organism to behave in a particular way should be zero as well.

motivation. Usually, both concepts are incorporated in a theory, but the relative emphasis on either varies from one theory to another.

Drive reduction theories

Other theorists began to study behavior to identify the needs we experience as drives. Murray (1938), for example, postulated 28 unique needs. These included the needs for achievement, order, exhibition, seclusion, dominance, deference, and nurturance. We mention Murray because his work also provided a basis for some of the contemporary theories we shall study. Maslow, for example, began his work by identifying and classifying needs.

Maslow's hierarchy of needs

One of the classic theories in the field of motivation is the hierarchy of needs postulated by Abraham Maslow (1970). According to this theory, all people have the same needs—the needs for physiological essentials (food, shelter, sex, and so on), safety, love and belongingness, self-esteem and group esteem, and self-actualization. Self-actualization, according to Maslow, is the "... self-fulfillment of the idiosyncratic and species-wide potentialities of the individual person." The need to self-actualize, then, is the need to become all that one is potentially.

Each need in the hierarchy depicted in Table 9-1 becomes prepotent when two conditions are present: (1) when deprivation of the need is sufficient for "wanting" to occur and (2) when the needs below it in the hierarchy have been fulfilled to a "tolerable" level. With respect to the first condition, Maslow argues that needs are not likely to affect behavior until deprivation produces an awareness of them—a drive, in Hull's terms. We all need water, but do not experience constant thirst. Thirst occurs only after the body's supply of water has fallen below a threshold. Regarding the second condition, Maslow contends that unfulfilled lower order needs predominate over unfulfilled higher order needs. An individual will not be motivated to fulfill a need for safety until physiological needs have been fulfilled to some degree—a starving person will risk physical well-being to obtain food. Similarly, fulfillment of the need for love and belongingness will be sought only after the individual's physiological and safety needs have been met.

TABLE 9-1
Maslow's need hierarchy

Self-actualization
Self-esteem and group esteem
Love and belongingness
Safety
Physiological essentials

The need for esteem becomes prepotent once the needs below it have been minimally fulfilled. Finally, the need to self-actualize will be experienced only after some degree of success in fulfilling all the needs that precede it.

Maslow suggests that few individuals have fulfilled their needs for self-actualization. Zaleznik and others (1958) elaborate this observation by describing processes that serve to impede movement through the need hierarchy. First, fulfillment of each successive need is likely to require the sacrifice of fulfillment of lower order needs. For example, the quest for self-esteem may entail a loss of peer acceptance if nonconforming behavior is prerequisite to its fulfillment. Many individuals seem unwilling to seek gratification of their higher order needs at the expense of their lower order needs. Second, many of the environments that we have created for ourselves lack the potential to fulfill higher order needs. Similar to the organizational setting described by Argyris (Chapter 3), these environments thwart self-actualization and lead to elaborations of lower order needs. Hence, individuals engage in seemingly endless pursuits of status, group acceptance, and security. Furthermore, Maslow sees self-actualization as the work of a lifetime. It is unlikely for an individual prior to middle age to have had the wealth of experiences that are essential to self-actualization. If these assumptions are correct, it should come as no surprise that self-actualization, unlike the other needs for which we have an understanding based on our experience, is a somewhat alien concept and, therefore, difficult to describe.

The validity of the hierarchy of needs

For some reason, the work of Maslow seems to have great intuitive appeal. Perhaps this is because the theory describes life as we have come to understand it. Certainly, we can find events in history that lend support to this view of motivation. The themes that pervade Stone Age art, for example, deal with fertility and the hunt. Given the marginal existence that prevailed in those times, we can safely assume that prehistoric people's lowest needs were rarely fulfilled to a degree that allowed them to become engrossed in more than the quest for food and survival. Similarly, in recent times there have been instances in which individuals, faced with starvation, have resorted to cannibalism. Does such gruesome behavior suggest that needs for self-respect and love lose their potency in the face of the compulsion to eat and remain among the living?

As for evidence of the other extreme of the need hierarchy, we find that many people experience a subtle longing for something more than what life seems to offer. Is this longing the tentative perception of an emerging need for self-actualization or merely a generalized feeling of dissatisfaction? Is self-actualization a concept that is founded in reality or part of a collective delusion of grandeur? Unfortunately, turning to empirical data is of little help in resolving the issue raised here. To date research has not yielded conclusions that would either validate or discredit Maslow's theory. Neither the hierarchy nor the need for self-actualization has been verified (Wahba and Bridwell, 1975, 1976).

Alderfer (1969, 1972), however, has proposed a similar but abbreviated theory for which there seems to be impressive empirical support. In Alderfer's work, Maslow's five needs are replaced by three: the needs for existence, relatedness, and growth.

A theory of need hierarchies

Although we should remain somewhat skeptical about the validity of hierarchical need theories, it is possible to construct a theoretical explanation of how such hierarchies can occur. David McClelland (1955), noted for his study of the need for achievement, extended Murray's work by postulating the role of *learning* in the motivational process. McClelland reasoned that a motive is a strong affective (emotional) association that arises from the individual's reaction to anticipated goal attainment. It is based on past associations of certain cues with pleasure or pain. An emotion per se (for example, fear or satisfaction) is not a motive. Neither are cues (for example, stomach contractions that follow fasting). However, when cues are associated with changes expected to result from the pursuit of goals, the presence of a motive can be inferred.

McClelland suggests that the persistence of a motive is a function of (1) the frequency of the cue-pleasure (pain) association, (2) the generality of this association and the ease with which it can be extinguished, (3) the intensity of pleasure or pain experienced at the time the association was formed, and (4) the age of the individual at the time the association was first learned. We can reasonably argue that the lower order needs described by Maslow are likely to generate cues that are both more persistent and more likely to trigger associations than are the higher order needs (Ullrich, 1972). Consequently, something on the order of a need hierarchy may well evolve in the growing individual. However, an individual's attention may be engaged in the short run by associations that relate to the higher order needs and prevent the formation of motives arising from the lower order needs. Thus, we have a conceptual explanation of the hierarchical theory of needs that can explain deviations from the hierarchical tendency as well.

The two-factor theory

The theories of Maslow and Alderfer primarily are based on Hull's notion of drive reduction. Going beyond Hull, though, they postulate psychological growth as a uniquely human need. A third, related theory was developed from empirical studies of workers rather than through abstract reasoning.

Frederick Herzberg and others (1959) explored workers' motives by asking subjects to describe their own experiences. Specifically, interviewees were asked to recall times when they felt particularly good (or bad) about their jobs and to describe those episodes. The anecdotes thus collected contained three basic components: (1) job-related factors that led to the episodes described, (2) the attitudes the episodes produced, and (3) the effects that interviewees attributed to their attitudes. Analysis of these interviews suggested that factors related to the work itself (for example, achievement, responsibility, and recognition), which are called *intrinsic factors,* are more likely sources of motivation than of dissatisfaction. Conversely, elements of the work setting that are extrinsic to the work itself (for example, working conditions, supervision, and company policies), the so-called *extrinsic factors,* are more likely sources of dissatisfaction than of motivation.

To explain these findings, Herzberg relied on the psychological growth model that, as we have seen, is so prevalent in the literature. He concluded that the factors related to the work itself lead to job satisfaction and increased motivation ". . . because of a need for growth and self-actualization" (1966, p. 75). Thus, one finds a rationale for relating the results of the Herzberg study to Maslow's heirarchy of needs, as illustrated in Figure 9–1.

Job enrichment

The practical application of Herzberg's *two-factor theory* is known as *job enrichment.* According to the theory, attempts to increase the motivation and, therefore, the productivity of employees will be more fruitful when intrinsic factors are improved than when extrinsic factors are improved.

FIGURE 9–1
A comparison of the two-factor theory* and the hierarchy of needs†

Herzberg's two-factor theory	Maslow's hierarchy of needs
Intrinsic factors Achievement Recognition Responsibility The work itself Advancement The possibility of growth	Higher-order needs Self-actualization Self-esteem and group esteem
Extrinsic factors Company policy and administration Technical supervision Working conditions Interpersonal relations—superiors Interpersonal relations—peers Interpersonal relations—subordinates Personal life (effects of the job on) Status Security Salary	Lower-order needs Love and belongingness Safety Physiological (food, water, shelter, sex, etc.)

* Herzberg et al. (1959).
† Maslow (1970).

A report of work conducted in Imperial Chemical Industries, Ltd., by Paul and others (1969) provides an example of apparently successful job enrichment. Among several experiments reported, Paul discusses job enrichment for a group of experimental officers. These individuals were responsible for the implementation of experimental programs designed by scientists in research and development units of the firm. Basically, their tasks were to set up apparatus for experiments, record data, and to supervise laboratory assistants who carried out simpler operations. At the time of the experiment, the subjects had apparently reached dead ends in their careers. The average age of the group was advanced, and approximately one quarter had reached the maximum salary for the position they held. They lacked the formal education and terminal degrees needed to advance into the ranks of scientists. Alternatively, promotions into the plant were unlikely due to the increasing technological complexity of the manufacturing operations. The group's morale, as measured by a job reaction survey, was low.

Paul separated the experimental officers into control and experimental groups and attempted to keep from both the knowledge that an experiment was in progress. Extrinsic job factors for both groups were held constant, while intrinsic factors were improved for the experimental group. To the existing job, the following tasks were added:

1. Subjects were encouraged to write final laboratory reports (formerly the sole responsibility of research scientists), which carried their names along with those of scientists.
2. Officers were free to decide whether to have their reports checked by scientists.
3. They were given full responsibility for answering queries arising from these reports.
4. Officers were given opportunities to participate in the planning of projects and experiments.
5. They were given time, on request, to conduct their own research, even when these projects went beyond the unit's research objectives.
6. They were authorized to requisition materials, equipment, analyses, and services such as maintenance.
7. The officers were made responsible for the design and implementation of training programs for their junior staff.
8. Senior officers were allowed to interview candidates for the position of laboratory assistant.
9. The officers became the first assessors of their own assistants.

As illustrated in Table 9-2, these changes restructured the officers' jobs to bring them into contact with the entire research process, as opposed to a limited segment of it.

As the two-factor theory predicted, the changes led to increased productivity. Laboratory research reports of both scientists and experimental offi-

TABLE 9-2
An example of successful job enrichment

Staff development	Production	Research and development
Interview job candidates	Participate in planning projects and experiments	Individual research (if requested)
Devise and implement training programs for subordinates	Requisition materials and services	
Evaluate subordinates	Set up experiments* Record data Supervise assistants	
	Write laboratory reports Respond to queries	

* Elements within the box indicate the job prior to job enrichment.
Source: Adapted from Paul et al. (1969).

cers were graded by an independent authority who did not know who wrote them. All but three of the research reports written by experimental officers were within the performance range of the scientist. Furthermore, the same individual wrote all three substandard reports. Of the remaining 31 reports written by experimental officers, none was worse than the worst submitted by a scientist and 3 were judged to be as good as the best of the scientists' reports. Encouraged by their success in designing and implementing training sessions for their subordinates, the experimental officers initiated one for themselves. Finally, one of the original research ideas from the experimental group resulted in an important discovery for the company.

To compare the performance of experimental and control groups, members of each were asked to write monthly progress reports. These reports of activities were graded; the mean scores of the experimental group exceeded those of the control. Midway through the experiment, the control group was subdivided into two smaller groups. One of these subgroups remained as a control while the other was subjected to job enrichment identical to that applied to the original experimental group. Following this change, the mean scores on monthly progress reports of the second experimental group increased for several months until they became comparable to those of the original experimental group. Mean scores for the remaining control group declined.

Limitations to the generality of job enrichment

The prediction that job satisfaction of the experimental subjects would increase significantly was not borne out in the experiment. Yet, this is a minor point on which to fault job enrichment. More telling data from other studies give us reservations about the general applicability of job enrichment. More important, these other studies cast doubt on the validity of the psychological growth model of motivation, at least as it is described by Herzberg.

One questionnaire survey shows that 81 percent of the firms responding were not using job enrichment (Reif and Schoderbeck, 1969). Of the 19 percent that were (41 firms), only 4 indicated "very successful" experiences. More optimistic, but in the same vein, is the finding that of 19 job enrichment studies conducted at AT&T, nine were rated "outstandingly successful," one was considered to be "a complete flop," with the remaining nine deemed "moderately successful" (Ford, 1969). A more recent survey (Luthans and Reif, 1974) finds that only five out of 132 of the top 300 firms in *Fortune*'s 1,000 industrials make any formal attempt to enrich jobs.

These research findings let some questions of major importance go begging. Namely, are the occasional failures of job enrichment due to inappropriate designs, implementation strategies, or measurement techniques inherent in the studies in question, or do systematic forces in the workplace render job enrichment appropriate under one set of circumstances and inappropriate under another?

Herzberg's work remains a paradox. Whereas criticisms of his work have been numerous (for example, House and Wigdor, 1967; Vroom, 1964) and, for the most part, intuitively appealing, applications of the two-factor theory have had apparent good results (for example, Paul, Robertson, and Herzberg, 1969). Furthermore, his findings bear resonable consistency with many of the works previously described. Then again, replications of his study and applications of his remedies frequently produce unexpected results.

Why should interpersonal relations with peers, superiors, and subordinates not produce feelings of satisfaction and motivation as does recognition for achievement, when recognition stems primarily from one's interactions with others? What is so unhealthy about aspiring to work in a physical environment that is both comfortable and aesthetically pleasing? In answer to questions such as these, it has been argued that the methodology used to generate the two-factor theory biases the data on which the theory is built (Vroom, 1964); that is, in responding to the interviewer's questioning, the interviewees are prone to exercise defensive behavior by attributing satisfactions to their own performance and dissatisfactions to characteristics of coworkers or the work environment.

In a secondary analysis of data collected in Herzberg's study and replications, House and Wigdor (1967) rank order the intrinsic and extrinsic factors according to the frequency with which they were mentioned as sources of dissatisfaction. Interestingly, the factors, achievement and recognition, were reported to cause more dissatisfaction than either working conditions or interpersonal relations with superiors.

These criticisms and numerous others are compelling but far from conclusive. Yet, Herzberg's theory seems to have collapsed under the weight of criticism. Please bear in mind, though, that Vroom's comments on methodological bias are unsupported by empirical data. Thus, even if we reject Herzberg's theory out of hand, we will not have explained away his findings, but merely swept them under the rug.

There are additional grounds on which the two-factor theory can be faulted, however. For one thing, it ignores the possibility of satiation. Rather than being a source of motivation and positive job attitudes, excessive responsibility, for example, was mentioned as a major source of dissatisfaction in a Herzberg-type study of nurses (Ullrich, 1978). Moreover, by postulating the universal appeal of intrinsic job factors and the ubiquity of growth needs among workers, the theory ignores subcultural and individual differences, topics we shall turn to next.

Motives and subcultural differences

A study conducted by Turner and Lawrence (1965) attempted to classify attributes of a variety of jobs and to measure workers' responses to jobs containing different attributes. In their study, job factors such as autonomy, responsibility, interaction opportunities, variety of task, and requisite knowledge and skill were aggregated to provide what they term the *requisite task attribute index*. The study hypothesized that job satisfaction will be high among workers whose jobs have a high index rating (that is, that are high in autonomy, responsibility, and so on) and low among workers whose jobs are low on these dimensions. Similarly, absenteeism will be low on jobs rated high on these dimensions and high on jobs rated low. The two hypotheses were generally supported, but ambiguities in the data led the researchers to pursue their investigation further.

The research sample consisted of 470 workers from 47 jobs in 11 organizations. When this sample was subdivided into subjects from *urban* and small *town* (rural) subcultural groups, the researchers found a positive relationship between job satisfaction and the task attribute score for the town subgroup, while this relationship was negative for the city subpopulation. Furthermore, index scores were negatively related to absenteeism for workers in the town subsample; for workers with urban backgrounds, no such significant relationship was found. From these findings, Turner and Lawrence reasoned that the favorable responses of town workers to complex jobs and urban workers to simple jobs can be explained by the observation that urban and rural workers learn different predispositions toward work. In this vein, it is postulated that the town workers in the Turner and Lawrence study held traditional values regarding work and work-related achievement and, consistent with the Protestant ethic, responded positively to more complex jobs (Hulin and Blood, 1968). Urban workers, who were perhaps alienated from these Protestant, middle-class values, did not respond favorably to complex tasks, but preferred simpler ones. Subsequent data indicate that the more individuals subscribe to the Protestant ethic, the more they will be satisfied with their work and with life in general (Blood, 1969).

Whatever its merits, the Turner and Lawrence study may have overstated its results, for several alternative interpretations of the findings are plausible. For one thing, the sample populations were not heterogeneous. Originally, 470 workers were studied—244 from urban locations and 226 from small towns. The small-town subjects were predominantly Protestants; only 65 were Catholic. The urban subjects ultimately used in the study were all Catholics; 107 additional urban subjects classified as "mixed" (who for some reason could not be classified as either Protestant or Catholic) were dropped from the study.

Turner and Lawrence report that these 107 subjects showed no consistent pattern of response to requisite task attributes. "It was as though for them the subculture was too diffuse or disorganized to be exerting a strong influence on the manner in which they responded to work" (1965, p. 72).

Thus, the differences attributed to urban and rural subcultures were measured for an urban sample of workers who were all Catholics and a rural sample that was more than 70 percent Protestant. While it was noted that the responses of the 65 Catholic workers from small towns were more similar to those of Protestants in the rural sample than to those of urban Catholics, it can be argued that as a minority these individuals may have become acculturated to the majority (Protestant) attitudes toward work.

Are we saying that the differences noted by Turner and Lawrence had more to do with religion than community size? Not necessarily, for the problem is further complicated by the fact that the Protestants and Catholics seem to have had dissimilar ethnic origins. For example, the Protestants were identified as descendants of English and Scandinavian ancestors while the Catholics were of French, Italian, and Irish origins. Thus, the differences observed between the two groups could have been reflections of ethnic as opposed to religious affiliations. In any event, dichotomies such as urban-rural or Protestant-Catholic tend to obscure the effects of individual differences on motivation.

Motives and individual differences

Wanous (1974) explored differences within dichotomies by examining the contributions of (1) urban-rural settings of early socialization, (2) degree of adherence to the Protestant work ethic, and (3) higher order need strength to the relationship between job characteristics on the one hand and satisfaction with specific job facets, overall job satisfaction, and job behavior on the other hand. Wanous found that the relationship is explained best by higher order need strength, followed by belief in the Protestant work ethic. Place of early socialization contributes least to the relationship. Wanous's interpretation of these findings is that belief in the Protestant ethic is likely to contribute to the strength of higher order needs and is more likely to be learned in rural settings than in cities. However, both are merely proximate measures of the causal variable, higher order need strength.

Contemporaneous influences on motives and aspirations are also observed as part of ongoing organizational processes. For example, Wernimont et al. (1970) report that "The supervisor seems to have an impact on motivation primarily as he modifies or intensifies 'expectancies.'" Such influences seem to align motives with opportunities in the long run, regardless of whether they are intentional or incidental. Research evidence in support of this position has been fairly consistent over time. For example, the early works of Gardner (1940), Hilgard et al. (1940), and Irving Child and Whiting (1949) are consistent with the observation of Iris and Barrett (1972) that individuals in unsatisfactory job situations who de-emphasize the various aspects of their jobs appear to be satisfied with their jobs and life in general.

These and other studies raise serious questions about the usefulness of the so-called drive reduction theories. It seems unrealistic to expect needs, even if they are universal, to produce uniform motives and behavior in the work force. Thus, we turn to a school of thought that emphasizes the role of learning in motivation.

Achievement motivation

Earlier we said that motives are neither drives nor behaviors; they are forces experienced by the individual to behave in one way or another. According to McClelland and associates (1953) motives, as such, are acquired. In consequence, individuals' motives differ according to the variety of experiences from which they are learned. As we mentioned, McClelland based his work on the needs postulated by Murray—the needs for achievement, power, seclusion, succorance, and the like. The primary focus of his research, however, is on the need for achievement.

As a result of certain child-rearing practices and other socialization processes, children learn to associate cues related to opportunities to achieve with positive affective states. When this happens, according to the theory, the need for achievement is acquired. For example, positive parental attitudes and expectations concerning a child's accomplishments, coupled with supportive behavior and relatively few restrictions that limit independence, are associated with high needs for achievement in children. The opposite parental attitudes and behaviors are associated with relatively lower levels of this need.

Once formed, such motives systematically affect behavior, according to McClelland (1961); for example, subjects with high needs for achievement, relative to subjects with low needs for achievement, are found to have better recall of incompleted tasks, to be more active in college and community activities, to choose experts over friends as working partners, to be more resistant to social pressures, and to perform better on experimental tasks.

The last observation needs to be qualified, since superior performance is not associated with a high need for achievement in all cases. In a series of experiments reported by Elizabeth French (1955), subjects classified as having either high or low needs for achievement were asked to perform decoding tasks. When subjects merely were asked to cooperate in an experiment designed to "find out what kinds of scores people made on these tests," the subjects high in need for achievement did not do significantly better than the others. However, in a similar experiment, subjects were informed that their performance at the task would measure a critical ability related to their intelligence and future careers. In this situation, the high need for achievement subjects did significantly better than subjects with low needs for achievement. According to McClelland (1961, p.44), "The 'highs' perform better only when performance has achievement significance for them." Finally, a third group of subjects was told that the highest performers would be released from the experiment while the remaining subjects stayed on to practice the task and take more tests. In this situation, the low need for achievement subjects performed somewhat better than the "highs"—presumably to get out of working.

Achievement motivation and economic development

McClelland's most intriguing proposition is that widely shared, culturally determined child-rearing practices can affect the need for achievement in entire populations. Furthermore, these effects subsequently manifest themselves in the culture's rate of economic achievement and growth (McClelland, 1961).

An argument such as this must be tested against economic data that span generations, since cultural child-rearing practices are slow to change, and such changes must be compared with resulting trends in the culture's rate of economic growth. Obviously, surrogate measures of both economic growth and child-rearing practices are needed in studies of civilizations for which the appropriate data are unavailable. In the case of economic performance, indices such as tonnage of shipping and size of trading area were used as estimates of gross national product (GNP) in studies of medieval Spain and the pre-Christian Athenian civilization.

The problem of identifying changes in child-rearing practices in these early civilizations is even more difficult. However, evidence of such practices is passed down through history in the form of literature—the stories, ballads, legends, and accounts of history that children learn. Literature serves many purposes, including acculturation. According to McClelland, motives as well as mores are learned as part of an individual's cultural indoctrination. Thus, the themes that pervade the literature of a period will influence the motivation of its readers.

The literary theme of particular interest to McClelland is achievement imagery—accounts of successful individual performance. Such imagery is exemplified in the Horatio Alger stories that were popular around the turn of this century. McClelland reasoned that the popularity of such literature reflects the level of need for achievement in the culture as a whole. Furthermore, children are exposed to these tales because their parents, who find the achievement imagery consistent with their own motives, select them. In consequence, the child's need for achievement will come to resemble the parents' needs.

McClelland (1961) reports several studies that compare the economic performance of a culture with the level of achievement imagery in its literature. The findings suggest that growth and decline of achievement imagery (and, thus, need for achievement) parallel economic growth and decline.

Motivation and organizational structure

Related to the need for achievement is a broader, less well-defined motive discussed by John Morse and Lorsch (1970), Deci (1975), and others—the *competence motive*. Given a general level of competence motivation in the work force, we will find not only that motivation affects performance, but also that both motivation and performance are affected in turn by organizational structure, technology, and goals.

Although recent developments in organizational design such as System Four, participative-group organizations and high total influence systems are alleged to yield greater productivity than do more traditional forms of organization, their advocates do not mention the conditions under which these organizational forms succeed or fail. On the contrary, they are usually presented as generally applicable. In Chapter 4, we found that other schools of thought (for example, Perrow's and Woodward's) relate organizational productivity to the degree of congruence between the organization's technological processes and its structure. Chapter 6 presented organizational goals arising from and being congruent with structural and technological arrangements. The various theories presented so far in this chapter suggest that productivity in organizations increases with the organization's ability to satisfy the needs of its members, although these arguments generally are made in the absence of concern for variations in the goals or technologies that organizations employ. As we said, however, one of our major concerns is to understand the relationships that exist among organizational structure, technology, goals, and people.

Morse and Lorsch (1970) explored these relationships by relating organizational characteristics to productivity in four organizational units. Two organizations were used in the study: Company 1, which was engaged in the routine, predictable task of manufacturing, and Company 2, which was involved in the more unpredictable tasks of research and development. Within each of these companies, two organizational units were studied. In each pair of organizational units, one unit was more effective than the other. The Akron plant was the more productive of the two units studied in the manufacturing company, while the Stockton research lab was the superior of the two units studied in Company 2. A major finding in the Morse and Lorsch study is that the two effective performers had very different organizational characteristics.

Table 9–3 summarizes the characteristics of each organization as perceived by organizational members. Obviously, if we rated the two organizations according to high total influence systems, System One, Two, Three, or Four organizations, and the like, the Akron plant would score lower than the Stockton research lab in the majority of cases. Yet this observation is contrary to the arguments made by proponents of System Four, and high total influence: that organizations with these characteristics are more productive than traditional ones.

Morse and Lorsch find resolution of this contradiction in the following logic. Although all people may have similar needs, it is not necessarily valid to assume that they, therefore, have similar motives (see also Graen, Davies, and Weiss, 1968). However, even when widely different motives are found, *one motive that most people seem to share is that of competence. Yet, given that their other motives are dissimilar, different groups will attain fulfillment of*

TABLE 9–3
"Climate" characteristics in high-performing organizations

Characteristics	Akron	Stockton
1. Structural orientation	Perceptions of tightly controlled behavior and a high degree of structure	Perceptions of a low degree of structure
2. Distribution of influence	Perceptions of low total influence, concentrated at upper levels in the organization	Perceptions of high total influence, more evenly spread out among all levels
3. Character of superior-subordinate relations	Low freedom vis-à-vis superiors to choose and handle jobs, directive type supervision	High freedom vis-à-vis superiors to choose and handle projects, participatory type supervision
4. Character of colleague relations	Perceptions of many similarities among colleagues, high degree of coordination of colleague effort	Perceptions of many differences among colleagues, relatively low degree of coordination of colleague effort
5. Time orientation	Short-term	Long-term
6. Goal orientation	Manufacturing	Scientific
7. Top executive's "managerial style"	More concerned with task than people	More concerned with task than people

Source: Reprinted by permission of the *Harvard Business Review*. Exhibit III from "Beyond Theory Y," by John J. Morse and Jay W. Lorsch (May–June 1970). Copyright © 1970 by the President and Fellows of Harvard College. All rights reserved.

their competence motives in different organizational settings. For example, individuals in the Akron plant appear to differ from those in the Stockton laboratory in their attitudes toward uncertainty, authority, and relationships with their peers. Because of these different need patterns, each group was able to achieve fulfillment of its need for competence in a different kind of organizational setting. Therefore, the authors conclude that an organization should be designed to fit both its task requirements and membership needs. In failing to accommodate the requirements of task performance, the organization will lose some of its potential to provide workers with feelings of competence. Similarly, in failing to account for the needs of its members, the organization will fail to provide the kind of motivational setting in which competence can be exercised.

However, while considerable attention has been paid to the problem of matching individual motives and job attributes, far less has been devoted to the measurement of organizational needs. Sophisticated measures of individual abilities and motives found in industrial psychology are, as yet, unparalleled by techniques for making systematic appraisals of job requirements. Scientific management (time and motion study) and human factors psychology (for example, Chapanis, 1965) have examined specific, molecular elements of jobs, but no simple, systematic taxonomy for the more molar aspects of jobs is at hand.

Motivation and ability

If the concept of motivation is to be useful in understanding the behavior of people in organizations, it must be combined with individual ability, for performance is a function of motivation and ability. While a treatment of individual differences and selection techniques is beyond the scope of this book, we have discussed various organizational characteristics that aid or impede the application of individual abilities.

We have seen that job enrichment, System Four management, and the like can motivate individuals to greater organizational productivity *provided that they aspire* to the opportunities for need fulfillment inherent in the respective reorganizational strategies. The managerial problem suggested here is to create a fit between individual members and their organizational environment. Yet, as Blake and Mouton (1970) indicate, this fit will be optimal from an organizational standpoint when it matches concern for individual need fulfillment with concern for organizational productivity requirements. Furthermore, task-related needs and organizational requirements cannot be met unless the organization's design facilitates effective task accomplishment.

Equally important, and of particular relevance to our discussion of motivation, is the relationship between aspired need fulfillment and the organization's effect on the individual's ability to achieve such fulfillment.

Although this problem is acknowledged by the drive theorists, it is treated explicitly by a different class of theories—the so-called *expectancy theories* of motivation.

EXPECTATIONS AND BEHAVIOR

Work satisfaction and productivity

Most early research in the field of human relations focused on employee morale. At the time it was felt that improving interpersonal relations would increase morale, which in turn would lead to greater worker productivity. Subsequent research indicates that at least two different effects contribute to feelings of morale: satisfaction with the status quo and satisfaction derived from anticipation of future rewards (Ullrich, 1972). The latter source of work satisfaction may be associated with increased productivity, but only when activities that lead to increased satisfaction also lead to greater productivity. If an individual aspires to a greater sense of accomplishment, more peer recognition, and a higher salary and thinks that greater productivity will yield these rewards at a "reasonable cost," that person may work harder. In this case, the individual views increased productivity as *instrumental* to the attainment of these aspired sources of satisfaction. However, simply increasing the satisfaction of the work force will not necessarily improve its productivity (Robert Kahn, 1960). This does not suggest that employee satisfaction is inconsequential. A number of studies show that dissatisfaction correlates with labor turnover, absenteeism, and other undesirable consequences (Porter and Steers, 1973). Furthermore, satisfying employees (aiding in their pursuits of happiness) may be a desirable organizational goal in itself.

Sources of work satisfaction

In an analysis of studies of the sources and nature of work satisfaction, George Strauss (1974) reports that these studies almost invariably find the majority of workers to be satisfied with their work (see also Robert Kahn, 1972). There are exceptions, of course, but according to Strauss "... the best evidence from psychological surveys suggests that average levels of job satisfaction in this country have remained fairly stable since the early 1960s and that satisfaction today is higher than it was during the 1940s and 1950s" (1974, p. 23). While some observers point to recent problems evidenced by statistics on declining productivity and increasing labor turnover, absenteeism, strikes and accidents, Strauss argues that these can be attributed to changes in economic conditions and occupational and demographic characteristics of the work force (see, for example, Flanagan, Strauss, and Ulman, 1974; Wool, 1973).

Although there has not been much recent change in levels of overall satisfaction, there have been changes in the relative importance of specific job factors. Strauss suggests that job security is less important to employees than it was 20 years ago, while the intrinsic value of work has become more important. However, this generalization masks some interesting differences. For many individuals, especially blue-collar workers, pay and job security still assume equal or greater importance than interesting work (see, for example, Porter and Lawler, 1965). The reasons for this are fairly obvious.

Many individuals, especially blue-collar workers, do not see their jobs as their "central life-interest" (Dubin, 1956). Instead, they are community- and home-centered. Unlike managers and professionals who are assumed to view work and its challenges as sources of meaning in their lives, these individuals view their jobs as instrumental to the attainment of security and money with which to pursue various extra-work activities (Fein, 1973; Goldthorpe, Lockwood, Beckhofer, and Platt, 1968). Strauss (1974) carries this argument further:

> ... much dissatisfaction is caused by low income, job insecurity, inadequate fringe benefits, or tyrannical supervision. Indeed, to me, the evidence suggests that for many workers at all levels—even many managers and professionals—lack of challenge may be less oppressive than lack of income. Instrumental orientation is widespread ... wants grow as fast as paychecks, and economic motivation may not atrophy as fast as some psychologists suggest (p. 34).

The expectancy model of motivation

These statements suggest that work itself is not a source of need fulfillment, but a means to need-fulfilling ends. Carried further, this reasoning leads to an expectancy theory, which holds motivation to be a function of the individual's expectation (subjective probability) that an outcome can be attained and the valence (utility) of the outcome in question for that individual $[M = f(E \times V)]$. This approach has its roots in the works of Lewin et al. (1944), Edwards (1954), Vroom (1964), and others. Essentially a theory of decision making, the approach is ideographic. Behavior is assumed to be influenced by the individual's perceptions of the environment and that person's ability to interact successfully therein. Need theories such as Maslow's direct our attention to the forces that drive behavior. Expectancy theories explore the processes by which such forces are focused in certain directions and not in others (Campbell, Dunnette, Lawler, and Weick, 1970).

According to Vroom (1964) and others, individuals evaluate alternative courses of action in terms of the *valences of outcomes* these actions are expected to produce. Valued outcomes have positive valences, while undesirable ones assume negative valences. Where the individual is indifferent regarding a potential outcome, valence is zero. A course of action produces two different kinds of outcomes: *first-level outcomes* are valued for their consequences, which are termed *second-level outcomes* and are valued in and of themselves. Returning to our example, the individual may choose to be more productive because he or she thinks increased output will result in a sense of accomplishment, peer recognition, and a higher salary. Please note that these second-level outcomes can be instrumental to the attainment of still more outcomes. Furthermore, it is important to recall that all outcomes are not positive. Increased productivity may be associated with fatigue and foregone opportunities as well. In any event, the first-level outcome, increased productivity, has no value other than as a means to second-level outcomes.

The extent to which a first-level outcome is seen as instrumental in producing each second-level outcome varies according to the individual's perception of the situation. Perceptions can range from complete certainty that increased recognition will follow increased productivity, through uncertainty, to certainty that the first-level outcome will not result in increased recognition. Thus, the valence of a first-level outcome is hypothesized to be the sum of instrumentality times valences over all second-level outcomes.

$$V_j = f(\sum_{k=1}^{n} [V_k \times I_{jk}])$$

where:

V_j = Valence of performance level j.
V_k = Valence of the kth second-level outcome.
I_{jk} = Instrumentality at performance level j.
n = Number of outcomes.

According to this logic, the individual's predisposition to achieve a certain level of performance (j) will depend, in part, on perception of the valence associated with this first-level outcome.

There is an additional problem to consider. How does the individual know that increased effort will result in performance level (j)? The expectancy model goes on to state that the *force* on an individual to perform act (i) (invest a certain amount of effort, in this example) is a function of the *expectancy* that the act will be followed by the outcome (j). Expectancy is expressed as a subjective probability ($P \leq 1$). Thus, the mathematical statement of Vroom's model is as follows:

$$F_i = f(\sum_{j=1}^{n} [V_j \times E_{ij}])$$

where:

F_i = Force to perform act i.
V_j = Valence of outcome j.
E_{ij} = Expectancy that act i will be followed by outcome j.
n = Number of outcomes.

Increased effort may not always lead to an anticipated increase in performance. Reduced to its simplest terms, the model states that in considering a given amount of effort (i), the individual perceives different subjective probabilities of attaining different levels of performance (j). For example, by investing a given amount of effort one perceives that one will be able to produce no fewer than zero and no more than three widgets a day. The expectancies for each of these outcomes are as follows:

First-level outcome (widgets per day)	V_j	E_{ij}	$V_j \times E_{ij}$
0	−10	0.01	− .10
1	1	0.09	+ .09
2	10	0.60	+ 6.00
3	22	0.30	+ 6.60
		1.00	+12.59

As the individual considers investing more or less effort, expectancies associated with each first-level outcome change accordingly. The force on the individual is to invest the amount of effort that will maximize $\sum(V_j \times E_{ij})$.

Evaluation of the expectancy model

Although this and similar theories have been the subject of a considerable amount of research, reviews of this research do not provide assurance that the model's validity has been confirmed. The model has been used to make reasonably accurate predictions of satisfaction (from valences), but does not fare as well in predicting the direction in which effort will be channeled (Mitchell, 1974). One problem is that no investigator has correctly tested the complete expectancy model. Tests of the model sometimes indicate that one variable (for example, valence or expectancy) predicts just as well or better than the complete formula (Locke, 1975). It appears to some researchers that "the theory has become so complex that it has exceeded the measures which exist to test it" (Lawler and Suttle, 1973, p. 502). Experiments designed to test the expectancy model against other models of motivation have yielded mixed results.

Further questions have been raised in terms of the model's inadequacy as a description of individual decision-making processes (Behling, Schriesheim, and Tolliver, 1973; Behling and Starke, 1973a, 1973b). Review of the literature on decision making suggests that individuals are unable to store the amount of information the model suggests they use. Furthermore, they are incapable of making the myriad calculations called for.

In short, while there is some empirical support for the expectancy model, the evidence is by no means conclusive. Support also exists for alternative theories, though none of these has carried the day either.

Applications of the expectancy model

Just as the need theories found application in practices such as job enrichment, expectancy theory has valid uses in organizations. Relatively simple situations in which behavior-reward contingencies are unambiguous are conducive to rational, cognitive behavior that may be described by an expectancy model (see, for example, Graen, 1969). In more complex situations, where there are more unknowns and where complex social factors intervene, a less "rational" approach to understanding behavior may be appropriate (for example, see Chapter 8).

One area where expectancy theory seems particularly useful is in highlighting differences between individual and environmental determinants of motivation. Lawler (1973) has expanded the Vroom model by emphasizing the individual's expectancy regarding the consequences of one's *efforts* to perform at a certain level. This effort-performance probability lends insight to the growing field of attribution theory—the study of psychological mechanisms by which individuals attribute their successes and failures to themselves or outsiders (Weiner, 1972). In contrast to predominantly individual, psychological views of effort-performance expectancies, Lawler emphasizes the environmental (often organizational) origins of performance-reward relationships. The latter emphasis permits us to explore the ways in which reward systems shape expectancies and motivations.

Expectancy theory is especially useful in explicating incentive plans used in industry. Such plans generally make incentives directly contingent on the individual's performance. As Lawler (1973) indicates, individual incentive systems such as piece rates, merit raises, and the like seem to improve performance 10 to 20 percent above that experienced when rewards are not directly contingent on performance. However, the success of such systems depends, in part, on the participants' trust in management, perceptions of a close relationship between rewards and performance, and understanding of the system (Cammann and Lawler, 1973). Group incentive plans do not always improve performance, probably because rewards are not entirely contingent on individual performance. These schemes do tend to facilitate cooperation among group members who work at interdependent tasks and are useful in this regard. Please note that individual incentive plans may be dysfunctional when applied to group members working at interdependent tasks, since cooperation may give way to competition.

The expectancy model and person-job discrepancies

Some theories, such as Herzberg's, ignore the possibility of satiation. The expectancy theory does not, since the valence of an outcome is a subjective perception and theoretically can be negative in the case of satiating consequences. This is no small problem. Apparently, the effects of satiation can be as severe as those of lack of satiation.

A recent program of research provides information on the various strains (for example, physiological disorders) that can arise when job requirements are ill suited to individual motives and abilities. John French and colleagues (French, 1974, French and Caplan, 1973) asked individuals to rate their jobs according to the extent to which selected factors were present. These subjects also indicated the extent to which they would like these factors to appear in their jobs. Factors studied included responsibility for the work of subordinates, work load, responsibility for things, utilization of abilities, and opportunities for advancement.

Responses indicating that subjects desired either more or less of a factor than their jobs contained were termed person-job discrepancies. Work satisfaction was found to be highest for subjects (managers and professionals employed by NASA) reporting little or no discrepancy. Positive correlations were found between degree of discrepancy and variables such as perceived threat to health and well-being, anxiety, and work-related depression. Even physiological measures such as cholesterol level, systolic blood pressure, and blood glucose level increased with extent of discrepancy.

Such research findings emphasize the desirability of increasing our knowledge of the interrelationships among people and major organizational variables. Here, we have reached one of the frontiers of knowledge in organizational design and behavior. How to measure and improve the goodness of fit remains to be seen.

Combining the expectancy and need theories

In our introductory chapter, we remarked that the development of science is more accurately described by revolutionary changes in paradigms than by the assembly of research findings to complete an existing paradigm. Between such epoch-making revolutions, however, routine science works within the existing paradigm, looking for pieces to fit the puzzle. In this sense, routine science refers to what the majority of scientists do rather than to the development of science per se. As we have said, routine science ultimately paves the way for scientific revolution, for the pieces never quite fit together (Kuhn, 1957).

In the next few pages, we will sketch the outlines of a theory proposed by

Deci (1975) that attempts to piece together some of the major theories of motivation. Deci's theory is tentative and unvalidated. It is neither the first attempt to integrate theories, nor presumably the last. However, it is imaginative and quite interesting.

Intrinsic motivation

At the heart of Deci's theory is the distinction between intrinsic and extrinsic motivation. Extrinsic motives predispose the individual to engage in behaviors directed toward attaining external (extrinsic) rewards such as food, safety, or shelter. *Intrinsic motives* lead to activities for which there is no apparent reward other than the activity itself.[2]

This definition of intrinsic motivation is not completely adequate, though. To say that there is no apparent reward for behavior other than the behavior itself only suggests that we do not know why intrinsically motivated acts are rewarding. Thus, Deci's theory begins with an attempt to explain intrinsic motivation.

The behavior of children, adults, and the more intelligent animals suggests that novel stimuli can produce two distinctly different effects in an organism. Up to a point, the organism will seek out novel experiences and may even go to considerable pains in doing so. Beyond a point, however, the organism will avoid what appears to be excessive stimulation—perhaps because of fear of the unknown or sensory overload.

The explanation of these phenomena involves an assumption about the needs of the brain. According to various theorists, the brain needs to be taxed by stimuli to the right extent to function properly. In fact, it appears that the central nervous system cannot develop normally in an organism deprived of stimulation. For example, dogs raised in small cages and and isolated from contact with other animals or humans are both stupid and peculiar in the sense that they do not seem to experience pain and are hyperactive (Hebb, 1955).

These and similar observations lead to the conclusion that organisms seek out situations in which the potential for arousal is optimal. Paradoxically, when *arousal potential* (stimulus intensity) is optimal the *arousal of the organism* will be minimal (Figure 9–2).

When arousal potential is below the optimal level, the organism becomes aroused and will seek greater stimulation. If the arousal potential is too great, the organism also becomes aroused, but will either withdraw from the situation or explore the source of excessive stimulation. In the case of withdrawal, the response obviously is to seek a lower, more nearly optimal level of stimulation. The second case is more complicated. Novel situations be-

---

[2] Please note the conceptual distinction between intrinsic motivation and the intrinsic job factors proposed by Herzberg.

**FIGURE 9-2
The relation between arousal potential and arousal**

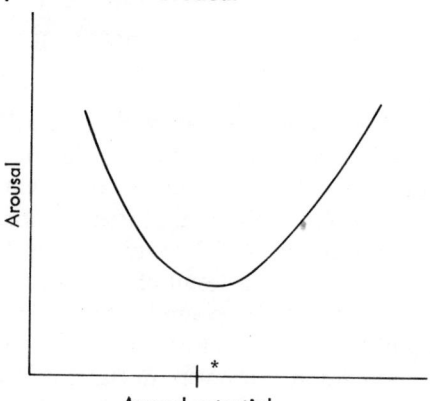

Arousal potential
* The vertical marker represents the optimal level of arousal potential.
Source: Deci, 1975, p. 47.

come less stimulating as we become familiar with them (or adapt to them). Thus, one way to reduce the arousal potential of a novel source of stimulation is to explore it to become familiar with it and, perhaps, even understand it.

Intrinsic motivation and central nervous system needs

There is a great deal more to this line of research than we have presented here. However, it should become clear that intrinsically motivated activities can be explained in terms of their effects on the central nervous system, that is, in terms of meeting the needs of the brain. However, this explanation does not satisfy Deci entirely, for people seem to seek novel, stimulating experiences on the one hand and explore, study, and ultimately master them on the other. In effect, they seek an optimal level of arousal, but then reduce it to a suboptimal level, and consequently become aroused and seek the optimum again. In everyday terms, we search for puzzles, problems, and novel experiences. Once we find them, we are motivated to master them. Once mastered, they are no longer puzzles, problems, or novelties. So the search begins anew. One interpretation of this observation suggests that the central nervous system needs to be exposed to novel stimuli and to be able to process them. In processing these stimuli, the organism learns, but such learning may entail mere familiarity with the sources of novel stimuli as opposed to an understanding of them. According to this logic, learning is merely an outcome of the need for stimulation. A second interpretation, which Deci favors, is that the tendency described implies a need to feel "competent and self-determining in dealing with [the] environment" (Deci, 1975, p. 100). Thus, the need for competence (learning) lies at the heart of intrinsic motivation.

Deci's theory

According to Deci, children are born with an undifferentiated intrinsic motivation to feel competent. As they mature, this need differentiates into specific intrinsic motives such as the need for achievement, the self-actualization need, or the need for intellectual mastery. Paralleling McClelland's description of the origins of the need for achievement, Deci argues that specific intrinsic motives develop as a result of learning.

Were it not for other needs, for example, those related to the safety and physical well-being of the organism, the individual would experience uninterrupted intrinsic motivation. However, intrinsic motivation is interrupted when drives for food, water, or safety engage the individual's attention, that is, when extrinsic motives emerge. According to Deci, extrinsic motivation is best described by expectancy theories. A simplified view of expectancy theory suggests that if there are two ways to achieve a desired outcome, the individual will select the easier way. This makes sense when extrinsic rewards are considered. However, the intrinsically motivated individual may choose the more difficult way, since mastery of challenge rather than extrinsic reward is the goal of such activities.

There is more to Deci's theory than this, but we have gone far enough to show how the works of Maslow, McClelland, Herzberg, Vroom, and others can be incorporated into a single theoretical perspective. Even individual differences in motivation are addressed, since specific motives develop as a result of the individual's learning.

The path not taken

Be that as it may, much of Deci's theory rests on the assumption of a need for competence. As we indicated, there is an alternative assumption, but Deci chose not to accept it. Choosing between the two, Deci says, is "to a large degree, a matter of preference" (p. 10). Fair enough, but out of curiosity we shall explore the path not taken.

Argyris (Chapter 3), Maslow, Alderfer, Deci, and still others view psychological growth in one form or another as a need. Similar to the physiological needs, deprivation of the need for psychological growth causes the individual to suffer and, in extreme cases, atrophy. One question to be raised at this point is whether psychological growth itself is a need or merely the outcome of behavior undertaken to fulfill another, unspecified need.

We can revise the growth-as-need proposition by observing that, under optimal environmental conditions, an organism will attain its potential. In doing so, we have described growth as an outcome rather than as a need. An analogy from horticulture will help to clarify this point. Among the 35,000 species of orchids is *Cattleya aurantiaca,* which typically produces two to three small, vivid orange flowers on each flower spike. Among members of a given species, however, genetic differences will be found, and in the case of *C. aurantiaca* some varieties produce large clusters of flowers, with a dozen or more on a spike. What we have described are two *genotypes* of a single species. If both genotypes, or varieties, are grown under optimal conditions, the second invariably will produce many more flowers than the first. However, if the second is grown under very poor conditions, it may produce fewer flowers than the first will when it is grown under proper conditions. Thus, differences in a plant's environment give rise to differing *phenotypes* for a given genotype. One phenotype of the second variety, resulting from inferior environmental conditions, may be indistinguishable from the first variety in terms of the number of flowers produced, while a second phenotype of the same variety may produce a dozen flowers. Neither variety, though, can exceed the limits inherent in its genotype, even under the best of conditions, for these limits are genetically determined.

The corresponding observation about humans, as Maslow suggests, is that a "good" environment will permit self-fulfillment of the idiosyncratic (genotypical) and specieswide potentialities of the individual, or in our terms optimal environmental conditions permit maximization of the phenotype within the constraints of the genotype.

Considering physiological characteristics of the organism, we can say that optimal growth within genotypic contraints occurs when the organism receives needed sustenance from the environment. Please note that while sustenance is needed, physiological growth is merely an outcome of the fulfillment of needs for sustenance. A similar argument can be made regarding psychological growth. The argument rests on two premises. First, genetic endowment and behavior are inseparable. According to Erwin Schrödinger, "You cannot have efficient wings without attempting to fly. You cannot have a modulated organ of speech without trying to imitate the noises you hear around you. To distinguish between the possession of an organ and the urge to use it and to increase its skill by practice, to regard them as two separate characteristics of the organism in question, would be an artificial distinction, made possible by an abstract language but having no counterpart in nature" (1969, p. 121). The second premise is similar to Schrödinger's, but applies specifically to the functioning of the brain. Theorists such as Berlyne (1966) maintain that the human brain is "designed" to handle a certain rate of stimulation and information. Too little stimulation (sensory deprivation) or excessive stimulation (sensory overload) can produce dire consequences in the organism. In Schrödinger's terms, you cannot have a good mind and not use it. However, the extent of stimulation required by a particular individual may be partly determined by genotypic variables. Beyond this, required stimulation may be determined by phenotypic variables; that is, the level of stimulation to which the individual becomes adapted and consequently needs in order to function is influenced by the environment in which the individual has matured. By environment, we mean not only physical and social surroundings, but also the inner world of mental functioning. An impoverished intellectual environment, no less than malnutrition, may produce a phenotype that fails to conform to the individual's unique genotypic potentialities.

In seeking out and subsequently processing needed stimuli, learning—that is, psychological growth—perforce occurs. Differences in the degree and kinds of stimulation sought will produce different kinds and amounts of growth. However, according to this logic, psychological growth is not a need, but a result of success in fulfilling the need for stimuli to be processed by the central nervous system.

DISCUSSION QUESTIONS

1. Can the same theory of motivation account for acts as dissimilar as stealing and studying?
2. What constitutes a good environment for people?
3. What are the implications of Deci's theory for the management of organizations?
4. How would you respond to a manager who asked you, "How can I motivate my workers"?

10

Organizational Roles and Norms

I. INTRODUCTION

In the last section, we attempted to explain why organizations are far more dynamic and complex than the rational view would have us believe. And yet something in our backgrounds still would have us ascribe more logic and programmed rationality to organizations than actually exists.

Imagine, for the moment, a psychiatric hospital. We see psychiatrists interviewing patients and diagnosing illnesses. Years of scientific training and experience permit the physicians to choose a course of therapy suited to the etiology of each patient's illness. Acting as a team, the physician, nurses, aides, orderlies, and housekeeping staff coordinate their activities to provide a comprehensive, rational treatment program. The organization, in fact, is a smoothly functioning system structured by formal rules and regulations and dedicated to meeting the patient needs determined by the application of modern science.

In any event, that is what we may think goes on in a psychiatric hospital. In actuality, according to sociologist Anselm Strauss, the functioning of such an organization is considerably less structured, orderly, or rational; for example, consider the following quotation from his article, "Healing by Negotiation: Speciality of the House":

Some psychiatrists in Michael Reese Hospital have established long-term understandings with certain head nurses, who know, almost without words, what is expected of them. A neurologist-psychiatrist generally tries to get his patients into the two wards where most electric shock treatment is done—and "his" nurses take it from there. We called this "speciality of the house"—as opposed to "a la carte"—treatment.

Once the negotiated arrangements are relatively stabilized, certain responses become almost automatic. Woe to the psychiatrist whose ideas of treatment are very troublesome to established routine and understandings, and who gets stubborn about it! He may suddenly find himself surrounded, perhaps hopelessly enmeshed, by an increasingly tight web of negotiation woven back and forth among nurses, administrators, and aides. When the furore in the ward is the greatest, the negotiation is most visible. Unless he has very powerful administrative support, he will sooner or later have to sue for peace (Strauss, 1964, p. 15).[1]

Chapter guide

1. How can it be that lower level personnel negotiate therapeutic matters with physicians, who presumably are solely competent to deal with these matters?
2. What are the "long-term understandings" mentioned in the quotation? How do they develop? Are they detrimental to health care over the long run?
3. What similar kinds of experiences have you had in other organizations with which you have been affiliated?

ROLES, NORMS, AND INDIVIDUAL BEHAVIOR

The fluid nature of organizations

In earlier chapters, we discussed the substance of organizations in terms of structure, goals, and technology. To be sure, these elements of organizations do much to shape the behavior that occurs within them. Yet, neither these elements nor the behavior that they shape are fixed. Rather, they are fluid, in the nature of processes; for example, goals may be formally stated and written down, but decisions frequently are made in the context of a variety of operative (sometimes conflicting) goals. Coalitions form and dissolve around important issues. The organization as a whole behaves differently over time as existing, internally established constraints are overcome and new ones are met.

---

[1] Published by permission of Transaction, Inc., from *Transaction*, Volume 1, no. 6. Copyright © 1964, by Transaction, Inc.

A negotiated order

Anselm Strauss and colleagues (1963) developed a model that portrays behavior in organizations as a *negotiated order*. Order, or a stable pattern of behavior, does not evolve solely because of formal structure in the form of job descriptions, rules, and regulations. Order is something that must be "worked at" and continually created and recreated. Certainly, rules and organizational goals foster agreement among an organization's members. Even so, disagreements arise due to differences in occupational roles, individual attitudes, goals, and styles of behavior.

In the psychiatric division of the hospital studied, Strauss and his colleagues found few formal rules. The rules that did exist were neither clearly stated nor seen as binding. Yet, work did go on; the staff was able to cite the kinds of behaviors that were likely to be encountered in the division and the consequences that these behaviors were likely to evoke, as if rules did, indeed, exist. Behavior within the division consisted of complex, although fairly predictable, activities.

This is not to say that rules were nonexistent; personnel did call on certain rules from time to time when such resort was to their advantage. Similarly, some rules and agreements between personnel were created as the situation warranted. But, while these rules may have been useful in a particular situation, they were not useful when the situation changed, rendering a rule less appropriate than before. In general, rules were cited selectively, broken, or ignored to suit the particular situation at hand or the needs of personnel. Even the hospital's administration did not rely on rules and regulations. Requests by new physicians for clarification of the hospital's regulations were resisted by the administrators for fear that overreliance on regulations would impede the innovation and improvisation believed essential to effective patient care.

Shared understandings

In the absence of formally stated rules, researchers found long-standing, shared understandings, or general "house rules" which were fairly clear. In addition, the organization had a goal, which was to discharge patients in better health than they enjoyed when admitted; however, this goal was admittedly ambiguous. The time-honored understandings that develop between personnel are essentially what we call *norms*. These expectations about behavior lead to more or less regularized behavior; for example, certain nurses, who interacted with certain physicians, in time came to understand what was expected of them. The physicians, in turn, came to know that their nurses knew what was expected of them. This state of events arose more or less informally. In fact, a physician might merely say, "Do the usual," though the usual had never been formally enunciated.

Understanding of this sort must be "worked at", but not always through conscious, formal action. The socialization of organizational members often results from unconscious social process wherein certain behaviors are reinforced and others are not; some are even met with negative sanctions. However, the socialization process does not automatically produce cogs that fit the organizational machinery. Individual personality differences, turnover among staff members, and changing situational variables limit the extent to which socialization can produce homogeneous behavior patterns.

Negotiating agreements

For this reason, explicit, temporary agreements and compromises become essential to the organization's functioning; for example, the staff may not wish to keep a troublesome, hyperactive patient on the ward, but may agree with the physician to try a new course of treatment for a limited period of time. If the treatment does not seem effective by the end of the set period of time, both sides may agree to negotiate further, possibly deciding to change the treatment in some way. However, the temporal aspect of such an agreement allows the physician and the staff to compromise.

In addition to explicit agreements, a number of tacit contracts exist in the form of understandings, as indicated above. For example, a registered nurse may suggest to a practical nurse that a treatment not permitted by hospital rules be administered, with the implicit understanding that the registered nurse, who is the superior, will take the blame if this infraction of the rules is discovered. In the absence of such an understanding, the subordinate may press the superior, through indirect or even explicit questioning, about how the consequences will be borne if the infraction is discovered.

A minimum amount of trust and a minimum number of tacit understandings are necessary if the organization is to run smoothly. In their absence, complicated negotiations and clarifications of intentions are required each time a new activity is encountered. Trust and understanding are especially needed in organizations like hospitals that bring the talents of diverse professionals and technicians to bear on specific tasks.

Strauss and colleagues suggest that this process of establishing order, by negotiating and reaching agreements, applies particularly to organizations with vague goals or a multiplicity of purposes. We argued in Chapter 6 that most organizations, in fact, fit this description. Consequently, we expect to find this dynamic, processual phenomenon in most organizations. The extreme example described here exists where different professionals strongly adhere to specific subgoals and to different means for their achievement.

However, as organizations increase in complexity and employ staffs with diverse professional backgrounds, they tend to use processes and negotiated orders more and to rely less on the kind of mechanical, formally structured order described in Chapter 3. We argue that most organizational behavior is processual, and whatever formal structure exists serves mainly as a constraint to prevent the process from destroying the organization by moving it too far in one extreme direction or another. However, we will move into a discussion of norms, roles, and power at this point, since these concepts provide a foundation for further discussions of organizational processes.

Informal structure

First, we shall elaborate on the concept of informal structure, which we introduced briefly in Chapter 2 as part of our discussion of bureaucracy and the Hawthorne studies.

By structure, we mean patterns of relationships among roles. These patterns comprise relatively enduring and often repeated forms of behavior that can be classified as being either formally or informally produced. *Formal* structure is planned and specified via official channels of communication with the intent that it will be used by the organization's members. *Informal* structure is unspecified, unwritten, and unplanned. Such structure can be viewed as arising out of, and in reaction to, formal structure.

As we indicated in Chapter 2, the system view of organizations focuses on the actual behavior of individuals, rather than on deliberately created formal structures. The early human relations movement grew in response to research findings that suggested that formally specified relationships were often amended or violated by the individuals to whom they were intended to apply. A typical illustration is an incentive scheme that establishes both a production standard for workers (for example, 20 widgets per day) and a piece rate for production attained in excess of the standard amount. The intent of this type of incentive scheme is to provide workers with a measure of financial security by paying them a fixed amount for production that falls below 21 widgets per day and to motivate them to produce more than that amount by paying an incentive rate for work produced above the minimum. What often happens under such incentive schemes is that work groups decide to limit their production to 22 or 23 widgets per day because they fear that management will increase the minimum while maintaining the old base rate if it becomes apparent that the workers can produce 25 or 30 units per day. From production statistics, we find that the data cluster around 22 to 23 units of production per day and that the distribution of data appears to be similar to a normal curve. The peak of the curve describes the work group's production norm. The productivity of individual workers tends toward the norm because deviations from the norm are met with sanctions of various kinds by the work group.

J-shaped distribution of behavior

One finds normative structure in many aspects of social life. Observe, for example, the behavior of motorists at stop signs. Most people come to a complete halt and, assuming the way is clear, start up a fraction of a second later; a few come to a "moving stop." A few halt for more than a fraction of

FIGURE 10-1
Distribution of individual productivity

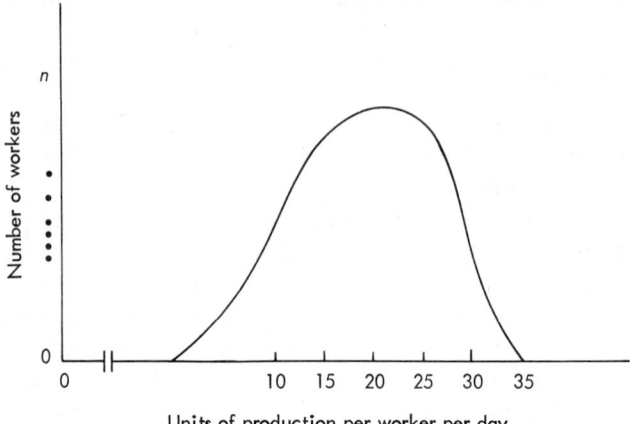

a second, but the majority halt for just a fraction of a second. This, in fact, is the norm for most drivers. However, in cities where the police are unable to enforce this traffic law and where this situation is generally recognized by motorists, the norm is apt to become a "moving halt" of two to three miles per hour, with exceptional individuals either halting completely or slowing down only to five or six miles per hour. A similar phenomenon will be found when one observes arrival times at work. If the factory whistle blows at eight o'clock, people will arrive very close to eight o'clock, and only a few individuals will arrive before or after.

Actually, distributions of data around norms such as those described above are not *exactly* normal shaped. They are what we might call J-shaped (Allport, 1934). This is to say that the majority of individuals (mode) behave at the norm, and some individuals operate away from the norm in one direction, but very few individuals, if any, operate away from the norm in the other direction. Behavior tends to conform to the J-shaped distribution because sanctions are more strictly applied to one side of the range of behavior than they are to the other. If an individual is conspicuously late to work, the supervisor is likely to consult the company's rules and apply whatever sanction is appropriate. The individual who arrives at work conspicuously earlier than fellow workers risks the disapprobation and sanctions that peers may apply, but the sanctions in this case are not specified and tend to be applied inconsistently. What we have illustrated is an example of how individuals shape their behavior to avoid sanctions. If sanctions are to be endured, individuals select the lesser of two evils.

So far, we have dealt with norms that arise from reactions to formal structures such as work standards, traffic laws, and company regulations. There are also informal norms that arise directly from informal behavior;

**FIGURE 10-2
Arrival times at work**

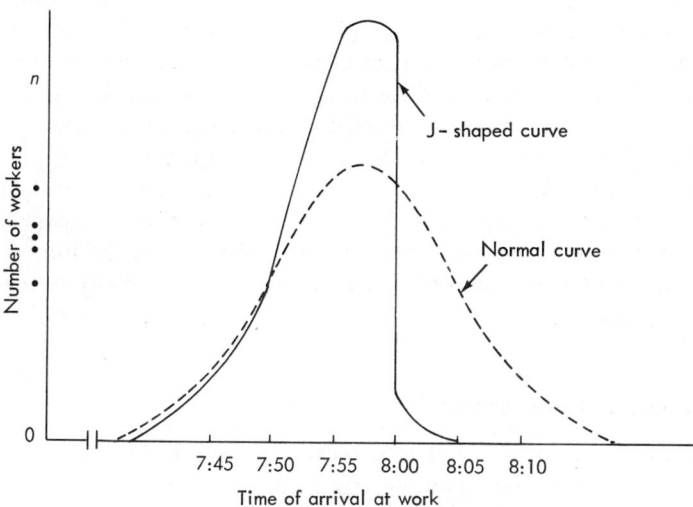

for example, work groups may decide among themselves that no more than one member of the group at a time can be absent from a work station during company time. Although there may be no official company regulation to this effect, workers will attempt to discipline themselves in this way if they agree that more than one of their number absent at a time makes them look bad in the eyes of their supervisor. Another example concerns a group of physicians who agreed not to resuscitate cardiac arrest patients above a certain age. Having established an informal norm, the doctors decided to make the norm part of the hospital's formal structure. They posted the rule where it came to the attention of the general public who, in turn, fought to have it rescinded. However, this is not to say that the physicians ceased to behave according to the norm that they had established for themselves. The informal norm may still exist unless sanctions have been brought to bear against it.

Internalized rules

Norms are internalized rules, or internalized structure, that create regularities in behavior (Thibaut and Kelley, 1959). These predictable responses are taught to give the individual an indication of how one is expected to behave in different kinds of situations. The adherence to, or the divergence from, certain social norms provides sources of information that in some elements of society are meaningful indices of an individual's background, status, and general worth. Norms operate because of a feeling of obligation to adhere to them and a sense of guilt when one is violated. Such norms are reinforced by sanctions for non-conformity.

Roles

A role consists of a set of norms that specify the behavior of an individual within a specific position in society (Thibaut and Kelley, 1959). Viewed more broadly, a role appears as a set of norms that prescribe the expected behavior and personal relationships of an individual with respect to other individuals who maintain other, related social positions; for example, the norms that apply to leaders of small, informal groups specify not only how the leader is expected to behave with respect to other members of the group and leaders of other groups, but also how group members are expected to relate to their leader. Within a small group, roles tend to be informal. In larger organizations, informal roles are augmented by formally stated rules and regulations.

Roles, norms, and role senders

Following Robert Kahn et al. (1964) and Katz and Kahn (1978), we shall describe a model for understanding how roles function, how shared understandings are created, how conflicts arise, and how a negotiated order develops. Organizations consist of numerous different positions or offices that are related to one another according to work flow, technology, and authority. The positions that are related directly to a particular role (the *focal role*) are said to comprise the *role set* of the focal role. The various members of an individual's role set depend on that person's performance in some way: (1) they expect the individual to use what they produce, (2) they themselves use what the individual produces, (3) they are subordinate to the individual and are expected to follow their superior's orders, (4) they are at the receiving end of the individual's reward system, and so on. The various members of the role set have expectations and attitudes concerning what should or should not be done by the occupant of the focal role. These expectations may be idiosyncratic or they may be agreed on by several individuals—i.e., they may be group or even organizational norms.

The expectations that are communicated to the occupant of the focal role are termed the *sent role*. Organizational members holding and communicating these expectations are called *role senders*. In other words, role senders communicate their expectations and thereby try to influence the behavior of the occupant of the focal role in specific ways; for example, young faculty members will learn their occupational role from both the senior faculty and their students. Both groups communicate their expectations, which sometimes conflict, concerning the manner in which a new instructor is supposed to behave.

The occupant of the focal role, however, perceives the sent role with varying degrees of accuracy, perceptions of the sent role, called the *received role,* are prone to be conflicting and to some extent inaccurate. For example, a professor, acting as a role sender, may expect the students to defer in speaking and to be attentive. Students who perceive their (received) role in this way will be deferent and attentive. Students who do not may appear pushy, arrogant, or insubordinate to the professor. As we shall see, lack of agreement about roles can provide the basis for conflict.

The structure of norms

Jackson (1966) provides a model, called the *return potential model,* which represents some of the more important structural aspects of norms. We can illustrate the model through a familiar example. Friendliness is expressed in varying degrees depending, not only on personal feelings of affection, but also on the norms that govern this kind of behavior in specific social settings. In many situations, established norms limit what are felt to be excessive displays of friendship as well as unfriendly behavior.

For the moment, let us imagine a continuum of behavior that ranges from overt hostility at one extreme to effusive demonstrations of affection at the other. On an 8-point scale, the former behavior can be placed at 0 and the latter at 8. The midpoint of the scale, 4, will represent indifference. Now, in a given social setting the behaviors described by different points on the continuum will be evaluated differently. Generally speaking, friendly behavior will be evaluated positively and hostile behavior negatively. These two dimensions, range of behavior and evaluation of behavior, provide the basis for Jackson's return potential model. Interestingly enough, we will find that not all *friendly behavior* is received with enthusiasm.

Using the two dimensions, we can plot a return potential curve that shows the extent to which approval or disapproval for different kinds of behavior registers along the entire range of possible behaviors. The curve in Figure 10–3 can be used to illustrate a hypothetical norm concerning friendliness between students and faculty members at a particular university.

The curve suggests that a hostile response on the part of students, no matter how slight, will be met with disapproval by faculty members. Students giving neutral, indifferent responses to faculty members (point 4 on the scale) will be met with a neutral response. Faculty members, however, will show approval of moderately friendly gestures on the part of students (around 5 and 6 on the scale). These might consist of short exchanges of pleasantries that are sufficient to display one's genuine pleasure at meeting. More effusive displays (points 7 and 8), however, will be disapproved, for at this point students will have transgressed a social barrier that maintains differences in status within the organization and will have acted out of keeping with their sent role.

The return potential model also shows that the norm of friendliness between students and faculty members confines the individuals to a relatively small range of acceptable behavior; that is, only a small portion of the horizontal dimension of behavior is approved. In addition, the norm is associated with considerable intensity of feeling, since much of the possible

FIGURE 10-3
The return potential model of norms

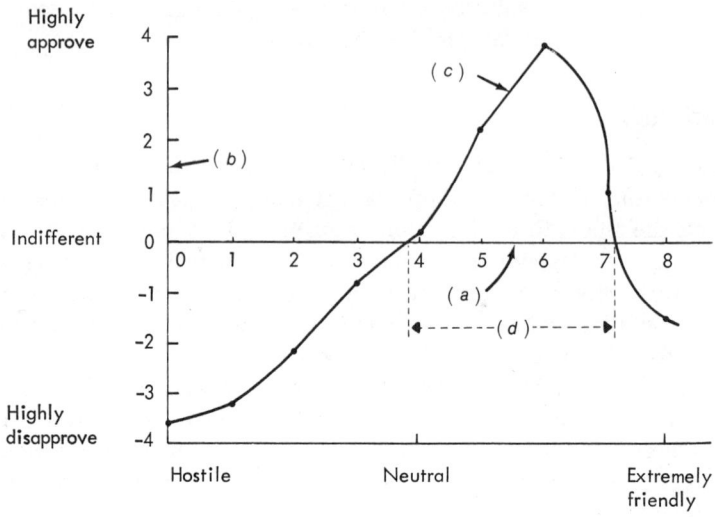

Schematic diagram showing the *return potential model* for representing norms. (a) A *behavior dimension;* (b) an *evaluation dimension;* (c) a *return potential* curve, showing the distribution of approval-disapproval among the members of a group over the whole range of behavior; (d) the range of tolerable or approved behavior.

Jay M. Jackson, "Structural Characteristics of Norms," in B. J. Biddle and E. J. Thomas, eds. (New York: John Wiley & Sons, 1966). Copyright © 1966 John Wiley & Sons, Inc. Reprinted by permission.

range of behavior is either highly approved or highly disapproved, rather than being met with milder reactions or indifference. Such norms concern matters of considerable importance in the organization. Similar norms might be found in organizations in which interpersonal relations bear directly on task accomplishment; for instance, in "people processing" organizations, such as schools and churches, relations among staff members and between staff members and "clients" are critical means to the organizations' ends. In contrast, norms concerning behavior that is less vital to the organization will be flatter, when diagrammed, illustrating less intense feeling about wider ranging behavior.

Effects of normative situations

Jackson describes norms in terms of their approval-disapproval ratio, which is the ratio of the range of behavior that is approved to the range of behavior that is disapproved. Where norms constrict the range of tolerable behavior, opportunities for learning are constrained. In this situation, one attends continually to one's behavior and limits it to a narrow range of variation, rather than be exposed to disapprobation. Consequently, we find that initiative, willingness to experiment, and creativity will be diminished by excessive concern for what others think of one's behavior.

Another interesting characteristic of norms is their tendency to *crystallize*. The return potential curve illustrated in Figure 10-3 represents average responses to behavior in the organizational unit under study. Although not shown by the curve, individual differences undoubtedly yield variations around the average. The average response to behavior described by point 3 on the friendliness behavior scale in Figure 10-3 will be mild disapproval (−1 on the vertical approval scale). However, the individual reactions from which the average is computed may range from indifference (0 on the scale) to relatively intense disapproval (−2 or −3). To the extent that the return potential curve depicts consistency (or low variation) around the average, the normal is said to be crystallized. The opposite of crystallization—where reactions to a particular behavior are random and, in the aggregate, lack a central tendency—implies a situation in which a norm does not exist.[2] The presence of a norm implies some regularity in expectations.

Ambiguous norms

In instances where the central tendency is weak and considerable variation is experienced, the norm is said to be ambiguous. This can occur when individuals fail to communicate their expectations effectively or when they disagree about the appropriateness of the behavior in question and, consequently, communicate mixed expectations. We alluded to this in remarking that young instructors sometimes receive conflicting sent roles from the student body and senior faculty. In situations of this kind, there may be a high degree of consensus within each subgroup. Considered singly, the subgroups will have fairly crystallized norms, and the return potential curve for each subgroup will be distinctive. However, when the curves for both subgroups are averaged (see curves *a, b,* and *c* in Figure 10-4), the resulting curve may be relatively flat. In fact, this average curve, *c*, masks considerable intensity of approval and disapproval of different behaviors and specificity regarding which behaviors are approved and which are not—both of which vary according to subgroups. To the receiver of such sent roles, the norm will seem unclear, not because of ambiguity of a lack of information, but because of conflicting information.

Variance in expectations about behavior is likely to be substantial in the early stages of a group's or organization's development. However, the development of shared norms is likely with the passage of time. The negotiated order that was discussed earlier results, in part, through the establishment of clear and unambiguous norms.

---

[2] Measures of *central tendency* seek to measure some central value of a distribution that is characteristic of it.

FIGURE 10-4
The return potential model of norm ambiguity

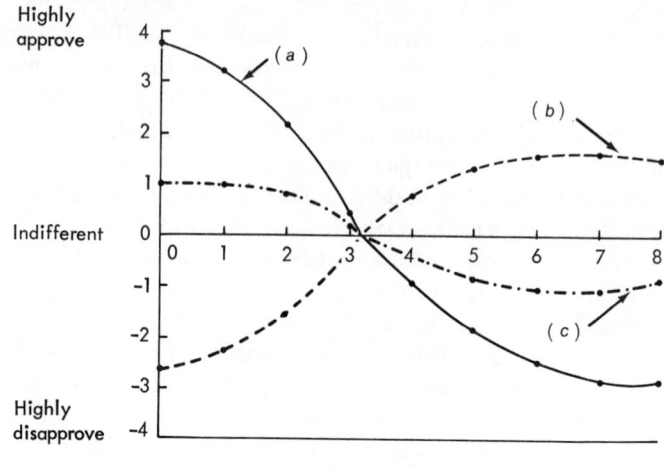

Schematic diagram for representing the *ambiguity* of a norm. In this situation there are two distinct return potential curves: (a) curve representing feelings of one subgroup; (b) curve representing feelings of a different subgroup; (c) return potential curve for a total group where norm has high ambiguity.

Source: Jay M. Jackson, "Structural Characteristics of Norms," in B. J. Biddle and E. J. Thomas, eds. (New York: John Wiley & Sons, 1966). Copyright © 1966 by John Wiley & Sons, Inc. Reprinted by permission.

A final source of influence that helps shape a role is found in the expectations that individuals in the focal role have for their own behavior. These expectations are the basis for what is termed the *own role*. The focal role holder's own role comprises expectations about how one ought to behave in the pursuit of organizational goals, one's own personal goals, or some combination of the two. According to Katz and Kahn (1978), individuals are *self-senders,* role sender to themselves.

The role episode

The expectations of role senders and the means by which they are communicated, together with the focal person's perceptions of these communications and that person's consequent behavior, can be viewed as a sequence or, as Katz and Kahn (1966) term it, a *role episode*. The nature of this sequence is illustrated in Figure 10-5.

The left half of the diagram represents the role sender, and the right half the focal person. The left half of each box (sections I and III) represents the individual's perceptions, concepts, and motives. The right segment of each box (sections II and IV) portrays the individual's overt responses.

FIGURE 10-5
A model of the role episode

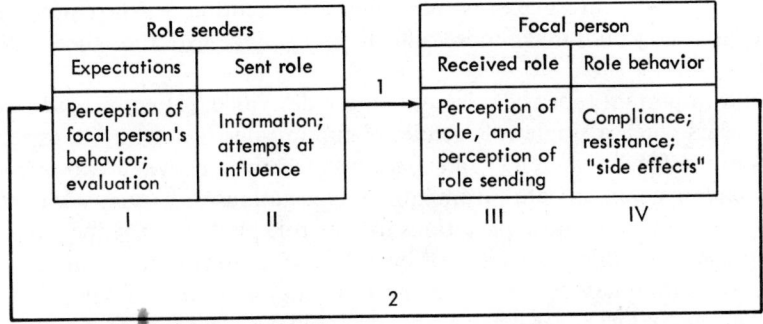

Source: Katz and Kahn (1966, p. 182). Copyright © 1966 John Wiley & Sons, Inc. Reprinted by permission.

The direction of the arrow from the role sender to the focal person is quite temporary, for the next role episode may well consist of the original focal person acting together with colleagues as a role sender to a focal person who had originally served in the other capacity. Thus, individuals occupy a focal role during the time they receive role expectations from other members of their role set. In the next instant, they may themselves become role senders. According to Katz and Kahn, "the on-going life of a large organization involves many continuous cycles of sending, receiving, responding, evaluating, and sending again by persons in many overlapping role sets" (1966, p. 183).

In Figure 10-5, the short arrow between the sent role and the received role indicates the process of role sending. The long feedback loop between the role behavior of focal persons and the expectations of role senders indicate the process whereby role senders consider how much compliance has been gained in response to the sent role, as well as the process by which they prepare to initiate another cycle of sending and hoping for compliance. Katz and Kahn provide the following overview of role episode:

> ... the role episode is abstracted from a process which is cyclic and ongoing: the response of a focal person to role-sending feeds back to each sender in ways that alter or reinforce his expectations and subsequent role-sending. The current role-sendings of each member of the set depend on his evaluations of the responses to his last sendings, and thus a new episode begins (Katz and Kahn, 1966, p. 183).

Role conflict

In addition to oversimplifying an ongoing process by describing a single episode, Figure 10-5 understates the complexity of the situation by omitting the fact that numerous role senders may have inconsistent and conflicting expectations of the focal person. Katz and Kahn define *role conflict* as the "simultaneous occurrence of two (or more) role sendings such that compliance with one would make more difficult compliance with the other" (1978, p. 204).

Four important types of role conflict are described. (1) *Intra-sender conflict* occurs when a single role sender communicates incompatible expectations to the focal person. (2) *Inter-sender conflict* results when two or more role senders communicate incompatible expectations. (3) *Inter-role conflict* is experienced when the expectations for one role played by the focal person are in conflict with one or more of his other roles (for example, an individual's work role may conflict with the roles that arise from home life). (4) *Person-role conflict* arises when sent roles are in conflict with the individual's own needs and values.

Occupational role conflict is a major problem, according to a survey conducted by Robert Kahn et al. (1964). Interviews were conducted with a probability sample of some 725 adults representing the labor force in the United States. Forty-eight percent of the sample reported being "caught in the middle" between two sets of people who had conflicting expectations of them. Fifteen percent reported this to be a frequent and serious problem. Thirty-nine percent said that not being able to satisfy these conflicting demands "bothered" them.

Furthermore, the investigators linked these subjective feelings of conflict to various affective and overt responses. Role conflict was associated with low job satisfaction, low confidence in the organization, and a high degree of job-related tension. Workers experiencing role conflict frequently attempted to withdraw from the perceived sources of conflict.

Role ambiguity

In connection with our preceding discussion of the clarity of norms, survey respondents to Kahn and associates also reported considerable role ambiguity. Four different kinds of ambiguity were cited as being disturbing and troublesome to focal persons. These consisted of uncertainty about (1) the way one's work would be evaluated by a supervisor, (2) opportunities for advancement, (3) the nature and extent of one's responsibilities, and (4) other people's expectations for one's performance.

The study showed that each of the four areas of ambiguity presented a problem for about one third of the respondents. Approximately 40 percent of the focal persons felt that they possessed insufficient information to perform their jobs adequately. Ambiguity produces significant undesirable results similar to those associated with role conflict, namely, low morale, job satsifaction, and self-confidence, and high feelings of futility and levels of tension.

Sources of role ambiguity

Kahn and associates (1964) observe that three general conditions contribute to role ambiguity. First, modern organizations have grown in size and complexity to the extent that a single employee cannot comprehend more than a small portion of the organization's functioning. Second, the rate of organizational change is increasing as a result of growth (and various attendant kinds of structural changes such as reorganization), changes in technology, and personnel turnover. Third, ambiguity often is associated with a managerial philosophy that restricts communication. The rational model of organization suggests that individuals specialize, learn only their own jobs, and look to their superiors for coordination. Even when interdependencies between jobs are recognized by management, communication is based primarily on what subordinates *need* to know rather than on what they would *like* to know. This is not to say that subordinates do not also restrict information since this is one of the few techniques available to them for influencing their superiors.

Some writers have specified a general psychological need for clarity (for example, Cohen, Stotland, and Wolfe, 1955; Robert Kahn, Wolfe, Quinn, Snoek, and Rosenthal, 1964). The survey by Kahn and associates, as well as a more recent study of registered nurses (Lyons, 1971), show that even individuals having relatively low needs for clarity experience more tension in ambiguous jobs than in those that are unambiguous.

MANAGING ROLE CONFLICT

Organizational roles, innovation, and adaptation

In our description of role conflict and ambiguity we cited consequences for the focal person. It seems that low levels of tension are found where roles are clear. However, a number of theorists suggest that motivation and satisfaction increase as organizational roles become less specific (Argyris, 1960; Likert, 1961; McGregor, 1960). Less role specification may allow individuals more discretion to work in ways that allow them to meet their own needs as well as those of the organization. An even stronger argument for the importance of discretion is provided by Frank (1963–64), who suggests that ambiguous and conflicting role definitions are useful in organizations that emphasize initiative and innovation.

Frank (1963–64) differentiates organizations according to whether they are (1) underdefined, (2) well-defined, or (3) overdefined. The classical formal approach to organizational design described in Chapter 3 typifies the well-defined organization (which comprises well-defined roles). Frank suggests the Hoover Commission Report on Organization of the Executive

Branch of the Government as a typical example, advocating an orderly, clear grouping of government functions into major departments and agencies, the establishment of clear lines of control from the chief executive to department and agency heads and thence to their subordinates, and so on. Managers who complain of overlaps between roles or lack of clear assignments of responsibility, and who long for clearly defined roles, are acting in this tradition. However, it is not well-defined roles but rather those that are under- and overdefined that lead to adaptability and innovation in organizations.

Underdefined roles permit individuals to take initiative and define roles for themselves or others. This, of course, leads to a changing, adapting, and innovating organization. Underdefined roles typically are found in new organizations and at topmost levels of management (see Chapters 8 and 12). With the passage of time, of course, the tendency is for underdefined roles (and organizations comprising these roles) to become either well-defined or overdefined.

The well-defined role limits individual initiative and may foster ritual performance. The organization with well-defined roles appears bureaucratic and tends to be stable when compared to an under- or overdefined role configuration. It follows that to have an organization that is creative or innovative, one ought to create a new organization comprising underdefined roles, rather than attempt to change a well-defined role configuration; for example, Frank describes how his university attempted to foster research and innovative teaching, which required underdefined roles, by setting up an entirely new college rather than changing roles in the ongoing organization.

The third kind of role configuration is the overdefined role. Excessive role expectations, or role overload, are associated with one form. The other, more common configuration is typified by role conflict, in which conflicting standards or norms prevent complete role performance. Excessive and conflicting role expectations allow incumbents discretion in defining their roles, since they obviously cannot perform the entire set of role requirements. In this respect, the overdefined role is similar to the underdefined role.

Sources of role conflict

Kahn and associates found three types of roles that were often characterized by conflict: *boundary roles, innovative roles,* and *supervisory roles.*

Boundary roles place the individual in contact with role senders outside of the organization. Generally, the more frequent and important an individual's contacts outside of the organization, the more role conflict that person experiences, although this was not true at the extreme. For those individuals having continuous outside contacts, some compensating factors served to ameliorate role conflict.

In any event, the focal persons have limited influence over the outsiders with whom they interact. Despite this, they are likely to be blamed by their co-workers for problems created by these outside contacts. Similarly, their outside contacts are likely to blame them for the shortcomings of others in their own organization. The study also showed that internal boundaries (boundaries between departments and divisions) also had implications for conflict and tension.

Roles demanding innovative problem-solving activities were the second major source of role conflict and tension. Such *innovative roles,* in which one attempts to bring about change, place one in conflict with those who stand to profit from maintaining the status quo (who in addition, often enjoy greater seniority and power than does the change agent). Furthermore, change agents experience conflicts arising from their involvement in nonroutine activities, as this involvement competes with their routine, administrative activities.

Supervisory roles were the third major source of role conflict. The common belief that the first-line supervisor is "caught in the middle" and subject to unparalleled conflict was not entirely borne out by the study. Instead, Kahn and associates found that the higher they looked in an organization, the more conflict they found. This is because increased status usually requires the manager to have more contacts outside the department, to assume more supervisory responsibility, and to engage in more innovative problem solving. This increasing stress continued through the middle-management level, where conflict tended to be highest. Kahn and associates suggest that the somewhat lower level of role conflict experienced by the highest levels of management is due, in part, to the fact that those executives had already achieved their career aspirations.

The more immediate causes of role conflict and tension were examined in the context of interpersonal relations. Specific kinds of relations with role senders (or sources of power) were found to be associated with high levels of conflict. In general, high pressure and high conflict were generated by individuals who were (1) in the same department as the focal person, (2) superior to the focal person, or (3) sufficiently dependent on the focal person to worry about that person's performance, but not so dependent that they were unable to influence the focal person. Colleagues who were some distance from the focal person in the organization applied the least amount of pressure.

Kahn's study also shows that different kinds of pressure are applied by different kinds of role senders. Superiors in the organization use legitimate authority, rewards, and coercive power. However, coercive power is used sparingly, since its application produces undesirable consequences which, over time, come to reflect poorly on the superiors themselves. In contrast, subordinates tend to use coercive power since they lack both legitimate power and rewards. The coercive power indicated here includes withholding of assistance and information, both of which can have detrimental effects on organizational performance.

Close ties between the focal person and role senders (in terms of work dependence, power, and communication) intensify the effect of an existing conflict. Withdrawal from the conflict by reducing the amount of communication or denigrating the power of role senders is a common, but not particularly effective, coping mechanism. Avoidance of conflict may not only fail to eliminate its causes, it may also lead to increased pressures by role senders, leading ultimately to even more conflict.

Managing role conflict

Robert Kahn and colleagues (1964) suggest measures that managers can employ in dealing with role ambiguity and conflict. This is not to suggest that either can be eliminated in an organization. Rather, they argue that some degree of role conflict is inevitable. The manager's options, then, are limited to reducing levels of conflict so that they become tolerable, or channeling the conflict in directions that are more positive for the organization and the individuals involved.

Four different approaches to reducing conflict and ambiguity are suggested. (1) Structural changes can be made within the organization. Some of these changes, discussed below in some detail, will produce configurations that are similar to Likert's "linking pin" structure (Chapter 3) and are termed *role-set management*. (2) Criteria for the selection and placement of personnel can be redefined to improve the fit between the requirements of a particular role and its incumbent. (3) Programs designed to increase the coping abilities and tolerance levels of employees in particularly stressful roles can be undertaken. Typically, these programs require the expertise of professional counselors. (4) Similar programs can be employed to change and strengthen the interpersonal bonds among personnel (for example, certain organization development interventions).

According to Likert's linking pin theory, the stresses that are experienced by the incumbent of a particularly difficult role can be dealt with effectively through the joint efforts of overlapping groups of peers, subordinates, and superiors. An even better approach, according to Kahn and associates, begins with the identification of the incumbent's role set. A group can be assembled from the incumbents of roles that are interdependent with the focal role (in terms of either work flow or hierarchical structure), and this group will probably be competent to deal with the problems of the focal role. This is not to say that the full set of role senders ought to convene to consider all problems relating to the focal role. "Whether a meeting of the entire set, consultation with subsets, or mere information will suffice depends upon the significance of the proposed action for their own needs and behavior" (Robert Kahn et al., 1964, p. 391).

Given this strategy, which particular positions within the organization should be identified as candidates for attention and, perhaps, modification? As we have seen, boundary or liaison positions, supervisory and middle-management positions, positions that require innovation, and those that are functionally related to and interdependent with other positions are all significant sources of role conflict and ambiguity.

What is suggested is a balanced approach in dealing with the dilemmas that are always present in organizations. In Chapter 6, we elaborated the dilemma of conflicting organizational goals. However, if one does not always expect optimum performance in attaining every goal, then perhaps extreme stress can be avoided. Another dilemma exists in the choice between containing sources of stress within one or a few roles or attempting to spread them out over a number of positions. A third dilemma cited by Kahn and associates arises in choosing between one stress and another, since eliminating a particular source of stress often produces side effects in the form of new tensions elsewhere in the organization.

Managing stress in boundary roles

Kahn and associates suggest that organizations make explicit and emphasize the importance of boundary roles. In addition to organizational recognition, such positions must have power and auxiliary services that are commensurate with the responsibilities that they bear. Wherever possible, multiple rather than single boundary and liaison roles should be established to diffuse role conflict and avoid focusing what may be crippling stress within an important organizational function.

It is also suggested that formal procedures be established for maintaining agreement and understanding between the incumbents of boundary and more internally focused roles. The means toward this end suggested by Kahn and associates include job rotation schemes wherein role senders within the organization are exposed to the received roles of boundary positions; for example, a dean may encourage faculty members to serve rotating tours of duty as associate deans to learn of the pressures that arise from attempts to mesh the expectations of faculty members with those of a university's administration. George Strauss (1962), in another example, explains how active and aggressive purchasing agents maintain and even expand their functions and responsibilities by bringing holders of internal roles, such as engineers, into contact with sales personnel from external vendor organizations.

Role stress tends to increase as the size of the organization increases (Robert Kahn et al., 1964). Organizational growth increases the requirements for coordination, since the number of subunits and relationships between subunits increase with size (Graicunas, 1937). Thus, requirements for coordination can be minimized by making organizational subunits as independent of one another and of top management as possible.

Of course, the very nature of organizations requires connections between roles, but such connections between positions in subunits must be examined carefully to determine that they are essential to effective performance. If centralized leadership is advocated merely because it is a principle of good management, an investigation of a more decentralized structure as an alternative would be in order. Similarly, flat rather than tall organizational structures and laterally autonomous or federated units rather than integrated units may be preferred, assuming that their introduction will not hinder organizational efficiency or effectiveness.

Influence, power, and bases of power

Modifying another person's behavior through role sending implies that the role sender is able to influence the focal role in one way or another. By *influence,* we mean an interpersonal relationship in which one actor affects the behavior of a second actor to cause a change that would not have occurred otherwise. *Power* refers to the ability to influence. Below, we shall speak of bases of power, which are various means that may be employed to influence and, thereby, cause compliance. *Authority* refers to legitimate power that is vested within a role or office; it is lawful power that is recognized by others in the organization. Finally, one has *control* over another to the extent the other behaves as one desires, and influence attempts are successful. Not only does the role sender influence the other person, but the influence is sufficiently strong so that counterinfluence and resistance are overcome (for example, see Katz and Kahn, 1978).

Power may be achieved through various means. John French and Raven (1959) described five bases of power. *Legitimate power* is based on the authority vested in a role or office, as we have said. *Reward power* is based on the various positive rewards or sanctions that an individual may employ in the pursuit of influence. *Coercive power* is based on negative sanctions or threats of harm or punishment. *Expert power* is based on knowledge or information that is accepted as accurate and correct. Finally, *referent power* is based on attractive personal characteristics that may lead others to like and emulate the referent person.

This categorization seems to indicate that power emanates from the possession of one or more bases. However, power and influence are characteristics of relationships. It is an oversimplification to speak of bases of power which the power wielder possesses (Patchen, 1974); for example, expert power requires both an individual possessing expert information and a person who lacks and needs this information. Similarly, the wielder of referent power possesses characteristics that are attractive to another individual. In similar fashion, the rewards, sanctions, and legitimate authority of the power wielder are only of value when the target of influence desires and lacks certain rewards, wishes to avoid certain punishments, and has internalized a moral obligation to obey the authority and wishes to fulfill that obligation.

Bases of compliance

Thus, we must consider not only bases of power, but also bases of compliance (Bachman, Bowers, and Marcus, 1968; Etzioni, 1961). This distinction allows us to describe attempts at influence, in which the power wielder consciously mobilizes particular bases of power that are successful merely because different bases of compliance are operating. For instance, one may attempt to influence by offering rewards, but influence may be gained because of some attractive characteristic of the power wielder, because of that person's referent power. In this case, one would speak of an attempt to influence on the basis of reward power and compliance gained on the basis of referent power.

Table 10–1 provides a separate listing of the characteristics and resources of persons attempting to influence, as opposed to the characteristics and needs of the targets of attempted influence. In this table, Patchen (1974) systematically describes the French and Raven bases of power and the corresponding bases of compliance. To this list is added the power base of stakeholders (Chapter 6) along with corresponding forms of compliance based on organizational norms that stakeholders should have influence over decisions affecting them. This notion is discussed in greater detail below.

The power of lower participants

In a paper entitled "Sources of Power of Lower Participants in Complex Organizations," Mechanic (1962) describes common situations in which authority does not suffice to explain the power and influence relationships in organizations. Certainly, supervisors and managers use their legitimate power to control the behavior of subordinates. However, lower participants circumvent or manipulate the organizational hierarchy by using various forms of power that are not legitimate. A major source of such power is the control of resources on which others are dependent; for example, members of a planning staff possess important information about potential future directions for the organization and are able to parlay this information into a variety of forms of influence. An executive's secretary controls access to an important individual and can use this resource to influence others. Mechanic also cites attributes such as likability, attractiveness, and charisma as sources of power. Finally, lower level personnel may obtain power through the control of instrumentalities or various aspects of the organization's physical plant or resources (for example equipment, machines, and cash).

Our analysis here follows that presented in Chapter 6 where power was viewed as the obverse of dependence. To the extent that a person is dependent on another, that person is subject to the other person's power. One can make others dependent on oneself by controlling their access to information, persons, and instrumentalities, as defined here.

TABLE 10-1
A framework for analyzing social influence,* with some examples

	Person exerting influence		
Kinds of influence	Characteristics	Resources	Decision role with respect to target
Expert	Expertise: special training, special experience, etc.	Knowledge about how to reach certain goals.	Investigates, makes tests, gives information to others.
Reward	Occupies important position in hierarchy.	Control over material rewards (money, promotion, etc.).	Makes request, coupled with promise of reward of compliance.
Coercive	Occupies important position in hierarchy.	Control over material penalties (fines, demotions, etc.).	Gives order, coupled with threat of punishment for noncompliance.
Referent	Strong: successful; has attractive qualities.	Approval.	States own opinions, preferences.
Legitimate	Occupies legitimate position of authority; secured position by legitimate methods.	Symbols of legitimacy; label of others' action as right or wrong.	Announces decision; asks for support.
Stakeholder	Is affected by certain decisions (by virtue of work needs, responsibilities, etc.).	Own cooperation; (may also have some resources listed in other rows).	Vigorously makes preference known to others.

*This framework may be expanded to include (a) the motivation of influencers to use their resources and (b) the perception by targets that the influencers will use their resources.
Source: Patchen (1974, p. 197).

Mechanic describes how the secretarial staff in a university often enjoys considerable power to make decisions about the purchase and allocation of supplies, the allocation of secretarial services, the scheduling of classes, and so on. Some of these powers may have been formally delegated, but often they exist because the secretarial staff takes initiative and exerts effort in areas where other, higher ranking participants are reluctant to act. A department leader may easily remove the scheduling activity from the jurisdiction of a secretary, but this can only be done if the department head or another faculty member is willing to do the scheduling.

Generally, evidence that lower level personnel are wielding illegitimate power to obstruct or frustrate certain higher level personnel is difficult to find, since these obstructive activities usually are not covered by specific rules. If the worst occurs and conflict emerges between higher and lower

Target(s) of influence			
Characteristics	Needs	Decision role with respect to influencer	Effect of influencer on target
Unexpert	Wants to find best ways to reach goals.	Reviews information presented by experts.	Sees new options; sees new favorable or unfavorable consequences following various actions.
Occupies less important position in hierarchy.	Wants rewards controlled by influencer.	Decides whether to accede to requests of others.	Compliance seen as means to rewards.
Occupies less important position in hierarchy.	Wants to avoid punishment but maintain self-esteem.	Decides whether to accede to order.	Compliance seen as way of avoiding penalty but may be seen as blow to self-esteem.
Less strong, less successful.	Wishes to be similar to, approved by, influencer.	Hears opinions, preferences of influencer.	Sees compliance as way of being similar to, approved by, influencer.
Occupies position of subordination; accepts legitimacy of other's position.	Wishes to fulfill moral obligations.	Gets request from authority.	Sees conformity in requested action as morally correct.
Peers or final decision-making authority.	Wants high level of cooperation from influencer.	Decides whether to accept recommendation	Sees accepting recommendation as leading to future cooperation by influencer.

level participants, the lower level staff may resort to "working to rule" or following to the letter those rules that do exist and thereby create mild chaos and a major backlog of work. Finally, since the process of gaining access to information, persons, and instrumentalities is time consuming, we can generalize that the power obtained by lower level participants increases with the amount of time the employee spends in the organization.

Even in prisons, the lower participants, or prisoners, have sufficient power to create difficulties for prison guards when they choose to do so (Sykes, 1958). Human behavior is complex, and every single move cannot be anticipated or controlled, even by a prison guard. Guards depend on the inmates to show initiative in activities such as working in the prison shop, cleaning their cells, and even moving from place to place in the prison according to the daily routine. Of course, it is possible to use formal sanctions against inmates to force compliance. However, extended use of these sanctions would make the guards look bad in the eyes of their superiors. For these reasons, then, exchange relationships develop in which guards give favors and overlook infractions of certain rules in return for the inmates' cooperation.

Interestingly enough, these exchange relationships seem to be inflationary in that more and more favors and increased immunity from rules are expected by prisoners in return for their cooperation. This inflation persists until the inmates have parlayed their power to the extent that the guards would lose their jobs if it were recognized by higher ups in the organization (or to outsiders, such as the press). At this point the guards crack down, sometimes at the risk of provoking a prison riot. Such is the power of lower participants, even in prisons. Yet, the balance of power is overwhelmingly in favor of the guards, the threat of prison riots notwithstanding. In addition to their legitimate, coercive, and reward power, they have an added advantage. Many prisoners come to believe (that is, internalize the norm) that guards are to be obeyed.

The normative element and power

We find that the various bases of power have normative elements. Norms may play an important part in causing compliance with influence attempts that are based on more rational and coercive bases of power. We may be influenced by an expert, not only because we need that knowledge, but also because the influencer *is an "expert."* We may even accept expert advice that does not make sense to us because we are influenced by the norm that expert advice is to be followed.

This is an important point, since our discussion of norms might leave the false impression that they constrain the individual's behavior and, in turn, limit the individual's power. While it is true that certain norms limit behavior, they may also contribute to the power of the focal role. This is evident in the extreme case illustrated above, and we will have more to say about this in the next chapter. It is also evident in the everyday affairs described below.

NORMS AND ORGANIZATIONAL BEHAVIOR

Power and decisions

Of particular interest are the ways in which norms and influence processes affect decision making in organizations. Do decision makers gather all available information and base their decisions primarily on the weight of such evidence? Certainly, the formal hierarchy of authority in organizations permits this. Or, is the decision maker moved by the power of various role senders in the organizations? If the latter is the case, what norms determine who is to have power in a particular decision?

Patchen (1974) explored these questions by examining nonrepetitive purchasing decisions made in 11 different manufacturing firms. On the average, 15 different individuals took part in a typical decision; for example, in a company manufacturing automobile parts, the decision to use zinc rather than aluminum for a particular product involved personnel from engineering, sales, manufacturing, and purchasing, as well as from other organizational units.

An attempt was made to discover the bases of power used to influence the decisions studied. The individuals involved in specific decisions were unable to agree on who had the most power. Generally, no single decision maker was identifiable. Decisions were formed through processes of accommodation and consensus. Power was rarely attributed to the sanctioning power of an individual—to that person's ability to reward or punish others. Formal authority was mentioned by respondents, but not very frequently (about 5 percent of the time). In addition, there was an almost total lack of reference to bargaining or coalition formation.

Power of stakeholders

As one might expect, power was attributed to expertise, but only by about 22 percent of the respondents. Equally important to expertise as a source of power was the extent to which an individual would be affected by the outcome of the decision in question; for example, the traffic supervisor in one firm was influential in a decision to purchase a tractor truck. In addition, individuals had power because they were responsible for a product that involved the use of the item under consideration. In one company, the plant engineer cited the sales manager as the most influential in the decision to buy a new piercing press for manufacturing because he could not have fulfilled his sales goals without it. Please note that the power described here by and large was independent of formal authority to make the decision.

Finally, some individuals were seen to have power over decisions because these decisions were their responsibility. The buyer in a firm that manufactures musical instruments was seen as influencing the choice of a mold used in making organ parts because it was his function to influence these kinds of decisions, given the way the firm operated. Patchen suggests that such responsibility may be delegated as a way of dividing up the work, but that it is unlikely that individuals having power because of delegated responsibility will override the power of those having a stake in the decision's outcome. Decision making, then, should be viewed as a *process* involving a variety of individuals having varying degrees of power over the decision by virtue of the organization's norms.

Normative power and decisions

Of special interest to us are the ways in which norms regarding the power of stakeholders stabilize a process that is both dynamic and complex. The most dynamic kind of decision-making process can be characterized as including extensive bargaining, coalition formation, and direct influence by means of persuasion, threats, and the like. But Patchen's study showed that understandings were found in place of conflict. As we indicated, norms can arise in dynamic situations because negotiating and bargaining are time consuming and disagreeable because of the conflict and hostility they are likely to generate. In making behavior more automatic, norms save time and energy and reduce interpersonal strife (Thibaut and Kelley, 1959).

The norm that provides stakeholders with power in the decision-making process is useful because it conserves the effort involved in negotiating a decision *and* because it has the potential to add to the satisfaction of those who will be affected by the decision. The stakeholders, who have desires and feelings about the outcome of a decision, will also possess information that is useful (and sometimes vital) to the success of the decision-making process. As we indicated in Chapter 3, participation in decision making is desirable, not only for motivational reasons, but also because it allows the specialized knowledge of subordinates to be incorporated in the process. Perhaps the most important reason for advocating this norm is enlightened self-interest. As Patchen suggests, it is a simple matter of logrolling; if I back you on what is important to you, you are likely to back me on what is most important to me.

Where several individuals have strong interests in a decision, their abilities to influence probably will depend on their respective intensities of interest as well as their degrees of power. Jockeying for position and negotiation will be common, depending on the amount of effort each participant is willing to expend and the kinds of sanctions that are available.

Where strong sanctions exist—sanctions such as the ability to withhold cooperation, needed resources, or one's services through terminating one's employment—norms are quite likely to emerge over time. Individuals may come to *internalize* the threat of sanctions and to behave as if the sanctions would follow if desired behavior was not forthcoming (Kelman, 1961; Thibaut and Kelley, 1959). Similarly, rewards may lead to the emergence of norms. Individuals may behave in ways that are rewarding (for example, in mutually satisfying exchange relationships), which in time become normative.

As indicated above, the extent of one's interest in a particular decision helps to determine whether or not one will try to influence the process. We cannot influence each and every decision in our organization. Those that are unimportant to us may be treated as giveaways. In others, we may wish to stake our claim. Bauer (1968) makes the point as follows:

In any ongoing institution, the ability to get important things done is dependent on maintaining a reservoir of good will. The person who fights every issue as though it were vital exhausts his resources including, most especially, the patience and good will of those on whom he has to depend to get things done. Therefore, it should be considered neither surprising nor immoral that, when an issue is of low salience the sensible individual may use it to build good will for the future, or pay off past obligations, by going along with some individual for whom the issue is of high salience (p. 17).

Normative structure and political processes

This study of purchasing decisions in business organizations shows normative structure to be important for organizational functioning. The psychiatric hospital described in the introduction to this chapter was less stable and illustrated more conflict and bargaining along the path to a negotiated normative order. Professional organizations are likely to display political processes in the service of norm-building. This is because professional organizations, such as the psychiatric hospital, serve a multiplicity of purposes and employ nonroutine technologies requiring the exercise of judgment and compromise. In addition, their external environments are constantly changing. In light of these problems for normative development, how do professionals organize?

Professional norms are found in these kinds of organizations, but in point of fact these norms are quite limited. There are norms regarding standards of expertise and knowledge and norms about using such knowledge/expertise in the client's service. However, while professional knowledge tells practitioners how to do their jobs, it does not tell them how to organize or how to structure their relations with others.

Bucher and Stelling (1969) suggest that when professionals are in control, they create distinctive social organizations quite different from those described by bureaucratic theory. On the basis of their observations of various kinds of hospitals and professionals, they describe the professional organization in terms of political processes and emphasize negotiation and shifting alliances as concepts for understanding the nature of these organizations.

Role negotiation

Professionals make claims to competence in particular areas. Professional expertise is not acknowledged automatically by others, but must be demonstrated in relation to others of one's own profession and of other professions. The professionals must show that they possess skills for defining problems, determining means for their solution, and judging the success of actions undertaken in their area of expertise. To the extent that the professional is able to substantiate such claims in relation to other professionals, autonomy and influence are achieved.

Professionals typically must build their roles in the organization as opposed to taking up a previously defined role. Role creation proceeds through negotiation with relevant individuals in the organization. For instance, Bucher and Stelling (1969) note that:

> In the medical school ... we have never seen a case in which a new faculty member took over the role of his predecessor. Even within the same discipline, faculty members differ in their conceptions of their responsibilities, their interests, and their ways of organizing their time.... One of our respondents requires a room in which temperature can be held constant. Another needs animal quarters where light can be held constant or varied by design. A third, engaged in dream research, needs a suite of rooms, *and* control of temperature. In all three of these cases, also, the researcher must have control of his time once the research begins—else the experiment is lost. Hence the new faculty member negotiates for work space and resources, and proceeds to set up his work as he conceives it (page 5).

Professionals differ from others in this negotiating behavior in that it often is conducted covertly. The negotiation is likely to be based on professional considerations. Even in the cases where one professional has authority over another, the superior will deal with the subordinate, not in terms of orders or directions, but rather in the guise of professional or technical considerations. The technically right thing will be discussed and argued for. The same kind of negotiation is found in the negotiated order in the psychiatric section of the hospital described above. In that setting, much of the negotiation took place between different kinds of professionals, especially in the context of teams of different professionals.

In such teams of different but interdependent professions, negotiation may become quite intense. Despite appeals based on the good of the patient, it may be that different professionals lack common goals and are interested in doing different things for different parts of the patient. In terms of the paradigm of James Thompson and Tuden (1966), lack of agreement on goals leads to decision making by bargaining and compromise (see Chapter 6).

Participation in a team can be fateful for the professional. It is an arena of action in which the work spaces of the different team members overlap. The work of one person is likely to affect that of another. In contrast to the bureaucratic organization, these groupings emerge from the impetus of the professionals themselves as they define roles and groups of roles.

This differentiation, of course, can generate competition and conflict in the organization. The emerging groups require resources that are always limited. Consequently, there will be competition and conflict over the budget and other resources such as space. Bucher and Stelling describe how the curriculum in a professional school becomes an important arena for competition. Emerging specialities attempt to require students to devote time to their areas and are resisted by the more traditional specialities.

Political processes

Of course, interaction among professionals comprises more than conflict and competition. Structure does develop, for the organization must mobilize its resources in a coordinated effort. While large, complex organizations such as medical centers may appear to be congeries of feudal fiefdoms, in fact they do maintain some semblance of integration with regard to organizational goals.

The point made by Bucher and Stelling and others (for example, Baldridge, 1971) is not that professional organizations are disorganized, but that these organizations must be understood in terms of political processes. Rather than authority, other bases of power are critical in professional organizations. Most critical is the process—the different tactics used at different points in time in cooperating and competing with other organizational members. In short, we suggest that the professional organization and also other organizations with multiple goals and nonroutine technologies are characterized by processes in which roles emerge and are created through negotiation and differentiation, by competition and conflict, with integration arising from the political processes.

Still, this is a matter of degree, for all organizations, even bureaucracies, are typified by internal competition and conflict. And this observation brings us to our next chapter.

DISCUSSION QUESTIONS

1. What do we mean by role conflict? In what sense is it inevitable?
2. What role conflict have you experienced?
3. To what extent do norms enter into decision making in a university?
4. How might decision making in a university differ from similar activity in a business firm?

11

Power and Conflict

INTRODUCTION

When one of the authors took his M.B.A. some 15 years ago, the behavioral portion of the curriculum was called "human relations." Surprisingly, the text used then made no references to problems associated with power and conflict in organizations. Why do you think that might have been?

As nearly as we can tell, no human organization has ever avoided conflict in one form or another, nor has one existed in the absence of power. Although humans have always sought and used power, these activities somehow are viewed as antithetical to deep-rooted American cultural norms. We sometimes pretend that they do not exist.

Niccolò Machiavelli was born before Columbus sailed for America. He wrote a handbook for those who seek practical means for increasing their power. According to Gauss (1952), Hitler read the book at bedtime and Mussolini chose it as the subject of his doctoral thesis. Lenin and Stalin, too, were versed in Machiavelli.

Although the past decade has seen a revival of interest in *The Prince*, most of us look askance at Machiavelli's advice. To be sure, the book is bitter, reflecting the author's failure and 15 years in exile. What seems worse, however, is his candid discussion of power and self-interest. It is almost as if the practices Machiavelli describes are unfit for public discussion, even though we recognize that they still are the substance of human affairs; for example, note below that Machiavelli would have us manipulate those whose advice we seek.

> ... by taking counsel with many, a prince who is not wise will never have united councils and will not be able to bring them to unanimity for himself. The counsellors will all think of their own interests, and he will be unable either to correct or to understand them. And it cannot be otherwise, for men will always be false to you unless they are compelled by necessity to be true. Therefore, it must be concluded that wise counsels, from whoever they come, must necessarily be due to the prudence of the prince, and not the prudence of the prince to the good counsels received (1952, p. 117).*

Chapter guide

1. A contemporary analogy to Machiavelli's statement is that the quality of advice received from subordinates is a function of the executive's skill in manipulating the way in which such advice is given. Do you agree?
2. Elsewhere, Machiavelli suggests that we seek advice, but only when it is our wish to be advised, not when others wish to advise us. Why do you think he recommends this?
3. In what sense is this ancient writing relevant to life in contemporary organizations?

SOURCES OF CONFLICT

Power as a source of conflict

Conflict is intimately related to power. It is said that, "Power inevitably begets conflict, in some form and in some degree" (Robert Kahn, 1964, p. 2). But we argue that the link between power and conflict is not necessarily inevitable. The exercise of power may produce cooperation, circumvention, or withdrawal as well (Halpert, 1974). The manner and degree in which conflict is expressed depends on the reciprocal power of the person who is the target of the initial change attempt. For example, targets may use their power to resist attempts to change their behavior. Alternatively, if their own power is great enough, they may counter with an attempt to change the other person.

Another source of conflict is found when individuals are dissatisfied with the status quo, but disagree on either the means for changing the organization or the ends these changes would produce. The greater the conflict in a

---

* Source: Niccolo Machiavelli, *The Prince* by permission of Oxford University Press.

situation of this sort, the more the individuals will desire power to render the particular change that they favor.

Are there not some organizations in which the seeking of power and the resultant conflict are mostly absent? Are there organizations in which individual members tend to think alike and go about their pursuits without resorting to the use of power and inadvertently producing the conflict that ensues?[1] Robert Kahn (1964) suggests that disagreements over goals and means are typical of human organizations, and it is only because power is unequally distributed among members that the organization is able to function by suppressing, containing, and in other ways managing potential conflicts that would otherwise lead to anarchy.

Power enables the control of organizational resources and consequently, the control of people. Because of asymmetries in dependence and power, some members are able to control the organization in a relatively systematic fashion, free from resistance and diversions by those who would prefer to exercise autonomy.

Now, it is often the case that power, which was initially sought as an instrument or means toward the attainment of specific and limited ends, becomes valued for its own sake and becomes an end. Power is generally found to be so useful that, with the passage of time, it may become sought in its own right.

> If a person seeks power only for instrumental purposes, we can predict that his search will be bounded; he wishes to control other people only in so far as that control will contribute to the attainment of other goals. If, on the other hand, he finds the experience of controlling others intrinsically rewarding, there may be few limitations on the number of people over whom he will strive for power, the magnitude of power to which he will aspire, or the kinds of activity over which power will be sought (Kahn, 1964, pp. 5–6).

We may distinguish between *specified* and *relative* power (Kahn, 1964). An individual may seek specified power as an instrument with which to attain defined and limited aspirations. Alternatively, the individual may seek power that is greater than the powers possessed by certain other individuals. This is relative power, the quest for which maximizes potential for conflict.

Having specified power, an individual can attempt to influence the behavior of another, although the other individual's reciprocal power may be sufficient to enable that person to resist, seek a compromise, or act in some other way that the power-willer did not intend. The target's behavior is still said to be influenced, although not wholly or perhaps even partially as intended. However, given sufficient relative power, the power-willer may overrule or control the other person. The target is influenced wholly in the

---

[1] We can note that friendship groups and families, which might be assumed to be relatively free of the exercise of power and the experience of conflict, in fact, are the sources and victims of an appalling amount of conflict and even violence.

direction desired by the power-willer. The threat of such loss of autonomy is likely to provoke extreme conflict.

Conflict also arises because organizations typically lack a single goal to which all members subscribe. Not only do members of a single organization strive toward different goals, they may also have different values and different perceptions of the means appropriate for realizing even goals and values that they hold in common. Thus, power is employed as a means for coordinating activities that would otherwise be conflicting and, perhaps, chaotic.

The process of conflict

Conflict can be viewed as a dynamic process consisting of a sequence of episodes (Pondy, 1967). These conflict episodes tend to follow a format: (1) conditions arise having the potential for conflict; (2) these conditions and their implications are perceived by participants; (3) perceived conflict results in felt conflict that evokes emotional reactions; (4) emotions give rise to overt behaviors of various kinds; and (5) finally, the episode reaches a conclusion that affects the course of succeeding conflict episodes.

According to Pondy, the first stage of the conflict episode, *latent conflict*, is thought to arise from three major sources: drives for autonomy, divergence of subunit goals, and competition for scarce resources. These three basic sources of conflict have been termed, respectively, *bureaucratic, systems,* and *bargaining conflicts*. We shall discuss each type in the remainder of the chapter.

The second stage, *perceived conflict,* is comparable to role conflict (Chapter 10) in which the incumbent of the focal role perceives some variance between self-role and the roles and norms that are sent to the incumbent by others. Two types of misperception are possible here. First, conflict may be perceived where none exists, as happens frequently when people do not communicate effectively. Second, the opposite may occur. Real conflict may be denied as a result of various defensive behaviors. Even when perceptions of conflict are accurate, an organization typically contains too many sources of conflict to be dealt with effectively, given the time and resources available. Hence, Pondy suggests that the manager's normal reaction is to focus on only a few of the existing conflicts at any one time and to limit that focus to those for which short-run, routine solutions are available.

The third stage, *felt conflict,* is one in which individuals sometimes deal with perceived conflicts in a relatively rational manner, without what Pondy calls "personalization," or the experiences of conflict-related anxiety, tension, or affect. However, feelings *are* brought into conflict situations frequently. These may stem from a condition of basic anxiety from which the individual suffers or from frustrations and hostilities that have developed in the context of other interpersonal relations unrelated to the present conflict; that is, feelings are *projected* from one source of conflict to another. Obviously, these feelings may also result from frustrations that are a direct result of the conflict situation in question.

The next stage, *manifest conflict*, sometimes is characterized by overt behaviors such as verbal or physical aggression. In organizations, however, the manifestations of conflict are more likely to be covert. Examples of these covert behaviors are apathy and the ploy of "working to rule" discussed in Chapter 10 in connection with the power of lower participants. They serve to thwart aspirations of others without appearing aggressive. In any event, when conflict becomes manifest and apparent to other members of the organization, interventions are made in an attempt to resolve, or at least to confine, the issues.

Finally, *conflict aftermath* sets the stage, as it were, for subsequent conflict episodes. Whether the initial conflict is genuinely resolved or merely suppressed and unresolved will bear on the nature of subsequent episodes. This notion is similar to the role-conflict model presented in the last chapter. As we saw, behavior emerges from perceptions and feelings and is perceived and acted on by role senders in yet another cycle of events. Depending on the behavior exercised and its effect on interpersonal relations or organizational conditions, the role sender will act somewhat differently in the next cycle of role sending.

Effects of conflict

Before examining sources of conflict and some mechanisms for its management, it will be useful to gain an appreciation of the effects of conflict. Traditionally, conflict has been viewed as undesirable. It is unpleasant for most individuals and leads toward psychological withdrawal or aggressive and hostile behavior. It may also lead to the falsification of data and distortion of reality. The effects on organizations have been viewed as negative, too. The rational approach to management suggests that we design and manage organizations in a way that limits conflict. The epitome of this approach is a clearly stated organizational objective pursued by means of logically articulated, harmonious tasks. The system model, too, with its stress on dynamic homeostasis views conflict as a temporary disequilibrium to be rectified. Conflict between the system and its environment is ameliorated through adaptation. Finally, the human relations approach, growing out of the rational theories, recognizes the continuing existence and great importance of conflict and seeks to reduce its toll on members of the organization.

In some contrast, however, recent views of motivation indicate that mild levels of stress or conflict are more desirable than the complete tension reduction suggested by the attitude balance, classic drive reduction, and learning theories. McClelland (1951) suggests that mild stimulation has positive emotional effects, and White (1959) tells us that the competence drive and curiosity compel individuals to submit themselves to new, tension-arousing situations.

Furthermore, some individuals even come to enjoy high levels of conflict. Conflict may remove boredom and, in extreme cases, may be exhilarating and provide a source of meaning for the individual (Fanon, 1967). Conflict also may be valued as a means toward specific ends. As Pondy (1967) suggests:

> One of the tactics of successful executives in the modern business enterprise is to create confusion as a cover for the expansion of their particular empire, or, as Sorenson observes, deliberately to create dissent and competition among [their] subordinates in order to ensure that [they] will be brought into the relationship as an arbiter at critical times, as Franklin D. Roosevelt did. Or, conflict with an out-group may be desirable to maintain stability within the group (p. 310).

Finally, conflict may be viewed as an unavoidable cost of the pursuit of one's aspirations. Where the net result of this pursuit is perceived to be positive, conflict will be endured as a necessary evil.

On the whole, our culture views conflict as undesirable, to be avoided whenever possible. Harmony and uniformity tend to be valued highly, and tolerance for divergence generally is lacking. And yet, recent works have challenged these cultural assumptions. While conflict is stressful and dissatisfying for most individuals, greater openness to conflict and confrontation has developed in organizations and in our society generally. Bach and Wyden's book, *Intimate Enemy: How to Fight Fair in Love and Marriage* (1969), as well as Sennett's book, *The Uses of Disorder* (1970) and Alinsky's various works (1946, 1971) exemplify this trend. Confrontation is seen to be valuable, and the important question is: How can one manage conflict without sweeping it under the rug or allowing it to run to pathological extremes?

The effects of bureaucratic conflict in different organizations

There is evidence (Clagett Smith, 1966) that bureaucratic conflict, that is, conflict between organizational levels, may produce different effects in different kinds of organizations. Smith found that conflict was negatively associated with effectiveness in three out of four kinds of business organizations studied. Following Litwak (1961), Smith argues that conflict in the traditional bureaucratic or hierarchical organization (such as those studied) detracts from effectiveness by making coordination more difficult. This is especially true in organizations that are complex and differentiated, requiring considerable coordination from top levels of management. In this kind of organization, conflict, particularly between different echelons in the organization (for example, conflict due to lack of compliance), will impede coordination and, therefore, effectiveness.

In contrast, a study of four union locals and 112 units of a voluntary organization revealed conflict to be positively associated with effectiveness. Smith suggests that these organizations, unlike business firms, are typified by basic agreements among members, and among different echelons, regarding the interests and goals of members and of the organization as a whole. Conflict between members of different echelons tends to be constructive because it centers around means more than ends. Such conflict causes periodic reevaluation and improvement of means.

More important, Smith argues that the consequences for organizational effectiveness are dependent on the techniques used to manage conflict. Whatever the amount of conflict in an organization, the use of certain techniques, such as the appeal to general rules, will detract from effectiveness. Other mechanisms for resolving conflict (for example, initiating structure [Chapter 12], supportive leadership, or mutual influence systems) permit conflict to have more positive effects.

A study of conflict in top management

Before studying conflict in further detail, we shall examine the management of conflict in one portion of an organization. How do top executives in major corporations (2,000 to 50,000 employees) handle differences that arise in making policy decisions? Stagner (1969, 1970), in a study of corporate vice presidents, provides a description of a decision-making process that contrasts with Patchen's report of decision making at lower levels in the organization, where norms about stakeholder power were common (Chapter 10).

Stagner's study provides a view of decision making in the context of conflicting pressures. It should be emphasized that the observed conflict was dissimilar to that usually found in small group settings, wherein individuals react solely to each other and to their immediate setting—to communications, aggressive persuasion, personal likes and dislikes, and perceptions of confidence. This dissimilarity is due primarily to the fact that top executives, unlike subjects in small group studies, represent, depend on, or make use of individuals external to the group as well as their goals and the resources they provide (Kotter, 1978).

By the same token, Stagner found that the economic or rational model of decision making did not apply to his findings either. Economic considerations such as increased profits did not play major roles in either decision making or the resolution of conflict. Although economic terminology was used to frame the arguments of both parties to controversy, it was found to serve primarily as a cover-up for other, noneconomic criteria. Profit projections, for example, are not precise; the trade-offs between short-term and long-term profitability are virtually unknowable. Stagner suggests that conflicts are resolved, not by appealing to the logic of economics (that is, expert power), but by resorting to power based on rewards and authority. Individuals having common interests form coalitions that pursue their own interests first, and those of the firm second.

Observing the behavior of decision-making groups, Stagner found that problems were discussed partly in terms of economic considerations, but also in terms of the ways in which the different executives perceived each situation. The functions (for example, marketing or production) and the disciplines (for example, accounting or law) in which participants were trained, determined whether they shared a common frame of reference. A chief executive with training in economics seemed to agree with the points of view of economists rather than those of individuals whose backgrounds included training in other functions or disciplines.

These differences in perceptions and potentials for conflict are likely to diminish as individuals come to know each other better. Socializing outside of office hours helps improve communications and, subsequently, mutual understandings. As we saw in Chapter 6, the clarity of goals is enhanced by social contact. Yet, the socialization process is lengthy. This accounts for Stagner's observation that in one of the companies studied, it took about five years for an individual to become a member of the management team.

The power of the boss

Stagner found the power of the chief executive to be the most potent and widely recognized influence in the settlement of conflict. Despite decentralization and democratization, the boss is still the boss. Executives reported that when a conflict attained certain proportions, they would take their disagreement to the boss for decision.

There are, however, several roles that the chief executive can play in attempting to resolve organizational conflicts. Some chiefs act as mediators (go-betweens), others are arbitrators (judges). Stagner reports that mediation fosters an open expression of views, helps conflicting parties seek agreement, and generally is effective. The chief executive using this technique effectively will conceal personal preferences to avoid being perceived as an arbitrator.

In other instances, the chief executive, serving purely as an arbitrator, hears out the principal contestants separately and decides the issue. Arbitration seems to provide the advantage of avoiding open confrontation and unpleasantness and offers opportunities to apply behind-the-scene, face-saving techniques. However, losers can be left with the feeling that they did not have a fair hearing.

A variation of this technique was found in the practice of having the executive vice president serve as arbitrator. This allowed the chief executive to play the role of referee in the event that one of the parties to the arbitration challenged the decision and requested an appeal. Both approaches, however, seemed to give less satisfaction to participants than the open hearing with participatory decision making.

The power of the chief executive seemed to be the most effective pressure for securing agreements in the organizations studied. Direct appeals to authority were common occurrences. Subjects told Stagner that when they could not agree, they took the problem to the president, who settled it. Also prevalent was the indirect pressure of authority that caused individuals to anticipate actions of higher-ups and perhaps the embarrassment of having to resort to arbitration, and in so doing contained their conflict.

Shared goals and pressures for conflict resolution

The second most important approach to resolving conflict, according to Stagner, is the development of shared goals, especially superordinate goals. If contestants share a superordinate goal, a basis for compromise or other form of agreement exists. Superordinate goals include the profitability and viability of the firm; for example, the heads of production and marketing will agree that, whatever their particular interests, these interests are subordinate to the goals that they hold in common.

Peer pressure is reported to be the third most effective impetus to conflict resolution. In addition to managing separate departments, the executives in Stagner's study also functioned as a team. An example of peer pressure was found in a situation in which the chief executive requested all vice presidents to submit their proposed budgets. Consolidation of the departmental budgets revealed that their total exceeded the total budget of the firm. Rather than confront the vice presidents with the need to pare their own budgets, the president asked the vice presidents to solve the problem as a group. In this way, all executives were exposed to the pressures of their peers as their inflated budgets constrained the resources available to others.

Individual persuasion was found to be the least effective of the four means of resolving disagreements. "Are vigorous, aggressive, persuasive individuals more likely to 'win' controversies than less colorful persons? The consensus was negative. Two executives estimated that such personalities might be effective 20 percent of the time, but in 80 percent of the cases power of the division or status in the company would decide the issue. All respondents agreed that it would be rare for a persuasive man in a lower echelon to win out over a less fluent but higher placed objector" (Stagner, 1970, p. 94).

The importance of power in resolving conflict

Stagner's findings argue that to be effective in resolving high-level conflict, one ought to rely, first, on the power of the chief executive; second, on one's ability to highlight or create shared goals; third, on available peer pressure; and finally, on individual persuasion. According to the role-sender model, a focal role must cope with the demands of many different role senders. It seems that a single role sender is not very potent—unless that person is the boss. One way to understand Stagner's findings is to note that in the ten major corporations studied, power seems to reside primarily in the chief executive's office. At lower organizational levels, power is more diffuse and equal among members of the same rank. Presumably, this is not true for all organizations. Sensitivity to the locus of power in an organization should provide the observer with working hypotheses about the ways in which conflict is resolved.

Conflict among Stagner's executives was resolved as if the nature of the organization did not permit lateral conflicts. Although coalitions and pressure groups did form around important issues, Stagner notes that factionalism was muted for the most part. These findings lead Stagner to view the corporation as "... a collection of pressure groups trying to arrive at compromise solutions.... For the most part, however, overt 'factionalism' in top management is muted. It is perhaps significant that in the only company in my survey where two vice presidents were known leaders of competing factions, one was fired before the year was out. This suggests that covert power struggles are permissible but open conflict is settled by eliminating the weaker" (Stagner, 1970, pp. 90-95). In short, the corporations studied appear to be rational, hierarchically coordinated organizations, but in reality they are collections of conflicting, competitive fiefdoms held in check by hierarchical power.

Earlier, we mentioned Pondy's (1967) three models of organizational conflict: the bureaucratic, systems, and bargaining models. Stagner undoubtedly observed mostly bureaucratic conflict—conflict arising from attempts to obtain compliance with rules, orders, and organizationally prescribed attitudes, and behaviors. This is our next topic for discussion.

BUREAUCRATIC CONFLICT

Autonomy and conflict

Members of an organization may come into conflict with their superiors for various reasons. Generally speaking, we find that the individual's desire for autonomy conflicts with the organization's need for coordination. Organizations can legitimate their requests for coordination through the use of authority, and subordinates generally accept requests that appear legitimate. However, superiors sometimes overstep their limited authority and engender resistance in their subordinates. In Chapter 6 we saw that rules can be used as impersonal means of coordination. However, because they are impersonal and inflexible, they may also engender conflict. Let us examine a number of mechanisms for dealing with subordinates' resistance and their drives for autonomy and power. These are part of what sociologists term "mechanisms for social control," since they are means employed by those in authority to control deviations and to maintain the social system at the status quo.

Activation of commitments and obligations

Some elements of authority are not used fully by managers. We generally feel some commitment and sense of obligation to those for whom we work. Superiors can tap this commitment to gain compliance and resolve conflicts. Commitment and feelings of obligation are especially evident in the normative organizations described in Chapter 5, but are present in most other organizations as well.

Such commitments have been demonstrated by attempts to cause individuals to violate them; for example, Jerome Frank (1944) designed a series of experiments in which subjects performed disagreeable and nonsensical tasks. For instance, subjects were asked to balance a marble on a small steel ball. They continued to attempt this impossible task for an hour without demonstrating overt resistance. Pepitone (1958) had subjects sort the contents of a wastebasket (cigar butts, dirty paper and rags, pieces of glass, damp kleenexes, and the like). Subjects performed the task without strong protest. More recently, Orne and Evans (1965) asked experimental subjects to pick up a harmless lizard, a harmless green snake, a poisonous snake, and even a coin that was in acid. Many subjects complied fully. Milgram (1963, 1964, 1965), in a widely publicized series of experiments, had subjects administer electrical shocks (ranging from 15 to 450 volts) to another "subject." Even when the "subject," who was not really shocked, pounded on the wall after an "application" of high voltage, the experimental subjects continued to honor their presumed obligation to the experimenter, despite their own obvious distress. Milgram reports:[2]

> I observed a mature and initially poised businessman enter the laboratory smiling and confident. Within twenty minutes, he was reduced to a twitching, shuddering wreck who was rapidly approaching a point of nervous collapse. He constantly pulled on his earlobe and twisted his hands. At one point, he pushed his fist into his forehead and muttered, "Oh, God. Let's stop it." And yet he continued to respond to every word of the experimenter and obeyed to the end (1963, p. 373).

An explanation of these observations is that people feel general obligations to "research" and "science," and when students are used as experimental subjects, to the expectations of faculty members as well. As Gamson suggests:

> Perhaps the most powerful and common means of social control is simply the conveying of expectation with clarity and explicitness coupled with clear and direct accountability for the performance of such expectations. As long as legitimacy is accorded in such situations, individuals will regard their noncompliance as a failure and any interaction which makes such a personal failure salient is embarrassing, unpleasant, and something to be avoided (1968, p. 134).

---

[2] What ethical considerations arise in experiments such as this?

Integrating individual and organizational goals

As we have said, bureaucratic conflict arises when individual and organizational goals (or means) are in conflict. Barrett (1970) describes three mechanisms for achieving integration of these goals: *socialization, accommodation,* and *exchange.* In socialization, integration is achieved by moving the individual's goals toward those of the organization. Socialization is a long-term process wherein individuals come to value what is valued in their environment. Goals that are in conflict with those of the organization are given up by the individual. If socialization is effective, individuals learn to want to perform activities that are required of them. Matters that once were external, rational, and calculative are internalized by the individual and take on moral connotations. The organization's objectives and the individuals' values become congruent.

Accommodation is a process by which the individual's goals are incorporated into those of the organization. Thus, Barrett describes how some attempts at job design configure technology and structure in ways that are compatible with the worker's objectives. Obviously, participative management is required if personal goals are to be introduced into decision-making and policy-formulation processes. As individuals participate and determine the organization's goals, these goals become their own goals.

The third mechanism, exchange, places less emphasis on goal integration than the other two. The organization offers incentives related to the individual's personal goals in exchange for performance of activities that contribute to organizational objectives. Rather than integration, this mechanism seeks a quid pro quo. Conditional reinforcement and extrinsic reward are pertinent here. Frederick Taylor's advocacy of a piecework incentive system of payment and March and Simon's (1958) *inducement-contributions* theory are examples.

Socialization as a means for resolving bureaucratic conflict

Socialization is a pervasive and essential societal process. Through this process the child becomes a social being, learning the proper habits, skills, beliefs, ethics, and morals of culture, as befitting that child's social class, ethnic group, and even local community. Parents as well as other family members, schools, and churches aid in this process.

Organizations, too, socialize their members. This may be seen quite clearly in the purposeful way medical schools go about inculcating an impersonal and objective approach in their medical students' dealings with patients. Students are shocked by their first view of a cadaver but soon come to be fairly unemotional and objective in dealing with the human body. It is essential that their professional judgment remain unclouded by emotions. In the same way, nursing schools emphasize deference toward physicians, universities emphasize academic honesty, and research laboratories emphasize standards of careful, systematic, objective reporting of experiments. In all of these examples, the organization, and particularly superiors within the organization, purposefully and consciously create a system whereby members are socialized to have the proper attitudes, values, and habits.

Socialization of attitudes and values

Organizations socialize rank-and-file employees, too. Such socialization may be purposeful and conscious (as in training courses), but usually is informal and even unplanned. Sigelman (1973) and Breed (1955) describe the process whereby journalists come to report the news more or less in the way their paper's owner and publisher see it. This is a most interesting example of socialization because the superiors in this case of bureaucratic conflict (namely the publisher and the editors) adhere to an ethical standard that prevents them from commanding subordinates to follow policy. Journalists, too, subscribe to ethical journalistic norms regarding objective reporting. How is it, then, that journalists whose attitudes and values vary and who are also somewhat more "liberal" than their publishers (Breed, 1955) come to subscribe to their newspaper's policies?

As Sigelman and Breed describe it, there is a subtle but pervasive socialization process at work. First of all, "anticipatory socialization" causes the new reporter who desires to "get on" and perhaps even move up to focus on role models provided by veteran reporters. The new reporters will say to themselves, "The senior reporters behave in certain ways and that's the way I'll behave when I have made it." The roles are learned as they interact with senior reporters and read their own newspaper every day and note the approach taken to reporting.

Leading control mechanisms

Editorial actions and especially revisions are useful mechanisms for controlling reporters' deviations from the attitudes and values of the organization. Reporters may submit what they feel is a fair and accurate account of events, but find that there are consistent blue pencil changes in their copy. In time they come to anticipate the kind of reporting that will avoid editorial revision.

The editorial conference, open usually to the most senior, most experienced reporters, also provides an opportunity for socialization. Veteran reporters and management discuss news coverage at these meetings. Here the desired approach to reporting is made quite clear, but for veterans, of course, years of socialization probably render much of the conference material superfluous.

Management, including the newspaper reporter's direct superiors, does not tell the reporter how to bias the news, but in myriad ways the news does become reported according to the policies of the newspaper. Superiors decide which stories will be covered, and therefore which will not. They decide which particular reporter will cover the story. Furthermore, an assignment often specifies the degree of importance the story will merit and the perspective from which it will be reported. Add to this the built-in quality control check in which editors examine and edit submitted copy (which most reporters argue entails only stylistic and not content changes), and one obtains a fairly tight system to control subordinate deviation from newspaper policy.

These control mechanisms are imbedded in the socialization process to the extent that it is difficult for newspaper reporters to perceive major conflicts between the policies of their publisher and editors and their own views. As Sigelman sees it, the reporter-newspaper relationship is not antagonistic or inherently conflict ridden. He suggests the relationship entails a tension-avoidance process. Sigelman emphasizes that these processes are structured so that senior newspaper personnel and reporters can interact in ways that avoid conflict.

The job of news reporting requires expert judgment and, as Perrow would indicate (Chapter 4), autonomy. Despite autonomy and resulting possibilities for deviation from newspaper policy (according to professional standards or the individual goals of particular journalists) socialization and the associated mechanisms for social control help eliminate conflict.

Selective recruitment

The relative ease with which the socialization process appears to work is somewhat misleading. Additional mechanisms foster integration of the individual's goals with those of the organizations. As Sigelman indicates, the employee selection process ensures that certain reporters will join certain newspapers. Sigelman found that reporters employed by two politically dissimilar newspapers tended to have the same political views as their employers. Despite the fact that the newspapers were located in the same building and were similar in other ways, only those reporters who were amenable to the policies of the newspaper joined its staff. Hence, the socialization and social control mechanisms were not required to overhaul completely the recruits' values or political beliefs. Socialization was limited to "cueing the recruit to matters of organizational style—developing in him a sense of limits of organizational tolerance, a more or less explicit theory of how people 'make it' in the organization, and a general conception of organizational purposes or methods . . . along with building the recruit's sense of belonging, of group solidarity" (Sigelman, 1973, p. 140). Interestingly, the selection process mentioned was neither formal nor purposive. It consisted of self-selection by the recruit. Those who were politically inclined to the left tended to gravitate to the leftward leaning paper and vice versa. Thus, as in the case of socialization, the selection process made no overt attempt to manage or bias news reporting arrangements. In point of fact, though, the newspaper organization developed in such a way that subordinates came to have values, goals, and attitudes congruent with those of top management.

Participation as a social control mechanism

Participation in decision making is a double-edged mechanism of social control. Participation, of course, has been advocated on the basis that it improves the motivation, understanding, and commitment of participants in the decision-making process. But there is a social control aspect to participative decision making as well. By participating in decisions about proposed alternatives, one becomes vulnerable to persuasive techniques. As Mulder (1971) suggests, when individuals participate but lack adequate information or expert power, their participation causes them to lose power (by being open and subject to influence), and they are worse off than had they not participated.

Gamson suggests that a ploy used by hard-pressed authorities is to involve a number of groups in participation, particularly rival groups. Such participation may appear to give increased power to each group, but authorities can point to the increased power of one rival group and say to the other group that pressures from the first group prevent them from taking action desired by the latter group and vice versa. Each group can be led to appreciate the constraints applied by the other group. It is said that President Roosevelt used this ploy with his cabinet members. He involved them in various (conflicting) assignments, thereby obtaining more information from a broader perspective, but at the same time maintaining power for himself.

The accommodation mechanism for individual and organizational integration

Interestingly enough, Barrett (1970) found in his study of 1,700 managerial and nonsupervisory employees in a large refinery that accommodation was most highly associated with integration of individual and organizational goals. The socialization approach was less highly related, and the exchange approach generally was ineffective in creating high levels of integration. The organization that moves toward the individual creates the most integration, as indicated by responses to survey questions measuring the extent to which individuals satisfy their personal needs and meet organizational objectives simultaneously.

According to the data, the socialization approach to integration was nearly as successful as accommodation. The combination of socialization and accommodation reminds one of the mutual influence system described in Chapter 3. Barrett suggests that these approaches to goal integration are compatible with the participative or democratic management systems proposed by Argyris, Likert, and others (Chapter 3). In contrast, the delimited exchange approach to integration seems most compatible with the traditional method of organization advocated by Gulick, Urwick, and Taylor (Chapter 2). Barrett provides evidence that participative-democratic management is more effective, if one takes as one's criterion of effectiveness the integration between individual and organizational goals.

The importance of Barrett's study can be ascertained by recalling our discussion of normative organizations in Chapter 5. Members make significant, encompassing emotional investments in such organizations. In addition, power, coordination, and organizational functioning in general are based on the norms, values, and goals that members hold in common. Normative organizations can be contrasted with more rational, calculative organizations that are typified by segmented, delimited relationships with their membership. Barrett describes such relationships in his exchange approach to integration. These two kinds of organizations correspond to a basic distinction made in sociology regarding societal relations.

Primary and secondary relations in organizations

Primary relations (diffuse, whole-person, emotional relations) are found in primary groups such as families or friendship groups. Secondary relations are more rational and calculative. Typically, they involve individuals interacting contractually with regard to specific interests. A number of sociologists have used variations of this distinction to describe different social relations: Toennies (1940) referred to "community" and "corporation," Durkheim (1947) to "organic" and "mechanical" solidarity, for example.

If one values primary relations as ends in themselves, one will prefer organizations that emphasize integration based on participation and socialization. This is not to say that these organizations necessarily are more effective in terms of productivity.

In point of fact, we suggest that much of the controversy in the study of organizations arises from the value orientations of theorists. Some value primary relations as ends in themselves while others do not. However, the trade-offs between primary relations and productivity or survival are unclear (Chapter 6).[3] Related to this distinction between primary and secondary relations is a general distinction between internal and external mechanisms for control that were discussed in Chapter 5.

---

[3] Barrett found that the mechanisms for integration did not work equally well for all individuals. This was least true of the accommodation model, which facilitated individual-organizational goal integration regardless of employees' individual differences (for example, differences in educational level, tenure, rural or urban background, managerial or nonmanagerial status, or production-administrative-research function membership). Socialization, however, showed the most effectiveness in creating goal integration in organizational units employing mostly rural workers. While the exchange model did not have much effect on the level of goal integration achieved, it did have some positive effect in units employing individuals of lower social status, low educational attainment, and nonmanagerial status. These findings remind us of the points made in Chapter 6 regarding individual differences, motivational structure, and the need for corresponding organizational practices.

SYSTEMS CONFLICTS

Subgoals and conflicts

The systems model of conflict derives from the observation that organizations are differentiated—that division of labor and task specialization are employed as means toward increased efficiencies and economies of scale (see March and Simon, 1958, pp. 112–35). The systems model explains conflict arising among functionally interdependent units that pursue conflicting goals or activities instead of acting in a coordinated fashion.

Because work flows laterally in an organization, the goals of one subunit may serve as constraints for another and vice versa. Furthermore, rather than adhere to the constraints of another unit, a particular unit often will emphasize its own goals at the expense of meeting these constraints. In Chapter 2, we described Selznick's criticism of the bureaucratic model, which suggests that delegation leads to local adaptations and, ultimately, to conflicting subgoals and suboptimization. This is what is meant by systems conflict.

Thus, the two major approaches to reducing conflict in lateral relationships, according to Pondy (1967), lie in (1) reducing goal differentiation by modifying incentive systems or selection, training, and assignment procedures, and (2) reducing functional interdependence arising from competition for resources, from scheduling and sequencing problems, and from requirements for consensus among subunits.

Goal and style differentiation

In addition to conflicting goals and competition for resources, one finds that the modus operandi of many subunits vary, and that these different "styles" often become ends in themselves and, therefore, sources of conflict within the organization; for example, college professors may come to view scholarly activities as the bases of a meaningful way of life instead of as means toward the acquisition of knowledge. This is not to say that they cease to produce knowledge, but rather that the activities can become as highly valued as the knowledge they seek. In Chapter 4, we discussed the structural requirements of different kinds of technologies. These ranged from structures that were bureaucratic and achieved coordination via plans and rules to those that were "organic," that vested more authority in lower levels and achieved coordination via feedback. The problem is that most large organizations have both routine and nonroutine tasks to perform, and the structures, interpersonal relations, and modes of cooperation associated with each must be combined and articulated somehow.

Lawrence and Lorsch (1967), also cited in Chapter 4, found that subunits such as R&D, sales, and production differed in their attitudes toward the environment and orientations toward time, as well as in terms of their requirements for different kinds of organizational structure. If they are to be effective in performing their allotted tasks, these units *must* be differentiated. However, the units also must be integrated if the organization is to be effective in performing all of its allotted tasks. Below we shall describe various integrative techniques that enable an organization to differentiate and specialize effectively while avoiding the conflict that differentiation is likely to produce.

Superordinate goals

Hampton and colleagues (1973) advocate the introduction of *transcendent objectives*—goals that are more important to members of the organization than those of the subunits to which they belong and that require the cooperation of the subunits for their attainment. A related means of unifying the goal-directed activities of subunits is found in the use of scapegoats or external enemies. Similarly, a leader may highlight serious internal problems common to conflicting subunits and severe enough that the long-term viability of the organization is dependent on their resolution.

Daniel Katz (1964) argues that the larger structure of the organization and its goals should be made to appear more salient when decisions that have organizationwide implications are pending.

> In setting up committees to handle an organizational problem, a common procedure is to name members who report to some top officer rather than to their department heads. In this way, the context of the committee's operation is the organization's problem, not the specialized interest of competing sub-groups. The members thus assume a set of responsibilities as citizens of the larger structure. It is not so much that there is communication across people from subgroups with varying specialized backgrounds as it is a matter of communication on issues essential to the goals of the organization (p. 112).

Moving conflict within units

The differentiation of goals by subunits and the resulting conflict between units may also be handled by moving conflict down to lower levels in the organization, according to Katz (1964). Goal differentiation may be increased so that the differentiation occurs *within* groups or even within individuals rather than between groups, thus avoiding polarization at the higher level. Conflict between two units is dependent on each unit mobilizing the efforts of its members in a unitary fashion. This cannot be done if there is internal conflict within the warring groups (March and Simon, 1958).

Katz describes how an organizational structure based on functional specialization can obscure the purpose of the organization because each functional unit identifies with its own particular concerns, rather than with the organization as a whole. It is suggested that departmentalization by product as well as multiple group membership for individuals in the various functional specialties be incorporated in the organization's design.

The general point is that the structure and, thus, the arrangement of power should not be congruent with any particular kind of task specialization. Rather, decision-making power should be based across several specializations. For example, Walker and Lorsch (1968) provide evidence that reorganization from a functional to a product structure will reduce the amount of conflict between functions, but increase the amount of conflict faced by each individual manager within a product department, since each manager will need to relate to other functional managers in working on a particular product. The question here, as we mentioned earlier, revolves around the manner in which one redistributes conflict. Conflict at very high levels will have direct, critical effects on the organization's effectiveness, while lower level conflict can be compensated for and dealt with as the efforts of lower level units are coordinated in the directions set by higher levels of the organization.

The crisscrossing of membership advocated by Katz has been cited as one of the reasons for the relative lack of severe political conflict in the United States. The major political parties consist of both Protestants and Catholics, WASPs and other ethnic groups, members of every economic class, and so on. Thus, when an issue arises, it is not dealt with by members of a single economic class, a single ethnic group, or a single religion, but by a heterogeneous membership. This may be contrasted with the situations in Quebec and Belgium where political conflicts can become quite polarized. In Quebec, the Catholic, French-Canadian, and generally lower-class population is sometimes arrayed against the Anglo-Protestant, middle- and upper-class population. In Belgium, the Flemish-speaking, Catholic, lower-income population in Flanders is often arrayed against the Walloons—the French-speaking, anticlerical, higher-status population in the south of the country.

The analogy can be extended readily to business organizations. If there is excessive conflict between functional departments, reorganization to a product structure should be considered as a way of reducing the polarization in which, for example, manufacturing personnel see themselves in conflict with members of the sales department. In a product structure, production experts will find themselves arrayed against other production experts from time to time when problems arise in allocating resources among different products. At other times, however, they will find themselves in conflict with members of other functional specialities (sales or R&D, for instance) within their own product group. Such conflict will not tend toward polarization, but will be more diffuse, sometimes in relation to one manager and sometimes in relation to another. Thus ingroups and outgroups tend not to develop. Since problems arise in relation to specific issues, conflict tends to remain limited.

Incentive systems

Goal differentiation can also be reduced through the use of incentive systems designed to reward activities that benefit the larger system, as opposed to those that are primarily in the interest of subunits. It may be recalled from Chapter 4 that the longwall approach to coal mining used three shifts of workers who specialized in mining, loading the conveyor, and moving the equipment up to the coal face. Each of the three shifts was paid separately according to a criterion appropriate to the shift's task. The resulting conflict was due in part to the reward system that encouraged suboptimization.

In contrast, the shortwall method of coal mining employed a small group of six men, two to a shift, who were effective in coordinating activities across shifts. In part, this was thought to have come about because they were paid as a group, rendering it in the interest of each member to do whatever was necessary on his shift to coordinate his own efforts with those of other shift workers, and in so doing to enhance the group's productivity. The Tavistock researchers recommended the composite longwall arrangement that coupled the advantages of mechanization with the behavioral attributes of the shortwall method. Most important for our purposes here, the researchers proposed a group incentive system that treated all three shifts as members of one group. It should be noted that the voluntary participation of workers in the composite longwall system together with the elimination of status differences among workers complemented the incentive system in reducing conflict between shifts. Groups, too, can be effective in socializing their members to desirable norms and obtaining conformity to superordinate goals.

Of course, there is a limit to the applicability of group incentive systems (Marriott, 1949). In large, complex organizations, the individual or small group of workers may feel that their contribution is insignificant to the attainment of major objectives. They fail to see relationships between their efforts and the unit's effectiveness. Since increased productivity on the part of a single individual will have an imperceptible effect on organizational performance, companywide incentive systems may not generate intended increases in motivation. Furthermore, task complexity, intangible results, and changing interdependencies hinder the development of criteria for assessing worker performance. When this is the case, it is difficult for individuals to understand, let alone evaluate, their efforts as those efforts relate to the goals of the larger system.

Perhaps the most to be hoped for in introducing incentive systems to reduce conflict is the elimination of existing (frequently individual-based) reward systems that inadvertently produce conflict of an unproductive nature. It is not uncommon to find situations in which two individuals or subunits have goals that cannot be met simultaneously. These are called *zero-sum* or *win-lose situations* (Litterer, 1966). Quality control inspectors, auditing departments, police departments, and the like commonly are subject to win-lose episodes. The job of quality control inspectors, for example, is to find errors, and they are rewarded accordingly, but the errors they find are potential sources of negative sanctions for another person.

Litterer makes the general point that win-lose situations exist where the reward system is based on individual performance that is contingent on interdependencies. He cites, as an example, a conflict between two managers in a major airline. In this case, the sales manager tried to increase sales volume by providing additional services for customers. The sales manager's incentive was to achieve a bonus computed from sales volume. These efforts to increase services were resisted by the service manager, since they would add to the service manager's budget. Ironically, the service manager anticipated a bonus that was based on cost reduction.

Another possible approach to reducing conflict that attends goal differentiation is found in the work of Likert (Chapter 3). Group management in an organization made up of overlapping groups may avoid the extreme individualism and conflict sometimes found in more traditional organizations. Overlapping membership between groups may serve to reduce between-group competition. In fact, this aspect of Likert's work is very similar to the crisscrossing of membership advocated by Katz.

Because organizations must perform a variety of activities to fulfill system needs (or to pursue conflicting operative goals, depending on one's point of view), no *single* incentive or reward system is likely to be effective. For that matter, as we have said, conflict cannot be avoided entirely. Landsberger (1961) identifies several basic dilemmas that evoke unavoidable conflicts: the need for flexibility and stability; the importance of both measurable and intangible results; the importance of short-run productivity vis-à-vis the need to trade off short-term gains for long-term efficacy. Thus, the problem is not to select an incentive system that will eliminate organizational conflict, but rather to decide which specific areas of conflict deserve attention and then to design the incentive system accordingly.

Reducing functional interdependence

In addition to the reduction of goal differentiation, a second general approach to dealing with the causes of systems conflict is to reduce functional interdependencies. We have already mentioned one source of interdependency that stems from sharing limited resources such as physical space, equipment, personnel, or funds. In competing for limited resources, interdependent units focus on the accomplishment of their own tasks, sometimes to the exclusion of realizing concern for larger organizational objectives. Such competition is likely to poison relationships between subunits and lead to conflict in still other areas. In short, the net result is suboptimization rather than coordinated, joint problem-solving endeavors.

A simple, although not always feasible, solution for conflicts arising from dependence on limited resources is to establish slack—to provide a supply of resources that is at least adequate to the needs of both subunits. Also possible is mediation of conflict by a third party, leading perhaps to the establishment of rules and agreements for equitable sharing. By their impersonality, rules so established may alleviate the more damaging, personal effects of conflict.

Interdependencies based on sequential work or information flows are somewhat more complex. Walton and Dutton (1969) discuss them in terms of *task-related symmetries and asymmetries*. In Chapter 10, we mentioned that the dependency of purchasing agents on engineers led them to attempt to influence the requisitions made by the latter individuals. In this manner, the agents developed symmetrical dependencies, wherein mutual influence was exerted. Asymmetrical interdependencies arise when the individual who is depended on has little incentive to cooperate or coordinate activities with those of the dependent individual. Such situations are likely to have adverse consequences for the organization.

Dealing with sequential dependencies

One approach to reducing sequential interdependencies is to loosen schedules. Another is to introduce buffers such as inventories or contingency funds. Where the output of one unit flows directly into another, the latter unit's work is subject to initiation by the former unit. This dependency is ameliorated when the first unit's output flows into an inventory from which the second unit draws. When maintained at a sufficient level, the inventory will buffer the second unit against variations in the quantity of output of the first unit. Another example is found in Whyte's (1949) order spindle (Chapter 4). Please recall that the spindle buffered higher status cooks from work initiated by lower status waitresses, thus reducing the dependence of the former on the latter and the conflicts that the initial situation created.

Just as dependence on a common pool of resources can be reduced by rules or resource duplication, so sequential interdependence can be reduced through facility duplication. For example, R&D can be provided with its own small production plant for pilot runs as an alternative to depending on the whims of the production department for access to facilities. Similarly, production can be provided with its own engineers for developmental projects and troubleshooting instead of depending on the goodwill of the engineering department.

Occasionally, sequential conflicts are reciprocal, consisting of two-way dependencies. Rather than duplicating facilities or investing in inventories, a somewhat more effective barrier to this kind of work flow conflict is established through the use of mediators or liaisons, who can eliminate personal contact between conflicting parties. The cost of hiring such buffer personnel may be considerable, but given the cost of major conflict between groups adjacent in the work flow, the expense may prove worthwhile. Sometimes, a low-status (and fairly passive) individual or group may serve as a communications link between conflicting units. For example, the go-between may be an individual who is near retirement age, and having little possibility for promotion, presents no threat to either of the conflicting parties. Examples of liaison personnel are field engineers who come between customers and design engineers, development engineers who buffer research scientists and design engineers or production managers, and public relations representatives who come between political leaders and the press or public (Hampton and colleagues, 1973).

A more extreme approach to reducing functional interdependence is decentralization. This provides for a more complete separation of formerly pooled resources and jointly held goals. Of course, decentralized units must be integrated by top management and through the efforts of liaisons. When this is accomplished, suboptimization may be transformed into a virtue. Furthermore, Daniel Katz (1964) suggests that the assignment of overall coordination to top management directs attention to major issues and avoids overloading top-level staff with problems arising from minor, less important conflicts.

Reducing pressures for compliance

A final approach to reducing the causes of systems conflict lies in reducing the functional interdependence arising from various pressures for compliance. Not all of the compliance required in organizations is essential to effective operation. Even in cases where compliance is essential, the pressures generated can be reduced by giving those expected to comply a voice in defining the situation to which their conformance is sought. Participative decision making permits subordinates to suggest the means for compliance that are consistent with the constraints under which they function.

Most of the solutions suggested for the problem of excessive functional interdependence have consisted of structural changes. An alternative approach is found in staff development. Victor Thompson (1961) speaks of *person specialization* as opposed to task specialization. Task specialization leads to differentiated tasks that are linked systemically, and thereby generate functional interdependencies. Person specialization leads to the training and education of individuals who can deal with an entire task, thereby eliminating some of the interdependencies mentioned above. Job enrichment, as discussed in Chapter 9, is one approach to this end. Participative management is another.

BARGAINING CONFLICTS

Limited resources and conflicts

We move now to the *third* model of organizational conflict, the bargaining model. Rivalry and the potential for conflict will arise among groups who compete for scarce resources. Typical of these are labor-management relations and the processes of capital and governmental budgeting (Pondy, 1964; Walton and McKersie, 1965; Wildavsky, 1964). Conflict in the bargaining model takes the forms of *integrative* and *distributive* processes. Integrative bargaining seeks to increase the total amount of resources available to competing factions. Distributive bargaining engages participants in the division of whatever resources are available.

Bargaining may be either explicit or implicit (Hampton et al., 1973). In contrast to explicit bargaining wherein both parties are aware that each is attempting to influence the other, implicit bargaining occurs when at least one party is unaware of the process. In a typical case, the manipulator creates a situation in which the manipulator is of service to the second party and then takes advantage of the situation by threatening to withdraw from it. Implicit bargaining may also be used as a supplement to formal authority. "A paternalistic manager who gives turkeys and bonuses at Christmas or builds an employee recreation park is often, consciously or unconsciously, attempting to manipulate subordinates into giving the firm greater loyalty" (Hampton et al., 1973, p. 758).

In distributive bargaining, one uses threats and bluffs, and presents the image of being immune to the power and threats of the other party. One withholds information about one's real strength, real desires, and minimum requirements. At the same time, one attempts to acquire valid information on the strengths and desires of one's adversary.

This is in contrast to the process of integrative bargaining wherein a free exchange of information is essential to solving the problem at hand. Here, the emphasis is not on using power to increase one's share of limited resources, but on cooperative problem solving that is intended to increase the resources available to all parties. This, in fact, was the idea behind Frederick Taylor's scientific management, which attempted to improve worker efficiency to increase productivity and, thereby, the returns to both management and labor.

Distributive bargaining tactics

As Pruitt (1972) sees it, the most general approach to bargaining is coercion of one's opponent into granting concessions while conceding as little as possible oneself. Two basic motives seem to affect all who engage in bargaining—to win concessions from the opponent and to resolve dispute by reaching some kind of agreement. Furthermore, he suggests two basic dilemmas that arise from various tactics used in bargaining—the tactics used to resolve dispute frequently are incompatible with the aim of gaining concessions, and tactics adopted to elicit concessions often subvert the aim of resolving dispute. As we shall see, these dilemmas encourage parties in conflict to rely on norms.

Pressure tactics

Pruitt categorizes pressure tactics as threats, punishment sequences, and positional commitments. *Threats* are understood generally. Bargainers frequently attempt to enhance their credibility, since the party to be influenced must believe that punishment will follow noncompliance. To make a strike threat credible, a union may make ostentatious arrangements for strike funds. At the same time, the party threatened may attempt to reduce the credibility of the threat. For example, management may arrange for supervisory stand-ins for striking workers, demonstrating that they cannot be hurt by the threatened strike.

A *punishment sequence* occurs when a party in conflict applies a negative sanction and promises to stop when compliance occurs. A student sit-in in the administration building, with an offer to move out when negotiations begin, is a punishment sequence.

Punishment sequences are more credible than ordinary threats because they are evidence of harm that can be continued. However, by giving the opponent a taste of what is in store if compliance is not forthcoming, this tactic also gives the opponent an opportunity to learn from the experience how to cope with the punishment and thereby blunt its effect.

The third pressure tactic described by Pruitt is *positional commitment.* By making a commitment and indicating inflexibility (by specifying nonnegotiable demands), one may pressure one's opponent into conceding, provided the demand is in an area where the opponent is willing to make concessions. The problem, of course, lies in determining whether the opponent's area of acceptable concessions includes the nonnegotiable demand.

But pressure tactics often are only partially successful. They may merely serve to delimit the outer boundaries of a solution to the problem—to delimit the points beyond which each party cannot be pushed. They rarely lead to specific solutions.

Concessions

Pruitt suggests that the next action in the bargaining process may be a substantial, unilateral concession or series of concessions. The problem here is that although a concession may move the dispute toward resolution, it usually requires that one move away from one's own position. In addition, concessions imply giving up something that could be used later in the process as part of a trade. Finally, a concession may be interpreted as a sign of weakness and may thus encourage the adversary to take a more rigid stand or to use pressure tactics even more vigorously.

Because of this, one may attempt other tactics that are more balanced with respect to the dilemma of seeking concessions and ending the controversy; for example, one may attempt an exchange of concessions (that is, a compromise). Pruitt suggests that most exchange-oriented tactics can be useful in resolving conflicts. If concessions are exchanged, fears of seeming weak or of rigidity on the part of the opponent are mitigated, since both parties appear "weak" and both are flexible. A proposal to exchange concessions may not resolve the bargaining dilemma, however. The proposal to start a negotiated exchange may be interpreted as a sign of weakness. Thus, indirect communication and the use of intermediaries may be appropriate to mitigate the risks of appearing weak or being rejected.

Tacit communication

Tacit communication, a type of indirect communication, takes a number of forms; for example, a negotiator may take too many words to say "no." This can be interpreted as a signal that the "no" will become a "yes" if a particular concession is forthcoming from the opponent. Other forms of tacit communication are more direct. A negotiator may tell the opponent: "This is the way we look at it. If we find something wrong with our position, we will change it. We will negotiate." The advantage of tacit communication is that an offer of flexibility and concession is ambiguous and may be withdrawn. The negotiator's image can be protected by giving contrary signals later.

Informal conferences

If the issues in conflict are particularly complex and ambiguous, an informal conference (for example, discussion over a cup of coffee) may enable movement toward compromise. Informal conferences give negotiators freedom to express their ideas. They may propose concessions informally, without risking loss of position if agreement does not result because of the norm that negotiators will return to the originally stated positions in the formal meeting. Such conferences may entail some loss of image in terms of flexibility but such losses are suffered by both sides equally.

According to Pruitt, the norms governing informal conferences are *(a)* what is said in conference will be confidential, *(b)* it will *not* be necessary to adhere to the rule that concession cannot be withdrawn, *(c)* parties will be willing to make concessions if the opponent makes them, and *(d)* agreements reached in informal conferences will be honored when the formal meetings reconvene. Negotiators typically make use of informal conferences if they trust their opponent to adhere to these norms. The more trustworthy the opponent seems, the more open a negotiator can be in such informal conferences. Pruitt suggests that informal negotiation (in which there is open discussion of goals, interests, flexibility, and possible concessions), seems to resemble the bargaining between friends or family members. It is a form of bargaining that develops over time, as one comes to know one's opposite number well and develops mutual trust.

Informal meetings may be held between subordinates of the negotiators or between intermediaries. In both cases, failure to reach agreement will lead to disowning the actions of subordinates or intermediaries, thus saving the negotiators from loss of position or image. If the parties are hostile, suspicious of each other, or likely to be embarrassed by mutual contact, intermediaries are particularly useful, since face-to-face meetings will be unlikely to be productive in such cases.

Intermediaries

A mediator is a neutral figure who communicates with both parties and tries to find a formula for agreement. These individuals can be useful in a variety of ways. "They can educate an inexperienced negotiator, arrange a meeting, give strategic advice, aid in reality testing, urge that a concession be made, recommend a known option, devise a new integrated option, guarantee compliance to an agreement, or help undo a commitment" (Pruitt, 1971, p. 229). Mediators can serve as channels of indirect communication between the negotiators. The mediators may interview the negotiators to determine concessions each is able to make and the conditions governing them. They will use this information to persuade each party to accept the largest concession the other seems willing to make. Since the negotiators, themselves, are not offering to make the concessions, they risk no loss of position or image. A mediator typically presents a possible concession in terms of a prediction of what the opponent will accept, saying, "If you will take this position, I think I can sell it to them." Just as there are important norms in tacit communication and informal conferences, mediations are governed by norms as well. These norms typically require the mediators to be impartial, to respect confidences, and to avoid publicizing their dealings with negotiators. Reciprocal norms require negotiators to be honest with mediators when indicating readiness to make concessions (Peters, 1955) and to have the flexibility to make concession when agreeing to employ a mediator (Stevens, 1963).

The importance of normative structure

While there is less risk of loss of position and image in indirect communication than in direct communication, a negotiator must still exercise caution, since these exchanges are dependent on the normative structure in the situation. Regardless of whether tacit communication, informal conferences, intermediaries, or mediators are employed, relevant norms must exist to provide security and channel interactions so that the probability of successful compromise is sufficiently high to compensate for the risks involved. Norms are built up over time and through repeated interactions between individuals. Pruitt emphasizes the importance of having skilled negotiators on the opposing side.

> ... a poorly qualified opponent will often not understand, and hence not respond to, a negotiator's efforts to coordinate an agreement. [In addition] ... such a negotiator can often not be trusted to observe the norms that regulate tacit communication because he doesn't know them or the implications of breaking them. The practical advice to which this reasoning leads is threefold: *(a)* be wary of making accommodative moves when the opponent is untutored, especially if he is anxious to win and thus likely to take a short-sighted exploitative outlook on these moves; *(b)* when ready to move toward accommodation, insist that an experienced negotiator ... represents the opposing side; *(c)* if the just prior advice seems unrealistic, take steps to *educate* one's opponent and make him into a skilled negotiator (Pruitt, 1971, pp. 237–38).

In conclusion, the indirect approaches to coordinating exchanges are useful because they reduce the risks of image and position loss in attempts to coordinate exchanges and also because they help begin the whole process of compromise and conflict resolution. In the final stages of bargaining, when there is considerable pressure for resolution of the conflict, when available pressure tactics have been tried, and especially when there is evidence that the adversary is ready to exchange concessions rather than exploit evidences of weakness, then one or more of the exchange-oriented tactics may prove successful.

Integrative bargaining

A mutually acceptable compromise, however, must be available if agreement is to be reached. If no such compromise is available, new options must be found. The concept of *integrative bargaining* (Walton and McKersie, 1965) is appropriate here: (1) state one's position in terms of a problem to be solved rather than a solution to be accepted by the adversary, (2) retain one's flexibility to refraining from commitment to a fixed position, (3) make every effort to understand the adversary's viewpoint, and (4) present an accurate picture of one's needs and motives to the adversary so that the adversary can derive options that satisfy the needs of both parties.

The problem, of course, is that while these tactics may foster resolution of conflict, they may also thwart the second aim of the bargainer, namely eliciting concessions from the adversary. Tactics (1) and (2) prevent negotiators from commiting themselves to a position favorable to their own interests. Tactic (3) is incompatible with the use of an intermediary, who knows little about the issues and has no authority to make concessions. Tactic (4) gives away the negotiator's minimal aspirations.

Just as integrative tactics favor the solution of conflict at the expense of eliciting concessions from the adversary, the reverse is true of pressure tactics, which tend to lend more weight to getting one's way than to resolving the conflict. Pressure tactics tend to interfere with integrative bargaining, which may lead to resolution of the conflict by development of a mutually acceptable solution.

Dealing with conflict sequentially

There may be some value in attempting to sequence integrative and distributive bargaining over time. According to Walton and McKersie (1965) this approach works in union-management negotiations. A cooperative attempt to enlarge the pie is made *first* (for example, an attempt to develop new work arrangements that benefit both the company and workers). Then competition emerges in which participants vie to split the enlarged pie. The reverse of the mixed model sequencing does not seem to work as well, since the initial competition tends to poison further negotiations and relations.

A similar kind of sequencing entails combining attitude change with distributive bargaining (Walton, 1969). Instead of relying solely on distributive bargaining (building power, using threats, and conveying misleading information), the participants build on possibilities for mutual attraction and trust, to establish more cooperative attitudes. This strategy entails minimizing perceived differences between the groups in conflict and their goals; avoiding threats and harmful actions; emphasizing mutual dependence; building positive, rewarding contacts between as many members of the groups as possible; and being trustful and trying to empathize. In short, one attempts to socialize the opponent.

The attitude change strategy can be made compatible with distributive bargaining through sequencing. For example, Soviet and U.S. relations have vacillated, freezing and thawing, apparently as a result of this dual strategy. Threats and warnings are followed by positive approaches (trade concessions, cultural exchanges, and negotiations aimed at relationship building). Walton indicates that the leader can engage in both kinds of behavior and still be credible so long as the cycle is sufficiently long and the initiatives and overtures are perceived to be genuine. Agreeable, but oppressive, supervisors who from time to time remind workers of their legitimate authority and ability to apply coercive sanctions use this alternating approach.

Second, these contradictory strategies can be implemented by different groups. Emissaries for scientific and cultural exchange may pursue harmony, while government representatives in Berlin issue threats and warnings. Finally, one may select particular actions with regard to their impact on the alternative strategy. One may issue threats strong enough to win concessions, but not severe enough to rupture relationships. One may provide concessions for relations building, but with the clear signal that these are not to be taken as a sign of weakness. In other words, one always remembers to negotiate from a position of strength, not from pure trust that prevents subsequent use of the distributive strategy.

Content specific and equity norms

We can argue that both distributive and integrative tactics are inadequate when used singly or jointly to deal with dilemmas and problems that arise in attempts to resolve differences of interest. Pruitt suggests that bargaining has other drawbacks as well, including the time and effort required and the uncertainties entailed. Norms of various kinds reduce the severity of such drawbacks.

Content specific and equity norms serve this purpose. *Content specific norms* specify the nature of the issues in question. For example, in some families the husband takes out the garbage. Norms that assign such unpleasant tasks to various household members eliminate the need to argue over who is to do what. *Equity norms* bring fairness and reciprocity to the bargaining process. The family in our example may have a norm that dessert is shared equally among members.

The problem with equity norms, according to Pruitt, is that although we all favor fair play, we have difficulty operationalizing the concept. We may differ in our opinions of what is fair. In addition, these norms may be insensitive to the needs of the parties. For example, a norm specifying a 50–50 split is not very helpful when one party needs the thing to be divided more than the other. A norm based on reciprocity will not be of much use to those who have little to give. The problem with content specific norms is that they tend to become sacred and inflexible, and may lag behind changes in the needs of the parties.

The norm of mutual responsiveness

In answer to some of these problems, Pruitt advocates a *norm of mutual responsiveness*—the willingness to help the other party satisfy that party's needs. The norm involves ". . . a kind of unwritten contract which [one individual] may have with [another] that requires each party to exhibit a certain level of responsiveness to the other's needs" (Pruitt, 1972, p. 147).

While norms of mutual responsiveness avoid the dilemmas involved in bargaining, they require certain preconditions. Pruitt suggests that both parties must feel *dependent* on one another—that each must believe the other capable of providing favors in the future. In addition, *trust* must be sufficient to allow one party to view the other as *willing* to provide these favors and to *represent self-needs honestly*.

PARTISANS

Two perspectives on conflict: Social control and partisans in the subsystem

In this last section, we turn to a rather different view of conflict. Gamson (1968) suggests that there are two different perspectives in behavioral science theory and research on conflict. One view, the one presented here (which is most popular in recent decades), is that of the "authorities." This viewpoint, which subsumes most of our discussion of systems, bureaucratic, and bargaining conflict, emphasizes the process by which goals of the system as a whole are achieved through the compliance of lower level individuals.

The second, less common, view is that of potential partisans—the point of view of those without power who attempt to organize and thereby influence the decisions of authorities. This view is also characterized as a conflict view of society. It is derived from Marxian theory, which describes the different interests of different groups in society and the resulting pervasive conflict (the dialectic). Rather than ask how conflict can be reduced and harmony and effectiveness achieved in the system, Marxian and conflict theorists focus on subsystems and their strategies for achieving their own ends. Conflict is viewed as an opportunity, rather than as a danger to the system as a whole. This view is the antithesis of the former social control perspective, which views conflict as something to be managed and contained in the interest of organizational effectiveness.

Getting power

We turn now to an examination of conflict from the perspective of the *partisan*—the individual or group desiring to obtain power. *How does one obtain power and use it effectively to get what one wants?* Such aspirations may, and probably will, create conflict. Gamson (1975) studied 53 groups (including the American Federation of Teachers, the National Urban League, the Bull Moose Party, and the American Student Union) that attempted to gain recognition and various political ends. Activist groups that were willing to use violence (either to initiate a fight or to fight back) were more successful than those that were passive. However, it should be added that violence usually was an ancillary part of a program that included strikes, bargaining, and propaganda. Furthermore, willingness to fight had to be supplemented by ability to fight, namely organization and discipline (centralization and bureaucratic structure) if the group was to be successful in achieving acceptance and advantages for its members. Bureaucracy in these groups was indicated by the existence of a constitution or charter with purposes and rules, a formal membership list, and at least three structural subunits. Centralization was indicated by a single leader or central committee, with local chapters having little autonomy. The anarchist's dream of organizational life, free of structure and authority, was not conducive to gaining power and implementing the group's ends.

Discussing power in more conventional organizations, McMurry (1973) says, "He [the executive] must stay in power by tactics that are mostly political and means that are in large part Machiavellian" (p. 140). McMurry provides a number of recommendations based on what he terms the "fruit of thirty years of observation of a great number of executives managing a variety of enterprises" (p. 141).

(1) The executive should employ subordinates who combine technical competence with reliability, dependability, and loyalty to guard against vulnerability to sabotage by underlings. In theory, the executive should be backed up by a competent lieutenant who can move in if the manager is promoted. Of course, a strong second in command is a threat. Therefore, McMurry suggests that the politically astute top executive seeks *subordinates who are loyal.* Such individuals tend to be security-conscious and dependent on their chief. (2) It is useful for the executive to have a *compliant board of directors.* Inside directors are better than outside directors since they are more malleable. (3) As in diplomacy, the most important stratagem of power in business is to *establish alliances.* The more alliances the better. Thus the executive should establish alliances with superiors, peers, and subordinates. (4) The *power of the purse* should be recognized. Thus, the astute manager "seeks as quickly as possible to position himself where he approves all budgets." In addition, McMurry enumerates supplementary ploys—personal styles employed by politically astute executives. (Please note the similarity of this advice to that of Machiavelli presented in the introduction to this chapter.)

1. Use caution in taking counsel. Advice can be useful, but can easily become pressure.
2. Avoid too close superior-subordinate relationships—the door may be open, but not too far.
3. Maintain maneuverability—don't commit yourself completely and irrevocably.
4. Use passive resistance when necessary. Stall or initiate action in such a way that the undesired program suffers delays and ultimately fails.
5. Don't hesitate to be ruthless when to be so is expedient—"no one really expects the boss to be a 'nice' guy at all times. If he is, he will be considered to be a softy or a patsy and no longer deserving of respect" (McMurry, 1973, p. 144).

6. Limit what is to be communicated. Many things should not be revealed if they will create anxieties or conflicts between parts of the organization.
7. Recognize that there are seldom any secrets. Don't reveal matters "in confidence."
8. Don't place too much dependence on a subordinate unless it is clearly in the latter's personal advantage to be loyal.
9. Compromise on small matters to obtain power for further movement.
10. Be skilled in self-dramatization and salesmanship. Be an actor, capable of influencing audiences emotionally as well as rationally.
11. Radiate self-confidence.
12. Give outward evidence of status, power, and material success.

Trust and distrust

A key to understanding the use of power against those who are more powerful and the responses of those in power is the nature of the trust relationship between authorities and partisans (Gamson, 1968). A climate of *trust* or confidence, support, allegiance, and satisfaction may be contrasted with one of *distrust,* discontent, alienation, dissatisfaction, or disaffection. Trust is essential in social systems. Decisions must always be made under uncertainty. Therefore, if authorities are to act effectively (without engaging in constant negotiation with subordinates), the trust and commitment of those in the social system are essential. "In war time," Winston Churchill told his critics, "if you desire service, you must give loyalty" (Churchill, 1962, p. 352). As Gamson says,

> ... for authorities to be effective, they must have a good deal of freedom to commit resources without the prior consent of those who will be called on ultimately to supply those resources. Such freedom to invest or spend the resources they have "borrowed" from members allows leaders to generate additional resources and thus, in theory, provide the lenders with a generous return in the form of public goods or increased resources.... Within certain limits, effectiveness depends on a blank check. The importance of trust becomes apparent: the loss of trust is the loss of system power, the loss of a generalized capacity for authorities to commit resources to obtain collective goals (1968, p. 43).

Gamson provides an example of the use of such power and the consequent loss of credit resulting because power was used unwisely. In 1964, the Johnson administration enjoyed a great deal of trust and credit. As a result, Congress gave President Johnson considerable authority to commit the United States to war in Vietnam. The president made use of this credit and his ability to make commitments, and involved the United States in a war that ultimately led to a loss of confidence by Congress and others. As a result, the president became increasingly constrained in his freedom to take action. He lost trust and credit and, paradoxically, lost power which would have enabled him to regain trust and credit. Distrust created powerlessness and, as a result, conditions engendering further distrust.

A well-functioning government is like a well-functioning bank. Both would prove insolvent at any given moment if individuals insisted on their formal rights. However, both are trusted, and individuals do not demand immediate delivery of that which is owed them. But let there be a loss of confidence or trust, and one will observe a run on the bank.

Usefulness of distrust

From the partisans' point of view, trust is less desirable. Trust seems to indicate that individuals are satisfied and unmotivated to change the status quo. Voting research, for example (Lipset, 1960), shows that as German voters became increasingly dissatisfied with the Weimar Republic, voter participation increased and led to Hitler's electoral victory. Apparently, some people did not vote earlier because they were satisfied. It seems that trust in authorities implies a lack of motivation to influence them. With this in mind, organizers of revolutionary groups attempt to create dissatisfaction, distrust, and readiness to organize among potential members. Much of the activity of community organizers such as Alinsky, which seemingly is bent on stimulating the powerless to make useless, ineffective attempts to influence authorities, really is aimed at increasing their dissatisfaction and polarizing the situation. This, in turn, may lead to mobilization of support for the activist organization.

Confidence, neutrality, and alienation

Gamson suggests that trust (distrust) relationships take three distinct forms. We have *confidence* in authorities when we trust them to have our interests at heart. *Neutrality* arises from the belief that in any decision the authorities have a 50–50 chance of deciding in our favor. Finally, *alienation* stems from the perception that authorities are *not* going to decide in our interest.

According to Gamson, a *confident* group tends to rely on *persuasion* as a means of influence. Authorities are assumed to be committed to the group's goals. Thus, influence is achieved by appealing to the authorities' goodwill by presenting information and arguments, by drawing on existing friendship and loyalty, and by activating commitment to the values shared by the authorities and the group. In short, goal congruence and trust permit the use of a psychological approach to influence. Other means of influence are avoided, since they will have adverse effects on the relationship between a confident group and authorities; for example, inducements may be defined as bribes. Gamson makes an analogy to the relationship between close friends. Such relationships entail diffuse, reciprocal obligations, and any particular action carried out in the spirit of friendship does not imply a quid pro quo. To offer a specific inducement to a friend is to violate the norms of friendship. "If one offers a quid pro quo for a favor, it implies that one also expects a *quid pro quo* when he performs a similar favor. In general, it implies a different relationship in which each act of influence becomes a separate transaction creating credits or debits for the parties involved" (Gamson, 1968, p. 167). Thus, if a partisan offers an inducement to authorities, the latter's expectations may be that in comparable situations additional inducements will be forthcoming.

In other words, the situation may become more nearly that of a *neutral partisan group* attempting to influence authority with inducements, which is appropriate under neutral circumstances. In this situation, authorities *do not* share the goals of the group, but have their own set of goals that may conflict with or complement those of the group. The partisans, however, do not perceive a systematic bias against them. Here it will take more than information to influence authorities to act in one's favor. *Inducements* are necessary. In the absence of common goals, influence has to be active, and focused on the desired behavior. But this use of power should not be violent or coercive and unnecessarily antagonizing to the authorities. Because they are neutral, a properly selected inducement may do the job—even in the face of differing or conflicting ends.

Finally, a partisan group that is *alienated* from authorities will tend to rely on coercion as a means of influence. Such groups, unlike the others, have little to lose by coercion. The probability of favorable outcomes is already low, and the resentment of authorities is of little consequence. In such situations, the prevailing sentiment may be that "the only thing they understand is force."

Reactions by authorities

We have seen that a partisan group is liable to use different influence strategies according to its trust relationship with authorities. The tactics used will involve the various bases of power described in Chapter 10. How, then, will authorities react?

Reactions depend on the relative strengths of the two parties. The discussion of bureaucratic conflict earlier in this chapter may be recalled. Accommodation may be in order if relatively weak authorities are faced by a strong, organized partisan group. Alternatively, the authorities may appear to yield, but really stall until the situation is calmed down, the resources and organization of the partisans dissipated, and the strength of the authorities regained. Conflicts occurring in a university near the end of the school year may be handled in this fashion.

When the balance of power is reversed, bureaucratic conflicts may be handled by mechanisms of social control in which those in power (the authorities) influence those without sufficient power to force changes. All other things being equal, the existence of high levels of trust is desirable from the authorities' point of view. Trusting subordinates give authorities the power to mobilize resources in the directions they select.

In contrast, under conditions of neutrality, authorities will tend to rely on sanctions and particularly inducements as means of social control. Although desirable, persuasion is difficult to use with a neutral group. Constraints, if used, might alienate the group and induce reciprocal actions.

Finally, Gamson suggests that authorities tend to rely on insulation to control alienated groups. By insulating an alienated group, authorities are protected from its use of constraints. Authorities will find such groups unreasonable to bargain with and insatiable with respect to inducements. " 'Give them an inch and they will take a mile,' is the classic expression of such attitudes toward alienated ... groups" (Gamson, 1968, p. 182).

Pitfalls in confrontation and participation

To continue our analysis of the partisan's role in conflict episodes, we suggest that attempts at conflict resolution that involve openness and participation as advocated by Likert and others are fraught with dangers. When subordinates deal with their superiors, interests clash (Dahrendorf, 1958). The superior's formal authority generally is unmatched by the bases of power on which subordinates rely. Even more important is the unequal distribution of knowledge and information between the two parties.

Mulder's (1971) research illustrates how participants in problem-solving situations suffer loss of influence and are persuaded to change their positions when they possess substantially less relevant information than others. Individuals who are disadvantaged by relative ignorance find that the decision to enter into participative decision making is harmful to them, in terms of their subsequent loss of power. A comparable situation is found in the Yugoslav Workers Council, a formal arrangement in which workers (who are relatively disadvantaged in terms of expertise and information) participate with top executives in the management of their organizations (Chapter 3). Observations of council meetings show that the executives retain the bulk of power, even though they are elected by the workers and bound by law to share decision-making authority with them. The proposals of executives, rather than those of workers, tend to be accepted by the council (Kolaja, 1965). In the vernacular, "Them as has, gets."

Our earlier discussion of the premise-setting behavior of top management may be recalled at this point (Chapter 6). The lower-level participants in decision making may be ignorant of potential alternatives. The premises they have come to accept may limit their exploration of feasible alternatives. The relative ignorance produced by these premises must be remedied if participation is to be used as anything more than a mechanism of social control. It is interesting to note that blue-collar workers appointed to the boards of directors of some Swedish firms are now being sent to management schools (*Business Week,* 1973).[4]

In any event, we are led to suggest that participation be limited to the areas of decision making in which all participants enjoy knowledge and expertise. Otherwise, lacking the ability to contribute to decisions, the participant will find individual future potential to influence eroded. Workers can participate effectively in shop floor matters, but not in those concerning the board of directors (Mulder, 1971). Similarly, managers can contribute to decisions related to their jobs, about which they possess knowledge and expertise. To extend participation to areas in which some participants are disadvantaged by virtue of their training and experience is unsound on purely logical grounds and, as we have seen, not in the best interests of the disadvantaged.

Participation's usefulness to the partisan

In Chapter 3 we saw that participation sometimes is conducive to organizational effectiveness. In some cases, organizations having high total influence were found to be more effective than those characterized by low total influence. Presumably, influence was enjoyed within the participants' areas of competence. Otherwise, we would expect participation to have left lower level members without power, as Mulder's reasoning suggests.

Thus, we are moved to advise members of organizations (potential partisans), who are faced with opportunities to participate with superiors in problem solving and decision making, to assure themselves that the areas within which they will participate fall within their competencies. Failing caution in this regard, the partisan may lose whatever power he or she enjoyed prior to becoming a participant.

A similar caution can be raised with regard to what Gamson terms "confidence," where goal congruence is assumed. If the partisans feel confidence in those with whom they will participate, relatively trusting behavior would appear to be in order. In Chapter 6, we suggested that various organization members and stakeholders often have different and sometimes conflicting goals. Here authorities are likely to use socialization and participation to control lower level members. In a general way, then, individuals must consider the trade-offs involved: Are they prepared to be socialized (How much?) to share in the rewards (How much?) of membership? Alternatively, the organizational model used by authorities may be on the order of Barrett's exchange model described above. Here the lower level participants must weigh the specific contributions they make against the inducements they receive.

More specifically, individuals must weigh the extent to which opening

---

[4] One is led to speculate, however, whether these workers, as business school alumni, will continue to represent the work force. It is conceivable that their education will socialize them according to the values and attitudes of management.

themselves to influence will lead to the danger of being influenced in directions they do not want to go and (from Mulder's experiment) the danger of losing power and subsequently being less able to prevent undesirable influence in the future. However, participation may prove worthwhile even after the subordinates weigh the (usually unanticipated) consequences noted above.

Many studies of participation have focused only on its benefits for the organization or on satisfactions reported by workers, and do not include a thorough analysis of the gains and losses of the individual worker. One wonders whether the Coch and French (1948) study of women machine operatives at Harwood (Chapter 3) fully accounted for possible losses of power of the participating workers. As Mulder observes:

> When someone's boss gives orders to him, he can resist. He can think, "what the boss doesn't see won't hurt him," or he can prevent the order from being carried out. He can also critically talk with others about it. But the mechanisms of resistance, obstruction, and catharsis are excluded from the participatory group after the decision has been made. The person is committed to the decision, and has to follow it without reserve (1971, p. 36).

Partisans will do well to determine whether structured protections are available to prevent their being manipulated. William Scott (1965) proposes the creation of formal appeals systems for white-collar workers—systems in which grievances regarding unfair behavior of supervisors are taken up the managerial hierarchy. As we saw in Chapter 5, rules and impersonality, as found in bureaucracies, may serve to protect the individual, just as informal norms can structure behavior and provide security through predictability and through the legitimacy inherent in such structured expectations.

A study by Kohn (1971) supports the argument that formal structure provides protection against "premise setting" and other forms of manipulation of the participating employee. He found that bureaucrats enjoyed more protections in terms of tenure, seniority guarantees, and formal grievance procedures than nonbureaucrats. Consequently, the former (especially the blue-collar workers in bureaucracies) were more open to change, felt more personal responsibility, and were more intellectually flexible.

The prospective partisan must look beyond formal protections for participation. Tannenbaum and colleagues (1974) found higher total influence in Yugoslav firms having worker's councils than in firms in Italy or Austria, which lacked workers' councils. However, influence curves were still higher for U.S. firms. The latter curves were high, despite the lack of formal provision for participation at the board level, because informal relations between superiors and subordinates were conducive to openness and to the development of relatively high degrees of influence and participation by subordinates (Chapter 3).

The prospective partisan must consider the expected rewards to be gained by participation. Some of these rewards take the form of shares taken from someone else (from distributive bargaining conflicts). This suggests the need for a careful diagnosis of the situation. In addition to considering one's own preferred goals and means, and those of authorities, the potential partisan must consider where rewards are to come from. A possible bigger pie is one thing, and a zero-sum situation (such as a cutback in jobs or budget) is another.

In conclusion, we have raised these issues in part to redress what appears to be an imbalance in the literature. Participative management sometimes is advocated without due regard to the well-being of either the organization or its participants. As we move on to even more controversial topics, please bear in mind that theoretical positions often are based on political predispositions that sometimes bias perception and reason. This observation applies to all of us to one extent or another. We have our biases, too. Please bear this in mind as well, as we continue our study of organizations.

DISCUSSION QUESTIONS

1. List some of the more apparent sources of conflict for faculty and students in your school.
2. Can you categorize them as bureaucratic, systems, or bargaining conflict?
3. Are these sources of conflict unavoidable? If not, how can they be avoided?
4. Describe the power of the student body, the faculty, and the administration.
5. How are these different forms of power exercised?
6. Americans seem prone to meet conflict with violence. Is the rate of violent crime higher in America than in England? How do you account for your answer?

12

Leadership

INTRODUCTION

Many contemporary, scientific observations of social organizations can also be found in the rich, archaic literature handed down to us throughout history. This is neither surprising nor a condemnation of the contemporary behavioral sciences. Sensitive and reasonable men and women throughout the ages have reflected on the affairs of society and generalized from their experiences.

Leadership has posed questions for reflective minds throughout recorded history. Let us, then, look to history for a moment and consider the advice provided would-be leaders by the sage, but oft-maligned, Machiavelli in his book *The Prince* (1952, pp. 48–50):

> I say then that in new dominions, where there is a new prince, it is more or less easy to hold them, according to the greater or lesser ability of him who acquires them. And as the fact of a private individual becoming a prince presupposes either great ability or good fortune, it would appear that either of these things would in part mitigate many difficulties. Nevertheless those who have been less beholden to good fortune have maintained themselves best. The matter is also facilitated by the prince being obliged to reside personally in his territory, having no others. But to come to those who have become princes through their own merits and not by fortune, I regard

as the greatest, Moses, Cyrus, Romulus, Theseus, and their like. And although one should not speak of Moses, he having merely carried out what was ordered him by God, still he deserves admiration, if only for that grace which made him worthy to speak with God. But regarding Cyrus and others who have acquired or founded kingdoms, they will all be found worthy of admiration; and if their particular actions and methods are examined they will not appear very different from those of Moses, although he had so great a Master. And in examining their life and deeds it will be seen that they owed nothing to fortune but the opportunity which gave them matter to be shaped into what form they thought fit; and without that opportunity their powers would have been wasted, and without their powers the opportunity would have come in vain.

It was thus necessary that Moses should find the people of Israel slaves in Egypt and oppressed by the Egyptians, so that they were disposed to follow him in order to escape from their servitude. It was necessary that Romulus should be unable to remain in Alba, and should have been exposed at his birth, in order that he might become King of Rome and founder of that nation. It was necessary that Cyrus should find the Persians discontented with the empire of the Medes, and the Medes weak and effeminate through long peace. Theseus could not have shown his abilities if he had not found the Athenians dispersed. These opportunities, therefore, gave these men their chance, and their own great qualities enabled them to profit by them, so as to ennoble their country and augment its fortunes.

Those who by the exercise of abilities such as these become princes, obtain their dominions with difficulty but retain them easily, and the difficulties which they have in acquiring their dominions arise in part from the new rules and regulations that they have to introduce in order to establish their position securely. It must be considered that there is nothing more difficult to carry out, nor more doubtful of success, nor more dangerous to handle, than to initiate a new order of things. For the reformer has enemies in all those who profit by the old order, and only lukewarm defenders in all those who would profit by the new order, this lukewarmness arising partly from fear of their adversaries, who have the laws in their favour; and partly from the incredulity of mankind, who do not truly believe in anything new until they have had actual experience of it. Thus it arises that on every opportunity for attacking the reformer, his opponents do so with the zeal of partisans, the others only defend him half-heartedly, so that between them he runs great danger. It is necessary, however, in order to investigate thoroughly this question, to examine whether these innovators are independent, or whether they depend upon others, that is to say, whether in order to carry out their designs they have to entreat or are able to compel. In the first case they invariably succeed ill, and accomplish nothing; but when they can depend on their own strength and are able to use force, they rarely fail. Thus it comes about that all armed prophets have conquered and unarmed ones failed; for besides what has been already said, the character of peoples varies, and it is easy to persuade them of a thing, but difficult to keep them in that persuasion. And so it is necessary to order things so that when they no longer believe, they can be made to believe by force.*

Chapter guide

Machiavelli observes that a prince's success in ruling new dominions depends on both his ability to wield power effectively and the existence of an opportunistic situation. In Chapter 6, we considered problems that arise when organizational members disagree on both the nature of the goals to which they should aspire and the means by which they will attain any of the goals in question.

1. What parallels exist in these two observations?
2. From what source(s) does a contemporary prince (executive) derive power?
3. Do you think that Machiavelli contradicted himself in suggesting that the followers who no longer believe "... can be made to believe by force"?
4. What forces are brought to bear on deviant members of democratic, participative organizations?

LEADER BEHAVIOR AND GROUP PERFORMANCE

Changing views of leadership

Some of the earliest studies of leadership attempted to identify personality traits of leaders that set them apart from followers and contributed to their leadership skills. As we shall see, this approach was fruitless, and was abandoned in favor of the view that specific types of leader behavior affect subordinates' performance regardless of the leader's personality. Encouraged by early research results, management theorists began to advocate certain management styles over others, because some styles seemed to evoke more desirable subordinate behaviors than others. However, the credibility of this approach came into question as the inadequacy of related, rational theories of management became apparent.

An outgrowth of dissatisfaction with the one-best-way approach of the rational theorists was the so-called contingency theory, which suggested that the appropriate leadership style is determined by crucial contingencies in the leader's task and work group environment. Many such theories have been proposed—some have been quite elaborate and well conceived. How-

---

* Source: Reprinted from Niccolò Machiavelli, *The Prince* by permission of Oxford University Press.

ever, all are related, in that leadership activities are thought to influence the behavior of subordinates. Hence, desired subordinate behavior can be elicited by adopting the appropriate leadership style or by altering contingencies in the work environment to make them compatible with a particular leadership style.

A more recent, somewhat compatible, view is that the behavior of a leader is affected by the leader's power in the organization. Relatively powerful managers are able to engage in relatively successful leadership behaviors because they are powerful. Less powerful individuals adopt less successful leadership styles because they lack the power to do otherwise. This leads to the conclusion that ineffectual leaders cannot improve their performance by altering their styles of management or by altering crucial contingencies in the workplace. To improve their performance as leaders, management must give these individuals greater power in the organization. But who is willing to increase the power of the ineffectual? We shall explore this view as well as others in this chapter.

Preliminary definitions of leadership

Leadership typically refers to behavior (undertaken within the context of an organization) that influences the ways in which other organizational members behave. Leadership sometimes is thought of as charisma, but we argue that a variety of behaviors, including authoritarianism, are appropriately considered under this rubric. As we shall discover, the efficacy of one type of leader behavior as opposed to another varies according to the characteristics of the situation in which it is enacted.

Leadership can be defined to include the sources of power that are built into a position in an organization's hierarchy. These include the ability to apply organizationally sanctioned rewards and punishments, as well as referent and expert power. However, some individuals seem to enjoy power that exists over and above that provided by their role in the organization.

We will focus our attention on the essence of leadership, that is, those incremental sources of power that go beyond routine organizational functioning and tap bases of power in excess of those that are organizationally decreed. Edward Hall (1972) envisages leadership as the abilities to persuade other individuals and to be innovative in decision making. Obviously, if stewardship over the routine activities in an organization is all that is required of a supervisor, precedents and existing structures will obviate the supervisor's need to innovate. As we shall see, this is sometimes the case. On the other hand, more ambiguous, less structured work situations require the definition of novel problems, selection of appropriate solutions, and the coordination of those responsible for enacting solutions. In this light, Bavelas (1960) defines leadership acts as those that help a group meet its objectives. Of particular importance among these activities are making choices and helping others to do so, especially in situations that help the group reach a desired state. In the most general terms, this sort of leadership consists of uncertainty reduction, which entails making the kinds of choices that permit the organization to proceed toward its objectives despite various kinds of internal and external perturbations.

Two factors in leadership

A number of studies have examined the effects of leader behavior on subordinate performance. One of these studies (Fleishman and Harris, 1962) examines the effects of elements of leadership behavior that are called *consideration* and *initiating structure*. Consideration refers to behavior that increases mutual trust, respect, warmth, and rapport between the leader and the group. More than superficial friendliness, consideration emphasizes concern for the needs of group members, participative decision making, and two-way communications.

Thus defined, the degrees of consideration exhibited by supervisors were compared to the grievance and turnover rates of their subordinates. As illustrated by Figure 12–1, turnover rate and the rate at which subordinates expressed grievances were found to diminish as the amount of consideration demonstrated by their supervisors increased. However, this observation appears to be valid only within limits, for beyond a certain point, increased consideration was not found to affect grievance or turnover rates materially.

The second variable studied, initiating structure, was defined to include the supervisor's behavior in assigning tasks, planning, deciding how things should be done, and pushing for productivity. Initiating structure embodies overt emphasis on the achievement of organizational goals. As in the case of consideration, the degree to which different supervisors initiated structure was plotted against the average rates of grievance and turnover of their subordinates.

Figure 12–2 shows that turnover and grievance rates varied directly with the degree to which structure was initiated by supervisors. Furthermore, as was the case above, this observation holds under limited conditions; beyond a certain point, decreases in initiating structure were not accompanied by associated decreases in grievance or turnover rates.

When consideration and initiating structure were examined jointly (Figure 12–3), grievance rates were found to be highest for supervisors low in consideration, regardless of whether they were ranked high or low on initiating structure. Similarly, supervisors ranked high on consideration produced low grievance rates despite differences in initiating structure. Supervisors rated moderate in consideration and low on initiating structure produced relatively low grievance rates. However, for supervisors rated moderately considerate, increases in initiating structure produced increases in grievance rates.

As was the case with grievances, it was found that supervisors who were ranked relatively low on consideration experienced the highest employee

FIGURE 12-1
Relationships between grievance and turnover rates and consideration

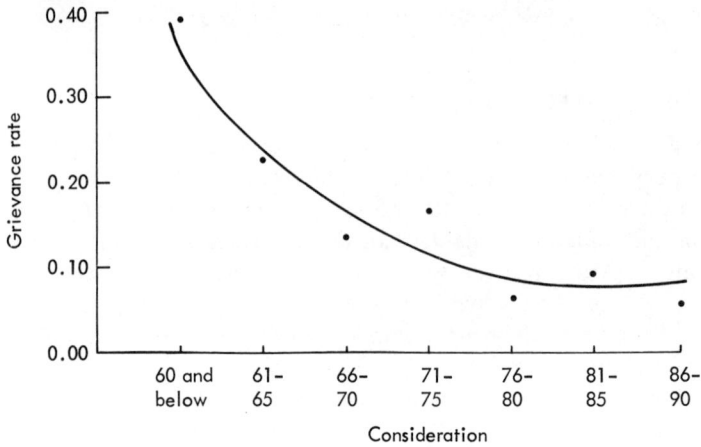

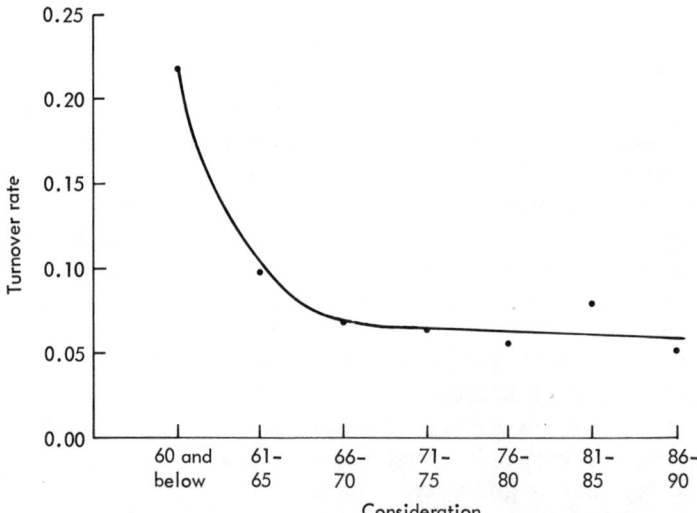

Source: Fleishman and Harris (1962, pp. 47–51).

turnover rates. Although the rate, in this case, varied directly with initiating structure, consideration seemed to be the overriding factor. Few differences in turnover rates were found to exist between supervisors who were high and medium on consideration. Furthermore, meaningful differences were not found to accrue from changes in initiating structure exhibited by the latter two groups of supervisors.

Other researchers have observed phenomena that appear similar to those described above; for example, Bales (1958) studied small discussion groups

FIGURE 12-2
Relationships between grievance and turnover rates and initiating structure

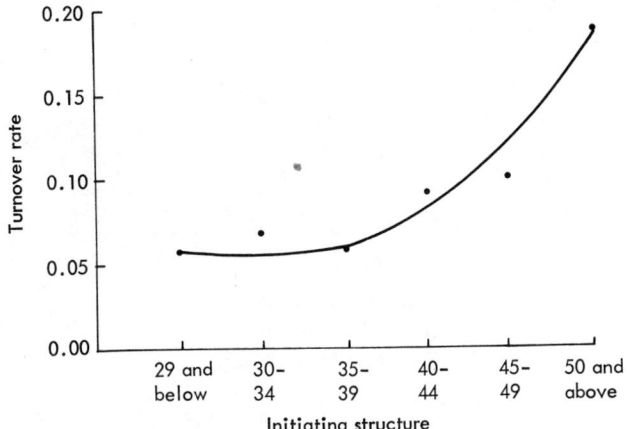

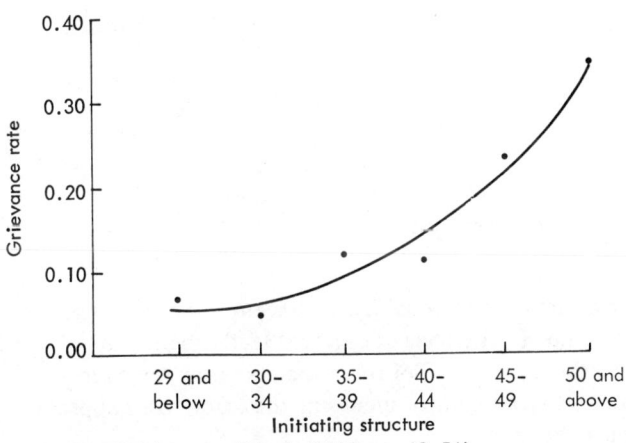

Source: Fleishman and Harris (1962, pp. 48–51).

and found that influential group members (leaders) were rated relatively high on the dimensions of task ability and likability, which is to say that they were "task leaders" and "maintenance leaders." The leaders who performed task functions helped their groups to get on with their jobs. The maintenance leaders (who were sometimes the same individuals as the task leaders) appeared to be good at dealing with interpersonal tensions and conflicts and at helping to maintain individual satisfaction at levels that were high enough to ensure continued group functioning.

FIGURE 12-3
The combined effects of consideration and initiating structure on grievance and turnover rates

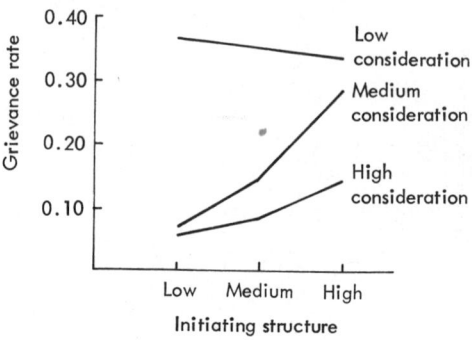

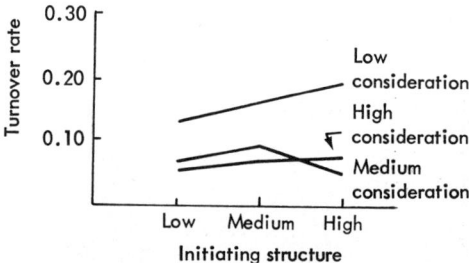

Source: Fleishman and Harris (1962, pp. 50-52).

Initiating structure and consideration seem to be useful concepts for understanding some of the effects of different leader behaviors. We shall return to emphasize the importance of these factors, after reviewing some alternative approaches to leadership—including the leader trait approach and some more complex theories.

Leader traits and group needs

Much of the early research on leadership focused on the personality characteristics and traits of leaders (Gibb, 1968). While some traits have been found more consistently among leaders than among others, the possession of these traits appears neither necessary nor sufficient to leadership. Dominance, intelligence, self-confidence, and empathy are often possessed by leaders, but they vary in importance according to the circumstances in which the leader must act; that is, one trait or another may be important depending on the goal sought by the group being led, the nature of the problems faced, the composition of the group, and so on.

A current view in the psychological literature is that leaders meet group needs. Furthermore, because different individuals may each contribute to fulfilling a particular group need and because different needs may be met by different individuals, leadership usually is not confined to a single individual. Rather, it is useful to speak of "leadership functions" or of activities carried out by various individuals to enhance the progress of the group and the fulfillment of its needs.

Four theories of leadership

A study by Mott (1972) compared four fairly general theories of leadership. The first of these is Likert's System Four approach to management, which we have already discussed (Chapter 3). The three other theories to be discussed here are based on the work of Bowers and Seashore, Mann, and Katz and Kahn. Later in the chapter, we shall examine still other approaches to leadership.

On the basis of an extensive review of leadership studies (including those of Fleishman and Harris [1962], Likert [1961], and others), Bowers and Seashore (1966) concluded that there are four basic dimensions of leadership: support, emphasis on goals, facilitation of interaction, and facilitation of work. *Support* is similar to consideration and to Likert's concept of supportive management. It is behavior that enhances someone else's feelings of personal worth and importance. We have already encountered *emphasis on goals* in Likert's System Four theory of management. This is the stimulation of enthusiasm for achieving high performance levels. *Facilitation of interaction* involves encouraging group members to develop close, mutually satisfying relationships. Finally, *facilitation of work* is stimilar to Fleishman and Harris' dimension of initiating structure. It is behavior that promotes the attainment of goals through activities such as scheduling, planning, coordinating, and providing resources.

We have already proposed the view that requisite management skills and activities differ from one hierarchical level in the organization to another. In a similar vein, Mann (1965) proposes a *skill-mix* model of leadership that takes such differences into account. At lower organizational levels, *technical skills* (the ability to use pertinent knowledge, methods, techniques, and equipment in performing and directing work activities) are most important. Less important at lower levels are *human relations* skills (the ability to work effectively with people), and least important are *administrative skills* (the ability to plan, schedule work, make job assignments, monitor work flows, and coordinate the work of one unit with the work of other units). Moving upward in the hierarchy, administrative skills increase in importance relative to the others. Human relations skills also increase in importance, but beyond middle management they again become relatively less important.

According to Mann's recent theorizing (Mott, 1972), a fourth requisite skill emerges at top-management levels—*institutional skill* (the ability to create and formulate policy, handle relationships with outside organizations, and manage the organization's mission vis-à-vis the political, social, and economic environment).

A fourth theory of leadership, and one which is similar to Mann's in that it illustrates the appropriateness of different managerial behaviors at different levels of the organization, is the three-pattern approach to leadership (Katz and Kahn, 1978). *Origination* (creating, changing, and eliminating structure), *interpolation* (supplementing and piecing out structure), and *administration* (using structure as it already exists) are management concerns of importance to top, middle, and lower levels in the hierarchy, respectively. Each of these three leadership patterns has both an affective and cognitive component.[1]

The cognitive component of *origination* is found in the leader's systematic perspective—awareness of the organization's relationship with its environment and of the interrelationships among subsystems within the organization—and in the leader's ability to change or create new structures. The emotional component of *origination* is charisma. This is the aura surrounding a leader that derives from a special gift for affecting individuals in an emotional way.

Interpolation, the managerial behavior thought to be appropriate at middle-management levels, has a subsystem perspective as its cognitive component. Middle managers need both an upward and downward orientation to implement policy directives emanating from above and to coordinate various interdependent subsystems. The middle manager must be a good problem solver and coordinator and be influential with both superiors and subordinates. The affective component of *interpolation* is found in the ability to integrate what sociologists have called primary and secondary relationships. The manager must be able to establish warm human (primary) relations with employees and integrate them with the more impersonal (or secondary) organizational elements that exist outside of the primary work groups. The manager must integrate individual needs with organizational requirements.

The *administrative* pattern has as its cognitive component the technical knowledge of a job and knowledge of organizational roles. The affective component is fairness, which enables rules to be applied equitably.

All four of these theories of leadership (Likert, Bowers and Seashore, Mann, and Katz and Kahn) were tested in a study of leadership effectiveness conducted in the Office of Administration at NASA headquarters in Washington (Butterfield, 1968; Mott, 1972). Twelve divisions of the Office of

---

[1] Note the similarity to the work of Bales (1958) wherein task and maintenance functions can be considered as, respectively, cognitive and affective in nature. Similar observations can be made about the dimensions of structure and consideration in the Fleishman and Harris (1962) study.

Administration (dealing with security standards, financial management, management information systems, personnel, transportation, and so on) and 28 branches within the divisions comprised the study population. Using a complex array of analytic techniques, Butterfield found that each of the theories had limited predictive power. Division effectiveness (measured according to Mott's questionnaire items described in Chapter 14) was generally predictable from the behavior of the division director, but branch (subunit) effectiveness could not be predicted from the behavior of heads of branches. It was not clear whether the criterion data used for branch-level analyses were improper, or whether the lack of findings was attributable to other causes.

Applying the skill mix theory at the division level, the best predictor of division effectiveness found was the degree to which human relations skills were used by division heads. Using the four-factor theory at this level, facilitation of work proved superior as a predictor to the other three. Application of the three-pattern theory demonstrated that integration and subsystem perspective correlated with effectiveness. Finally, of the components of System Four, supportive relationships was the best predictor. None of the four theories received complete validation in the study. Only some of the factors in a particular theory worked. Furthermore, taking all of the factors in a single theory simultaneously and comparing the theory in question to other theories so considered, none stood out as a superior predictor of effectiveness. Reviewing the variables that successfully predicted effectiveness, the familiar and simple *task* and *maintenance* factors account for most of the findings.

STRUCTURAL VARIABLES AND LEADER BEHAVIOR

Conditions and intervening variables in leadership processes

Comprehensive review of research undertaken to determine the roles that the two above-mentioned factors play in the leadership process shows that, taken singly or jointly, neither predicts leadership effectiveness consistently. A number of writers suggest that greater emphasis must be placed on the conditions under which a leader operates, and that different leader behaviors will be differentially effective under different kinds of circumstances. As a theoretical model by Yukl (1971) suggests, some of these conditions may be intervening variables that can be controlled by the leader. These variables include subordinate motivation, task-role organization (job assignment and the technical quality of task decisions), and subordinate skill levels (which can be increased through training). In Yukl's model (Figure 12–4), leader consideration affects subordinate motivation directly, while initiating structure affects motivation as well as task-role organization and

FIGURE 12–4
A multiple linkage model of leader effectiveness

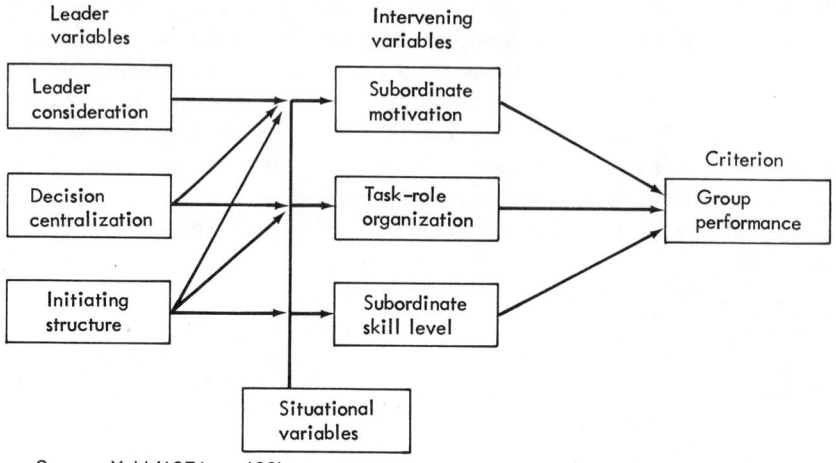

Source: Yukl (1971, p. 423).

subordinate skill levels. Yukl's model has a third leader variable termed "decision centralization" (or participation), which affects both motivation and task-role organization.

An important aspect of this model is the assumption that leadership behavior indirectly determines the effectiveness of the group as a whole by means of certain other, intervening variables that affect group performance directly. Study of these intervening variables should provide us with information about the ways in which leadership behavior can be improved to increase the output of group members.

Yukl's first intervening variable is motivation. We have already seen how leader consideration can increase motivation to improve group performance and also (in Chapter 3) how decision decentralization or participation can affect motivation and coordination among various roles.

The skill level of subordinates may be improved through on-the-job instruction and training and through improved communications of task-relevant information. These are all elements of the component of leadership called initiating structure, and they explain how initiating structure affects group performance. Even highly motivated employees will not perform well if they lack prerequisite knowledge and skills.

Task-role organization refers to the efficient utilization of subordinates' skills in the pursuit of the group's assigned tasks. The adequacy of task-role organization depends on how well job assignments and work-method selections are made. If jobs are highly specialized, if each job demands the exercise of different skills, and if there are differences in the skills possessed by subordinates, then decisions concerning job assignments will bear major consequences for group performance. When job assignments are poorly made, some workers will be underutilized while others will be unable to perform their jobs adequately. Decisions concerning the selection of work methods become important whenever tasks can be performed in a number of different ways, and some ways are better than others.

We have indicated that leaders who are high on initiating structure will attempt to improve the efficiency of their groups, and if they have the proper organizing skills and technical knowledge, they will affect performance by means of task-role organization. In addition, however, subordinates' knowledge and skills of task-role organization can be tapped by means of participative decision making (in Yukl's model, decentralizing decisions). But where pressures exist to organize task roles quickly, participative decision making may be dysfunctional. In this event, unilateral or centralized decision making is advocated, assuming that the leaders possess the requisite knowledge and skills to do so.

Fiedler's "favorableness" of the situation for leadership

Fiedler (1967) conducted an extensive program of research on the relative effectiveness of different leadership styles in different situations. He suggests that "... we must recognize that training people is at best difficult, costly, and time consuming. It is certainly easier to place people in a situation compatible with their natural leadership style than to force them to adapt to the demands of the job" (Fiedler, 1965, p. 121). Executives should learn to recognize and diagnose group task situations to place their subordinates in jobs suited to their leadership styles. In addition, because appropriate placement is not always possible, Fiedler (1967) suggests that organizations attempt to engineer jobs to fit the persons. All of these points have to do with the factors labeled situational variables in Yukl's model (Figure 12-4).

Fiedler found that the favorableness of the work situation will determine the effectiveness of a particular leadership style. Permissive (considerate) and authoritarian (controlling) styles of leadership are both effective, but each is effective in different kinds of work situations.

The favorableness of a work situation is defined in terms of three characteristics: the quality of leader-member relations, the extent to which the task is structured, and the extent of the leader's power. Of the three factors, leader-member relations is the most important, followed by task structure and power of the leader, respectively. The most favorable situation is one in which a leader enjoys good interpersonal relations with subordinates, supervises a highly structured task, and exercises considerable power over the group. The most unfavorable situation is described by poor leader-member relations, an unstructured task, and relatively little power vis-à-vis followers.

A considerable number of studies conducted in a variety of work groups, including basketball teams, surveying parties, military combat groups, steel furnace crews, and boards of directors, show that the more directive and controlling leaders perform best when their group situation is either rela-

FIGURE 12-5
How style of effective leadership varies with the situation

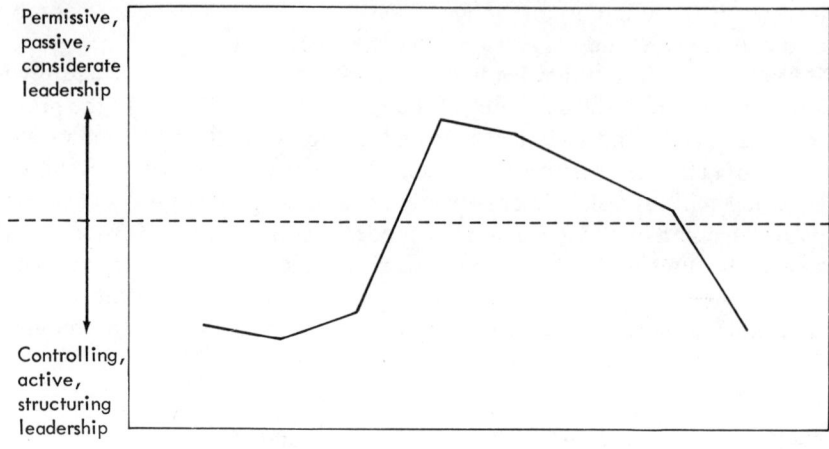

Leader-member relations	Good	Good	Good	Good	Poor	Poor	Poor	Poor
Task structure	Structured		Unstructured		Structured		Unstructured	
Leader position power	Strong	Weak	Strong	Weak	Strong	Weak	Strong	Weak

Data below the midpoint of the vertical axis indicate that, under the circumstances described, task-controlling, managing leadership styles were more effective than permissive, nondirective, and human relations-oriented leadership styles. The opposite is true for situations in which data points occur above the midpoint.

Source: Reprinted by permission of the *Harvard Business Review*. Exhibit II from "Engineer the Job to Fit the Manager" by Fred E. Fiedler (September–October 1965). Copyright © 1965 by the President and Fellows of Harvard College. All rights reserved.

tively unfavorable *or* relatively favorable, but not in between. In contrast, nondirective, human relations-oriented leaders are more effective in situations that are neither favorable nor unfavorable as defined here.

In more specific terms, the directive leaders performed best in basketball and surveying teams, and in open-hearth shops, as well as in military combat crews (provided the leader was accepted by the group) and as company managers. In contrast, the nondirective leaders tended to perform best in decision- and policy-making teams and in groups having a creative task (provided that the group liked the leader or that the leader felt that the group was pleasant and free of tension).

Summarizing a variety of different leadership studies, Filley and House

(1969) provide specific conclusions about the conditions under which supportive leadership behavior is most effective. These conditions seem to parallel and amplify Fiedler's view. Supportive leadership is effective when:

1. Decisions are not routine in nature.
2. The information required for effective decision making cannot be standardized or centralized.
3. Decisions need not be made rapidly, allowing time to involve subordinates in a participative decision-making process.

And when subordinates:

4. Feel a strong need for independence.
5. Regard their participation in decision making as legitimate.
6. See themselves as able to contribute to the decision-making process.
7. Are confident of their ability to work without the reassurance of close supervision (Filley and House, 1969, pp. 404–5).[2]

There seem to be several parallels here with the work of Fiedler, particularly regarding the degree of structure in tasks and also, to some degree, the relationships and differential needs of leader and subordinates.

The path-goal theory of leadership

A systematic treatment of leadership and its effects on Yukl's first intervening variable, motivation, has emerged in the path-goal theory (House and Mitchell, 1974). Building on the expectancy model of motivation, it emphasizes the leader's effects on subordinates' perceptions of personal and work goals and the paths leading to them (see also Evans, 1970, 1974; House, 1971: Nebeker and Mitchell 1974). Leaders increase motivation by clarifying paths to subordinates' goals and by strengthening and clarifying contingencies between subordinates' performance and valued outcomes. Motivation also is increased to the extent that the relationship between an individual's intention to perform and the actual performance is enhanced—by coaching and direction and even the removal of frustrating obstacles. Finally, the level of desired rewards may be manipulated directly; for example, by the superior increasing the amount of recognition provided.

According to House and Mitchell (1974), two major classes of situational variables affect leadership. One includes the nature of environmental demands determined by the task, the authority structure, and peer relations, all of which can affect motivation, clarify paths, and so on. The second class of variables concerns personal characteristics, especially individual differences in motivation. As one might expect from the discussion in Chapter 5, individuals predisposed to internal control are more satisfied with participative

---

[2] From *Managerial Process and Organizational Behavior,* by Alan C. Filley and Robert J. House. Copyright © 1969 by Scott, Foresman and Company. Reprinted by permission of the publisher.

leadership. Also, individuals who perceive themselves to be competent to perform the required task are more satisfied with participative leadership than are those who are predisposed to external control or perceive their ability to be low.

The environment affects the relationships between leadership and subordinate motivation and satisfaction through its effects on the paths and goals and their outcomes for the individual. For example, subordinates performing ambiguous tasks are likely to prefer more directive leadership because such leaderships can foster goal achievement and subsequent achievement of related rewards. But in a structured task, the less directive the leadership the better. Since the path-goal relationship is already clear, directive leadership does not enhance motivation or satisfaction.

While both environmental and personal characteristic variables moderate relationships between leader behavior and motivational and affective outcomes, the environmental variables seem to have overriding importance (House and Mitchell, 1974). At lower levels of the organization, where tasks are routine, directive leadership may be preferred by relatively closed-minded, authoritarian individuals while nondirective leadership may be preferred by more open-minded, nonauthoritarian workers. At higher levels in the organization, where work is more nonroutine and ambiguous, directive leadership may be preferred by both authoritarian and nonauthoritarian subordinates. In other words, both the nature of the task and subordinate personality seem to determine the preferred kind of leadership, but task characteristics seem to have the greater effect.

In Chapter 3, we discussed Likert's suggestion that managers emphasize high-performance goals. The path-goal theory helps us understand how, and under what circumstances, such leadership behavior is effective. Leadership behavior that emphasizes achievement may affect subordinates' levels of aspiration vis-à-vis their tasks. Such emphasis also is likely to affect subordinates' confidence in their abilities and their perceptions of effort-performance probabilities (Chapter 9). Some confirmation of the theory is found in a study, described by House and Mitchell (1974), showing that for subordinates performing ambiguous, nonrepetitive tasks, there was a positive association between the leaders' emphasis on achievement and subordinates' expectancies that their efforts would lead to effective performances. But for subordinates performing more repetitive, less ambiguous tasks, leader emphasis on achievement did not seem to create higher expectancies that effort would lead to performance. Unfortunately, the possible effects of personality differences in the situation were not studied. (The same kind of qualification of Likert's emphasis on supportive management is found in House and Mitchell's review. In nine out of ten studies, subordinates were most satisfied with supportiveness *when they had to work on stressful and frustrating tasks.*)

A final example of the usefulness of the path-goal theory of leadership, provided by House and Mitchell, pertains to the effects of participative leadership. This kind of leadership may be expected to improve motivation in a number of ways, including helping subordinate) (1) clarify path-goal contingencies (that is, they learn about the organization by actually doing things and observing the results), and (2) select goals of higher value (because of the influence provided by participation). This increased motivation, together with the autonomy provided by participation, may be expected to lead to higher performance. However, there are studies that show that some individuals prefer autonomy and self-control more than others (for example, Vroom, 1959). Some individuals may prefer not to have autonomy, thus reducing the potential effects of participative leadership. Even more important, however, is the effect of the environment (that is, the task) on the leadership-performance relationship. There is evidence that in ambiguous and ego-involving tasks, subordinates prefer participative to nonparticipative leadership, regardless of their personality differences. But for repetitive and less ego-involving tasks, personality makes a difference—nonauthoritarian subordinates prefer participation more than authoritarian individuals.

While the path-goal approach to leadership is largely untested, it is promising because it focuses on both the individual and the environment. The leader can be seen as mediating between the individual and the organization (its technology, structure, and goals). The leader can have important effects on the motivation of subordinates, in terms of the rewards and paths to rewards provided, and important effects on performance for the organization, by affecting the perceptions of contingencies that are important in motivation.

The varying effects of leadership

In contrast to the preceding discussion of the effectiveness of leadership styles in different situations, a number of studies suggest that an even more significant question needs to be addressed. Namely, to what extent (or when) does leadership have any effect at all?

Earlier, in discussing the relationships between technology and structure proposed by Perrow (Chapter 4), we saw that coordination by feedback is appropriate for nonroutine technologies while coordination by planning is appropriate for routine technologies. This typology suggests that for highly structured technologies there is not much leeway for supervision or different supervisory styles.

In fact, no supervision at all may be appropriate in such highly structured technologies. A case in point is Woodward's (1965) study of technology, which shows that mass-production systems provide considerably more routinization and structure for management than do either batch or continuous process systems. The supervisor of a team performing batch production, as well as the supervisor of a maintenance crew for a continuous process technology, will have opportunities to affect the productivity of their workers, for better or worse, depending on the supervisory style used. This is in some contrast to the supervisor on the assembly line, where the task is so highly structured the use of either a human relations style or a more directive approach to supervision makes relatively little difference to the productivity of the work unit.

Norms as well as technology may serve to structure the task (Mott, 1972). As indicated in Chapter 10, informal norms may produce just as much or more regularity in behavior as formal rules and regulations. Thus, a situation characterized by a restrictive normative structure (whether formal rules as in a bureaucracy or informal norms as in a work group) may be one in which different supervisory styles make little difference for the effectiveness of the group.

From his NASA study, Mott (1972) found that as one moves upward in the organizational hierarchy and as tasks become less structured, variations in leadership styles seem to have more effects (for better or worse) on the productivity of the division under study. Respondents in the study were asked whether their supervisors had any effect on their performance, and answers varied considerably according to the respondent's level in the organization. One third of the respondents low in the hierarchy (GS levels 1 to 7) agreed with the statement that supervisors have very little effect on the work they perform, in contrast to none of the respondents at high levels (GS level 12 or higher). That is, at lower GS levels, supervision's contribution to subordinates' performance was not as apparent as it was at higher levels. Those at lower levels felt the factors that *did* have an impact on their work included the stage at which work arrived, whether or not it arrived on time, the clarity of job requests, and whether or not equipment was working properly. The individuals in question were performing highly structured, repetitive batch work, and their productivity depended primarily on effective coordination, rather than on the nature of their supervision. The supervisory behavior that they perceived as helpful included the application of technical skills, certain techniques of administration, fairness, and effective communication.

In contrast, respondents at the GS 12 or higher levels viewed supervision as important. They also mentioned a different set of supervisory skills. These consisted of task- and support-oriented skills that include the following: (1) good human relations skills, (2) willingness to stand up for subordinates with other, higher level supervisors, (3) openness to employee influence in decision making, (4) willingness to discuss work-related problems with employees, (5) the possession of authority adequate to their responsibility, and (6) good administrative and planning skills.

Generalizing from his findings, Mott (1972) suggests that the more closed a system is and the more it is routinized, the less effect leadership behavior has on the system's effectiveness. In the NASA study, respondents at higher organizational levels exercised their leadership within relatively unstructured (open) circumstances, while those at lower levels worked within systems that were more nearly closed. Mott goes on to suggest that leadership styles effective for higher level management are similar to those that are effective in the management of research laboratories, although the hierarchical positions of the managers and research directors may differ considerably. Both kinds of managerial endeavor occur within relatively open systems where feedback loops providing information for control purposes are long.

Mott also argues that the importance of leadership increases as the interdependence of tasks is increased. Unfortunately, this hypothesized relationship was not amenable to direct observation in his study. However, an indirect form of analysis did lend some support to the notion. The NASA divisions staffed by highly trained professionals, who were performing work that came from outside clients to whom they were assigned by the division director, experienced little need to share client information. In these divisions, supervisory behavior had little effect on performance. In contrast, leadership behavior was found to affect productivity in divisions wherein the work activities were closely interrelated.

Leadership in changing situations

Some factors affecting leadership effectiveness are not amenable to manipulation by the manager. However, awareness of their importance can enable managers to deal with them appropriately. A number of these factors concern change—changes in the situation of the group or organization.

The effects of crises on leadership have been studied in small groups (Hamblin, 1958). Each group in the study was assigned a complex task and allowed time to learn the rules under which the task was to be performed. After the groups were functioning smoothly, Hamblin exposed them to crisis situations in which the rules were changed radically. Leadership in the experimental groups was affected in two ways: (1) group members were more willing to follow a strong leader than a weak one, and (2) leaders who did not respond to the crisis rapidly and decisively were rejected and replaced by other leaders.

Occasionally, groups change leaders quite systematically as they move between situations that are alternatively crisis ridden and "normal." Shepard (1967) studied a World War II raiding unit that alternately operated as an organic system, with open interaction among all participants, and as a more mechanical system, with strict hierarchical command. In the organic system, leadership was widely shared when ideas and plans for upcoming raids were generated and as completed raids were reviewed and evaluated. However, during the execution of a raid, a strict command structure was followed, with leadership confined to the top of the hierarchy.

Time pressures and other forces that evoke a need for directive leadership, as opposed to more participatory forms of leadership, can be observed in organizations as complex as national governments. For example, the British rejected Chamberlain as the threat posed by Nazi Germany increased and turned to Churchill, only to turn away from their great war hero to Attlee when the crisis passed.

Mann (1965) describes how demands for supervision changed in an electrical utility during the introduction of an electronic data processing system. In addition, he found that the skills demonstrated by supervisors in six different power plants (which ranged from being new or in the process of being rebuilt to being obsolete and about to be retired) varied considerably according to the stage in the life cycle of each of their plants.

Lippitt and Schmidt (1967) view organizations as having different critical concerns and issues as they progress from origination to maturity, much as (in Chapter 6) the critical tasks performed over the history of a hospital studied by Perrow changed. Initially, the organization's members are concerned with creation and survival, while at later stages concern shifts to matters of stability, reputation, and to organizing, reviewing, and evaluating performance. Finally, as organizations mature, members become concerned with attaining organizational uniqueness, maintaining adaptability, and making contributions to society. According to the investigators, early stages of organizational growth require technical and administrative skills, while later stages require the exercise of human relations skills to a greater extent.

Leadership and organizational constraints

Organizational norms may severely constrain the use of a particular leadership style or changes in leadership behavior. Merei (1949) conducted an experiment on a large number of children's groups in which children identified as followers were placed together in special rooms. After these groups had sufficient time to function and to create their own rules, habits, and traditions, a child identified as a leader in previous settings was placed in each group. The leader, usually an older child who tended to give orders more often than to follow them and who tended to be imitated more often than to imitate was usually forced by the group to accept their traditions, as opposed to being able to lead the group. The leader's own proposals were either rejected by the group or accepted only after being made congruent with existing group traditions. Usually the leader was able to modify means that were employed by the group, but not the group's ends. Jay (1971) describes a similar attempt to change the organizational culture of an English school through the introduction of new teachers. They, too, were quickly absorbed by the school's normative structure.

As Tannenbaum and Schmidt (1958) indicate supervisors must fit their behavior to the job at hand. The concept of fit implies that the leaders must not only be "true" to themselves and their personalities, but also to subordinates in their work groups. An elaboration of this thought is found in Hollander's (1958) work on *idiosyncrasy credits*. As leaders begin to conform to the norms of their groups, they build up idiosyncrasy credits with group members. These credits allow the leaders to behave idiosyncratically, and in so doing to lead the groups in different and creative directions. A related finding is reported by John Andrews (1967) from a study of two Mexican firms—one of which was highly achievement oriented, progressive, and expansion minded, while the other was oriented more toward power relations. It was found that the most regularly promoted managers in both firms had power and achievement motives congruent with the values of the organization in which they were employed, but not necessarily with the formal goals of the organization. In short, the leader and the group may be viewed as engaging in an interpersonal process in which the leader may influence others in exchange for being influenced by them in some way. Fiedler's "favorableness" may be amenable to influence since leaders may not only initiate structure but also affect the interpersonal processes that occur with the structure (Hollander and Julian, 1969). Our description of the process of role-sending (Chapter 10) is quite relevant here, for leaders may attempt to influence followers' conceptions of their roles, as well as their expectations of the leaders' own behavior. The research described above seems to indicate that such attempts at influence by leaders are not always successful.

In a study of English hospitals, Revans (1964) demonstrates that one leader characteristic, authoritarianism, may be a systemwide phenomenon—as was evidenced by a situation in which student nurses were afraid to ask questions of their supervisors who, in turn, were reluctant to behave openly with other nurses or physicians. Revans suggests that behaving openly is difficult in a climate characterized by anxiety and defensiveness. To ameliorate this system and the consequent anxiety and blocked communication it produced, Revans (1972) attempted to alter the behavior of top leadership in the hospital—senior nurses, physicians, and administrators. It was felt that to change the normative structure of the organization, the influence of those at the top of the hierarchy would be essential. In fact, in hospitals where the top leadership "bought" the action program, the system did seem to change, opening up and showing increased efficiency in patient care, even at the ward level (Revans, 1976; Wieland and Bradford, 1979).

Another study demonstrating the impact of relations across hierarchical levels was conducted by Fleishman (1953) who found that the leadership behaviors of supervisors were correlated with those of their bosses. People who work for considerate superiors were reported more considerate of their own subordinates than were others who worked for less considerate individuals. A similar correlation was found for the dimension of leadership behavior we termed *initiating structure*. The notion that organizational climate can constrain behavior is evidenced by the observation that supervisors tend to practice what they have learned in human relations training programs only when their own supervisors maintain a supportive climate. On returning from such training programs, supervisors who work for superiors low in consideration tend to revert to former patterns of behavior. A. J. M. Sykes (1962) found that supervisors trained in human relations became frustrated when top executives were unwilling to practice what they preached or had encouraged their subordinates to learn. Furthermore, the supervisors, who previously had been rated highly successful, became dissatisfied and on occasion left the organization because of their frustration.

In addition to a large number of *small group* studies that show that group members prefer leaders who show consideration, Pelz (1952) found in his studies of *organizations* that workers prefer supervisors who identify closely with higher levels of management. This does not imply that workers are indifferent to the amount of consideration that their supervisors give them. In addition to consideration, however, workers value the power their supervisors enjoy in interactions with high levels of management. Supervisors who have good relations with superiors will be able to supervise those under them in a more considerate fashion by virtue of their ability to work at satisfying subordinates' needs without interference from above.

While the scarcity of research findings in this general area prevents us from drawing definitive conclusions, it seems clear that the supervisor's power and leadership style may be circumscribed both by normative structure and by the distribution of power in the organization.

Leadership and decision making

Alternatively, a more profitable approach to understanding leadership may emerge if we redefine the problem in light of some of the constraints noted above. If we return to our earlier view of leadership, we can argue that leadership entails two sets of decisions. First, there is the question of what should be done; that is, What is the task, and how is it to be accomplished? Second, the leader must decide how subordinates are to be involved in performing task-related activities.

Obviously, the leader can initiate structure without consulting others and can exert legitimate authority to obtain subordinates' compliance in performing task-related activities. Thus, if we ask whether or not some form of subordinate participation would be appropriate in this situation, we really are asking whether (or under what conditions) participation will lead to better decisions regarding the task and enhanced commitment to its accomplishment. Furthermore, we must ask what degree of participation will enhance the quality of decisions and commitment, for it is obvious from what we have said so far that neither authoritarianism nor full participation is advisable in all cases.

Degree of participation

Vroom (1960) defines participation as a process of decision making engaged in by two or more people. The degree of participation enjoyed by

TABLE 12-1
Decision methods for group decisions

Property of decision-making process	Group problems	
Autocratic	AI.	You solve the problem or make the decision yourself, using information available to you at the time.
	AII.	You obtain the necessary information from your subordinates, then decide the solution to the problem yourself. You may or may not tell your subordinates what the problem is in getting the information from them. The role played by your subordinates in making the decision is clearly one of providing the necessary information to you, rather than generating or evaluating alternative solutions.
Consultative	CI.	You share the problem with the relevant subordinates individually, getting their ideas and suggestions without bringing them together as a group. Then *you* make the decision, which may or may not reflect your subordinates' influence.
	CII.	You share the problem with your subordinates as a group, obtaining their collective ideas and suggestions. Then you make the decision, which may or may not reflect your subordinates' influence.
Group-centered	GII.	You share the problem with your subordinates as a group. Together you generate and evaluate alternatives and attempt to reach agreement (consensus) on a solution. Your role is much like that of chairman. You do not try to influence the group to adopt "your" solution, and you are willing to accept and implement any solution that has the support of the entire group.

Source: Adapted from *Leadership and Decision-Making* by Victor H. Vroom and Philip W. Yetton by permission of the University of Pittsburgh Press. © 1971 by University of Pittsburgh Press.

each individual is related to the extent of that person's power to affect decisions. Since participation is a property of one's role in a decision-making process, Vroom and Yetton (1973) argue that one can "... define leader behaviors representing clear alternative processes for making decisions that can be related to the amount of participation each process affords the manager's subordinates" (1973, p. 12). A taxonomy of leader behaviors rank ordered according to the amount of participation they afford participants is presented in Table 12-1.

Choosing the appropriate degree of participation

Table 12-1 lists typical leadership activities that range from authoritarian at one extreme to group-centered leadership at the other. Which of these activities is appropriate in a particular decision situation is contingent on the subordinates' potential to contribute to the quality of the task decision and the effect of participation in enhancing commitment to its successful implementation. The contingencies that may be encountered in any situation are indicated in Figure 12-6 in the form of questions requiring yes or no answers. In essence, each question is designed to indicate the presence of a crucial contingency for the leader.

FIGURE 12-6
Decision process flowchart

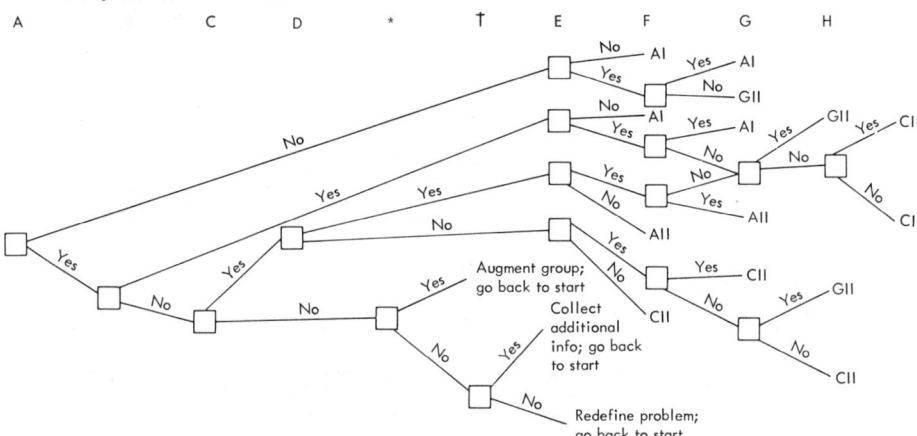

A. If decision were accepted, would it make a difference which course of action were adopted?
B. Do I have sufficient info to make a high quality decision?
C. Do subordinates have sufficient additional info to result in high quality decision?
D. Do I know exactly what info is needed, who possesses it, and how to collect it?
* Is necessary additional info to be found within my entire set of subordinates?
† Is it feasible to collect additional info outside group prior to making decisions?
E. Is acceptance of decision by subordinates critical to effective implementation?
F. If I were to make the decision by myself, is it certain that it would be accepted by my subordinates?
G. Can subordinates be trusted to base solutions or organizational considerations?
H. Is conflict among subordinates likely in preferred solutions?

Source: Reprinted from *Leadership and Decision-Making* by Victor H. Vroom and Philip W. Yetton by permission of the University of Pittsburgh Press. © 1971 by University of Pittsburgh Press.

In answering each question in turn, the leader presumably can analyze the situation in terms of the crucial contingencies likely to be encountered. Furthermore, answers to each question lead as through a decision tree that ultimately suggests the appropriate leadership behavior.

Leadership and power

We begin this chapter by defining leadership as behavior that influences the ways in which other organizational members behave. Accordingly, leadership can be described as the successful exercise of power. This fairly simple observation raises a number of serious concerns about the usefulness of Vroom and Yetton's contingency approach to leadership. Merely to suggest that a particular kind of leadership activity is appropriate in a given situation ignores the possibility that the leader may not have the power to act in the manner suggested. A further discussion of power and organizational politics will amplify this point.

Access to adequate resources is a prerequisite to successful performance of organizational tasks. Yet, an organization's resources typically are scarce. Thus, organizational members compete for power to obtain needed resources by employing various political strategies. Both the rational and system views seem to have minimized the ubiquity of power and politics in organizations. On one hand, bureaucracies are portrayed as using their immense powers to constrain individuals to the performance of their tasks, thereby minimizing power struggles. The system view, on the other hand, is biased toward viewing cooperative effort as the natural outcome of an adequately managed system—but for no apparent reason.

Recently, however, a number of theorists have attempted to construct models of organizations that incorporate power and conflict as inherent properties of the system (Benson, 1977; Collins, 1975). In this view, power is seen as the mechanism for influencing major organizational choices, including the choice of goals. Even highly structured bureaucratic organizations are described as having a strong latent potential for political behavior that arises from differences between individuals' self-interest and the interest of the organization. Zaleznik (1970) provides an illustration.

> If an individual (or group) is told that his job scope is reduced in either absolute or proportional terms for *the good of the corporation,* he faces a conflict. Should he acquiesce for the idea of common good or fight in the service of his self-interest? Any rational man will fight.... His willingness to fight increases as he comes to realize the intangible nature of what people think is good for the organization (p. 50).

The quest for power in organizations leads to a number of unforeseen, but not always adverse, consequences. According to Kanter (1977), organizational members acquire power by undertaking activities that are extraordinary, visible, and relevant to crucial organizational problems. "Neither persons nor organizations get 'credit' for doing the mandatory or the expected" (p. 177). However, while undertaking projects for which they receive "credit," individuals gain not only the power to command additional resources, but also the means to increase their power still further (Kotter, 1978). New activities, for example, will create new contingencies for other members of the organization who subsequently become dependent on the activity's originator. Such activities also may employ additional personnel, and they too become dependent on the manager in question. Thus, success in gaining power paves the way for gaining even greater power.

Powerful managers can engage in particular leadership activities merely because they are powerful. We noted, for example, that subordinates value their superiors' ability to stand up for them with other superiors and generally to influence higher levels of management. Powerful leaders, undertaking new projects, have less time for managing routine activities and consequently tend to delegate these to subordinates, thus providing them with opportunities to participate. In a similar vein, these managers are likely to be upwardly mobile, and will delegate responsibilities to their subordinates to develop successors in anticipation of their own promotion (Kanter, 1977).

The leadership activities of less powerful managers are quite different. "People held accountable for the results produced by others, whose formal role gives them the right to command but who lack informal political influence, access to resources, outside status, sponsorship, or mobility prospects, are rendered powerless in organizations" (Kanter, 1977, p. 186). Constrained to perform merely routine, unexceptional tasks, these individuals cannot enlarge their base of political support or provide additional rewards for their subordinates. Furthermore, delegation of responsibilities may be viewed askance, for in the absence of new challenges to meet, such delegation could leave the supervisor with little to do. Kanter suggests that in extreme cases powerless supervisors concentrate their power needs on those over whom they have authority. As a defense against feelings of helplessness, inferiority, or insignificance, these managers become critical, controlling, and bossy. The result is the authoritarian style of leadership that has been criticized so widely in the literature.

Kanter goes on to suggest that these individuals cannot alter their behavior easily, to act as if they were among the organization's power elite. Rather, their behavior is a result of their powerlessness, and for behavior to change, power must be increased. Yet, management understandably is reluctant to increase the power of the ineffectual. However, nothing less is required.

LEADER BEHAVIOR AND ORGANIZATIONAL PERFORMANCE

Top management and leadership

Most of the research cited has used lower and, occasionally, middle-level managers (as opposed to executives) as subjects. We have seen from Mott's research in NASA that the higher one moves in the organization, the greater difference leadership behavior can make for organizational effectiveness. However, the highest level of management studied by Mott consisted of division heads, who essentially performed staff functions and were considerably below the top-management level. This may explain, in part, why Katz and Kahn's three-pattern theory did not predict, in its entirety, the effectiveness of units at various levels of the organization. The best predictors in the Katz and Kahn theory were *subsystem perspective* and *integration,* both of which are second- or middle-level patterns. In Mann's skill mix theory, human relations skills were most effective in predicting unit effectiveness. These skills, too, are supposedly more important at middle levels of the organization than at higher or lower levels. Therefore, we conclude that neither of the two theories was tested completely since neither was applied to top-level executives. Unfortunately, little exists in the way of systematic study of top-level management. Consequently, we are limited in our discourse to what are essentially case studies.

The role of top management is viewed as encompassing "institutional skills" (Mann), a "systematic viewpoint," and a "charismatic affective capability" (Katz and Kahn). Similarly, the major functions of top management have been viewed as reducing uncertainty in turbulent environments and making value judgments or acts of appreciation (McWhinney, 1968). These functions consist of perceiving reality and making value judgments that correspond to the cognitive and emotional components of top-level leadership described by Katz and Kahn. Top management must be aware of the environment and of potential domains for the organization's activities (see Chapter 7) and must make value-laden decisions. Vickers (1965) has called the latter "appreciative decisions."

Selznick's perspective of institutional leadership

These views of leadership at topmost levels of organizations are derived from the seminal work of Philip Selznick (1957). From Selznick's perspective, leadership entails dealing with organizations as "institutions" (see Chapter 2) and with the related phenomena of "organizational character" and "distinctive competence." Leadership at the top of an organization encourages the transformation of an "engineered" or technical arrangement of parts into a social institution, and, in these terms consists of more than selecting means that can be applied efficiently toward given ends. Leadership consists of selecting ends and means that are efficient and in keeping with these ends. Decisions related to attaining efficiency in operations are distinguished from more critical decisions that involve choices affecting the basic character of the enterprise. In addition to distinctive goals, organizations may come to have cultures, including values and ideologies, that are unique.[3]

---

[3]Increasing efficiency in an inefficient organization may itself become a top-management goal that requires, for its realization, the exercise of creativity and choice and a re-

We have viewed organizations, in part, as rational means toward goals—as technical instruments. These technical instruments also are social entities. Individual members and the organization as a whole may come to take on distinctive ways of making decisions and unique commitments to aims, methods, or clienteles. To some extent, these aspects of the organization can become ends in themselves, rather than remaining wholly rational and therefore completely modifiable elements of a technical instrument (Gouldner, 1959). The process whereby rational organizations become infused with values is termed *institutionalization* (Selznick, 1957). Institutional leadership assumes importance as the organization changes from a wholly rational instrument to a social institution.

The main responsibilities of leaders in top-management positions, therefore, are not found in technical, rational administration but rather in the creation and maintenance of organizational character and instutional integrity. In Selznick's view, integrity is achieved when organizational form and policy become congruent. A unity emerges in which social orientations imbue the organization so that all that is done reflects this orientation to one degree or another. The embodiment of organizational purpose with institutional character can, under favorable conditions, render the organization uniquely competent in its particular undertakings.

This transition from organization to institution goes on unconsciously and inevitably whenever leeway exists in the technical and rational system. Katz and Kahn and others argue that such leeway exists in all organizations by virtue of their openness and reliance on human members.

Leadership can consciously guide this transition from organization to institution. The history of the *New York Times* provides an example of a conscious effort of this sort. The ideals of objectivity and public instruction have been inculcated throughout the organization by means of staff selection and education, controlling the pace of work, managing relationships with advertisers, and defining the paper's role in relation to other newspapers.

An institutional perspective allows the manager to analyze existing and proposed procedures in terms of their expected or actual facilitation or hindrance of the enterprise's attempts to maintain and further its distinctive role and character. Some of the activities undertaken by an organization may be considered neutral in this regard, but they are probably fewer than is commonly thought. At the very least, an activity or technique can be considered neutral when it is suitable for a variety of institutions, while the most desirable activity or technique would be uniquely suited to the character of the enterprise.

As we saw in Chapter 6, organizations move through stages wherein dif-

---

shaping of fundamental organizational perspectives and relationships. But this kind of decision regarding organizational efficiency should not be confused with routine, efficiency-related administrative decisions that are made in lower-level, more rationalized units of the organization.

ferent needs, problems, and environmental relations exist. Top management must examine the historical origins and the growth stages of the organization to determine whether organizational pressures to resist changes in basic character, as well as changes in particular procedures, personnel, and technologies, are appropriate to contemporary problems or if they are aftereffects of earlier situations. Yet, in so doing, management must recognize that basic character and organizational integrity cannot be changed wholly. In some cases, it may be better to start a new organization than to attempt drastic alterations of an old one.

Opportunism and utopianism

Good leaders are known as much for the things they do not do as for what they actually do. Selznick suggests that effective leaders avoid both *opportunism* and *utopianism*. Opportunism is the pursuit of immediate and short-run advantages in the absence of consideration of their ultimate consequences. Utopianism is the flight into abstractions and overgeneralizations that enables leaders to avoid limiting their aspirations according to the strengths, weaknesses, values, and aims of the organization.

To avoid opportunism, leaders must look to the long-run consequences of present advantages to conjecture the effects of present alternatives on the institution's future identity. This, of course, implies that leadership has attended to the prerequisite activities of goal-setting and mission definition, rather than letting the institution drift, whether through a laissez-faire policy or opportunistic maximization of short-run advantages.

The dangers of opportunism are (1) that undertaking short-run, partial adaptations will affect the organization in such a way that in the long run there are unanticipated changes in its character and (2) that the aggregation of opportunistic responses will not result in the attainment of long-range goals. Given the diffuseness of opportunistic leadership, organizational character may become attenuated or confused. According to Selznick, attenuation of character is found in tendencies toward vagueness, in abstraction of the organization's set of predispositions for distinctive competence, and in the consequent inability of this distinctive competence to influence the work of the staff and operating divisions. In actual practice, attenuation of character arises when the formulation of institutional goals is an afterthought or a way of rationalizing activities undertaken in the spirit of opportunism. Selznick describes an organization with a confused character as one possessing a combination of unordered and disharmonious capabilities that render the organization incapable of acting with unity in any particular task.

Opportunism can also result from excessive adaptation to external pressures. Management needs to respond to external pressures, but it must limit its responses to demands that are potent threats to the organization.

Less severe pressures can be reduced through intervention, as is the case when the organization forms coalitions within the environment to counteract these forces.

Leadership must test the environment and ascertain the true strength of threats, rather than respond opportunistically to all and sundry. The lesser threats probably can be ignored without undue consequences. When adaptation to external pressures or opportunities comes to dominate an organization's strategic responses to the environment, the organization ceases to be independent and, as a result, loses its unity and distinctive identity. Of course, sources of external pressure can be co-opted (see Chapter 7), but there is a difference between entering into such relationships consciously, bearing in mind the expected consequences on organizational integrity, and reacting blindly to external stimuli.

The danger of utopianism lies in the tendency for leaders to be seduced by flights into abstractions and away from the necessity of making difficult and often disagreeable choices. In taking flight, they can avoid the critical functions and consequent psychological burdens of leadership. According to Selznick, one source of utopianism is the overgeneralization of organizational purpose. The goal of "making a profit" can be stated so generally as to allow opportunistic reliance on quick returns, easy liquidation, and highly flexible tactics. These behaviors can be undertaken without regard for institutional responsibilities and specific institutional purposes. To rely on overgeneralized purposes is, in fact, to rely on very little. Where the organization's mission has not been defined, decisions will still be made. However, in this event the criteria that enter the decision-making process will do so in an uncontrolled fashion. When this occurs, the organization will be threatened with the disintegration of its basic character.

Another form of utopianism is what Selznick calls the "retreat to technology"—the hope or belief that institutional problems will be resolved through technological advances. The retreat to technology is known as the "technological fix" by environmentalists; it is the belief that advances in technology will alleviate the problems leading to overpopulation, pollution, and the like (see Meadows, Meadows, Randers, and Behrens, 1972). Another example is the tendency of soldiers (such as MacArthur) to advocate military solutions to problems that are in reality political in nature (as former President Truman and others saw it). Selznick terms this *adventurism*—the willingness to commit an organization as a whole to a course of action on the basis of some partial assessment of the situation derived from limited professional or technical perspectives.

In short, responsible leadership attempts to operate between the extremes of utopianism and opportunism. It provides the organization with directions that are in keeping with the organization's basic character and limitations. It seeks to transcend mundane survival concerns by encouraging actions that promote the distinctive identity of the organization.

Leadership and creativity

In addition to the reasoned conservatism that Selznick feels is a sine qua non of responsible leadership, he emphasizes a concern for organizational change and reconstruction. We alluded to this more creative side of top management earlier as "the institutional embodiment of purpose." Establishment of internal policy (the in-building of purpose) entails transforming individuals and groups from neutral, technical units into participants who have a particular set of capabilities, orientations, and commitments. Basically, this is an educational process in which the leader interprets the role and character of the enterprise and develops models through which other organizational members can gain the perspective of the organization as a whole.

There is, unfortunately, little research on this vital function of top management. Hollander and Julian (1969) advocate a reexamination of the Freudian concept of identification in which the leader serves as a conscience for group members and inculcates them with values and ideas. Hollander's research on voting behavior shows that agreement with the president on issues and views of conditions leads to loyal voting behavior; for example, regardless of the actual economic status of voters, if they agree and identify with the president's views on the economic prospects of the nation, they will continue to be loyal in their voting behaviors.

We should emphasize, however, that Selznick's description of the creation of internal policy and the education of organizational members has cognitive as well as emotional elements. The intent of the educational process is to orient members of the organization in such a way that their support of organizational policy has a basis in reason. This consists of more than mechanical or even authoritarian loyalty. Members who come to understand and embody institutional purposes (who intelligently assess long-run goals and the consequences of alternative choices available in the present) will be likely to abide by and support reasoned policy decisions.

Selznick speaks of the usefulness of elaborating and socially integrating these educational processes. A fairly explicit institutional philosophy may be developed that exemplifies the organization's ideals in a rather direct way. Clearly, this creative and constructive educational activity can be a vital aspect of leadership.

DISCUSSION QUESTIONS

1. Discuss the respective functions of leaders of assembly-line workers and members of a planning task force. What similarities and differences would you expect to find?
2. What personality traits do successful leaders hold in common?

3. Give examples of utopianism and opportunism. Is it possible for a leader to err in both extremes? How?
4. People frequently exercise leadership functions even though they lack the formal authority to do so. Can you provide examples of this phenomenon? Do the functions of these informal leaders differ from those of formal leaders?

13

Behavioral Consequences of Organizational Architecture

INTRODUCTION

Similar to environmentalists, who anguish over humanity's careless use of the biosphere and forewarn possible dire consequences, a small but growing number of behavioral scientists have begun to study the effects of the fabricated environment humanity has created. Little is known for certain, and the literature is rife with contradictions. As we have seen, for example, Herzberg and associates (1959) find working conditions a source of dissatisfaction when they are poor, but when they are perceived as good, they do not affect their inhabitants positively. In contrast, R. Buckminster Fuller (1969) envisions a properly structured environment permitting humans to become what they potentially are.

> Don't attempt to reform man. An adequately organized environment will *permit* humanity's original, innate capabilities to become successful. Politics and conventionalized education have sought erroneously to *mold* or *reform* humanity, i.e., the collective individual (p. 320).

Students of organizations are amply motivated to join the search for understanding in this area since average adults spend the bulk of their waking hours within the physical confines of one organization or another. Beyond this, however, this problem interests increasing numbers of scholars, presumably for its intrinsic qualities. Few other areas of study simultaneously unfold the wonderment of humanity's aesthetic nature on one hand and concern for things that are mean and petty on the other. Few other topics lead us to consider problems as complex as the design of cities, neighborhoods, factories, and schools and, at the same time, to discover phenomena of interpersonal behavior from observations of everyday occurrences such as how furniture is arranged in offices. In this light, consider the following quotation from the article "The Top-Down Society: Spatial Decisions in the Organizational World" by F. I. Steele (1971):

> When it comes to physical facilities, the dominant pattern of decision-making in organizations is clearly a top-down, high-control one in which power is seldom shared. This is true of both large and small scale decisions. Large scale decisions about location, general layout, type of decor for offices as a whole, and relative locations of people to one another, are nearly always made at the very top management level. Most influence is exerted by the president and his staff (who control the decisions about facilities) and the maintenance staff (since a major criterion for design is usually whether something will be easy for them to clean). Those at the in-between and lower levels have relatively less influence over their own settings.
>
> Many organizations require that members get clearance before making changes in individual offices or spaces. A case in point: a middle-level manager decided that his desk had faced the door of his office for too long. So he turned it around to face a side wall. Next day he found a memo on his desk from the president's assistant saying that it had been found that the most effective way for managers to arrange their offices was with the desk facing the door so others would feel welcome. He was instructed to return his desk to its old position, with the implied threat of no longer being considered an effective manager if he did not. He later discovered that there was only one exception to the desk-to-the-door rule—and that was the president's office!
>
> At one level, the message our friend received was that he had encroached on the symbolic territory of the president, namely the desk arrangement itself. More importantly, however, he also received a higher-level message: "What I noticed most was not that our desks were so different, but that our freedom to arrange our desks was so different. Can you imagine him (the president) getting a memo because he moved his stuff around?"
>
> This message of lack of control over one's own work surroundings is often institutionalized by company policy. One major national company had a famous design firm create a new building for them, including an "integrated" interior design for all executive offices. A rule was established in writing that no changes could be made in any of the executive offices without the approval of the president.
>
> The pattern of top-down facilities decisions needs changing, because its costs to the organization and its members are relatively high. If organizational development specialists[1] fail to consider the physical system aspect of

---

[1] Namely, change agents, behavioral scientists, and others whose role is to help organizations restructure and adapt, in order to become more responsive to changing needs, changing markets, the changing environment, and so on.

organizational change as well as the social side, their clients' physical systems may drag down efforts for necessary change rather than support them.

Chapter guide

As indicated above, employees frequently lack the authority to arrange the work space to suit their needs.

1. What reasons would management have for withholding this authority?
2. In what ways could the rearrangement of furniture improve an individual's performance?
3. Think of the last several offices you have visited. Can you think of reasons for their layouts?
4. Try to imagine a space in which you could perform your work (or studies) more satisfactorily than you do in the location you ordinarily use. What does this space look like? How large is it? Do you occupy it alone? What kinds of furnishings does it have? How are they arranged? How is it decorated? What kinds of equipment are present? What facilities are nearby? How is it different from the space you generally use? If you can imagine a better place in which to work, how is it that your present facilities are inferior to what they could be?

ARCHITECTURE AND BEHAVIOR

Environmental determinism

In the discussion of technology and power relationships in Chapter 4, we reported that tensions arise when waitresses directly initiate work orders to cooks (Whyte, 1949). Many restaurants, it was noted, reduce the magnitude of this problem by using barriers such as counters or spindles on which waitresses place their written orders for the cooks, who select orders in a sequence that allows them to control the pace at which they work. What is described here, in essence, is an architectural solution to a behavioral problem. The notion that desired behavioral responses can be induced by characteristics of the fabricated physical environment is known as environmental determinism (for example, Perin, 1970).

One of the assumptions of this school of thought is that perceived attributes of the physical environment serve as cues that evoke fairly predictable behavioral responses; for example, an individual's behavior in a church, classroom, or drugstore differs in each of these settings and, to some extent, is predictable. Similarly, one receives and interprets cues on entering nightclubs, conference rooms, and vestry rooms that rigidly define what may or may not be said or done. Ruesch and Kees (1970) explain this observation by asserting that the designers and users of settings endow them with specific meanings through what they term *object language*—"that which is communicated by the incorporation and arrangement of physical objects."

As we shall see, numerous attributes of the physical environment can influence the behavior enacted therein. At this point, however, we will deal with only two attributes: size and location. Size is, perhaps, the most readily discernible feature of architectural structures, and one that produces easily recognizable behavioral responses. The sheer enormity of the interior space in a cathedral can give the individual a sense of insignificance or powerlessness in the broader scheme of celestial events. Hence, it is postulated, feelings of awe and wonder give rise to hushed and respectful behavior. These reactions of people who enter cathedrals are so predictable, in fact, that we have come to expect them. Now, the argument can be made that the behavior manifested is in response to religious sentiments that the place evokes rather than to size per se. While one could argue that religious edifices evoke religious attitudes and behavior in some people, it is also true that similar behavior is evoked by monumental structures that are secular in origin. The Nazi architect, Speer (1971), made effective use of this phenomenon in his creation of a "cathedral" of searchlights under which party members were commemorated before a mass meeting.

The phenomenon described above may also account for our tendency to commemorate significant historical events with statues of monumental proportions. Again, size is assumed to convey a sense of the viewers' own insignificance in comparison with the individual whose likeness towers above them. Architectural design can produce similar effects. The authors are familiar with a suite of executive offices, the doors to which are 14 feet high. The impression on entering these portals is that the events that transpire within are of greater importance than the men and women who participate in them. These doors, as we might expect, lead to the office of the organization's top executives.

The literature provides no conclusive evidence to explain why the scale of an edifice produces the feelings and behavior indicated above, or even that such responses occur in a consistent fashion in the population as a whole; one can speculate that familiar objects constructed larger than those to which we are accustomed evoke memories and responses from childhood. We stand in relation to the 14-foot-high door as adults in much the same way that we stood in relation to ordinary doors as children. This abrupt exposure to oversized objects may serve as a source of cues that trigger the feelings of insignificance, awe, wonder, and insecurity that we felt as children but have outgrown as adults.

Size of work space and group cohesiveness

Size seems to have more complex effects on behavior than those described above. Wells (1972) studied 295 employees working in large and small office spaces of an insurance firm in Manchester, England. While all of these individuals worked on the same floor, 214 of them were housed in a single, open work area while the remaining 81 were distributed among three smaller offices. Social cohesion, one of the variables examined in the study, was measured by determining the number of reciprocal friendship choices among workers in both types of work settings. The findings showed (1) reciprocal friendship choices were directly related to the proximity of workers; (2) workers from the small offices were more likely to prefer co-workers from the same office than from other offices; and (3) social isolates, that is, individuals who were not chosen as workmates by any of their colleagues, occurred more frequently in the smaller spaces than in the larger one. Wells suggests that, social isolates notwithstanding, group cohesion tends to be greater in smaller work spaces than in larger ones.

Research findings such as these provoke skepticism that leads us to question the validity of environmental determinism as a sole guiding principle for environmental design. The environmental deterministic school of thought, oversimplified, suggests that small work spaces foster work group cohesion among other things and, thus, provide us with both means and ends for office design. However, let us explore, in turn, the desirability of the ends suggested and the efficacy of the means. Does group cohesion necessarily lead to the fulfillment of individual and organizational objectives? Perhaps, but how desirable is this outcome when it is brought about in a way that limits communications among different segments of the organization and increases the percentage of social isolates? Obviously, we cannot answer these questions at this point, but only raise them to anticipate the direction our line of inquiry will lead. Let us return, then, to the second reservation expressed in connection with environmental determinism, namely, the efficacy of architectural means in producing desired behavioral outcomes.

Westgate and Regent Hill

An analysis of the proximity of dwelling units as a determinant of social behavior has been provided by Festinger (1972). The focuses of the studies reported here were two housing projects: Westgate, which housed graduate students, and Regent Hill, which formerly housed shipyard workers and subsequently housed a variety of different workers. The student residents of the Westgate project were enthusiastic about their environment and enjoyed active social lives. Dwellings were arranged in U-shaped courts leading off a road. The units at either end of the U, being closest to the roadway, were built to face the road rather than the court, which the others faced. Friendships that developed within the housing project were influenced by two architectural factors according to Festinger—the distances between houses and the directions the houses faced. People tended to establish friendships with next-door neighbors. As the distance between houses increased, the likelihood of friendships diminshed; friendships between residents separated by four or five other houses were rare. Second, residents tended to interact with households that faced theirs. Consequently, individuals living in the end houses, which faced the roadway, tended to have half as many friends in the project as did those whose dwellings faced the court.

Confounding social variables

This finding is startling in itself. Imagine—your social life can be enhanced or diminished by a factor as impersonal as the location of your house, apartment, or dormitory room! Yet, the second study, dealing with the Regent Hill project, contains findings that weaken the case for environmental determinism and cause us to question the efficacy of purely architectural solutions to social problems. Regent Hill was constructed as a government housing project for shipyard workers in 1942. At the time of the study, 40 percent of the residents were old-timers who stayed on after World War II. The rest of the project's inhabitants chose to live there after the war in a time of acute housing shortage when few alternatives were available. According to Festinger, most residents felt that the circumstances that caused them to live in Regent Hill were beyond their control, stemming either from shipyard employment and other war-related conditions or from the housing shortage. Many residents reported that they expected not to like the kinds of people found living in a government housing project and assumed them to be of lower class origin. As a result, residents tended to avoid one another. Forced to choose between associating with neighbors perceived as lower class and social isolation, residents chose the latter.

We found similar dynamics in early attempts to foster better attitudes among whites and blacks by increasing their contacts with one another. At the time, many of us felt that such contacts would break down the stereotypes in which whites cast black people. We assumed that actual face-to-face contact with blacks, rather than the reliance on information from the mass media, friends, family, or white work associates, would remedy these stereotypes.

Considerably subsequent research has shown that contact alone is not sufficient for these purposes. For instance, specially created integrated housing projects did little to change attitudes concerning neighbors of different racial origins. Individuals entered into social contacts with existing beliefs and attitudes intact. Consequent interactions flowing from these social contacts tended to support and confirm existing attitudes and beliefs. This is not altogether surprising; for example, southern whites traditionally had numerous and frequent contacts with blacks without developing more favorable attitudes toward them. In the North, increasing job opportunities for blacks and consequent on-the-job contacts between blacks and whites similarly did little to change attitudes. The contact situations were predefined as interactions between high- and low-status individuals, with influence flowing one way. Only when job-related and other social contacts were established in which blacks had high status could interactions serve as an impetus for attitude changes.

Here, then, evidence suggests that proximity alone does not induce social cohesion, that architectural characteristics do not automatically determine behavioral responses, and that people are not as conditioned by their environment as some would believe. Other individuals form part of one's environment, and the social processes that emerge between them create, as well as derive from, the environment.

Need fulfillment in the environment

Having expressed our reservations about the limitations of environmental determinism, we need to affirm our view that, while physical surroundings exert something less than complete control over the individual's behavior, their influence is substantial. Proshansky and others (1970) observe that people's behavior in a given physical setting is relatively enduring and constant over both time and situation. However, changes in behavior patterns within the setting can be induced by changing either the physical, social, or administrative attributes of the setting. In addition, note that although the physical environment influences behavior, individuals also modify their physical surroundings to accommodate their own need-fulfilling activities. And yet, this distinction is not as clear as it would appear. Arranging one's work setting to enhance the likelihood of certain needs being met, such as the need for esteem, may create conditions that convey status symbols to others and thus elicit desired responses from others. Furthermore, the trappings of power, status, and authority may in turn cause the occupant to experience increased esteem and status and react accordingly. Finally, changes in the physical environment may convey the intentions of such changes (Proshansky, Ittelson, and Rivlin, 1970); when a change in behavior follows alteration of the physical environment, we must inquire whether behavior was altered in response to the changed surroundings per se or in response to the actors' assumptions concerning the behaviors these changes were intended to produce (Ruesch and Kees, 1970). Does the subordinate show more deference to a manager with a large office than to a second manager with a smaller one because size induces deference or because size is a symbol that tells the subordinate how to behave?

We need not belabor these points, but merely emphasize them as indications of the interrelationships that can exist among the physical, social, technical, and other characteristics of the work setting. Having made these points, let us explore the functions that physical environments can serve in the processes of need fulfillment. For this purpose, we will use a taxonomy of needs already described in some detail, Maslow's need hierarchy (1970).

The physiological needs

The observation that physical environments are designed, in part, to provide for the fulfillment of certain physiological needs is obvious. Office buildings protect inhabitants from the elements and provide adequate lighting, drinking and washing water, rest rooms, and, on occasion, restaurants and coffee shops.

Less obvious is the notion that behavior can be predisposed in part by the inclusion or omission of elements in the physical environment that serve the lower order needs. The exclusion of drinking fountains, lavatories, or resting places tends to limit the amount of time that an individual is willing to spend in an environment. For example, shops whose customers are expected to browse and take their time selecting purchases may include comfortable furniture and a coffee urn. Alternatively, other business establishments encourage a high turnover of clientele by eliminating access to lavatories and resting places.

The need for safety

Attempts to fulfill the need for safety (or security) are apparent in the incorporation of locks, fire escapes, sprinkler systems, closed-circuit television monitoring systems, and similar security and safety features in offices, schools, and factories.

Concerns for security, however, range beyond attempts to minimize the potential for physical harm and include regard for organizational and social protections as well. For example, some factories and laboratories use elaborate security measures to protect their products and processes from industrial espionage. Similar measures frequently are used to shield certain organizational activities from clients and even other members of the organization.

There has been a growing awareness among both architects and managers of the interdependence of social and physical factors in providing protection from physical harm. Despite extensive security arrangements, banks and merchants are robbed and apartment dwellers are mugged and raped. Jane Jacobs in *The Death and Life of American Cities* (1969) discusses the need for social density as a protection against crime. Criminals are reluctant to act where there are many people about because of the increased likelihood of apprehension. The movement of slum dwellers from areas with small shops open at all times to antiseptic urban-renewal projects is a case in point. In the latter surroundings, there may be no shopkeeper or stream of customers to see a mugging or to notice a loitering stranger.

The importance of the social parts of social density—requiring both proper physical arrangements (for example, in Westgate) and social arrangements (discussed below under "The Needs for Love and Belongingness")—has been illustrated by shocking cases of crimes observed by many people (even 50 or more in the case of Kitty Genovese in New York City), none of whom apparently was socially involved enough to help or even call the police! The high crime rates in high-rise urban renewal buildings supposedly are due to this lack of *social* density. In contrast, if a building is only four or five stories (and houses only 100 or so people), there is sufficient social density to ensure that strangers are noticed and that there is sufficient commitment to others to foster protective actions.

Erving Goffman (1959) provides a fascinating description of the elaborate measures that are undertaken to control access to interpersonal processes in physical and social settings. Part of the substance of everyday life, according to Goffman, is the management of the roles that we play in various social situations. As was mentioned in Chapter 10, social roles prescribe the expected behaviors and personal relationships of individuals with respect to other individuals who maintain other, related social positions. The management of a role consists of controlling the ways in which we express our role to others. This expression is both "given" through verbal communications and "given off" by the setting in which the role is enacted, mode of dress, physical gesture, and other nonverbal behavior.

Physical environments frequently are designed to provide decor and props that support (give off) the roles that are to be enacted therein, segregated areas where incompatible roles can be assumed, unnoticed by the inhabitants of other areas, and "backstage" areas where the "actors" can relax their roles, repair their appearances, and engage in additional behaviors unrelated to those of the "front stage." In this manner, the arrangement of physical space isolates various roles from their respective audiences and, in so doing, establishes subtle regions of security.

The needs for love and belongingness

As was illustrated by the study of the Westgate and Regent Hill housing projects, the proximity and physical orientation of architectural spaces can both encourage and impede the formation of interpersonal bonds. Similarly, Wells's study of cohesion in large and small office spaces indicates that the physical dimensions of work areas may bear directly on the social relations housed therein.

The factors in the physical environment that help and hinder the development of social interactions may be as gross as the inclusion or exclusion of suitable places in which to congregate. Alternatively, characteristics of meeting places as subtle as the arrangement of seats and tables may, to a lesser extent, serve the same ends; for example, Robert Sommer (1969) provides evidence that individuals seated in line, next to one another, are less likely to converse than when they are seated facing one another across the corner of a table. Sommer describes an old-age home in which the location of furniture required residents to seat themselves in rows with their backs to a wall. After introducing tables and locating the chairs around them, Sommer observed that the rate of interactions nearly doubled.

However, this change, which was obviously to the benefit of the elderly residents, was resisted by staff and service personnel. The new arrangement gave the dayroom a "cluttered" look and made it more difficult to clean than it had been when the chairs were arranged in rows. Furthermore, carts and trays, which previously had been moved through the center of the room, had to be rerouted, causing the staff an inconvenience. This observation is similar to that of Steele (1971) who, at the introduction of this chapter, is quoted as follows: "Most influence is exerted by the president and his staff (who control the decisions about facilities) and the maintenance staff (since a major criterion for design is usually whether something will be easy for them to clean)."

The need for self-esteem and group esteem

Each of us is surrounded by an invisible sphere that Edward Hall (1966) and others call *personal space*. The size of this sphere and the kinds of people admitted within it vary from one culture to another.

Beyond the sphere of personal space is another zone that we usually use unknowingly to establish our status vis-à-vis second and third parties. This second space is measured in terms of social distance (Edward Hall, 1966, 1972; Sommer, 1969); that is, the difference in status between two people is roughly proportional to the distance that they maintain between one another (social distance) during an interaction. Colleagues who are on good terms with one another will tend to stand closer together than will either of the individuals with a superior.

Office designs frequently employ social distance to regulate the status relationships of occupants. We have indicated that the size of an individual's desk relative to those of others usually is taken as an indication of status. Yet, beyond the visual cues provided by the proportions of office furniture, size provides a means for establishing social distance. The larger an individual's desk, the further the visitor must remain from the officeholder, and consequently, the greater the social distance both parties experience. The authors are familiar with the office of an executive whose desk is of monumental proportions and is constructed in the shape of a hexagon with the back side removed for access. Enclosed by the desk as he is, the executive gives the appearance of being remote and completely unapproachable.

Height is similarly used to convey status in our culture. "Higher ups" in organizations occasionally have their desks mounted on platforms that elevate them above those who are seated before them. The effect achieved in this manner may be similar to that described above in the discussion of the oversized door.

The more expensive the furnishings of an office, the more status we attribute to its occupant. "A title on the door rates a Bigelow on the floor." Access to "private" spaces such as executive washrooms, elevators, faculty lounges, and dining rooms renders inferior status to those denied entry. The security of the office itself—giving privacy and distance—is important. Finally, individuals who are free to control and manipulate their own surroundings and those of others are perceived to have greater status than individuals who lack these freedoms.

These acts, as well as others, have acquired symbolic meanings in our society and fall into the general category of status symbols. Other status symbols include having one's own company car, secretary, titles, industry and company certificates (for example, "one-million club," "Admiral of the Flagship Fleet"), and the like.

The need for self-actualization

According to Maslow (1970), individuals who are fulfilling their need for self-actualization are becoming what they are potentially. This implies that they are learning, but what is more, according to Maslow; "Self-actualizing individuals (more matured, more fully human), by definition, already suitably gratified in their basic needs, are now motivated in other higher ways, to be called 'metamotivations' " (1971, p. 299).

Maslow postulates that metamotives (unlike those associated with the fulfillment of the needs described in the hierarchy below self-actualization) are experienced as metaneeds and become prepotent in the self-actualizing person. Metaneeds include the needs for truth, goodness, beauty, wholeness, uniqueness, perfection, justice, playfulness, and self-sufficiency among others (Maslow, 1971, pp. 133–36). What sorts of physical environments are needed to permit the self-actualizing individual to experience goodness, truth, and beauty? Although we cannot answer this question directly, we can learn of the effects of physical environments on learning processes and of aesthetic qualities of the environment on the average individual's behavior.

The fact that our surroundings affect our ability to learn has been demonstrated by Tognoli (1973) in a study that relates an individual's ability to remember data with attributes of the surroundings in which these data are learned. Tognoli found that the presence or absence of windows and other embellishments in a room were correlated with the occupant's ability to recall what had been learned therein.

The effects of the aesthetic qualities of environments on the behaviors of subjects have been studied in an experiment by Maslow and Mintz (1972). The experimenters furnished three rooms, rendering one of them beautiful (in the eyes of the experimenters), the second ugly, and the last in-between or "average." Interviewers, who were unaware of the true intent of the study in question, met with subjects in each of the three rooms. The interviewers showed each subject ten negative print photographs of human faces that were to be rated on two six-point scales. Subjects rated each face according to the degrees of fatigue/energy and displeasure/well-being that the face seemed to express.

The subjects in the beautiful room gave significantly higher ratings (that is, rated the faces as being expressive of more energy and greater well-being) than did subjects in either the average or ugly room. Average-room scores were also higher than those obtained in the ugly room, but not significantly so. While the findings obtained in the average room were consistently in the predicted directions, the lack of significance noted above leads to speculation that average rooms and offices produce effects that are more like those produced by ugly surroundings than by beautiful ones.

While the experiment described above was in progress, a second experiment was under way, one in which the interviewers served as unknowing subjects (N. L. Mintz, 1972). On the basis of direct observation and observational notes, it was found that interviewers spent less time in the ugly room (finished their testing more rapidly) than they did in the beautiful room. Furthermore, observational notes indicated that, when working in the ugly room, interviewers experienced monotony, fatigue, headache, discontent, irritability, and hostility, and tended to avoid the room. Conversely, when working in the beautiful room they experienced feelings of comfort, pleasure, enjoyment, importance, energy, and the desire to continue their activity. From these findings, Mintz concludes that:

> ... visual-aesthetic surroundings (as represented by the "beautiful room" and the "ugly room") can have significant effects upon persons exposed to them. These effects are not limited either to "laboratory" situations or to initial adjustments, but can be found under naturalistic circumstances of considerable duration (1972, p. 227).

One final observation is that individuals tend to seek fulfillment of their needs in ways that are consistent with the values they hold (Ullrich, 1972). When people are free to arrange and decorate their work spaces to suit their needs, one finds a tendency for the physical appearance of the work space to reflect the values of its occupant; for example, values related to power and politics will manifest themselves in furniture arrangements, posters, and the like. Similarly, the aesthetic values will become apparent in the works of art with which some people choose to decorate their offices. It may be argued that, within practical limits, individuals who are able to give expression to their values in their work will be better able to fulfill their needs consistent with these values than will those who are inhibited in such expression. Organizations that do not permit the occupant of a work space to alter its arrangement and decorum to suit one's needs and values may inadvertently frustrate that person's need-fulfilling activities.

DESIGNING WORK SPACES

Guidelines for the design of work environments

Although it has not been possible in the limited space of this chapter to provide readers with sufficient information to make them designers of schools or factories, we have suggested ways in which intelligent modifications can be made to limit areas in the workplace. By way of illustration, we can turn to the problem of office design.

The guidelines that we suggest for making systematic use of the material presented above are relatively simple.

1. Ascertain the objectives that are sought in a given workplace (for example, an office).
2. Determine the activities undertaken to produce these outcomes.
3. Rate the physical environment according to its contribution to
   a. supporting these activities.
   b. fostering the ends to which these activities are addressed.
4. Alter the workplace to improve the two criteria mentioned above.

To illustrate a method for using these guidelines, we will consider some rather elementary modifications to the office space of a college professor. Professors engage in a variety of activities in their offices. Obviously, they prepare lectures, write books and articles, counsel students, give tutorial help, and collaborate with colleagues on research projects, committee agenda, and other matters of business. They also read, reflect on theoretical and practical problems, daydream, engage in informal bull sessions, drink coffee, gripe, and involve themselves in a host of other activities. In actual practice, we would list the objectives that are sought by the officeholder and rank order them according to their relative importance. (An example is provided in Table 13-1.) This implies that the planner will work cooperatively with the officeholder, for it is unreasonable to assume that the former will, a priori, take into account the idiosyncratic needs of the latter.

Having rank ordered objectives, the planner in collaboration with the officeholder will identify the activities associated with the pursuit of each. Next, the physical attributes to the office will be rated according to the extent to which they impede or enhance the execution of these activities and the extent to which these activities, as modified by their physical surroundings, serve the officeholder's objectives. Less-than-satisfactory ratings will become the focus for office modification, with the bulk of effort applied to the higher priority objectives.

By way of illustration, let us return to the problem of the college professor's office. For the sake of simplicity, we will limit the number of objectives sought at work to three: teaching, lecture preparation, and writing.

TABLE 13-1
Objectives and activities

Rank-ordered objectives	Associated activities
1. Teaching	Tutorial instruction
	Small group instruction
2. Lecture preparation	Reading
	Thinking
	Writing
	Preparing visual aids
3. Writing	Reading
	Thinking
	Small group discussion
	Writing
	Drawing

In Figure 13-1, office layout 1 represents the work space assigned to one of the authors several years ago. Office layout 2 represents one possible improvement to the original layout that has been designed to foster the attainment of the three objectives listed above. In actual fact, the original layout remained unchanged by the author. This was primarily because of two factors. At the time, the author was unfamiliar with the literature on the design of physical facilities and consequently insensitive to both the limitations of the office and its potential. Second, the author was subject to a common misperception, namely, that of viewing the office as a "Pseudo-Fixed-Furniture Space" (Steele, 1973). In other words, we tend to take existing furniture and the like as fixed when, in fact, they are readily movable.

In any event, office layout 1 was experienced as being unsatisfactory even though no active steps were undertaken to remedy the sources of dissatisfaction. In the first place, the arrangement of the furniture was unsuitable for tutorial and small group instruction. The room contained no blackboard on which ideas could be represented and explained. Students seated across the desk from their teacher could not view materials on the latter's desk. What is probably most important, a rather great social distance was established between the students seated in chairs 2 and 3 and the teacher in chair 1. Teaching consists of helping others to understand concepts and procedures. Yet, it is difficult at best to help those whom one intimidates. The prestige of college professors and the social distance they maintain from students can inhibit the open and free expression of ideas.

For these and other reasons, the desk has been moved in layout 2 to a side wall, and a round table has been introduced. With chairs located around the table, the officeholder is afforded the following options in arranging social interactions. The professor can invite students to sit in chairs 2 or 3 and move chair 1 to join them at the table. The professor can indicate to a visitor to sit in chair 4, placing the student at a greater social distance than in the former case, or can move chair 4 up to the desk so that the visitor can look over the professor's shoulder, so to speak. The last option provides the least

FIGURE 13–1
An illustration of office redesign

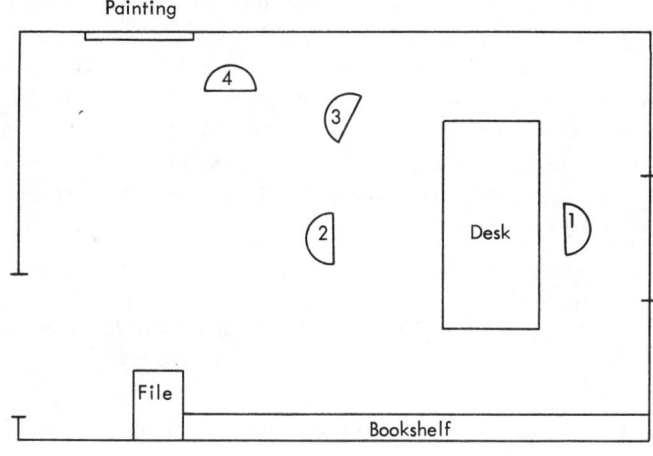

Office layout 1

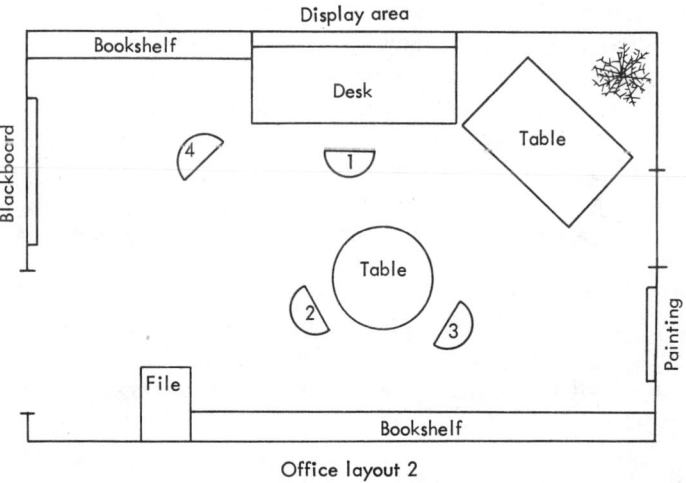

Office layout 2

social distance. A blackboard has been introduced as an aid to both teaching and thinking.

The problem of reconfigurating the environment to foster the preparation of lectures is addressed in part by moving the desk to the side of the room. Thinking is aided by the presence of cues that bring to mind informaiton that is relevant to the problem under consideration. For this reason, the wall above the desk has been converted to a display area onto which can be attached charts, lists, graphs, pictures, and the like. This space over the desk, which is normally unused, thus becomes an information display area. As Propst (1968) says:

> The suppression of relevant display is one of the most serious deficiencies in our present office culture and one of the factors most assuredly due for correction.... An office with no relevant visual display deprives the human performer of a spectacular recall tool: the human eye as a receptor for the mind (p. 21).

A second bookshelf has been added to the left of the desk for the same reason. The spines of books bearing their titles remind us of their contents. The addition of the blackboard also aids activities that support this objective. Outlines often are worked out at a board rather than on paper. For one thing, the option to work standing up is a valuable one, once discovered. Thinking may be invigorated by changes in posture and activity. Hemingway and Churchill frequently worked while standing at their desks.

A table has been added to provide a second work station. Different tasks require different supporting facilities and semipermanent work stations often are needed for separate activities. The production of a book or article is a lengthy process for the author. In addition to work spaces that are used for a number of changing activities, the author requires a station that can be permanently set up with the accouterments of the trade—a typewriter, papers, drawing equipment, and a good dictionary.

Here, then, is a modest scheme for improving the physical environment of a college professor. Obviously, teachers pursue activities and objectives other than those used to illustrate the design guidelines put forth here. Consequently, our exercise has been less extensive than would be the case in actual practice. Yet, the point is that improvements to the design of physical facilities are well within the scope of ability of the average manager.

Physical design in the larger organization

The individual manager probably will find fewer opportunities to design large spaces. Major physical plants often are perceived as an especially visible sunk cost. Not only is the organization viewed as being stuck with the present design, it is also difficult to make a strong case that a new physical design will, by itself, improve organizational effectiveness. In contrast to common beliefs in the importance of good communications or good social relations, a good executive lounge or a good building for a sales or marketing department is seen as less important. While there has been little systematic study of the effects of physical arrangements on organizational effectiveness, we have cited some case studies as well as anecdotal evidence above, and shall provide some preliminary notes here on how physical designs may be important for the large organization.

A contingency approach to design

Here we shall assume a contingency model of the role of physical elements in relation to technology, structure, goals, or environment. An appropriate physical design matches the other impinging elements, and these relationships are conducive to effective organizational functioning. Above we suggested that physical arrangements that fit people variables will be conducive to effectiveness (or at least satisfactions that encourage participation in the workplace, if not the motivation to produce more). Similarly, there must be a good fit between the physical arrangements and technological and environmental dimensions.

A major problem lies in defining the dependent physical variables—developing a taxonomy of organizational variables that have some systematic relation to one another. Because there is no accepted theory of physical design, we must rely on interpretations of physical variables in terms of social variables such as communication, liking, and status.

While physical size itself may not have readily understandable implications for behavior in organizations, we may interpret size in terms of social cohesiveness, discuss the fit of size with the degree of cohesiveness required for the attainment of a certain goal, and then judge whether the existing fit is conducive to organizational effectiveness.

Technology clearly has implications for architectural design, and vice versa. A mass-production technology requires large-scale physical arrangements, while certain craftwork may be undertaken in smaller facilities. Mass production or routine technologies generally have special work flow requirements, too. The programmed search and low variability that characterize routine technology enable high degrees of operating efficiency through rationalization of work processes. In our discussions of the longwall method of coal mining and the waitress versus cook conflict (Chapter 4), we found that such dependencies may have destructive effects on social relations if power and status are not carefully articulated with these dependencies. Alternatively, assembly-line operations have made workers dependent on their assembly line—on the *physical* work flow and only indirectly on other people. That is to say, workers on an assembly line are isolated from one another because noise and the demanding pace of work prevent communication. They coordinate their work with the activity of the conveyor belt and its materials.

At the extreme, such mass-production technology makes the worker a cog in a machine. It requires that the worker act as an object interacting with other objects, rather than as a social being having the various needs we have discussed above. Of course, these needs must be met, and it would seem that one important question is whether they are met primarily away from the assembly line (on a 5-minute coffee break or a 30-minute lunch period) or whether they are met on the job, too. We have already discussed job enrichment as a means whereby technology can be changed to accommodate some of the people variables. However, the manipulation of physical variables offers an additional way in which some needs can be met, perhaps without changing the routine nature of the technology and losing its advantages. The use of piped-in music, stimulating paint schemes, and alcoves for social interaction at the work site are examples.

The congruence between physical arrangements and formal (and informal) structure is important, too. In discussing formal structure, we described different arrangements of departments by function, product, process, or geography to emphasize one kind of coordination over the other. As described above, physical arrangements can foster organization by product by ensuring that distances are minimal between the members of different functions who are assigned to the same product line. However, such changes do not always produce the results intended, for example, Kover (1963) describes how an advertising agency reorganized from function to product. The account executives began to work with their own creative staff along product or account lines, and the assignment of offices was changed accordingly. Instead of working in a department consisting wholly of creative personnel, the artists and writers found themselves parceled out to various different product lines or accounts. According to Kover, the physical inability of creative staff to interact with one another, to exchange ideas and social support, was a major factor leading to a high level of turnover. This is understandable in light of Lawrence and Lorsch's (1967) report that managers in a product-organized firm appeared to be more effective in coordinating the work of different functions around the particular product line, but showed higher levels of tension and irritation than managers in a similar, less effective firm organized by function. This firm afforded the security and support of working with members of one's own function who possessed similar values, orientations, and styles of behaving. If, in fact, the physical arrangements in the advertising reorganization were a major factor in creating turnover, we wonder if supplemental physical arrangements, such as a lounge for coffee breaks or separate lunchrooms enabling a certain minimal amount of interaction among creative staff, might have alleviated the problems encountered.

Let us examine next an example of the interrelations between technology, structure, and physical arrangements. From Perrow's analysis in Chapter 4, we recall that a nonroutine technology requires coordination by feedback within both middle and lower hierarchical levels, as well as interdependence within groups. This type of social system is created by means of the mutual influence found in Likert's cohesive groups (Chapter 3) or in the autonomous work groups described by the Tavistock researchers. We have seen how physical arrangements can be designed to enhance this kind of social structure and, thereby, the functioning of an organization with a nonroutine technology. When a research institute headed by Rensis Likert was given an opportunity to design its own new building, it did in fact design a building with a great deal of open floor space conducive to high social density—one in which the staff could interact and get to know one another. Each floor had perhaps a dozen courtyards or open spaces around which a program director and a number of study directors or assistant study directors had offices, all facing inward onto the open space. A corresponding number of secretarial, clerical, and computational staff members had desks in the courtyard. The entire arrangement encouraged interaction across hierarchical levels within a project, as well as between staff members who were on the same level, but working on different projects. Furthermore, in walking from the central elevators to one's courtyard and workplace, one had to pass through the courtyards of other related programs. These programs comprised a research center within the institute. The arrangement thereby fostered additional, but less intensive, contacts with those in related programs. Finally, all of the institute staff used the same entrance, elevators, lunchroom, and library. Thus, contacts and identification with the institute were enhanced. A possibly serendipitous arrangement was achieved by locating the various business or administrative offices on the first floor, between the entrance and the elevators, encouraging contacts between administrative and professional staff and possibly fostering harmonious relations between these two often-warring functional groups.

Physical designs for diagnosis

While the manager may have little opportunity to design the physical arrangements for an entire organization, knowledge and awareness of physical components are useful diagnostic tools. We have suggested that congruency between physical arrangements and technology, structure, people, goals, and environment can lead to organizational effectiveness. If this is true, it is also likely that there will be *some* existing congruency in these elements. We suggest that effective organizations grow and acquire resources (see Chapter 3) and use these resources to arrange the organization in ways that are still more effective. For this reason, congruence between physical layout and other organizational variables is likely, and physical layout may provide a quick diagnosis of these variables.

Let us try out this reasoning. Take a business school. One might ask where the dean's office is located—secluded from others at the top of a large high-rise building, similar to that of the head of a large corporation, or is it next to the main office, which includes the secretarial pool, student admissions office, and the like, as a chief development engineer's office might be located near the offices and workplace of the engineering staff and supporting technicians?

The first physical layout would suggest that the former business school is structured in some ways like a business and has a relatively routine technology. Hierarchical differences are emphasized; students have relatively little power; analyzable search programs and a homogeneous student body may be emphasized. There will be many rules and work will be done by the book. Students may be treated more or less alike. The second school places less distance between its dean and its staff and students, and its structure and technology may render it more like a research institute than the first business school.

Of course, many of the physical accouterments have symbolic values determined by the local culture. Consequently, the outside observer cannot readily discern the meaning of all of the arrangements perceived. However, valid diagnostic signs, other than the location of the top executive's office, generally can be found. We can cite the arrangement of parking spaces—whether assigned by name or category of staff, or first come, first serve, or perhaps by some differential arrangements across hierarchical levels, or by departments or professional groups. The same applies to the number and arrangement of different lunchrooms, sport facilities, and the like, and their assignment.

Two interesting studies have been made of the physical diagnostic signs found in financial institutions (Coffey, Athos, and Reynolds, 1975; Wolf, 1971). Wolf describes a number of physical dimensions that enabled him to distinguish the goals and organizational character of two savings and loan associations. One was situated in a shopping center in a modern, functional building, draped with a large banner advertising the current interest rate. The chief executive had a modern desk with a "clean" top, clear of papers. The lunchroom for the staff was small and spartan. The other savings and loan association was located in an older, downtown neighborhood and housed in an older, more traditional, relatively unobtrusive building. The interior was richly furnished with statuary and portraits of the founders. There were flowers on desks and beautiful wood paneling on walls. Staff facilities were comfortable.

As one might expect, the former bank emphasized profitability and had a brash, growth-oriented strategy, while the latter bank had a goal of carrying on traditions with an emphasis on security. Its character included a strong component of the workplace as a home away from home.

Physical designs in time and space

Finally, we may observe that physical arrangements can be designed to transcend the organization's boundaries and its present existence. Exemplifying the time dimension, Sears designed its new Chicago headquarters building, now the tallest in the world, so that it can lease out space it will need later as the firm grows in the remaining decades of this century. It has arranged office suites so that it can expand easily by taking over contiguous and integrated facilities from leaseholders.

Geographic location, including proximity to important markets and supplies, is important, too. This is even true in the mass-market publishing industry that does not rely on geographically delimited suppliers or markets. One reason for demise of the magazine *Saturday Review* may have been its movement away from New York and the stimulation and information provided by other editorial and management personnel found primarily there. In contrast, the editor of *Transaction* (now *Society*), Irving L. Horowitz, argues that movement from Washington University, St. Louis, to Rutgers University, New Brunswick, New Jersey, 35 miles from New York, was useful in providing physical access to New York and the relevant personnel found in sufficient and critical numbers only there.

These examples support the argument that face-to-face contacts cannot be replaced entirely by use of letters or telephones. It is said that the growth of Chicago's O'Hare airport and the demise of Midway airport, despite strenuous opposition by Mayor Daley, was due to the need for executives from different parts of the country to fly in and talk face-to-face and then fly out, all in the same day. O'Hare has the airline connections plus the meeting facilities for this face-to-face contact. Midway is closer to downtown but does not have the meeting facilities and connections. O'Hare airport serves as a "conference room" for geographically widespread firms or firms with geographically extensive contacts with other organizations. A firm with these needs does well to site its headquarters and branch operations in towns with good airline connections to a centrally located airport that may serve as its "conference room."

DISCUSSION QUESTIONS

1. What is meant by the term *object language?* Select a room such as the one in which you live or an office and prepare a glossary of the object language found therein.
2. How does the architecture of the room selected for the prior question enhance or impede behavior? Are these intended consequences of the architecture or unforeseen results?
3. Redesign this space to make it more functional without making major structural changes (for example, without moving walls, doors, and so on).
4. How practical are such redesign efforts in ongoing organizations? How desirable are they?

SECTION IV

Criteria for Evaluating Organizations

Chapter 14
Criteria for Evaluating Organizations

PREMISE

Organizations are evaluated daily. For example, while colleges and universities are evaluated periodically by accrediting agencies, they are also evaluated by organizations that fund research or engage in philanthropy, by prospective faculty members and administrators, and of course by prospective students. Business organizations, health-care institutions, and governmental agencies similarly are evaluated by other organizations and members of the general public.

As a manager, you may be called on to evaluate potential vendors, customers, competitors, or candidates for merger or acquisition. More important, you will need to evaluate your own organization to assess its performance and to identify areas in need of improvement. As we shall discover in the next chapter, this is exceedingly difficult to do, for the criteria typically used to evaluate organizations leave much to be desired.

14

Criteria for Evaluating Organizations

INTRODUCTION

Our interest in organizations will lead us back to detailed examinations of processes that occur within them. For the present, however, we shall step back and view them as complete entities again to gain a measure of perspective. While gaining perspective at this point will provide a framework for our concluding discussion of organizational change, it will not be a simple task. The more we aggregate phenomena (the more comprehensive our study becomes), the more abstract we must be. Furthermore, systematic, scientific study becomes more difficult as the objects of study increase in complexity. For this reason, we will marshal fewer facts and, indeed, arrive at fewer conclusions in our analysis of organizations as social entities than we did, for example, in our study of individual behavior in organizations.

Let us begin by asking how we can evaluate an organization as a social entity. At first glance we may respond that the successful attainment of the organization's goals is the sole criterion by which to measure effectiveness. Profitability for business firms and the delivery of quality health care for hospitals are examples of hallmarks that come to mind. For a beginning, let us test the notion that effectiveness can be measured by goal attainment. The following portion of a recent *Fortune* article will cast some doubt on the notion:

> ... By 1970, too, the leasing companies were depriving I.B.M. of substantial rental revenues. Back in the late 1960s the lessors went on a buying spree, purchasing almost $3 billion worth of 360 computers—or about 12 percent of the 360s installed. Those purchases contributed to the big earnings bulge that I.B.M. registered in 1967 and 1968, but they came at the expense of future rental revenues. The sales-to-rental formula is generally four to one—i.e., a computer that sells for $1 million rents for $250,000 a year. In the long run, rentals obviously bring in a lot more money than outright sales. At least, that has been the experience in the past. (There are still about 3,900 I.B.M. Series 1400 computers out on rental that were manufactured in the late 1950s.) With the introduction of the 360, the leasing companies started getting under I.B.M.'s skin, and Tom Watson demanded that a strategy be formulated to combat them.
>
> ... The 370 [computer] was designed to accomplish a number of diverse goals, all of which would lead to restoration of I.B.M.'s customary high profitability while achieving a tightening of control over I.B.M. installations. When I.B.M. introduced its 360 computers in 1965, according to Watson, the company realized a net income gain of 20 percent on an installation basis by replacing older computers. It expected to repeat that performance with the 370. At the same time, 370 computers were designed to be compatible with the 360 machines in terms of software, so that the users' huge investment in programming would be protected. The 370 in essence was intended to make 360 programs run faster; the transition to the new machines was to be painless compared to the disruptive way the 360 had been introduced.
>
> Because of its price and design, the 370 packed a two-pronged wallop at those old enemies—the leasing companies and the small manufacturers. To thwart peripherals makers, controls for disk drives were built into the main frames of two 370 models. And the leasing companies were surprised to find that the sales price made re-lease of the new machines unattractive. The 370 is intended to be around for perhaps a decade. So I.B.M. wanted most users to rent the machines—from I.B.M. "As long as we operate legally and fairly," says Watson, "it's not incumbent on us to price our machines to allow the leasing companies to take away our inventory." For rival mainframe manufacturers like Honeywell and Burroughs the surprise in the 370 was the use of semiconductor main memories in two of its five models. Finally, the 370 was viewed by I.B.M. as a stimulant to its own sales force. Says Watson: "You have to keep feeding them new things to keep their morale up."
>
> This carefully laid strategy, however, boomeranged. The 370 hit hardest of all, not I.B.M.'s competitors, but I.B.M.'s own rental base. To start with, the timing of the 370 proved disastrous; announced in June, 1970, and first delivery was made in January, 1971, squarely in the middle of the recession. The timing depended to a large extent on the fact that by 1970 most of the

370 building blocks were in hand, for development had begun as far back as 1965. "We had invested a few hundred million dollars in the 370," says Watson. "Actually, we could stop any product a month before we plan to announce it. But we were reckoning that the economy was going to resume its growth, and it took us a long time to recognize that we were in a serious recession."

... As for those archenemies—the leasing companies—they may eventually disappear, but right now they are doing a lot of damage to I.B.M. The 370 forced the leasing firms into a scramble. Leases on many of the machines they acquired in the 1960's are now expiring, and they are eager to farm out these computers on "second" leases, usually at exceedingly low rates, or even to sell them for half their original price. "Nobody is going to rent 360's from I.B.M. anymore," says one computer user. "The leasing company now comes in and says that they'll give you the same central processing unit you are paying $15,000 for in rentals for $8,000 a month."

Similarly, the strategy against the independents turned out to be far from a resounding success, even though Learson predicts that some of I.B.M.'s competitors in peripherals will "go under." The independents haven't yet matched I.B.M.'s new 370 peripherals with their own models. But they continue to offer attractively priced devices that further enhance the value of the 360's to sophisticated users. Observing the 370 versus 360 clash, one executive remarks: "I.B.M. now has its first real competition in the computer business—and the competition is I.B.M."

Looking back, Watson says he is sure that "if we had to do it over again, I would do the same thing. We were committed and the decision had been made." As so often happens with the introduction of a new product, in the case of the 370 the marketing executives won the early round over the engineers. Technical men at I.B.M. would have preferred to have equipped the whole range of 370 computers with semiconductor memories at the same time. That would have made the 370 series more versatile, more powerful, and technologically far ahead of any other computer. But I.B.M.'s marketing men wanted to rush to the customers with the first available new product. Frank Cary puts the reasoning this way: "In the rental business, you either replace yourself or someone else will do it for you." The upshot was that I.B.M.'s two major objectives, to maintain its dominant position in the industry and to make the maximum profit while doing so, clashed painfully (Bylinski, 1972).

Chapter Guide

IBM is an unparalleled organization in many ways and has affected the lives of all of us in one way or another. As awesome as the company is, however, it resembles other organizations, even schools, hospitals, and grocery stores. Before examining characteristics that determine an organization's effectiveness as a social entity, we need to raise some questions.

1. Is continued growth a goal of the IBM Corporation? Is it a goal of all organizations? What are the limits to organizational growth?

2. In what ways does the firm's environment seem to be changing? How did the introduction of the 370 attempt to deal with this change?
3. Is the morale of salesmen a company goal? Is it a goal in the same sense that profitability may be?
4. The story concludes with the statement that "I.B.M.'s two major objectives, to maintain its dominant position in the industry and to make the maximum profit while doing so, clashed painfully." Is it rational to have objectives that clash? Is this phenomenon common? How does a firm go about maximizing profits? How, in fact, does it know at any point in time that it is (or is not) maximizing profits?

INTERNAL CRITERIA

The rational and system models

Our earlier discussions of two dissimilar models of organizations provide a starting point for evaluating organizations. The rational model of organization suggests an evaluation in terms of efficacy in achieving stated goals. In contrast, the system model suggests that survival of the system and consequently the optimal articulation of efforts and resources to satisfy system needs (including environmental contingencies) are important criteria. We will attempt to resolve these conflicting approaches to evaluation. However, please bear in mind that the means with which to evaluate organizations will elude us. The concept of organizational effectiveness "... is an underlying construct that has no necessary and sufficient *operational* definition but that constitutes a model or theory of what organizational effectiveness is" (Campbell, 1977, p. 18). Yet, as is the case with other theories, the construct will lead us in potentially useful directions.

A goal view of organizational effectiveness

If we follow the rational model of organizations, we must develop measures of goal attainment. At first glance, this appears a simple task. Profitability and return on investment (ROI) calculations are readily available. However, as we saw in Chapter 6, the goals of business organizations range far beyond profitability and ROI. Some business organizations are concerned primarily with stability (or risk); some want quantity of production (or quality). Furthermore, statistics comparable to profitability calculations generally are unavailable in other kinds of organizations such as hospitals, schools, and governmental agencies. For these reasons, we are impelled to learn more about other kinds of organizational goals and to develop corresponding measures of achievement.

Criterion measures

An apparently successful method poles organizational members and qualified outsiders for their perceptions of the organization's goals and its performance in attaining them. One such technique was developed by Georgopoulos and Mann (1962) for a study of community general hospitals and later elaborated for use in a variety of different organizations (Price, 1972). Georgopoulos and Mann asked the following question of hospital staff members:[1] "On the basis of your experience and information, how would you rate the quality of *overall care* that the patients generally receive from this hospital?" This question was followed by seven alternative responses: (1) outstanding, (2) excellent, (3) very good, (4) good, (5) fair, (6) rather poor, and (7) poor. The researchers found that hospitals differed significantly in the quality of overall care they provided as rated by this questionnaire item, as well as in the quality of medical care and nursing care as rated in similar items for relevant groups of professional staff. To demonstrate that the evaluations of overall care were characteristic of the organization as a whole and not affected differentially across subgroups within the organizations, the researchers aggregated the ratings for each hospital by work group characteristics such as raters' shift of work, division, medical specialty, and status as full- or part-time employee. Ratings thus categorized were not significantly different from those obtained from the larger organizational unit. Therefore, answers to the questions apparently reflected organizational effectiveness as a whole and not merely subgroup effectiveness.

The validity of this sort of measure of organizational effectiveness has been demonstrated by correlations with other volunteered comments about the organization (for example, "I would send my family here"), as well as by correlations with other relevant questionnaire items (Price, 1972). Subsequent research shows that the measurement of medical care using these kinds of questions is significantly correlated with "harder," more objective data from hospital records, for example, data on whether patients with a diagnosis of diabetes receive a urine analysis within 24 hours of admission—a practice that experts judge to constitute good medical care (Basil S. Georgopoulos, personal communication).

Multiple goals

A major shortcoming of dealing with evaluation in this way is that the organization is likely to have a variety of goals rather than a single, overriding one. In a study of the goals of top executives in 145 businesses, Dent (1959) found that the goals most frequently mentioned were three: profits, public

---

[1] Hospital staff was defined to include medical staff, registered nurses, lab and X-ray technicians, various administrators, and members of the board of trustees.

service (in the form of producing quality products), and employee welfare. It is interesting to note that only about one third of Dent's sample mentioned profits. Even when individuals who mentioned goals other than profits, public service, or employee welfare were eliminated from the sample, only half of the remaining managers cited profitability. We might infer that two thirds of the managers in the sample did not consider profitability an important goal. As Anthony (1960) suggests, profit-maximization may be viewed by business managers as too difficult to attain, unrealistic, and immoral.

Having been assured that their interviews would be held in complete confidence, Dent's subjects can be assumed to have been candid; their emphasis on goals other than profit can be attributed to more than platitudes in the interest of good public relations. Limiting our focus to the first three of the aims voiced by each manager, we find that nearly 40 percent of the respondents cited "providing a good service or a public service." A similar percentage of the sample cited "providing for the welfare of employees—a good living, security, happiness, good working conditions." Other important goals mentioned were growth, efficiency, meeting competition, and operating the organization. Furthermore, one sixth of the managers cited more than three goals. Clearly, there is no single goal that one can use as a criterion, even for an evaluation of a single organization.

As Seashore (1965) observes:

> Most organizations have many goals, not one. These goals are of unlike importance and their relative importance changes. Problems arise because these goals are often competing (i.e., have tradeoff value), and sometimes incompatible (negatively correlated). A strategy of optimal realization of goals cannot be determined unless there exists some conception of the dimensions of performance, their relative importance, and their relationships with one another. These relationships may be of causation, of simple correlation, of interaction; they may be linear and compensatory or nonlinear and noncompensatory (Seashore, 1965, p. 26).

A further problem in measuring effectiveness in terms of goal attainment is that different individuals or goups in an organization often have different expectations concerning its goals. A study of 97 small businesses (Friedlander and Pickle, 1968) shows that the needs and demands of owners, employees, and interested third parties (for example, governments, customers, suppliers, and creditors) generally are not fulfilled concurrently. Very few positive relationships were found among employee, owner, and societal interests (see also Pickle and Rungeling, 1973). As we said in Chapter 6, many organizations encompass numerous different groups having goals that are incompatible or inconsistent to varying degrees. The use of goals as the sole criterion for evaluating organizations does not provide a simple or straightforward solution.

Empirical approaches to evaluation criteria

The goal approach starts with an a priori model of organizational behavior that is used as a rationale for selecting criteria. Alternatively, we may take a more inductive approach to the problem. Starting with a great many measures of organizational performance (ratings, judgments, statistical records, and so on), we can attempt to establish the existence of functional relationships among the various measures and possibly correlations with some basic overall judgment about the organization's effectiveness.

In an early study that compared various methods of evaluation, Georgopoulos, Indik, and Seashore (1960) found that an empirically developed model predicted overall effectiveness about as well as did other, more theoretically based models. Subsequently, Seashore and Yuchtman (1967) studied the 11-year history of 76 different kinds of records data (taken from an original source of 200 items) which were obtained from 75 insurance sales agencies located throughout the United States. The application of a statistical technique known as factor analysis reduced these 76 categories of data to 10 general factors (see Table 14-1), which showed fairly consistent relationships to one another over the 11-year period. Seashore and Yuchtman (1967), however, did not interpret the ten factors as organizational goals, since some were clearly means toward other goals. The common denominator in all the factor was "... that they represent the acquisition of resources for organizational functioning from the organizations' environments" (p. 392).

From the vantage point of the system model, the results of the Seashore and Yuchtman study suggest that one should judge organizations, not on the basis of goal attainment, but on their performance in exchanging scarce and valued resources with their environments. In this light, organizational effectiveness is viewed in terms of the organization's strengths in bargaining for scarce resources: "We define the effectiveness of an organization as its ability to exploit its environment in the acquisition of scarce and valued resources to sustain its functioning" (Seashore and Yuchtman, 1967, p. 393). We shall return to this definition later.

Limitations of the empirical approach

Other investigators have used empirical approaches to generate useful intermediate criteria. Mahoney (1967) studied 114 criteria that were developed for 283 organizational units which were subordinated to 84 managers in 13 companies. Some 24 "midrange" criteria were found by factor analyzing the 114 items. Table 14-2 shows the more important of these factors. Further analysis indicated that of these, the most important factors (the most highly correlated with ratings of overall effectiveness) were (1) productivity-support-utilization, (2) planning, (3) reliability, and (4) initiation.

TABLE 14-1
Performance factors in insurance agencies

Factor	Assigned name	Number of assigned variable	Indicator variables
I	Business volume*	Ia	Number of policies in force (year's end)
		Ib	New insurance sold (dollar volume)
		Ic	Renewal premiums collected (dollars)
		Id	Number of lives insured (year's end)
		Ie	Agency manpower (number of agents)
II	Production cost	IIa	Production cost per new policy
		IIb	Production cost per $1,000 of insurance
		IIc	Production cost per $100 of premium
III	New member productivity	IIIa	Average productivity per new agent
		IIIb	Ratio of new agent versus old agent productivity (new agent less than five years of service)
IV	Youthfulness of members	IVa	Ratio of younger (under 35) to total membership
		IVb	Ratio of productivity of younger members to total members of agency
V	Business mix†	Va	Average premium per $1,000
		Vb	Percentage of new policies with quarterly payments
		Vc	Percentage of business in employee trust
VI	Manpower growth	VIa	Net change in manpower during year
		VIb	Ratio of net change to initial manpower
VII	Management emphasis	VIIa	Manager's personal commissions
VIII	Maintenance cost‡	VIIIa	Maintenance cost per collection
		VIIIb	Maintenance cost per $100 premium collected
IX	Member productivity	IXa	Average new business volume per agent
X	Market penetration	Xa	Insurance in force per capita
		Xb	Number of lives covered per 1,000 insurables

* Including both accumulated volume and current increment in volume.
† Many low-value transactions versus fewer high-value transactions.
‡ Refers to maintenance of accounts, not of physical facilities.
Source: Seashore and Yuchtman (1967, p. 383).

Using the 24 dimensions described on the following page, Mahoney and Weitzel (1969) studied 103 R&D units associated with four companies. Ratings by 32 managers indicated a somewhat different model for R&D departments (see Figure 14-1, 14-1B), with the most important dimensions being (1) reliability, (2) cooperation, and (3) development.

Therefore, the empirical approach does not seem to yield a single, small set of criteria of effectiveness in different kinds of organizations. It may be

TABLE 14-2
Dimensions of organizational effectiveness with standardized regression coefficients*

Dimension	Model General business	Model Research and development
Flexibility. Willingly tries out new ideas and suggestions, ready to tackle unusual problems.	.07	−.19
Development. Personnel participate in training and development activities; high level of personnel competence and skill.	.08	.23
Cohesion. Lack of complaints and grievances; conflict among cliques within the organization.	.07	.00
Democratic supervision. Subordinate participation in work decisions.	.03	.01
Reliability. Meets objectives without necessity of followup and checking.	.13	.27
Selectivity. Doesn't accept marginal employees rejected by other organizations.	.02	−.16
Diversity. Wide range of job responsibilities and personnel abilities within the organization.	−.02	−.03
Delegation. High degree of delegation by supervisors.	.04	−.09
Bargaining. Rarely bargains with other organizations for favors and cooperation.	−.05	.01
Emphasis on results. Results, output, and performance emphasized, not procedures.	.01	.14
Staffing. Personnel flexibility among assignments; development for promotion from within the organization.	.06	.01
Coordination. Coordinates and schedules activities with other organizations, utilizes staff assistance.	−.08	−.08
Decentralization. Work and procedural decisions delegated to lowest levels.	−.01	.19
Understanding. Organization philosophy, policy, directives understood and accepted by all.	−.08	−.04
Conflict. Little conflict with other organization units about authority or failure to meet responsibilities.	−.09	−.01
Personnel planning. Performance not disrupted by personnel absences, turnover, lost time.	−.04	−.06
Supervisory support. Supervisors support their subordinates.	−.12	−.04
Planning. Operations planned and scheduled to avoid lost time; little time spent on minor crises.	.25	.31
Cooperation. Operations scheduled and coordinated with other organizations; rarely fails to meet responsibilities.	.11	.33
Productivity-support-utilization. Efficient performance; mutual support and respect of supervisors and subordinates; utilization of personnel skills and abilities.	.43	.12
Communication. Free flow of work information and communications within the organization.	−.07	−.27
Turnover. Little turnover from inability to do the job.	.01	.17

TABLE 14-2 (continued)
Dimensions of organizational effectiveness with standardized regression coefficients*

	Model	
Dimension	General business	Research and development
Initiation. Initiates improvements in work methods and operations.	.09	.12
Supervisory control. Supervision in control of progress of work.	.03	.08
Multiple correlation, R	.76	.79

* Standardized regression coefficients are estimates of relationships between the dimensions and ratings of effectiveness.
Source: Mahoney and Weitzel (1969, p. 358).

possible to discover a small number of criteria that can be applied to specific types of organizations, but this remains to be seen.

Efficiency

In addition to the goal and empirical approaches, a third approach to evaluating organizations, which is also derived from the rational model, used measures of efficiency as criteria. Under this rationale, one disclaims goals and attends instead to the efficacy of organizational means in pursuing ends that are "given." Efficiency is measured by the ratio of organizational output to input. Much of the psychological literature on supervisory practices and work group arrangements uses productivity as a dependent variable and as an efficiency criterion of sorts. This kind of research commonly focuses on such questions as; what leadership style will allow supervisors to get the most productivity from their work group?

Katz and Kahn (1978) speak of "energic" efficiency or the ratio of the energy produced by an organization to the energy it consumes in the process. Unfortunately, supplies, equipment, people, money, and information are not readily convertible to units of energy. Furthermore, overhead, indirect costs, and the like are difficult to measure systematically. However, Katz and Kahn argue that they can examine the relative efficiency of an organization if not its absolute efficiency; they can determine whether an organization consumes more resources and energy than another in producing a similar level of output.[2]

---

[2] In viewing organizations as producers and consumers of information as well as of other commodities, one comes to find fault with the use of energy as an efficiency measure. If information is an output, then organizations need not run down as would be suggested by the Second Law of Thermodynamics. Culture or informational complexity may be built up, giving the organization antientropic properties (Buckley, 1967; Fuller, 1969).

FIGURE 14–1
Diagram of relationships of midrange criteria of organizational effectiveness to overall effectiveness in (A) general business model and (B) research and development model

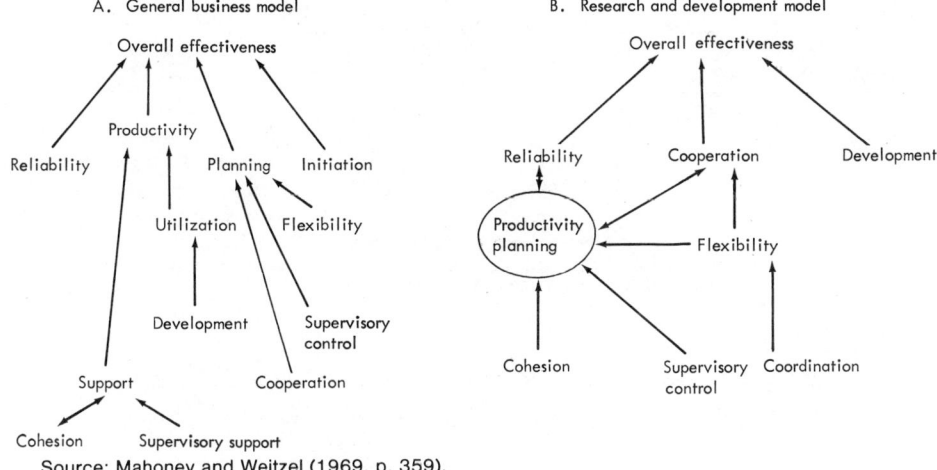

Source: Mahoney and Weitzel (1969, p. 359).

Potential and actual efficiency

It is useful to make a distinction between "potential" and "actual" efficiency (Katz and Kahn, 1978). So far, we have described efficiency in terms of the ratio of the value of output to its costs of production. This concept can be refined by distinguishing between the potential efficiency conjectured for a particular organization and the actual efficiency experienced when the organization operates under a variety of different conditions in an environment where things sometimes go wrong. Katz and Kahn suggest that some organizations are more capable of actualizing their potential than other organizations having equal potential that seem to be "fragile" or "accident-prone." Potential efficiency is a concept with origins in the rational model of organization. The concept of actual efficiency admits to the importance of complex and sometimes unknown factors in both the organization and its environment and, in so doing, approaches the system model of organization. Of the two, actual efficiency is more useful to the middle manager who deals with day-to-day problems. The concept of potential efficiency is useful to top management as an indication of the extent to which management intervention can improve ordinary practice. Potential efficiency, in short, may serve as a goal for the organization as a whole.

The efficiency approach to evaluating organizations is based ultimately on the notion that an organization of parts is better (more efficient) at producing desired outcomes than is a disorganized aggregation of the same parts. According to this logic, individuals will tend to remain organized because of the advantages of this efficiency. It is but a short step from this view

FIGURE 14-2
Three views of organizational effectiveness

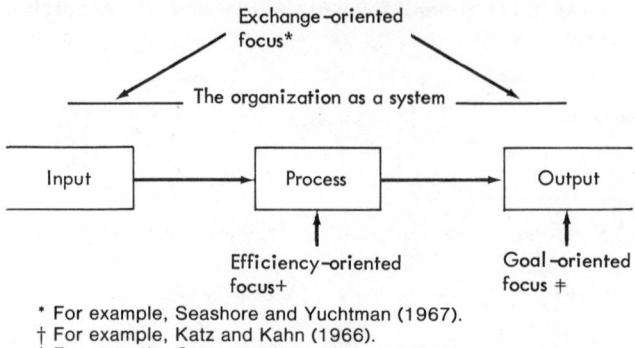

* For example, Seashore and Yuchtman (1967).
† For example, Katz and Kahn (1966).
‡ For example, Georgopoulos and Mann (1962).

of organizations to the system approach, a point of view that is similar to Gouldner's natural-system model of organizations (Etzioni, 1960).

The system approach to evaluation

A fourth approach to evaluating organizations, the system approach, uses system need variables as criteria. System analysis begins, not with organizational goals, but with a model of the system that is capable of achieving these goals. In developing a model, one identifies various independent subcomponents of the system and specifies for each a set of prerequisite operating requirements (needs). Next, one ascertains the extent to which these various system needs are being met and whether the balance of organizational effort has been optimally distributed among the subcomponents according to their specific needs. Sometimes an organization's members are not conscious of all the needs of the system to which they belong. Nevertheless, if we view organizations as natural systems rather than as rational tools, we must argue that the fulfillment of system needs is prerequisite to organizational success. An organization that devotes all of its resources and efforts to goal attainment, and in so doing neglects some of its system needs, may eventually prove ineffectual in achieving its goals. It may even fail to survive (Etzioni, 1960).

A study of the theoretical requirements of an organization as an open system and empirical investigations of a variety of different organizations, including especially hospitals, has yielded a list of seven basic organizational problems (Georgopoulos, 1973):

> (1) The ability of the organization to adapt to the external environment and carry on an effective interchange with it at all times. This includes ability to respond successfully to relevant changes in the outside world; to obtain resources and personnel; to maintain advantageous relationships with

outside interest groups; to project a creditable image and maintain a favorable reputation in the community; and generally to influence the environment in ways that benefit the system and its members in relation to all aspects of organization-environment articulation.

(2) The ability of the organization to deploy and allocate available resources, facilities, funds, and personnel in the most appropriate manner; to handle related problems of access to, and distribution of, authority, rewards, and information among the participants; and to solve problems concerning work specialization and the allocation of tasks and functions among departments, groups, and members.

(3) The ability to articulate and constantly coordinate, in time and space, the many diverse but related roles and interdependent activities of its many different staffs and members, so that the energies and efforts of all the participants always converge toward the solution of system problems and the attainment of organizational objectives.

(4) The ability of the system to integrate itself. This includes all necessary, functions associated with the problem of integrating individual members into the system and securing their cooperation and compliance, and the problem of integrating all parts of the social system with one another so that the total organization can achieve a certain overall social-psychological unity and coherence. Generally, it involves the development of common organizational values and shared norms, attitudes, and mutual understandings, which can serve to provide a common universe of discourse for the different groups and members, and to socialize and bind the members securely into the system.

(5) The ability to minimize and resolve the tensions and conflicts which arise within the organization; particularly frictions and confrontations among interacting groups, and members and among equal status participants, and to manage and control stress and strain throughout the system.

(6) The ability to reach and maintain high levels (in terms of quantity, quality, and cost) of output, e.g., patient care and health service to its clients, at all times. This involves the ability to maximize efficient and reliable performance by all departments, groups, and members, at all levels, and is in turn dependent upon maximization by the system of opportunities for personal goal attainment and job satisfaction on the part of the members.

(7) The ability of the organization to preserve its identity and integrity as a distinct and unified problem-solving system, or to maintain itself and its basic character and viability, regardless of changes which are constantly occurring within and outside it, including potential disruptions and threats to the survival or well being of the organization (pp. 126–27).

The system approach to evaluation seems to be more complex and, therefore, more difficult to apply than the goal approach described at the beginning of this chapter (Schulberg, Sheldon, and Baker, 1969). Organization theorists have not yet agreed on a single list of system needs. Furthermore, the differing lists of the various theorists tend to be quite long and complex. On the other hand, by relying on a variety of system needs, this approach may be less prone to bias than the goal approach, which uses organization-defined criteria that are based on one goal (or at most, a few) as they are reported by one or more individuals (Etzioni, 1960). In other words, the system approach seems to be more comprehensive and, therefore, more balanced. However, proponents of the system approach, who look for balance in what presently exists in an organization, are accused of being more conservative than the advocates of the goal view, who focus on ideals and the potential to improve on the status quo. But, in fact, the goal view can tend toward Utopianism or unrealistic expectations for achievement, since goals are relatively easy to state in a neat, clear, and idealistic fashion. The system approach seems more realistic in that it highlights the difficulties that can be anticipated in operating and changing the organization (Etzioni, 1960).

Our position on the matter is that although the system view is complex and unwieldy, certain basic system needs can be isolated and incorporated into the goal approach to evaluation. Later, we will pursue this notion under a discussion of the system resource approach to evaluating organizations.

EXTERNAL PERSPECTIVES

Profit: Efficiency and political effectiveness

For the most part, our discussions of efficiency and system need criteria have focused inside the organization, so to speak. The efficiency model, of course, is most useful internally, where management has sufficient control (through the buffering out of external uncertainties) to attempt a rational arrangement of means in the service of known ends (James Thompson, 1967). The system model directs our attention toward prerequisites for system survival and the attendant needs for organizational adaptation. However, the specific elements in most of these models tend to describe characteristics of the internal organization. Next, we shall look at the organization's relationships with other entities in the environment as evaluation criteria.

Our earlier discussion of the concept of energic efficiency becomes relevant here. An inefficient firm can be profitable, but not as profitable as another firm that is similar to the first in other respects, but more efficient. However, profit is determined by more than efficiency.

Some costs of production will be borne by the organization, but profitable management sees to it that as many costs as possible are borne by its personnel and outside groups—not by the organization per se. Costs borne by outside groups include pollution and degradation of the environment, which are costly to undo or repair. These are termed externalities by economists. Employees also bear costs of production, such as tensions, frustration, and the psychosomatic illnesses that work can bring on. In dealing with externalities and human costs so as to strike an advantageous balance between costs borne by the organization and by others, management evidences what is terms political effectiveness (Katz and Kahn, 1978).

Managers also exercise political effectiveness when they influence suppliers and customers (or clients) to enter into transactions that are advantageous to their organization. The value of the organization's outputs is thereby enhanced. Additional ways of increasing political effectiveness include advertising and lobbying for favorable legislation, subsidies, and tariffs (see Figure 14–3).

FIGURE 14–3
A system view of organizations

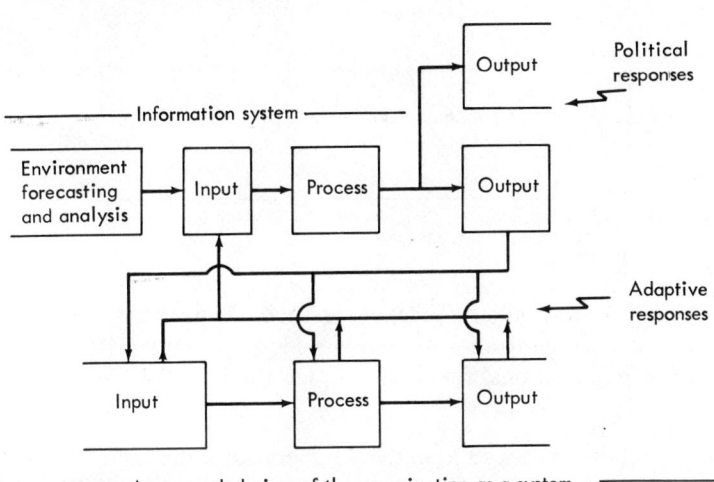

Through various forms of persuasion, negotiation, and the exercise of power, the organization maximizes its return at the expense of other organizations or individuals. These political means of gaining advantages entail shifting costs to other entities; efficiency involves gaining advantages through shifting internal arrangements to reduce costs and increase outputs. Both approaches contribute to profitability—returns to the organization by economic and technical means (efficiency) and by political means.

Long-run efficiency

In observing efficiency and political effectiveness, we must also note how these attributes affect the organization over time. Attempts to increase efficiency may entail the creation of inventories, the acquisition of advanced technology, or organizational growth undertaken to achieve economies of scale. These strategies clearly are geared to long-run efficiency. Similarly, attempts to apply political pressure to outside groups and organizations may result ultimately in a measure of control over the environment. These out-

FIGURE 14-4
Economic efficiency and political effectiveness: Vehicles for profit and survival

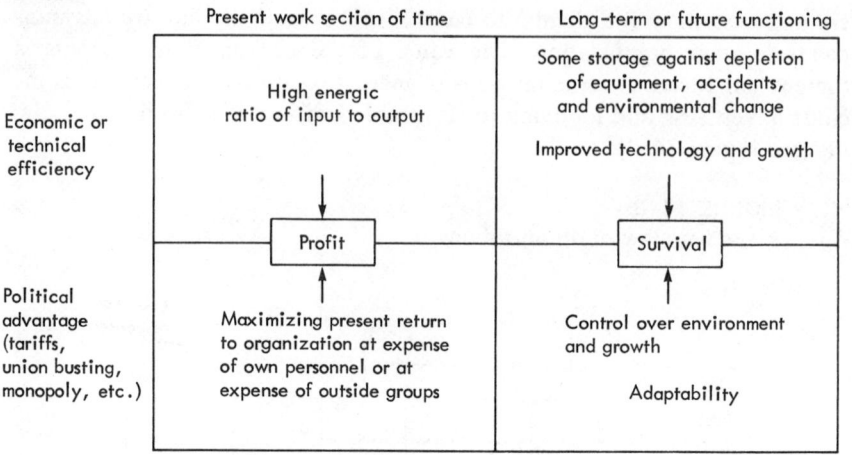

Source: *The Social Psychology of Organizations* by D. Katz and R. Kahn. Copyright © 1978, John Wiley and Sons, Inc. Used by permission.

comes of long-term political effectiveness and efficiency will enhance the probability of the organization's *survival,* which is often used as an ultimate criterion for organizational functioning. (See Figure 14-4.)

Organizational effectiveness from the perspective of the larger system

We have viewed the transactions between an organization and its environment primarily in terms of advantages to the organization. Study of the problem at a higher level of aggregation is also useful. For the moment, let us inquire about the kinds of organizational designs and organizational functioning, including the nature of exchanges with the environment, that are most efficient for the larger system (organization and relevant environment) *as a whole.*

There are a number of valid reasons for studying the larger system of which the organization is merely a part or subsystem. We are becoming increasingly interdependent with organizations in our own society, as well as with various segments of other societies. Increasing differentiation and specialization of social units constitute a major impetus toward interdependence (Durkheim, 1947). Also, in the near future at least, competition for natural resources may assume the characteristics of zero-sum games rather than variable-sum or increasing-sum situations (Meadows, Meadows, Randers, and Behrens, 1972). This appears particularly valid in light of the rising expectations of lesser developed countries. Furthermore, individuals throughout the world are becoming increasingly aware of the larger system through mass media, with the result that both interdependence and expectations for social progress are increased (see, for example, McLuhan and Fiore, 1967).

If we adopt a larger system, perhaps societal, perspective, we will consider whether the organization is effective *as a component of the larger system*. Following the thinking of Katz and Kahn (1978), we can inquire whether the organization contributes to the efficiency, environmental control, and survival of the total system, which includes the organization in question. We might ask whether the functioning of General Motors, IBM, the League of Women Voters, and the Committee to Re-elect the President, each of which may be an effective organization, also contributes to the efficiency of the United States of America of which these organizations are a part. In short, the criteria developed by Katz and Kahn can be applied, at least in theory, to the organization's contribution to the larger system.

The goal approach to evaluating organizations also corresponds to the larger system level. Parsons (1956) suggests that we try to analyze the special functions or contributions of the organization as they apply to the larger society. For example, we saw in Chapter 6 that a sample of university administrators and faculty members believe that the top two goals of the university ought to be to (1) protect the faculty's right to academic freedom and (2) train the students in methods of scholarship and/or scientific research and/or creative endeavor. However, we cannot accept these stated goals without question. The university contributes differently to different segments of the larger system. For instance, the local business community may view the contribution of the university as providing a pool of well-trained young people for entry level managerial and professional positions and may see the university as most useful in training students for positions in a business organization, and less useful in educating for scholarship or scientific research as the faculty sees it. Because these conflicts are perceived by different groups, we argue that the goal or function of a subsystem in relation to the larger system can be identified most readily in terms of the mutual expectations that system components have of one another.

Domain consensus

Transactions with the larger system can be identified where these contributions have been "legitimated" (Parsons, 1956)—that is, where consensus exists among organizational members and members of the public at large that the organization "ought to be doing one thing or another." James Thompson (1967) refers to this state of affairs as "domain consensus," (Chapter 6). In studying relationships among health care agencies in the community, Levine and White (1961) refer to domain as the "claim which an organization stakes out for itself in terms of (1) diseases covered, (2) population served, and (3) services rendered." To the extent that other organizations in the environment accept the organization's domain, domain consensus exists. A hospital may stake out a domain of certain kinds of patients, who receive certain kinds of treatment and who are drawn from a certain portion of the community. Physicians, other hospitals, and health care agencies support the hospital's domain by referring to it appropriate patients, rerouting inappropriate patients, providing backup support in emergencies, lending equipment or staff, and so on. The important point here is that domain consensus can be used to identify the criteria by which an organization is judged—criteria regarding contributions to the larger system.

Domains as subsystems

Given the great complexity of the larger system (society), legitimation of goals, or domain consensus, may be relatively circumscribed—that is, limited to a portion of the larger system. In a particular community, only other hospitals, physicians, welfare agencies, and the like will clearly recognize the domain of a particular hospital and refer patients to it appropriately. If this is true, then one is still left with primarily a subsystem frame of reference, as provided by Katz and Kahn. In this case, the subsystem is larger than the organization under study, but considerably smaller than the entire system. A domain may consist of little more than a federation or combination of organizations, and one may consider the effectiveness of a member organization in relation to its contributions to the confederation.

At a higher level of aggregation, one may also consider the effectiveness of organizations that comprise the federation vis-à-vis the federation's environment, namely other organizations, groups of organizations, and unorganized groups in the still larger social system. For example, instead of evaluating a municipal hospital on the basis of the number of patients it handles for the city welfare department, one may evaluate the city's combined health care delivery systems to determine how they enable the city to compete with other cities for new industry. Competition will be based, in part, on the quality of health care that the city provides. Success in attracting new industry may increase the city's tax base and, in turn, provide additional resources for the improvement of existing health care delivery systems as well as other services. Thus, we have evaluated the municipal hospital in terms of its contributions (both legitimated and not legitimated) to the city which comprises the municipal government, city dwellers, private industry, and so forth. Obviously, a large system perspective is essential for certain planning purposes.

Organizational contributions to the general good

Extending the direction of our line of inquiry, we can examine the role of a particular organization in terms of its contributions to the effectiveness of the largest system, the society of which it is a part; for example, we may inquire whether the organization in question specializes appropriately vis-à-vis other organizations, given their respective capabilities, opportunities, and the like. Inquiry such as this, in the largest sense of the word, led the Soviet Union to request that Romania emphasize agricultural production and that East Germany (German Democratic Republic) focus on industrial production for the good of the Soviet bloc (Comecon) nations as a whole. From this perspective, a single organization's political effectiveness (in Katz and Kahn's sense of the term) is not relevant. Success in forcing others to bear costs is not efficient for the system as a whole. This assumes, of course, both the presence of an overall goal for the society in question and the opportunity to arrange means toward that end. However, political effectiveness defined in terms of an organization's ability to force costs on organizations that are *outside* of the society in question can contribute to the political effectiveness of the larger system.

There is no consensus about the general good. There are no agreed goals for systems larger than the single organization; for example, Romania has taken a more independent stand than other members of the Soviet bloc and has since moved toward industrialization. In fact, as we saw in Chapter 6, clearly defined goals often are lacking at the organizational level as well. Rather, what we find in society is a concern for the politics of subsystems, a concern for who gets what, when, and where (Lasswell, 1936). This observation is not merely a reflection of Western values and their emphasis on the individual or the subsystem; it is a reflection of fact and a result of the descriptive analysis of current behavior around us.[3]

The normative point we raise here is that a larger system perspective is undesirable as long as there are major disagreements and conflicts over the rationale for distributing valued resources. A rational approach that evaluates an organization in terms of its contribution to the efficiency or effectiveness of the larger system assumes that there is some ultimate goal in relation to which relative efficiency is appropriate. At the subsystem level, one would evaluate a university in terms of the numbers and quality of educated students graduated. But, at the larger system level, government officials must decide on the goals of society, and it is not yet clear how much education, not to mention how much good health, we should enjoy. If the "pursuit of happiness" is our goal, perhaps good health is more important than education. If this is the case, we should have fewer universities and more hospitals.

---

[3] It has been observed that much of present-day descriptive sociology provides an invitation to join the conservative party (Dahrendorf, 1958). Considering whether subsystems or supersystems should be given top priority involves us, among other things, in assumptions about human nature. Given the pessimistic, Hobbesian view of humanity's potential, one becomes concerned about the possible harm that can befall individuals if human nature is not constrained. Hence, one will be led to focus on the subsystem and its protection. A more liberal view of the inherent goodness of human nature will lead one to speculate about the gains that will be realized from the actualization of human potential. Here, one will be led to stress the advantages of joining together and working in trusting collaboration. One's focus will become the supersystem so as to enhance outcomes for all and ultimately for each individual, too.

But how many hospitals and how few universities? In Chapter 6, we suggested that instead of a rational approach to these matters, a "muddling through" approach may be better. At this point it is sufficient to observe that the larger system viewpoint seems to raise more questions than it answers.

A FRAMEWORK FOR EVALUATION

Operative goals and system needs

This is all quite complex. The goal approach leaves questions of efficiency begging. Furthermore, official goals may not be the real goals of the organization. Different groups within an organization may profess different, often conflicting goals. The efficiency approach attends to a very limited portion of the organization's behavior. The system need approach is complicated and quite difficult to pursue if one is to evaluate the performance of an actual organization rather than an abstract system. Finally, the larger system perspective raises the question of *which* larger system one should select for evaluation: The organization's domain, some related subset of society, or society at large?

An increasingly common response in the literature (Ansoff and Brandenburg, 1971; Richard Hall, 1972; Mott, 1972; Perrow, 1970; Yuchtman and Seashore, 1967) is to throw up one's hands in the face of these problems and to settle for some set of operative or intermediate goals that correspond fairly well to some basic system needs. Yuchtman and Seashore (1967) have proposed a system resource approach that builds on the Katz and Kahn view that organizations are open systems which must be politically effective and thus compete and bargain for resources with the environment. In this sense, an organization is effective according to its "ability . . . in either relative or absolute terms, to exploit its environment in the acquisition of scarce and valued resources" (Yuchtman and Seashore, 1967, p. 898). However, Yuchtman and Seashore differ from Katz and Kahn in postulating that only the "ability to exploit the environment" is maximized, not the actual resource acquisition, since the latter might lead to dangers of various kinds. The organization attempts to optimize (rather than maximize) its resource procurement so as to avoid "depletion of its resource-producing environment or the devaluation of the resource, or . . . stimulation of countervailing forces within that environment" (p. 902). It will be recalled that the Standard Oil trust tried to maximize resource procurement, with the result that the government attacked and broke it up with antitrust legislation.

We can simplify the views of Yuchtman and Seashore (1967) and postulate that organizations are effective to the extent that they acquire power over their environment. Organizations must engage in transactions with the environment to acquire resources which, in turn, foster the organization's goal attainment. The needed resources may be of various kinds, and the kinds of relationships in which power can be used to acquire them are many. Hence, there is no single criterion with which to measure effectiveness. However, according to this line of reasoning, all of the relevant measures of effectiveness fall under the general rubric of power to acquire resources. As Yuchtman and Seashore (1967) argue, factors such as business volume, market penetration, productive efficiency, and member productivity are all either resources obtained from the environment or means to attain such resources.

A number of other investigators have proposed operative goals that also seem to fall under the general rubric of power. We saw in Chapter 3 that Ansoff and Brandenburg (1971) describe an evolution of the organizational designs of business firms undertaken to meet the following process criteria: (1) steady state efficiency, (2) operating responsiveness, (3) strategic responsiveness, and (4) structural responsiveness. Mott's (1972) concept of organizational effectiveness is similar: "... the ability of an organization to mobilize its centers of power for action—production and adaptation" (p. 17). He suggests that effective organizations "produce more and higher-quality outputs and adapt more effectively to environmental and internal problems than do other, similar organizations" (p. 17).

These are all rather general statements of commonly articulated goals for the ongoing operations of organizations (operative goals). They are also examples of commonly stated system needs, although they do not by any means comprise the full list of such needs usually given by system theorists. This apparent convergence between the goal and system approaches to evaluation argues that a combination of the approaches will yield a practical means for evaluating organization designs.

Some suggestions for evaluating designs

Let us spell out a full-fledged goal model for evaluating organizations, then add elements from the system model; this combination then provides a comprehensive, although unwieldy approach to evaluating designs. Suchman (1967) makes use of a process model in his evaluation of various social change programs, such as Headstart and X-ray screening programs for tuberculosis. An important component of the process model is the concept of a sequence of goals—immediate (or short-range), intermediate, and ultimate (long-range) goals (see Figure 14-5). Immediate goals or sets of goals result from attempts to implement various elements of a project. The immediate goals, in turn, have consequences for the achievement of intermediate and ultimate goals; for example, in pursuing an immediate goal such as increasing *the productivity and efficiency of subordinates,* managers may alter some characteristics of the organization that are under their control (for example, the degree to which they are supportive of subordinates). Such actions and results in turn can affect an intermediate goal such as *profitability.* Changes

FIGURE 14-5
The goal sequence in a process model of evaluation

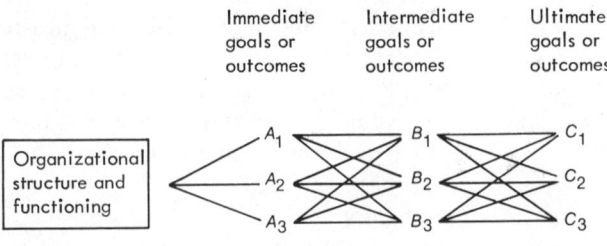

in the organization's rate of profitability, furthermore can affect one of the firm's ultimate goals, *survival.*

Relevance of selected criteria

A common error in managerial thinking is the assumption that the attainment of an immediate goal will lead automatically to the realization of subsequent goals in the hierarchy. Managers must examine and assess goal relationships as far down this entire hierarchy as is possible. Many of the earlier human relations studies focused on the satisfaction of individual workers under the assumption that productivity is a function of work satisfaction. Subsequently, this assumption proved valid only under very special conditions (Robert Kahn, 1956). In light of such observations, we clearly ought to verify the assumed causal relationships among goals at various points in the hierarchical sequence. This line of questioning, furthermore, should be pursued until a goal state is reached that is of unquestioned value in and of itself, rather than being valuable only as a doubtful means to some even further end. If an ultimate goal of a hospital tuberculosis screening unit is detection of cases in the community, an evaluation of the unit based on numbers of cases may be insufficient. The assumption that the cases found at the hospital will reduce the community TB rate may be false. The cases turning up at the hospital may be ones readily found by a number of procedures, and the hardcore TB population in the community—the ultimate criterion—may not be affected at all.

Furthermore, the stated official goals of the organization cannot always be taken at face value as criteria. Rather, we would do better to study the organization's actual behavior and infer its real goals from the ways in which it acts. These actions may be only means toward the ends of particular individuals or groups, but as Simon (1964) suggests, such means or agreed constraints for interactions between groups may serve to guide the behavior of the organization as a whole (see Chapter 6).

In relating organizational means to ends (immediate to ultimate outcomes), we might also consider whether there are alternative means to these ends. This is a matter of efficiency. Some of these alternatives may be unknown to members of the organization. The analyst, however, through the ability to conceptualize organizations as systems and identify requisite system needs, views the organization as flexible in some areas and thus capable of altering its structure and functioning and of using alternative means in the pursuit of particular ends.

In developing this model, we must accept no single criterion for assessing the performance of an organization. An ultimate criterion may exist in principle, but it would measure performance over such a long period of time that we must settle for more intermediate criteria, or what have been termed *mid-range criteria* (Mahoney, 1967). If we used still more immediate criteria, the task would become quite complex, involving a great number of variables in complicated and dynamic relationships (Seashore and Yuchtman, 1967). Our assumption is that intermediate criteria consist of several indicators that are generally useful across different organizations and over time, as well.

As we saw above, Seashore and Yuchtman (1967) derive a relatively small number of criteria from their study of insurance agencies, as did Mahoney (1967) in his study of units in a business firm. However, no single, small list of criteria is available at this time for use across a variety of different organizations. At this point, it is partly a matter of choice which of several lists of penultimate criteria to use. We feel similarly about the use of the goal or system approach to evaluation. The goal approach allows specific tailoring of criteria to the characteristics of the organization under study. The system need approach is more general and may force one to recognize some critical but often overlooked dimensions. A combination of criteria from both approaches appears most useful at this time.

Some operative criteria

For this reason, we suggest evaluation in terms of a small number of intermediate outcomes that are selected from both operative goals and system characteristics—outcomes such as efficiency, productivity, adaptability, and innovativeness. We expect that performance in these areas will contribute to the organization's ultimate effectiveness, including especially the organization's system-resource position (or its power position vis-à-vis the environment) as we have termed the Yuchtman-Seashore view.

Mott (1972, p. 20) provides a useful outline of criteria of the kind we have proposed:[4]

    A. Organizing centers of power for routine production (productivity)
        1. The quantity of the product.
        2. The quality of the product.
        3. The efficiency with which it is produced.

---

[4] Questionnaire items used by Mott to measure these criteria of effectiveness are found in Figure 14–6. An earlier version of this kind of approach may be found in Georgopoulos and Tannenbaum (1957).

B. Organizing centers of power to change routines (adaptability)
    1. Symbolic adaptation
        a. Anticipating problems in advance and developing satisfactory and timely solutions to them.
        b. Staying abreast of new technologies and methods applicable to the activities of the organization.
    2. Behavioral adaptation
        a. Prompt acceptance of solutions.
        b. Prevalent acceptance of solutions.
C. Organizing centers of power to cope with temporarily unpredictable overloads of work (flexibility).

Productivity, adaptability, and flexibility

Each of these three areas of concern is a basic component of the list of operative criteria we wish to propose. We have discussed *productivity* in the first section of this chapter under a goal view, and it was illustrated by the questionnaire items used by Georgopoulos and Mann to measure the quality of patient care in hospitals. Also relevant to productivity is the subsequent discussion based on the Katz and Kahn view of efficiency as the ratio of output to input. Our second operative criterion, *adaptability*, was touched on when we mentioned the Seashore and Yuchtman view of organizations engaging in exchanges with the environment and, more important, when we discussed the Katz and Kahn view of political effectiveness. These often require the organization to make internal changes as well as external changes. Adaptability may be viewed as synonymous with problem-solving ability. As indicated by Mott's breakdown of adaptability into two parts, the organization must first become aware of problems and formulate solutions, and second, implement these solutions in a timely fashion and with sufficient breadth and depth of adjustment. *Flexibility* is a special case of adaptation. It is an unpredictable and time-limited (or temporary) adjustment that must be made.

In addition to Mott's list of productivity, adaptability, and flexibility, there are two other major sources of operational measures that we wish to cite. Price (1968, 1972) provides a useful list of measures of organizational effectiveness that includes productivity, morale, adaptation, and innovation. Second, Ansoff and Brandenburg (1971) provide broad categories of criteria with which to measure steady state efficiency, operating responsiveness, strategic responsiveness, and structural responsiveness in business firms.

Price (1968) defines productivity in much the same manner as Mott (see Figure 14–6). Price defines morale as the degree to which individual motives are gratified. Absenteeism and turnover rates can be used as indicators of morale (see also Lyons, 1972). A number of investigators (for example, Price, 1972; Ullrich, 1972; Vroom, 1964) have differentiated several kinds of behavioral criteria for organizations, with *work satisfaction* or an emotional state (indicated by turnover and absenteeism) differentiated from motiva-

FIGURE 14-6
Mott's questionnaire items used to measure criteria of effectiveness

Every worker produces something in his work. It may be a product or a service. But sometimes it is very difficult to identify the product or service. Below are listed some of the products and services being produced in the Office of Administration.*

- Typed pages
- Delivered mail
- Dispatched automobiles
- Staff papers and studies
- Coding systems
- Recommended policies and procedures
- New programs
- Classified jobs
- Supplying new equipment
- Contracts

These are just a few of the things being produced.

We would like you to think carefully of the things that you produce in your work and of the things produced by those people who work around you in your division.

(Production: Quantity)
Thinking now of the various things produced by the people you know *in your division*, how much are they producing?
_____(1) Their production is very low.
_____(2) It is fairly low.
_____(3) It is neither high nor low.
_____(4) It is fairly high.
_____(5) It is very high.

(Production: Quality)
How good would you say is the *quality* of the products or services produced by the people you know *in your division*?
_____(1) Their products or services are of poor quality.
_____(2) Their quality is not too good.
_____(3) Fair quality.
_____(4) Good quality.
_____(5) Excellent quality.

(Production: Efficiency)
Do the people in your division seem to get maximum output from the resources (money, people, equipment, etc.) they have available? That is, how *efficiently* do they do their work?
_____(1) They do not work efficiently at all.
_____(2) Not too efficient.
_____(3) Fairly efficient.
_____(4) They are very efficient.
_____(5) They are extremely efficient.

(Adaptation: Anticipating Problems and Solving Them Satisfactorily)
How good a job is done by the people in your division in *anticipating* problems that may come up in the future and preventing them from occurring or minimizing their effects?
_____(1) They do a poor job in anticipating problems.
_____(2) Not too good a job.
_____(3) A fair job.
_____(4) They do a very good job.
_____(5) They do an excellent job in anticipating problems.

(Adaptation: Awareness of Potential Solutions)
From time to time newer ways are discovered to organize work, and newer equipment and techniques are found with which to do the work. How good a job do the people in your division do at keeping up with those changes that could affect the way they do their work?

FIGURE 14-6 (continued)

_____(1)	They do a poor job of keeping up to date.
_____(2)	Not too good a job.
_____(3)	A fair job.
_____(4)	They do a very good job.
_____(5)	They do an excellent job of keeping up to date.

(Adaptation: Promptness of Adjustment)
When changes are made in the routines or equipment, how *quickly* do the people in your division accept and adjust to these changes?

_____(1)	Most people accept and adjust to them very slowly.
_____(2)	Rather slowly.
_____(3)	Fairly rapidly.
_____(4)	They adjust very rapidly, but not immediately.
_____(5)	Most people accept and adjust to them immediately.

(Adaptation: Prevalence of Adjustment)
What *proportion* of the people in your division readily accept and adjust to these changes?

_____(1)	Considerably less than half of the people accept and adjust to these changes readily.
_____(2)	Slightly less than half do.
_____(3)	The majority do.
_____(4)	Considerably more than half do.
_____(5)	Practically everyone accepts and adjusts to these changes readily.

(Flexibility)
From time to time emergencies arise, such as crash programs, schedules moved ahead, or a breakdown in the flow of work occurs. When these emergencies occur, they cause work overloads for many people. Some work groups cope with these emergencies more readily and successfully than others. How good a job do the people in your division do at coping with these situations?

_____(1)	They do a poor job of handling emergency situations.
_____(2)	They do not do very well.
_____(3)	They do a fair job.
_____(4)	They do a good job.
_____(5)	They do an excellent job of handling these situations.

* The names of other agencies were substituted when appropriate.
Source: Mott (1972, pp. 21–24). Copyright © 1972 by Paul E. Mott. Reprinted by permission of Harper & Row Publishers, Inc.

tion. *Motivation* usually is measured by the amount of effort put forth by workers or by their degree of commitment to the organization and its goals (Lodahl and Kejner, 1965; Patchen, 1965).[5]

We have already discussed what Price terms adaptation, including Mott's adaptability and flexibility measures cited above. A somewhat related and important criterion from Price, but one not often treated because it presents both conceptual and measurement difficulties, is *innovation*. Innovative behavior is change inducing, as is adaptive behavior, but the change, in the

---

[5] Related to the study of satisfaction and motivation, mainly by psychologists, is the study of "alienation," or the extent to which work entails a feeling of meaninglessness, separation, isolation, powerlessness, or apathy (Blauner, 1964; Miller, 1967; Pearlin, 1962; Seeman, 1959).

former case, is in a novel direction. Forehand (1963) suggests that "innovative behavior includes the development and consideration of novel solutions to administrative problems, and evaluation of them in terms of criteria broader than conformity to preexisting practice . . ." (p. 206). Price (1972), following Becker and Whisler (1967), defines innovation as "the degree to which a social system is a first or early user of an idea among its set of similar social systems" (p. 118). Examples of measures of innovativeness include questionnaire items that are designed to determine workers' interests in work-related innovation and their attitudes toward changes introduced to their jobs (see Patchen, 1965).[6]

Until recently, relatively few systematic scientific studies have been conducted at the organizational level of analysis, wherein the organization per se is evaluated as a source of innovation (*Trans-action*, 1970). Much of the extant work is based on analogies with creativity in small groups of scientists (Gary Steiner, 1965). However, a useful discussion of bureaucracy and its effects on innovation is presented by Victor Thompson (1965). The literature on diffusion of new technologies (hybrid seed corn to farmers, drugs to physicians, and so on) is also useful (Coleman, Katz, and Menzel, 1966; Havelock, 1971; Rogers, 1962; Rosner, 1968).

Further criteria

Many of the criteria discussed above are found as overt organizational goals, or at least as subgoals of individuals within the organization. However, as one becomes more specific in defining these criteria, they shade off into the system needs described by Georgopoulos. When evaluating an organization, it is useful to view these criteria as an additional checklist for matters that are vital to the organization over the long run, but that may be, and often are, overlooked in the short run. It may be recalled that the Georgopoulos list included (1) adaption, (2) allocation, (3) coordination, (4) integration, (5) tension management, (6) productivity, and (7) integrity. As we have indicated, consensus does not exist among students of organizations on the exact nature of these critical system needs. Be that as it may, the Georgopoulos list seems both comprehensive in terms of existing theoretical models and also relatively practical, as is indicated by its usefulness in studies of hospitals (Georgopoulos and Mann, 1962; Georgopoulos and Matejko, 1967; Georgopoulos and Wieland, 1964).[7]

---

[6] Of related interest as sources of criteria for innovation are the many studies of scientists and engineers that use as criteria such things as patents, publications, and ratings by peers or superiors. However, inventiveness and creativity do not always lead to innovation as it has been defined here (Doctors, 1970). See Pelz and Andrews (1966), Smith (1970), Andrews and Farris (1967), Gordon and Marquis (1966).

[7] Examples of other criteria of effectiveness include Price's (1968) "conformity" (the extent to which performance corresponds to institutional norms or the extent to which organizational decisions are supported by the environment), Georgopoulos and Tannen-

Another potentially useful set of operational criteria is found in the Ansoff-Brandenburg (1971) lists of measures for evaluating organizational designs. It is of interest to note the parallels that exist between these and Mott's operational criteria. Of further interest is the fact that Ansoff and Brandenburg point to another criterion that can be added to those of Mott.

Ansoff and Brandenburg's (1971) concepts of steady state efficiency, structural responsiveness, and operating responsiveness are assumed to be included under Mott's criteria of productivity, adaptability, and flexibility, respectively. The concept of *strategic responsiveness* is novel. We shall add this to our list of six operative criteria discussed above. It may be recalled that this criterion refers to an organization's "... ability to respond to changes in the *nature* (rather than volume) of its throughput, such as obsolescence of products, changes in product technology, emergence of international markets, opportunities to enter new lines of business, [and] changes in legal and social constraints under which the organization is forced to operate. Firms typically respond to these by changing [the] composition of their products and markets, acquisition of other firms, or divesting from parts of existing operations" (Ansoff and Brandenburg, 1971, p. 711).

External criteria

Most of the criteria examined so far concern internal organizational functioning. This is particularly true of efficiency (or productivity) criteria, which assume external goals and direct our energies toward the optimal, rational arrangement of means toward these ends. Criteria that are concerned with adaptation or flexibility are less internal since they deal with the organization's behavior in relation to a dynamic and changing environment. However, these models essentially view the organization as adapting in a reactive way to the environment. Characteristics of the organization, rather than the organization's effects on its environment, serve as criteria.

A further task for the evaluator is to operationalize what Yuchtman and Seashore have termed the *system-resource position* vis-à-vis the environment. We shall refer to the *political effectiveness* of the system, for this eighth and final addition to our list of operative criteria (see Figure 14–7). Relevant here are the organization's exchanges with the environment including, in the case of business firms, profitability as a measure of the efficacy of these exchanges.

It can be argued that even the system-resource view of organizational effectiveness focuses attention within the organization. Admittedly, our attention is drawn to the organization's power to act and to its history of past interactions. For this reason, we propose the use of operative goals as criteria

---

baum's (1957) criterion of the absence of intraorganizational strain or tension, and Caplow's (1964) "integration" ("the organization's ability to maintain or increase the total volume of interaction among its positions or, negatively, to control internal conflict") p. 123.

FIGURE 14-7
Evaluating organizations: Operative criteria, system needs, and values

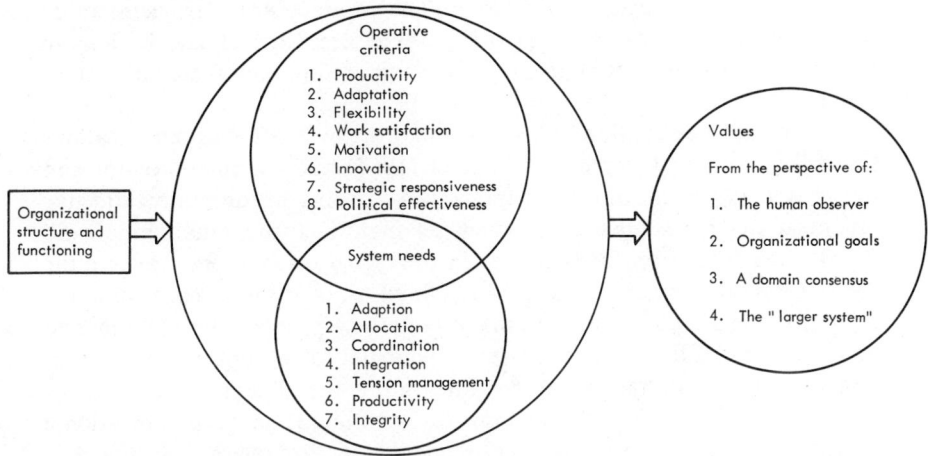

Note: The above list of operative criteria and system needs provides a set of overlapping criteria which measure outcomes of the structure and functioning of the organization. The outcomes, furthermore, have implications for the organizational values; values taken from a variety of perspectives—the individual, the organization's goals and domain, and the larger system.

that will serve as correctives in the process of evaluation. Operative goals of interest to the evaluator include those of the dominant coalition in the organization and also those of groups in the environment who control crucial contingencies. The groups on which the organization depends for resources, for supplying inputs or taking outputs, are groups with significant power over the organization. The degree to which exchanges are advantageous for the organization (and the extent of the organization's political effectiveness) will be determined by the extent to which organizational goal attainment is congruent with the expectations that these groups have of the organization. We have discussed this in Chapters 6, 7, and 8.

No single criterion: Trade-offs and suboptimization

Different organizational arrangements may be needed to meet the two basic kinds of criteria we have discussed—efficiency criteria (for internal functioning) and political criteria (for relations with the environment). Any single arrangement may have to be chosen on the basis of the trade-offs one desires to make. Certainly there is evidence that some of the criteria we have discussed are in conflict; for example, Ansoff and Brandenburg's operating responsiveness conflicts with organizational attempts to achieve steady state efficiency. Mott (1972) provides empirical evidence that flexibility (responsiveness to emergencies in hospitals) is negatively associated with adaptation or problem solving in these hospitals. Walker and Lorsch (1968) find that two closely matched factories differ primarily in whether they were organized by product or function. The result they found is a trade-off between productivity and manager satisfaction. The product structure yields more conflicts between managers and a high level of stress in exchange for a more dynamic, increased level of productivity compared to the functionally organized plant.

In view of these conflicts, we suggest that the evaluation of organizations take a leaf from the Lawrence and Lorsch (1967) study of differentiation and integration in organizations (Chapter 3). According to this study, effective organizations have subsystems (such as manufacturing, marketing, and R&D) that differ from one another in their goal orientations. Despite the conflict produced by dissimilar goal orientations, or in fact because of it, the organizations are effective (in terms of growth of profits, sales volume, and new products). Effectiveness, however, is achieved through the incorporation of various special means for integrating the dissimilar subsystems. Thus, efficiency alone, or some rational configuration of organizational parts to achieve system needs, is insufficient to realize overall effectiveness. What is needed, in addition, is a certain amount of tension or conflict between subsystems and operative goals and organizational practices that allow the optimization of conflicting goals to be realized through various integrating mechanisms.

Suboptimization as a virtue

In a study of universities in which he illustrates the rather different goals held by different subgroups or stakeholders, Edward Gross (1968) suggests that such conflicts are similar to the phenomenon economists have termed *suboptimization* (Chapter 6). Suboptimization also is likely to be found in organizations that include groups of craftsmen or professionals. Similarly, Merton (1957) describes the bureaucratic personality who rigidly adheres to a rule rather than to the end which the rule addresses. A certain amount of this, however, may be desirable. Oftentimes, considerable attention must be given to activities that are indirectly related (or even unrelated) to overall organizational goals. Gross thus introduces the notion of support goals, or what we have termed *system needs*. If the plumbing of a university is so much in need of repair that the health department is threatening to close it down, then some organizational unit (plant operations) must devote its entire attention to the task of improving the plumbing system, even to the extent that concerns for efficiency are temporarily cast aside.

Suboptimization is not necessarily a temporary matter. After the university in our example encourages plant operations to suboptimize at the possible expense of faculty and student needs, it may encourage the engineering school to do so because of falling student enrollments, and so on. But the actual situation often is worse than the one we have described. Besides sequentially attending to matters that seem to require suboptimization, the university devotes major resources to a number of efforts that conflict with one another. Attempts to meet maintenance goals (our system needs) frequently conflict with attempts to achieve output goals. This can be the case when athletic programs that are intended to secure alumni loyalty and, consequently, financial support for the university compete with academic programs for the organization's limited resources. Although suboptimization in the extreme clearly is dysfunctional for the organization, we would argue that limited and intelligently managed conflict must be determined in part by the ultimate values of the organization and its top management (see, for example, Guth and Tagiuri, 1965; Miner, 1968).

Values

This leads us to a final set of criteria for organizational effectiveness. We have seen that criteria for internal functioning (efficiency criteria) must be supplemented with criteria for the relationship between the organization and its environment (political effectiveness criteria). But, efficiency and power over the environment are only means to an end. They may be sufficient to allow us to make judgments about the effectiveness of an organization if we accept a machine model of organizations, but not if we are to deal with them as social entities. People are the essential components of organizations, and people concern themselves with alternatives over and above those that deal with efficiency and power over the environment.

We submit that the latter criteria are necessary but not sufficient to the task of judging an organization to be effective or ineffective. We must also subject organizations to criteria derived from human values. An organization, as a creation of society, is subject to evaluation in terms of the values of the society in which it resides.

This point becomes clear if we envision a Briton in 1940 contemplating the very efficient and politically effective Third Reich across the English Channel—an organization that stood for values antithetical to England's own. A more problematic situation—one that calls for a very careful examination of our values and the trade-offs and risks that we are willing to undertake—confronts us in evaluating an organization that realizes enviable profits through the production and sale of hardcore pornography. Such also is the case with arms manufacturers who, while improving our balance of trade, sell their merchandise to under-developed nations that cannot really afford them. Finally, if one values the compact car because of its conservation of materials and energy, should one not judge the less profitable and less powerful (in system-resource terms) American Motors to be more effective than the more profitable and powerful General Motors? In this connection, our earlier discussion of contributions to the larger system is appropriate.

As we saw in our discussion of leadership (Chapter 12), a vital function of top management is to decide the directions that the organization takes and, consequently, to mold its character, including its values. If this is not undertaken consciously, a diffuse, confused, or even undesirable organizational character may result. In short, a considerable amount of an organization's activity is directed toward matters that are not covered by the rational model. An organization is far more than an efficient arrangement of means or even an effective source of political power. It has implications for human values and for the values embodied in organizational goals, in the organization's domain, and in the larger system (see Figure 14–7).

We argue that the evaluator must go beyond mere technicality. Organizations, whether by design, error, or oversight, reflect value choices that bear directly on the lives of people (including you and me) and on what these people want, cherish, and esteem.

DISCUSSION QUESTIONS

1. How do the concepts of effectiveness and efficiency differ? Can an organization be efficient but ineffective?
2. What are system needs? What are some examples?
3. Under what circumstances would you be willing to sacrifice organizational efficiency for flexibility? Are there limits to such trade-offs?

SECTION V

Changing the Organization

Chapter 15
Introduction to Organizational Change

Chapter 16
The Process of Change in Organizations

Chapter 17
The Future: Some Ways of Thinking

PREMISE

As we look at our society, we cannot help but sense frustration. So many aspects of contemporary life could be improved! We seem to possess the means with which to change for the better, and surely there are ends on which we all agree. Why, then, are improvements so long in coming?

We have made modest suggestions for improving organizations throughout our text. These range from the trivial (changing relationships between people) to the monumental (changing an organization's technology or goals). However, we have not yet dealt systematically with the problems encountered in introducing even trivial changes to organizations. The problems associated with changing complex organizations together with tentative solutions for these problems constitute the substance of our final chapters.

15

Introduction to Organizational Change

INTRODUCTION

Throughout preceding sections of this text we have suggested changes that can improve organizational performance. However, it is one thing to understand the nature of desirable changes and quite another to know how to make them. Introducing successful organizational change is an extremely difficult task—one that requires a great breadth of knowledge and skill. We have devoted the remaining section of our text to the study of change processes for this reason.

We indicated that, in theory, strategic change is an organizational response made in anticipation of substantial environmental changes. We also attempted to provide convincing evidence that the process of strategic change is less rational and more political than is sometimes thought. The evidence also compels us to assume that strategic changes are more often reactions to discontinuities in the environment than anticipations of such changes. For reasons to be investigated in this section, individuals and organizations seem to adhere to the status quo, even after changing circumstances render such behavior inappropriate. It sometimes appears as if organizations forestall needed adaptations until impending crises force the issue.

For example, consider the plight of higher education in America today.

As the last member of the post-World War II baby boom receives a sheepskin, the wave of young adults for whom existing educational facilities were expanded will have passed through the system. Although many schools experienced increased enrollments in the 1970s because of the high rate of unemployment, we can predict with certainty that the number of 18-year-olds applying for admission to colleges and universities will decline over the next decade. This trend is elaborated in the following *Time* article:

The Student Shortage

For graduating high school seniors, the once-traditional spring/summer struggle to get into college—any college—appears to have gone the way of the draft and campus demonstrations. With fall sessions at some schools only weeks away, the National Association of College Admissions Counselors reported last week that there are still about 500,000 openings for freshmen and transfer students at colleges and universities across the country. The figures mark the second straight year of declining college enrollments. California alone has at least 40,000 vacancies. Even in New England, some 25,000 places are going begging, although the area's Ivy League and other prestigious schools can still pick and choose as much as they please.

Officials attribute the decline to a number of factors. The 1970s have brought both the close of the postwar baby boom that swelled the ranks of college-age youth in the 1960s and the end of the Viet Nam conflict, which drove many young people to seek shelter on campus from the Selective Service. Vocational schools are becoming more popular, while fewer parents are willing or able to cope with rising college costs (the current annual average at private four-year schools: $3,504).

Many institutions, especially state colleges, overexpanded in the 1960s. They now find themselves underutilized. Says Nancy Barber of the Western Interstate Commission on Higher Education: "Colleges will have to find other ways to put their facilities to use. Hopefully there will be more recruitment of the poor, minorities and the elderly" (*Time*, 1974, p. 86).[1]

Chapter guide

1. Although estimates vary, it is common to hear that 200 to 300 colleges and universities will close their doors within the next decade. Do you think that this form of societal divestment will be the result of strategy or merely a reaction to circumstances?
2. Is it desirable to change the purposes of universities, if this is essential to keep them from closing?
3. Changes in the university's environment include decreases in student demand for higher education and increases in the numbers of candidates for faculty positions. What organizational responses may be appropriate under these circumstances? What forms of resistance are to be

---

[1] Reprinted by permission from *Time*, The Weekly Newsmagazine. Copyright Time, Inc.

expected when these responses are made? What dilemmas are raised by alternative responses?

DETERMINANTS OF ORGANIZATIONAL CHANGE

Some determinants of change in organizations

As our discussion of organizational change unfolds, it will become evident that most work in the area comes from psychologists, whose studies emphasize the behavior of individuals in organizations. Equally important from our point of view is the study of the organization as a whole. The major, systematic sociological study of this sort is the work of Hage and Aiken (1970), to which we shall devote a considerable part of this chapter.

Hage and Aiken are concerned with the rate at which organizations change themselves and the factors that foster or impede this rate of change. Why is it that some organizations are quick to adopt even untested ideas while others are slow to implement changes that have withstood the test of time? Although General Motors and Ford faced comparable circumstances during the 1920s, the former successfully developed a number of new products while the latter did not. Why do organizations with the same general objectives and comparable environments seem to differ in terms of the rate at which they change themselves? This is the question addressed by Hage and Aiken.

The focus of their study is *program change,* which they define as the addition of new services or products. Please bear in mind that these were the only kinds of changes studied and that, furthermore, the ultimate success or failure of these change efforts was not considered.

Hage and Aiken focus on seven organizational variables: (1) degree of complexity, (2) centralization, (3) formalization, (4) stratification, (5) production, (6) efficiency, and (7) job satisfaction. These particular aspects were selected because they were well studied in the literature and found to be related in one way or another to the rate of program change. Other aspects were considered but discarded when found to be more or less unimportant in determining the rate of change in organizations.

We shall take each of these variables in turn and examine evidence that suggests its relationship to the change process. Much of this evidence comes from Hage and Aiken's survey of 16 welfare agencies that provided services in the areas of physical rehabilitation, mental rehabilitation, or psychiatry.

Complexity

Complexity refers to (1) the extent of knowledge and skill required of occupational roles and (2) their diversity. Organizations employing many different kinds of professionals are highly complex. One way to measure complexity is to determine the *number* of different occupations within an organization that require specialized knowledge and skills. An organization can be considered complex when it employs numerous kinds of knowledge and skills (occupations) and when these occupations require sophistication in their respective knowledge and skill areas. A general hospital is a complex organization. Typically, members of 50 different occupational groups will appear on the wards in the course of 24 hours. One will find a variety of nurses (having different amounts and kinds of training), dieticians, X-ray technologists, laboratory technologists, a variety of physicians of different specialties, occupational therapists, orthopedic therapists, medical social workers, psychiatric social workers, chaplains, ward clerks, housekeepers, janitors, engineers, various kinds of administrators, and others.

Organizations employing professionals of a single kind (or a few kinds) are less complex. An elementary school is of moderate complexity. Relatively few occupations are employed, and required levels of knowledge and skills within occupations are relatively modest. At the low end of the scale of complexity, one finds organizations such as automobile factories that employ a relatively homogeneous, unskilled, and unknowledgeable work force.

Hage and Aiken measured complexity in their sample of welfare agencies in terms of the number of occupational specialties employed, the length of professional training required by each specialty, and the extent of employees' involvement in professional societies and activities. It was found that the greater the complexity, the greater the rate of program change. The rationale for this relationship seems clear. In addition to their formal training, professionals engage in constant study to remain abreast of advances in their respective fields. Acquisition of new knowledge paves the way for change. Professionals may work themselves into new professions eventually. Alternatively, they may recognize the need for new kinds of professionals who can aid in the pursuit of their objectives. Social psychologists are results of the first kind of change, and media specialists who support faculty teaching are results of the latter. The professional's service ideal also contributes to the high rate of change in complex organizations. To be of service implies seeking the best ways to meet client needs. Obviously, improvements to existing service delivery practices frequently take the form of program changes.

Centralization

Centralization (Chapter 5) is a measure of the distribution of power within the organization. According to Hage and Aiken, the fewer the occupations participating in decision making and the fewer the areas of decision making in which they are involved, the more centralized the organization.

Hage and Aiken find that the higher the organization's degree of centralization, the lower its rate of program change. An explanation of this finding is that a centralized organization, with power concentrated in the hands of a few individuals, tends toward the status quo because their power enables them to protect their own interests and to veto changes that are likely to threaten them. Michel's iron law of oligarchy describes the situation well.

In a decentralized organization, where decision-making power is more widespread, a variety of different views will emerge from different occupational groups. This variety of opinion can lead to conflict, but also to successful resolution of conflict and to problem solving. In any event, decentralization appears to foster the initiation of new programs and techniques that are proposed as solutions to various organizational problems. However, Hage and Aiken suggest that these organizations will be slow to implement the changes initiated. In a decentralized organization, it takes time for suggested changes in products and services to receive approval of all individuals party to the decision to implement them. A centralized organization may produce fewer new ideas, but once an idea is put forth its implementation is fairly straightforward. Lines of communication are clear and direct. The route to top management for ultimate approval or disapproval is traveled quickly. Nevertheless, in the long run, it is likely that the decentralized organization will experience more initiation of change and a greater number of actual program changes than the centralized organization. This, in fact, is what Hage and Aiken found in their study of welfare agencies.

Formalization

Formalization represents the extent to which jobs are governed by rules and specific guidelines. It may be recalled that this aspect of organization is typical of bureaucracies. Measures of formalization can be attempted in a number of ways. One may count the number of rules that apply to *jobs,* as these are found in formal job descriptions, rules manuals, or staff handbooks. In fact, the mere existence of such documents suggests a relatively high degree of formalization. Alternatively, one may count the number of rules and regulations that operate in the *organization* as a whole. These may be codified or unwritten as in the case of norms.

As one would expect, Hage and Aiken found that the greater the degree of formalization, the lower the rate of program change. Rules and norms discourage search for better ways of doing things. Furthermore, they rigidify the organization and promote homogeneity among its various units. Thus, implementation of change is made difficult, since even a minor change may impact on extensive portions of the organization. Rules, regulations, job descriptions, and the like serve to stabilize an organization's behavior—to make it reliable and predictable. Obviously, they militate against change.

A recent study of the Teacher Corps, however, provides an example of how formalization (as well as centralization) can foster change (Corwin, 1972). The aim of the Teacher Corps is to promote educational reforms in low-income schools through innovative teacher training programs. Corwin found that in the 42 schools studied, innovations (such as team teaching, introduction of black history, and mixed-age grouping) were associated with the organizational control exerted by the schools. Those with centralized decision-making procedures, stress on rules and procedures, and emphasis on pupil discipline were schools that innovated.

The contrast with the Hage and Aiken study is explained by the observation that implementation, not initiation of innovations, was studied in these organizations. While the universities and interns provided ideas, the administrators and their staff selected and implemented them. In the Corwin study, formalization and centralization fostered change. In this situation teachers *had to change* the way they were teaching. Rather than tacking a new program onto ongoing programs, a fairly simple matter for Hage and Aiken's professionals, top administration was responsible for selecting innovations and then seeing that they were implemented properly. A centralized administration with control of resources and the ability to formulate and enforce rules and regulations was able to enforce and also to *help* the process of innovation. (See also Gross, Giacquinta, and Bernstein [1971] for further evidence, and Wilson [1966] and Zaltman et al. [1973] for a similar argument.) In sum, where emphasis is on implementation rather than initiation of innovations, centralization and formalization may be assets.

For each of the above—complexity, centralization, and formalization—Hage and Aiken found evidence (in both the research literature and their own study) of relationships with program change. Several further aspects of organizations discussed below, however, receive less support from the literature and the study, and they are to be viewed somewhat more tentatively as characteristics that influence an organization's propensity to change.

Stratification

Rewards are distributed fairly equally among members in some organizations and differentially in others. Stratification is a measure of this phenomenon. When some employees receive higher salaries, greater status, and more fringe benefits than others, their organization is said to be highly stratified. A second dimension of stratification concerns mobility between different parts of the organization. An organization is *not* considered highly stratified when employees are free to move vertically and horizontally among jobs, even when the rewards associated with these jobs differ markedly. Barriers to mobility (advancement), as well as heterogeneity in rewards, contribute to stratification.

According to Hage and Aiken, the greater the degree of stratification, the lower the rate of program change. Here again the iron law of oligarchy seems to apply. Where rewards are distributed unequally, those receiving the largest share resist changes that threaten their advantage. Now, one might argue that differences in rewards will motivate individuals at lower levels of the organization to work their way up in the hierarchy and that, consequently, they will seek improvements over the status quo to gain recognition that eventually will result in promotion. While this may occur, suggestions for change will be muted to the extent that they are perceived as criticisms of higher level employees. Thus, advocacy of change is undertaken reluctantly.

In general, high stratification discourages accurate upward communication. Lower-level employees tend to tell their superiors what they want to hear. It has been argued that much of the distorted information in the Vietnam War was attributable to this phenomenon. Inflated body counts were reported because they were met with approbation by superiors. What evidence there is suggests that stratification blocks interaction and communication and, therefore, retards not only the initiation of change, but also its implementation.

Production

As used by Hage and Aiken, production measures organizational emphasis on *volume* of output rather than *quality*. The number of units produced (or clients served) varies from one organization to another. Some automobile manufacturers engage in mass production of cars just as large state universities offer their services to a large number of students. These can be contrasted with manufacturers of limited production cars (for example, Jensen and Jaguar) and small, private universities that employ low student-faculty ratios.

Hage and Aiken argue that the higher the volume of production, the lower the rate of program change. Their rationale is that emphasis on speed of production and volume, rather than on quality, leads management to resist interruptions of the productive process such as program changes are likely to entail. High-volume production permits the realization of economies of scale. Steady state efficiency becomes valued more than operating or strategic responsiveness (Chapter 3). Success attained in operating the implied kind of technology will militate further against change. It is difficult to argue in favor of altering a system that produces satisfactory results.

Organizations with these characteristics can be contrasted with others emphasizing quality of production. The latter orientation will direct management's attention toward means for improving production standards or, at least, for preventing their deterioration. Research and development activities will be directed toward product (or service) improvement. These improvements often are found in the form of program changes.

Efficiency

The sixth variable studied, efficiency, measures the relative cost of producing the organization's product or service. Some organizations are more concerned with costs than others; for example, research institutes generally are less concerned with operating efficiently than are the organizations that apply knowledge generated by the former.

A review of the literature provides some evidence that the greater the emphasis on efficiency, the lower the rate of program change. As Hage and Aiken suggest, new programs incur additional costs, some of which are unpredictable. Additional costs, especially those which are uncertain and, thus, uncontrollable, are unattractive to managers whose orientations are toward cost reduction and operating efficiencies. Of course, some innovations are sought as a means toward cost reduction. Necessity is the handmaiden of invention, as we say, and problems accompanied by high costs may lead to innovations directed toward their improvement. A close examination of such innovations, however, suggests that costs are *not* reduced in many cases. The application of computer technology to paper work problems is a common example of innovation that does not necessarily improve costs. Furthermore, cost-cutting innovations seems to be rarer than other kinds aimed at improving quality or providing hitherto unavailable services. In short, the efficiency-seeking organization is likely to play a wait and see game—to be a follower rather than an innovator in its industry.

Job satisfaction

The final variable studied by Hage and Aiken is job satisfaction. Overall job satisfaction usually is assumed to be related to satisfaction with a variety of specific factors such as pay, fellow workers, supervision, working conditions, and the like.[2] One index of job satisfaction is the rate of employee turnover. Dissatisfied employees tend to leave their organizations in search of better jobs.

Hage and Aiken found a moderate relationship between job satisfaction and the rate of program change. The more satisfaction, the greater the rate of change. Apparently, satisfied employees become committed to their organizations. This commitment entails a desire to improve organizational effectiveness and a willingness to explore new ideas and try out the suggestions of others.

Systemic qualities of the variables studied

Hage and Aiken's most important point is that the seven variables and rate of program change seem interrelated. In static organizations the rate of program change is low and *all* of the seven variables seem to be arranged to contribute to organizational stability. Organizations that do not change their programs frequently also seem typified by high degrees of (1) centralization,

---

[2] The nature of this relationship, though, is anything but clear. See, for example, Wanous and Lawler (1972).

(2) formalization, (3) stratification, and (4) emphasis on high-volume production, and (5) efficiency and low degrees of (6) complexity and (7) job satisfaction.

In other words, these seven characteristics are *systemic qualities* of organizations. If one variable changes, the others tend to change as well in directions that are compatible with the change in the first. Hage and Aiken carry this analysis further. First, they argue that dynamic and static organizations arise in different kinds of environments. The dynamic organization arises in an unstable environment and the static organization in one that is stable. This analysis is useful since it enables us to anticipate changes in an organization based on our perceptions of changes in its environment. Second, Hage and Aiken suggest that changes in certain variables induce conforming changes in the remaining variables. A dynamic organization is most likely created by increases in its *complexity*. Alternatively, an organization can be rendered more stable by increasing its degree of *centralization*. These two observations provide us with levers, as it were, with which managers can attempt to move their organizations in desired directions. However, we must be careful to note that changes in these variables do not cause the organization to change. Rather, they are assumed to affect the organization's propensity to change.

Before examining the characteristics of static and dynamic organizations in greater detail, we are compelled to emphasize that neither kind is superior to the other. In general, it is appropriate to view the organization's degree of change propensity in terms of its adequacy in meeting environmental demands. Therefore, it is important to understand how both kinds of organization evolve, since it may be necessary for management to move the organization first in one direction and then in the other as its environment changes.

Dynamic organizations

As the knowledge employed by an organization increases in quantity, complexity, and diversity, it becomes increasingly difficult for a few top managers to maintain a monopoly on power. As organizations become knowledge intensive, they make decisions on the basis of the combined inputs from experts and specialists. *Complexity* seems to require decentralization of power to make or influence decisions. Furthermore, as we noted in Chapter 10, experts and specialists seem to work best on a relatively informal basis. Gaining external control of professional activities is difficult, if not at times impossible. Generally, professionals require freedom sufficient to deal with problems that cannot be programmed in any simple fashion with rules, regulations, job descriptions, or plans. Knowledge-based organizations tend to rely on the quality of their professionals' training to control their behavior and ensure adequate job performance rather than on rules or programs. In consequence, the relative absence of rules and programs together with the associated distribution of decision-making power foster horizontal as well as vertical communication. Reliance on others for help in the coordination and execution of one's own tasks fosters teamwork and tends to diminish status differences among interrelated occupations. In other words, stratification is reduced.

As we saw earlier, highly trained employees may emphasize quality and service to the client as opposed to efficiency, corner-cutting, or cost reduction. Finally, highly trained employees (whose training is utilized in their occupations) seem to derive more satisfaction from their jobs than do employees possessing and using lesser skills. This may result from their power to demand or negotiate better, more satisfying conditions of work. In general, then, it seems that although each of the variables can affect the others, *complexity* is of paramount importance in determining the dynamic properties of the organizational system.

Static organizations

Let us turn now to static organizations. The less complex an organization, the more it depends on unskilled employees who perform simple, specialized tasks. Similarly, these organizations do not depend on the knowledge and training of such employees to the extent indicated above. Such organizations tend to be highly *centralized.* Centralization (control from the top) implies that behavior in the rest of the organization is controlled via formalization, the use of job descriptions, rules manuals, evaluation systems, records, and the like. Also flowing from centralization is stratification—differences in rewards and low mobility in the organization.

The general policies of such organizations are likely to stress quantity of production and efficiency. As we indicated earlier, quantity is a less costly criterion of effectiveness than quality, which may require continual changes in the productive processes. Finally, external control, inequality of rewards, simple-minded jobs, and poor working conditions are likely to affect employee satisfaction adversely. In short, the qualities mentioned are likely to conform to one another in static organizations. Apparently, the critical factor among these is centralization, which seems to affect the others directly.

Stable and dynamic environments

Hage and Aiken suggest that the environment becomes unstable (dynamic) as a result of increases in knowledge. Growth in knowledge can affect both the demand for products and services and the technologies used to produce them. As knowledge increases, new products become available and the demand for older products diminishes. When this happens, the organization must adapt accordingly, seeking innovations to replace services and products for which demand is waning and installing technologies capable of producing them.

Changes in technology sometimes require the addition of new occupations spawned by the technology itself; for example, consider the number of computer programmers and systems engineers employed today and recall that these occupations were not found in businesses, governmental agencies, or hospitals 30 years ago. Major organizational changes have resulted from the introduction of computer technology which, in turn, resulted from acquisition of knowledge in the information sciences. In summary, this suggests that environmental instability stems from increased knowledge, which in turn requires organizations to become more complex. As we have suggested, increased complexity produces corresponding changes in other organizational qualities that allow the organization to become more change prone.

This can be contrasted with a relatively stable environment in which organizations experience constant or steadily changing (predictable) demand for their products and services. Since knowledge develops slowly, technology changes gradually. Under these conditions, there is little need to launch new programs to produce new products or services, nor is there need to introduce new technologies and occupations. In a stable environment, organizations can pursue the modus operandi suggested by the rational school of thought (Chapter 2). When goals are clear (for example, market share in an unchanging market) and when means toward the achievement of these goals are stable (for example, technology), the organization can centralize and structure itself to produce as efficiently as possible. From this follow the other characteristics of stable organizations, including low rates of program change.

Diversification

The environment can encourage or force diversification in a number of ways (Chapter 7), and through diversification, complexity is increased; for example, governments may force diversification through antitrust proceedings. Declining markets may encourage similar changes, although more subtly. As indicated at the beginning of this chapter, colleges are seeking to diversify their services in the face of declining student populations.

The important point is that the addition of products and services requires employment of additional occupations that add to complexity. As we have noted, increases in complexity are likely to affect change propensity through the remaining variables. Diversification also seems to encourage decentralization. Problems of coordination increase as heterogeneous elements are added to the organization. The resulting overload of top management is ameliorated when decentralized profit centers are established (Chapter 5). These centers are responsive to local circumstances and free top management's time for matters of strategic concern.

Similar to the effects of diversification are those of interorganizational programs. When organizations collaborate to produce a product or service, different occupational groups may be brought into contact. It follows that the creation of joint programs can increase organizational complexity.

Scientific management

A number of variables in addition to the seven identified by Hage and Aiken seem to affect the organization's propensity to change. The first of these might be termed *rationalism,* as exemplified by scientific management (Chapter 2). Victor Thompson (1969) suggests that application of scientific management techniques may hinder the organization's propensity to change.

Bureaucracy is a rational form of organization emphasizing formal rules and a hierarchy of authority that can be ascended by only the most competent employees. The higher one rises in the organization, the greater the rewards and power one enjoys. Scientific management contributes a second dimension of rationality to bureaucracy—economic rationality, which Hage and Aiken term *efficiency.* Going beyond structural arrangements, scientific management addresses problems of efficiency in decision making. Formulas and programs are sought to provide optimal solutions to problems of middle and top management as well as to the problems of shop floor employees, which were studied in Taylor's early work.

The so-called Planning, Programming, and Budgeting System (PPBS) of control developed by the Department of Defense under Secretary McNamara is a modern elaboration of Taylor's line of thought. Under this system, the organization identifies its goals and objectives, elaborates various means for their attainment, and estimates the results to be expected from each alternative for each dollar spent over a period of, perhaps, several years. If all costs and benefits are measured for all feasible alternatives, an optimal arrangement will be found. This logic assumes that organizational effectiveness is a function of rational management.

Thompson's point is that even when such approaches to management work, they are liable to have drastic effects on the organization's propensity to change. Furthermore, there are many situations in which the approaches will not work at all. Most organizational problems include human factors that cannot be measured adequately, and, therefore, cannot be entered into a formula. Another area of difficulty concerns goals. Most organizations pursue multiple goals. The optimal strategy to achieve one goal (supposing it can be identified) may prove detrimental to the attainment of a second, equally important, goal. Yet, it is impossible to consider these goals simultaneously—to determine an indifference schedule that permits identification of trade-offs of progress toward one goal at the expense of another—given the present state of the art.

An obvious example is found in the American government that pursues the following goals among others: national security; an adequate (if not affluent) standard of living for all; justice; and equality. Unfortunately, there is no calculus for determining the point at which we should trade increments in standards of living for increases in national security. For such problems, rational methods have not been devised, and the application of existing techniques may produce results that are misleading.

In fact, we find that PPBS has been a failure of sorts (Hoos, 1972). It has not worked well when transferred from the Department of Defense to other departments. One might even question its degree of success in defense. Vietnam provides a tragic example of the limitations of such rational approaches. True to the principles of scientific management, we sought the "biggest bang for the buck" in Vietnam. Studies of kill ratios were conducted to determine the amount of destruction wrought by different weapons systems. Records were maintained on the tonnage of bombs dropped on North Vietnam and the Ho Chi Minh Trail. These data were plugged into formulas devised to allow the United States to pursue an effective war effort.

Such rational approaches tend to ignore the human element. Thus, an inverse relationship was assumed between enemy morale and tonnage of bombs dropped. In light of evidence developed during World War II, the opposite assumption would seem more appropriate. A major finding of that war was that the tonnage of bombs dropped on German cities was positively related to the morale of residents of the cities (United States Strategic Bombing Survey, 1947). Only when the tonnage of bombs approached extreme amounts did morale begin to decline.

This limitation of bombing is noted in Speer's (1971) book, which details the ways in which Germans overcame most of the effects of bombing. Only late in the war, when precision bombing stopped production in certain aircraft factories and petroleum refineries, did morale deteriorate. Until that time, morale was unaffected and even improved by bombing and seemed to compensate for the material inconveniences wrought by destruction.

Similarly, the Ho Chi Minh Trail continued to operate efficiently despite numerous bomber attacks. The morale of the North Vietnamese, an imponderable to PPBS, presumably remained unaffected. When important variables are left out of an organization's decision-making process, the organization cannot react appropriately to negative feedback. Such organizations cannot adapt to the environment successfully. In short, overreliance on rationalism, or any other managerial viewpoint that excludes attention to important variables, impedes appropriate organizational change.

Organizational affluence

Another factor that seems to contribute to change propensity is the organization's affluence. Organizations having surplus resources seem to innovate more than those constrained by lack of funds. As Hage and Aiken suggest, money is essential to the development of new programs and techniques. Yet, their survey did *not* show that affluence caused innovation. They asked heads of the welfare agencies studied what they would do if additional funds became available. Responses varied considerably. Some agency heads indicated they would expand existing services to increase the number of clients served or reduce the staff's case load. Quantity in the former case and quality in the latter were emphasized. Other agency heads said they would use additional funds to add new programs or services. Hage and Aiken infer from these findings that affluence is a necessary but not sufficient condition for innovation and change.

Other research shows that affluence, or *organizational slack* (Cyert and March, 1963), bears a low, positive relationship to innovation (Mohr, 1969; Rosener, 1967). This relationship may arise in part through the indirect effect of affluence on other variables, which affect innovation. According to Wilson (1966), these other variables include some of those studied by Hage and Aiken. Wilson suggests that organizations, such as railroads or gold-mining firms, that suffer from a scarcity of resources, tend to suppress conflict, maintain hierarchical controls, and proclaim the supremacy of certain explicit organizational goals. More affluent organizations tend to avoid conflict, relax hierarchical controls, proliferate new products and processes, and engage in the elaboration of vaguely defined goals.

Two folk sayings attempt to resolve this problem of innovation and affluence. First, necessity is said to be "the mother of invention." However, it appears that necessity often makes for hierarchical controls and concerns for costs and efficiency. These concerns, in turn, appear related to a low rate of program change or innovation.

The other saying is that "the devil makes work for idle hands." Organizational affluence may lead to relaxation of hierarchical controls, greater decentralization, and less formalization and stratification. These changes, in turn, are conducive to organizational change. But, not all change is good. Let us give the devil his due!

"Everyday" change

Thus far, we have dealt with change as if it were an extraordinary event for organizations. Of course, change is ever present. The organization is never the same from one month to the next. A useful way to visualize the manager's job was presented in Chapter 8. While managers do have general goals and strategies, they usually react to events, for example, attempting to maintain production despite problems of absenteeism, material shortages, line imbalances, and the like. The manager makes "changes" by dealing with these everyday problems.

Another source of everyday change not readily apparent is turnover of personnel. Each change in staffing provides new human inputs to the organization (attitudes, motivations, expectations regarding norms, and so on). To some extent newcomers will be socialized to conform to the requirements of the organization, but it is also true that they can affect and come to change the organization, since each individual is a role sender as well as a recipient of sent roles.

McNeil and Thompson (1971) refer to "regeneration of organizations"— a measure of personnel change akin to the half-life of radioactive elements. Examining faculty records at two universities, during the middle and late 1960s, they find a half-life of about four to five years; that is, at the end of four or five years, old-timers are matched by newcomers. For one university, which had a growth rate (increase in faculty size) of 26 percent, the half-life was about five years; for the other, which had a greater rate of growth (42 percent), the half-life was reached in four years or less.

The significance of regeneration arises in part because of the need to socialize newcomers. If the half-life is too short, the socialization process may require excessive organizational effort. High rates of turnover in typing pools, or on assembly lines, require that time be spent inducting and socializing members. In many cases, management may not devote sufficient time to the socialization processes, but socialization will take place anyway— through the efforts of peers, with the possible result that undesirable norms will be inculcated.

McNeil and Thompson suggest that regeneration may be especially disruptive if it outpaces the normal production process. If a bachelor's degree takes four years and the half-life of the faculty is three years, then students will become the old-timers watching the faculty come and go. To the extent that the school employs an intensive technology (Chapter 4) to socialize students into certain attitudes and values, a high rate of faculty turnover will render it ineffective.

On the other hand, a high rate of regeneration offers some advantages— primarily for the achievement of organizational flexibility. In discussing individual motivation and attitudes, we emphasized the difficulties involved in changing behavior. Instead of requiring veterans to unlearn old behavior and attitudes, one can hire newcomers having desired predispositions. It is said that science progresses in major steps (as from the Aristotelian-Ptolemaean tradition to the Copernican view of the universe), not so much by persuading the old guard to see the truth, but rather by replacing the old guard with a new generation of scientists who have grown up accepting the new view as natural (Kuhn, 1957).

This aspect of organizational regeneration is significant in leadership succession. New leaders commonly ensure that their accession is accompanied by major organizational regeneration by replacing existing personnel, adding to existing personnel, or both. This tactic is useful if the new leader is to have an impact on the organization, for as we saw in Chapter 12, leaders by themselves do not always find that they can lead and influence the organization more than the organization leads them.

Growth

At a number of points in the text, we allude to organization growth, a seemingly ubiquitous phenomenon. Its apparent pervasiveness renders this phenomenon a source of "everyday" change. Perhaps organization growth is ubiquitous because it has been viewed, until very recent times, as either an end or a means to other ends. In Western industrial society, growth seems to be valued as a symbol of achievement and success. Where organizational effectiveness is especially hard to measure, as in nonprofit organizations, attained size has been employed as a surrogate criterion measure. Starbuck (1965) lists a number of different goals for which organizational growth constitutes either the means for achievement or a side effect of such achievement. Individuals may be motivated by the desire for adventure—they may wish to gamble on new activities and to expand the organization; they may desire the prestige, power, and job security that comes from managing large numbers of people; and they may desire higher salaries. Research shows that salaries of top executives sometimes are not correlated with profit, but with sales volume (Roberts, 1956, 1959). Starbuck further suggests that increased size results from the manager's desire for stable jobs and an organization that has a high probability of survival, leading to diversification, the wherewithal to affect the environment, and large amounts of slack. Finally, organizational growth is pursued as a means to increase profits by reducing costs (economies of scale), and increasing revenues (through sales volume).

Consequence of growth

In Chapter 11, we saw that one apparent consequence of growth is increased structuring of the organization, for example, as indicated by formalization. Starbuck suggests that members of new organizations are committed to the organizations' goals. These are primary relations focusing on goals, to use our terminology of Chapter 11, while means are less sacrosanct. This comes to be less true as the organization ages and increases in size. With organizational growth, individuals transfer their commitments from goals to means and social structure. This is because (*a*) friendships and interpersonal loyalties spring up; (*b*) the organization itself tries to create loyalty to its structure, rather than to specific goals or products; and (*c*) individuals with such loyalties tend to move into central, policy-making positions. Weber describes this general process in terms of the "routinization of charisma" (Demerath and Hammond, 1969; Weber, 1964). When a new, charismatic leader passes from the scene (and even before), personal and emotional bonds between organizational members are replaced by less emotional ties that are supported by structure—by rules, norms, and other aspects of formalization. The disciples create a church, as it were, to replace the leader and hold the organization together.

The formalization accompanying growth and the associated gain in flexibility with regard to goals (compared to inflexibility regarding survival) might be viewed as undesirable, but there is a positive side to formalization as we indicated in Chapter 5.³ Formalization may result from organizational learning (Starbuck, 1965). The organization learns to ignore unimportant problems as it develops causal models that indicate critical variables. Trivial, reoccurring problems are assigned routine solutions. The young organization requires intense loyalty to goals and must select its members carefully, according to their attitudes, motivations, and potential internal controls. The older, more formalized organization can be more rational, divesting goals when they have been achieved or when the environment changes, and less careful in selecting members, since the external controls in the structure can be relied on.

However, formalization alone may not be adequate to deal with the added complexity in the growing organization. A general research finding is that larger organizations tend to have lower morale as well as higher absenteeism, turnover, and accident rates. The study of role stress by Robert Kahn and colleagues (Chapter 9) showed role stress to increase with size, leveling off in organizations of 5,000 or more members. A nationwide survey of hospitals similarly found that pressures on individuals and tensions between groups increase with organizational size (Wieland, 1965).

As a trade-off, of course, the large, bureaucratic organization offers its members resources and security, as well as freedom, as we saw in Chapter 5. A move to decentralized units within the larger organization may provide a way to avoid these dilemmas so that such trade-offs become unnecessary.

Organizational life cycles

Related to growth are phenomena associated with organizational aging. Lippitt and Schmidt (1967) described six stages of organizational development.

1. Creating a new organization.
2. Surviving as a viable system.
3. Gaining stability.
4. Gaining reputation and developing pride.
5. Achieving uniqueness and adaptability.
6. Contributing to society.

Of major concern in the first stage, organizational creation, are planning and decision making regarding resources and manpower risked, and in the second stage, the sacrifices to be made in terms of deferred activities. The

---

³ Richard Hall, Haas, and Johnson (1967) suggest that increasing size may lead to increasing formalization, if the technology is routine (for example, mass production). If it is not, growth may lead to the use of more professionals, in which case additional formalization may not result. However, if the increase in size comes about in the administrative component of the organization, then formalization probably will increase (Meyer, 1968).

third stage, achievement of stability, is concerned with organizing members and leading them to accept and enforce discipline (see also Sarason, 1972). Lippitt and Schmidt provide the following description of problems encountered at this stage, including those of formalization, described above:

> As an organization grows, the original leaders undergo varying degrees of trauma in surrendering personal leadership; the expanding hierarchy breeds factions and results in complicated politics; the maintenance of records becomes ever more burdensome; and there is a certain loss of freedom. It becomes hard to decide between further development, with concomitant stability and resilience, and the retention of close relationships and control.
>
> In the birth stage, there is excitement in creation and challenge in survival. The youthful stage is far less dramatic; the organization is accommodating itself to its environment and adjusting its internal operations. Here is where the concept of what we have called a socio-technical system becomes *functional*.
>
> As the outside pressures (e.g., market uncertainties, creditors demands) on such a system diminish, the internal defects become more evident. Interpersonal or intergroup tensions which could be overlooked in the early stage now clamor for attention. Differing expectations of the founders, managers, and workers are freely expressed. Compensation for sacrifices made earlier is demanded in the struggle to distribute recognition, rewards, and profits. Motivation is complicated by the conflicts between short-term personal gain and long-term organizational gain. Management faces problems of training and retraining personnel, developing a team spirit, stabilizing a core clientele, and developing a long-range plan.
>
> Willingness to accept and enforce discipline means recognizing that expansion is not synonymous with success, that larger gross sales may not mean larger net profit. It also involves the wisdom required to avoid overcommitment of resources; this is a time for solidifying gains before launching into large arenas of action (1967, p. 106).*

Thus, we see that in the normal course of growing, the organization generates internal forces that make change inevitable.

Two stages of organizational change

Having begun this survey of change with a study of organization structures and characteristics that enhance or hinder change, we have reviewed many of the elements of the contingency model of organizations. The evidence presented suggests that organizations shaped according to the rational, mechanical model do not foster change as readily as those fashioned after the system model. However, at several points we suggested that organizational characteristics, such as centralization, have differential effects on the rate of program change, depending on whether the change process is in

---

* © 1967 by the President and Fellows of Harvard College. All rights reserved.

the initiation stage or the implementation stage. This point must be amplified, for identification of the different stages in the process of organization change is essential to understanding the nature of change.

Most conceptualizations of change can be simplified as follows: Initially there is a process of creativity and subsequently there is a process of gaining acceptance of these ideas from key individuals and the organization generally. Much of the literature dealing with the first half of this sequence has a cognitive, rational emphasis. The focus is on communication—on getting new information to the right individuals. Chin and Benne (1969) term this the *rational strategy for change*. Examples of this literature concern the diffusion or acceptance of new drugs among physicians (Coleman, Katz, and Menzel, 1966). These studies identify opinion leaders—key individuals who keep abreast of innovations and who disseminate this information to followers in their profession (Elihu Katz and Lazarsfeld, 1955).

The second half of the change sequence, dealing with implementation, is addressed by a somewhat different body of literature—the "planned change" literature, which is concerned with emotional and structural problems involved in changing the behavior of individuals in organizations (Benne, Bennis, and Chin, 1969). This literature emphasizes that communication of ideas is necessary but not sufficient to the change process. Resistance to change and the multitude of problems encountered in changing individuals and their informal structures must be overcome.

The distinction between the rational-cognitive view of change and the *emotional-structural approach* is greatly oversimplified and overgeneralized here, but serves a useful purpose in reminding us that, in the rather under-researched field of organizational change, basic assumptions and perspectives are very important and somewhat controversial. Below, we shall cite literature from both perspectives.

DILEMMAS IN THE PROCESS OF CHANGE

Determining the need for change

Hage and Aiken (1970) view the change process as comprising four different stages: (1) determining the need for change, (2) initiation, (3) implementation, and (4) routinization.[4] During the first stage, the organization becomes aware of problems that suggest the inadequacy of the status quo. Perhaps goals are not being met as adequately as in prior periods, or as projected by forecasts. In any event, perception of a gap between desired and actual performance initiates the process of organizational change.

---

[4] Hage and Aiken term the first stage *evaluation*. We have changed their terminology, since we use the term in a different sense elsewhere.

An external consultant might think of this as the diagnostic phase of the process. However, from management's point of view, this term is not exactly appropriate. Most organizations have ongoing surveillance and monitoring procedures as well as programs for gathering information in nonroutine situations. Identification of gaps between actual and intended performance is a routine activity. When interpreted according to the theories, constructs, or paradigms employed by management, these gaps suggest both the sources of problems and tentative remedies for them.

An interesting question at this stage concerns the extent of consensus about the need to change. Need for change is indicated by the perception of gaps between intended and actual performance, as we have said. But we have also said that organizations typically pursue a number of goals which occasionally are in conflict. Goals and shorter run objectives constitute statements of intended performance. Depending on the goals most salient to managers and the accuracy with which performance toward them can be measured, conflicts may arise due to different perceptions of the need for change. The processes by which these perceptions are communicated to top management as well as the negotiation and compromise strategies that lead to consensus should interest us here. Unfortunately, these aspects of the change process have received little attention from behavioral scientists, perhaps because they occur so early in the change process that they precede the scientists' interventions. One description of the process is provided in Chapter 8. A modified rational theory of perception of the need for organizational change is found in March and Simon (1958) and more recently in Downs (1967). The interested student may wish to pursue these theories for a view of how the first stage of the change process would look if managers behaved "rationally."

One dilemma facing management during the early part of the change process is whether to engage in a large-scale or modest change effort. Modest changes are relatively simple to make and bear proportionate risks. Large-scale changes are more difficult to bring about, more costly, and riskier, although more likely to remedy serious problems. One way to analyze the magnitude of a change effort is in terms of its depth of intervention (Downs, 1967). Relatively shallow structural changes modify a limited portion of the organization; for instance, a university may create a new associate dean's position in its school of business in response to administrative overload. A deeper change affects the organization's rules for decision making. At this level, the university in our example may alter the formula by which funds are allocated to its various schools. Still deeper are changes in the organization's structural arrangements for making and enforcing rules. This depth of change would be observed in a university that granted students a vote in decisions to tenure faculty members. Finally, the deepest level of change modifies the purposes of the organization and would be found in a university that divested its traditional goals to become a training center.

Different managers and consultants have different predilections for shallow and deep changes. Some will prefer to operate at shallow levels, while others will be attracted to more dramatic efforts. Similarly, different individuals will entertain different theories of organizational behavior and change. These will give rise to contrasting opinions of the ends and means of change efforts. Please bear in mind that these differences are based on attitudes and predilections as well as on objective scientific experience. Thus, a series of dilemmas can arise. We shall introduce some of these dilemmas in the present chapter and attempt to elucidate them throughout the remainder of the text.

Initiation of change

The initiation stage of the change process arises when it is decided that change is necessary and when one alternative solution is perceived to be more desirable than competing alternatives. At this stage, management must decide *who* is to conduct the remainder of the change process. Should the organization employ external consultants or rely on the talents of its own employees? Using insiders is preferable if management wishes to avoid major disruptions. However, because of existing obligations, loyalties, preconceptions, vested interests, and the like, insiders may find themselves unable to bring about major changes. The opposite is true of outsiders, of course, who can bring new ideas and directions for change to the organization, but who are likely to create conflict and resistance in the process.

A second dilemma concerns the source of financial support for the change effort. Use of existing resources will curtail other planned or ongoing activities. Thus, reallocation of a fixed budget is likely to engender conflict or at best a lack of wholehearted cooperation from segments of the organization adversely affected. Going outside the organization for financial support will create dependency on the source of funding. The various arrangements described by James Thompson (1967) are relevant here: namely, cooptation and cooperation. The form of dependency experienced will depend on the nature of the arrangement; for example, a bank loan will be accompanied by the bank's insistence on safeguards such as limitations on the organization's activities, the right to certain kinds of surveillance, and the right to specific reports.

The need to identify the starting point for a change program gives rise to another series of dilemmas. An organization contemplating changes in its branch offices has a choice of targets for its initial change attempts. Should the parent organization begin the change program in units that are weak or powerful? Should it begin with independent units or those that are linked with other units? Should integrated, cohesive units be selected, or should the program begin with personnel who are not so closely knit?

A stronger effort is required to change powerful, integrated, or cohesive units than to achieve the same initial results with those that are relatively weak, independent, or fragmented. However, the long-run effectiveness of the change program may be enhanced by starting with units having the former characteristics. Powerful and cohesive units may serve as models for others. The latter may follow the lead of the former to the extent that changes will be emulated. Interrelated units must remain compatible. A change in one unit will create pressures in the others to change accordingly. Where this is the case, change tends to be diffused throughout the organization more readily.

The degree of risk inherent in the intended change is an important factor in the decision to select a particular starting point. If the change is modest and experience suggests that attendant risks are slight, it is probably well to begin with the more difficult units. When the change program is envisaged to be difficult or to portend substantial risks, it is appropriate to begin with a pilot project in a unit separate from the others and weak enough to offer minimal resistance to change. Having demonstrated the effectiveness of change in the pilot unit, management can turn its efforts to more difficult areas of the organization.

Implementation of change

Top management tends to operate on its own without involving others throughout the first two stages of the change process. In the implementation stage, lower-level personnel must become involved as well. Awareness of a need for change and exploration of alternative courses of action tend to disrupt (unfreeze) top management's habitual ways of thinking and acting. We shall examine the phenomenon of unfreezing habitual behavior in Chapter 16. At this point, it is important to note that lower level participants must be unfrozen as well.

Habits, rules, structures, and procedures contribute to organizational stability. The more stable the organization, the more readily its steady state activities can be predicted and controlled. This situation can be described as one of equilibrium. Hage and Aiken note that the implementation of change increases organizational disequilibrium. At this point, more of the staff have become unfrozen. In the utopian world of the rational school of thought, this is the point at which a plan for change is implemented, behavior refrozen, and equilibrium reestablished. In actual pratice, we find this stage to be a prolonged period of muddling through.

Management cannot make complete plans for change. For one thing, they lack a science of organizational change. For another, they lack vital, detailed information residing at lower levels of the organization. Furthermore, intended changes may be resisted by various personnel. When organizational objectives and the self-interest of participants conflict, employees appear perverse, unpredictable, and stubborn. The behavioral sciences are inexact. We cannot predict all responses to change accurately. As these and other shortcomings compound the situation, mistakes are made. Thus, the change process must proceed gradually, using feedback to correct mistakes and accommodate unforeseen contingencies. The organization must be unfrozen for the initiation of change and *remain* unfrozen for the duration of the change.

Hage and Aiken note that conflict is prone to arise during the implementation stage. Units undergoing change or newly created by change frequently demand additional resources, authority, and changes in rules. However, these demands can affect other units adversely. Resources may be taken directly (or indirectly) from the budgets of other units. Changed rules may impede their functioning. Newly acquired authority may encroach on established turfs. If top management does not accede to legitimate demands of this sort, the change effort may die on the vine. If it does accede, it may disrupt the organization and possibly limit its effectiveness.

A related dilemma concerns the extent to which change programs should be made participative. Should all parties affected be allowed to participate, as human relations practitioners suggest? An expected result of such participation is increased commitment to the process. Another expected outcome is that participants will express their desires and change the program to suit their own ends, possibly hindering or curtailing those of top management. Cooperation is bought at the price of alterations to the change program envisaged. Alternatively, the integrity of the change effort may be maintained at the cost of resistance to change and conflict.

Top management may decide to make structural changes unilaterally, expecting that in the long run interpersonal conflicts and adverse attitudes will die out—that eventually behavior will conform to new structural arrangements. Alternatively, behavioral scientists may be brought into the organization to alter behavior prior to making structural changes. Changing people is costly, risky, and occasionally subject to question on ethical grounds. However, appropriate changes may foster intended structural modifications.

Another dilemma arises in attempting to decide whether to use a highly structured or unstructured change effort. On the one hand, management can plan changes in considerable detail beforehand and then proceed to implement its plan systematically. On the other hand, it may be decided that planning is infeasible, or too costly. In this event, change will be implemented and coordinated by feedback. The advantage of planning is that it provides a degree of security when it can be done effectively. Contingencies are foreseen, costs projected, and pitfalls perhaps avoided. Management can determine its progress by comparing actual to planned results at any point in time. Anxieties of those responsible for implementation may be reduced to the extent that the direction of the effort is foreseen. The existence of a plan, similar to the existence of rules, may reduce potential for interpersonal conflict.

However, flexibility is lost in the process. In relatively deep change efforts containing risk and uncertainty, mistakes in the initial planning effort are difficult to correct. The mere existence of a detailed plan may cause those charged with its implementation to become relatively insensitive to feedback. Accomplishment will be measured in terms of executing the plan rather than in terms of the achievement of objectives which may entail modifying what has been planned.

Routinization of change

A problem arising in both the implementation and routinization stages concerns identifying the point at which changes will be consolidated. One strategy is to prolong the unfrozen state and to work numerous changes simultaneously—to move from one change to the next without attempting to freeze behavior. The alternative strategy is to consolidate each change as it is accomplished. An advantage of the latter approach is that management can devote its attention to other portions of the organization without worrying about backsliding in previously changed units. This outcome may be offset by the very attributes that make it seem advantageous. Interdependent units must remain compatible despite changes undergone. We may find that a change in unit 2 requires modification of unit 1. If unit 1 was previously changed and refrozen, it must be unfrozen, changed, and refrozen once again if resistance to change is to be overcome. At the extreme, the situation becomes expensive, frustrating, and baroque.

This may be contrasted with the strategy of leaving change efforts unfrozen temporarily. As change proceeds in one unit, interdependencies will affect other, unfrozen units influencing them to change appropriately and reinforcing them for these responses. In fact, the situation can be mutually reinforcing. Changes made in the second unit reinforce and stabilize those made in the first. The problem with this approach is that it disperses the attentions of management across numerous units. Although the total change effort may be substantial, the effort directed to any one unit may be meager.

The timing of efforts to consolidate changes is contingent on the degree to which changes have been completed. Ideally, consolidation occurs after the gap between intended and actual performance is eliminated. In reality, it may be impossible to measure this gap precisely. Alternatively, the gap may have shrunk as a result of organizational change, but not completely. In this case, the question arises whether major or minor effort is required to complete the process. Continued major effort is costly and time consuming. Oftentimes, the costs of change are salient while the benefits are not. Time and money spent, conflict and anxiety suffered, and inefficiency and confusion endured are readily identified with attempts to change organizations. Benefits, such as improved morale, are intangible. Improvements such as organizational growth and survival are remote in time from changes intended to cause them. In short, when costs are more apparent than benefits, change efforts may be terminated prematurely.

Resistance to change

As the manager contemplates and initiates change in the organization, one theme is likely to emerge time and again—resistance to the change process. These reactions have been emphasized in the psychological literature, perhaps overly so (Neal Gross et al., 1971), but resistance to change is a major problem that can develop at any point in the change process. As Gross indicates, there is little research on the actual process of change or overcoming associated resistance to change. For this reason, we are forced to rely primarily on the day-to-day experience of change agents, who work with management to bring about organizational change.

The organization members' responses to change depend on their perceptions of the proposed change and, of course, on the effects they think the change will have on their needs and aspirations (Mann and Neff, 1961). If they experience ambiguity, individuals may engage in search behavior that may appear as resistance from the perspective of those initiating change. Also related to search behavior are the individuals' perceptions of their ability to control the situation and their general trust in those in charge of proposed changes (see Figure 15-1). Ambiguity may not lead to resistance if individuals are permitted a degree of control over their destiny, as is the case when they are encouraged to participate in the change process. Participation in the planning phases of change, of course, provides not only the opportunity for control, but also clarity about the nature of the intended change. Trust also affects the degree to which the individual views prospective changes positively. Mann and Neff suggest that information, participation, and the organizational culture determine the individual's perception of a proposed change by operating through the mediating variables of ambiguity, control, and trust. Participation is useful in overcoming resistance to change because of its potential for increasing the accuracy of perceptions and extent of control, and for reducing ambiguity. However, trust may or may not increase, depending on what is observed in the act of participation. The individual's perception of participation as a facade, used to increase manipulation (see Chapter 11), or as an opportunity openly granted, with openly stated risks and trade-offs, is likely to affect trust.

This is basically a rational model in which individuals respond to change situations by considering the implications and acting in their self-interests. Ambiguities and anxieties enter into the model by coloring perceptions. It is assumed that individuals react either positively or negatively, depending on how the change is presented. Sometimes, however, we can expect to find individuals with basic predispositions toward change—who view either change or the status quo as an end in itself (Barnes, 1967).

If one perceives change to be compatible with one's personal goals and management concurs in this estimate, there are few problems. However, if the individual's perception is inaccurate (for example, if change is seen as

428   V.   Changing the organization

FIGURE 15-1
A model for understanding an individual's response to change

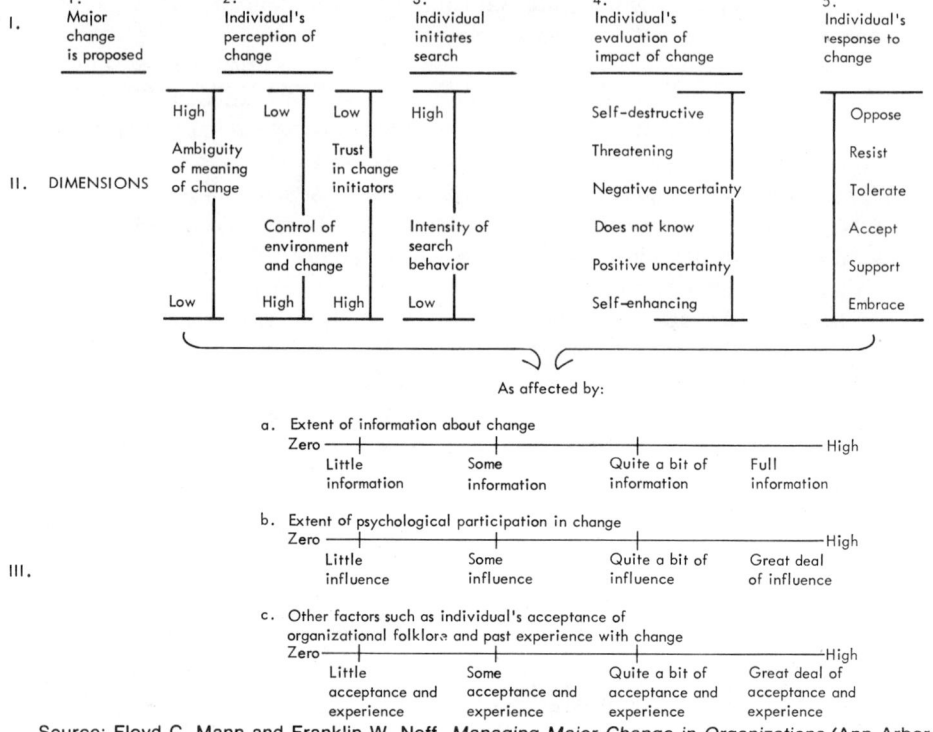

Source: Floyd C. Mann and Franklin W. Neff, *Managing Major Change in Organizations* (Ann Arbor, Mich.: Foundation for Research on Human Behavior, 1966).

compatible when it is not), management will need to clarify the situation even though the individual's resistance may increase as a result. If management were to mislead employees deliberately, the longer-range effects on trust and acceptance of future changes (even those clearly within the individual's interest) would be costly.

When management experiences resistance from individuals who perceive changes to be incompatible with their goals, even when management's view is to the contrary, increased communication is also advised, although the climate of trust may be such that perceptions of negative implications of change cannot be altered. Mann and Neff suggest that management emphasize its *actions* when these are compatible with individual goals, and that the proposed change be differentiated from other, past changes.

When individuals see change as incompatible with their goals and management concurs in this view, then Mann and Neff suggest that management must review the objectives of the change and either alter them or proceed with the original change program (assuming that the wherewithal to overcome resistance is available, and that the various costs of change do not outweigh its benefits).

Sometimes, management is uncertain about the effects of a proposed change. Here the offer of employee participation may be in order. When employees are involved in decisions concerning change, its implications for both management and employees become clearer.

In general, Mann and Neff suggest that the management of change can be improved by giving those affected more information and allowing them to participate in the change process.[5] While these are useful suggestions, we shall explore change phenomena in greater depth, developing more detailed, specific approaches to organizational change.

Dilemmas in perspective

Throughout this chapter we have raised major issues without resolving them. As we move into more detailed analyses of change phenomena, we shall address them as best we can. Be forewarned, however, that science cannot provide precise resolutions for these issues. Yet, every organization faces them at one time or another, resolves them in one way or another, and continues to play its role in society. This is an area in which theory lags behind practice. Thus, we shall pursue these few remaining chapters cautiously, treading as it were on the frontiers of knowledge.

ALTERNATIVE CHANGE STRATEGIES

Rational and emotional aspects of change

For the most part, we have been concerned with the rational aspects of organizational change. The emotional aspects of change are examined in the field of organizational development. T-groups, personal growth labs, and a host of other techniques attempt to deal with emotions, attitudes, and values as these affect organizational performance and change. While the field of organizational development is beyond the scope of our text, we shall address the rational-emotional dichotomy in somewhat more detail below.

We sometimes believe that people are so rational that if one provides reasons for behaving differently they will do so, or if one supplies more and better information they will make better decisions. However, emotions, values, and attitudes are not developed rationally or logically. Behavior and decisions based on emotions, therefore, are not likely to be altered by appeals to logic or reason. One's aversions to snakes and spiders, for example,

---

[5] For a theoretical treatment of the role of participation in planned change, see Ullrich, 1976.

are not likely to be altered by knowledge that these are generally useful creatures, nor is one's behavior toward these creatures likely to change.

Emotions and feelings are difficult to change, but once altered they may become stable. Furthermore, it is believed that overt behavior is more closely linked to feelings and emotions than to ideas or thoughts. This is the reason psychoanalysts lead their patients to reexperience the emotional situations and stimuli that are sources of their apparent maladjusted behavior. By relearning emotionally, the patient comes to behave more adaptively.

Depth of intervention

Harrison (1970) labels attempts to change a person's values (that are central to one's sense of self) as *deep change strategies*. *Shallow change strategies* are those more formal and public attempts to change ideas, technologies, and the like. The operations research analyst, in redesigning tasks and roles to fit a rational model, uses shallow strategies. Psychological readjustments do not enter into the design for change.

Harrison argues that the depth of intervention ought to be as shallow as the problem permits. Intervention strategies can be arrayed on a continuum of depth. The choice of a particular change strategy will be determined by two criteria: (1) the depth to which one must go to locate information that must be exchanged to improve organizational performance, and (2) the level of intervention that is acceptable to the client.

At the shallow end of the continuum of change strategies one finds *cognitive and rational* problem-solving techniques such as those used in operations research, managerial accounting, and the like.

Somewhat deeper are the practices of *industrial psychology,* which include methods for employee selection, placement, and appraisal. Here the focus is on individual performance as it can be predicted by education, work experience, biographical data, personality characteristics, and other dimensions that are measured, but not changed. Using these kinds of measurements, industrial psychologists advise management on hiring, promotion, and dismissal decisions. Other change strategies at a comparable level include job enrichment and management by objectives. In neither case is personality change sought.

A still deeper, *instrumental* or work style, approach to change is exemplified by the Blake and Mouton (1970) *managerial grid.* Using a two-dimensional rating scale, managers rate themselves and their colleagues on their orientations toward people and production. By analyzing their own ratings and those given them by others, managers are helped to alter their managerial styles, attitudes, and work-related behavior. Some managers are encouraged to give more emphasis to productivity, others to attend more to the needs of employees, and still others to increase their emphases of both. These changes in emphasis are manifested in increased delegation of authority, enhanced concern for employees' needs, better planning, and increased use of feedback in the control and support of subordinates. Change at this instrumental level is deeper than interventions made using management by objectives (MBO) and similar techniques. Job enrichment and MBO alter task-related behavior and the objectives to which it is addressed. The Blake and Mouton approach attempts to change attitudes and social orientations as well, but only insofar as these are instrumental to effective task performance.

The next level down, according to Harrison, deals with *interpersonal relations* and is exemplified by some of the so-called human relations training programs. These change strategies bring to light the feelings, attitudes, and perceptions that individuals have about one another. The focus here is not only on instrumental behavior, but also on the quality of interpersonal experiences. T-group sessions that emphasize trust, openness, and authentic behavior are designed to produce changes at this level.

Finally, Harrison cites *intrapersonal analysis* as the deepest level at which change is commonly sought. Psychoanalysis is a situation in which the patient's attitudes, values, and conflicts concerning ability to function effectively, identity, and existence are examined. Some of the most extreme T-groups operate at this level, such as marathon groups that probe to the very basis of the individual's psychological makeup.

Depth of intervention and client dependency

Harrison suggests that the deeper change strategies make the client *dependent* on the change agent. Deep changes are *difficult* to bring about and carry *considerable risks* for the client (Lieberman et al., 1973). Furthermore, it is hard for the client to *transfer* the benefits of these change efforts to other members of the organization.

If a change effort is shallow, the change agent will be able to teach the practices to the client; for example, when a consultant employs an operations research technique to solve a problem, the client will gain some understanding of the technique and its applications. In fact, the client can learn to solve such problems and teach others what has been learned. At deeper levels, change efforts are less readily communicated. It is difficult for a trainer to explain what a T-group is going to be like to potential participants. Even after experiencing a T-group, the clients will be at a loss to explain what has happened to them. Furthermore, they may have trouble imagining themselves ever acquiring the skills to train others. The T-group experience does not equip participants to act as trainers.

Because of this, clients tend to become dependent on consultants using deep change strategies. This, of course, has its consequences. Dependency is costly, since the consultant's role cannot be reduced as clients learn the consultant's skills. Furthermore, change will spread slowly in the organization. Unlike shallow change attempts, which can snowball as clients begin to impart their newly gained knowledge to others in the organization, deep change generally is limited to those who participate in exercises with the consultant. In general, dependence makes it difficult for the consultant and client to terminate their relationship. Clients may find they are hooked on the help of the change agent. As a result of this dependency, the change agent comes to have considerable power over clients. Being unable to provide, let alone understand, the process through which help is given, the client must depend on, and even accept strong influence from, the change agent.

At this point, the reasoning behind one of Harrison's criteria for determining the depth of intervention should be apparent. Because costs increase with the depth of change sought, one ought to go no deeper than necessary. Ideally, the client and consultant will examine the situation in which changes are sought and agree on an appropriate depth of intervention; for example, it may be found that bottlenecks in the work flow can be eliminated by the application of techniques from industrial engineering. Morale and productivity may be improved through the introduction of job enrichment schemes. Sources of conflict may be ameliorated through redesign of work roles. Each of these change efforts, although relatively shallow, may be sufficient for the problem to which it is addressed and may spare the organization the costs of deeper efforts.

The second criterion states that the depth of intervention should be limited by its acceptability. According to Harrison, the consultant must investigate the client system's norms, values, fears, and resistance to deep interventions. The consultant will need to ask: Do the clients resist discussing their management styles, personalities, or innermost feelings? How much of this sort of information can be discussed, examined, and acted upon legitimately? This varies considerably from one organization to another and among individuals within a single organization. It is particularly important for the change agent to ascertain whether there are group or organizational norms that are likely to be violated by a deep intervention strategy. For example, if there is a norm that one should refrain from discussing personal matters at work (such as one's feelings about the boss or the personalities of co-workers), then one would assume that deep strategies such as T-groups will effectively violate the norm.

Deep intervention strategies and social norms

Because deep change strategies tend to make clients dependent on consultants, the latter are able to influence the former; that is, the change agent can exercise power over the client to overcome organizational norms. Despite the existence of a norm of the sort described above, the T-group trainer can establish norms to the contrary. However, Harrison suggests that in doing this, the trainer is likely to become counterproductive. While the change agent may have considerable power vis-à-vis individuals and small groups, that person does not have such power over the organization as a whole. In the larger organization, established norms are more powerful. Thus, individuals leaving the sheltered T-group setting will revert to their former behavior once their newly learned attempts to reveal their feelings and change the feelings of others are met with sanctions or organizationwide norms to the contrary.

Harrison describes how change agents working at the interpersonal and deeper levels tend to adopt a resistance-oriented approach to change. Some consultants seem to take pride in confrontation, in dramatically violating organizational norms, and in pressuring organizational members into departing from them. He cites the marathon T-group as a case in point wherein the irritability and fatigue that attend prolonged contact and lack of sleep move participants to deal with one another more emotionally, personally, and spontaneously than they would normally.

Harrison's point is substantiated by the study of encounter groups by Lieberman and colleagues (1973) in which it was found that the type of group technology (sensitivity training, gestalt therapy, transactional analysis, marathons, and so on) did not affect the individual outcomes achieved. In fact, what went on in groups of the same type was usually not very similar, and groups supposedly of different types often had fairly similar processes and outcomes.

What did make a difference in terms of outcomes, and especially casualty rates, was the behavior of the leader. Leaders who pushed the individual participants (regardless of the readiness of participants to confront their problems and deal with the perceptions of the group) produced high casualty rates.

The practice of inducing clients to behave in ways of which they would not approve otherwise is subject to question on ethical grounds. In addition, Harrison judges it to be ineffective since existing organizational norms will tend to reverse changes attained in this fashion.

This problem may be likened to that of the community developer in an underdeveloped nation who, by virtue of personal influence over certain villagers, succeeds in convincing them to dig a well or build a school, which upon the developer's departure, quickly falls into disuse. In situations such as this, the change agent fails to integrate improvements into the social structure of day-to-day life. Although successful in solving an immediate problem (or perhaps in removing a symptom of a more basic problem), the community developer fails. To succeed, the change agent must develop new norms supporting the use and maintenance of the improvements and overcome existing norms that impede this progress. In the absence of the latter activities, community development may even be counterproductive to the extent that it discourages future projects of a similar nature.

The change agent who must work at a level of intervention that is deeper than organizational norms permit must create new norms, and this is no easy task. It is better, Harrison suggests, to establish the level of intervention at the *level of the system's felt need for changes.* Certain problems of communities and organizations are given high, conscious priorities by their members. Individuals and groups generally are willing to invest time and energy in dealing with these felt needs. Conversely, needs that are experienced solely by the outside consultant (experienced because of the consultant's values or power to achieve specific kinds of changes) are unlikely to spur the cooperation of the community or organization. In short, the consultant must take the role of collaborator in the client's attempts to solve problems that are important to the client, and in so doing mobilize existing motivations.

Here, then, we have summarized the reasoning behind Harrison's second criterion for choosing an intervention strategy: intervene no deeper than the level at which the client desires change. In attempting to meet this criterion, the change agent will examine the norms of the organization to determine whether they will legitimate the depth of intervention being considered. Furthermore, the change agent will devise change strategies that are clearly relevant to the consciously felt needs of the organization's members.

The consultant's dilemma

Unfortunately, it appears that these two criteria can be contradictory when applied in practice. The first criterion suggests intervention at a level deep enough to obtain information with which to diagnose the problem and subsequently rectify it. This level is sometimes deeper than the level at which an individual or a group is willing to invest energy and resources. Harrison refers to this discrepancy as the *consultant's dilemma.*

Ideally, the dilemma is resolved by intervening first at a level that generates support from organizational norms, the power structure, and the felt needs of members. As time passes and the consultant gains trust and support from within the organization, intervention at deeper levels can begin—levels at which particularly important forces may be operating. This, however, is no simple matter to accomplish. To quote Harrison:

> I believe we should always avoid moving deeper at a pace which outstrips a client system's willingness to subject itself to exposure, dependency, and threat.... [I]f the dominant response of organization members indicates that an intervention violates system norms, ... then one has intervened too deeply and should pull back to a level at which organization members are more ready to invest their own energy in the change process. This point of view is thus in opposition to that which sees negative reactions primarily as indications of resistances which are to be brought out into the open, confronted, and worked through as a central part of the intervention process (Harrison, 1970, p. 199).[6]

In short, Harrison encourages consultants to accept the client's felt needs and problems and to work on them at the level where the client can serve as

---

[6] From "Choosing the Depth of Organizational Intervention" by Roger Harrison, *Journal of Applied Behavioral Science,* 1970, 6, 181–202. Reproduced by special permission.

a confident and willing collaborator. He generalizes from his own experience that the level of intervention most likely to permit collaboration and feelings of legitimacy falls somewhere between interventions at an instrumental level and those at the interpersonal relations level. Deeper levels of intervention are likely to produce hostility, passivity, and dependence in clients.

In Harrison's words:

> If I intervene directly at the level of interpersonal relationships, I can be sure that some members, and often the whole group, will react with anxiety, passive resistance, and low or negative commitment to the change process. Furthermore, they express their resistance in terms of norms and values regarding the appropriateness or legitimacy of dealing at this level. They say things like; "It isn't right to force people's feelings about one another out into the open"; "I don't see what this has to do with improving organizational effectiveness"; "People are being encouraged to say things which are better left unsaid."
>
> If I then switch to a strategy which focuses on decision making, delegation of authority, information exchange, and other instrumental questions, these complaints about illegitimacy and the inappropriateness of the intervention are usually sharply reduced. This does not mean that the clients are necessarily comfortable or free from anxiety in the discussions, nor does it mean that strong negative feelings may not be expressed about one another's behavior. What is different is that the clients are more likely to *work with* instead of *against* me, to feel and express some sense of ownership in the change process, and to see many more possibilities for carrying it on among themselves in the absence of the consultant (Harrison, 1970, pp. 200–201).[7]

In light of the controversy that surrounds some techniques of organizational development, the risks to which clients are sometimes exposed by practitioners, and the uncertain results, we generally subscribe to Harrison's conclusions and guidelines. His argument does not completely solve the dilemma he posits, though. The problems of an organization very often rest at levels deeper than the client is willing to go. But Harrison argues that to stay at the more shallow level, where collaboration is feasible, is in the long run more productive than moving to deeper strategies.

However, even if relatively deep interventions are found to be somewhat effective, we must still consider questions of values and ethics prior to advocating their use. For example, how shall we weigh the right to privacy and respect for the desires of others in our decision to impose deep change techniques to solve organizational problems? Can we ignore the rights of participants and subject them to problem-solving methods of questionable efficacy?

As we see it, organizational development, broadly conceived, must utilize flexible approaches that allow the consultant to produce both cognitive and

---

[7] Ibid.

emotional changes that are linked together by the problem's solutions. Depth of intervention should be limited by the informed consent of participants and by the practitioner's competence to deal effectively with the psychological and social forces released by such practices. Above all, we advocate caution in the face of uncertainty.

DISCUSSION QUESTIONS

1. We have discussed numerous attributes that foster or hinder change in organizations. Using these attributes, formulate organizational designs appropriate to stable and dynamic environments.
2. How do these designs compare with those discussed in Chapter 3?
3. Should all organizations be made change prone? Why?
4. What ethical issues arise in the application of deep change strategies?
5. What are the major limitations of shallow change strategies?

16

The Process of Change in Organizations

INTRODUCTION

One of the foundations of classic economic thought is the assumption that each individual will act in his or her own best interest if allowed sufficient freedom of behavior. In the aggregate, individuals' pursuits of their self-interests contribute to the well-being of society. Thus, the capitalistic system is guided by an *invisible hand:* enlightened self-interest. Or, so it was thought by Adam Smith.

Much of the classic thought in Smith's germinal work has been replaced by contemporary economic theory. Unfortunately, belief in the individual's ability to act in self-interest lingers on in one form or another. Management tends to diagnose many problems as products of poor communications and assumes that workers will cooperate with their supervisors once they understand such cooperation will be in their eventual self-interest. Carried to the level of policy formulation, this assumption suggests that the availability of programs designed to enhance the well-being of participants is sufficient to engage their interest and cooperation.

For reasons to be investigated in this chapter, people often do not act in their own best interests. In some cases this seeming perversity has its roots in personality disorders or other forms of pathology. In other cases, perhaps the vast majority, individuals simply are unable to implement the kinds of change that will improve their lot. For example, consider the following:

> ... as surely as we can say that people shape their environments, we can also state that people's environments, in turn, shape their behavior. A vivid example of the latter phenomenon is provided by Guest (1962). Of his research with automobile workers, he remarks:
>
> "One theme expressed as often as any other concerned the hopelessness of making any plans for the future or having any strong aspirations whatever...."
>
> The following interview data which support Guest's observation do not seem to have come from the men who have never had ambitions, but from men who have come to the pathetic realization that their previous ambitions are irrelevant to their foreseeable futures.
>
> "I don't know. I've been there for 14 years and I haven't accomplished a thing."
>
> "I'll be on the (assembly) line 15 years in July and I think I can last another 15, if I take care of myself. Then I'll get a job off the line ... maybe a sweeper's job. Wouldn't that be something, to end my years at [plant Y] in a blaze of glory as a sweeper?" (Ullrich, 1972, p. 153)

Chapter guide

1. The sources of the dissatisfaction expressed in Guest's quotations should be apparent from what we have said in other chapters. What forces keep individuals who experience such dissatisfactions from seeking better jobs?
2. Have you been in dissatisfying situations that you were unable to improve or leave? What kept you in these situations? What made you want to leave? What kept you from altering the situation?
3. Think of a situation you would like to change. Can you change it? What resistance to change must be overcome? Why does the situation remain as it is?

THEORETICAL VIEWS OF CHANGE PROCESSES

Behavioral equilibrium

Lewin's (1952) *unfreezing-changing-refreezing* model provides a useful vehicle for understanding change processes. According to this model, behavior is determined by the net effect of an elaborate set of contemporaneous forces. A crude analogy, if you will, likens these forces to fields of magnetic flux within which an iron particle is trapped. In some configurations of flux, the particle will move. In all static configurations, it will eventually come to rest at a point where each force on the particle is met by an equal and opposite force.

It is helpful to view behavior in terms of analogous forces. We can imagine forces that move individuals to change their behaviors, but we must also recognize similar forces that restrict deviations from habit or the status quo. Some of these forces emanate from within the individual and include needs, attitudes, and habits. Others flow from second and third parties who respond to the focal individual's behavior with rewards or punishments.

The focal individual experiences these forces as they are perceived. While perceptions may be valid or not, Lewin argues that they are real to the individual, who responds to them regardless of their actuality; that is, imagined threat is experienced as realistically as actual threat and is responded to accordingly. Thus, the forces described by Lewin are psychological forces.

It probably is impossible to comprehend all of the forces acting on an individual in a situation. No wonder human behavior seems unpredictable. Yet, we admit that behavior is fairly predictable within reasonable limits. This is most often true when dealing with groups of individuals whose norms are well understood. The study of group dynamics follows Lewin's early work. Particularly studies of group norms and group pressures follow his original theoretical directions. We shall examine Lewin's work in terms of group work norms and behavior.

Lewin's model can be applied to a group norm specifying level of worker productivity. Where such norms exist, individuals' behavior will conform fairly closely to the norm. Yet, there are forces working on individuals that, by themselves, would cause them to deviate in one or the other direction. Obviously, group pressures limit deviation in either direction. Slight deviations are met with mild sanctions, such as half-joking, half-critical comments from co-workers. Major deviations evoke more severe sanctions; for instance, the informal group leader may rebuke the offending worker, other group members may threaten action, and ultimately physical violence may erupt. The latter sanction is a rare, but not unknown, penalty for violating important group norms.

Several motives can cause a work group to establish and maintain norms such as the one discussed here. First, output above the norm is likely to signal to management that it has established unrealistically low output requirements. One likely consequence is that the requirements will be restudied with the result that workers eventually find themselves working harder for the same hourly wage. This can be especially threatening to older members of the work group who would have difficulty keeping a faster pace of work. Output below the norm is also sure to attract management's attention. A consequence to be anticipated in this event is increased pressure from supervision. Our discussion of psychological work contracts in Chapter 3 suggests that interaction with management in any form may be undesirable from the workers' point of view.

We have looked at two kinds of forces limiting deviation from the norm and serving to maintain behavioral equilibrium. In addition to forces emanating from the work group are those solely within the individual; for example, fatigue serves to limit the individual worker's rate of productivity. Counteracting this force to some extent are psychological forces that stem from the need for achievement or the Protestant ethic. Work-related aspirations, anxieties about the state of the economy and employment security, and pressures and inducements applied by the organization may also enter into the balance.

According to Lewin, the net effects of these forces are stabilized behavior and social equilibrium. However, the resulting equilibrium is dynamic rather than static and, thus, is termed *quasi-stationary equilibrium*. It is dynamic in the sense that it can be altered by a number of possible changes in the balance of forces.

Unfreezing behavior

For convenience, Lewin terms forces hindering movement from the existing equilibrium *restraining forces*. Opposing forces which direct behavior away from the status quo are called *driving forces*. Now, to cause change, one must upset the balance of driving and restraining forces; that is, *unfreeze* the quasi-stationary equilibrium. There are, of course, three ways to unfreeze the situation: (1) increase the driving forces, (2) decrease the restraining forces, or (3) accomplish some combination of the first two strategies. We shall examine these change strategies in order.

Driving forces can be increased through manipulation of positive and negative incentives; for example, management may inform the work force of impending layoffs that can be avoided only by increases in employee productivity. Alternatively, an incentive payment scheme can be implemented. The success of neither approach is guaranteed. In the first case, workers are led to fear that their present level of productivity will result in unemployment. Even so, they may think that in yielding to these pressures they will encourage management to seek further changes in the same manner. In the second case, workers may fear that increased productivity motivated by incentive payments will lead management to restudy the job (Whyte, 1955). Both attempts appear to produce additional restraining forces inadvertently.

Thus, increasing driving forces can produce or increase restraining forces, especially as movement is made away from the previous equilibrium. In the event that the increased driving forces are of sufficient magnitude to overcome existing and newly created restraining forces (which is not true in all-cases), behavior may reach a state of equilibrium at a new level. Whether or not a new equilibrium level is reached, the individual will experience greater tension. This occurs because both driving and restraining forces have been increased. Were this not the case, behavior would change endlessly in the direction of the driving forces. Obviously, this cannot occur, for fatigue, if nothing else, will restrain behavior ultimately.

Increased tension of this sort creates additional dynamic potentialities in the situation, which imply greater instability and unpredictability. A minor fluctuation in one of the major driving or restraining forces may create widely fluctuating behavior. Large forces are not maintained effortlessly and are more likely to change than are smaller forces. This produces a tendency toward instability. In psychological terms, the individual experiencing pressures from two directions is in a conflict situation. That person may expend considerable energy monitoring the conflicting pressures and making tentative moves, first in one direction, then in the other.

Because of this, it appears more reasonable to unfreeze behavior by removing restraining forces. In the previous examples, we described restraining forces arising from labor's distrust of management. To continue the example, we note that these forces can be reduced by assurances that such distrust is unfounded. This may, of course, require effort over and above giving assurances. Trust between workers and management must be established, possibly by some tangible evidence that such restraining forces are unwarranted. Other avenues of progress include redesigning work to reduce worker fatigue and reformulating group norms.

In the event that management is successful in reducing or removing certain restraining forces, existing driving forces may be sufficient to change behavior in the desired direction; that is, forces already in the situation, such as need for achievement, can drive performance higher and in so doing unfreeze the situation. Furthermore, the new equilibrium will contain less tension since a smaller set of opposing forces results.

From this observation, we find the two major advantages of the second change strategy over the first. First, it takes less effort to remove forces than to add them. Adding driving forces may create opposing restraining forces. Thus, further driving forces may be needed. Reducing restraining forces permits existing forces to effect change. Second, given the same degree of change, the latter strategy produces a more psychologically healthy and, in managerial terms, more controllable situation than does the former. This occurs because the reduction in forces yields lower tension, more stability, and greater predictability.

The third strategy, increasing driving forces while reducing restraining forces, probably is the most advantageous of the three. The addition of driving forces can provide further impetus for change in the desired direction. Furthermore, the unfreezing effect may be more pronounced as positive motivations are increased. Theoretically, the increased tension experienced at the new equilibrium may be justified by the arousal of positive motivation. Not all tension is undesirable or unpleasant.

Changing behavior

The second stage in Lewin's model is the *changing stage,* which we have already begun to discuss. Unfreezing sometimes elicits change as the addition and reduction of forces drive behavior away from the initial point of equilibrium. However, this is not always the case. Despite a reasoned alteration of the force field, new forces may come into play as existing ones are manipulated. We might think of this in terms of people's willingness to tolerate uncertainty and ambiguity rather than move in directions they do not wish to travel.

When unfreezing does not produce adequate change, management is left with the task of analyzing and reshaping the force field. Returning to our former example, we may find that production has increased somewhat but is limited by employee fatigue. Management will deal with this restraining force, perhaps by redesigning the job or employing superior equipment. These actions, in turn, can evoke additional restraining forces. We resist change in principle because it can lead to unanticipated consequences and requires additional effort. Thus, the change process must be supported by psychological as well as material improvements. In our example, workers will need assurances that change will not work to their detriment.

Refreezing behavior

Typically, behavioral changes gained even through the expenditure of considerable resources and effort dissipate over time; for example, the manager whose attitudes and behavior have changed as a result of recent management development activities may revert to old habits shortly after returning to the organization from the classroom. This occurs when the *refreezing stage* of the change process has been dealt with inadequately.

Following change, a new quasi-stationary equilibrium must be established by an appropriate, balanced configuration of driving and restraining forces. The unfreezing and change stages of the process usually are enhanced by psychological support and inducements applied by the change agent. These forces tend to disappear once change has been accomplished and management loses interest in the problem, assuming that its remedy has been found. Indeed, the maintenance of these forces over the long run may prove infeasible. Yet, as they are removed, they must be replaced by other forces if the new equilibrium is to be maintained. Failing this, behavior may return to its former state.

Change programs are likely to be accompanied by forces arising from the attentions of management and other novel influences that may disappear once the process of change appears to have been completed. The refreezing stage is advocated in recognition of this phenomenon. Basically, this stage consists of the systematic replacement of temporary forces with more permanent ones. In some cases, the technique used to create change can be continued as a vehicle for its maintenance; for example, if the change program was structured around a particular technique, the same technique can be employed to investigate problems and performance arising from the new equilibrium point. In other cases, it may suffice to formalize the changed situation through revisions of rules, regulations, and procedures. These activities can lend organizational authority as well as legitimate sanctions to the new state of equilibrium and thus maintain it temporarily until norms evolve to sustain it in a more permanent fashion.

Change and the larger organization

Thus far we have restricted our view of the change process to individuals and small groups. Lewin's model can also be applied to problems of organizational change—to the diffusion of change from one group to another, and from subsystem to subsystem throughout the organization. If one subsystem is unfrozen and changed, other, related parts of the system will be affected. Furthermore, the effect of subsystem A on adjacent subsystem B is likely to produce a countereffect wherein B affects A. We noted managers' tendencies to revert to habitual behavior on reentering their organization following management development activities. This may be due in part, to their inability to sustain newly learned attitudes and behaviors as members of subsystems that expect their former behavior of them. Specifically, the returning manager's altered behavior affects that person's group and perhaps other, adjacent groups as well. But, these subsystems have not undergone corresponding changes that would enable them to incorporate the manager's newly acquired behavior successfully. Consequently, they fail to reinforce this behavior and, in some cases, sanction against it. These acts can shift the manager's behavior back to its prior form.

Similarly, changed work groups can experience frictions with other groups with which they no longer fit; for example, our workers, who now produce at a higher rate, pass their increased output downstream to other groups in the production process. These interdependent groups, feeling pressured by increased supplies of work in process, may react adversely, having been inadvertently unfrozen. Whyte (1955) describes a change program that was curtailed by this phenomenon. Employees working at one station of a production line were encouraged to organize their own work and to enrich their jobs by combining delimited individual tasks into a group operation. The increased motivation thus tapped caused an increase in productivity. However, the increased productivity of one group entered the work flow of the next group in the process. Unfortunately, the second group could not be reorganized as the first had been to handle the increased work required of them. In Lewin's terms, the second group became unfrozen by the output of the first. Restraining forces in the situation prevented them from adapting to the new driving forces (increased work in process inventories). Ultimately, they were successful in resisting change, and the experiment with the first group was discontinued.

Of course, pressures and discomfort experienced by adjacent subsystems can provide an entree for the change agent in attempts to move the change effort through the organization. The change agent's potential to help with uncomfortable, unsettling problems can elicit cooperation from other subsystems, paving the way for additional changes that are congruent with changes made in the initial subsystem. Furthermore, by decreasing the resistances of adjacent subsystems, refreezing (maintenance of change) in the initial subsystem is enhanced.

A process for consultants

The intervention of a consultant complicates the change process somewhat. Ronald Lippitt and collegues' (1958) amplification of Lewin's model clarifies the role of the consultant in bringing about organizational change.[1] The first of seven phases in the change process described by Lippitt is *the development of a need for change* and is the essence of Lewin's unfreezing stage. The second phase, *the establishment of a change relationship*, creates the basis for all subsequent phases of the change process. The third through fifth phases have to do with change itself; phase three is *the clarification of the client system's problems,* phase four is *the examination of alternative means and ends and the choice of those to be implemented,* and phase five is *the transformation of intentions into actual change efforts.* The sixth phase concerns *the generalization and stabilization of change* and is comparable to the refreezing stage of the Lewin model. Peculiar to the consultant's role in the change process, the seventh phase directs effort toward *ending the relationship.* This phase is essential since dependence on the consultant throughout the change process must be dissipated prior to the consultant's departure if change is to be permanent.

Developing a need for change

Stress or disruption within a system or between the system and its environment must be translated into actual problem awareness (desire for change) before the process of organizational change can begin. Oddly enough, this does not occur naturally in all cases. In some instances, management is unaware of existing problems. In other cases, awareness has not advanced to a level at which problems are conceptualized and thus meaningfully viewed as needing (and being amenable to) change; for example, existing problems may seem to be inevitable. Alternatively, they may be viewed as being prohibitively expensive to correct. However, even when awareness of problems is accompanied by knowledge of potential sources of help, an additional form of resistance must be overcome. Seeking help is admitting to failure, in a sense. It admits to problems beyond the capabilities of management.

---

[1] This model is based on a great variety of observations of work by consultants with individuals, groups, organizations, and communities, and is a distillation of what seems to be effective in helping the client to change.

Now, it is quite likely that these elements in the first phase of the change process will be resolved in the absence of a consultant. Even so, the change agents may find that the problems they are asked to address are symptomatic of others of which management is unaware. In this instance, the change agents will eventually work at several phases in the process concurrently, progressing on one problem and developing the need for change on others.

Establishing change relationships

Initial relationships between the consultant and client serve as levers for subsequent change in the organization. For this reason, the second phase can be critical to the consultant's role in the process of planned change. First impressions are important. Consultants, as professionals, must be competent and trustworthy. Furthermore, they must *appear* so to members of the client organization. The change agents must convey evidence of their skills and knowledge and the ability to employ them successfully. At the same time, they should appear similar to clients—as people who will understand their roles and problems and respect their organization's needs and values.

A critical element of the second phase is *clarification* of the consultant's relationship to the client. Each party must learn of the effort and participation expected by the other. This admittedly is difficult, coming as it does before a thorough diagnosis of the organization's problems. The change agent must communicate realistic, though general, goals for the change program as well as a realistic assessment of the effort that will be demanded of the client. The issue of depth of intervention should also be raised at this point to establish joint norms regarding appropriate and inappropriate areas in which to pursue change.

Because organizations comprise a variety of subsystems, the change agents need to clarify their relationship vis-à-vis each subsystem with which they will work. Although this cannot be accomplished in any detail at this preliminary stage, the consultants will at least touch base with important sources of power. In light of the tentative nature of arrangements at this point in the change process, the consultant and client may agree to a shakedown period of finite duration, giving both parties an option to withdraw from the relationship should this appear warranted by events of the trial period.

Clarifying the problem

The substance of this phase of the change process will be determined by techniques employed by the consultant. One format will be used for survey approaches while other formats will accompany techniques such as management by objectives. In general, the format will be collaborative regardless of the particular techniques employed. The client possesses information that the consultant needs. The consultant has a range of diagnostic skills that can aid the client. Wherever possible, we advocate that the consultant help the client learn these diagnostic skills so that collaboration can occur. For instance, using survey techniques, the client may be called on to design and implement means for data collection and analysis with the help of the consultant (see, for example, Wieland and Leigh, 1971).

The diagnostic phase also serves to unfreeze further the client's organization. Analysis of data may show that problems are more numerous and more threatening than had been expected. The need for change may be seen as more pervasive or as affecting more subsystems than was originally thought. At this point, the change agent may guide the process of diagnosis to prevent the client from becoming overly impressed with the problems involved, fatalistic about them, or convinced that their solution can only be achieved by experts such as the consultant. Numerous problems can be brought to light by the diagnostic phase. Balance is achieved as alternative change strategies are considered for each problem as it is brought to light. Rather than an inventory of problems lacking solutions, the process yields an assortment of problems in various stages of resolution as management considers alternative actions and definite intentions to change in specified ways (Ronald Lippitt et al., 1958).

Choosing from alternatives

At this point, the fourth phase has begun. Evaluation and choice are cognitive, rational processes ostensibly. As we saw in Chapter 8 on "Strategy Formulation," the actual process is likely to deviate from these expectations to one degree or another. Satisficing behavior may supersede optimization by necessity. One or at most two custom-made solutions may be considered rather than a broad array of feasible alternatives.

Equally important as the cognitive aspects of alternative selection is a motivational process accompanying this phase of the process, for at this point the organization must marshal commitment to act and carry out the programs of change selected. This is accomplished in large measure by the collaborative nature of the change process as the client develops commitment to the solution he or she helped design.

Transforming intentions into change efforts

As we indicated earlier, many client-consultant relationships terminate at the conclusion of the previous phase when alternatives are selected and described in report form. This is unfortunate when it occurs, for the present phase is at the heart of the change process, so to speak. It is at this point that the consultant's expertise can be critical to the entire process of change. As we indicated in discussing Lewin's model, the change agent's expertise can be of value in aligning an adequate configuration of forces and maintaining a favorable imbalance in the force field throughout the change period. In a sense, the consultant helps the client progress through a series of cycles in the change process in which: (1) preliminary moves are made, (2) gains are consolidated and compared to desired outcomes, and (3) depending on the nature of this comparison, further consolidation is effected or further changes are sought.

Stabilizing change

The sixth phase of the process concerns diffusion of change throughout the client organization. As we indicated in our discussion of Lewin's model, a change in one subsystem often necessitates corresponding changes in adjacent subsystems. In helping the client achieve this, the consultant serves a second purpose, namely, providing an external and fairly objective evaluation of progress. Added to the client's own evaluation, the consultant's opinion can provide reinforcement for the efforts and results obtained.

Stabilization also can be achieved as the consultant helps the client diffuse change to adjacent subsystems. As converts to a better way of life reinforce their own conversions by proselytizing new converts, so do managers reinforce their newly learned skills and behaviors by helping others acquire them.

Ending the relationship

When change is realized and stabilized, the consultant's role has been discharged. To the extent the change agent involved the client in participation and transferred the agent's skills to the client's organization, difficulties in terminating the client-consultant relationship will have been reduced. Be that as it may, they still may be substantial. By seeking expert help, the client became dependent, although perhaps not as dependent as he or she might have been had the consultant behaved differently. The consultant attempts to reduce this dependence as the change program draws to completion. If the consultant has been successful in transferring skills to the client's organization, the problem may entail little more than reinforcing the client's confidence by demonstrating the organization's newly acquired competence.

DESCRIPTIVE VIEWS OF CHANGE PROCESSES

Descriptive studies of change processes

March and Simon's (1958) observation that people rarely achieve the degree of rationality to which they aspire is reinforced throughout the literature in organizational behavior. We are not surprised, then, to find discrepancies between normative and descriptive views of organizational change. It appears that the clinical rationality described in Lippitt's work represents a model for organizational change that is rarely, if ever, achieved.

Greiner (1967) began a descriptive study of the change process by identifying relatively successful and unsuccessful planned-change programs in complex organizations. The former numbered 11 and the latter 7. The 11 successful change programs included Blake and Mouton's managerial grid study of a factory (Blake and Mouton, 1964), Guest's (1962) study of a factory, Jaques's (1951) study of Glacier Metal, Rice's (1958) Ahmedabad experiment discussed in Chapter 4, and Seashore and Bower's (1963) implementation of Likert's System Four management. Each of the 18 change programs dealt with substantial, complex changes that were monitored by systematic, objective evaluation. Greiner (1967) found that successful programs seemed to comprise identifiable steps undertaken in the following order.

Problem recognition

Successful change programs were found in organizations whose top management was under considerable pressure to change. Furthermore, pressures emanated both from the environment and from within the organization. In contrast, unsuccessful change programs were launched in response to pressures originating either internally or externally *but not both*.

Furthermore, it should be emphasized that these pressures were quite serious from top management's point of view. Typical sources of external pressure were stockholder discontent, decreasing sales volumes, and breakthroughs by competitors. Internal pressures emanated from strikes, low worker productivity, rising costs, and interdepartmental conflict. Greiner emphasizes the probable significance of the simultaneous existence of internal and environmental pressures. Pressure from one source or the other by itself can be rationalized as temporary or even inconsequential, as is likely to happen, for instance, when low employee morale is accompanied by high profits. Such rationalization is less likely when poor morale and declining profits are experienced together. If Greiner's observations are valid, one is led to question whether the consultant alone will be able to develop a need for change.

Search for solutions

The second stage observed in successful change programs involves top management's search for solutions. Presumably, success at this stage precludes the next stage. In any event, we postulate that problem-solving activities of top management are approximated by our discussion of strategic decision making in Chapter 8. However, these activities do not arise automatically in response to problems. Even under severe pressure, management may rationalize its problems by blaming them on the union, government, or other entities over which they lack control.

Arrival of a change agent

Failing to react successfully to pressures, management will seek out (or have thrust on them) the services of an outsider, known for the ability to improve organizational functioning. Sometimes organizations in dire straits find their top management replaced by a "manager of the hour." More frequently, existing management employs a consultant. The newcomer's position is advantageous. Having no vested interests in the organization or historical loyalties to one manager or another, the consultant can provide a relatively objective appraisal of the organization. Furthermore, the consultant's reputation (or aura) as a change agent will provide leverage to influence top management's behavior.

Commitment of top management

The fourth stage involves the newcomer's attempts to commit top management to one change strategy or another. Dealing with top management appears to be critical to success, since changes are most likely to come about if the organization's power structure is behind them. In successful change programs, the newcomer encourages top management to examine past practices and current problems. The power structure is encouraged to suspend temporarily its preconceptions and accustomed ways of viewing problems. In this vein, management is led to original perceptions of the causes of organizational behavior.

Collaboration

Successful change efforts tend to involve the head of the organization and the immediate subordinates in extensive reexaminations of past practices and current problems. After having secured the collaboration and support of top management, fact-finding and problem-solving discussions are begun in lower levels of the organization. Top-management support is important at this stage, since it enables subordinates to view their own efforts as legitimate, having the backing of important people in the organization. Greiner (1967) suggests that subordinates have evidence that top management is willing to change, since they are involved in the diagnosis and change efforts. They have evidence that important problems are being acknowledged and faced up to and furthermore that ideas from lower levels are being valued by upper levels.

Creativity

At some point, management may become convinced that its problems, as they have been redefined, defy solution using available techniques. Here, the change agent's function is to provide new ideas and methods for developing solutions. Management generally is involved in learning and practicing new forms of behavior that permit creative problem solving. As unique solutions are generated, top management's commitment increases. Greiner notes that none of the less successful change programs reached this particular stage of development. The seeds of failure, sown in previous stages, grow into severe resistance to change prior to this. As this occurs, top management usually gives up or regroups for another effort.

Reality testing

Solutions developed in the previous stage are tested on a pilot basis to determine their efficacy. This is observed in successful change efforts prior to attempts to broaden the scope of change to larger problems and the entire organization. Difficulties are nearly inevitable in the pilot run. Rather than presenting problems, they serve as opportunities to modify solutions and enhance their effectiveness.

Diffusion

Following pilot testing, adequate solutions are introduced on a larger scale. With each successful implementation, management support grows and the change is gradually absorbed into the organization's way of life. This final phase of the change process seems identical to our prior discussions of diffusion and reinforcement of change.

Greiner's findings may be disturbing to some students of organizational change, for they contradict the ideologies of many organizational development theorists. Some writers advocate democratic, grass-roots change strategies that bring about change by first involving lower level members of the organization. Clearly, Greiner's findings do not provide empirical support for such a belief. Other scholars make much of the change agent's ability to cause change—to move the organization in anticipation of problems rather than in reaction to them. Yet, Greiner suggests that awesome pressures, perhaps near-calamities, must arise before management will consider changing their organization substantially. We also observe in Greiner's work an emphasis on formal authority as a prerequisite to change. This too runs contrary to schools of thought emphasizing organizationwide collaboration in the absence of formal sanctions. As we have indicated, the field of organizational development is rife with controversy based on ideology as well as fact. The field is relatively young, even in comparison to the field of organization theory.

An example of organizational change

The most common approach to organizationwide change is to change the organization itself directly, by changing its structure, technology, people, and perhaps even goals according to some predetermined plan for accomplishing specified outcomes. Top management may plan and organize mergers, reorganizations of existing structures, or divestments of existing programs, for example.

Rigorous scientific study of this kind of organizational change is rare. Especially rare are applications of experimental methodologies to the change phenomenon. This is understandable, given the magnitude of the phenomenon and its complexity. One example of this sort of research is Morse and Reimer's (1956) study of a large insurance company that modified its authority and decision-making structures.

The objective of the experiment was to alter role structures with respect to decision making and related activities, to give employees at lower hierarchical levels adequate power and authority to conduct more of the organization's work. It was felt that the human relations approach, with its emphasis on group involvement and participatory management, would prove inadequate unless the groups to which it was applied were given authority to make decisions and power to implement them. Hence, the human relations approach was augmented with a planned change in the organization's power structure that was to be accomplished through decentralization.

General support for this change strategy was found in a study by Pelz (1952), who noted the conditions under which human relations training tended to be effective or ineffective. The success of such training, that is, its usefulness to the trainee's organization, seemed to be influenced directly by the trainee's power and authority within the organization. Trainees having sufficient authority and power were able to delegate decisions to their subordinates and to back these decisions in the larger organization. Those in weaker positions were unable to provide subordinates with the breadth of responsibility participatory decision making requires.

To alter existing patterns of authority and responsibility, the experimenters worked with top management to restructure the firm's production department. The intent of this change was to give rank-and-file employees the wherewithal to discharge not only their previous functions, but also those of first-line supervision. In turn, first-line personnel were to assume responsibility for running the division. Displaced by supervisors, division managers were made responsible for their departments. Finally, the department head was to assume some of the executive vice-president's functions, specifically the coordination of the production department and other departments.

Thus, the change program entailed moving authority and responsibility for decision making downward in the hierarchy, not only at lower levels, as is done in some job enrichment schemes, but at upper levels of the organization as well. In contrast to individual or group changes, the experiment encompassed systematic changes in the organization's structure from the shop floor to the department head. The latter kind of change is more likely to endure the passage of time, since changes to individuals and groups that do not cause subsequent adjustments in the remainder of the organization are likely to be reversed.

Elements of organizational change

Katz and Kahn argue that although organizational characteristics are difficult to change since so much must be changed in the process, it is important to alter these characteristics directly. Failing to do so may incur even greater costs and effort in the long run as unchanged elements of the system exert pressure on changed elements to revert to their former states.

Now, this does not mean that acting on systemic variables precludes the use of individual and group change techniques. In fact, they are used, although they are not the focuses of change. Rather than individual or group behavior, interdependent structural aspects of the organization are selected as targets of the change effort. Management may become convinced of the efficacy of structural changes through participation in surveys or group sessions, but the intent of these activities will not be to change managers' attitudes about themselves or others, but to change their understanding of the relationships between systemic variables and organizational performance.

In the present study, this was accomplished by providing the executive vice-president with survey results indicating that higher-producing sections in the firm were less closely supervised and more involved in decision making than were lower-producing sections. For instance, clerks in the higher-producing sections helped one another in addition to discharging their own duties. Similarly, supervisors of higher-producing clerks gave them more freedom within their own tasks.

Employees at various levels of the organization were prepared for the anticipated change by involvement in group discussions. These discussion sessions attempted to prepare supervisors for their new roles as well. As the discussions progressed, intended structural changes were introduced as official policy changes, which were presented and explained to employees by the firm's executive vice president. Finally, group decision making was implemented as the firm's routine mode of operation for rank-and-file and supervisory employees.

Results of the organizational change

As these changes were introduced, a second, unrelated group of employees was selected as a control. The control group received the opposite treatment, more or less. Further centralization was implemented. Measures of morale and productivity were taken in both the experimental and control groups before and after the experiment. The experimental manipulations were successful in changing the intended systemic variables. Clerical work groups on the decentralized unit made decisions on matters that were important to them, such as recess periods, the handling of tardiness, and work methods and processes. In the control group, all decisions were made by management, and most were made at least one level above first-line supervision.

The results were generally as expected. Self-actualization, as measured in the study, increased among employees in the decentralized unit and decreased under centralization.[2] Relations with supervisors improved under the decentralized program and deteriorated in the control group. Unfortunately, measures of productivity left something to be desired. Only clerical time and costs could be measured against throughput of work. Both groups showed significant increases in productivity in terms of the clerical costs associated with output. However, the centralized unit achieved greater productivity than the experimental unit. Morse and Reimer explain this finding by observing that employees in the centralized unit experienced more dissatisfaction than their counterparts in the experimental unit. Consequently, greater labor turnover was also experienced. However, new personnel were not hired to replace those who terminated their employment. Rather, the work was distributed among fewer remaining employees. Since the work flow was nearly constant, the reduction in the work force decreased clerical cost per unit of work. It can also be argued that since measurement was made shortly after the change, productivity measures may have noted short-run effects that would not have lasted over the long run.

Katz and Kahn (1966) also observe that the rate of work flow was nearly constant for both groups. This implies that the cooperative group spirit engendered in the decentralized group could not be expressed fully in terms of increased productivity without disrupting the group. Under these conditions, increasing group productivity would have required decreasing the group's size. Specifically, clerks would have had to declare one or more of their number redundant and request that they be transferred to another group. This is a difficult step for a cohesive group to take.

A more general explanation of the decentralized group's failure to realize greater productivity is that human relations programs may be inappropriate for certain technologies such as assembly lines and other routine functions such as the clerks performed. According to theorists such as Perrow (1970), productivity results from effective organization achieved when structure and technology are matched appropriately (Chapter 4). Yet, this raises additional questions. One may introduce participative management and other human relations techniques for reasons other than improving productivity. As we noted, productivity in the experimental unit exceeded its prior level. We may be satisfied with this outcome and not seek ultimate performance provided we value gains in employee satisfaction and the dignity of work as well. As indicated in Chapter 14, productivity is but one of the criteria to be used in assessing organizational effectiveness.

---

[2] Given the lack of evidence that a need for self-actualization exists, we question what actually was measured (see Chapter 9).

The point of reviewing this experiment is not so much to evaluate its end results as it is to explore organizationwide change attained by altering basic structural variables. To continue in this vein, we shall review a second example to indicate the great variety of activities required in changing an organization.

Reorganizing

Service unit management (SUM), a relatively new structural design for hospitals, brings a manager into the wards to work with nurses, ward orderlies, housekeepers, and clerks. Problems encountered introducing SUM together with the arrangement's operating characteristics were examined by a multidisciplinary research team. The team focused its attention on eight hospitals employing SUM and also conducted a nationwide survey of hospitals. Their work is described by Jelinek, Munson, and Smith (1971).

Advocates of SUM claim that it addresses two major problems in hospitals. First, the continuing shortage of nurses is aggravated by the amount of administrative and supervisory work required of them, which removes them from activities for which they are trained—direct patient care. In fact, the more skilled the nurse—the greater the training and experience—the greater the likelihood of assignment to administrative and supervisory duties. This leaves patient care to the less skilled and inexperienced. Second, most nurses are not trained managers. Therefore, it would seem reasonable to separate professional and managerial activities and assign the latter to those uniquely qualified to discharge them.

The role of the service unit manager was designed to subsume managerial functions on the hospital ward and consequently free nurses' time for patient care. In addition, cost savings were anticipated. Presumably, the service unit manager would assign some of nursing's unskilled tasks to less skilled personnel. Furthermore, the management orientation of the service unit manager was expected to be more effective in reducing costs than the more professional orientations of nurses. The reorganization was expected to increase the work satisfaction of various personnel on the ward. Nurses, freed from "paper shuffling," would have opportunity to exercise more of their professional skills and, presumably, increase their satisfaction in the process. Finally, the manager's training was expected to result in better quality supervision and fewer related employee dissatisfactions.

Typical service unit managers order equipment and supplies from various hospital departments. Similarly, they schedule required maintenance service for the ward. They supervise the ward clerk, who answers phones, greets visitors, schedules appointments, and maintains patient records. They coordinate requests for charts and records, lab and X-ray information, and supervise the various clerical activities that arise from these and associated tasks. Other activities of the service unit managers include coordinating food, laundry, and housekeeping services on the ward. Supervision of patient feeding and transportation frequently are delegated to the managers as well.

There are two common procedures for locating the service unit manager in the organizational structure. In both cases the manager enjoys status equal to that of the head nurse, or the senior nurse on the ward. In one case, both the head nurse and the manager are located in the nursing division and report to the director of nursing who, in turn, is subordinate to the hospital administrator. In the second case, the head nurse is subordinate to the director of nursing. The manager, though, reports directly to the hospital administrator. Another variation is found in the number of units or wards managed. Typically these range from one to three (the latter comprising about 80 beds). Further variations occur across shifts. In some hospitals, service unit managers are employed around the clock. In others, the manager's responsibilities revert to the head nurse between the hours of 5:00 P.M. and 8:00 A.M. Obviously, these and related variations must be decided on prior to implementation of this form of management.

Introducing structural change

Major problems arise as changes of the magnitude described here are introduced to the organization's traditional structure. As Robert Smith (1971) and Jelinek and colleagues (1971) indicate, organizational change creates problems at numerous levels in the hierarchy. At the *individual level,* the manager must be particularly concerned with employees' feelings of security. He or she will need to anticipate potential reactions of head nurses, who may view their administrative skills as having been rendered obsolete and their status as having diminished accordingly. At the extreme, ambiguities arising from the transition period and attendant insecurities may lead to conflicts, to disruptions, and to staff turnover.

New patterns or relationships will be created at the *unit level* by the creation of the service unit manager's position. Existing patterns of interaction and status will be altered. Left to themselves, these alterations may produce undesirable consequences; for example, the head nurse may use the time once spent on administrative matters to supervise licensed practical nurses more closely. This change in the relationship between superior and subordinate may result in a decrease in the latter's job satisfaction.

Problems also arise at the *system level.* The service unit manager will replace the head nurse as liaison with other hospital units. Consequently, relations between nursing and other departments will change. In addition, the service unit manager will need to forge new relations with other units to discharge the boundary role.

It is possible to eliminate the causes of some of these problems in the planning phase of the change effort. The process whereby unfreezing is achieved and motivations mobilized can be structured to minimize resistance and anxiety. Here, of course, the whole area of participation in planning is relevant. Individuals who will be most involved and affected can participate in planning for change. Those whose involvement will be merely tangential ought to have the opportunity to provide input. Finally, various other individuals will need to be kept informed, at least.

Training can also pave the way for change. The study in question showed lack of training to be a source of serious problems—especially in the case of the service unit manager. When the manager was inadequately trained for the tasks associated with the role, nurses and others were reluctant to relinquish their control and pass their authority on to the newcomer. Where justified, this concern implied the service unit manager's striving for undeserved status. The training advocated here should focus on the development of interpersonal skills as well as technical competence. If the manager is sensitive to potential conflict areas and competent to deal with them, the service unit manager will be free to perform the technical aspects of the job more easily. This is equally true for the head nurse and ward staff.

Phases of change processes—Development of the role

According to Robert Smith (1971), the change process can be divided into three phases, each concerning problems relevant to the three levels discussed above. The first phase concerns *development of the role,* the second *unit integration,* and the third *system integration.*

Problems facing the head nurse are acute, since the nurse must not only learn a new role, but unlearn an old one as well. The former role consisted of stabilized sets of role expectations together with skills and attitudes consistent with the former. This integrated set of skills, attitudes, and behaviors is disrupted by the change, and the nurse will be required to learn new responses to events on the ward.

Smith suggests three approaches to preparing the head nurse as well as other nursing personnel for the anticipated changes. First, they can be made aware of the problems associated with role changes—the need to unlearn and suppress old behaviors before new behaviors can be learned. Second, they can be provided emotional support throughout the period of transition. Admittedly, this is difficult, but at the very least, nurses should be provided opportunities to express their feelings and be reinforced as they demonstrate progress in adapting to their new roles. Third, and most important, is to provide the nurses with role models they can emulate. It is not enough to inform them of tasks that will no longer be required and to assume that they will use their free time effectively. What is required is a model, or description, of the new role—one that is integrated and makes sense in terms of the nurses' training, skills, and function in the hospital.

Please note that other case studies indicate the importance (and usual lack) of role models and support in moving into new roles. New educational programs, for example, may attempt to change the teacher's role from lecturer to resource person. Teachers can be unfrozen by learning the shortcomings of the lecture method and of the possible harm it does as it creates dependency in the student. Teachers can be persuaded to adopt new roles, but these experiments frequently meet with failure. If the new role is not clearly defined, the teacher will not *know how* to be a resource person. If adequate training in the role is not provided, the teacher will lack the *skills* of a resource person. Even when these are provided, the teacher will need additional resources in the form of materials and supplies as well as psychological support.

Unit integration

As progress is made in the first stage (as roles are learned), new problems come to the foreground. In the second phase of the change process one finds inter-role conflict. What was formerly a single role (head nurse) has now become two separate roles (head nurse and service unit manager). Other individuals must therefore reorganize their roles vis-à-vis the two major changes. This is descriptive of the integration phase.

Smith describes how the new arrangement (the creation of roles that are highly interdependent and physically close) creates potential for conflict. Role conflict emerges as individuals solve the problems of learning their new roles. Power plays are symptomatic of role conflict. Typically, management and nursing will attempt to influence their superiors to pressure the rival group to conform to specific role expectations; for instance, management may court the hospital administrator's support in laying claim to an area of authority that is also claimed by nursing. Distrusting one another, the two groups resort to power plays, defensiveness, and rigidity, rather than confront the disagreement directly. Cooperation may be perceived as a sign of weakness and subservient status.

The change agent must be aware of the potential for role conflict and, in this situation, reinforce the individuals' perceptions of equal status. It is particularly important that role overload be avoided at this point in the change process. Overload is likely to heighten the intensity of existing conflict. Excessive work-related demands cause the individual to suffer tension and frustration which frequently lead to aggression and aggravate existing difficulties in interpersonal relations. Furthermore, excessive tasks absorb organizational slack which could have been used to explore and remedy sources of conflict.

Another potential source of conflict is found in differences between the nurses' and managers' roles. The orientation of the nurses' role is professional while the manager's is efficiency-seeking. Thus, managers are likely to value stability as a means to steady state efficiency, while nurses value flexibility as a precondition to individualizing health care according to the patient's needs. The change agent may alleviate this source of conflict by devising performance measures that evaluate the ward as a total entity, as opposed to constructing separate measures of management's and nursing's performance. Thus, attention is focused on a superordinate goal. Pressures to suboptimize performance are reduced to the extent that incumbents of each role perceive cooperation as essential to goal attainment.

System integration

The third phase of the change process, system integration, becomes salient as problems encountered in unit integration are stabilized. At this point, the manager becomes caught between the demands of nursing (which the manager has come to view as legitimate in the second phase) and those of other departments such as housekeeping, dietetics, or the lab. Typically, these departments do not adapt automatically to changes on the ward. According to Smith, their unresponsiveness has its roots in their ability to maintain the status quo without suffering undue consequences; for example, lab employees can continue old ways of behaving toward people on the ward. They will still contact nurses when problems arise with respect to a patient's test, rather than follow the new lines of communication. Consequences of this behavior will be borne on the ward, but not in the lab. Thus, even after relationships and roles are established on the ward, they will be threatened by elements of the system that have not articulated with these novel roles.

This is probably the lowest point in the change process. The act of solving problems on the ward level has created new problems elsewhere in the hospital, which impede the service unit manager's effectiveness. One possible remedy for problems of system integration is the temporary assignment of an assistant administrator to oversee relationships between service unit management and the various ancillary departments. A second remedy is to establish a task force, comprising department heads and representatives of service unit management, to establish guidlines for interaction. Either way, formal authority is brought to bear in one form or another on recalcitrant department members.

It is entirely possible that problems arising in the third stage of the change process may never be solved. Alternatively, it may be that as one set of problems is resolved another is created. Hospitals, indeed, all complex organizations, are systems. Changes to one part of a system must be met with adaptation in the remainder of the system for interdependencies to remain viable. Furthermore, each of these changes is temporary in the sense that each can be altered by feedback and adaptation. Thus, phase three may never come to an end. As radical as this notion may seem when made explicit, we suggest that it is one with which most of us are familiar and comfortable. Organizations and societies are never freed of their problems by acts of humans or nature. Rather, they alleviate the severity of those most intolerable and, in so doing, create new ones.

Evaluation of the change effort

Of final interest is whether the introduction of service unit management improved patient care and reduced its costs in the eight hospitals surveyed. It turns out that the quality of nursing and nonnursing patient care improved overall. However, there is no evidence that the change reduced personnel costs. Job satisfaction increased for both professional and nonprofessional employees. One might conjecture that, because of this, labor turnover will be reduced, constituting one form of cost reduction.

One interesting finding is that while the change provided head nurses with more time to devote to improving the quality of patient care, the greatest improvements were made by nonprofessionals. Nurses generally failed to take full advantage of the opportunities provided by the service unit management system. This may have been due to the failure of many of the hospitals to provide adequate training and support for nurses whose roles changed. In short, one major conclusion of the present study is that service unit management is productive but can be made even more productive if sufficient attention is paid to the implementation of the nurses' role. Obviously, there is more to changing an organization than changing its structure, and that is what this book has been about.

Sequencing changes in technology, structure, and people

The outline of our text provides a useful framework within which attempts at planned organizational change can be analyzed. Since technology, structure, people, and the like are interdependent, a change in one may require changes in the others. Observing this, one is led to wonder whether there is an optimal sequence for organizational change; that is, whether it is better to permit people to adapt to a change in the formal structure of their organization, or whether structural changes should follow change efforts focusing on employee behavior.

We have described numerous ways of changing organizations at various points throughout the text. Beginning with the rational view of organizations, we examined alternative formal structures. Major structural changes are found in reorganizations (for example, from a functional structure to a decentralized divisional structure or a matrix organization). The service unit management program in hospitals is another example.

Technological change can include applications of scientific management, work measurement techniques, time and motion study, job classification schemes, and various industrial engineering techniques. Operations research seems similar to these, but appears to be more applicable to managerial tasks (for example, selecting media in an advertising agency, controlling inventories, and scheduling production runs).

Now we are led to ask, what are the relationships between these structural and technological approaches to organizational change and the behavioral approaches described in the organizational development literature? Structural and technological changes often have been implemented without concern for people variables; for example, when reorganization follows a decision to implement a more appropriate formal structure, employees are moved to "new sets of boxes" on the organizational chart. Similarly, when technological changes follow the determination of more efficient production methods, tasks are reassigned to employees accordingly. These are oversimplifications, of course. Training programs and shakedown periods are employed frequently. Furthermore, a change in structure or technology often is sold to lower-level staff. However, these practices suggest that attempts to change structure (or technology) precede attempts to change people.

The Tavistock study of the change to the longwall mining system (Chapter 4) is a case in point. However, the sequence did not operate as planned, and the technology did not take. Structural and people change had to proceed apace with a redesign of the technology. We might say that it was necessary to match the social system to the technological system.

Here, we are developing a loose and informal argument for a contingency approach to organizational change. Yet, there is an argument to the contrary—that external, unilateral change efforts involving technology or structure may be cheaper. If they are sufficient in and of themselves, they can be used alone. Furthermore, it can be argued that attempts to change people often do not work. Even when they do work, their effects may be unpredictable.

On the one hand, we note problems in change attempts such as those reported in the Tavistock study. On the other hand, we can refer to countless structural and technological changes (for example, installation of computer systems) that were not accompanied by the application of behavioral science techniques. While the debate goes on, we profess to have no answer to these arguments at this time.

Postscript

Introduction of service unit management seems a relatively modest change, particularly when the substance of the change is viewed in the context of the hospital, an extremely complex organization. And yet, as Smith indicates, even as simple a change as the addition of one individual to the ward structure must accommodate complex social and technical interdependencies that comprise the organization.

We have tried to unravel these interrelationships and to examine each in its context in the organization. Yet, we have only scratched the surface in doing so. Each chapter of this text represents a field of inquiry in which scientists and scholars pursue their careers. We hope we have been fair and accurate in reporting and integrating the fruits of these labors and that in so doing we have given you something of value, of use in your careers in a complex and changing society.

DISCUSSION QUESTIONS

1. Can Lewin's force field analysis of behavioral change be used as a tool for problem solving in organizations? How?
2. What are the limitations of the force field analysis?
3. The force field analysis is an analogy to physical systems. What are some limitations of all such analogies?
4. Identify some of the interdependencies that exist between your school and other parts of the university. How would these be affected by a hypothetical change in your school's modus operandi?

17

The Future: Some Ways of Thinking

INTRODUCTION

What will life be like 5, 10, or, say, 25 years from now? How will organizations change? How much of what we have covered in this text will be relevant in ten years?

Looking into the future—once the pastime of wool-gatherers and the occupation of science fiction writers and occultists—is now an accepted and lucrative trade. According to one estimate, one out of every five firms in the *Fortune* 500 employs futurologists of one sort or another (Gallese, 1975). Major works in the area of futurology are reported in the popular press and scientific journals. As the rate of change in society increases, futurology may rival history as a source of inspiration and direction, or so it seems.

Our intent in this concluding chapter is not merely to lay out the various utopias and horrors that futurology presents as alternative futures, but to review the bases of these predictions, to examine some of their limitations, and to suggest the use of genotypic variables in forecasts of this sort. In essence, we shall present some ways of thinking about forecasts and their use in organizations. One way to begin is to examine the premises—the hidden assumptions—on which works of this sort are based. What follows is the preface to a research proposal written by one of the authors some years ago. What assumptions are made about the future?

Educators have always tried to prepare their students for "tomorrow." But technology and society have undergone such rapid changes in the last third of this century that the tasks of the teacher, and the student, have never been more complex. Moreover, our colleagues the world over have begun to resurrect and revise Parson Malthus' gloomy prophecy. Resource depletion, pollution, and unchecked population growth are expected to contribute to a world-encompassing catastrophy by the middle of the next century. The discovery of additional resources and increments to existing technology will not ward off the impending disaster, they tell us, but will merely postpone or, in some cases, hasten its eventuality. The only remaining hope for contemporary society lies in our being able to alter our values and ways of living. We must husband our remaining resources and produce services in place of numerous consumer durable and semi-durable goods. We must limit population growth and learn to desire national growth along dimensions other than economic stature. We will need to develop and learn to value the abilities to ration, recycle, and ephemeralize. In short, we will need to produce a society which bears a symbiotic relationship to its environment and is both satisfying to its members and supportive of their personal growth. From what has been reported to date, one is led to imagine that art, philosophy, psychology, and the life sciences will guide and direct the application of physical and engineering sciences in this symbiotic society. But our various learning disciplines do not seem to be supplying the proper responses to the challenges of Today and Tomorrow (Ullrich, "Experimental Learning Community," 1971).

Chapter guide

1. What are the author's assumptions about the role of technology in the solution of future problems? What are possible sources of these assumptions?
2. In what sense must values change to accommodate the future? Have the author's values colored the premises of his argument? Is it possible to make value-free forecasts?
3. If you were to write a comparable paragraph about the future, how would it differ from the one presented above?
4. How could a college respond to the problems raised by the author? Would you advocate making these organizational responses? What difficulties might arise if these responses were to be implemented?

MAJOR APPROACHES TO FUTUROLOGY

The inevitability of mishap

In 1964, Slater and Bennis published a paper entitled "Democracy is Inevitable" in which they predicted the coming demise of bureaucracy. Unsuited to the demands of contemporary society, bureaucracy would be made obsolete by new organizational forms based on humanistic-democratic ideals. Bennis's subsequent experience, however, led him to recant in a follow-up article entitled "A Funny Thing Happened on the Way to the Future" (Bennis, 1970a). This denouement is instructive, since it parallels the fate of many such forecasts and illustrates the origins of their inaccuracies.

As Slater and Bennis saw it, bureaucracy could not endure the pressures building in society. Applications of human relations techniques, System Four management, and the like would relieve some of these pressures, but bureaucratic structures inherently were ill-equipped to survive the rapid growth of science and technology and unable to adapt to increasingly turbulent environments. Bennis's many years of experience as a leading organizational development practitioner led him to conclude that bureaucracies were unable to meet changing human needs as well. For these reasons, he expected bureaucratic structures to be replaced by "... adaptive, problem-solving, temporary systems of diverse specialists, linked together by co-ordinating and task evaluating specialists in an organic flux ..." (Bennis, 1970b, p. 14).

As a high-level university administrator, Bennis had the opportunity to implement organizational forms of the type he advocated. This experience gave rise to his doubts expressed in the second paper. Specifically, he admits that the democracy of the small group does not transfer readily to the large-scale organization, which comprises subsystems having differing interests. Moreover, he suggests that the earlier paper underplayed power of all types and emphasized the management of conflict while ignoring the strategy of conflict. His more recent writings continue to reflect doubt that large-scale organizations can be made more democratic. In fact, he wonders aloud whether complex organizations such as the university are governable at all.

Earlier enthusiasm for utopian organizations such as communes provides another example of prediction gone wrong. A tremendous upwelling of interest among young people led to the creation of thousands of these organizations during the late 60s and early 70s. There were concomitant predictions that the counterculture values of these organizations' founders would soon characterize most of Western society (see, for example, Roszak, 1969). The process through which this would occur became known as the "greening of America" (Reich, 1971).

As these predictions were being made, Peter Drucker (1971) noted the imminent demise of the counterculture. He suggested that the upwelling of emphasis on humanistic values was caused by demographic factors that were soon to change and, in so doing, dissipate the counterculture. Although many people assumed that young people would retain these values as they moved into later stages of adulthood, Drucker pointed out that the demographic characteristics of the situation were unique and temporary. From 1948 to 1953 the number of babies born rose by nearly 50 percent. Consequently, the percentage of the population in the 17-year-old group increased proportionately from 1965 to 1970. In addition, because of low birthrates during the Great Depression and World War II, the sudden increase of postwar births caused the center of gravity of the U.S. population to shift from the 35 to 40 age group in 1960 to the 17-year-old age group in 1965. Thus, each 17-year-old group was larger than the previous one for the next seven years. Because this age group marks the transition from family control to self- or peer-control, it played a critical role in the development of the counterculture. As Drucker indicates, it has been the age of rebellion for centuries.

Because the baby boom crested in 1955, 17-year-olds have become less numerous and have less effect on societal values. In fact, the 1960–67 baby bust will decrease the numbers of 17-year-olds even further in the 1980s. Drucker interprets this to mean that youth will have even less influence in society in the future. If we assume that the most numerous group in society has the most impact on its values, we can expect 21- to 35-year-olds to shape the course of history over the next 15 years. According to Drucker, this group will be concerned primarily with concrete problems, not addicted to causes, intoxicated with ideas, or in search of identity. His view is that the values of these individuals will concern jobs, economic performance, and productivity.

While population dynamics cannot explain all of the psychology or economics of the future, Drucker seems to have made a case for viewing demographics as a factor of some importance. Not to incorporate such genotypic variables in forecasts is to invite mishap, as we have just seen.

Genotypic variables in the social system

One problem with the kinds of prognostications cited above is that they often are based on projections, or extrapolations, of short-term trends for phenotypic (superficial) variables. To improve the accuracy of prediction, we must identify genotypic (basic) variables *and* their relationships to the system for which predictions are sought (Emery, 1967). We shall investigate the nature and importance of several genotypic variables later in this chapter. For the moment, we shall focus on the degree to which various approaches to futurology emphasize societal ends and the means of achieving those ends.

Approaches to futurology

The major approaches to futurology can be categorized according to two dimensions: (1) specification of system goals, and (2) specification of strategies or means. First, futurologies differ according to whether they define or specify future societal goals and values. Often futurologists take their own values for granted, neglecting to specify them and ignoring those of others; for example, the dominant technological, materialistic values in our society frequently are implicitly accepted without conscious choice. Second, futurologists may specify and delineate the means or strategies to achieve their values, or they may neglect the problem of change strategies, perhaps in favor of the value question. This categorization scheme is depicted in Figure 17–1. *Surprise-free futurology,* the most common form of futurology, does not specify the goals or values desired of the system in question. It does accept and extend current, usually materialistic and technological, strategies into the future, thereby yielding surprise-free futures. Reduced to its simplest form, this approach to forecasting takes the system where it seems to be headed. Writers such as Bell (1960, 1973), Herman Kahn and Wiener (1967), and Toffler (1970) tend to see humanity converging on a single future, a "post-industrial society" that is determined by the continuation of past trends. The directions of the engines of change—economic growth and technological development—are easily plotted, and the derived expectations often have been validated. For example, Ayres (1969) has stated: "... if the envelope curves for macrovariables representing the state of the art of a given technology show a definite trend, there already exists an internal dynamics which tends to continue the trend more or less straight ahead (on the appropriate scale) until some constraint is reached" (pp. 114–15).

FIGURE 17–1
Orientations of futurology

System means specified	System goals specified	
	No	Yes
Yes	Surprise-free (Toffler)	Strategy formulation (Lodge)
No	Crisis (Meadows)	Value-critical (Reich)

Source: Adapted from Hake (1973, p. 6).

The limitations of surprise-free forecasting are numerous. We may not wish to go where society seems to be headed. What alternative ends are available to us? How are we to select from among possible alternative futures? How are we to change society to reach a preferred alternative?

In contrast to the emphasis on current, existing societal strategies, the *crisis futurologists* have indicated that we may not achieve the surprise-free future plotted for us. There are limits to growth because the earth is a closed system—resources are finite. This approach to futurology has provided a useful criticism of the emphasis on current materialistic, technological, and growth-oriented strategies, but it suffers from the same limited view of possible societal values and a negativistic approach to strategies. If measures for avoiding catastrophe are suggested, they generally consist of more of the same technological answers, but better, more efficient ones: population control, recycling, conservation, pollution control, and the like. The main thrust of this approach is a negative one; that current strategies will not work. Little attention is given to social or political strategies. As Hake (1973) suggests, the approach demonstrates political naïveté about the implementation of any technological reforms that might be proposed.

A third school of futurology rests on dissatisfactions with present societal values and goals. These *value-critical futurologists* focus on alternative values and goals and the need to go beyond our current predominant values. The problem is that means to desired ends are not considered. As Hake (1973) suggests, "New social ideals do not in themselves create a new society. Idealistic utopian thinking, divorced from the action of social groups, is no more viable as a creator of change than ... technological determinism ..." (p. 7). Thus, while Reich (1971) advocates the "greening of America," he does not examine the workings of our society to determine whether and how such ends are attainable.

The limitations of futurology noted above can be overcome in theory by an approach akin to *strategy formulation* (Chapter 8). This approach attempts to specify alternative goals and values for society as well as the means by which these can be achieved. There is an emphasis on the process by which both ends and means jointly can be more clearly articulated. Lodge's *The New American Ideology* (1975) is an example of this approach to futurology.

Unfortunately, there are limits to what we can expect from social strategy formulation. In the world system, everything is related to everything else. Political and social factors affect technological and economic factors, and vice versa. These interrelations are too numerous and complex to be understood in their entirety, and the result is a very imperfect forecasting technique. Yet, this approach probably holds more promise than the others. As Hake indicates: "We cannot know the future, but we can know alternative possibilities and the means of their attainment and we can act to produce one or another of these concrete utopias" (1973, p. 7).

It is interesting to note that when we assume both consensus regarding goals and the knowledge with which to select appropriate means, forecasting and planning become inseparable. Social strategy formulation, similar to organizational strategic planning, may seem to imply omnipotence. As we saw in Chapter 8, though, this is hardly the case. We do not mean to imply that either perfect knowledge of the system or complete consensus regarding goals is ever attained. Rather, we have described an approach to planning and futurology that allows muddling through to take on purpose.

SOME GENOTYPIC ORGANIZATIONAL VARIABLES TO CONSIDER

Many reports of futurologists omit analysis of organizational variables. To our way of thinking this is unfortunate, for prediction must include some notion of the limits to organizational capabilities and responsiveness. For this reason, we shall describe organizational phenomena that may circumscribe the alternatives available to society.

Rationality in organizational life

Rationality is critical to Weber's description of bureaucracy. In these terms, the coming "death of bureaucracy" touted by Bennis and others is far from imminent, for rationality of the technical core (James Thompson, 1967) increases with the complexity of technological processes. As technologies become more complex, we can expect organizations to become more rational. Protecting the rationality of the technological core from environmental and human uncertainty may constitute a prime organizational problem in the future.

While this may sound contradictory in the face of growing interest in the human relations movement, we agree with William Scott (1969) that organizational development, job enlargement, and the like often are based on values similar to those espoused in Taylor's scientific management. Viewed from one perspective, the human relations movement is merely the behavioral scientist's approach to management science. Observing a credibility gap between the pronouncements of the human relations movement and the goals of its various programs, Scott remarks that management generally installs human relations projects where they are consistent with economic values; that is, with better, more efficient functioning of personnel. Thus, organizational development and other practices serve as intended means to even greater organizational efficiency, productivity, and rationality.

As rationality increases and as the environment becomes more complex, management's problems are magnified. In Chapter 7 we discussed buffering, smoothing, anticipating, rationing, exchange, acquiring prestige, and more direct uses of power as ways of dealing with uncertainty. Strategic planning (Chapter 8), as well as planned change (especially Chapters 15 and 16), are also useful in this regard. However, as problems become more acute, more drastic steps may become appropriate.

One apparent response in large organizations has been for organizational roles to become increasingly specified and segmented. James Thompson's (1973) scenario of organizations in the year 2000 illustrates this. By then, he suggests, we are likely to work for more than one organization. Technical reps employed by private contractors to work with government personnel, as well as university professors who pursue research funded by external agencies, are prototypes of tomorrow's workers according to Thompson. Please note that the kinds of role conflict described in Chapter 10 are likely to be intensified by such arrangements. Second, organizations (including managers and clientele) are likely to be located in widespread, changing networks, as are present-day firms that subcontract parts of various projects from the federal government. In this case, interorganizational relations such as those described in Chapter 7 are likely to become more important in day-to-day organizational functioning. Finally, Thompson suggests that individuals and organizations will cease to work under unitary authority systems. He cites the war on polio as an example which:

> ... involved the activities of 3,100 local chapters, each of which raised funds through solicitations by volunteers, with 50 percent of those funds to be retained locally for treatment of local polio victims. But it motivated the pooling of the remaining 50 percent nationally, both as insurance against local outbreaks which might overrun local funds and for research and education purposes. In 20 years the Foundation spent $315 million on patient care, $55 million on research and $33 million on fellowships and scholarships ... (1973, pp. 330–31).

The limits to rationality

At this point we must ask whether the average person will be able to survive the fragmentation of the work role that results when such drastic attempts to increase rationality are made. While the increased tempo of change and the temporary character of relationships may provide the individual greater freedom and opportunity (see, for example, Bennis and Slater, 1968), a person's ability to adapt, let alone stay in control of the situation, will be taxed severely. At present we have limited, but compelling, evidence that excessive life changes produce somatic illness and psychological distress (Moss, 1973).

Taking a larger perspective, it would seem that increasing rationalization can destroy the organization per se. The essence of organization is the dedication of its parts to some ultimate purpose. Excessive rationality questions everything with an eye to efficiency. Nothing is held sacred. Everyone is assumed ultimately flexible, adaptable, and malleable. We wonder how the ultimately rational organization can be coordinated to act with unity of purpose. We suspect that organizational character (Chapter 12) and trust are dissipated by fragmentation and excessive change.

PREDICTIONS BASED ON GENOTYPIC VARIABLES

Having explored the bases of futurological works, we shall summarize a variety of such predictions below. Please bear in mind that these works have been selected as examples and do not necessarily reflect our own beliefs about the future or our preferences for the kind of world we would like our children to inherit.

Theoretical biases toward growth and consensus

Both the system and rational views of organizations may become increasingly inappropriate paradigms, since both implicitly rely on organizational growth to obtain individual commitment to the organization and to achieve concerted organizational action (William Scott, 1974). Conflict between individuals and the organization, as well as between subunits, is avoided by using surpluses achieved through organizational growth (Chapter 5). This implicit premise raises some important questions for the future of organizations.

According to system theory, subsystems are evaluated according to their contributions to the larger organization. Adopted from the field of biology, the system view does not readily conceive of one subsystem (organ) acting in conflict with the total system (organism) (Peery, 1972). Rather, it is assumed that the parts work harmoniously for the sake of the whole. However, social systems are typified by conflict.

Any approach to understanding organizations that includes conflict as more than an addendum must fight a tradition that views equilibrium, order, conflict reduction, and, ultimately, organizational consensus as both feasible and desirable. Taylor spoke of "mutuality of interest," whereby rational management leads to increased productivity and, consequently, to greater rewards for all members of the organization. By the same token, Simon views the organization as obtaining individual or subunit contributions by providing similar inducements. Human relations and organization development theorists, as we have seen, have also taken individual-organization integration to be a necessary and desirable condition of organizational functioning.

Perhaps the theoretical bias toward reducing conflict and emphasizing consensus developed concomitantly with the general prevalence of growth in organizations. Because growth provides an increasing pool of resources for management to distribute, the resulting organizational slack can be used to reduce the potential for subsystem conflict.

In addition to viewing growth as a means for achieving subunit consensus, however, Peery considers growth to be a basic principle of system theory.

As indicated in Chapter 2, system survival is achieved by importing more than the organization exports and by differentiation and elaboration that enable the organization to adapt to a complex, changing environment. Viewed in this light, system survival implies growth.

Is economic growth inevitable or desirable?

Indeed, growth has characterized Western civilization for the past two centuries and especially for the last quarter century. But now we are approaching simultaneously the limits to a host of resources—petroleum, natural gas, and other sources of energy; a variety of minerals; fresh water; agricultural land; and the waste-absorbing capacity of the environment (Harman, 1976). Population growth is placing tremendous pressures on renewable resources as well. Too much demand for too little supply shows up in the worldwide tendency toward inflation.

The problems that accompany excessive economic growth also affect less tangible, but very real, aspects of the quality of life and, according to some, the moral basis of society. Within the United States, many people claim that the quality of life has deteriorated in a variety of ways despite increased affluence. Growth has meant increased change rather than the social stability that some favor. It has also resulted in a reduction of durable, nonsuperficial interpersonal relationships. Change and the impersonality of relationships:

> ... may contribute to the decline of customs and behavioral rules which have in the past helped to reduce many external costs that people would otherwise have inflicted on each other. At best there is a serious free-rider mentality problem involved in people's decisions as to whether to be friendly or courteous, to take garbage cans to the rear of the house, to serve as witnesses, to refain from making noise and even to be honest. Why should I do my bit, which is just a drop in the bucket, when other people may not reciprocate (McKean, 1973, pp. 213-14)?

The alternative to growth, however, is not utopia. If we could stop the momentum of growth in our society, we would face severe distributional problems. Without an ever-expanding GNP, the economic progress of the poor would be made at the expense of the middle class and the wealthy. No one would gain, except at the expense of someone else. Finally, governmental or other collective action would surely increase—to regulate growth and bring it to a halt (Olson, 1973). But as Olson observes, even democratic government, with majority rule, is a gross, "meat cleaver" approach to resolving conflicts and meeting societal needs. It is not clear whether a large, diverse population such as ours would benefit from increased governmental services.

A benign decrease in economic growth

In any event, such concerns about growth may be unfounded. According to Herman Kahn's (Kahn et al., 1976) recent projections, we need apply only "a modicum of intelligence and good management" to current problems to sustain continued growth. First, we can count on the evolution of knowledge and technology to increase resources. Kahn provides an impressive account of potential breakthroughs in various stages of development that will avert predicted crises in energy, raw materials, and food supplies and in environmental damage. More important, Kahn discerns the beginning of a decrease in population growth. The demographic transition to lower birthrates took 150 years (from 1775–1925) in the most advanced societies, such as in the United States and Western Europe, but is taking place more rapidly in later, more quickly developing countries. A definite decline in birthrates seems to have occurred in 15 developing nations during the 1960s, and there is partial evidence of a similar decline in a number of other developing countries (Salas, 1978). Thus, Kahn sees the growth of world population at an inflection point.

Kahn envisages a consequent slowing of economic growth, too. In this sense, he agrees with the crisis futurologists, but according to his forecast, the slowing of growth will result from a decline in demand rather than from difficulties in meeting increasing demand

> ... the gradual leveling-off tendency will be a social consequence of the proliferation of such factors as modernization, literacy, urbanization, affluence, safety, good health and birth control, and governmental and private policies reflecting changing values and priorities (accompanied by the increasing desire of vested interests to protect their status quo from external pressures for expansion) (p. 8).

Kahn sees us approaching a great transition. Unlike the previous 200 years of accelerating economic growth, the next 200 years will result in an eventual leveling off at an average world per capita production of two to three times the current U.S. level.

An important factor in future economic development will be a change in the nature of the growth process itself. Historically growth occurs first in the primary sector of the economy (for example, the extractive industries) and then in the secondary (industrial) sector. In the present U.S. economy, the tertiary (service) sector is growing at the expense of other two. In time, growth will shift into what Kahn calls the quaternary sector—where services are produced for their own sake; for example, in the future individuals will work at intrinsically motivating tasks in the pursuit of self-actualization.

If Kahn is right, organization theorists and managers will need new theories to replace the rational and system views—but not for a while. Rather than the conflict-based paradigm suggested by the crisis futurologists such as Scott, the emergent view will account for the great human transformations to come—about which we will have more to say below.

The social limits to growth

The critical limits to growth, however, may be social rather than material. We have already raised several objections to growth that are based on various social and moral values. Such objections are predicated on the assumption that continued growth will precipitate a radically different society—one that is characterized by social conflict, rather than by the degree of consensus that accompanied growth in the past.

In his book *The Social Limits to Growth,* Hirsch (1976) argues that as affluence comes to more and more people, the goal of competition among individuals will change. When everyone can go to the beach, no one will win, and all will be worse off in the crowding and pollution that result. Similarly, increased use of personal automobiles will result in jammed freeways and packed national parks. Hirsch looks to political allocation processes, perhaps even socialism, as a possible remedy.

The problem noted above is that economic growth may stimulate demand that exceeds the supply of social amenities and leads to a special kind of competition in society—competition for the power to have what others cannot have. In a sense, such competition is evident today in the form of contests for professional and managerial positions—the result of such competition is that the winners get not only the jobs, but also power over the losers. Desirable jobs obviously provide good salaries, but in addition, they give the position holder authority over others. Success in this kind of competition, whether for jobs or material goods, implies constantly keeping up and looking over one's shoulder. Success can never be assured, for it is measured in relative terms and depends on getting more than others get.

The growth of individualism and self-interest

Such observations suggest a rise in individualism and self-interest in modern society. A major exposition of this view is provided by Daniel Bell (1975, 1976), who expresses concern over individual aspirations that are becoming increasingly hedonistic. The trend toward self-interest, according to Bell, appears to be without moral underpinnings, for it implies goal selection in the absence of concern for the betterment of society. In a sense, this trend has resulted from a basic contradiction in the capitalistic system. Workers are exhorted to work hard, conform, and produce, but they are also exhorted to indulge themselves off the job—to consume the wealth of goods and services produced in the economy.

The result is ironic, for individuals are led to value equality of outcome over equality of opportunity.[1] This observation is reminiscent of deTocqueville's prescient conclusion that the natural effect of equality is to make people individualistic and selfish. Be that as it may, demands for equality, or entitlement, ultimately are thrust on the government, which has come to assume the responsibility "to redress all economic and social inequalities" (Bell, 1975, p. 100). In the depression era, the federal government assumed responsibility for the general health of the economy. During and after World War II, government's interests were broadened to include the development of science and technology. Since the middle 1960s though, the gov-

---

[1] Please note the philosophic distinction between the meaning of equality of outcome as it is used here and as it was used in Chapter 3.

ernment has become responsible for the general well-being of its citizenry through programs related to health, housing, welfare, and even the environment. At the same time, government spending at all levels has risen to the point where it now exceeds one third of GNP.

As competing interest groups have demanded entitlements and fought for government largesses, the government has become enmeshed in litigation and other forms of conflict. The consequence of rising demands for entitlements, according to Bell, has been a crisis of belief, a loss of legitimacy for societal institutions, and a loss of *civitas:* "... that spontaneous willingness to obey the law, to respect the rights of others, to forego the temptation of private enrichment at the expense of the public weal" (p. 102).

What is needed is agreement on a definition of the common good—a definition of societal needs and ends that permits adjudication of conflicting demands for entitlements. Once accepted, such an agreement would take precedence over the "hedonistic emphasis on satisfaction of private appetites"—while retaining a "concern for individual differences and liberty" (p. 182). Ultimately, such agreement would fill the "need for some transcendent tie to bind individuals sufficiently for them to make the occasional necessary sacrifices of self-interest" (Bell, 1975, p. 185).

The time frame of the observations

Bell's analysis does not provide much in the way of time frame, and this may crucial. The upsurge of both individualism and conflict in the governmental arena that Bell observes may be merely temporary disturbances that have arisen as the cohort of postwar babies grows into adulthood. Perhaps other temporary factors have been at work as well. Analysts a few years hence may well emphasize the subsequent benign trends in society. Huntington (1975), a political scientist, reminds us that there have been a number of periods in our history noted for similar emphases on participation and equality and associated challenges to authority, especially that of the government. Just as this emphasis in the Jacksonian and Progressive eras subsided, so, too, will what Huntington terms the *distemper* of the 1960s and 70s.

A shift toward communal concerns

For an analysis that proclaims a turning point in the social crisis, we shall turn to George Cabot Lodge's (1975) recent study of ideology—the ideas that explicate the nature of the good community. Lodge sees the United States undergoing a basic shift in its ideology: from individualism to communitarianism, that is, from emphasizing the rights of property to stressing those of community membership, and from using consumer demand as the basis for resource allocation to using community need in this regard. In general, America seems to be returning to the communal norms of the ancient and medieval worlds, according to Lodge. Most important, Lodge not only identifies the change in social consensus that Bell calls for, he also describes explicit mechanisms through which such changes are occurring and by which they can be enhanced. In this regard, the government will play a critical role as it expands its present, limited functions to engage in comprehensive planning in society. Communitarianism, the concern for society as a whole, can be seen developing today in such trends as the increasing emphasis placed on participation in the workplace and in the redefinition of the concept of justice to include equality of outcome. Concern for community membership as opposed to individual property rights is implicit in recent legislation aimed at protecting the environment, in the legal guarantee of rights (that is, Bell's "entitlements") due all regardless of their position in society, and in the replacement of individual stockholders by mutual and pension funds, insurance companies, and bank trust departments. Individual demand is replaced, with the help of government, by community need as a basis for decision making, as for example in the case of the automobile, by the government requiring pollution controls and safety features such as seat belts. Lodge predicts that in the future corporations will be made more legitimate and responsive by mechanisms such as shareholder democracy, worker participation and codetermination, as well as by specified state interventions. Future corporations will be chartered and given their basic purposes by an appropriate level of the government—neighborhood, city, state, regional, national (and even world)—not by the state of Delaware. They also will be regulated in specific undertakings by representatives of the communities affected.

The state as a mechanism for changing values

In the past, government was viewed in terms of its ability to mediate and regulate the interplay of interest groups. Political action was tactical and shortsighted. The emerging view of government's legitimate role is similar to one that has only been known before as a temporary expedient in wartime. During World War II, the federal government became, for a time, a centralized, long-range planning agent for the entire nation. In the future, Lodge argues, the state (which is to say, the federal, state, and local governments) will define public interests and resolve trade-offs among competing community needs. The federal government will engage in comprehensive long-range planning, and will intervene, as appropriate, when the actions of private parties jeopardize the implementation of such plans. It will also charter the 2,000 or so largest publicly held corporations. However, little government intervention, if any, will be required in industries typified by a low degree of industrial concentration.

In addition, Lodge envisages a proliferation of organizations similar to TVA, COMSAT, and the Port of New York Authority, that result from joint ventures of private capital and public funds. Initial financing, overall planning, and the terms of public accountability will be provided by the government. In turn, management will be responsible for operations, R&D, and the marketing and distribution of products and services.

Japan as a model

Throughout his book, Lodge refers to Japan as an example of the future toward which the United States is moving. In this regard, he cites the deliberate symbiosis between the Japanese government and business and, in general, the spirit of harmony, cooperation, and sacrifice that seems to typify the worker's commitment to communal aims.

Instead of individualism and equality, the Japanese emphasize the individual's relationships with others and membership in a group. Belonging to a group and sharing common feelings, understandings, and experiences take precedence over individualism. Property is considered to be held in trust for a group—for the family or for society as a whole. It is not for single individuals to do with as they will. There is competition between firms, as there is in the United States, but such competition is tempered by cooperation within the firm and by cooperation between firms in matters of interest to the nation as a whole. Competitiveness is subordinated to the good of the whole because cooperation and harmony are major values in the Japanese culture. In keeping with these values, the role of the Japanese government is not as limited as that of the U.S. government. Rather, the government is viewed as a supporter and coordinator of business cooperation and consensus, for the good of all.

In Japan, most workers and managers in large, technologically advanced firms generally are hired on the basis of a commitment to life-time employment. Turnover is negligible. Salaries are based primarily on seniority—young workers receive approximately one third of what they will earn as they near the retirement age of 55. In general, employers and employees are bound by shared understandings. There is a normative commitment on the part of employees to work hard (that is, to take work home at night and work during vacations) while, in return, the firm provides many paternalistic fringe benefits that may include free or subsidized housing, free membership in leisure clubs, and company-sponsored outings.

Compared to U.S. corporations, there is a high degree of employee participation in Japanese firms. Some of this is based on a formal system in which only middle management takes initiative for decision making (including policy decisions). Only after middle management acts are such matters passed on to higher levels of management. However, much of the participation is informal, occurring between individual employees and their immediate superior, who shows interest in their ideas and is receptive to suggestions. Tannenbaum and associates (1974), in their study of Italian, Austrian, U.S., Yugoslavian, and Kibbutz organizations, found that informal participation, rather than participation through formal structures such as the Yugoslavian workers' councils, leads to high levels of total influence (Chapter 3) and to a variety of positive outcomes such as high job involvement and initiative, low alienation, and relatively few symptoms of psychosomatic illness.

The Japanese employee typically has a relatively strong emotional commitment to the firm. Such commitment generally takes precedence even over commitments to relatives. The firm provides a major source of identification for the average Japanese employee, who works with almost moral fervor. This relationship seems to be enhanced by communal rituals, company songs, and reverence for the historical origins of the firm.

Generally, employees are organized into informal groups, or *batsu,* that are similar to the autonomous work groups described by the Tavistock researchers (Chapter 4). Below the top levels of an organization, there are no individual boxes on the organization chart, only departments or formal groupings. The *batsu* operate either within or coterminously with these formal groupings. Usually, assignments are made the responsibility of a group, rather than an individual. Thus, group members can assume roles that are best for the group (and that often are best for the individuals in the sense that they are likely to choose to do what they are good at), rather than roles that are limited by formal job descriptions.

Power and value changes

While we have emphasized the role of power in organizations throughout our text, we find that it has been overlooked in most of the futurological writings cited above. The various works of Neil Chamberlain are an exception, however, for Chamberlain (1973) examines the effects of power in national and international affairs on cultural values that in turn affect the future.

According to Chamberlain, most periods in history are typified by the ascendancy of a single group that influences the nation through its governmental structures. Power is used by such groups to develop congruence between the group's and the nation's welfare. Thus, the group's values tend to become those of the nation. The dominant groups that Chamberlain describes generally emerge from one or another of society's three major institutions—the military, religious, and economic institutions.

The dominant group's status is problematic, however. To preserve its status, the group continually must exert influence in governmental and other societal structures such as educational and related socializing institutions. In doing so, the dominant group attempts to socialize the population according to its values.

A transition to a new societial value system occurs when a challenger group gains ascendancy by taking advantage of major changes in society, such as changes in the state of the economy, alterations of technology, shifts in demographic characteristics, changes in the bases of authoritative knowledge, or political change. Chamberlain calls these challenger groups *thruster groups*.[2]

The dominance and decline of business

According to Chamberlain's view of American history, the dominance of the early patrician groups waned in the 19th century and was replaced by the dominance of business interests. The latter interests evolved over the years, and presently represent national and multinational corporations. However, corporate power in society is waning as well. Work, itself, is no longer esteemed as a widely held social value. For many, it represents merely the means to consumption and material welfare. The authority of business, as well as materialistic values, are under attack from the young, the intellectuals, and the upper middle class. In short, while large corporations still dominate American values, their power to do so is being eroded.

Extrapolating from the declining influence of corporate interests on societal values, Chamberlain projects three alternative scenarios for the future. First, the decline of corporate power may not be accompanied by a concomitant rise to power of another group that could instill a new set of values in society. In this event, values will become increasingly diffuse and social disorder will prevail. The weakening of society that accompanies a loss of shared values will be particularly evident in America's declining influence in international affairs.

New thruster groups

Alternatively, thruster groups may emerge to fill the void left by the decline of corporate power. One likely candidate as a successor to corporate interests is what Chamberlain calls the "social technocrats." This group may achieve dominance in society by exploiting the emerging need for control and coordination of vital services. To this end, the social technocrats will establish large, integrated organizations, having control systems that span political, geographic, and industrial boundaries and are chartered to coordinate complex services such as transportation, education, and crime control. These organizations will be characterized by a high degree of centralized planning and by their emphasis on efficiency. Joint ventures with private corporations will be common. In return for an opportunity to ex-

---

[2] Chamberlain's focus on thruster groups and their rise to power in society is not without a basis in sociological research. For example, we remarked in Chapter 11 that Gamson (1975) studied 53 groups that challenged the status quo—groups such as the National Urban League, the American Federation of Labor, and the Federal Suffrage Association. Successful groups were observed to employ (1) bureaucratic structures (for example, cadres of reliable workers and well-coordinated tasks); (2) centralized power (for example, unity of command); and (3) violence (for example, strikes or other physical manifestations of power).

pand into the public service sector and to profit therein, the vestige of corporate power will be co-opted by the social technocrats.

> ... Today's highly professional manager, eyes fixed on profit performance, operating with excellent controls and within strict rules in the glare of a public scoreboard, needing growth opportunities, and not limited by conventional business boundaries, may be the most promising recruit for solution of the crises in our public service. (Eli Goldston, quoted in Chamberlain, 1973, p. 309).

Chamberlain's third scenario develops as follows: as the power of corporate interests declines, the American middle class will see material success slipping from its grasp and will react repressively. America's weakness in international affairs will provoke challenges from other nations (for example, nationalization of American assets) that injure national pride. At the same time, other nations will lay claim to the role in international leadership that America can no longer play. The initial responses of the American public will be to emphasize national defense and to preserve traditional values.

In consequence, an increasing percentage of GNP will be devoted to the military budget. As in wartime, government controls will be established. Individual conspicuous consumption, once valued, will be replaced by a program of austerity that will benefit the nation as a whole. Hierarchical control and conformity will be valued above individualism and self-development. In response to domestic and international needs, as well as to an opportunity to seize power, a military thruster group will emerge. Under this regime, urban turmoil and other forms of social disorder will not be tolerated. Finally, rank and associated privileges, rather than social equality, will govern the allocation of resources to individuals.

The trouble with futurology

Our sample of futurological works was not determined by the kinds of predictions they offer, but the way in which these predictions were made. In each case, changes in genotypic variables were related to predicted changes in society. The variables studied include rationalization and technological efficiency; economic and population growth; social limits to change, including individualistic competition; self-interest versus communal concern; the role of the state in planning; and the power of dominant and thrusting groups—and nations. The brief summaries presented above represent attempts to identify key variables and to record apparent trends, usually by simple extrapolation, but in some cases by the use of more dynamic, dialectic models incorporating a number of genotypic variables. Still to be developed are models of the future that systematically incorporate most of these basic factors.

An encouraging trend in this direction is exemplified by the work of Jay Forrester (1978). According to Forrester: "More and more, we realize that everything is connected to everything else. But the multiple interconnections are not easy to understand" (p. 379). Forrester's latest work is a systems dynamics national model of the political and economic factors in our national economy. The model provides preliminary evidence of what economists term *long-wave* or Kondratieff cycles, which cover 50 years or so, as well as evidence of the well-known, short-term (three to seven years) business cycles. The Kondratieff cycle is characterized by a rapid expansion of capital investment that is followed by a fairly rapid collapse—and a depression. The crest of this long wave is characterized by a decline in capital investment, a decline in the growth of labor productivity, falling rates of return on investment, and reduced innovation resulting from the maturation of the current wave of technology. Forrester likens our current economic conditions to the crest of the cycle.

In the past, depressions have been deflationary. Thus, they have provided a way, through defaults, of erasing overextended indebtedness and permitting a new wave of investment to begin. Forrester hedges his statements about a future depression, however, by noting the present, extraordinary rate of inflation. Depreciating our currency may provide an alternative way of erasing debt. One hopes that Forrester also will incorporate international economic factors into his model to assay the role of U.S. indebtedness for OPEC petroleum and the like. We exist in a world economy, and differential inflation rates, floating currencies, and balances of payment have important influences on the functioning of our national economy.

Transformation to a new paradigm

We shall end this chapter on an optimistic note. In short, we shall take a brief look at the value-critical quadrant of Hake's table (Figure 17–1). As Lewis Mumford observed in *The Transformations of Man* (1968), Western society has progressed through a number of basic transformations. The fall of the Roman Empire and the founding of Christian society was one. Next, and of particular interest to us, the feudalistic Christian society of the Middle Ages was transformed into a society based on an individualistic and materialistic ethic. The rise of the Protestant ethic, with its emphasis on achievement as reflecting the grace of God, was a major element in this transformation. In America, a civil religion emerged—one in which the individual was free to engage in the pursuit of happiness. There emerged a vision of humanity's potential on the new continent, along with the belief that a cornucopia of material wealth could be made available to all. The resulting way of life, it was thought, would be a guiding light for the rest of the world.

But the vision of materialistic individualism may have lost its moral fervor, as we have indicated above. Among important elements in society (the educated upper middle class), a spiritual vision is beginning to take shape in the form of a "reemergence of the age-old spiritual quest for inner awareness and a deeper understanding of man's relationship to the Universe about him" (Harman, 1976, p. 29).

We have discussed some of the origins of this trend—the profound dissatisfaction with material achievement and competition and the loss of a sense of community. In fact, the present malaise and social disorder may be a necessary step in the process of changing social paradigms—of relinquishing old commitments and questioning old premises and world views.

The Copernican revolution, as well as the industrial revolution, entailed paradigm changes, and these were part of the basic transformation from feudal to Western, rational-materialistic society. Today's societal malaise seems so great as to foreshadow another major transformation. The coming transformation may well entail a major shift from rationalism and materialism to very different, fundamentally new social values. Pitirim Sorokin (1937–41), one of the major sociologists of the 20th century, has characterized the nature of society after a major transformation as ideational—that is, characterized by an idea that galvanizes individuals and society as a whole. Such transformations entail the rejection of an increasingly sensate society—one that is secular, hedonistic, and empirical—in favor of one that is spiritual, ascetic, and idea oriented. As long as the new idea maintains vitality, the transformed society remains coherent, purposeful, and flourishing.

As Harman sees it, such transcendent ideas played a vital role in the founding of America. We need only look at the back of a one dollar bill to see the truncated, unfinished pyramid surmounted by the all-seeing eye. It proclaims that the works of humans are not complete unless they incorporate divine insight. For today, its message is that our society must recreate a transcendent image of itself if it is to survive and flourish.

A new transcendent paradigm

Let us examine Harman's view of the future, for it is similar to the views of Lodge and others who have attempted to discern the coming transformation. The social paradigm of the future will be based on two major ethical views: (1) *An ecological ethic*—humans will identify with the whole of nature, with all of humankind, and with the evolutionary processes leading to future generations. (2) *A self-realization ethic*—the proper end of all individual experience will be seen as growth in awareness, as well as the further evolutionary development of the human species. According to Harman, both ethics have been around for a long time, becoming salient at some moments in history and waning in others. Throughout history, though, they are at "... the center of highest consciousness discoverable in one's own inner experience ..." (1976, p. 120).

The future social paradigm that Harman envisages also entails a *new knowledge paradigm*—one that goes beyond the scientific paradigm to encompass "... subjective as well as objective experience, entering domains previously the realm of religion, philosophy, literature, and the arts" (Harman, 1976, p. 123). Rather than seeking reductionistic explanations, the new knowledge paradigm would accept that "... a teleological cause may complement rather than contradict a mechanistic cause" (Harman, 1976, p. 123).

Finally, the dominant theme or objective of society would be neither material nor technological progress. These would be replaced by a *central project of learning and planning,* "... promoting individual growth in awareness, creativity, adaptability, curiosity, wonder, and love; evolving social institutions to more effectively foster such individual growth; and participating as a partner with nature in the further evolution of the human species on earth" (Harman, 1976, p. 125).

Progress toward this new transformation will not be easy. There will be extensive social disruption. We will have to explore new institutional forms such as those cited by Lodge as well as many more. We will have to manage our organizations with efficiency and effectiveness in mind while we develop and integrate the new human and social considerations.

Reprise

It probably takes more courage to predict the future than to postulate a scientific theory, for unlike many theories, all predictions ultimately are tested completely as the future becomes the present. One of the more courageous predictions we have read was made by John Maynard Keynes, and published shortly after Black Tuesday—the onslaught of the Great Depression. It is worth quoting Keynes at length.

> I draw the conclusion that, assuming no important wars and no important increase in population, the economic problem may be solved, or be at least within sight of solution, within a hundred years. This means that the economic problem is not—if we look into the future—the permanent problem of the human race....
>
> I see us free, therefore, to return to some of the most sure and certain principles of religion and traditional virtue—that avarice is a vice, that the exaction of usury is a misdemeanour, and the love of money is detestable, that those walk most truly in the paths of virtue and sane wisdom who take least thought for the morrow. We shall once more value ends above means and prefer the good to the useful. We shall honour those who can teach us how to pluck the hour and the day virtuously and well. The delightful people who are capable of taking direct enjoyment in things, the lilies of the field who toil not, neither do they spin.
>
> But beware! *The time for all this is not yet.* For at least another hundred years we must pretend to ourselves and to everyone that fair is foul and foul is fair; for foul is useful and fair is not. Avarice and usury and precaution must be our gods for a little longer still. For only they can lead us out of the tunnel of economic necessity into daylight.[3]

---

[3] John Maynard Keynes, "Economic Possibilities for Our Grandchildren." In Vol. IX of the Royal Economic Society edition of the *Collected Writings of John Maynard Keynes,* pp. 365–66, 371–72. Italics added.

Keynes' predictions, made some 50 years ago, bear striking resemblance to many of the futurological works described above. Be that as it may, he assumed away World War II and the population growth that alarms us so today. Half his hundred years have come and gone, and the solution to the economic problem still eludes us. In fact, Keynes' theory seems to become ever more inappropriate in the light of contemporary economic problems.

But, as he said, "The time for all this is not yet." Let's give Keynes another 50 years, at least. There is still much to be done, and there still is time to do it. If the problems seem too great and the time to solve them too short, a look into the past will be reassuring.

Our parents remember gaslights in their homes, horse-drawn carts, and crystal radio sets. They recall the Wright Brothers, the Model T, icemen, blacksmiths, and chimney sweeps. As young adults, they made their way through the Great Depression and World War I. World War II came in their early middle age, the Korean War in their 50s, and the Viet Nam War in their retirement. They have also seen the sunrise on Mars!

From gaslight to space flight in a single lifetime, despite wars, recessions, and economic collapse—that is the bench mark of progress. There is much to be done in *our* lifetime.

DISCUSSION QUESTIONS

1. Of what value is futurology to managers?
2. Is it always the fault of the forecaster if the prediction turns out wrong?
3. What is your scenario for organizational life in the year 2000?

References

Aiken, Michael. The distribution of community power: structural bases and social consequences. In Michael Aiken and Paul E. Mott (eds.), *The structure of community power.* New York: Random House, 1970. Pp. 487–525.

Alderfer, Clayton P. An empirical test for a new theory of human needs. *Organizational Behavior and Human Performance,* 1969, *4,* 142–75.

Alderfer, Clayton P. *Existence, relatedness, and growth.* New York: Free Press, 1972.

Alinsky, Saul. *Reveille for radicals.* Chicago: University of Chicago Press, 1946.

Alinsky, Saul. *Rules for radicals.* New York: Random House, 1971.

Allison, Graham T. *Essence of decision: explaining the Cuban missile crisis.* Boston: Little, Brown, 1971.

Allport, Floyd H. The J-curve hypothesis of conforming behavior. *Journal of Social Psychology,* 1934, *5,* 141–83.

Allport, Gordon W.; Vernon, Philip E.; and Lindzey, Gardner. *A study of values.* Boston: Houghton Mifflin, 1960.

American Management Association. At Emery Air Freight: positive reinforcement boosts performance. *Organizational Dynamics,* 1973, *2,* 3, 41–50.

Andrews, Frank, and Farris, George. Supervisory practices and innovations in scientific teams. *Personnel Psychology,* 1967, *20,* 497–515.

Andrews, John D. W. The achievement motive and advancement in two types of organizations. *Journal of Personality and Social Psychology,* 1967, *6,* 163–69.

Anshen, Melvin. The manager and the black box. *Harvard Business Review,* 1960, *62,* 5 (November–December), 85.

Ansoff, H. Igor. *Corporate strategy.* Harmondsworth, Eng.: Penguin, 1965.
Ansoff, H. Igor; Avner, Jay; Brandenburg, Richard G.; Portner, Fred E.; and Radosevich, Raymond. Does planning pay? The effect of planning on success of acquisition in American firms. *Long Range Planning,* 1970, *3* (2), 2–7.
Ansoff, H. Igor, and Brandenburg, Robert G. A language for organization design, Parts I and II. *Management Science,* 1971, *17,* B705–31.
Ansoff, H. Igor; Declérck, Roger P.; and Hayes, Robert L. From strategic planning to strategic management. In H. Igor Ansoff, Roger P. Declérck, and Robert L. Hayes (eds.), *From strategic planning to strategic management.* London: Wiley, 1976. Pp. 39–78.
Anthony, Robert N. The trouble with profit maximization. *Harvard Business Review,* 1960, *38,* 6 (November–December), 126–34.
Anthony, Robert N. *Planning and control systems; a framework for analysis.* Boston: Division of Research, Harvard Business School, 1965.
Argyris, Chris. *Personality and organization.* New York: Harper & Bros., 1957.
Argyris, Chris. *Understanding human behavior.* London: Tavistock, 1960.
Asch, Solomon. *Social psychology.* Englewood Cliffs, N.J.: Prentice-Hall, 1952.
Ayres, Robert U. *Technological forecasting and long-range planning.* New York: McGraw-Hill, 1969.
Azim, Ahmad N., and Boseman, F. Glenn. An empirical assessment of Etzioni's typology of power and involvement. *Academy of Management Journal,* 1975, *18,* 680–89.
Bach, George R., and Wyden, P. *Intimate enemy: how to fight fair in love and marriage.* San Diego: Morrow Pubs., 1969.
Bachman, Jerald G.; Bowers, David G.; and Marcus, Philip M. Bases of supervisory power: a comparative study in five organizational settings. In A. S. Tannenbaum (ed.), *Control in organizations.* New York: McGraw-Hill, 1968.
Baldridge, Victor J. *Power and conflict in the university: research in the sociology of complex organizations.* New York: Wiley, 1971.
Bales, Robert F. Task roles and social roles in problem-solving groups. In E. Maccoby, T. M. Newcomb, and E. L. Hartley (eds.), *Readings in social psychology.* 3d ed. New York: Holt, Rinehart & Winston, 1958. Pp. 437–47.
Ball, Robert. Volkswagen gets a much needed tune-up. *Fortune,* 1972, *85,* 3 (March), 85–105.
Barkdull, C. W. Span of control—a method of evaluation. *Michigan Business Review,* 1963, *15,* 3 (May), 25–32.
Barnes, Louis B. Organizational change and field experimental methods. In V. H. Vroom (ed.), *Methods of organizational research.* Pittsburgh: University of Pittsburgh Press, 1967.
Barrett, Jon H. *Individual goals and organizational objectives: a study of integration mechanisms.* Ann Arbor, Mich.: Institute for Social Research, 1970.
Bauer, Raymond A. The study of policy formation. In R. A. Bauer and K. G. Gergen (eds.), *The study of policy formation.* New York: Free Press, 1968. Pp. 1–26. Copyright © 1968 by The Free Press, a division of the Macmillan Company.
Bavelas, Alex. Leadership: man and function. *Administrative Science Quarterly,* 1960, *4,* 491–98.
Becker, Selwyn W., and Whisler, Thomas L. The innovative organization: a selective view of current theory and research. *Journal of Business,* 1967, *40,* 462–69.

Behling, Orlando; Schriesheim, Chester; and Tolliver, James. Alternate cognitive formulations of the work-effort decision. Paper presented at the Midwest Academy of Management meeting, Chicago, 1973.

Behling, Orlando, and Starke, Frederick A. The postulates of expectancy theory. *Academy of Management Journal,* 1973, *16,* 374–88. (a)

Behling, Orlando, and Starke, Frederick A. Some limits on expectancy theories of work motivation. Paper presented at the Midwest AIDS meeting, East Lansing, Michigan, 1973. (b)

Bell, Daniel. *The end of ideology.* Glencoe, Ill.: Free Press, 1960.

Bell, Daniel. *The coming of post-industrial society: a venture in social forecasting.* New York: Basic Books, 1973.

Bell, Daniel. The revolution of rising entitlements. *Fortune,* 1975, *91,* 4 (April), 98–103 ff.

Bell, Daniel. *The cultural contradictions of capitalism.* New York: Basic Books, 1976.

Bell, Gerald D. Determinants of span of control. *American Journal of Sociology,* 1967, *73,* 90–101.

Benne, Kenneth D.; Bennis, Warren G.; and Chin, Robert (eds.). *The planning of change.* 2d ed. New York: Holt, Rinehart & Winston, 1969.

Bennis, Warren G. A funny thing happened on the way to the future. *American Psychologist,* 1970, *25,* 595–608. (a)

Bennis, Warren G. Beyond bureaucracy. In Warren G. Bennis (ed.), *American Bureaucracy.* Chicago: Aldine, 1970. Pp. 3–16. (b)

Bennis, Warren G., and Slater, Philip E. *The temporary society.* New York: Harper & Row, 1968.

Benson, J. Kenneth. Innovation and crisis in organizational analysis. *Sociological Quarterly,* 1977, *18,* 3–16.

Berlyne, Daniel E. Exploration and curiosity. *Science,* 1966, *153,* 25–33.

Blake, Robert R., and Mouton, Jane S. *The managerial grid.* Houston, Tex.: Gulf Publishing, 1970.

Blake, Robert R., and Mouton, Jane S. with Barnes, Louis B. and Greiner, Larry E. Breakthrough in organization development. *Harvard Business Review,* 1964, *42,* 6 (November–December), 135–55.

Blau, Peter M. *Bureaucracy in modern society.* New York: Random House, 1956.

Blau, Peter; Heyderbrand, Wolf F.; and Stauffer, Robert. The structure of small bureaucracies. *American Sociological Review,* 1966, *31,* 179–91.

Blau, Peter M., and Meyer, Marshall. *Bureaucracy in modern society.* 2d ed. New York: Random House, 1971.

Blauner, Robert. *Alienation and freedom: the factory worker and his industry.* Chicago: University of Chicago Press, 1964.

Blood, Milton R. Work values and job satisfaction. *Journal of Applied Psychology,* 1969, *53,* 456–59.

Bower, Joseph L. *Managing the resource allocation process.* Boston: Harvard University, Graduate School of Business Administration, Division of Research, 1970.

Bowers, David G., and Seashore, Stanley E. Predicting organizational effectiveness with a four-factor theory of leadership. *Administrative Science Quarterly,* 1966, *11,* 238–63.

Braybrooke, David, and Lindblom, Charles E. *A strategy of decision.* New York: Free Press, 1963.

Breed, Warren. Social control in the newsroom: a functional analysis. *Social Forces,* 1955, *33,* 326–35.

Bucher, Rue, and Stelling, Joan. Characteristics of professional organizations. *Journal of Health and Human Behavior,* 1969, *10,* 3–15.

Buck, Vernon E. A model for viewing an organization as a system of constraints. In James D. Thompson (ed.), *Approaches to organizational design.* Pittsburgh: University of Pittsburgh Press, 1966. Pp. 103–72.

Buckley, Walter. *Sociology and modern systems theory.* Englewood Cliffs, N.J.: Prentice-Hall, 1967.

Burns, Tom, and Stalker, G. M. *The management of innovation.* London: Tavistock Publications, 1961.

Business Week. When workers become directors. *Business Week,* 1973, *2297,* (September 15), 188–96.

Butterfield, Anthony. An integrative approach to the study of leadership effectiveness in organizations. Doctoral dissertation, University of Michigan, Ann Arbor, Mich., 1968.

Bylinski, Gene. Vincent Learson didn't plan it that way, but I.B.M.'s toughest competitor is—I.B.M. *Fortune,* 1972, *85,* 3 (March), 55–61, 145–50.

Cammann, Cortlandt, and Lawler, Edward E. Employee reactions to a pay incentive plan. *Journal of Applied Psychology,* 1973, *58,* 163–72.

Campbell, John P. On the nature of effectiveness. In P. S. Goodman, J. M. Pennings, and Associates (eds.), *New perspectives on organizational effectiveness.* San Francisco: Jossey-Bass Publishers, 1977. Pp. 13–55.

Campbell, John P.; Dunnette, Marvin D.; Lawler, Edward E.; and Weick, Karl E. *Managerial behavior, performance, and effectiveness.* New York: McGraw-Hill, 1970.

Caplow, Theodore. *Principles of organization.* New York: Harcourt, Brace & World, 1964.

Carey, Alex. The Hawthorne studies: a radical criticism. *American Sociological Review,* 1968, *33,* 403–16.

Carlisle, Harvard M. Are functional organizations becoming obsolete? *Management Review,* 1969, *58,* 1 (January), 2–9.

Carroll, Stephen J., and Tosi, Henry L. *Management by objectives: application and research.* New York: Macmillan, 1973.

Caves, Richard E. Uncertainty, market structure, and performance: Galbraith as conventional wisdom. In J. W. Markham and G. F. Papanek (eds.), *Industrial organization and economic development.* Boston: Houghton Mifflin, 1970.

Chamberlain, Neil W. *The place of business in America's future/a study in social values.* New York: Basic Books, 1978.

Chandler, Alfred D., Jr. *Strategy and structure: chapters in the history of the American industrial enterprise.* Cambridge, Mass.: M.I.T. Press, 1962.

Chapanis, Alphonse. *Man-machine engineering.* Belmont, Calif.: Brooks/Cole, 1965.

Chevalier, Michel. The strategy spectre behind your market share. *European Business,* 1972 (34) (Summer), 63–72.

Child, Irving L., and Whiting, John W. Determinants of level of aspiration and evidence from everyday life. *Journal of Abnormal and Social Psychology,* 1949, *44,* 303–14.

Child, John. Organization structure and strategies of control: a replication of the Aston study. *Administrative Science Quarterly,* 1972, *17,* 163–77. (a)

Child, John. Organizational structure, environment and performance: the role of strategic choice. *Sociology,* 1972, *6,* 2–22. (b)

Child, John. Predicting and understanding organization structure. *Administrative Science Quarterly,* 1973, *18,* 168–85.

Chin, Robert, and Benne, Kenneth D. General strategies for effecting changes in human systems. In W. G. Bennis, K. D. Benne, and R. Chin (eds.), *The planning of change.* 2d ed. New York: Holt, Rinehart & Winston, 1969. Pp. 32–59.

Churchill, Winston. *The second world war.* Vol. 4. New York: Bantam Books, 1962.

Cleland, David. Why project management? *Business Horizons,* 1964, *7,* 4 (Winter), 81–88.

Coch, Lester, and French, John R., Jr. Overcoming resistance to change. *Human Relations,* 1948, *4,* 161–84.

Coffey, Robert E.; Athos, Anthony G.; and Raynolds, Peter A. *Behavior in organizations: a multidimensional view.* Englewood Cliffs, N.J.: Prentice-Hall, 1975.

Cohen, Arthur R.; Stotland, Ezra S.; and Wolfe, Donald W. An experimental investigation of need for cognition. *Journal of Abnormal and Social Psychology,* 1955, *51,* 291–94.

Coleman, James S.; Katz, Elihu; and Menzel, Herbert. *Medical innovation: a diffusion study.* Indianapolis: Bobbs-Merrill, 1966.

Collins, Randall. *Conflict sociology: toward an explanatory science.* New York: Academic Press, 1975.

Corwin, Ronald G. Strategies for organizational innovation: an empirical comparison. *American Sociological Review,* 1972, *37,* 441–54.

Crozier, Michel. *The bureaucratic phenomenon.* Chicago: University of Chicago Press, 1964.

Crystal, Graef S. The manager's journal. *The Wall Street Journal,* Monday, Feb. 27, 1978, 16.

Cyert, Richard M., and March, James. *A behavioral theory of the firm.* Englewood Cliffs, N.J.: Prentice-Hall, 1963.

Dahl, Robert A. *Who governs?* New Haven, Conn.: Yale University Press, 1961.

Dahrendorf, Ralf. Out of utopia: towards a reorientation of sociological analysis. *American Journal of Sociology,* 1958, *64,* 115–27.

Dale, Ernest. *Organization.* New York: American Management Association, 1967.

Davis, Stanley M. and Lawrence, Paul R. *Matrix.* Reading, Mass.: Addison-Wesley, 1977.

Deci, Edward L. *Intrinsic motivation.* New York: Plenum Press, 1975.

Demerath, Nicholas J., III, and Hammond, Phillip E. *Religion in social context: tradition and transition.* New York: Random House, 1969.

Dent, James K. Organizational correlates of the goals of business management. *Personnel Psychology,* 1959, *12,* 365–93.

Dewey, John. *How we think.* Boston: D.C. Heath, 1910.

Doctors, Samuel I. *The management of technological change.* New York: American Management Association, Extension Institute, 1970.

Domhoff, William G. *Who rules America?* Englewood Cliffs, N.J.: Prentice-Hall, 1967.

Domhoff, William G. *The higher circles.* New York: Random House, 1970.

Downs, Anthony. *Inside bureaucracy.* Boston: Little, Brown, 1967.

Drucker, Peter. *The practice of management.* New York: Harper & Bros., 1954.

Drucker, Peter F. Business objectives and survival needs. *The Journal of Business,* 1963, *31,* 2 (April), 81–90.

Drucker, Peter F. The surprising seventies. *Harper's Magazine,* 1971, *243,* 1454 (July), 35–39.

Dubin, Robert. Industrial workers' worlds: a study of the "central life interests" of industrial workers. *Social Problems,* 1956, *3,* 131–42.

Duff, Raymond S., and Hollingshead, August B. *Sickness and society.* New York: Harper & Row, 1968.

Durkheim, Emile. *Division of labor in society,* trans. by George Simpson. Glencoe, Ill.: Free Press, 1947.

Edwards, Ward. The theory of decision making. *Psychology Bulletin,* 1954, *51,* 380–417.

Emery, Fred E. The next thirty years: concepts, methods, and anticipations. *Human Relations,* 1967, *20,* 199–236.

Emery, Fred E. Bureaucracy and beyond. *Organizational Dynamics,* 1974, *2,* 3 (Winter), 3–13.

Emery, Fred W., and Trist, Eric L. The causal texture of organizational environment. *Human Relations,* 1965, *18,* 21–31.

England, George W. Personal value systems of American managers. *Academy of Management Proceedings,* August, 1973, 81–87.

Engel, Gloria V. The effect of bureaucracy on the professional autonomy of the physician. *Journal of Health and Social Behavior,* 1969, *10,* 30–41.

Etzioni, Amitai. Two approaches to organizational analysis: a critique and a suggestion. *Administrative Science Quarterly,* 1960, *5,* 257–78.

Etzioni, Amitai. *A comparative analysis of complex organizations.* New York: Free Press, 1961.

Etzioni, Amitai. *Modern organizations.* Englewood Cliffs, N.J.: Prentice-Hall, 1964.

Evan, William M. The organization-set: toward a theory of interorganizational relations. In J. D. Thompson (ed.), *Approaches to organizational design.* Pittsburgh: University of Pittsburgh Press, 1966. Pp. 173–91.

Evan, William M. An organization-set model of interorganizational relations. In Matthew Tuite (ed.), *Interorganizational decisionmaking.* Chicago: Aldine, 1972. Pp. 181–200.

Evans, Martin G. The effects of supervisory behavior on the path-goal relationship. *Organizational Behavior and Human Performance,* 1970, *55,* 277–98.

Evans, Martin G. Extensions of a path-goal theory of motivation. *Journal of Applied Psychology,* 1974, *59,* 172–78.

Fanon, Frantz. *The wretched of the earth.* Harmondsworth, Eng.: Penguin, 1967.

Fayol, Henri. General principles of management. In H. F. Merrill (ed.), *Classics in management.* New York: American Management Association, 1960. Pp. 217–41.

Fein, Mitchell. The real needs and goals of blue collar workers. *Conference Board Record,* 1973, *10,* 2 (February), 28–33.

Festinger, Leon. *A theory of cognitive dissonance.* Evanston, Ill.: Row, Peterson, 1957.

Festinger, Leon. Architecture and group membership. In R. Gutman (ed.), *People and buildings.* New York: Basic Books, 1972. Pp. 120–34.

Fiedler, Fred E. Engineer the job to fit the manager. *Harvard Business Review,* 1965, *43,* 5 (September–October), 115–22.

Fiedler, Fred E. *A theory of leadership effectiveness.* New York: McGraw-Hill, 1967.

Filley, Alan C., and House, Robert J. *Managerial process and organizational behavior.* Glenview, Ill.: Scott, Foresman, 1969.

Flanagan, Robert F.; Strauss, George S.; and Ulman, Lloyd. Worker discontent and work place behavior. *Industrial Relations,* 1974, *13,* 2 (May), 101–23.

Fleishman, Edwin A. Leadership climate, human relations training, and supervisory behavior. *Personnel Psychology,* 1953, *6,* 205–22.

Fleishman, Edwin A. (ed.). *Studies in personnel and industrial psychology.* Homewood, Ill.: Dorsey, 1967.

Fleishman, Edwin A., and Harris, Edwin F. Patterns of leadership behavior related to employee grievances and turnover. *Personnel Psychology,* 1962, *15,* (Spring), 43–56.

Ford, R. N. *Motivation through the work itself.* New York: American Management Association, 1969.

Forehand, Garlie A. Assessments of innovative behavior: partial criteria for the assessment of executive performance. *Journal of Applied Psychology,* 1963, *47,* 206–13.

Forrester, Jay W. A great economic depression ahead? Changing economic patterns. *The Futurist,* 1978, *12,* 379–385.

Frank, Andrew Gunder. Administrative role definition and social changes. *Human Organization,* 1963–64, *22,* 238–42.

Frank, Jerome D. Experimental studies of personal pressure and resistance. *Journal of General Psychology.* 1944, *30,* 23–64.

Franke, Richard H., and Kaub, James D. The Hawthorne experiments: first statistical interpretation. *American Sociological Review,* 1978, *43,* 5, 623–43.

Freidson, Eliot. *Profession of medicine.* New York: Dodd, Mead & Co., 1970. (a)

Freidson, Eliot. *Professional dominance: the social structure of medical care.* New York: Atherton, 1970. (b)

French, Elizabeth G. Some characteristics of achievement motivation. *Journal of Experimental Psychology,* 1955, *50,* 232–36.

French, John R. P., Jr. Person role fit. In A. McLean (ed.), *Occupational stress.* Springfield, Ill.: Charles C. Thomas, 1974, Pp. 70–79.

French, John R. P., Jr., and Caplan, Robert D. Organizational stress and individual strain. In A. J. Marrow (ed.), *The failure of success.* New York: AMACOM, 1973. Pp. 30–66.

French, John R. P., Jr., and Raven, Bertram H. The bases of social power. In D. Cartwright (ed.), *Studies in social power.* Ann Arbor, Mich.: University of Michigan, Institute for Social Research, 1959.

Friedlander, Frank, and Pickle, Hal. Components of effectiveness in small organizations. *Administrative Science Quarterly,* 1968, *13,* 289–304.

Friedman, John, and Hudson, Barclay. Knowledge and action: a guide to planning theory. *American Institute of Planners Journal,* 1974, *40,* 2–16.

Fruhan, William W., Jr. Pyrrhic victories in fights for market share. *Howard Business Review,* 1972, *50,* 5 (September–October), 100–107.

Fuller, Richard Buckminster. *Utopia or oblivion: the prospects for humanity.* New York: Bantam Books, 1969.

Galbraith, Jay R. Organization design: an information processing view. In J. W. Lorsch and P. R. Lawrence (eds.), *Organizational planning: cases and concepts.* Homewood, Ill.: Dorsey, 1972. Pp. 49–74.

Galbraith, Jay R. *Designing complex organizations.* Reading, Mass.: Addison-Wesley, 1973 © 1973 Addison-Wesley. Reprinted with permission.

Galbraith, John Kenneth. *The new industrial state.* Boston: Houghton Mifflin, 1967.

Gallese, Liz Roman. The soothsayers: more companies use "futurists" to discern what is lying ahead. *The Wall Street Journal,* March 31, 1975, 1, 10.

Gamson, William A. *Power and discontent.* Homewood, Ill.: Dorsey, 1968.

Gamson, William A. *Strategy of social protest.* Homewood, Ill.: Dorsey, 1975.

Gantt, Henry L. *Work, wages, and profits.* Easton, Pa.: Hive, 1973.

Gardner, John W. The use of the term "level of aspiration" *Psychological Review,* 1940, *47,* 59–68.

Gauss, Christian. In Niccolo Machiavelli, *The prince.* New York: New American Library, 1952.

Georgopoulos, Basil S. An open system theory model for organizational research. In Anant R. Negandhi (ed.), *Modern organization theory,* Kent, Ohio: Kent State University Press, 1973, Pp. 102–31.

Georgopoulos, Basil S.; Indik, Bernard P.; and Seashore, Stanley E. Some models of organizational effectiveness. Mimeo. Ann Arbor, Mich.: Institute for Social Research, University of Michigan, 1960.

Georgopoulos, Basil S., and Mann, Floyd C. *The community general hospital.* New York: Macmillan, 1962.

Georgopoulos, Basil S., and Matejko, Alexander. The American general hospital as a complex social system. *Health Services Research,* 1967, *2,* 76–112.

Georgopoulos, Basil S., and Tannenbaum, Arnold S. A study of organizational effectiveness. *American Sociological Review,* 1957, *22,* 534–40.

Georgopoulos, Basil S., and Wieland, George F. *Nationwide study of coordination and patient care in voluntary hospitals.* Ann Arbor, Mich.: Institute for Social Research, The University of Michigan, 1964.

Gerstner, Louis V., Jr. Can strategic planning pay off? *Business Horizons,* 1972, *15*(6), 5–16.

Gibb, Cecil A. Leadership. In G. Lindzey and E. Aronson (eds.), *Handbook of social psychology.* 2d ed. vol. IV. Reading, Mass.: Addison-Wesley, 1968. Pp. 205–82.

Gilbreth, Frank B. *Bricklaying system.* Easton, Pa.: Hive, 1972. (a)

Gilbreth, Frank B. *Motion study.* Easton, Pa.: Hive, 1972. (b)

Ginsberg, Eli. The professionalization of the U.S. labor force. *Scientific American,* 1979, *240,* 3 (March), 48–53.

Glassman, Robert B. Persistence and loose coupling in living systems. *Behavioral Science,* 1973, *18,* 2 (March), 83–98.

Glueck, William F. *Business policy: strategy formation and management action.* New York: McGraw-Hill, 1972.

Goffman, Erving. *The presentation of self in everyday life.* Garden City, N.Y.: Doubleday, 1959.

Goffman, Erving. *Asylums: essays on the social situations of mental patients and other inmates.* Garden City, N.Y.: Doubleday, 1961.

Goldthorpe, John H.; Lockwood, David; Beckhofer, Frank; and Platt, Jennifer. *The affluent worker: industrial attitudes and behavior.* Cambridge: Cambridge University Press, 1968.

Gordon, Gerald, and Marquis, Sue. Freedom, visibility of consequences, and scientific innovation. *American Journal of Sociology,* 1966, *72,* 195–202.

Gouldner, Alvin W. *Patterns of industrial bureaucracy.* Glencoe, Ill.: Free Press, 1954.

Gouldner, Alvin W. Cosmopolitans and locals: toward an analysis of latent social roles. II. *Administrative Science Quarterly*, 1958, *2*, 444–80.

Gouldner, Alvin W. Organizational analysis. In Robert K. Merton, Leonard Broom, and Leonard S. Cottrell, Jr. (eds.), *Sociology today*. New York: Basic Books, 1959. Pp. 400–428.

Graen, George B. Instrumentality theory of work motivation: some experimental results and suggested modifications. *Journal of Applied Psychology Monographs*, 1969, 53, *2*, Pt. 2, 1–25.

Graen, George B.; Davies, Rene O.; and Weiss, David W. Need type and job satisfaction among industrial scientists. *Journal of Applied Psychology*, 1968, *52*, 286–89.

Graicunas, V. A. Relationship in organization. In L. Gulick and L. Urwick (eds.), *Papers on the science of administration*. New York: Institute of Public Administration, 1937. Pp. 183–87.

Greiner, Larry E. Patterns of organizational change. *Harvard Business Review*, 1967, *45*, 3 (May–June), 119–30.

Gross, Edward. Universities as organizations: a research approach. *American Sociological Review*, 1968, *33*, 518–44.

Gross, George R. The organization set: a study of sociology departments. *The American Sociologist*, 1970, *5*, 25–29.

Gross, Neal; Giacquinta, Joseph B.; and Bernstein, Marilyn. *Implementing organizational innovations: a sociological analysis of planned educational change*. New York: Basic Books, 1971.

Guest, Robert Henry. *Organizational change: the effect of successful leadership*. Homewood, Ill.: Irwin, 1962.

Guth, William D. Toward a social system theory of corporate strategy. Proceedings of the 16th Annual Midwest Management Conference, Academy of Management, Midwest Division, April 1973.

Guth, William D., and Tagiuri, Renato. Personal values and corporate strategy. *Harvard Business Review*, 1965, *43*, 5 (September–October), 123–32. © 1965 by the President and Fellows of Harvard College. All rights reserved.

Gutman, Peter M. Strategies for growth. *California Management Review*, 1964, *6*, 4 (Summer), 31–36.

Gutman, Robert (ed). *People and buildings*. New York: Basic Books, 1972.

Hage, Jerald T., and Aiken, Michael. Routine technology, social structure, and organizational goals. *Administrative Science Quarterly*, 1969, *14*, 366–77.

Hage, Jerald, and Aiken, Michael. *Social change in complex organizations*. New York: Random House, 1970.

Hage, Jerald, and Dewar, Robert. Elite values versus organizational structure in predicting innovation. *Administrative Science Quarterly*, 1973, *18*, 279–90.

Hake, Barry. Values, technology and the future. *Futures Conditional*, 1973, *1*, 6 (June), 6–7.

Hall, Edward T. *The hidden dimension*. Garden City, N.Y.: Doubleday, 1966.

Hall, Edward T. *The Silent Language*. Greenwich, Conn.: Fawcett Books, 1972.

Hall, Richard H. Professionalization and bureaucratization. *American Sociological Review*, 1968, *33*, 92–104.

Hall, Richard H. *Organizations: structure and process*. Englewood Cliffs, N.J.: Prentice-Hall, 1972.

Hall, Richard H. *Organizations: structure and process*. 2d ed. Englewood Cliffs, N.J.: Prentice-Hall, 1977.

Hall, Richard H.; Haas, J. Eugene; and Johnson, Norman J. Organizational size, complexity, and formalization. *American Sociological Review*, 1967, *32*, 903–12.

Halpert, Burton P. Interorganizational relationships: some theoretical and empirical notes on power, conflict and cooperation. Paper presented at The American Sociological Association meetings, Montreal, August 1974.

Hamblin, Robert C. Leadership and crisis. *Sociometry*, 1958, *21*, 322–35.

Hampton, David R.; Summer, Charles E.; and Webber, Ross A. *Organizational behavior and the practice of management*. Rev. ed. Glenview, Ill.: Scott, Foresman, 1973.

Harman, Willis W. *An incomplete guide to the future*. Stanford, Calif: Stanford Alumni Association, 1976.

Harrison, Roger. Choosing the depth of organizational intervention. *Journal of Applied Behavioral Science*, 1970, *6*, 181–202.

Harvey, Edward. Technology and the structure of organizations. *American Sociological Review*, 1968, *33*, 247–59.

Havelock, Ronald G. *Planning for innovation through dissemination and utilization of knowledge*. Ann Arbor, Mich.: Center for Research on Utilization of Scientific Knowledge, Institute for Social Research, University of Michigan, 1971.

Hebb, Donald O. *The organization of behavior*. New York: Wiley, 1949.

Hebb, Donald O. The mammal and his environment. *American Journal of Psychiatry*, 1955, *111*, 826–31.

Hellriegel, Don, and Slocum, John W., Jr. *Management: a contingency approach*. Reading, Mass.: Addison-Wesley, 1974.

Herzberg, Frederick. *Work and the nature of man*. New York: World, 1966.

Herzberg, Frederick; Mausner, Bernard; and Snyderman, Barbara B. *The motivation to work*. 2d ed. New York: Wiley, 1959.

Hilgard, Ernest H.; Sait, Edward S.; and Margaret, G. Ann. Level of aspiration as affected by relative standing in an experimental social group. *Journal of Experimental Psychology*, 1940, *27*, 411–21.

Hirsch, Fred. *Social limits to growth*. Cambridge, Mass.: Harvard University Press, 1976.

Hofer, Charles W. Some preliminary research on patterns of strategic behavior. Proceedings, Academy of Management, Division of Business Policy and Planning, 33d Annual Meeting, Boston, August 1973. Pp. 46–54.

Hofer, Charles W. Research on a contingency theory of strategic behavior: issues and methods. Paper given at Academy of Management Meetings, Seattle, August 1974.

Hollander, Edwin P. Conformity, status, and idiosyncrasy credit. *Psychological Review*, 1958, *65*, 117–27.

Hollander, Edwin P., and Julian, James J. Contemporary trends in the analysis of leadership process. *Psychological Bulletin*, 1969, *71*, 387–97.

Hoos, Ida R. *Systems analysis in public policy: a critique*. Berkeley, Calif.: University of California Press, 1972.

Horwitz, Murray. The recall of interrupted group tasks: an experimental study of individual motivation in relation to group goals. *Human Relations*, 1954, *7*, 3–38.

House, Robert J. A path-goal theory of leader effectiveness. *Administrative Science Quarterly*, 1971, *16*, 321–38.

House, Robert J., and Mitchell, Terence R. Path-goal theory of leadership. *Journal of Contemporary Business*, 1974, *3* (Autumn), 81–97.

House, Robert J., and Wigdor, Lawrence A. Herzberg's dual-factor theory of job satisfaction motivation: a review of the evidence and a criticism. *Personnel Psychology*, 1967, *20*, 369–89.

Hulin, Charles L., and Blood, Milton R. Job enlargement, individual differences, and worker responses. *Psychological Bulletin*, 1968, *69*, 41–55.

Hull, Clark L. Knowledge and purpose as habit mechanisms. *Psychological Review*, 1930, *37*, 311–25.

Hull, Clark L. *Principles of behavior*. New York: Appleton-Century, 1943.

Hunter, Floyd. *Community power structure*. Chapel Hill, N.C.: University of North Carolina Press, 1953.

Huntington, Samuel P. The democratic distemper. *The Public Interest*, 1975, *41* (Fall), 9–38.

Iris, Benjamin, and Barrett, Gerald V. Some relations between job and life satisfaction and life importance. *Journal of Applied Psychology*, 1972, *56*, 301–4.

Ivancevich, John M. A longitudinal assessment of management by objectives. *Administrative Science Quarterly*, 1972, *17*, 126–38.

Ivancevich, John M., and Donnelly, James H., Jr. Relation of organizational structure to job satisfaction, anxiety-stress, and performance. *Administrative Science Quarterly*, 1975, *20*, 272–80.

Jackson, Jay M. Structural characteristics of norms. In B. J. Biddle and E. J. Thomas (eds.), *Role theory: concepts and research*. New York: Wiley, 1966. Pp. 113–26. Copyright © 1966 John Wiley & Sons, Inc. Reprinted by permission.

Jacobs, Jane. *The death and life of American cities*. New York: Random House, 1969.

Jaques, Elliot. *The changing culture of a factory*. London: Tavistock, 1951.

Jasinski, F. J. Use and misuse of efficiency controls. *Harvard Business Review*, 1956, *34*, 4 (July–August), 105–12.

Jay, Anthony. *Corporation man*. New York: Random House, 1971.

Jelinek, Richard C.; Munson, Fred; and Smith, Robert L. *SUM (Service Unit Management): an organizational approach to improved patient care*. Battle Creek, Mich.: W. K. Kellogg Foundation, 1971.

Kahn, Herman; Brown, William; and Martel, Leon. *The next 200 years: a scenario for America and the world*. New York: William Morrow, 1976.

Kahn, Herman, and Wiener, Anthony J. *The year 2000: a framework for speculation on the next thirty years*. New York: Macmillan, 1967.

Kahn, Robert L. The prediction of productivity. *Journal of Social Issues*, 1956, *12*, 41–49.

Kahn, Robert L. Productivity and job satisfaction. *Personnel Psychology*, 1960, *13*, 275–87.

Kahn, Robert L. Introduction. In R. L. Kahn and Elise Boulding (eds.), *Power and conflict in organizations*. London: Tavistock, 1964. Pp. 1–7.

Kahn, Robert L. The meaning of work: interpretation and proposals for measurement. In A. Campbell and P. E. Converse (eds.), *The human meaning of social change*. New York: Russell Sage, 1972. Pp. 159–203.

Kahn, Robert L. Organizational development: some problems and proposals. *Journal of Applied Behavioral Science*, 1974, *10*, 485–502.

Kahn, Robert L.; Wolfe, Donald M.; Quinn, Robert P.; Snoek, J. Diedrick; and Rosenthal, Robert A. *Organizational stress: studies in role conflict and ambiguity.* New York: Wiley, 1964.

Kanter, Rosabeth Moss. *Men and women of the corporation.* New York: Basic Books, 1977.

Kast, Fremont E., and Rosenzweig, James E. *Contingency views of organization and management.* Chicago: Science Research Associates, 1973.

Katz, Daniel. Approaches to managing conflict. In R. L. Kahn and E. Boulding (eds.), *Power and conflict in organizations.* London: Tavistock, 1964. Pp. 105–114.

Katz, Daniel, and Kahn, Robert L. *The social psychology of organizations.* New York: Wiley, 1966. Copyright © 1966 John Wiley & Sons, Inc. Reprinted by permission.

Katz, Daniel, and Kahn, Robert L. *The social psychology of organizations.* 2d ed. New York: Wiley, 1978. Copyright © 1978 John Wiley & Sons, Inc. Reprinted by permission.

Katz, Elihu, and Lazarsfeld, Paul F. *Personal influence: the part played by people in the flow of mass communications.* Glencoe, Ill.: Free Press, 1955.

Kelman, Herbert C. Processes of opinion change. *Public Opinion Quarterly,* 1961, 25, 57–78.

Kerr, Norman D. The school board as an agency of legitimation. *Sociology of Education,* 1964, 38, 34–59.

Kevles, Daniel J. Robert A. Millikan. *Scientific American,* 1979, 240, 1, 142–51.

Keynes, John Maynard. Economic possibilities for our grandchildren. In Vol. IX of the Royal Economic Society edition of the *Collected Writings of John Maynard Keynes.*

Khandwalla, Pradip M. Mass output orientation of operations technology and organizational structure. *Administrative Science Quarterly,* 1974, 19, 74–97.

Klongan, Gerald E.; Paulson, Steven; and Rogers, David. Measurement of interorganizational relations: a deterministic model. Paper presented at American Sociological Association meetings, New Orleans, August 1972.

Kohn, Melvin L. Bureaucratic man: a portrait and an interpretation. *American Sociological Review,* 1971, 36, 461–74.

Kolaja, Jiri. *Workers' councils: the Yugoslav experience.* London: Tavistock, 1965.

Kotter, John P. Power, success, and organizational effectiveness. *Organizational Dynamics,* 1978, 6, 3 (Winter), 26–40.

Kover, Arthur J. Reorganization in an advertising agency: a case study of a decrease in integration. *Human Organization,* 1963, 22, 252–59.

Kuhn, Thomas S. *The Copernican revolution.* Cambridge, Mass.: Harvard University Press, 1957.

Landsberger, Henry A. The horizontal dimension in bureaucracy. *Administrative Science Quarterly,* 1961, 6, 299–322.

Lasswell, Harold D. *Politics: who gets what, when, and how?* New York: Peter Smith, 1936.

Lawler, Edward E., III. *Motivation in work organizations.* Monterey, Calif.: Brooks/Cole, 1973.

Lawler, Edward E., III, and Suttle, J. Lloyd. Expectancy theory and job behavior. *Organizational Behavior and Human Performance,* 1973, 9, 482–503.

Lawrence, Paul R., and Lorsch, Jay W. *Organization and environment: managing differentiation and integration.* Boston: Division of Research, Harvard University Graduate School of Business Administration, 1967.

Leavitt, Harold J. Applied organizational change in industry: structural, technical and humanistic approaches. In J. G. March (ed.), *Handbook of organizations.* Chicago: Rand McNally, 1965. Pp. 1144–70.

Levine, Sol, and White, Paul E. Exchange as a conceptual framework for the study of interorganizational relationships. *Administrative Science Quarterly,* 1961, *5,* 583–601.

Lewin, Kurt. Group decision and social change. In G. E. Swanson, T. M. Newcomb, and E. L. Hartley (eds.) *Readings in social psychology.* Rev. ed. New York: Holt, 1952. Pp. 459–73.

Lewin, Kurt; Dembo, Tamara; Festinger, Leon; and Sears, Pauline S. Level of aspiration. In J. McV. Hunt (ed.) *Personality and the behavior disorders.* Vol. 1. New York: Ronald Press, 1944.

Lewis, Helen L., and Franklin, Muriel F. An experimental study of the role of ego in work. II. The significance of task orientation in work. *Journal of Experimental Psychology,* 1944, *34,* 195–215.

Lieberman, Morton A.; Yalom, Irvin D.; and Miles, Matthew B. *Encounter groups: first facts.* New York: Basic Books, 1973.

Likert, Rensis. *New patterns of management.* New York: McGraw-Hill, 1961.

Likert, Rensis. *The human organization: its management and value.* New York: McGraw-Hill, 1967.

Lindblom, Charles E. *The intelligence of democracy: decision-making through adjustment.* New York: Free Press, 1965.

Lippitt, Gordon L., and Schmidt, Warren H. Crises in a developing organization. *Harvard Business Review,* 1967, *45,* 6 (November–December), 102–12. © 1967 by the President and Fellows of Harvard College. All rights reserved.

Lippitt, Ronald; Watson, Jeanne; and Westley, Bruce. *The dynamics of planned change.* New York: Harcourt, Brace & World, 1958.

Lippitt, Ronald, and White, Ralph K. The "social climate" of children's groups. In R. G. Barker, J. Kounin, and H. Wright (eds.), *Child behavior and development.* New York: McGraw-Hill, 1943. Pp. 485–508.

Lipset, Seymour Martin. *Political man.* Garden City, N.Y.: Doubleday, 1960.

Lipset, Seymour M.; Trow, Martin; and Coleman, James S. *Union democracy.* Glencoe, Ill.: Free Press, 1956.

Litterer, Joseph A. Conflict in organization: a re-examination. *Academy of Management Journal,* 1966, *9,* 178–86.

Litwak, Eugene. Models of organization which permit conflict. *American Journal of Sociology,* 1961, *67,* 177–85.

Locke, Edwin A. Personnel attitudes and motivation. *Annual Review of Psychology,* 1975, *26,* 457–80.

Lodahl, Thomas M., and Kejner, Mathilde. The definition and measurement of job involvement. *Journal of Applied Psychology,* 1965, *49,* 24–33.

Lodge, George Cabot. *The new American ideology.* New York: Knopf, 1975.

Lorsch, Jay W. Introduction to the structural design of organizations. In K. N. Wexley and G. A. Yukl (eds.), *Organizational behavior and industrial psychology.* New York: Oxford University Press, 1975. Pp. 256–67.

Luthans, Fred, and Reif, William E. Job enrichment: long on theory, short on practice. *Organizational Dynamics,* 1974, *2,* 3 (Winter), 30–43.

Lyons, Thomas F. Role clarity, need for clarity, satisfaction, tension, and withdrawal. *Organizational Behavior and Human Performance,* 1971, *6,* 99–110.
Lyons, Thomas F. Turnover and absenteeism: a review of relationships and shared correlates. *Personnel Psychology,* 1972, *25,* 271–81.
McClelland, David C. *Personality.* New York: Holt, Rinehart & Winston, 1951.
McClelland, David C. (ed.). *Studies in motivation.* New York: Appleton-Century-Crofts, 1955.
McClelland, David C. *The achieving society.* New York: Free Press, 1961.
McClelland, David C. *Motivational trends in society.* Morristown, N.J.: General Learning Press, 1971.
McClelland, David C.; Atkinson, John W.; Clark, R. A.; and Lowell, E. L. *The achievement motive.* New York: Appleton-Century-Crofts, 1953.
McGregor, Douglas. *The human side of enterprise.* New York: McGraw-Hill, 1960.
McKean, Roland N. Growth vs. no growth: an evaluation. In Mancur Olson, and Hans H. Landsberg (eds.), *The no growth society.* New York: Norton, 1973. Pp. 207–27.
McLuhan, Marshall, and Fiore, Quentin. *The medium is the message: an inventory of effects.* New York: Bantam Books, 1967.
McMurry, Robert N. Power and the ambitious executive. *Harvard Business Review,* 1973, *51,* 6 (November–December), 140–45.
McNeil, Kenneth, and Thompson, James D. The regeneration of social organizations. *American Journal of Sociology,* 1971, *36,* 624–37.
McWhinney, William H. Organizational form, decision modalities and the environment. *Human Relations,* 1968, *21,* 269–81.
Machiavelli, Niccolò. *The prince.* New York: New American Library, 1952.
Magnusen, Karl O. *Organizational design, development, and behavior.* Glenview, Ill.: Scott, Foresman, 1977.
Mahoney, Thomas A. Managerial perceptions of organizational effectiveness. *Management Science,* 1967, *14,* 76–91.
Mahoney, Thomas A., and Weitzel, William. Managerial models of organizational effectiveness. *Administrative Science Quarterly,* 1969, *14,* 357–65.
Mann, Floyd C. Toward an understanding of the leadership role in formal organization. In R. Dubin, G. C. Homans, F. C. Mann, and D. C. Miller (eds.), *Leadership and productivity.* San Francisco: Chandler, 1965, Pp. 68–103.
Mann, Floyd C., and Neff, Franklin W. *Managing major change in organizations.* Ann Arbor, Mich.: Foundation for Research on Human Behavior, 1961.
Mansfield, Roger. Bureaucracy and centralization: an examination of organizational structure. *Administrative Science Quarterly,* 1973, *18,* 477–88.
March, James G., and Simon, Herbert A. *Organizations.* New York: Wiley, 1958.
Marriott, R. Size of working group and output. *Occupational Psychology,* 1949, *23,* 47–57.
Marrow, Alfred J.; Bowers, David G.; and Seashore, Stanley E. *Management by participation: creating a climate for personal and organizational development.* New York: Harper & Row, 1967.
Maslow, Abraham H. *Motivation and personality.* New York: Harper & Row, 1970.
Maslow, Abraham H. *The farther reaches of human nature.* New York: Viking Press, 1971.
Maslow, Abraham H., and Mintz, N. L. Effects of esthetic surroundings: I. Initial

short-term effects of three esthetic conditions upon perceiving "energy" and "well-being" in faces. In R. Gutman (ed.), *People and buildings.* New York: Basic Books, 1972. Pp. 212–19.

Mattill, John I. The coming of automatic factories. *Technology Review,* 1975, *77,* 4 (February), 60.

Mattill, John I. Are we ready for the computerized factory? *Technology Review,* 1978, *81,* 2 (November), 21.

Meadows, Donella H.; Meadows, Dennis L.; and Randers, Jorgen, and Behrens, William W., III. *The limits to growth.* New York: Universe Books, 1972.

Mechanic, David. Sources of power of lower participants in complex organizations. *Administrative Science Quarterly,* 1962, *7,* 349–64.

Merei, Ferenc. Group leadership and institutionalization. *Human Relations,* 1949, *2,* 23–29.

Merton, Robert K. Bureaucratic structure and personality. *Social forces,* 1940, *18,* 560–68.

Merton, Robert K. *Social theory and social structure.* Glencoe, Ill.: Free Press, 1957.

Meyer, Herbert H.; Kay, E.; and French, John R. P. Split roles in performance appraisal. *Harvard Business Review,* 1965, *43,* 1 (January–February), 123–29.

Meyer, Marshall W. Automation and bureaucratic structure. *American Journal of Sociology,* 1968, *74,* 256–64.

Michael, Donald, N. *On learning to plan—and planning to learn.* San Francisco: Jossey-Bass, 1973.

Michels, Robert. *Political parties.* Glencoe, Ill.: Free Press, 1915.

Michels, Robert. *Political parties: a sociological study of the oligarchical tendencies of modern democracy.* New York: Dover, 1959.

Milgram, Stanley. Behavioral study of obedience. *Journal of Abnormal and Social Psychology,* 1963, *67,* 371–78.

Milgram, Stanley. Group pressure and action against a person. *Journal of Abnormal and Social Psychology,* 1964, *69,* 137–43.

Milgram, Stanley. Some conditions of obedience and disobedience to authority. In Ivan D. Steiner and Martin Fishbein (eds.), *Current studies in social psychology.* New York: Holt, Rinehart & Winston, 1965. Pp. 243–62.

Miller, George A. Professionals in bureaucracy: alienation among industrial scientists and engineers. *American Sociological Review,* 1967, *32,* 755–68.

Miller, James G. Information input, overload, and psychopathology. *American Journal of Psychiatry,* 1960, *116,* 695–704.

Miller, J. Wade, Jr., and Wolf, Robert J. The micro-company: organizing for problem-oriented management. *Personnel,* 1968, *45,* 4 (July–August), 35–43.

Miner, John B. Bridging the gulf in organizational performance. *Harvard Business Review,* 1968, *46,* 102–10.

Mintz, Morton. *The therapeutic nightmare.* Boston: Houghton Mifflin, 1965.

Mintz, N. L. Effects of esthetic surroundings: II. Prolonged and repeated experience in a "beautiful" and an "ugly" room. In R. Gutman (ed.), *People and buildings.* New York: Basic Books, 1972. Pp. 220–28.

Mintzberg, Henry. The science of strategy-making. *Industrial Management Review,* 1967, *8,* 71–81.

Mintzberg, Henry. Research on strategy-making. Proceedings, Academy of Management, 32d Annual Meeting, Minneapolis, Minn., August 13–16, 1972. Pp. 90–94.

Mintzberg, Henry. A new look at the chief executive's job. *Organizational Dynamics*, 1973, *1*, 3, 20–30.

Mintzberg, Henry, Rasinghani, Dury, and Theoret, Andre. The structure of "unstructured" decision processes. *Administrative Science Quarterly*, 1976, *21*, 246–75.

Mitchell, Terrance R. Expectancy models of job satisfaction, occupational preference and effort: a theoretical, methodological, and empirical appraisal. *Psychological Bulletin*, 1974, *81*, 1053–77.

Mohr, Lawrence B. Determinants of innovation in organizations. *American Political Science Review*, 1969, *63*, 111–26.

Mohr, Lawrence B. The concept of organizational goal. *American Political Science Review*, 1973, *67*, 470–81.

Mooney, James D., and Reiley, A. C. *The principles of organization.* New York: Harper, 1939.

Morse, John J., and Lorsch, Jay W. Beyond Theory Y. *Harvard Business Review*, 1970, *48*, 3 (May–June), 61–68. Copyright © 1970 by the President and Fellows of Harvard College. All rights reserved.

Morse, Nancy, and Reimer, E. The experimental change of a major organizational variable. *Journal of Abnormal and Social Psychology*, 1956, *52*, 120–29.

Moss, Gordon E. *Illness, immunity, and social interaction: the dynamics of biosocial resonation.* New York: Wiley, 1973.

Mott, Paul E. *The characteristics of effective organizations.* New York: Harper & Row, 1972.

Mulder, Mauk. Power equalization through participation. *Administrative Science Quarterly*, 1971, *16*, 31–38.

Mumford, Lewis. *The transformations of man.* New York: Harper & Bros., 1968.

Mumford, Lewis. *The myth of the machine.* Vol. 2, *The pentagon of power.* New York: Harcourt Brace Jovanovich, 1970.

Mumford, Lewis. Two views on technology and man. In C. A. Thrall and J. M. Starr (eds.), *Technology, power, and social change.* Lexington, Mass.: Lexington Books, 1972. Pp. 1–16.

Murray, Henry A. *Explorations in personality.* London: Oxford University Press, 1938.

Nebeker, Delbert M., and Mitchell, Terrance R. Leader behavior: an expectancy theory approach. *Organizational Behavior and Human Performance*, 1974, *11*, 355–67.

The New English Bible. The Oxford University Press, 1961, 1970. (Exodus 18:13–27.)

Newman, William H. Strategy and management structure. *Journal of Business Policy*, 1971, *2*, 56–66.

Nietzsche, Frederich. *The birth of tragedy and the genealogy of morals.* Garden City, N.Y.: Doubleday, 1956.

Odiorne, George S. *Management by objectives: a system of managerial leadership.* New York: Pitman, 1965.

Olson, Mancur. Introduction. In Mancur Olson and Hans H. Landsberg (eds.), *The no growth society.* New York: Norton, 1973. Pp. 1–13.

Orne, Martin T., and Evans, Frederick J. Social control in the psychological experiment. *Journal of Personality and Social Psychology*, 1965, *1*, 189–200.

Orwell, George. *Down and out in London and Paris.* New York: Harcourt Brace Jovanovich, 1972.

Parsons, Talcott (ed.). *Max Weber, the theory of social and economic organization* (trans. A. Henderson and T. Parsons). New York: Free Press, 1947.

Parsons, Talcott. Suggestions for a sociological approach to a theory of organizations. I. *Administrative Science Quarterly,* 1956, *1,* 63–85.

Parsons, Talcott. *Structure and process in modern societies.* New York: Free Press, 1960.

Patchen, Martin. *Some questionnaire measures of employee motivation and morale.* Ann Arbor, Mich.: Survey Research Center, University of Michigan, 1965.

Patchen, Martin. The locus and basis of influence on organizational decisions. *Organizational Behavior and Human Performance.* New York: Academic Press, Inc., 1974, *2,* 195–221.

Paul, William J.; Robertson, Keith B.; and Herzberg, Frederick. Job enrichment pays off. *Harvard Business Review,* 1969, *47* (2), 61–78.

Pearlin, Leonard I. Alienation from work: a study of nursing personnel. *American Sociological Review,* 1962, *27,* 314–26.

Peery, Newman S., Jr. General systems theory: an inquiry into its social philosophy. *Academy of Management Journal,* 1972, *15,* 495–510.

Pelz, Donald C. Influence: a key to effective leadership in first-line supervision. *Personnel,* 1952, *29,* 205–17.

Pelz, Donald C., and Andrews, Frank M. *Scientists in organizations: productive climates for research and development.* New York: Wiley, 1966.

Pennings, Johannes M. The revelance of the structural-contingency model for organizational effectiveness. *Administrative Science Quarterly,* 1975, *20,* 393–410.

Pepitone, Albert. Attributions of causality, social attitudes, and cognitive matching processes. In Renato Taguiri and Luigi Petrullo (eds.), *Person perception and interpersonal behavior.* Stanford, Calif.: Stanford University Press, 1958. Pp. 258–76.

Perin, Constance. *With man in mind: an interdisciplinary prospectus for environmental design.* Cambridge, Mass.: The M.I.T. Press, 1970.

Perrow, Charles. Organizational prestige. *American Journal of Sociology,* 1961, *66,* 335–41.

Perrow, Charles. Hospitals: technology, structure, and goals. In James G. March (ed.), *Handbook of organizations.* Chicago: Rand McNally, 1965. Pp. 910–71.

Perrow, Charles. A framework for the comparative analysis of organizations. *American Sociological Review,* 1967, *32,* 195–208.

Perrow, Charles. *Organizational analysis: a sociological view.* Belmont, Calif.: Wadsworth, 1970.

Perrow, Charles. *Complex organizations: a critical essay.* Glenview, Ill.: Scott, Foresman, 1972.

Peters, Edward. *Strategy and tactics in labor negotiations.* New London, Conn.: National Foremen's Institute, 1955.

Petit, Thomas A. Systems problems of organizations and business policy. *Proceedings,* Academy of Management, 32d annual meeting, Minneapolis, August 13–16, 1972. Pp. 103–7.

Pfeffer, Jeffrey. Merger as a response to organizational interdependence. *Administrative Science Quarterly,* 1972, *17,* 382–94 (a).

Pfeffer, Jeffrey. Size and composition of corporate boards of directors: the organization and its environment. *Administrative Science Quarterly,* 1972, *17,* 218–28 (b).

Pfeffer, Jeffrey. Size, composition, and function of hospital boards of directors: a study of organization-environment linkage. *Administrative Science Quarterly,* 1973, *18,* 349-64.

Pfeffer, Jeffrey, and Leblebici, Huseyin. Executive recruitment and the development of interfirm organizations. *Administrative Science Quarterly,* 1973, *18,* 449-61.

Pfeffer, Jeffrey, and Salancik, Gerald R. *The external control of organizations.* New York: Harper & Row, 1978.

Pickle, Hal B., and Rungeling, Brian S. Empirical investigation of entrepreneurial goals and customer satisfaction. *Journal of Business,* 1973, *46,* 268-73.

Pondy, Louis R. Budgeting and inter-group conflict in organizations. *Pittsburgh Business Review,* 1964, *34* (April), 1-3.

Pondy, Louis R. Organizational conflict: concepts and models. *Administrative Science Quarterly,* 1967, *12,* 296-320.

Porter, Lyman W., and Lawler, Edward E., III. Properties of organizational structure in relation to job attitudes and job behavior. *Psychological Bulletin,* 1965, *64,* 23-51.

Porter, Lyman W., and Steers, Richard M. Organizational, work, and personal factors in employee turnover and absenteeism. *Psychological Bulletin,* 1973, *80,* 151-76.

Pounds, William F. The process of problem finding. *Industrial Management Review,* 1969, *11,* 1-19.

Price, James L. *Organizational effectiveness: an inventory of propositions.* Homewood, Ill.: Irwin, 1968.

Price, James L. *Handbook of organizational measurement.* Lexington, Mass.: D. C. Heath, 1972.

Propst, Robert. *The office: a facility based on change.* Elmhurst, Ill.: The Business Press, 1968.

Proshansky, Harold M.; Ittelson, William H.; and Rivlin, Leanne G. The influence of the physical environment on behavior: some basic assumptions. In Harold M. Proshansky, William H. Ittelson, and Leanne G. Rivlin (eds.), *Environmental psychology.* New York: Holt, Rinehart & Winston, 1970. Pp. 27-37.

Pruden, Henry O., and Reese, Richard M. Interorganizational role-set relations and the performance and satisfaction of industrial salesmen. *Administrative Science Quarterly,* 1972, *17,* 601-9.

Pruitt, Dean G. Indirect communication and research for agreement in negotiation. *Journal of Applied Social Psychology,* 1971, *1,* 205-39. Washington, D.C.: V. H. Winston & Sons, 1511 K St., N.W.

Pruitt, Dean G. Methods for resolving differences of interest: a theoretical analysis. *Journal of Social Issues,* 1972, *28,* 133-54.

Pugh, D. S.; Hickson, D. J.; Hinings, C. R.; and Turner, C. Dimensions of organization structure. *Administrative Science Quarterly,* 1968, *13,* 65-105.

Pugh, D. S.; Hickson, D. J.; Hinings, C. R.; and Turner, C. The context of organization structures. *Administrative Science Quarterly,* 1969, *14,* 91-114.

Raia, Anthony P. A second look at goals and controls. *California Management Review,* 1966, *8* (4), 49-58.

Reich, Charles. *The greening of America,* New York: Bantam Books, 1971.

Reid, Samuel R. *Mergers, managers, and the economy.* New York: McGraw-Hill, 1968.

Reif, William E., and Schoderbeck, Peter P. *Job enlargement.* Ann Arbor, Mich.: Bureau of Industrial Relations, Graduate School of Business Administration, University of Michigan, 1969.

Revans, Reginald W. *Standards for morale: cause and effect in hospitals.* London: Oxford University Press, 1964.

Revans, Reginald W. (ed.). *Communication, choice, and change.* London: Tavistock, 1972.

Revans, Reginald W. *Action learning in hospitals: diagnosis and therapy.* London: McGraw-Hill, 1976.

Rice, Albert K. *Productivity and social organization: the Ahmedabad experiment* London: Tavistock Publications, 1958.

Richetto, Gary M. Organizations circa 1990: demise of the pyramid. *Personnel Journal,* 1970, *49,* 598–603.

Ringbakk, K. A. Long range planning in major U.S. companies. *Long Range Planning,* 1969, *2*(2), (December), 46–57.

Roberts, David R. A general theory of executive cooperation based on statistically tested proportions. *Quarterly Journal of Economics,* 1956, *20,* 270–94.

Roberts, David R. *Executive cooperation.* Glencoe, Ill.: Free Press, 1959.

Roethlisberger, Fritz J., and Dickson, William J. *Management and the worker.* New York: Wiley, 1964.

Rogers, Everett M. *Diffusion of innovations.* New York: Free Press, 1962.

Rosener, Marvin M. Economic determinants of organizational innovation. *Administrative Science Quarterly,* 1967, *12,* 614–25.

Rosner, Martin M. Administrative controls and innovation. *Behavioral Science,* 1968, *13,* 36–43.

Roszak, Theodore. *The making of a counter culture.* Garden City, N.Y.: Doubleday, 1969.

Rue, Leslie W., and Fulmer, Robert M. Is long-range planning profitable? Proceedings, Academy of Management, 33d Annual Meeting, Boston, August 1973. Pp. 66–73.

Ruesch, J., and Kees, W. Function and meaning in the physical environment. In Harold M. Proshansky, William H. Ittelson, and Leanne G. Rivlin (eds.), *Environmental psychology.* New York: Holt, Rinehart & Winston, 1970. Pp. 141–53.

Rumelt, Richard P. *Strategy, structure, and economic performance.* Boston: Harvard University Press, 1974.

Salas, Rafael M. World population growth: hopeful signs of a slowdown. *The Futurist,* 1978, *12,* 276–82.

Sarason, Seymour B. *The creation of settings and the future societies.* San Francisco: Jossey-Bass, 1972.

Sarnoff, Irving. *Personality dynamics and development.* New York: Wiley, 1962.

Schoeffler, Sidney; Buzzell, Robert D.; and Heany, Donald F. Impact of strategic planning on profit performance. *Harvard Business Review,* 1974, *52,* 2 (March–April), 137–45.

Schoettle, Enid C. B. The state of the art in policy studies. In R. A. Bauer and K. G. Gergen (eds.), *The study of policy formation.* New York: Free Press, 1968. Pp. 149–79.

Schrödinger, Erwin. *What is life?* Cambridge: Cambridge University Press, 1969.

Schulberg, Herbert C.; Sheldon, Alan; and Baker, Frank. Introduction in Herbert Schulberg, Alan Sheldon, and Frank Baker (eds.), *Program evaluation in the health fields.* New York: Behavioral Publications, 1969. Pp. 3–28.

Scott, Joseph W., and El-Assal, Mohamed. Multiversity, university size, university

quality and student protest: an empirical study, *American Sociological Review,* 1969, *34,* 708.
Scott, William G. *The management of conflict: appeal systems in organizations.* Homewood, Ill.: Dorsey, 1965.
Scott, William G. Organization government: the prospects for a truly participative system. *Public Administration Review,* 1969, *29,* 5, 43–53.
Scott, William G. Organization theory: a reassessment. *Academy of Management Journal,* 1974, *17,* 242–54.
Seashore, Stanley, E. Criteria of organizational effectiveness. *Michigan Business Review,* 1965, *17,* 26–30.
Seashore, Stanley E., and Bowers, David G. *Changing the structure and functioning of an organization.* Monograph No. 33. Ann Arbor, Mich.: Survey Research Center, 1963.
Seashore, Stanley E., and Yuchtman, Ephraim. Factorial analysis of organizational performance. *Administrative Science Quarterly,* 1967, *12,* 377–95.
Seeman, Melvin. On the meaning of alienation. *American Sociological Review,* 1959, *24,* 783–91.
Selznick, Philip. *TVA and the grass roots.* Berkeley, Calif.: University of California Press, 1949.
Selznick, Philip. *Leadership in administration.* Evanston, Ill.: Row & Peterson, 1957.
Sennett, Richard. *The uses of disorder: personal identity and city life.* New York: Random House, 1970.
Shepard, Herbert A. Innovation-resisting and innovation-producing organizations. *Journal of Business,* 1967, *60,* 470–77.
Siekman, Philip. Henry Ford and his electronic can of worms. *Fortune,* 1966, *73,* 2 (February), 116–19.
Sigelman, Lee. An organizational analysis of news reporting. *American Journal of Sociology,* 1973, *79,* 132–51.
Silverman, David. *The theory of organizations.* London: Heineman, 1970.
Simon, Herbert A. On the concept of organizational goal. *Administrative Science Quarterly,* 1964, *9,* 1–22.
Simon, Herbert A. *Administrative behavior.* 3d ed. New York: Free Press, 1976.
Skinner, B. F. *Walden two.* Toronto: Macmillan, 1970.
Skinner, B. F. *Beyond freedom and dignity.* New York: Knopf, 1971.
Slater, Philip E., and Bennis, Warren G. Democracy is inevitable. *Harvard Business Review,* 1964, *42,* 2 (March–April), 51–59.
Sloan, Alfred P., Jr. *My years with General Motors.* Garden City, N.Y.: Doubleday, 1964.
Smith, Clagett G. A comparative analysis of some conditions and consequences of intraorganizational conflict. *Administrative Science Quarterly,* 1966, *10,* 504–29.
Smith, Clagett G. Consultation and decision processes in a research and development laboratory. *Administrative Science Quarterly,* 1970, *15,* 203–15.
Smith, Robert L. Management of change. In Jelinek et al., *SUM.* Battle Creek, Mich.: W.K. Kellogg Foundation, 1971. Pp. 57–78.
Soelberg, P. O. Unprogrammed decision making, *Industrial Management Review,* 1967, *8,* 2 (Spring), 19–29.
Sommer, Robert. *Personal space: The behavioral basis of design.* Englewood Cliffs, N.J.: Prentice-Hall, 1969.

Sorokin, Pitirim. *Social and cultural dynamics.* 4 vols. New York: American Book Company, 1937–41.
Speer, Albert. *Inside the Third Reich.* New York: Avon, 1971.
Spranger, Eduard. *Types of men.* Halle (Saale): Max Niemeyer Verlag, 1928.
Stagner, Ross. Corporate decision making: an empirical study. *Journal of Applied Psychology,* 1969, *53,* 1–13.
Stagner, Ross. Conflict in the executive suite. In Warren G. Bennis (ed.), *American bureaucracy.* Chicago: Aldine, 1970. Pp. 85–95.
Starbuck, William H. Organizational growth and development. In J. G. March (ed.), *Handbook of organizations.* Chicago: Rand McNally, 1965. Pp. 451–533.
Steele, Fred I. The top-down society: spatial decisions in the organizational world. *Environment Planning and Design,* 1971, *1* (Summer), 24–30.
Steele, Fred I. *Physical settings and organizational development.* Reading, Mass.: Addison-Wesley, 1973.
Steiner, Gary A. Introduction in G. A. Steiner (ed.), *The creative organization.* Chicago: University of Chicago Press, 1965. Pp. 1–24.
Steiner, George A. *Top management planning.* New York: Macmillan, 1969.
Steiner, George A., and Miner, John B. *Management policy and strategy: text, readings and cases.* New York: Macmillan, 1977.
Steiner, George A., and Ryan, William G. *Industrial project management.* New York: Crowell-Collier and Macmillan, 1968.
Stevens, Carl M. *Strategy and collective bargaining negotiation.* New York: McGraw-Hill, 1963.
Strauss, Anselm. Healing by negotiation: specialty of the house. *Trans-action,* 1964, *1* (6), 13–15.
Strauss, Anselm; Schatman, Leonard; Ehrlich, Danuta; Busher, Rue; and Sabshin, Melvin. The hospital and its negotiated order. In E. Freidson (ed.), *The hospital in modern society.* Glencoe, Ill.: Free Press, 1963.
Strauss, George. Tactics of lateral relationships: the purchasing agent. *Administrative Science Quarterly,* 1962, *7,* 161–86.
Strauss, George. Job satisfaction, motivation, and job redesign. In G. Strauss, R. E. Miles, C. C. Snow, and A. S. Tannenbaum (eds.), *Organizational behavior: research and issues.* Madison, Wis.: Industrial Relations Research Association, 1974. Pp. 19–49.
Suchman, Edward A. *Evaluative research: principles and practice in public service and social action programs.* New York: Russell Sage, 1967.
Sykes, A. J. M. The effect of a supervisory training course in changing supervisors' perceptions and expectations of the role of management. *Human Relations,* 1962, *15,* 227–43.
Sykes, Gresham M. *The society of captives.* Princeton, N.J.: Princeton University Press, 1958.
Tagiuri, Renato. Value orientations and the relationships of managers and scientists. *Administrative Science Quarterly,* 1965, *10,* 39–51.
Tannenbaum, Arnold S. Control and effectiveness in a voluntary organization. *American Journal of Sociology,* 1961, *67,* 33–46.
Tannenbaum, Arnold S. Control in organizations: individual adjustment and organizational performance. *Administrative Science Quarterly,* 1962, *7,* 236–57.
Tannenbaum, Arnold S. *Control in organizations.* New York: McGraw-Hill, 1968.

Tannenbaum, Arnold S., and Kahn, Robert L. *Participation in union locals.* Evanston, Ill.: Row Peterson, 1958.
Tannenbaum, Arnold S.; Kavčič, Bogdan; Rosner, Menachem; Vianello, Mino; and Wieser, Georg. *Hierarchy in organizations.* San Francisco: Jossey-Bass, 1974.
Tannenbaum, Robert, and Schmidt, Warren H. How to choose a leadership pattern. *Harvard Business Review,* 1958, *36,* 2 (March–April), 95–101.
Tauskey, Curt, and Parke, E. Lauck. The mythology of job enrichment: self-actualization revisited. *Personnel,* 1975, *52,* 5, 12–21.
Taylor, Frederick W. The principles of scientific management. In H. F. Merrill (ed.), *Classics in management.* New York: American Management Association, 1960. Pp. 82–113.
The student shortage. *Time,* 1974, *104,* 3 (July 15), 86.
Thibaut, John W., and Kelley, Harold H. *The social psychology of groups.* New York, Wiley, 1959.
Thompson, James D. *Organizations in action.* New York: McGraw-Hill, 1967. Copyright © 1967 McGraw-Hill Book Company.
Thompson, James D. Society's frontiers for organizing activities. *Public Administration Review,* 1973, *33,* 327–35.
Thompson, James D., and Tuden, Arthur. Strategies and processes of organizational decision. In James D. Thompson et al. (eds.), *Comparative studies in administration.* Pittsburgh: University of Pittsburgh Press, 1956.
Thompson, Victor A. *Modern organization: a general theory.* New York: Knopf, 1961.
Thompson, Victor A. Bureaucracy and innovation. *Administrative Science Quarterly,* 1965, *10,* 1–20.
Thompson, Victor A. *Bureaucracy and innovation.* University, Ala.: University of Alabama Press, 1969.
Thornton, Russell. Organizational involvement and commitment to organization and profession. *Administrative Science Quarterly,* 1970, *15,* 417–26.
Thune, Stanley S., and House, Robert J. Where long range planning pays off. *Business Horizons,* 1970, *13* (4) (August), 81–87.
Toennies, Ferdinand. *Fundamental concepts of sociology* (trans. C. P. Loomis). New York: American Book, 1940.
Toffler, Alvin. *Future shock.* New York: Random House, 1970.
Tognoli, Jerome. The effect of windowless rooms and unembellished surroundings on attitudes and retention. *Environment and Behavior,* 1973, *5,* 191–201.
Trans-action. A symposium: the innovating organization. In Warren G. Bennis (ed.), *American Bureaucracy.* Chicago: Aldine, 1970. Pp. 135–63.
Trist, E. L., and Bamforth, K. W. Some social psychological consequences of the longwall method of coal-getting. *Human Relations,* 1951, *4,* 3–38.
Trist, E. L.; Higgin, G. W.; Murray, H.; and Pollock, A. B. *Organizational choice.* London: Tavistock Publications, 1963.
Turner, Arthur N., and Lawrence, Paul R. *Industrial jobs and the worker.* Cambridge, Mass.: Harvard University Press, 1965.
Udell, Jon G. An empirical test of hypotheses relating to span of control. *Administrative Science Quarterly,* 1967, *12,* 420–39.
Ullrich, Robert A. Experimental learning community. Unpublished manuscript, 1971.

Ullrich, Robert A. *A theoretical model of human behavior in organizations: an eclectic approach.* Morristown, N.J.: General Learning Corporation, 1972.

Ullrich, Robert A. Organizational design, employee motivation, and the support of strategic motivation. In H. Igor Ansoff, Roger P. Declérck, and Robert L. Hayes (eds.), *From strategic planning to strategic management.* London: Wiley, 1976. Pp. 199–216.

Ullrich, Robert A. Herzberg revisited: factors in job dissatisfaction. *Journal of Nursing Administration,* 1978, *8,* 10, 19–24.

United States Strategic Bombing Survey. *The effects of strategic bombing on German morale, Vol. 1.* Washington, D.C.: Government Printing Office, 1947.

Urwick, Lyndall. *The elements of administration.* New York: Harper, 1943.

Vancil, Richard F. The accuracy of long range planning. *Harvard Business Review,* 1970, *48,* 5 (October–November), 98–101.

Vickers, Geoffrey. *The art of judgment.* New York: Basic Books, 1965.

Vroom, Victor H. Some personality determinants of the effects of participation. *Journal of Abnormal and Social Psychology,* 1959, *59,* 322–27.

Vroom, Victor H. *Some personality determinants of the effects of participation.* Englewood Cliffs, N.J.: Prentice-Hall, 1960.

Vroom, Victor H. *Work and motivation.* New York: Wiley, 1964.

Vroom, Victor H., and Yetton, Philip W. *Leadership and decision-making.* Pittsburgh: University of Pittsburgh Press, 1973.

Wahba, Mahmoud A., and Bridwell, Lawrence G. A review of research on the need hierarchy theory. In Kenneth N. Wexley and Gary A. Yukl (eds.), *Organizational behavior and industrial psychology: readings with commentary.* New York: Oxford University Press, 1975. Pp. 5–11.

Wahba, Mahmoud A., and Bridwell, Lawrence G. Maslow reconsidered: a review of research on the need hierarchy theory. *Organizational Behavior and Human Performance,* 1976, *15,* 212–40.

Walker, Arthur H., and Lorsch, Jay W. Organizational choice: product versus function. *Harvard Business Review,* 1968, *46,* 129–38.

Walmsley, Gary L., and Zald, Mayer N. *The political economy of public organizations.* Lexington, Mass.: D. C. Heath, 1973.

Walton, Richard E. Two strategies of social change and their dilemmas. In Warren G. Bennis, Kenneth D. Benne, and Robert Chin (eds.), *The planning of change.* New York: Holt, Rinehart & Winston, 1969. Pp. 167–76.

Walton, Richard E., and Dutton, John M. The management of interdepartmental conflict: a model and review. *Administrative Science Quarterly,* 1969, *14,* 73–84.

Walton, Richard E., and McKersie, Robert B. *A Behavioral theory of labor negotiations: an analysis of a social interaction system.* New York: McGraw-Hill, 1965.

Wanous, John P. Individual differences and reactions to job characteristics. *Journal of Applied Psychology,* 1974, *59,* 616–22.

Wanous, John P., and Lawler, Edward E., III. Measurement and meaning of job satisfaction. *Journal of Applied Psychology.* 1972, *56,* 95–105.

Warner, W. Keith, and Havens, A. Eugene. Goal displacement and the intangibility of organizational goals. *Administrative Science Quarterly,* 1968, *12,* 539–55.

Warriner, Charles K. The problem of organizational purpose. *Sociological Quarterly,* 1965, *6,* 139–46.

Weber, Max. *From Max Weber: essays in sociology* (trans. Gerth and Mills). New York: Oxford, 1958.

Weber, Max. *The theory of social and economic organization* (trans. Henderson and Parsons). New York: Free Press, 1964.

Wells, B. W. P. The psycho-social influence of building environment: sociometric findings in large and small office spaces. In R. Gutman (ed.), *People and buildings.* New York: Basic Books, 1972. Pp. 97–119.

Weiner, Bernard. *Theories of motivation: from mechanism to cognition.* Chicago: Markham, 1972.

Wernimont, Paul F. A systems view of job satisfaction. *Journal of Applied Psychology,* 1972, *56,* 173–76.

Wernimont, Paul F.; Toren, Paul; and Kapell, Henry. Comparison of sources of personal satisfaction and of work motivation. *Journal of Applied Psychology,* 1970, *54,* 95–102.

When workers become directors. *Business Week,* 1973, *2297* (September 15), 188–96.

When workers manage themselves. *Business Week,* 1965, *1855* (March 20), 93–94.

Where being nice to workers didn't work. *Business Week,* 1973, *2263* (January 20), 98–100.

White, Robert W. Motivation reconsidered: the concept of competence. *Psychological Review,* 1959, *66,* 297–333.

Whyte, William F. The social structure of the restaurant. *American Journal of Sociology,* 1949, *54,* 302–10.

Whyte, William F. *Money and motivation.* New York: Harper & Bros., 1955.

Wieland, George F. *Complexity and coordination in organizations.* Doctoral dissertation, University of Michigan, 1965.

Wieland, George F. The determinants of clarity in organization goals. *Human Relations,* 1969, *22,* 161–72.

Wieland, George F., and Bradford, Amos. Action and understanding for improving management. Paper presented at the Academy of Management meetings, Atlanta, Georgia, August 1979.

Wieland, George F., and Leigh, Hilary (eds.). *Changing hospitals: a report on the hospital internal communications project.* London: Tavistock, 1971.

Wildavsky, Aaron. *The politics of the budgetary process.* Boston: Little, Brown, 1964.

Wildavsky, Aaron, and Hammond, Arthur. Comprehensive versus incremental budgeting in the department of agriculture. *Administrative Science Quarterly,* 1965, *10,* 321–46.

Wilson, James Q. Innovation in organization: notes toward a theory. In James D. Thompson (ed.), *Approaches to organizational design.* Pittsburgh: University of Pittsburgh Press, 1966. Pp. 193–218.

Wolf, William. Address at Southern Management Association meetings, Miami Beach, November 1971.

Woodward, Joan. *Industrial organization: theory and practice.* London: Oxford University Press, 1965.

Wool, Harold. What's wrong with work in America—a review essay. *Monthly Labor Review,* 1973, *96* (3) (March), 38–44.

Work in America. Report of a special task force to the Secretary of Health, Education and Welfare. Cambridge, Mass.: The M.I.T. Press, 1973.

Worthy, James. Organizational structures and employee morale. *American Sociological Review,* 1950, *15,* 169–79.
Wrapp, Edward H. Good managers don't make policy decisions. *Harvard Business Review,* 1967, *45,* 5 (September–October), 91–99.
Yuchtman, Ephraim, and Seashore, Stanley E. A system-resource approach to organizational effectiveness. *American Sociological Review,* 1967, *32,* 891–903.
Yukl, Gary. Toward a behavioral theory of leadership. *Organizational Behavior and Human Performance,* 1971, *6,* 414–40.
Zald, Mayer N. Comparative analysis and measurement of organizational goals: the case of correctional institutions for delinquents. *Sociological Quarterly,* 1963, *4,* 206–30.
Zald, Mayer N. Urban differentiation, characteristics of boards of directors and organizational effectiveness. *American Journal of Sociology,* 1967, *73,* 261–72.
Zald, Mayer N. The power and functions of boards of directors: a theoretical synthesis. *American Journal of Sociology,* 1969, *75,* 97–111.
Zald, Mayer N. *Organizational change: the political economy of the YMCA.* Chicago: University of Chicago Press, 1970.
Zaleznik, Abraham. Power and politics in organizational life. *Harvard Business Review,* 1970, *48,* 3 (May–June), 47–60.
Zaleznik, Abraham; Christensen, Carl R.; and Rothlisberger, Fritz J., with Homans, George C. *The motivation, productivity and satisfaction of workers.* Boston: Harvard Graduate School of Business Administration, 1958.
Zaltman, Gerald; Duncan, Robert; and Holbek, Jonny. *Innovations and organizations.* New York: Wiley, 1973.
Zeigarnik, Bluma. Veber das Behalten von erledigten und unerledigten Handlungen, III. The memory of completed and uncompleted actions. *Psychologische Forschung,* 1927, *9,* 1–85.
Zwerman, William L. *New perspectives on organization theory.* Westport, Conn.: Greenwood Publishing Company, 1970.

Name Index

A

Aiken, Michael, 93–94, 122, 183, 405–16, 424–25
Alderfer, Clayton P., 222, 242
Alinsky, Saul, 279, 307
Allison, Graham T., 196
Allport, Floyd H., 250
Allport, Gordon W., 210–11
Andrews, Frank M., 395 n
Andrews, John, 333
Ansoff, H. Igor, 43–46, 48, 51–53, 62, 70, 105, 125, 192, 212, 388–89, 392, 396–97
Anthony, Robert M., 190–91, 374
Argyris, Chris, 54–56, 221, 242, 259, 288
Aristotle, 10
Athos, Anthony G., 364
Ayres, Robert U., 466

B

Bach, George R., 279
Bachman, Jerald G., 265
Baker, Frank, 381
Bales, Robert F., 318, 322 n
Ball, Robert, 144, 145
Bamforth, K. W., 96
Barkdull, C. W., 41
Barnes, Louis B., 427
Barrett, Gerald V., 229
Barrett, Jon H., 285, 288–89
Bauer, Raymond A., 193, 270
Bavelas, Alex, 316
Becker, Selwyn W., 395
Beckhofer, Frank, 235
Behling, Orlando, 238
Behrens, William W., 342, 384
Bell, Daniel, 466, 473–74
Bell, Gerald, 80
Benne, Kenneth D., 421
Bennis, Warren G., 421, 463–64, 469
Benson, J. Kenneth, 337
Berlyne, Daniel E., 243
Bernstein, Marilyn, 408
Biddle, B. J., 254
Blake, Robert R., 233, 430–31, 448
Blau, Peter, 108, 110
Blauner, Robert, 394 n
Blood, Milton R., 4, 227
Bower, Joseph L., 196
Bowers, David, 65, 265, 321–22, 448
Bradford, Amos, 333
Brandenburg, Robert, 43–46, 48, 51–53, 62, 70, 105, 125, 388, 392, 396–97
Braybrooke, David, 193–94
Breed, Warren, 286
Bridwell, Lawrence G., 4, 222
Bucher, Rue, 271–73
Buck, Vernon E., 150
Buckley, Walter, 33, 378 n

Name Index

Burns, Tom, 83, 85, 87, 122 n
Butterfield, Anthony, 322, 333
Bylinski, Gene, 371

C

Cammann, Cortlandt, 238
Campbell, John P., 235, 372
Caplan, Robert D., 239
Caplow, Theodore, 178–79, 396 n
Carey, Alex, 23
Carlisle, Harvard M., 48–49
Carroll, Stephen J., 127
Caves, Richard E., 186
Chamberlain, Neil, 477–79
Chandler, Alfred D., Jr., 47, 195
Chapanis, Alphonse, 233
Chevalier, Michel, 213
Child, Irving, 229
Child, John, 110, 196
Chin, Robert, 421
Churchill, Winston, 306
Cleland, David, 49
Coch, Lester, 311
Coffey, Robert E., 364
Cohen, Arthur H., 259
Coleman, James S., 21, 395, 421
Collins, Randall, 337
Copernicus, 10, 78
Corwin, Ronald G., 407
Crozier, Michael, 100
Crystal, Graef S., 205
Cyert, Richard M., 138, 150, 153–54, 156, 416

D

Dahl, Robert A., 183
Dahrendorf, Rolf, 309
Dale, Ernest, 38, 41
Davies, Rene O., 232
Davis, Stanley M., 53
Deci, Edward L., 231, 240–42
Declérck, Roger P., 212
Demeroth, Nicholas J., III, 418
Dent, James K., 373–74
Dewar, Robert, 211
Dewey, John, 105
Dickson, William J., 22
Doctors, Samuel I., 395 n
Domhoff, William G., 183
Donnelly, James H., Jr., 41
Downs, Anthony, 422
Drucker, Peter, 126, 137, 141, 464–65
Dubin, Robert, 235
Duff, Raymond S., 114
Dunnette, Marvin, 235
Durkheim, Emile, 288, 384
Dutton, John M., 295

E

Edwards, Ward, 235
Einstein, Albert, 4, 8, 10–11
Emery, Fred W., 121, 169–71, 465
Engel, Gloria V., 114
England, George W., 211
Etzioni, Amitai, 118, 129–31, 139–40, 164, 263, 380
Evan, William N., 179–80
Evans, Frederick J., 284
Evans, Martin G., 327

F

Fanon, Frantz, 279
Farris, George, 395 n
Fayol, Henri, 17, 24–25
Fein, Mitchell, 235
Festinger, Leon, 213, 349
Fiedler, Fred E., 325–27
Filley, Alan C., 326, 327 n
Flanagan, Robert F., 235
Fleishman, Edwin A., 317–21, 322 n, 333
Ford, R. N., 226
Forehand, Garlie A., 395
Forrester, Jay, 479–80
Frank, Andrew Gunder, 259
Frank, Jerome, 284
Franke, Richard H., 23 n
Franklin, Muriel F., 95
Freidson, Eliot, 114
French, Elizabeth, 229
French, John R. P., Jr., 127, 239, 264, 311
Friedlander, Frank, 374
Friedman, John, 193
Fruhan, William W., Jr., 213
Fuller, R. Buckminster, 345, 378 n
Fulmer, Robert M., 192–93

G

Galbraith, Jay, 122–26, 129, 131, 201
Galbraith, John Kenneth, 196
Gallese, Liz Roman, 462
Gamson, William A., 288, 304, 306–9
Gantt, Henry L., 16
Gardner, John W., 229
Gauss, Christian, 274
Georgopoulos, Basil S., 116, 373, 375, 380, 391 n, 392, 395
Gerstner, Louis V., Jr., 212
Giacquinta, Joseph B., 408
Gibb, Cecil A., 320
Gilbreth, Frank B., 16
Ginsberg, Eli, 112
Glassman, Robert B., 153
Glueck, William F., 192
Goffman, Erving, 353
Goldston, Eli, 479

Goldthorpe, John H., 235
Gordon, Gerald, 395 n
Gouldner Alvin W., 19–20, 28, 115, 340
Graen, George B., 232, 238
Graicunas, V. A., 263
Greiner, Larry E., 448–50
Gross, Edward, 135–36, 398
Gross, George R., 178
Gross, Neal, 408, 427
Guest, Robert Henry, 438, 448
Gulick, 289
Guth, William D., 194, 211, 399
Gutman, Peter M., 212

H

Haas, J. Eugene, 419
Hage, Jerald, 93–94, 122, 211, 405–16, 421, 424–25
Hake, Barry, 466–67, 480
Hall, Edward, 316, 354
Hall, Richard, 112–14, 172–73, 388, 419 n
Halpert, Burton P., 275
Hamblin, Robert C., 331
Hammond, Arthur, 194
Hammond, Phillip E., 418
Hampton, David R., 296–97
Harman, Willis W., 471, 481–82
Harris, Edwin F., 317–21, 322 n
Harrison, Roger, 430–35
Harvey, Edward, 87–89, 122 n
Havelock, Ronald G., 395
Hayes, Robert L., 212
Hebb, Donald O., 4, 240
Hellriegel, Don, 42
Herzberg, Frederick, 222–23, 226, 239, 242, 345
Higgin, G. W., 95
Hilgard, Ernest H., 229
Hirsch, Seymour, 423
Hofer, Charles W., 192–93, 212
Hollander, Edwin P., 332–34
Hollingshead, August B., 114
Hoos, Ida R., 415
Horowitz, Irving L., 365
Horwitz, Murray, 95
House, Robert J., 192–93, 226, 326–28
Hudson, Barclay, 193
Hulin, Charles L., 4, 227
Hull, Clark L., 219–20, 222
Hunter, Floyd, 183
Huntington, Samuel P., 474

I–J

Indik, Bernard P., 375
Iris, Benjamin, 229
Ittelson, William H., 351
Ivancevich, John M., 41, 127

Jackson, Jay M., 253–54, 256
Jacobs, Jane, 352
Jaques, Elliot, 448
Jay, Anthony, 332
Jelinek, Richard C., 454
Johnson, Norman J., 419
Julian, James J., 333, 343

K

Kahn, Herman, 466, 471, 472 n
Kahn, Robert L., 28–33, 53, 62, 70, 138, 141, 151, 164, 234, 252, 256–58, 260–64, 275–76, 321–22, 339–40, 378–80, 383–86, 388, 390, 392, 419, 452–53
Kanter, Rosabeth Moss, 337–38
Kast, Fremont E., 195
Katz, Daniel, 28–33, 53, 62, 70, 138, 141, 151, 164, 252, 256–58, 291–92, 294, 296, 321–22, 339–40, 378–80, 383–86, 388, 392, 395, 452–53
Katz, Elihu, 421
Kaub, James D., 23 n
Kay, Andrew, 217–18
Kay, E., 127
Kees, W., 347, 351
Kejner, Mathilde, 394
Kelley, Harold H., 140, 153–54, 251–52, 270
Kelman, Herbert C., 270
Kennedy, John F., 196–97
Kerr, Norman D., 183–84
Kevles, Daniel J., 4
Keynes, John Maynard, 482–83
Khandwalla, Pradip M., 111–12
Klongan, Gerald E., 185
Kohn, Melvin L., 311
Kolaja, Jiri, 309
Kotter, John P., 280, 337
Kover, Arthur J., 362
Kuhn, Thomas, 5–8, 11, 239, 417

L

Landsberger, Henry A., 294
Lasswell, Harold D., 387
Lawler, Edward E., III, 235, 237–38, 410 n
Lawrence, Paul R., 4, 53, 71–73, 76–77, 85–86, 88–89, 94, 151, 227–28, 290, 362, 398
Lazarsfeld, Paul F., 421
Leavitt, Harold J., 101
Leblebici, Huseyin, 178, 179 n
Leigh, Hilary, 446
Levine, Sol, 385
Lewin, Kurt, 235, 438–41, 443–44, 446–47
Lewis, Helen L., 95
Lieberman, Morton A., 431, 433

Likert, Rensis, 56–60, 62–63, 66–67, 83, 94, 150, 259, 262, 288, 294, 309, 321–22, 328, 363, 448
Lindblom, Charles E., 193–94
Lindzey, Gardner, 210–11
Lippitt, Gordon L., 332, 419–20
Lippitt, Ronald, 100, 444, 446
Lipset, Seymour M., 21, 307
Litterer, Joseph A., 293–94
Litwak, Eugene, 279
Locke, Edwin A., 237
Lockwood, David, 235
Lodahl, Thomas M., 394
Lodge, George Cabot, 467, 474–75
Lorsch, Jay, 71–74, 76–77, 85–86, 88–89, 94, 151, 231–32, 290, 362, 397–98
Luthans, Fred, 226
Lyons, Thomas F., 259, 392

M

McClelland, David, 222, 229–31, 242, 278
McGregor, Douglas, 259
Machiavelli, Niccola, 274–75, 305, 315
McKean, Roland M., 471
McKersie, Robert B., 157, 297, 301–2
McMurry, Robert N., 305
McNamara, Robert, 414
McNeil, Kenneth, 417
McWhinney, William H., 339
Magnusen, Karl O., 92–93
Mahoney, Thomas A., 375–76, 378–79, 391
Mann, Floyd C., 116, 321–22, 332, 339, 373, 380, 392, 395, 427–29
Mansfield, Roger, 111
March, James G., 19–20, 149, 151, 153–56, 200, 285, 290–91, 416, 422, 447
Marcus, Philip M., 265
Marquis, Sue, 395 n
Marriott, R., 293
Marrow, Alfred J., 65, 94
Maslow, Abraham, 3, 12, 220–23, 242–43, 351, 355
Matejko, Alexander, 395
Mattill, John I., 79
Mayo, Elton, 22
Meadows, Dennis L., 342, 384
Meadows, Donella H., 342, 384
Mechanic, David, 265–66
Menzel, Herbert, 395, 421
Merei, Ferenc, 332
Merton, Robert K., 19, 149, 398
Meyer, Herbert H., 127
Meyer, Marshall W., 108, 419
Michels, Robert, 20–21, 139
Milgram, Stanley, 284
Miller, George, 116, 394 n
Miller, James, 80
Millikan, Robert A., 4, 8, 11
Miner, John B., 189, 399

Mintz, N. L., 12, 355–56
Mintzberg, Henry, 191–92, 200–204, 206–10, 214
Mitchell, Terrance R., 237, 327–28
Mooney, James D., 17
Mohr, Lawrence B., 416
Morse, John, 231–32
Morse, Nancy, 451, 453
Mott, Paul E., 321–22, 330–31, 339, 388–89, 391–94, 396–97
Mouton, Jane, 233, 430–31, 448
Mulder, Mauk, 288, 309–11
Mumford, Lewis, 78, 89, 480
Munson, Fred, 454
Murray, H., 95, 220, 229

N–O

Nebeker, Delbert M., 327
Neff, Franklin W., 427–29
Nietzsche, Friedrich, 178 n
Nixon, Richard, 191
Odiorne, George, 126
Olson, Mancur, 471
Orne, Martin T., 284
Orwell, George, 99

P

Parsons, Talcott, 26, 33, 112, 167, 169, 190, 385
Patchen, Martin, 264–66, 269–70, 280, 394, 396
Paul, William J., 224–26
Pavlov, Ivan, 219
Pearlin, Leonard I., 394 n
Peery, Newman S., Jr., 470
Pelz, Donald C., 334, 395 n, 451
Pennings, Johannes M., 77
Pepitone, Albert, 284
Perin, Constance, 347
Perrow, Charles, 28, 87, 90–94, 98–99, 108–9, 116–17, 140–43, 149, 151, 156, 160–62, 164, 176, 195, 287, 329, 362, 388, 453
Petit, Thomas A., 33, 199–200
Pfeffer, Jeffrey, 171–78, 179 n, 181–87, 213
Pickle, Hal, 374
Platt, Jennifer, 235
Pollock, A. B., 95
Pondy, Louis R., 107–8, 277, 279, 283, 290, 297
Porter, Lyman W., 234–35
Pounds, William F., 202
Price, James L., 373, 392, 394
Propst, Robert, 360
Proshansky, Harold M., 351
Pruden, Henry O., 181–82
Pruitt, Dean G., 297–301, 303
Pugh, D. S., 110

Q-R

Quinn, Robert P., 259
Raia, Anthony P., 127
Randers, Jorgen, 342, 384
Raven, Bertram H., 264
Raynolds, Peter A., 364
Reese, Richard M., 181–82
Reich, Charles, 464, 467
Reid, Samuel R., 186
Reif, William E., 226
Reiley, A. C., 17
Reimer, E., 451, 453
Revans, Reginald W., 333
Rice, Albert K., 97, 448
Richardson, Elliot L., 3
Richetto, Gary M., 53
Ringbakk, K. A., 192
Rivlin, Leanne G., 351
Roberts, David R., 418
Robertson, Keith B., 226
Roethlisberger, Fritz, 22
Rogers, Everett M., 395
Rosener, Marvin M., 416
Rosenthal, Robert A., 259
Rosenzweig, James E., 195
Rosner, Martin M., 395
Roszak, Theodore, 464
Rue, Leslie W., 192–93
Ruesch, J., 347, 351
Rumelt, Richard P., 212
Rungeling, Brian S., 374
Ryan, William G., 51

S

Salancik, Gerald R., 171–77, 181, 183–87, 213
Salas, Rafael M., 472
Sarason, Seymour B., 420
Sarnoff, Irving, 55 n
Schmidt, Warren H., 332, 419–20
Schoderbeck, Peter P., 226
Schoeffler, Sidney, 193
Schoettle, Enid C. B., 193
Schriessheim, Chester, 238
Schrödinger, Erwin, 243
Schulberg, Herbert C., 381
Scott, William, 311, 468, 470, 472
Seashore, Stanley, 65, 321–22, 374–76, 380, 388, 391–92, 448
Seeman, Melvin, 394 n
Selznick, Philip, 20, 142, 290, 339, 340–43
Sennett, Richard, 279
Sheldon, Alan, 381
Shepard, Herbert A., 331
Siekman, Philip, 143
Sigelman, Lee, 286
Silverman, David, 33

Simon, Herbert, A., 19–20, 25, 149, 151–53, 200, 285, 290–91, 390, 422, 447, 470
Skinner, B. F., 127
Slater, Philip E., 463–64, 469
Sloan, Alfred P., Jr., 47
Slocum, John W., Jr., 42
Smith, Adam, 142, 437
Smith, Clagett, 279–80, 395 n
Smith, Robert L., 454–57
Snoek, J. Diedrick, 259
Soelberg, P. O., 214
Sommer, Robert, 353–54
Sorokin, Pitirim, 481
Speer, Albert, 348, 415
Spranger, Edward, 210
Stagner, Ross, 280–83
Stalker, G. M., 83, 85, 87, 122 n
Starbuck, William H., 418–19
Starke, Frederick A., 238
Steele, F. I., 346, 354, 358
Steers, Richard M., 234
Steiner, Gary A., 51, 395
Steiner, George A., 106, 189
Stelling, Joan, 271–73
Stotland, Ezra S., 259
Straus, Anselm, 245–48
Strauss, George, 234–35, 263
Suttle, J. Lloyd, 237
Sykes, A. J. M., 334
Sykes, Gresham, M., 267

T

Tagiuri, Renato, 211, 399
Tannenbaum, Arnold, 60–61, 63, 65, 67–69, 75, 77, 83, 94, 150, 311, 332, 391, 395 n, 396 n, 476
Taylor, Frederick Winslow, 14–17, 103, 285, 289, 297, 414, 468, 470
Thibaut, John W., 140, 153, 251–52, 270
Thomas, E. J., 254
Thompson, James, 24–27, 29, 80–83, 100–101, 117–19, 121–22, 129, 131, 141, 155–58, 168, 178, 181, 185, 187, 197–99, 204, 212, 272, 382, 385, 417, 423, 468–69
Thompson, Victor, 296, 395, 414
Thornton, Russell, 115
Thune, Stanley S., 192
Tocqueville, Alexis de, 473
Toennies, Ferdinand, 289
Toffler, Alvin, 466
Tognoli, Jerome, 355
Tolliver, James, 238
Tosi, Henry L., 127
Trist, E. L., 95–96, 169–71
Trow, Martin, 21
Tuden, Arthur, 155, 157–58, 197, 204, 272
Turner, Arthur N., 4, 227–28

U-V

Udell, Jon G., 41
Ulman, Lloyd, 235
Ullrich, Robert A., 117, 222, 227, 234, 356, 392, 438, 463
Urwick, Lyndall, 17, 289
Vancil, Richard F., 192
Vernon, Philip E., 210–11
Vickers, Geoffrey, 339
Vroom, Victor H., 226, 235–36, 242, 329, 334–37, 392

W

Wahba, Mahmoud A., 4, 222
Walker, Arthur H., 292, 397
Walmsley, Gary L., 182
Walton, Richard E., 157, 295, 297, 301–2
Wanous, John P., 228, 410 n
Warriner, Charles K., 118, 139–40
Weber, Max, 18, 155, 418, 468
Weick, Karl E., 235
Weiner, Bernard 238, 466
Weiss, David W., 232
Weitzel, William, 376, 378–79
Wells, B. W. P., 348, 353
Wernimont, Paul F., 229
Whisler, Thomas L., 395
White, Paul E., 385
White, Ralph K., 100
White, Robert W., 278
Whiting, Jon W., 229
Whyte, William F., 99, 101, 295, 347, 440, 443
Wieland, George F., 80, 149, 333, 395, 419, 446
Wigdor, Lawrence A., 226
Wildavsky, Aaron, 194
Wilson, James Q., 150, 408, 416
Wolfe, Donald W., 259
Woodward, Joan, 84–86, 88, 111, 122 n, 329
Wool, Harold, 235
Worthy, James, 41
Wrapp, Edward H., 208, 210
Wyden, P., 279

Y-Z

Yetton, Philip W., 335–37
Yuchtman, Ephraim, 375–76, 380, 388, 391–92
Yukl, Gary, 323–25
Zald, Mayer N., 139, 162, 182–83
Zaltman, Gerald, 408
Zeigarnik, Bluma, 95
Zwerman, William L., 87

Subject Index

A

A&P, 144
Ability, 233-34
Accomodation, 285, 288-89
Achievement motivation, 229-30
   child-rearing practices, 230-31
   economic development, 230-31
Adaptability, 392
Adaptation, 392-94
Adaptive subsystems of organization, 30
Administration pattern of leadership, 322
Administrative planning, 190
Adventurism, 342
Alienation, 308
Ambiguous norms, 255-56
Anticipation, 168
Arousal, 240-41
Arousal potential, 240-41
Assembly line, 54, 361
Authoritarian organization, 62
Authority, 18, 264
   concentration, 110
   delegation of, 20
   hierarchy of, 38-39, 60-62, 107
   line of, 26-27
Authorization, 204-5
Autonomy, 95
   organizational transactions, 184-85
   professionals, 144

B

Bargaining conflict, 277, 297-304
   concessions, 298-99
   distributive processes, 297-98
   informal conferences, 299-300
   integrative processes, 297, 301-2
   mediators, 300
   pressure tactics, 298
   sequencing, 302-3
   tacit communication, 299
Batsu, 476-77
Behavior in organizations
   formal structure, 249
   informal structure, 249
   J-shaped distribution, 249
   negotiated order, 247-49
   norms, 247, 249-51
   physical environment, 347
   rules, 247
Behavioral equilibrium, 438-40
Behavioral modification, 128-29
Benevolent authoritative management systems, 63-64
Beyond Freedom and Dignity, 127
Boards of directors, 182
Boundary roles, 181, 260
   management of stress, 263-64
Buffering, 111, 168
   personnel, 295-96

516 Subject Index

Bureaucratic conflict, 277, 279, 283–89
  accomodation, 285, 288–89
  autonomy, 283
  commitment, 284
  control mechanisms, 286–87
  effects, 279–80
  exchange, 285
  integration of individual and organizational goals, 287–88
  participation as social control mechanism, 288
  primary relations in organization, 289
  secondary relations in organization, 289
  selective recruitment, 287–88
  socialization, 285–88
  sources, 277
Business policies, pyramid of, 105–6
Bureaucracy, 18, 31, 414
  dysfunctions, 19–20
  functions, 19
  future role, 464
  individual freedom, 20–21
  legal-rational authority, 18
  line of authority, 26–27
  rationality, 18–19, 468
  rules, 109

C

Centralization, 111, 406–7
Centralized functional form of organization, 46–47
Centralized organizational structure, 92
Change processes in organization
  alternative change selections, 446
  behavioral equilibrium, 438
  changing behavior stage, 441
  collaboration, 449
  consultant, 444–47, 449
  contingency approach, 460
  creativity, 449–50
  diagnostic phase, 445–46
  evaluation, 459
  example of, 450–54
  implementing, 446–47
  larger organization, 443
  need for change established, 444, 448
  reality testing, 450
  refreezing behavior stage, 442
  results of, 452–54
  role development, 456
  search for solutions, 448
  sequencing, 459
  stabilizing, 447
  structural changes, 455
  subsystems relationships, 445
  system integration, 458
  top management commitment, 449
  unit integration, 457–58
Charisma, 418

Chief executive officer (CEO), 205, 209–10
  conflict settlement, 281–82
Closed system of organization, 24–26, 29, 31–32
Closure, 95–96
Coal mining study, 96–97
  longwall system, 96, 293
Coercive organization, 129
  alienative compliance relations, 130
Coercive power, 264
Cognitive dissonance, 213
Commitment, 284
Communes, 464
Communitarianism, 474–75
Community power structures, 183
Competence motivation, 231–33
Competition, 76–77
Complexity, 405–6
Comprehension cycles, 207
Compulsory advice, 42
Computer technology, 413
Concentration of authority, 110
Conceptual economy, 6
Concessions, 298–99
Concurring authority, 42
Confidence, 308
Conflict
  autonomy, 283
  bargaining; see Bargaining conflict
  bureaucratic; see Bureaucratic conflict
  effectiveness, 279–80
  effects of, 278–79
  felt, 277
  latent, 277
  manifest, 278
  organizational change, 425
  partisans; see Partisans
  perceived, 277
  power, 275–77, 282–83
  resolution of, 281–83
  subsystem, 470
  systems; see Systems conflicts
  top management, 280
Conflict aftermath, 278
Consultative management system, 63–64
Content specific norms, 303
Contingency theory of leadership, 315
Control, 103, 264
  definition, 105
  external, 104–5, 126
  internal, 104–5, 126–28
  locations, 122–23
Co-optation, 183–84
Coordination, unprogrammed, 116
Cosmology, 5–6
Cosmopolitan orientation of staff, 115, 198
Craft industries, 90–92, 116–117
Crisis futurology, 466–67
Cuban missile crisis, 196–97

Subject Index 517

Cue, 222
Cyclical problem-solving behavior, 201

D

The Death and Life of American Cities, 352
Decentralized divisional form of organization, 47–49
Decentralized organizational structure, 92
Decision-communication process, 206
Decision control process, 206
Decision making
  compromise, 157
  computation, 155, 204
  constraints, 152–53
  goals as determinants, 155
  group involvement, 57
  inspiration, 157–58
  judgment, 156, 197–98, 204
  norms affecting, 270–71
  participation, 334–36
  power affecting, 268–69
  rationality, 151
  strategic: *see* Strategic decision making
Deep change strategies, 430
  social norms, 432–34
Defensive behavior, 55
Demographics, 464–65, 471–72
Departmentalization, 39
  by function, 39
  by location, 40
  by process, 40
  by product, 40
Deterministic system, 24–25
Disjointed incrementalism, 193–94
Distrust, 306–7
Disturbed-reactive environment, 170
Diversification, 186, 413–14
Divisional form of organization, 47–49
Domain consensus, 181, 385–86
  subsystems, 386
Dominant coalition, 141, 161, 197–98, 212
  inner circle, 198
Drive reduction theories, 219–20
Driving forces, 440–41
DuPont Co., 47
Dysfunctional elements in organization, 19
Dynamic homeostasis, 32

E

Eastern Airlines, 143–44
Ecological ethic, 481
Economic growth, 470–72
  systems theory, 470
Economic rationality, 414
Efficiency, 16
  economic, 384
  evaluation of organization, 378–80
  long-run, 383

Efficiency—*Cont.*
  organizational change, 407–10
  potential or actual, 379–80
  scientific management, 414
Elements of Administration, 17
Emery Air Freight, 128
Emotion, 222
Employee participation, 56
Encounter groups, 433
Energic efficiency, 378, 382
Engineering technologies, 118
Entitlements, 474–75
Environment, physical; *see* Physical environment
Environment of organization
  causal texture, 169–71
  definitions, 166, 171
  interdependencies, 169
  interorganizational relationships, 172–74, 176, 187–88
  negotiated, 177
  organization set, 171
  stability, 412–13
  uncertainty reduction, 168–69
Environmental determinism, 347, 349–50
Equality of opportunity, 67, 473
Equality of outcome, 67–68, 473, 475
Equifinality, 32
Equity norms, 303
Evaluation/choice, 204
Evaluation of organization, 372
  criterion measures, 373
  efficiency measures, 378
  empirical approach, 375
  external criteria, 396–97
  external perspectives, 382–88
  goal view of effectiveness, 372–74, 389
  internal criteria, 372–82
  larger system perspective, 384–88
  midrange criteria, 391
  multiple goals, 373–74
  operative criteria, 391–97
  political criteria, 396–97
  process model, 389
  rational model, 372
  system model, 372, 380–82
  system need variables, 380
  tradeoffs, 397–98
  values, 399–400
Exchange, 288
Exodus, Book of, 36–37
Expectancy model of motivation, 235–40
  applications, 238–39
  evaluation, 237–38
  need theories, 239–40
  person-job discrepancies, 239
  satiation, 239
Expert power, 264
Exploitive authoritative management system, 63–64

F

Failure cycles, 207
Feedback delays, 206
Felt conflict, 277
Flexible, centralized organizational structure, 92
Flexible, polycentralized organizational structure, 92
Flexibility, 392, 394
Focal role, 252, 261–62
Food and Drug Administration, organization set, 180
Formalization, 110, 407–8
Functional analysis
Functional interdependence, 294–96
  asymmetrical, 295
  sequential, 295
Functional staff arrangement, 42
Futurology, 462
  corporate power decline, 478
  crisis, 466–67
  demographic factors, 464
  genotypic variables, 465, 468–83
  growth, 470–73
  Japan as an example, 476–77
  power, 477–79
  predictions, 469–82
  rationality, 468
  specification of strategies, 465–67
  specification of system goals, 465–66
  strategy formulation, 467
  surprise-free, 466
  value changes, 477–79
  value-critical, 467

G

General Motors, 40, 47
Genotypes, 243
Genotypic variables, 465
  communal concern, 474–75
  growth, 470–72
  individualism, 473–74
  power of dominant groups, 477
  rationalization, 468
  self-interest, 473–74
  state role in planning, 475
Goals; see Organization goals
Governmental planning, 475
Group esteem, 354–55
Growth
  economic, 471–72
  organization, 470
  population, 471–72
  social limits to, 472
  systems theory, 470

H

Harwood Manufacturing Company studies, 64
Hawthorne studies, 21–24
Hierarchy of authority, 38–39
Hoover Commission Report on Organization of the Executive Branch of the Federal Government, 259
Horizontal differentiation, 41
Horizontal integration, 185
Hospitals
  behavior in organization, 247
  boards of directors, 182
  goals, 161–63
  organizational changes, 454–59
  Veterans Administration, 182–83
Human relations, 22–23, 468
Human resources, 45–46

I

I.B.M., 370
Ideational nature of society, 481
Idiosyncrasy credits, 332–33
Imperial Chemical Industies, Ltd., 224
Individualism, 473–74
Inducement-contribution theory, 285
Industrial concentration, 177, 185–86
Industrial psychology, 430
Influence, 264
Influence graph, 60–62, 69–72
Informal conferences, 299–300
Information overload, 80
Information processing
  capacity, 123
  requirements, 122–23
Innovation, 392, 394–95
  organizational affluence, 415–16
Innovative organizational structure, 52–53
Innovative roles, 261
Institutional leadership, 339–41
Institutionalization, 340
Instrumental perfection, 81
Integration of individual and organizational goals, 287–88
Integration of organizational subunits, 72–77
  definition, 72
Intensive technology, 81–83
Interorganizational relations, 172–74
  autonomy and dependency, 184–85
Interpersonal analysis, 431
Interpolation pattern of leadership, 322
Interrupts, 206
Interstate Commerce Commission, organization set, 180
The Intimate Enemy: How to Fight Fair in Marriage, 279
Intrapersonal analysis, 431
Intrinsic motivation, 240–42
  arousal potential, 240
  central nervous system needs, 241
  definition, 240

Iron Law of Oligarchy, 20–21, 407
Israel, participative management, 66–69

J

Japan, 476–77
Job complexity, 80
Job enrichment, 128, 223–27
Job satisfaction, 221
  behavioral criteria for measuring, 392
  organizational change, 410
  productivity, 234
  sources of, 234–35
  subcultural differences, 227–28
Joint ventures, 184
Judgment, 156, 204

K-L

Kibbutzim, 66–69
Knowledge paradigm of the future, 481
Kondratieff cycles, 480
Latent conflict, 277
Lateral relationships, 125
Leadership
  authoritarianism, 333
  changing situations, 331–32
  consideration, 317–18, 320
  contingency theory of, 315
  creativity, 343
  decision making, 334
  definition, 316
  effect of, 329–31
  favorableness of work situation, 325
  facilitation of interaction, 321
  facilitation of work, 321
  goals, 321
  initiating structure, 317, 319–20, 330
  institutional, 339–41
  intervening variables, 323
  motivation, 324
  opportunism, 341–42
  organizational constraints, 332
  path-goal theory, 327–29
  skill level, 324
  skill-mix model, 321, 323
  support, 321
  task-role organization, 324–25
  three-pattern theory, 322
  top-level management, 339
  utopianism, 341–42
League of Women Voters, 62
Legal rational authority, 18
Legitimate power, 264
Life cycle of organizations, 419–20
Limited company authority, 42
Line of authority, 26–27, 41
Line and staff relationships, 41–43
Linking pins, 57–58
  role conflict reduction, 262

Local orientation of staff, 115, 198
Long-linked technology, 81–83
Long-wave cycles, 480
Longwall approach to coal mining, 96, 293, 361, 460
Love and belongingness needs, 353–54
Lower level personnel, power sources, 265

M

Maintenance subsystem, 30
Management
  lower, 27
  middle levels, 27
  systems, 63
  top level, 27
Management, principles of, 16–17
Management by exception, 123
Management by objectives, 126–127, 431
Management by Participation, 64–65
Management systems, 63–65
Managerial grid, 430
Managerial subsystems, 30–31
Manhattan Project, 49
Manifest conflict, 278
Mass production technologies, 85–86, 361–62
Mechanistic organization, 85
Mediating technologies, 81–83
Mediators, 300
Mergers, 186
Metamotivation, 355
Middle management, 39, 199
Modeling, 117–18
Morale, 392
Motivation, 219
  ability, 233–34
  achievement, 229–31
  competence, 231–33, 242
  expectancy model, 235–40
  individual differences, 228–29
  intrinsic; *see* Intrinsic motivation
  learning, 222
  measuring, 394
  need theories, 220–23
  organizational characteristics, 231–33
  subcultural differences, 227–28
  two-factor theory, 222–23
Motive, defined, 222
Mutual responsiveness, 303–4

N

Need hierarchies, 220–23
Negotiated environment, 177
Negotiated order, 247
Neutrality of partisans, 307–8
The New American Ideology, 467
Nonroutine technologies, 90, 92–93, 116

Normative organizations, 129
  normative-moral compliance relationships, 130
Norms, 247, 249
  ambiguous, 255
  approval-disapproval ratio, 254
  content specific, 303
  crystallization, 255
  decision making, 268-69
  equity, 303
  informal, 250
  internalized rules, 251
  mutual responsiveness, 303
  professional, 271
  return potential model, 253-54
  structure, 253-54

O

Object language, 348
Office design, 357
  contingency approach to, 361-63
Oil companies, organization structure, 82
Oligarchy, 20-21
Open system view of organization, 25, 31-32
Operating responsiveness of organization, 44-45, 396, 409
Opportunism, 341-42
Organic organization, 83, 90, 156-57
Organization
  bureaucracy; *see* Bureaucracy
  change; *see* Organizational change
  closed system perspective, 25-26
  contingency approach, 24
  environment; *see* Environment of organization
  evaluation; *see* Evaluation of organization
  input and output, 28-29
  institutional level, 168, 261
  managerial level, 26, 167-68
  objectives, 43
  open system perspective, 25-26
  process criteria; *see* Process criteria
  rational view, 15-25
  social systems view, 33-34
  strategy; *see* Strategy formulation
  structure; *see* Organizational Structure
  subsystems; *see* Subsystems
  system model; *see* System view of organization
  technical level, 26-27, 167
  theories of, 14
Organization set, 171-73
  prestige, 178
Organizational affluence, 415-16
Organizational change; *see also* Change processes in organization
  affluence of organization, 415-16

Organizational change—*Cont.*
  centralization, 406-7, 411-12
  change agent, 433-36
  complexity, 405-6, 411-12
  depth of intervention, 422, 430-36
  determining need, 421-23
  diversification, 413-14
  emotional aspects of, 429-36
  emotional-structural view, 421
  environmental stability and instability, 412-13
  everyday, 416
  formalization, 407-8
  growth, 418-19
  implementation of, 424-25
  initiation of, 423-24
  intervention strategy, 430-36
  life cycles, 419-20
  personnel, 416-17
  planned, 421
  process of: *see* Change processes in organizations
  production, 409
  program change, 405
  rational-cognitive view, 421
  regeneration, 417
  resistance to, 427
  routinization, 426
  scientific management, 414-15
  stratification, 408-9
  technology, 412-13
Organizational effectiveness; *see* Evaluation of organization
Organizational goals, 129, 137
  behavioristic versus rationalistic study of, 139-40
  clarity, 149
  communication, 149-50
  conflicting, 150, 153
  constraints, 153
  controlling elites, 161
  decision making, 155-58
  derived, 145
  formal, 138
  measures of attainment, 372-74
  multiple goals, 159
  operative, 140-41
  output, 142-43
  product, 144
  rationalistic study of, 139-40
  sequential attention, 155
  side payments, 153
  system, 143-44
Organizational interdependence
  management of, 119-21
  pooled, 118-20
  reciprocal, 119
  sequential, 118-19
Organizational politics, 205-6
Organizational slack, 124, 416

Subject Index

Organizational structure, 28
  centralized functional form, 46–47
  decentralized divisional form, 47–49
  definition, 38
  departmentalization; *see* Departmentalization
  employee participation; *see* Participative organization
  horizontal differentiation, 39
  innovative, 52
  line and staff, 41–43
  matrix organization, 50
  process criteria; *see* Process criteria
  project management structure, 49
  span of control, 41
  system view; *see* System view of organizational structure
  vertical differentiation, 38
Organizational vocabularies, 151–52
Origination pattern of leadership, 322

P

Participation
  decision making, 334–36
  Japan, 476
  organizational changes, 427–29
  social controls, 288
Participative organization
  bureaucracy compared, 69–70
  comparative study, 65–70
  group in decisions, 57
  performance characteristics, 62–63
  performance goals, 58
  supportive relationships, 56
Partisans
  alienation, 308
  coercion, 308
  confidence, 307
  neutrality, 307–8
  participation in conflict resolution, 309–12
  persuasion, 307
  power, 304
  relations with authority, 308–9
  trust and distrust, 306
Path-goal theory of leadership, 327–29
Perceived conflict, 277
Person-job discrepancies, 239
Person specialization, 296
Personal space, 354
Personalization, 277
Personnel exchange, 178–80
Persuasion, 307
Phenotypes, 243–44
Physical environment
  behavior, 347
  need fulfillment, 351
    group esteem, 354–55
    love and belongingness, 353–54

Physical environment—*Cont.*
  need fulfillment *Cont.*
    personal space, 354
    physiological, 352
    safety, 352
    self-actualization, 355–56
    self-esteem, 354–55
    social density, 3652–53
    work spaces, 348, 357
Physiological growth, 242–44
Physiological needs, 352
Placid, clustered environment, 170
Placid, randomized environment, 169–70
Planet, 7–8
Planning, Programming and Budgeting System (Department of Defense), 414–15
Population growth, 471–72
Positional commitment, 298
Positive reinforcement, 127–28
Power, 264
  bases of, 264
  conflict, 275–77
  compliance bases, 265
  decision making, 268–69
  futurology, 477–79
  leadership, 337–38
  lower level participants, 265–68
  partisans, 304–38
  relative, 276
  specified, 276
  stakeholders, 269–70
Prestige sets, 178
The Prince, 274, 313
Principles of Organization, 17
Process criteria, 44, 46
  operating responsiveness, 44–45
  steady state efficiency, 44
  strategic responsiveness, 45
  structural responsiveness, 45
Process technologies, 86
Production, 409
Production subsystem, 29–30
Production systems
  mass, 84–85
  process, 84
  unit, 84
Productivity, 292–93
Professional autonomy, 114
Professional norms, 271
Professional organizations, 271
  political processes, 273
Professionalization, 112
  cosmopolitans, 115
  locals, 115
Professionals
  complexity of organization, 406
  role negotiation, 271–72
Profitability, 372, 382
Program change, 405

Subject Index

Progressive differentiation, 29, 33, 70
Project management, 49–52
  matrix organization, 50–51
Psychological growth, 242–44
Psychological work contracts, 56
Punishment sequence, 298
Pyramid-shaped organization, 39

Q–R

Quasi-stationary equilibrium, 440
Quota system, 103–4
Rational strategy for change, 421
Rational view of organizations, 15–25
  evaluation, 372
Rationalism, 414
Rationality, 18
  futurology, 468
Rationing, 168
Received role, 252
Referent power, 264
Regeneration of organizations, 417
Regent Hill housing project, 349–50
Requisite task attribute index, 227–28
Resources, 172–74
Restaurant study, 99, 295, 347, 361
Restraining forces, 440–41
Retreat to technology, 342
Retrograde motion, 8–9
Return on investment (ROI), 372
Return potential model of norms, 253
Role ambiguity, 258–59
Role conflict, 257–58
  boundary roles, 260
  innovative roles, 261
  management of, 262
  sources of, 259–62
  supervisory roles, 261
Role episode, 256–57
Role negotiation, 271–72
Role senders, 252, 256
  focal person, 261–62
  self-senders, 256
Role set, 252
  management, 262
Role stress, 263, 419
Roles, 252
  boundary, 260
  conflict; *see* Role conflict
  focal, 252, 256
  innovative, 261
  overdefined, 260
  own, 256
  received, 252
  sent, 252
  supervisory, 261
  underdefined, 260
Routine technology, 90, 92–94, 117
Routinization of charisma, 418

Rules of organization, 108–10
  internalized, 251
  interpersonal conflict, 110
  invisible, 108
  shared understandings, 247

S

Safety need, 352–53
Sales representative, 181–82
Satiation, 239
Satisficing, 151, 200, 203, 446
Scheduling delays, 206
Science, 8–11
  routine, 8
Scientific management, 14–17
  behavioral science, 468
  organizational change, 414–15
Screening, 204
Securities and Exchange Commission, organization set, 179–80
Selective recruitment, 287–88
Self-actualization, 3–4, 221–22
  environment affecting, 355–56
Self-esteem, need for, 354–55
Self-interest, 473–74
Self-realization ethic, 481
Self-sender, 256
Sent role, 252
Sequential attention, 154–55
Sequential dependencies, 295–96
Service unit management (SUM), 454–60
Shallow change strategies, 430
Side payments, 153–54
Skill-mix theory of leadership, 321, 323
Smoothing, 168
Social control
  participation, 288
  socialization, 286–87
Social density, 352–53
Social Limits to Growth, 473
Social system view of organization, 33–34
Social systems, 31, 33
Social technocrats, 478
Socialization, 285–88
  control mechanisms, 286–87
  integrating goals, 287
  participation, 288
  selective recruitment, 287–88
Societal value system, 477–78
Span of control, 41
  job complexity, 80
  technology, 84–85
Specialization, 110; *see also* Departmentalization
Staff, 41–43
  functional arrangement, 42
Staff advice, 42
Stakeholder, 146

Subject Index

Stakeholder expectations, 146
  conflict, 146–47
  mixed, 148
  reinforcing, 148
  unsupported, 148–49
Standardization, 110
Static organizations, 412
Status symbol, 355
Steady state efficiency, 27, 32, 44, 396, 407
"Storming the quota", 103–4
Strategic decision making, 200–207
  analyses, 204
  authorization, 204–5
  comprehension cycles, 207
  computational, 204–5
  crisis, 202–3
  development phase, 203
  evaluation/choice, 204
  failure cycles, 207
  feedback delays, 206
  identification phase, 201–3
  interrupts, 206
  organizational politics, 205–6
  schedule delays, 206
  screening, 204
  selection phase, 203
  timing delays and speedups, 206
Strategic leniency, 108
Strategic responsiveness of organization, 45, 396, 409
Strategy, definition, 189, 191
Strategy formulation
  behavior of managers, 208–10
  cognitive dissonance, 213
  contingency approach, 194–96
  disjointed incremental approach, 194–94
  futurology, 467
  management, 212–13
  normative approach, 192
  related to performance, 192–93
  values, 210–12
Stratification, 408–9
Stress, 263
Structural response of organization, 45, 396
Structuring of activities, 110
Suboptimization, 141, 398–99
Subsystems, 29
  adaptive, 30
  competition, 76–77
  conflict, 470
  differentiation, 70–75
  domains, 386
  influence, 75–76
  integration, 72, 470
  interdependence, 118
  location in organizational hierarchy, 32–33
  maintenance, 30

Subsystems—Cont.
  management of, 75–76
  managerial, 30–31
  organization in society, 31
  production, 29–30
  support, 30
  system theory, 470
Supervisory management, 39
Supervisory roles, 261
Support subsystems, 30
Surprise-free futurology, 466
Synergy, 44
System Four organization, 63–67, 321
System needs, 32, 380–82, 395, 397–98
System-resource position, 396
System view of organization, 25–34, 70–77
  competitive issues, 76
  evaluation of subsystems, 470
  growth, 470
  social systems, 31
  subunit differentiation, 70–72
  subunit integration, 72–77
Systemic qualities of organizations, 411
Systems conflict, 277, 290–96
  functional interdependencies, 294–96
  goal differentiation, 290–94
  reducing pressure for compliance, 296
  subunits, 290

T

T-group, 431
Tacit communication, 299
Task force, 125
Task-related symmetries and asymmetries, 295
Task specialization, 296
Tavistock Institute, 95
  coal mining study, 96–97, 460
  organizational control, 121
  textile mill study, 97–99
Teacher Corps, 407–8
Technical core of organization, 27
  anticipation, 168
  buffering, 168
  production subsystems, 29
  rationality, 468
  rationing, 168
  reducing uncertainty, 168
  smoothing, 168
Technical diffuseness, 87
Technical specificity, 87
Technological fix, 342
Technology, 78
  architectural design, 361
  diffuseness, 87, 89
  humanism, 94
  intensive, 81–82
  interpersonal relations, 99–101

Technology—Cont.
  long-linked, 80–81, 83
  mediating, 81–83
  problem-solving, 89–90
  routine and nonroutine, 90–94
  specificity, 87, 89
  subunit differentiation, 89
  task variability, 89–91
Textile mills study, 97–99
Theory, 5
  functions in everyday life, 6–7
  revolutions in, 8–11
  systematic modifications, 7–8
Threats, 298
Three-pattern approach to leadership, 322
Thruster groups, 478–79
Timing delays and speedups, 206
Top level management, 39
  commitment to organizational change, 449
  conflict, 280–82
  leadership, 338–39
  stategic formulation, 199–200
Transcendent objectives, 291
The Transformation of Man, 480
Triage, 168
Trust, 234, 306–7, 427
Two-factor theory of motivation, 222–23
  job enrichment, 223–27
Two-sphere theory of cosmology, 6–7
Turbulent fields, 170

U

Uncertainty, 168–69, 177
  organizational growth, 186–87
Unfreezing-changing-refreezing model, 438–47
  changing behavior, 441–42
  driving forces, 440
  restraining forces, 440
Unit-production technologies, 86
Universities, goals, 135
Unprogrammed coordination, 116

The Uses of Disorder, 279
Utilitarian organizations, 129
  remunerative-calculative compliance relationships, 130–31
Utopianism, 341–42

V

Valences of outcome, 235–37
Value-critical futurology, 467
Values
  criteria for organizational effectiveness, 399–400
  futurologists, 465–66
  socialization of, 286
  societal system, 477–78
Vertical differentiation, 41
Vertical information systems, 125
Vertical integration, 82, 111–12, 185
Veterans Administration hospitals, 182
Volkswagen, 144–45

W

Weldon Company study, 64
Westgate housing project, 349
Win-lose situation, 293–94
Work
  extrinsic factors, 223
  intrinsic factors, 222
  motivation, 222–23
  satisfaction; *see* Job satisfaction
Work in America, 3–4
Work group
  autonomy, 95
  closure, 95–96
  control, 121–22
  participative organization, 57–60
  personal relations, 95
  Tavistock study, 95–98
  Zeigarnik effect, 95–96
Work methods, 15–16

Y–Z

Yugoslavia, participative management, 65–66
Zeigarnik effect, 95–96
Zero-sum situation, 293